SEP 0 1 2021

AFTERSHOCKS

AFTERSHOCKS

· · · · ·

PANDEMIC POLITICS AND
THE END OF THE
OLD INTERNATIONAL ORDER

COLIN KAHL AND
THOMAS WRIGHT

ST. MARTIN'S PRESS
NEW YORK

First published in the United States by St. Martin's Press, an imprint of St. Martin's Publishing Group

AFTERSHOCKS. Copyright © 2021 by Colin Kahl and Thomas Wright. All rights reserved. Printed in the United States of America. For information, address St. Martin's Publishing Group, 120 Broadway, New York, NY 10271.

www.stmartins.com

The Library of Congress Cataloging-in-Publication Data is available upon request.

ISBN 978-1-250-27574-5 (hardcover)
ISBN 978-1-250-27575-2 (ebook)

Our books may be purchased in bulk for promotional, educational, or business use. Please contact your local bookseller or the Macmillan Corporate and Premium Sales Department at 1-800-221-7945, extension 5442, or by email at MacmillanSpecialMarkets@macmillan.com.

First Edition: 2021

10 9 8 7 6 5 4 3 2 1

Colin dedicates this book to Rebecca, Nora, and Rylan.

Tom dedicates this book to Karen and Senan.

CONTENTS

PART IV
TOWARD A POST-COVID WORLD

AUTHORS' NOTE

In researching this book, we conducted over sixty interviews with senior officials from the United States, Europe, Asia, Australia, Israel, and the World Health Organization. Most of these interviews were conducted "on background," meaning that we could use the information and quote the source directly but not attribute it to them by name without prior approval. Given the politically sensitive nature of many of our conversations, this was necessary to get as full and frank a picture as possible. Throughout the book, wherever we say "an official told us" something or that a specific official said or thought something, and no citation to another work is provided, it came from one of these interviews. In each case where we use information from one of these interviews, the official had direct knowledge of the events being discussed. In most instances, we do not provide endnotes referencing interviews conducted for the book; we only do so when the source of the information is not otherwise clear from the text.

AFTERSHOCKS

Introduction

Donald Trump was a natural unilateralist. He was elected on an "America First" platform that rejected seventy years of U.S. global leadership and viewed alliances, treaties, and trade deals as attempts by the rest of the world to trick the United States out of its money and power. Nevertheless, his core team understood early—in fact, earlier than European governments—that the novel coronavirus that emerged in Wuhan, China, in December 2019 could be a game-changer, a national security challenge that would define his presidency. But it took weeks to get Trump's attention. After what felt like an eternity, on January 31, 2020, Trump's national security and health teams convinced him to take action by banning travel from China. It was an important, though insufficient, step—the ban still allowed tens of thousands of Americans and others from China to fly back to the United States, which would require a significant program of testing and contact tracing that was never put in place. Crucially, the virus was already circulating in America.

The next day, Robert O'Brien, the U.S. national security advisor, began asking other countries to follow suit. The virus could be contained only if everyone acted swiftly, but was it already too late? The Australians had barred travel from China and the Japanese were on board. But O'Brien was frustrated with the Europeans. Each capital refused to move individually; they preferred a united response by the whole of the European Union (EU), and that was unlikely, especially since many European governments were wary about alienating Beijing. As the virus took hold in

Italy, O'Brien tried to convince European national security advisors to impose travel restrictions within the Schengen Area, a free-travel area encompassing twenty-six countries, but they would have none of it. In Washington, O'Brien and his deputy, Matthew Pottinger, pushed the president to make a case for an international response to the pandemic, but Trump was unpersuaded. "Why aren't the Europeans doing anything?" he fired back. That was the moment, some administration officials felt, when the opportunity for allies to work multilaterally on an unfolding and potentially unprecedented crisis evaporated.

From the time Trump first heard of the dangers posed by the virus, his instinct was to minimize it. He had just signed a trade pact with China and was eager to portray himself as the dealmaker in chief in advance of his reelection bid in November. His opponents described him as a warmonger, but he hoped to roll out a number of agreements with foreign leaders. It would show that he was a tough operator who was fiery and furious in negotiations but also could close the deal. For example, Trump seemed to push the United States to the brink of nuclear war with North Korea in 2017, only to pull back and hold three made-for-TV meetings in 2018 and 2019 with the country's dictatorial leader, Kim Jong-un. It was mostly for show—but for Trump that was all that really mattered. In early 2020, the American economy was going strong, and the president worried about any action that would derail its progress. The travel ban was action enough, he believed, and everything was under control. That is what China's president, Xi Jinping, was telling him in a number of phone calls. But both the emerging pandemic and the economy were about to get much, much worse.

In early March, the markets went into free fall. The contagion—now known as COVID-19, shorthand for coronavirus disease 2019—was spreading across Europe. Trump's advisors warned that millions could die if he took no further action. So on March 11, Trump reluctantly agreed to shut the economy down for three weeks. It may not have been enough, but it was a start. For more than a month, O'Brien, Pottinger, and the administration's health advisors had struggled to convince the president that this was serious. But now the dam was breaking, and a national crisis loomed. Trump quickly turned on China (one of his favorite rhetorical targets, despite his warm personal relationship with Xi). His message to his aides was blunt: "These guys have fucked us and they fucked me personally." He began to call the pandemic "the China virus." In response, Beijing started to sow rumors that the U.S. Army had brought the virus to Wuhan. Trump had another phone call with Xi on March 26; this one was contentious, as they argued about the origins of COVID-19. For the remainder of Trump's term, the two men would not speak again.

By late March, all the world's wealthiest democracies were in lockdown, facing what appeared to be their most severe crisis since World War II. No one knew what the ultimate death toll could be, but a rough back-of-the-envelope calculation was terrifying. The U.S. Centers for Disease Control and Prevention (CDC) estimated that up to 1.7 million Americans could die. German officials worried that they could lose half a million people. Everyone had known some sort of global pandemic was possible; some countries had even planned for it. But now that one had arrived, many leaders were flying blind. To curb the spread, economies were deliberately shut down, but that triggered an unimaginable worldwide recession that rivaled that of the Great Depression of the 1930s (or so it seemed for a while). Each country, in its own way, worried that its population was not prepared, psychologically or materially, for what was about to happen.

International cooperation was effectively at a standstill. The World Health Organization (WHO), stymied by insufficient cooperation from China and overly deferential to Beijing, struggled to understand the evolving nature of the pandemic. As a result, it also found it difficult to offer coherent advice on how to contain it. Around the world, a competitive, self-help logic dominated national responses. Germany closed its borders, stranding thousands of its citizens who were abroad and could not return home. French authorities seized 6 million protective masks from a Swedish-owned distribution center in Lyon to prevent the masks from being exported to other European countries. Italian leaders warned that the crisis could break the European Union. The United States gained a reputation as a big spender, persuading medical suppliers around the world to divert to America shipments that had already been promised to other nations. In Asia, Japan and other nations struggled to comprehend how to care for thousands of passengers on infected cruise ships afloat in the Pacific.

In the United States, where by mid-March much of the country was being roiled by the crisis, Trump suddenly saw his reelection prospects slipping away. Though he generally despised multilateral meetings, he looked ahead to a consequential one planned for June. As chair of the Group of 7 (G7), the United States was scheduled to host a summit of leaders from other advanced democratic economies. The pandemic was forcing most international meetings to be held virtually. But there was reason at the time to believe that the virus might recede by the summer. And Japanese prime minister Shinzo Abe, U.K. prime minister Boris Johnson, and French president Emmanuel Macron told Trump that, with adequate preparation, they hoped to attend in person. Trump tweeted,

> Now that our Country is "Transitioning back to Greatness," I am considering rescheduling the G-7, on the same or similar date, in Washington, D.C., at the legendary Camp David. The other members are also beginning their COMEBACK. It would be a great sign to all—normalization![1]

Created in 1975 as a response to the oil shock and economic recession, what would become the G7 originally included just four countries: France, the United Kingdom, Germany, and the United States. Japan, Canada, Italy, and the EU joined later, as did Russia for a time (although it was expelled after its annexation of Crimea in 2014). As a club of the world's wealthiest democracies, it was a forum for leaders to deal with global crises as well as to make long-term improvements to the international order. Now the coronavirus pandemic had fallen on the club's doorstep.

THE "FUCK THIS" MOMENT

At forty-two years old, Macron was the youngest French leader since Napoleon. Whip-smart, he was extraordinarily ambitious and saw himself as a transformative leader who would push France and the EU to prepare for its twenty-first-century challenges. The COVID-19 crisis would put this ambition to the test.

Macron had a complicated relationship with Trump. After Trump became president, Macron engaged and flattered him, distinguishing himself from other European leaders who held Trump at arm's length. He invited Trump to be the guest of honor at France's Bastille Day military parade—an experience that so affected the American president that he began pressing for a similar military-style parade in Washington, DC. Later on, when it became apparent that Macron, despite his fawning, had received little of substance in return, the relationship between them cooled.

Nonetheless, the French president, who had chaired the G7 in 2019, pressed the group to act quickly during the early days of the pandemic. Macron had hoped that Trump would take the lead from there, but he quickly realized that the American president did not care for French input. That was not all that surprising, but what did come as a shock to French officials was that the White House had no ideas of its own. There was no plan. As the crisis worsened, Paris asked the White House for a call among G7 leaders. The White House agreed, but France would have to organize it. Paris took the lead, and the call went ahead on March 18 without incident. However, when a long-scheduled meeting of foreign ministers of the G7 convened virtually on March 26, the group was unable to agree on a joint declaration because of U.S. secretary of state Mike Pompeo's insistence that it relabel COVID-19 the "Wuhan virus." The French were astonished. Could the United States really be torpedoing the G7 over semantics? Nevertheless, Macron pushed ahead. These challenges had to be dealt with between leaders, face-to-face. He was encouraged by Trump's decision to hold the G7 summit in person and declared that he would attend. The French president also retained faith in his own ability to strike a deal with other leaders no matter the challenges.

Boris Johnson, Britain's prime minister, was also supportive of an in-person G7 summit. With his floppy blond hair, penchant for outrageous but funny statements, and embrace of populism, he was sometimes called Britain's Trump. It wasn't entirely fair: Johnson had spent a lifetime in politics, he read widely, and, unlike Trump, he accepted the threat of climate change, endorsed the Iran nuclear deal, and generally valued multilateral institutions (if not the EU). But it was also true that he would happily follow Trump's lead, in keeping with Britain's foreign policy tradition of backing American positions. The problem, from Johnson's point of view, was that there was no U.S. lead to follow. America was entirely absent from any attempt to craft a strategic approach to the pandemic. Nevertheless, Johnson persisted and backed Macron's push for a

G7 summit, which he hoped would spur the world's major powers to action. He wanted them to collectively engage with Gavi, the Vaccine Alliance, a public-private global health partnership funded in part by the Gates Foundation, and COVAX, the COVID-19 Vaccines Global Access initiative created in response to the pandemic. The British prime minister was also eager to coordinate effectively on the economic recovery and on assistance to the developing world, which was being hammered by the pandemic and the global economic shutdown.

When it came to Trump, Macron and Johnson were keen to engage, but the German chancellor, Angela Merkel, had no such desire. A scientist who grew up in East Germany under communist rule, she was empirical, cautious, and deliberate. In power since November 2005, she was set to step down in 2021. Merkel's relationship with Trump had never been congenial—indeed, at times it had felt downright absurd—but in 2019 she came to a startling realization about the American leader. Their tensions were not only about policy disputes. Nor were they about a clash of styles. Rather, she concluded that she simply embodied everything that Trump opposed: science, humility, intelligence, and multilateralism. That meant that any form of personal engagement with the American president brought out his absolute worst qualities. She was the red cape to his bull. When they spoke, he went off the rails. All she had to do was be in his presence. If Germany and the United States were to find common ground, Merkel believed it would never arise with her on one side and Trump on the other. Armed with this insight, Merkel felt liberated. In May 2019 she gave a commencement address at Harvard University. Every sentence had a double meaning, both articulating her own philosophy of multilateralism and repudiating Trump's personal brand of politics. She had no reason to be careful in her remarks; Trump already hated her and, in any case, was an unpersuadable force on the world stage.[2]

Merkel would participate in the G7 conference calls, but when the French president asked her to fly to Washington for the in-person G7 summit in June, she declined. At the time, German officials claimed Merkel's decision had everything to do with travel restrictions related to the pandemic. There was some truth to this: Merkel was extremely cautious and took the virus very seriously. In April she had received a flu vaccination shot from a doctor who subsequently tested positive for COVID-19, and upon learning this she immediately went into self-isolation for two weeks. She refused most foreign visitors. So it was no surprise that she did not want to travel to the United States, a global epicenter for the pandemic. Incidentally, this decision became public just hours after Trump announced he would break off ongoing talks with the WHO and, doubling down, would pull America out of the organization entirely.

But there was another reason she did not want to attend: Merkel did not want to be in the same room as Trump. It would not just be a waste of time; her oil-and-water relationship with the American president would make matters worse. She also saw the United States as an increasingly irresponsible actor and had no interest in giving Trump a photo op that he could leverage for his reelection bid or use in his cold war with China.

On May 28, 2020, Merkel spoke with Trump on the phone. She told him she would not be attending an in-person G7. Trump was taken aback; he had not expected her to pull out. Trump yelled at Merkel and after a tense exchange, he hung up on her. White House officials were furious with the chancellor. As they saw it, Merkel's refusal was not just a huge mistake that undermined America's hosting of the G7; the U.S. president had invited each of the G7 leaders personally. The two leaders had their differences, but he was also a gracious host, they felt, so Merkel's decision was an insult as well. It was, Trump's team thought, "a terrible fucking setback; Merkel had killed the G7." If they had met in person, they would have been able to shape something. Now, even though the Europeans portrayed themselves as the champions of cooperation, nothing would happen.

Trump, meanwhile, was in a rage. The summit now had to be rescheduled for after the U.S. election. "I'm postponing it because I don't feel as a G7 it probably represents what's going on in the world. It's a very outdated group of countries," he told the press.[3] Then he went even further. Trump wanted to include other nations—such as Australia, India, South Korea, and most controversially Russia—and would wait to reconvene the group until preparations were made to bring them on board. Trump had long wanted a way to cooperate with Vladimir Putin. He was fond of the Russian autocrat—expressing admiration for him during the campaign, frequently questioning why Russia was a foe, and taking his side of the narrative at the 2018 Helsinki summit when pressed about

Russian interference in the 2016 U.S. presidential election. He had raised the prospect of inviting Russia back to the G7 in the past but had been met with strong objections from other leaders, including Canada's Justin Trudeau. Now Trump resurrected the proposal to provide an alternative rationale to Merkel's snub for the cancellation of the G7 summit.

While French officials had always supported the idea of an in-person summit, they were not entirely upset by Trump's decision to postpone. They already had real reservations about whether the agenda would be at all substantive, and they did not think that the U.S. approach would be very effective in fighting the virus or helping the economy. As they saw it, the United States had little interest in mobilizing an international response to COVID-19; the Americans only seemed interested in blaming China for the original outbreak. The French assessment was not wrong. U.S. officials acknowledged that they saw the pandemic first and foremost as a China problem. The only U.S. response to that point had been a concerted effort to check Chinese power. The French also noted that after Trump canceled the G7 summit, nothing else happened. There were no American initiatives or requests on global public health, no bold thinking on the economic recovery. There was no plan to rally the world to jointly develop a vaccine or provide humanitarian assistance to millions suffering overseas. In other words, there was no leadership. Just silence.

Meanwhile, the British seemed particularly irked by Trump's play to bring Russia back into the G7. As London saw it, the G7 was supposed to be a grouping of democracies, and in March 2018 the Kremlin had attempted to assassinate a Russian dissident in the United Kingdom using a chemical agent, putting many people at risk. And, in any case, Moscow had little to offer to the COVID response, so what was even the point? It was a "fuck this" moment for Johnson's team. The American president was not serious, would do nothing, and would not lead an international response. So British officials gave up hope. Under Johnson, Britain would do its own thing—engaging in the COVAX initiative without the United States, hosting the Gavi summit, and becoming the largest bilateral donor to the WHO after the United States pulled back.

With the Europeans now fully estranged from the United States, for all practical purposes the G7 ceased to exist. As COVID-19 swept through every part of the world in 2020, it would be every nation for itself.

THROUGH THE LOOKING GLASS

Some years stand out in history: 1914 and 1939 for the outbreak of world wars and 1918 and 1945 for their end; 1929 and 2008 for international financial crises that hurt the livelihoods of hundreds of millions; 1989 and 2001 for the end of one global era and the beginning of another, one out of hope and the other in sadness. Even now, with so little distance from it, there is little doubt that 2020 will join the list. It is not just that the world was hit with the worst pandemic since the 1918–20 influenza a century before, resulting in tens of millions infected, nearly 2 million dead by year's end, and on track to do over $22 trillion in damage to the global economy by year's end.[4] There is never a good time for a pandemic, but the novel coronavirus hit the world at perhaps the worst possible moment, when international cooperation had largely broken down after a tumultuous decade. The fact that world leaders were hardly on speaking terms and could not even arrange to meet to discuss the pandemic is a stark illustration of this.

This book tells the story of how a highly interconnected world coped with a global contagion in an age of gross inequality, rising populism and nationalism, and escalating geopolitical competition. We argue that nationalistic impulses undermined much-needed collaboration and the U.S.-China rivalry overshadowed nearly everything, further complicating the international response. We show how COVID-19 was a truly global political crisis with repercussions far and wide, from undermining the European Union and locking down the global economy to reversing decades of poverty reduction in the developing world and eroding democracy and civil liberties. And we demonstrate how pandemic politics ultimately dealt the final blow to the old international order. Such a comprehensive look is necessary to understand what we all collectively experienced—and to better prepare for where we are headed in the years to come.

For the three decades prior to 2020, the world tended to work together during times of crisis—whether it was to deal with the aftermath of the collapse of the Soviet Union in 1991, the initial response to the terrorist attacks of 9/11 in 2001, the HIV/AIDS epidemic ravaging sub-Saharan Africa in 2003, the financial crisis of 2008–9, the Ebola outbreak of 2014, or the rise of the Islamic State in Iraq and Syria that same year—with the United States leading the way. The cooperation that occurred was often incomplete and imperfect, but it did make a difference. This cooperation had been fraying for several years, and in 2020 it was torn asunder. An international experiment ensued: What would happen in a global crisis if world politics was dominated by nationalist governments that refused, or were unable, to cooperate with one another? On the eve of the COVID-19 pandemic, the United States was led by President Trump, an avowed America Firster who saw international politics as a transactional zero-sum contest. Meanwhile, as the United States turned inward, Xi Jinping shattered hopes that China would become a responsible stakeholder in the global order as he quashed dissent at home and increasingly bullied other nations abroad. Brazil and India, once bastions of democracy and multilateralism, had taken an illiberal turn. Britain and the European Union were engaged in a bitter divorce. And while humanity was more interconnected than ever, a hyperglobalized world was also awash in economic, cultural, and political grievances and besieged by viral disinformation and conspiracy theories, courtesy of new technologies and willing accomplices, including some of the world's most powerful people.

This was the unforgiving geopolitical context in which COVID-19 unleashed a cascade of interlocking international calamities. Every country had to cope with an unparalleled public health emergency. Most countries failed. Some, such as Germany and Israel, did well at first but struggled once the second wave hit. A few, including Australia, New Zealand, South Korea, and Taiwan, performed consistently well, avoiding the national lockdowns that became commonplace in Europe. Instead, they relied on aggressive contact tracing, isolating the potentially infected, and imposing draconian restrictions on travel. Some of these nations enjoyed geographical advantages that made it easier to keep the virus at bay, but they generally had one other thing in common: they had experience mishandling recent epidemics, pandemics, or other national disasters, and had learned their lessons.

The coronavirus caused the worst economic downturn in modern times, and it also nearly triggered a massive financial crisis in the United States—averted only because of a timely and overwhelming response by the U.S. Federal Reserve. The pandemic exposed the vulnerability of global supply chains as countries experienced shortages of critical medical supplies and other goods. It tore at the fabric of the European Union—a coalition of twenty-seven countries supported by shared economic, social, and security concerns—as national border closings and the scramble for medical supplies unraveled its common purpose and raised questions about its very survival. The EU seemed to get back on track after several months, but then was thrown into crisis once more in the fall and winter of 2020, with new questions raised about its failure to contain the pandemic's second wave and how it handled the development and distribution of the vaccines.

The lockdown model worked in China and, at least initially, in parts of the West that sought to "flatten the curve" and buy time for other containment measures. But these same interventions proved disastrous in the developing world. Many low- and middle-income nations were not in a position to take advantage of the time afforded by stay-at-home orders and business closures to bolster health care capacity. They also lacked the resources to provide adequate assistance to people already living on the margins. As a result, COVID-19 gravely damaged already vulnerable people and economies. Even developing countries that had enjoyed considerable economic success over the past two decades were hit hard as debt mounted and tens of millions fell back into poverty and were pushed to the brink of starvation. Meanwhile, in fragile states in Africa, Central Asia, and the Middle East already suffering from violent conflict and displacement, the pandemic made conditions even more dire.

Illiberal leaders and autocrats also took advantage of the health crisis to consolidate power, game elections, further erode their citizens' freedoms, and crack down on dissent. In this they were aided by new digital technologies, including surveillance apps developed to stop the spread of the virus. In country after country the political arena was roiled by clashes between those who wanted to control the outbreak and populists who denied its severity, preferring an end to restrictions on economic activity and everyday life. Across the globe, in response to governments doing too much or too little to combat COVID-19 and its political and economic fallout, millions of people took to the streets to demand change.

THE SHADOW OF THE U.S.-CHINA COMPETITION

The coronavirus pandemic ushered in a global crisis with seismic effects that will have a long geopolitical tail. The story of what began in 2020 involves not just the struggling individuals and countries that will get left even further behind, the crushing fiscal effects on rich and poor nations alike, or the lingering health impact. At the heart of the 2020 story is a rivalry between two superpowers—China and the United States—that manifestly failed in their responsibilities.

China's slow response to the early signs was perhaps understandable. Many other governments were also slow to realize the threat that COVID-19 posed both at home and abroad. But what was inexcusable was Beijing's consistent refusal to cooperate with the international community once the magnitude of what was happening became apparent. The Chinese government prevented the World Health Organization from gaining access to the site of the outbreak, failed to share samples from the early cases of COVID-19 (something they were still refusing to do as of this writing), and actively repressed doctors and journalists who tried to alert the public. China had made significant reforms after the severe acute respiratory syndrome (SARS) crisis in 2002–3, aiming to improve transparency and effectiveness in combating future outbreaks. But the reforms inspired by SARS were largely swept aside as the country's medical authorities were sidelined and Xi Jinping took control of managing the crisis. This was the inevitable consequence of a regime that had become more dictatorial since Xi took power in 2012–13. Beijing did not want to tell its rivals more than it absolutely had to.

Domestically, this was not seen as a failure. On the contrary, after early talk on Chinese social media of a "Chernobyl moment," the regime turned 2020 to its advantage at home. It contrasted China's early success in containing the virus with the West's apparent inability to do so. This, they claimed, demonstrated the superiority of their governance model. The pandemic was also a geopolitical event that materially benefited China relative to the United States. By some estimates, China will now surpass the United States as the world's largest economy by 2027, arriving at the crossover point five years earlier than previously predicted because of China's ability to better weather the economic fallout from the virus. For the Chinese Communist Party (CCP), this was the second global crisis in the span of a dozen years (along with the global financial crisis) that allowed it to gain on the United States.

Overseas, China flexed its muscles almost as soon as the virus took root in Wuhan. Beijing waged a massive disinformation campaign against the West, alleging that the virus had come to China from the United States and casting doubt on American-made vaccines. Beijing capitalized on the pandemic to crush the protest movement in Hong Kong, effectively dissolving the "one country, two systems" model that had provided Hong Kongers with autonomy and freedom since the end of British rule in 1997. Employing "wolf warrior" diplomacy, China bullied countries that questioned Beijing's response to COVID-19, while using the offer of pandemic assistance to advance its geopolitical interests in Europe, Africa, and Latin America. This assertiveness would backfire, though, generating a counterreaction that left many countries looking for a different partner. Unfortunately, under Trump, the United States did not step up to play its traditional role and failed to seize this opportunity.

Contrary to the account that is most often given, some senior Trump administration officials, already suspicious of China, realized the magnitude of what was happening in Wuhan faster than any other government except Taiwan. However, throughout 2020 the administration largely viewed the pandemic through the prism of its rivalry with China, seeing it as emblematic of the threat that China's regime posed to the world, rather than as a global public health challenge requiring international collaboration, at the very least among like-minded countries. This put the United States at odds with other advanced democracies, especially in Europe, who shared some of the administration's skepticism of China but worried that public health could become collateral damage in an intensifying cold war. Beyond the Trump administration's attempts to target the world's collective ire at Beijing, it largely ignored the broader imperative to rally international cooperation to contain the pandemic and address the economic and humanitarian wreckage the disease was leaving in its wake. Instead of supporting the WHO's efforts around the globe and working from inside the organization to press for needed reforms, as some of his top officials wanted, Trump turned the WHO into a political football, which he used to wage his ongoing battle with China. Meanwhile, zero-sum competition between the United States and China paralyzed multilateral efforts in other forums as well, including the G7 and the United Nations Security Council.

In Geneva, the director-general of the WHO, Tedros Adhanom Ghebreyesus, knew that great-power rivalry would hugely complicate his job, and he was determined to avoid becoming embroiled in it. He would privately push China but offer public support and encouragement. It was the only way, he believed, that the WHO could get anything from Beijing at a time when they desperately needed China's cooperation. He had the same attitude toward the United States, but it put him on a collision course with Washington. U.S. officials wanted him to acknowledge that China was covering up the pandemic and refusing to cooperate adequately with the international community. They believed it was only through public pressure that Beijing would be persuaded to share vital information. But Tedros would not do this, setting the stage for the U.S. decision to withdraw from the WHO later in the spring. Tedros would later criticize China—in the spring of 2021—for a lack of transparency and cooperation on the investigation into the origins of the virus, this time angering Beijing.

Meanwhile, in the "competition of systems" with China, the Trump administration's efforts also fell short, largely because of its shambolic response to the pandemic at home. By the end of 2020, the United States had recorded 352,000 deaths from the coronavirus (compared to 4,800 reported in China). That stunning figure represented 20 percent of the world's COVID death toll despite the United States having only 4 percent of the global population. There simply was no excuse for one of the world's most powerful nations to be ranked the fourteenth-worst among all countries for deaths as a percentage of the population.[5]

Trump had failed to heed the advice of several senior officials in February 2020 to follow up on the travel ban on China with a series of measures to prepare for a 1918-style pandemic, including additional travel restrictions on hotspots like Italy and requesting funds for diagnostics, medical supplies, and therapeutics. Instead, the views of those who wanted to tread cautiously for fear of disrupting the economy had prevailed. February was a lost month. Medical and scientific expertise was sidelined. The Trump administration displaced most of the responsibility—and the blame—for handling COVID-19 to states and localities without providing adequate support or guidance. Studies showed that President Trump was the world's top purveyor of misinformation about the virus and public health, hawking unproven drugs and downplaying the pandemic's importance. And even basic precautions, such as whether to wear a mask or avoid mass gatherings, became heavily politicized. The Trump administration deserves credit for accelerating the development of vaccines through its Operation Warp Speed initiative, as well as for timely action to avert a total economic collapse. But these victories were overshadowed by its broader failure to manage the multiple catastrophes produced by the pandemic.

The election of Joe Biden as president of the United States was, of course, a profoundly important change. Since the new administration came into power in January 2021, the United States has reengaged international institutions and is taking COVID-19 seriously, both domestically and globally. But make no mistake: many of the aftershocks from 2020 have staying power and will likely define our world for the next decade if not longer. The pandemic marks the end of an old American-led international order where the United States and its democratic allies automatically had the upper hand in international institutions and where cooperation on transnational challenges, such as pandemics and climate change, were insulated from great-power rivalry. Looking ahead, America must prepare for a world in which we are hit more regularly by global shocks against a backdrop of deeply rooted major-power rivalry, particularly with China. The United States should certainly seek to cooperate with rivals on shared threats, but we must also acknowledge the real limitations on such cooperation, amply demonstrated by Beijing's behavior in response to the coronavirus. And America must prepare accordingly—by working more closely with other free societies and like-minded countries.

WRITING A FIRST DRAFT OF HISTORY

The two of us—Colin Kahl and Tom Wright—have been friends for over fifteen years. We were both trained as academics studying international relations, but we approached the subject from different angles. In the 1990s and early 2000s, Colin worked on how demographic and environmental stress can exacerbate civil and ethnic wars in the developing world.[6] After opposing the U.S. war in Iraq, he spent the better part of a decade working on it as an academic, as a political advisor, and then as a government official. He served in the Obama administration, first in the Pentagon as the top official focused on the Middle East and later at the White House as national security advisor to then–Vice President Biden. At the time of this writing, Colin is once again headed back to the Pentagon. Meanwhile, Tom has worked on U.S. relations with major powers and European politics at the Brookings Institution in Washington, DC. In 2017, he wrote the book *All Measures Short of War,* about how hopes for a cooperative international order were giving way to great-power rivalry.[7] We have worked together on a number of occasions—on political campaigns and in think tank and academic settings—trying to figure out some of the big changes under way and how the United States must adjust to deal with them.

Shortly after the coronavirus pandemic emerged, both of us penned long essays about its potential geopolitical impact.[8] One thing that struck us in the debate that began in the spring of 2020 was that it was often heavy on broad predictions about the implications for grand strategy and the

international system but light on what the world was actually doing—
and not doing—to address COVID-19. We decided to write this book because we wanted to uncover the empirical detail of what was transpiring
in front of our eyes—the pandemic politics that were gripping the globe,
its aftershocks, and the world's failure to come to grips with both. Only
then, we thought, would we be in a position to draw larger conclusions.
Despite the development of promising vaccines, COVID-19 continues to
plague much of the globe as we type these words. The events we analyze
in these pages continue to unfold. But we cannot afford to wait five or ten
years to start drawing lessons from the greatest international crisis in our
lifetimes. Some understanding is required now, not least because urgent
action is required to address the grave challenges barreling toward us.

We know that in 2020 billions of people around the world were focused on how this crisis affected them directly. Will the supermarkets
be fully stocked? When can schools and businesses reopen? How can we
protect our elderly relatives? How can we pay our rent or mortgage? How
can we get vaccinated? Many also experienced the pandemic firsthand,
either getting sick or knowing someone who fell ill. Countless others had
friends or family who died from the disease.

In America, the news in 2020 was dominated by Trump and what
COVID-19 was doing inside the United States. But this was a global event,
and it must be understood as one. Thus, in our discussion of U.S. policy we
focus much more on the international aspect of the Trump administration's
thinking rather than revisit every outrageous moment of Trump's behavior,
which was heavily covered by the press at the time. We also explore the
varied responses to the pandemic (and its consequences) around the globe,
discussing the dynamics at work in Europe, Asia, Africa, the Middle East,
and Latin America and sketching the struggles playing out in multilateral
organizations ostensibly designed to address the crisis across borders. Many
of these stories have flown under the radar but are crucial to understanding
the impact COVID-19 will continue to have on our world for years to come.

The book is divided into four parts. Part I zooms back in time to look at
the last great pandemic and its effects on world affairs. It tells the story of the
underappreciated impact the 1918–20 influenza pandemic had on the end
of World War I, President Woodrow Wilson's dreams for building a liberal
international order, and the cascading instability that followed during the interwar years. We recount this dark history because of its eerie parallels to our

current predicament—and the warnings it carries for contemporary policy makers. Part I concludes with an examination of the state of the world on the eve of COVID-19. We argue that today's once-in-a-century pandemic may prove even more consequential for international order than the last one because the coronavirus hit a world already teetering on the brink.

Part II examines national responses to the early phase of the pandemic. We describe the origins of COVID-19 in China and Beijing's efforts to pivot from its initial struggles to a position of strength on the world stage. We also discuss the Trump administration's response to the growing crisis at home and abroad. Part II then concludes with an assessment of how governments in Europe, East Asia, and elsewhere grappled with the contagion.

Part III dives deeply into the cascading crises that flowed from the pandemic. We describe the unprecedented global economic crisis set in motion by COVID-19. We examine the enormous stresses placed on the developing world and existing conflict zones. We analyze the impact of the pandemic on democracy and civil liberties around the world. And, as we do, we analyze how these aftershocks unfolded against a backdrop of accelerating geopolitical competition and floundering international cooperation.

Part IV looks at the global response to the second wave of the pandemic— a time when escalating infections around the world intersected with growing hopes that vaccines would finally bring the pandemic to an end. We conclude the book by drawing lessons from the experience of 2020, offering recommendations for American foreign policy in the post-COVID era.

The COVID crisis and the collapse of international cooperation coincided with the Trump presidency—but the old order will not be restored simply because Trump is no longer in the White House. Nationalism and geopolitical rivalry constrained and shaped the responses of governments and international organizations during the pandemic and they will continue to do so as the world moves beyond it. We have a very limited ability to change that. We can no longer assume the interests of major powers are broadly aligned, and we should not expect them to automatically work in concert with the United States to confront common challenges. Moreover, the lingering aftershocks of the pandemic will weaken key states and regions for years to come, producing new problems that will likely fragment the world further instead of unifying it.

For all these reasons, the old international order, already battered and bruised before COVID-19, is now gone. We must chart a new course that accepts the hard realities the current crisis has laid bare. America must re-engage the world and international institutions to address pandemics and other shared dangers, but it cannot invest all of its energy in responses that require unanimity. Even as we seek to reform critical organizations like the WHO, countries that have a shared commitment to transparency, accountability, and international cooperation must be willing to pool their resources and influence and move ahead on their own when they face resistance from China and other nations. Free societies must define their interests broadly enough to provide an affirmative and inclusive vision for the future—and they must stand together to fight for it.

PART I

· · · · ·

THE LAST PANDEMIC AND
THE COLLAPSE OF
INTERNATIONAL ORDER

1

The Great War, the Great Influenza, and
Great Ambitions for World Order

As MARCH TURNED to April in 1919, an unseasonable snow fell over Paris and a chill descended over the prospects for a just and lasting peace.

On April 3, the American president, Woodrow Wilson, became deathly ill, confined to his bed at the Hôtel Murat. His convulsive coughing fits, difficulty breathing, fever, and diarrhea were so severe that he was unable to move for several days. Even as the worst of Wilson's symptoms began to subside, those around the president observed notable differences in his demeanor. He tired more easily. His wits and memory faltered. He became increasingly irritated and prone to outbursts. He struggled with the ability to reason and seemed to suffer from delusions. His chief usher, Irwin "Ike" Hoover, remarked, "One thing was certain: he was never the same after this little spell of sickness."[1]

Precisely what befell Wilson remains a matter of dispute. But he was most likely stricken by the "Spanish flu," which had ravaged humanity the year before and was still rampaging through Paris in the spring of 1919. The timing of Wilson's illness—which arrived during a critical moment of negotiations aimed at building an enduring peace agreement following the devastation of World War I—could not have been worse. "The president was suddenly taken violently sick with the influenza," his personal doctor, Cary T. Grayson, wrote, "at a time when the whole of civilization seemed to be in the balance."[2]

Eleven weeks earlier, on January 18, delegations from every corner of the globe had gathered at the French Foreign Ministry at the Quai d'Orsay to open the Paris Peace Conference. Their charge was nothing less than to transform international politics—to build something better out of the ashes of the Great War, as World War I was then known. "You are assembled in order to repair the evil that it has done and to prevent a recurrence of it," French president Raymond Poincaré said in his welcoming remarks. "You hold in your hands the future of the world."[3] Harold Nicolson, a junior member of the British delegation whose treatise on the conference (*Peacemaking 1919*) remains a classic exposition on diplomacy, expressed the aspirations of many in attendance. "We were journeying to Paris, not merely to liquidate the war, but to found a new order in Europe," he wrote. "We were preparing not Peace only, but Eternal Peace."[4]

Many of these hopes and dreams were poured into the vessel of Wilson. The U.S. president was the world's most popular leader, and after years of unfathomable bloodshed he was seen by many across Europe as a savior. After a nine-day voyage on the USS *George Washington*, Wilson had arrived in the French port city of Brest on December 14, 1918. In Paris, and during brief visits to London and Rome, he was greeted by large and adoring crowds grateful for America's late but crucial entry into the war. Among the onlookers who crowded the streets to catch a glimpse of Wilson, some were still sick from influenza or were recovering from it. One such person was Private Harry Pressley, a military police officer in the American Expeditionary Forces, who had come to witness the president's arrival in Brest. He had contracted influenza in the fall, and his symptoms lingered for several months. "As my chest has remained sore, since I had the flu, it was quite hard on me," he remarked in a letter at the time. "I can hardly breathe this evening."[5] Pressley was not alone. "The war was over," the historian Alfred Crosby observes, "but Spanish influenza was not."[6] In Paris, the virus hung over the peace proceedings like Death's scythe. "There seems to be millions of throat germs going around, and a number of diplomats have lost their voices altogether," one of Wilson's aides commented. "This old world is badly germ-ridden. It is soaked with disease."[7]

Our world, too, is soaked with disease. As we grapple with the fallout from COVID-19, it is worth recalling that today's "once in a century" pandemic is not the first time that a contagion has touched people in every

corner of the globe and shaken the very foundations of international order. The 1918–20 influenza pandemic—or what the historian John Barry
dubbed "the Great Influenza"—affected the planet in profound and often
underappreciated ways. It not only killed tens of millions—it altered the
course of history. It changed the material fortunes and fates of great powers, sickened key leaders at inopportune moments, and sharpened the
underlying inequalities and grievances roiling many nations. By examining the geopolitical implications of the Great Influenza, we not only glean
insights into our past—we also gain a glimpse into our possible future.

THE GREAT WAR AND WILSON'S VISION FOR WORLD ORDER

World War I began on June 28, 1914, as a local crisis in the Balkans,
following the assassination of Archduke Franz Ferdinand and his wife
in Sarajevo. It quickly spiraled out of control: just thirty-seven days later,
the Triple Entente (France, Great Britain, and the Russian Empire) was
at war with the Central Powers (initially Germany and Austria-Hungary,
and later the Ottoman Empire and Bulgaria). Eventually, other world
powers (Italy, Japan, China, and the United States) were pulled into the
vortex, joining the Entente as Allies (or, in America's case, as an "Asso-
ciate"). The conflict was expected to be short, sharp, and decisive. It was
not. Instead, the world witnessed four grinding years of trench warfare,
poison gas, and blockades—resulting in the greatest concentration of
suffering and geopolitical upheaval to that point in human history. By
the end, tsarist Russia had been overthrown by the Bolshevik Revolution
and flung into civil war, the Austro-Hungarian and Ottoman Empires lay
in ruins, and the German Empire was defeated and dismembered.[8]

When the war first erupted in Europe, Wilson was reluctant to enter.
Although he had come close in 1915 after the infamous sinking of the
Lusitania by a German U-boat, he ultimately decided to keep the United
States neutral. During his reelection bid in 1916, Wilson even campaigned
on a platform of keeping America out of the conflict. Instead, as combatants slaughtered each other across the trenches of Europe, Wilson offered
to mediate a settlement, calling for "peace without victory." His primary
objective "was not to ensure that the 'right' side won in World War I, but
that no side did," the historian Adam Tooze notes. It was a matter of self-
interest. "Only a peace without victory . . . could ensure that the United

States emerged as the truly undisputed arbiter of world affairs."[9] Wilson also believed that any resolution to the war would prove unsustainable unless it was accepted by all sides. Any victory forced upon the loser, Wilson told the U.S. Senate in January 1917, "would be accepted in humiliation, under duress, at an intolerable sacrifice, and would leave a sting, a resentment, a bitter memory upon which terms of peace would rest, not permanently, but only as upon quicksand."[10]

Escalating German hostilities eventually posed a direct threat to U.S. interests, making it impossible for America to stay out. In early 1917, the interception of the Zimmermann telegram (a German offer to Mexico to help return territory lost in the Mexican-American War in exchange for assisting Germany against the United States) and Berlin's resumption of unrestricted submarine warfare (which threatened U.S. shipping) pushed Wilson and the U.S. Congress over the edge.

As Wilson pivoted away from neutrality, he faced the challenge of mobilizing a reluctant nation for war. In doing so, the president, a devoutly religious man, embraced a crusading tone. In his April 2, 1917, address to Congress requesting a declaration of war against Germany, Wilson told his countrymen that "the world must be made safe for democracy." He continued:

> It is a fearful thing to lead this great peaceful people into war, into the most terrible and disastrous of all wars, civilization itself seeming to be in the balance. But the right is more precious than peace, and we shall fight for the things which we have always carried nearest our hearts— for democracy, for the right of those who submit to authority to have a voice in their own governments, for the rights and liberties of small nations, for a universal dominion of right by such a concert of free peoples as shall bring peace and safety to all nations and make the world itself at last free.[11]

Once America entered the conflict, Wilson used a series of speeches to flesh out his ambitious agenda for winning the peace. He envisioned nothing less than sweeping away the old international order, dominated by multiple great powers jockeying for supremacy. After all, it was unending balance-of-power machinations that had produced the Great War and countless conflicts before it. On January 8, 1918, Wilson presented his famous "Fourteen Points," a mix of specific conditions placed on the Central Powers and broad ideals that all states needed to embrace to secure an enduring world peace. He then clarified and sup-plemented this initial framework with "Four Principles" (presented to Congress on February 11), "Four Ends" (delivered during an address at Mount Vernon on July 4), and "Five Particulars" (outlined in a speech in New York on September 27). Despite the apparent proliferation of objectives, Wilson's speeches embodied a set of common themes. These included the imperatives for free trade, freedom of the seas, and disar-mament. He called for an end to secret pacts, imperialism, and territo-rial annexation. He insisted on the realization of universal aspirations for self-determination and democratic government. And, as it related to Germany, he made clear that he was not out for revenge. His quarrel was with the atavistic militarism and autocracy embodied by Kaiser Wilhelm II's regime, not the German people, who deserved to be free from it.[12]

At the core of Wilson's vision for peace was the fourteenth of his Fourteen Points: the creation of a League of Nations, a new international mechanism for ensuring the territorial integrity and independence of all nations and for ending the threat of great-power war once and for all. The League would be designed to nurture a growing community of democ-racies, manage great-power relations, peacefully resolve disputes, and, through collective security commitments, deter armed aggression. Wil-son's plan for transforming the world was breathtaking in its ambition. He sought nothing less than to overturn the deeply ingrained system of European realpolitik—rooted in centuries of mercantilism, authoritari-anism, imperial conquest, and balance-of-power politics—and replace it with a new liberal international order.[13] He also sought to preserve some distance from the Allies, insisting on a more detached status as an Asso-ciate that would, in Tooze's words, "give him the freedom he needed to throw his weight on the scales, not behind London or Paris, but so as to restore America's role as the arbiter of global power."[14]

For Wilson, the grandness of this vision was necessary given the unprecedented destruction and human suffering unleashed by the war. Estimates suggest that around 10 million combatants were killed. Tens of millions of civilians also perished from the hostilities and, most especially, from the starvation and disease that stalked in the wake of the bloodletting.[15]

Most devastating, however, was the influenza pandemic, which struck like a thunderclap in the final year of the conflict.

THE GREAT INFLUENZA

The origins of the influenza pandemic of 1918–20 remain murky, although on some things there is consensus. It is widely accepted that the particular virus—an H1N1 subtype of influenza A that passed from birds to people—was probably around for years before it spread across the globe in 1918. There is also agreement that the "Spanish flu," as the virus was known at the time, did not originate in Spain. (The disconnect between the name and its origins appears to have been a byproduct of the fact that Spain, neutral in World War I, did not censor news of its influenza outbreak, creating the misimpression that the virus had originated there.) Beyond that, however, there remain competing views over where and how the pandemic started. One theory posits that patient zero lived in Shansi, China—a scenario eerily similar to the emergence of COVID-19 a century later. The virus then spread to Europe in 1918 as 100,000 Chinese laborers traveled to France to dig trenches and free up Allied forces for combat. Other researchers have suggested the possibility that the pandemic originated at a major Allied troop staging and hospital camp in Étaples, France. But the most widely accepted account is that the virus emerged in rural Kansas and then spread to Camp Funston in Fort Riley—a huge cantonment for U.S. troops preparing to deploy to Europe—in March 1918. From there, American soldiers brought the contagion with them to the Western Front.[16]

Whatever the flu's precise origins, the massive mobilization of U.S. workers and troops triggered by Wilson's decision to enter the war played a major role in its spreading. Millions of workers flocked to factories and cities, where inadequate housing forced them into tight quarters. Under these conditions, social distancing was an impossibility. Meanwhile, millions of other young men were crammed into military training camps, barracks, and trains, spreading the virus in their ranks and to neighboring civilian populations across North America. By May 1918, hundreds of thousands of U.S. soldiers were making their way in tightly packed troopships across the Atlantic each month, taking the flu with them to staging bases and the front lines in Europe.[17]

The pandemic swept the world in three waves. The first, comparatively mild wave spread from North America and Europe onward to Russia, North Africa, India, and China during the spring. The second, most deadly wave radiated outward from places as diverse as Freetown (Sierra Leone), Boston (United States), and Brest (France). From there, the virus again hopscotched across the planet, peaking in October and November, just as the Great War was winding down. As soldiers demobilized and returned home, superspreader events erupted around the globe as massive, packed crowds gathered to celebrate the end of the war. A third wave followed, running its course during the first half of 1919. While the disease eventually subsided in many regions, it did not completely disappear until late 1920.[8]

Unlike COVID-19, which left the very young largely unscathed while devastating older people, the influenza pandemic was indiscriminate. It did not just fell the very old; it also sickened and killed many of the very young and large numbers of people between twenty and forty years old.[19] The majority of those infected had typical flu symptoms. But for others, the virus was particularly nasty and deadly. In some people with robust immune systems (often young adults), the virus triggered an overly vigorous immune response. This could cause viral pneumonia and what we today call acute respiratory distress syndrome, visible signs of which are bluish discolorations of the skin stemming from a lack of oxygen. In other individuals, the virus created an opening for bacterial pneumonia.[20] Symptoms were sometimes so unusual and severe that the virus was misdiagnosed as dengue, cholera, or typhoid.[21]

All told, perhaps 500 million people—more than a quarter of the world's 1.8 billion people at the time—were infected during this period, with many becoming seriously ill. There were no effective therapeutic drugs or vaccines (the first influenza vaccine was not developed and authorized for use until the 1940s). Hospitals were inundated. Of those who became sick, estimates suggest that between 21 and 100 million people died, with the most widely accepted figure being 50 million fatalities—approximately 2.8 percent of the global population.

The United States was hit hard. The pandemic killed an estimated 675,000 Americans (out of a total population of around 103 million at the time). Notably, among those caught up in the first wave was Frederick Trump, the grandfather of future U.S. president Donald J. Trump, who

died from the flu in New York in May 1918 at the age of forty-nine. As the
second wave hit in the fall, the U.S. health system—already stretched thin
by the deployment of medical personnel for the war effort—was overwhelmed. In October 1918 alone, 195,000 Americans died of the virus.
The effect was so grim that average American life expectancy in 1918
was reduced by twelve years (the average for men fell from forty-eight
years to thirty-six; for women it fell from fifty-four to forty-two).[22]
As communities sought to contain the outbreak, schools, churches, and
theaters were closed, mass gatherings were banned, and measures were
taken to encourage hygiene and isolate sick individuals. Masks were mandated too, with newspapers providing instruction on how to make them
at home, and organizations such as the Red Cross distributing them.[23]
But, as with the U.S. response to COVID-19 a century later, almost all
these public health measures were initiated at the state and city levels,
and there was tremendous variation in how quickly and aggressively localities acted to contain the virus.[24]

Meanwhile, even more so than Trump in 2020, President Wilson in
1918 pretended that the pandemic did not exist. As the virus picked up
steam across America, "Wilson took no public notice of the disease, and
the thrust of the government was not diverted [from the war]," Barry
writes. "From neither the White House nor any other senior administration post would there come any leadership, any attempt to set priorities,
any attempt to deliver resources."[25] Like other warring parties, the United
States suppressed information on the toll the virus was taking on soldiers out of fear of undermining morale and support for the war effort.[26]
"So . . . the government lied," Barry notes. "National public health leaders
said things like, 'This is ordinary influenza by another name.' . . . As a
result, more people died than would have otherwise."[27]

THE VIRUS IN THE TRENCHES

It is indisputable that World War I helped to spread the virus. Less widely
recognized, however, was how crucial the pandemic would prove to be in
shaping the endgame of the war—creating aftershocks that would impact
the future of world politics for decades to come. In the conflict's final
year, death and debilitating sickness from influenza affected hundreds
of thousands of soldiers along the Western Front, undermining morale

and unit cohesion, disrupting logistics, and diverting precious attention and resources.[28] None of the warring parties was spared. But as the war reached its critical phase, the contagion fell hardest on the German army.

Beginning in March 1918, Germany's first quartermaster general, Erich von Ludendorff, launched a series of all-out offensives along the Western Front. After years of attrition, Ludendorff hoped to take advantage of Russia's withdrawal from the war following the February 1918 signing of the Treaty of Brest-Litovsk. Germany shifted more than forty divisions—roughly 1 million men and 3,000 guns—from the east to the west. By the spring, Germany outnumbered Allied divisions 191 to 178. It was a risky gamble. But Ludendorff saw it as Germany's best shot to deal a decisive blow against exhausted British and French troops before the United States could fully deploy its forces in the field.[29]

The aggressive tactics initially showed significant progress. In a war where military progress was often measured in feet, the Germans gained dozens of miles as they pushed west against British and French forces. At one point they came within artillery range, and a three days' march, of Paris. But by June the German offensives had stalled. Then a final make-or-break German push in July failed. Although the fighting would continue until November, July was the moment when the once-formidable German army cracked and the tide of the war irrevocably turned. American reinforcements were arriving en masse and the Allies counterattacked, driving back overstretched and increasingly demoralized German forces. In early August, as the Allies kicked off what was later known as the "Hundred Days Offensive," Ludendorff admitted to himself that the war was lost and the end near.[30] When asked by the kaiser what had happened, Ludendorff told him that German troops had lost their will to fight. They were too exhausted. And they were too sick.[31]

In his memoir of the war, Ludendorff pointed to the influenza pandemic as a major factor in Germany's reversal of fortunes. "Our army had suffered. Influenza was rampant," he later wrote about the summer offensives. "It was grievous business having to listen every morning to the chiefs of staffs' recital of the numbers of influenza cases, and their complaints about the weakness of their troops." Indeed, in Ludendorff's estimation, the effects extended beyond the immediate death toll or temporary removal of sickened forces from the battlefield. Even after the number of German influenza cases began to decline, "it often left a greater weakness in its wake than the doctors realized." He complained about the morale of his troops, "already weakened by influenza and depressed by the uniform diet." And in assessing the failure of the July offensive, Germany's last shot at winning the war, Ludendorff pointed to the "diminished strength of the divisions, the result partly of influenza."[32]

It would be easy to dismiss these claims as an excuse for Ludendorff's own considerable failures. Moreover, since the pandemic affected all sides, even some historians who take the flu seriously have downplayed its importance in shaping the final outcome of the war.[33] But a close look at the available evidence reveals that influenza did *not* affect all the combatants equally or at the same time. The German army suffered more and, crucially, bore the brunt of the contagion earlier. As the American military historian David Zabecki observes, the pandemic, which initially spread among Allied forces, "hit the Germans [in June]—except much harder because of the inferior German diet and their strained medical system."[34] The political scientist Andrew Price-Smith notes that "the pathogen-induced destruction was so profound, and the German physicians and nurses so overwhelmed by the dead and dying, that they were unable to keep track of the mortality as the first wave of the pandemic struck."[35] Thousands of men in each army division were afflicted during this period, and the trench strength of companies was significantly reduced.[36] In June and July, at least half a million soldiers—approximately a third of the total fighting force Germany had at the beginning of the spring offensive—were affected by influenza.[37] Given how overstretched their forces were across the Western Front at this critical juncture, the army could not afford that level of sickness in its ranks. All told, estimates suggest that between 700,000 and 1.75 million German soldiers were affected by influenza in 1918. Morbidity rates ranged from 16 to 80 percent of troops, depending on the unit, and the overall morbidity rate among German forces in 1918 was 683 percent higher than it was during the first year of the war. The army's medical service simply could not cope, and many less seriously injured or afflicted soldiers took the opportunity to go home. Demoralization, desertions, and shirking of duties mounted, and discipline collapsed.[38]

The impact was felt far beyond the trenches. Influenza also devastated German civilians, especially during the deadly second wave in the fall of

1918. The population had been primed for a public health disaster by the Allied blockade of foodstuffs, which left the average person with a poorer diet than even their underfed countrymen on the front lines.[39] As a consequence, in October and November, the country experienced its highest levels of civilian mortality of the entire war.[40] Mounting misery and the army's defeat created a social tipping point. Mutinies and mass unrest left the kaiser's abdication and the transition to a republic as the only means of restoring political stability.

The other Central Powers were unraveling as well. With the stunning failure of Ludendorff's offensives, the writing was on the wall. Meanwhile, pressures were growing at home to give up the fight. Here too, the pandemic may have played a role. Austria-Hungary was slammed by the Great Influenza in October and November 1918. The multinational empire was already under considerable strain after years of war and mounting demands from labor movements and ethnic minorities—demands exacerbated by the 1917 Russian Revolution and Wilson's support for national self-determination—and within two weeks of the final wave of influenza hitting Vienna, the empire collapsed. "It is quite certain that influenza was not the sole agent responsible for the dissolution of the empire," Price-Smith writes. "However, the influenza pandemic undoubtedly functioned as a powerful stressor to shatter the rotten and tottering foundations of the institutions of the empire, which had been successfully eroded by years of war."[41]

Of course, the flu affected the Allied war effort as well. One U.S. War Department report, for example, calculated that 340,000 members of the American Expeditionary Forces were hospitalized for influenza during 1918, roughly equal to the number of those wounded in combat on the Western Front that year. During the climax of the U.S. military surge into Europe in September, October, and November, 25 to 40 percent of soldiers in American training camps were hospitalized and 30,000 died before they ever made it to France.[42] The spread of the flu among U.S. troops was so pernicious by the fall that the draft was temporarily suspended in October as training bases were quarantined.[43] The British reported a similar number of sickened forces (around 313,000) in 1918. The total number of sickened French troops is less clear, but it was certainly greater than 100,000 and perhaps considerably so. In terms of deaths among Allied troops, Price-Smith estimates that the ratio of influenza fatalities to combat deaths was 1:1 for the Americans, 1:10 for the British, and 1:6 for the French during this period.[44]

In terms of the war's outcome, however, timing was everything. Available data suggests that influenza affected only tens of thousands of Allied troops during the critical May–July 1918 timeframe, compared with the hundreds of thousands of German soldiers stricken with the virus during that period. The brunt of the contagion's impact on British, French, and American forces occurred in the fall of 1918.[45] But by then the war was already won.

On September 29, 1918, the German Supreme Army Command informed the kaiser that the military situation on the Western Front was hopeless and that Germany needed to sue for peace. Ludendorff recommended the acceptance of Wilson's Fourteen Points as the starting point for negotiations. On October 5, the German government sent a message to Wilson to negotiate terms on those grounds. Wilson responded with a series of conditions, including the retreat of German forces from occupied territories, the end of submarine attacks, and—most critically— democratic regime change. Wilson made clear that he would be accommodating if the kaiser abdicated and Germany transitioned to a constitutional democracy. If not, he "must demand not peace negotiations, but surrender."[46]

Ludendorff bristled and contemplated a return to war. But it was too late. The kaiser fled to exile in the Netherlands on November 9, and Germany transitioned to a de facto democracy under a new civilian government. (What came to be known as the Weimar Republic was formally created the following year.) The new German government agreed to an armistice on November 11. By then, the other Central Powers had all separately sued for peace: Bulgaria in September, the Ottomans at the end of October, and Austria-Hungary at the beginning of November.

The Allies were shocked by this turn of events. Many had assumed the war would drag on until the summer of 1919, when American forces flowing to Europe were expected to reach their peak. Even as the Central Powers signaled their willingness to stop, there were voices on the Allied side pushing to continue the fight to ensure total surrender, including U.S. general John J. Pershing. But there were compelling factors pushing in the opposite direction, not the least of which was the impact of the influenza pandemic, which Hew Strachan, a professor of international relations at the University of St. Andrews, notes "was a material factor in the [Allied] armies' fitness to fight."[47]

Celebrations rang out across the globe as the armistices came into effect. The mass gatherings served to worsen the second wave of the influenza pandemic, but it was impossible to contain the outpouring of joy at the apparent end of a calamitous war. The arrangements with the Central Powers, however, were essentially fragile cease-fires. Crafting something more durable would be the mission Wilson and other world leaders would turn to in Paris.

WILSON AND THE GERMAN QUESTION

Influenza was still burning through the City of Light as foreign delegations arrived, with a few thousand Parisians dying each month as talks got under way. And as the virus crept into the inner sanctum of the negotiations, it would end up having a crucial impact on the outcome.

Invitations to the Paris Peace Conference had been sent to every country that could plausibly claim to be on the Allied side. More than thirty countries and nationalities showed up, although some major players were left out. Russia, an original member of the Triple Entente, was not invited because the new Soviet government had signed a separate peace deal with Germany a year earlier. There were no German representatives present either, largely due to concerns that they might exploit competing aims among the Allies.

Initially, the Council of Ten (so named because there were two delegates each from France, Great Britain, Italy, Japan, and the United States) met to shape the terms of the peace. But the most consequential deliberations happened between the "big four": French prime minister Georges Clemenceau, British prime minister David Lloyd George, Italian prime minister Vittorio Emanuele Orlando, and Woodrow Wilson. These four men met 145 times over the course of six months to decide the peace terms that were later presented to the assembled delegations from the "minor powers."

During the first three months of the conference, Wilson proved effective in advancing his agenda, most notably in getting agreement on his number one priority: the terms for the new League of Nations. Things became more contentious, however, as the Allies turned to the thorniest issue: what to do with German territory and colonies, and what to demand in terms of reparations and acceptance of responsibility for the war.

Wilson and Clemenceau were at loggerheads over the specific conditions to impose on Germany, clashing over Germany's borders and its responsibility to pay reparations to the Allies for war damages. Wilson had promised "peace without victory," but Clemenceau's primary objective was to ensure France's security by leaving Germany permanently weakened, both militarily and economically. Lloyd George, meanwhile, sought compromises between the two that would protect Britain's imperial interests and its desires for a continental balance of power. In pushing back against French and British demands on reparations, Wilson emphasized the importance of standing on principle. He told Lloyd George that "nothing would be finer than to be put out of office during a crisis of this kind for doing what was right." Wilson continued: "I could not wish a more magnificent place in history."[48]

On March 27, Wilson's physician, Dr. Grayson, recorded observations of the negotiations in his diary: "The situation continued [to be] extremely complicated because of the fact that the French were maintaining an attitude of bitter obstruction on the program suggested by the President." Asked by Grayson how the talks were going, Wilson expressed great frustration, saying, "After arguing with Clemenceau for two hours and pushing him along, he practically agreed to everything, and just as he was leaving he swung back to where he had begun." Grayson noted that Wilson had warned his colleagues that an unjust peace would "simply sow the seed for a further war and engender bitterness that would be hard to overcome later on."[49] By the end of March, talks were at an impasse and Wilson was fed up with the French premier's maximalism.[50] On April 2, Wilson told his press secretary, Ray Stannard Baker, that "we've got to make peace on the principles laid down and accepted, or not make it at all."[51]

The next evening, Wilson fell ill.

In a series of events that seemed to foreshadow the coronavirus outbreak in the Trump White House in 2020, Wilson was just one of many in his inner circle who were stricken. Wilson's closest advisor, "Colonel" Edward House, had contracted influenza three times, most recently in January as the peace conference got under way. Wilson's daughter Margaret contracted the flu in February, and in March, Wilson's wife, Edith, and a number of his staff were ill. Now the American president too was sick.[52]

Clemenceau, who barely survived an assassination attempt in February, had also been suffering from "colds" (perhaps the flu) ever since. In his case, it left the prime minister no less stubborn in pushing for French demands.[53] Wilson's condition, however, was much graver and its effects on the negotiations more profound. He was stuck in his sickbed for four and a half days. "In his absence," the historian Margaret MacMillan writes, "much of the groundwork had been laid for the subsequent agreements."[54] On April 6, Wilson told Dr. Grayson from his sickbed that he feared the consequences for the world if the French were "allowed to have their way and secure all that they claim France is entitled to."[55] He considered departing the conference early and sailing home rather than caving to French demands, but he remained. When Wilson finally returned to negotiations on April 8 (conducted at his bedside), he was notably depleted. The illness appeared to have weakened his faculties and softened his resolve.[56]

Over the coming days, an agreement on the basic German questions was reached. Wilson acceded to the imposition of onerous reparations on Germany without specifying a maximum amount. He agreed that the Rhineland would be demilitarized and occupied by Allied troops for fifteen years. The industrialized Saar Basin would be administered by the League of Nations—an organization Germany would initially be excluded from—and the valuable Saar coal mines would be awarded to France. All told, under the terms Wilson agreed to, Germany would lose 13 percent of its European territory and one-tenth of its population. It would also be stripped of its colonial possessions. Meanwhile, the German army and navy were reduced to rump forces, and the country was forbidden to have an air force, tanks, poison gas, and a general staff. The language in the Treaty of Versailles, which codified these agreements, also included what came to be known as the "war guilt clause," which read: "The Allied and Associated Governments affirm and Germany accepts the responsibility of Germany and her allies for causing all the loss and damage . . . as a consequence of the war imposed upon them by the aggression of Germany and her allies."[57]

"The terms of the peace appear immeasurably harsh and humiliating, while many of them are incapable of performance," Robert Lansing, the

U.S. secretary of state—who was sidelined for much of the negotiations in Paris—wrote in a memorandum at the time.[58] The famous economist John Maynard Keynes, who attended the Paris Peace Conference as senior British treasury advisor, argued in a 1919 assessment of the negotiations that Wilson wilted—that his vision of a just end to the war had been overtaken by Clemenceau's "Carthaginian Peace."[59] This may be a bit unfair to Wilson. All sides, including France, compromised. Nevertheless, Wilson bent considerably further and, as Barry observes, "suddenly abandoned principles he had previously insisted on."[60] About a dozen junior members of the American delegation resigned in protest. Among them was William C. Bullitt. In an open letter explaining his resignation, Bullitt rebuked Wilson directly. "That you personally opposed most of the unjust settlements, and that you accepted them only under great pressure, is well known," Bullitt wrote. "I am sorry that you did not fight our fight to the finish."[61]

Why did Wilson fold? It impossible to know for sure, but his deteriorating health appears to have been an important factor. By the end of the negotiations on the German issue, Wilson was a shadow of his former self. "I have never seen the President look so worn & tired," his press secretary, Baker, wrote. "He could not remember without an effort what the council had done in the forenoon."[62] Lloyd George noted the American president's "nervous and spiritual breakdown in the middle of the Conference."[63] And Wilson himself admitted to his wife during this period, "If I have lost the fight, which I would not have done had I been on my feet, I will retire in good order."[64]

The ripple effects from Wilson's compromises would be felt for decades. Nicolson, the young British diplomat, called the president's "collapse" at the Paris Peace Conference "one of the major tragedies of modern history."[65] The Germans had quit the war under the assumption that the peace would be guided by Wilson's Fourteen Points. They put a lot of faith (perhaps too much) in Wilson's ability to ensure that the peace terms would be mild and fair. And they especially believed themselves worthy of lesser penalties since they willingly acceded to the American president's demand for democratic regime change. In this context, Wilson's apparent capitulation was seen as a betrayal. "Where Wilson had been seen to this point as Germany's savior," MacMillan writes, "he overnight became the wicked hypocrite."[66] Indeed, Crosby concludes, more was done during the period immediately following the president's bout of influenza "to convince Wilson's most fervent admirers, in general, and Germans, in particular, that he was a traitor to his own principles . . . than in all the rest of the peace conference."[67]

The Paris Peace Conference changed the world. In addition to establishing the League of Nations, the Allies redrew the maps of Europe, the Middle East, Africa, and Asia. New national boundaries were created. Newly independent countries emerged from the wreckage of collapsed empires. And German and Ottoman overseas colonies were divvied up (mostly to Britain and France, but also, in the important case of China's Shandong Peninsula, to Japan). The conference also resulted in five treaties with the defeated Central Powers. The most consequential was the Treaty of Versailles, which was presented to Germany as a fait accompli and ultimately signed on June 28, 1919. In retrospect, historians now argue that the actual costs imposed on Berlin by the treaty were lower than many Germans believed. But perception, not reality, proved decisive.[68] The greatest legacy of the effort to forge a lasting peace would be a litany of German grievances and a deep reservoir of humiliation that would come back to haunt Europe and the world over the next twenty years.

The Germans were not the only ones disillusioned. Coming full circle on his idealistic hopes at the outset of the peace negotiations, Nicolson reflected:

> We came to Paris confident that the new order was about to be established; we left it convinced that the new order had merely fouled the old. We arrived as fervent apprentices in the school of President Wilson: we left as renegades. . . . We arrived determined that a Peace of justice and wisdom should be negotiated: we left it, conscious that the Treaties imposed on our enemies were neither just nor wise.[69]

BITTERNESS AND REVENGE

In the aftermath of the Weimar Republic's acquiescence to the Treaty of Versailles, an insidious conspiracy theory took hold in Germany, especially in military circles, to explain the country's shocking defeat. Germany had not been bested in battle, the theory went, but rather "stabbed in the back" by traitors at home. General Ludendorff, a champion of this myth, argued that Marxists, democrats, Jews, and other internal enemies had shattered the resolve of the German people, robbing the army of the victory it (and he) had fought so hard to achieve. Of course, this was all a convenient and particularly vile lie. An influenza-ravaged German army had been vanquished in the field. Military defeat, in turn, had contributed to revolution and democratic regime change at home—not the other way around.[70]

Among the most ardent subscribers to (and eventual peddlers of) the stab-in-the-back narrative was Corporal Adolf Hitler. The Austrian-born Hitler had enlisted in the German army in August 1914, enthusiastically taking part in some of the most ferocious fighting on the Western Front. In the final month of the war, he was wounded by a British mustard gas shell in Belgium. As the future Führer recovered in the Pasewalk military hospital, he learned of Germany's surrender. He later described his sense of betrayal as a formative moment. "I brought back home with me my experience at the front," Hitler recalled, and "out of them I built my National Socialist community."[71] As Ian Kershaw, perhaps the most authoritative biographer of Hitler, notes, "From the following year onwards, his entire political activity was driven by the trauma of 1918—aimed at expunging the defeat and revolution which had betrayed all that he believed in, and eliminating those he held responsible."[72]

Soon Hitler rose from obscurity to infamy. After the Great War, he became an increasingly prominent propagandist and beer-hall agitator in extreme right-wing circles. In 1921, he was chosen as the leader of the National Socialist German Workers' (Nazi) Party, which had been founded the previous year. In 1923, he took his first gamble for power. Against the backdrop of French and Belgian troops occupying the industrial Ruhr Valley in response to a dispute over German reparations payments and hyperinflation sweeping the country, Hitler joined with Ludendorff and other right-wing officers in a failed coup attempt in Munich. The "Beer Hall Putsch," as the revolt came to be known, was quashed. Ludendorff was acquitted, but Hitler was convicted of treason and sent to Landsberg Prison, where he dictated his autobiography and manifesto, *Mein Kampf* ("My Struggle"), outlining his genocidal views and expansionist ambitions.

Upon Hitler's release a mere nine months later, he reasserted his leadership over the Nazi Party and went to work to grow it into a mass

movement. The 1930 federal election, coming a year after Germany's economy was devastated by the shock of the Great Depression, made the Nazis
the second-largest party in the Reichstag, the German parliament. Two
years later, the Nazis became the largest party, although they still lacked
a majority. In January 1933, President Paul von Hindenburg named Hitler chancellor. Shortly after assuming the chancellorship, Hitler exploited
the February 1933 burning of the Reichstag to dismantle what was left of
German democracy. By the following summer, the Weimar Republic was
dead, replaced by the Third Reich: a fascist, one-party dictatorship with
Hitler as Führer.

As Hitler rose to prominence and power, he stirred the passions of an
increasingly desperate German populace by weaving together themes of
national victimization and racial superiority. The country's defeat, revolution, and rapid democratization had created space after World War I for
these ideas to grow. Germany's economic troubles in the 1920s and the
disaster of the Great Depression accelerated their appeal as the German
people looked for scapegoats to understand their predicaments.[73] Hitler
also rode to power on the backs of German industrialists, the press, aris-
tocrats, and disgruntled army officers who hoped to use him as a vehicle
to unshackle Germany from the Treaty of Versailles.[74]

In Hitler's mind, Jews, communists, and the "November Criminals"
(the civilians who led the democratic revolution against the kaiser and
then signed the November 1918 armistice) were responsible for Germany's plight. So too were the harsh terms of the Treaty of Versailles, which
he portrayed as falsely pinning the Great War on Germany, extracting
unjust reparations, stealing German land, and emasculating the country's patriotic armed forces. And in presenting this stream of injustices,
he made no secret of his willingness to take Germany to war again to
rectify them. "The day must come when the German government shall
summon up the courage to declare to foreign powers: 'The Treaty of Versailles is founded on a monstrous lie,'" Hitler told an audience in Munich in 1923. "We fulfill nothing more. Do what you will! If you want
battle, look for it!"[75] As chancellor, he blamed the treaty, especially its
demand for onerous reparations, for the country's economic hardships.
"All the problems which are causing such unrest today," he declared to
the Reichstag on May 17, 1933, "lie in the deficiencies of the treaty of
peace."[76] Eight years later, with the world once again at war and Hitler the

self-proclaimed Führer, he told 20,000 onlookers in Berlin: "No human being has declared or recorded what he wanted more than I. Again and again I wrote these words: 'The abolition of the Treaty of Versailles.'"[77]

There were many causes of Germany's descent into fascism, and one would be hard pressed to find historical accounts that would list the Great Influenza among them. Yet key effects of the influenza pandemic— from its role in Germany's defeat in World War I to the humiliating terms of the Treaty of Versailles agreed to by a sickened Woodrow Wilson in Paris—helped set in motion a chain of events that made the country more susceptible to Hitler's twisted vision. "Without the unique conditions in which he came to prominence, Hitler would have been nothing," his biographer Kershaw writes. "It is hard to imagine him bestriding the stage of history at any other time."[78]

What was true in Germany was true elsewhere. As we will see in the next chapter, the consequences of the 1918–20 influenza pandemic would continue to be felt for years to come.

Ripples Through Time

HISTORY UNFOLDS AT the intersection of underlying conditions, contingent moments, and human choices. This was apparent in the two decades following the Great War and the Great Influenza, commonly referred to as the "interwar years"—one of the most turbulent and consequential periods in modern times. The events of the interwar period are worth reflecting upon. As we saw in Chapter 1, the Great Influenza demonstrated the potential for global pandemics to shape international order by undermining the material capabilities of key states and by producing contingent historical events, such as the illness of Woodrow Wilson, that ripple through time. In the immediate postwar period, the hangover from the pandemic was not the sole—or in many cases the primary—driver of world events. But the contagion continued to produce important consequences across the international system. In particular, it laid bare, accelerated, and magnified the impact of underlying forces between and within countries, straining economies, worsening inequality, and contributing to social and political unrest. In so doing, the aftershocks of the influenza pandemic made an already tumultuous and conflict-prone world even more unstable.

As the 1920s and 1930s marched on, the geopolitical impact of the Great Influenza became harder to discern. And yet this history is no less important to consider in our current moment, because many of the factors that made the world so volatile, crisis-prone, and dangerous during the interwar period—mounting inequality, widespread civil strife, rising populism and xenophobia, growing economic nationalism and pressures to deglobalize, resurgent authoritarianism, backsliding democracy, escalating great-power rivalry, American retreat, brittle international institutions, and a free world in disarray—were *already* reemerging in our time during the years immediately before the coronavirus pandemic struck. And, as we detail in Parts II and III of this book, COVID-19 and the shock waves flowing from it have made all these problems worse.

As the coronavirus accelerates these preexisting conditions for global disarray, the interwar years offer a cautionary tale of just how bad things could get—and highlight the urgent need to change course. In particular, we see how easily international order can break down, with disastrous implications, when the world's leading democracies—and the United States in particular—fail to stand together in managing crises and confronting common challenges before it is too late.

WILSON AND THE DEFEAT OF THE LEAGUE

On June 29, 1919, Woodrow Wilson departed for his final Atlantic voyage, arriving in Hoboken, New Jersey, on July 8. Large, cheering crowds greeted him as his motorcade journeyed through New York City, and when Wilson's train arrived at Union Station in Washington, DC, at midnight that evening, an estimated 100,000 people were there to witness his return.

On July 10, Wilson held a press conference in the East Room of the White House, assuring the assembled media that he could secure the two-thirds majority of the Senate needed to ratify the Treaty of Versailles and the covenant for the League of Nations it contained. Wilson then formally delivered the treaty to the Senate. The world expected the United States to "make the triumph of freedom and right a lasting triumph," he told the senators. He then asked: "Dare we reject it and break the heart of the world?"[1] Wilson's rhetoric was no exaggeration, as the economic historian Adam Tooze writes, for "both the victors and the vanquished looked to the United States as the pivot of the new order."[2]

The president's confidence in ratification proved unfounded. Three factions within the Senate quickly emerged. At one end were internationalists, including most of Wilson's fellow Democrats, who favored deeper

U.S. engagement with the world and therefore supported the treaty. At the other end of the spectrum were the "irreconcilables," a modest-sized isolationist group composed mostly of Republicans plus a few Democrats, who opposed the treaty. The largest faction included strong and mild "reservationists" positioned somewhere in the middle. Led by the chair of the Senate Committee on Foreign Relations, Henry Cabot Lodge, these were mostly Republicans, plus a handful of Democrats; they would consider ratification, but only with caveats clarifying America's interpretations and obligations under the treaty. Laced through the debate among these factions were strong disagreements over several issues: national sovereignty; the implications of America's long-standing foreign policy traditions of exceptionalism, unilateralism, and aloofness from great-power matters; and the appropriate balance of executive and legislative power. Deep partisanship and bitter personal rivalries were also at work.

Among the major reservations to the Treaty of Versailles and the League covenant, three stood out. One involved the ceding of China's Shandong Peninsula (controlled by Germany) to Japan. In Paris, Japan had pushed for the inclusion of a statement of racial equality in the League covenant, but, as the historian John Cooper notes, "Wilson had bowed to his own country's and British white supremacist sentiments and vetoed the proposal."[3] Fearing that this decision might prompt Japan to refuse to join the League altogether, Wilson, who was still recovering from the flu, caved to Tokyo's demand to take possession of Shandong.[4] But given his stated opposition to imperialism and his defense of self-determination, the move opened the president up to scathing charges of hypocrisy at home. A second criticism centered on the fact that the League covenant allowed for separate votes for five of Britain's dominions (Australia, Canada, India, New Zealand, and South Africa), which gave the British Empire six votes in the League Assembly (although not in the League's decision-making body, the Council).

The strongest reservation, however, concerned the collective security obligations under Article X of the League covenant. These committed the United States, like all other members, to preserve the territorial independence and political autonomy of other countries, including through the possible use of military force. Irreconcilables saw this not only as an egregious violation of American sovereignty but as firmly at odds with the country's long-standing tradition, first articulated in George

Washington's Farewell Address, of staying out of foreign entanglements. Among those reservationists who could support the notion of collective security, the main concern was that Article X seemed to bypass Congress's sole authority under the U.S. Constitution to declare war.

Frustrated by opposition and the insistence of many senators on significant reservations, Wilson decided to take his case directly to the American people by arranging a cross-country tour.[5] In doing so, he overruled the advice of his personal physician, Dr. Grayson, who worried about the president's fragile disposition.[6] Wilson's health had failed him in Paris, and it would soon put his entire presidency in jeopardy. But he was insistent that he must present his case for the League to the public.

Wilson's train departed from Washington on September 3. Over the next three weeks, he crisscrossed the nation, giving forty speeches. His orations provided a passionate defense of the League and the liberal international order it represented, a point-by-point rebuttal to the main criticisms emerging in the Senate, and stark warnings of what would happen if America abandoned its commitment. Throughout, Wilson frequently invoked the dark specter of another global conflagration. Five days into his journey, in Omaha, Wilson made what would turn out to be a tragically accurate prediction. He told his audience that while there was "no absolute guarantee" against war if the United States joined the League, "I can predict with absolute certainty that, within another generation, there will be another world war if the nations of the world—if the League of Nations—does not prevent it by concerted effort."[7]

From the outset of the trip, Wilson's health was an issue. He suffered constantly from headaches and periodically from breathing troubles and extreme coughing fits, which his doctor described as "asthma attacks." By September 25, Wilson's health had deteriorated to the point that Grayson recommended canceling the remaining five stops of the trip. "The Doctor is right," Wilson told a close aide; "I have never been in a condition like this, and I just feel as if I am going to pieces."[8] Back in Washington a week later, in the early hours of October 2, Wilson suffered a massive stroke. It left him partially paralyzed down his left side and partially blind in his right eye, and he would end up disabled for the rest of his life. Looking back, it appears Wilson had an underlying neurological condition and may have suffered a series of mini-strokes over the course of several years. His case of influenza in Paris, in turn, may have triggered additional mini-strokes in the spring and summer, and the flu certainly made him more susceptible to the massive stroke that befell him in October.[9] "Although he would make a limited recovery over time," the historian Margaret MacMillan concludes, "he was not physically or mentally the man he had been. And while he continued to influence the debate in the Senate from his sickroom, Wilson never effectively functioned as president again."[10]

In Wilson's absence, the Senate debated numerous amendments and reservations. A vote on treaty ratification was eventually scheduled, including a package of fourteen reservations put forward by Lodge and the Foreign Relations Committee. (The number fourteen was somewhat ironic given Wilson's famous Fourteen Points.) Wilson issued a written statement from his sickbed arguing that the reservations essentially reflected a "nullification" of the treaty, and asked Democrats in the Senate to oppose them. The vote on ratification with reservations occurred on November 19. It was decisively defeated 39–55, with irreconcilables joining all but four Democrats in voting against. A vote on ratification without reservations then followed—and it too was defeated, 38–53, with only one Republican joining the majority of Democrats in support of unconditional approval.[11]

The issue was not yet settled, however. Four weeks after Wilson's initial defeat, he won the Nobel Peace Prize. Meanwhile, on Capitol Hill, the Senate continued to negotiate over the treaty. Strong reservations persisted, especially over the League's collective security provisions. Among those voicing concerns was Senator Warren G. Harding, who would go on to be elected U.S. president in November 1920. "Let us hesitate before we surrender the nationality which is the very soul of highest Americanism," Harding told his audience at the Ohio Society of New York on January 20. In doing so, he weaponized a phrase—"America First"—that Wilson himself had pioneered as a slogan in 1916 to claim credit for keeping the United States out of World War I. Harding insisted on the imperative to "safeguard America first, to stabilize America first, to prosper America first, to think of America first, to exalt America first, to live for and revere America first."[12] ("America First" would also be embraced by the isolationist movement in 1940, as we will see, and much later by the Republican U.S. presidential candidate Pat Buchanan in the 1990s and Donald Trump in the 2016 presidential campaign.)

At the same time, the opportunity for a possible compromise arose. A growing number of Democrats contemplated breaking ranks with Wilson, increasing the prospect for bipartisan agreement on softening the reservations somewhat, and potentially paving the way for ratification. Wilson's wife, Edith, his closest personal aides, and his secretary of state, Robert Lansing, all urged the president to accept some form of the deal as the last, best chance of salvaging American participation in the League. Meanwhile, Sir Edward Grey, who had served as British foreign secretary from 1905 to 1916, suggested that the Allies would understand U.S. reservations, even if they did not like them. If Wilson had followed this collective advice and compromised, Cooper writes, "he could have brokered a settlement that would have resolved the conflict differently."[13] But he would not.

In Paris the previous spring, influenza had taken Wilson away from negotiations for several days at a critical moment and, thereafter, appeared to have weakened his resolve to stand by his principles on the German question in the face of French demands. His stroke had a different effect. It was more debilitating, leaving him unable to engage in negotiations with the Senate for a month and, then, removing him from physical contact with all but a handful of participants in the talks. Physiologically, the stroke left Wilson incapable of adapting to changing circumstances and making sound political judgments. As his physical condition gradually improved, Wilson became increasingly prone to a kind of "euphoria" common among recovering stroke patients, which left him delusional about the prospects of achieving his objectives without the need for any accommodation. At other times, he suffered from mood swings and depression, often triggered by recurring bouts of the flu in January and February 1920. Ultimately, as Cooper concludes, "his condition rendered him incapable of compromise."[14]

In the absence of any presidential accommodation, another Senate vote was held on March 19, 2020, to ratify the treaty with essentially the same fourteen reservations as the previous fall. This time, in a sign of how far Wilson's fellow Democrats were willing to move, the vote was 49 in favor and 35 against (the official tally was 57–39, which accounted for the announced positions of a dozen absentees). There was now majority support for ratification with reservations—but it fell seven votes short of the two-thirds majority required. With his options in the Senate exhausted, Wilson was forced to concede defeat, though he was convinced he would be vindicated by history. The United States would not be joining the League.

AMERICA ON FIRE

As Wilson debated the future of world order with the Senate, the rest of the nation roiled. The U.S. economy experienced back-to-back recessions, a shock in 1918–19 that the country rapidly rebounded from in the second half of 1919, and then another in 1920–21, which stands as one of the deepest U.S. recessions on record (comparable in some ways to the severity of the Great Depression, albeit much shorter, and considerably sharper than the contraction experienced by Americans during the 2008–9 financial crisis). The pandemic played a role in the first recession, perhaps reducing U.S. gross domestic product (GDP) by about 1.5 percent, but not in the second.[15] Compared to the economic dislocation produced by COVID-19 a century later, the Great Influenza appears to have had a lesser impact on the U.S. economy, in part because a century ago far fewer Americans worked in jobs that required close social contact. The absence of widespread sick leave and unemployment insurance also meant that even workers who were ill could not afford to stay home, and many nonessential businesses stayed open.[16] Despite these important differences, there were also some similarities. One recent study found that in 1918–19, the contagion depressed the American economy through both supply-side and demand-side effects in the form of reduced productivity, labor shortages, and falling demand for retail goods. Contemporary newspaper accounts suggested that numerous sectors of the economy were adversely affected by the influenza pandemic, including coal and copper mining, shipbuilding, textile production, wholesale and (to a lesser extent) retail trade, and entertainment. It is also noteworthy, given controversies over COVID-19 lockdowns, that U.S. cities that took more aggressive public health interventions to contain the pandemic, such as Oakland, California, and Omaha, Nebraska, appear to have performed better economically than those that did not, including Philadelphia, Pennsylvania, and St. Paul, Minnesota.[17]

In 1919, the postwar, post-flu economic downturn unleashed a remarkable year of labor and racial unrest. Organized labor had grown in strength over the course of World War I, and afterward many unions demanded recognition, shorter hours, and wage increases to compensate for high food prices and inflation. In 1919, there were 3,300 strikes involving coal miners, textile workers, steelworkers, and others. All told, 4 million Americans—approximately one-fifth of the workforce—went on strike that year, one of the largest waves of labor agitation the country had ever experienced.[18]

Racial tensions also burned bright. Wartime production needs had sparked a boom in manufacturing, and those new jobs needed new workers. This contributed to the Great Migration of half a million African Americans from the rural South to cities in the North and Midwest during World War I (all told, around 1 million migrated between 1910 and 1920). The Black population in cities such as Chicago, Cleveland, Detroit, New York, and Philadelphia grew dramatically. When the war ended, many white servicemen came home to a recession, and many of the jobs they had left in factories, warehouses, and mills had been filled by newly arrived African Americans. Business owners also found it useful to employ Black laborers, who were willing to work for lower pay, to break strikes, undercut wages, and sow tensions within unions. Competition for jobs and housing mixed with deeply ingrained racist attitudes to create flashpoints for violence.[19]

The pandemic became intertwined with racial stereotypes and grievance as well. Historically, African Americans had been more susceptible to getting sick and dying from respiratory diseases. This was certainly true during the COVID-19 pandemic, in which Black Americans were much more likely to become infected and twice as likely to die as whites from the disease. But the picture was somewhat different during the influenza pandemic. Available data from the time suggests that African Americans were less likely to get sick during the pandemic, and consequently fewer Blacks died as a percentage of the population than whites. The cause for this disparity remains uncertain. But whatever the reason, case fatality rates (the proportion of deaths compared to the total number of people diagnosed with the disease) were still higher for Blacks. In other words, African Americans were generally less likely to get the flu, but those individuals who did were more likely to die from it (and associated pneumonia) than whites. This was likely a consequence of poorer living conditions and inadequate, highly segregated health care systems—systems that were quickly overwhelmed even by the lower levels of influenza emerging in Black communities.[20]

The lower overall rate of influenza among African Americans was observed and reported upon at the time, although more often by prominent Black newspapers such as the *Chicago Defender* and *Baltimore Afro-American* than by the mainstream press. This did nothing to derail widely held racist theories about the biological inferiority of Black people or overturn racist stereotypes that African American communities represented disease threats to whites.[21] In places such as Chicago, where some of the worst racial violence in 1919 transpired, Black migrants from the South had for years been portrayed as carriers of contagious disease. In that context, reported disparities in cases of the flu perversely exacerbated racial tension and added to the argument for segregation as a public health measure. "Even though African Americans were not carrying the deadly influenza virus," the historian Elizabeth Schlabach writes, "their bodies became the metaphorical vessels of transmission, and, therefore, in the eyes of whites African Americans were worthy of punishment and physical acts of violence."[22]

Beginning on April 13, lynchings and anti-Black mob violence in Jenkins County, Georgia, kicked off a rolling wave of anti-Black violence across the South, the Midwest, and the North, as well as in the nation's capital. Over eight intense months, targeted killings surged, at least fifty-two Blacks were lynched, and there were more than two dozen race riots and mob actions across the country. Small towns, entire counties, and large urban areas alike were swept up in the vortex. Cities as diverse as Washington, DC, Chicago, Knoxville, Omaha, and Elaine, Arkansas, were immobilized by race riots for days. All told, hundreds of people—most of them Black—were killed, while countless others were injured and tens of thousands were forced to flee their homes or workplaces. Similar events had happened before and would occur again (most notoriously the massacres targeting Blacks in East St. Louis, Illinois, in 1917 and Tulsa, Oklahoma, in 1921). But the scope and duration of what came to be known as the "Red Summer" of 1919 stand out as the worst period of nationwide violent racial unrest since the American Civil War.[23]

Also notable during the Red Summer was the fact that African Americans fought back with a determination rarely seen before. This was part of a broader postwar trend, led by organizations such as the National Association for the Advancement of Colored People (NAACP), founded in 1909, to assertively push for Black equality. These efforts produced struggles for justice in courtrooms and legislatures—but also self-defense measures in the streets to fight back against white mobs.[24] Black veterans, hundreds of thousands of whom were returning from Europe, played a key role. In a May 1919 essay, "Returning Soldiers," the prominent Black scholar and NAACP co-founder W. E. B. Du Bois argued that these veterans had an opportunity to serve as champions of a broader civil rights movement: "Make way for Democracy! We saved it in France, and by the Great Jehovah, we will save it in the United States of America, or know the reason why."[25] This charge resonated with many returning from the war. Having bravely served their country, Black soldiers justifiably believed they had earned the basic rights promised to them since emancipation. Yet they returned to an America that continued to deny them the very ideals they had supposedly bled for in Europe. Lacking adequate housing and jobs, facing segregation, mistreated by law enforcement, denied basic rights, and besieged by anti-Black violence, many African American veterans chose to resist and defend their communities.

By mid-July, the Red Summer reached Washington, DC, barely a week after Wilson had returned from the Paris Peace Conference. A white supporter of the NAACP wrote to Du Bois about his horror that a race riot should take place "in the very heart of our capital, where sits our illustrious and humane President, Mr. Woodrow Wilson, who only a few months ago . . . said America stood for justice and democracy. . . . Today he sits silent while mob rule sweeps the streets of our capital."[26]

The growing racial crisis laid bare a fundamental contradiction in Wilson's worldview. Despite the president's promotion of the rights of self-determination abroad, he held deeply racist views. The Virginia-born Wilson was the descendant of Confederate soldiers, and he favored a southern-oriented view of U.S. history. He saw slavery as relatively benign, was sympathetic toward the Ku Klux Klan, and saw Reconstruction as having been a disaster for the South. When Wilson ran for president, he courted Black leaders, but once in office he oversaw the resegregation of multiple federal agencies.[27]

As racial violence seized multiple cities in 1919, the president was mostly silent. In one of the rare instances where Wilson did comment, however, he acknowledged that whites were the primary instigators. During his tour to defend the League of Nations, he told an audience in Helena, Montana, on September 11, 1919, "I hope you won't think it inappropriate if I stop here to express my shame as an American citizen at the race riots that have occurred in some places in this country, where men have forgot humanity and justice and orderly society and have run amuck."[28] Still, Wilson took no federal action to quell the violence gripping the country, seeing it as a problem local authorities should handle. And as a series of anarchist bombings sparked a postwar "Red Scare" among federal law enforcement agencies and the media, Wilson seemed inclined to buy the false narrative that African Americans involved in racial unrest—particularly Black veterans returning from Europe—were susceptible to Bolshevism.[29]

In his provocative essay "The Souls of White Folk," written during the Red Summer and published a year later, Du Bois pointed out the deep hypocrisy at the heart of Wilson's progressive agenda, which held up an ideal for the world to follow but failed to augur change at home. He wrote:

> Conceive this nation, of all human peoples, engaged in a crusade to make the "World Safe for Democracy"! Can you imagine the United States protesting against Turkish atrocities in Armenia, while the Turks are silent about mobs in Chicago and St. Louis; what is Louvain compared with Memphis, Waco, Washington, Dyersburg, and Estill Springs? In short, what is the black man but America's Belgium, and how could America condemn in Germany that which she commits, just as brutally, within her own borders?[30]

All this turmoil served to reinforce long-held American instincts to remain at arm's length from the rest of the world. The lives lost in Europe, a wrenching pandemic, economic recession, and widespread labor and racial unrest all contributed to a growing feeling of regret among Americans about the country's participation in World War I. An exhausted nation wanted to return its focus to the home front. Americans had long sought to remain aloof from overseas entanglements, and "widespread disillusionment with the war . . . reinforced that conviction," the historians Norman Graebner and Edward Bennett write. "Not without reason,

[Americans] concluded that the United States had gained little more from its trans-Atlantic experience than Prohibition and the Spanish flu."[31]

"A LIGHTNING BOLT ACROSS THE GLOBE"

The world was no calmer beyond America's shores, and the pressures plaguing nations and driving them apart seemed to grow by the day.

In the decades prior to World War I, there had been a tremendous expansion in economic growth, commerce, and interdependence—what we would now describe as globalization—among nations. But the Great War and the Great Influenza were part of a complex chain of events— some connected, others distinct—that reversed these trends.[32] One recent analysis notes that, prior to COVID-19, the four most important negative macroeconomic shocks since 1870 were, in order of severity, World War II, the Great Depression, World War I, and the 1918–20 influenza pandemic. Of course, disentangling the independent effects of World War I and the influenza pandemic is extremely difficult since they overlapped. But the same study found that between 1919 and 1929, the Great War reduced GDP by 8.4 percent in the typical country, while the pandemic reduced GDP by 6 percent.[33]

In the immediate postwar period, the economies most directly affected by the conflict stagnated. Then, as industry bounced back, global overproduction became a problem, encouraging countries to resort to tariffs to protect their national industries. This initiated a protectionist trend that would come to characterize the interwar period. The enormous costs incurred by the combatants during World War I also produced huge debt obligations in Britain, France, and Germany—much of it owed to the United States. These burdens worsened in the conflict's aftermath as Allied countries attempted to recover and Germany was forced to pay reparations. Finding capital to finance these debts became harder. The gold standard was abandoned and then reinstated in a haphazard fashion. Inflation increased, with hyperinflation and currency crises hitting Germany and other central and eastern European countries in the 1920s.[34]

The postwar period was also a time of rising popular anxiety and accumulating grievances across Europe. This stemmed partly from ongoing changes in the structures of economies and societies. Rapid urbanization,

industrialization, revolutionary advances in technology and mechaniza-
tion, and assembly-line efficiencies during the interwar years continued
to produce enormous concentrations of wealth in the world's most advanced economies. But these forces of modernization uprooted many
traditional segments of society—including rural communities, small
shopkeepers, artisans, the landed gentry, and portions of the old conservative elite—and created significant economic inequalities.[35] The influenza pandemic, in turn, accentuated these challenges. Class differences
were reinforced by the perception that the rich and the poor had experienced the hardships of both the war and the pandemic differently, leaving an entire generation of Europeans deeply scarred.[36]

For similar reasons, anticolonial sentiment grew around the world.
The sense of exploitation and relative deprivation was worsened by the
fact that in many locations the Great Influenza disproportionately affected the colonized relative to the colonizers. As the science journalist
Laura Spinney observes, the flu "hurled a lightning bolt across the globe,
illuminating the injustice of colonialism."[37] In Korea under Japanese rule,
for example, ethnic Koreans and Japanese were sickened by influenza at
roughly the same rate, but disparate living conditions and health care
meant that Koreans were twice as likely to perish. A Korean independence movement against the Japanese ensued in March 1919, which
Japan violently crushed.[38]

Elsewhere, an expanding web of cracks emerged in imperial structures just as the British and French Empires reached their zenith. For
imperial powers, colonial possessions increasingly went from assets to
liabilities. In the 1920s and 1930s, France faced rising opposition, unrest, and nationalist movements in Algeria, French Indochina, Morocco,
Syria, and Tunisia. Great Britain confronted agitation for independence
in places as diverse as Egypt, Iraq, Ireland, and India.[39]

Across the British Empire, the pandemic played an important, albeit
often ignored, role in highlighting the fundamental inequalities intrinsic
to imperial rule. In Egypt, then a British protectorate, the death rate from
influenza was twice as high as it was in Great Britain itself. As many as
170,000 Egyptians (more than 1 percent of the population) may have
died, with most of those deaths occurring in the last two months of 1918.
The pandemic fell hardest on rural areas, and the hardships were one of
the factors contributing to the Egyptian revolt against the British in 1919.

(Egypt would gain independence three years later.)[40] In Ireland, where the pandemic killed at least 23,000 people, the influenza crisis "seemed to fester every sore exacerbating already difficult relationships or situations" during a critical moment in the push for Irish independence.[41]

No place on earth suffered more from the influenza pandemic, however, than India, at the time the crown jewel of Britain's empire. British and Indian troops fighting Ottoman forces during the Mesopotamian campaign are thought to have brought the contagion from Basra, Iraq, to Bombay in the spring of 1918. From there it spread throughout India in waves. Of the more than 250 million people in India at the time, an estimated 12–17 million (that is, at least 5 percent of the population) perished. The sheer volume of sickness and death overwhelmed India's poor health care infrastructure, which was already understaffed due to the diversion of the Indian Medical Service to the war effort in Europe. Although the virus itself did not discriminate between British authorities and the Indians they lorded over, the disparate impact was stark. Among sickened British troops in India, for example, 9.61 percent died; in contrast, the case mortality rate for Indian troops was 21.69 percent.[42]

The unfathomable human toll caused by the virus was compounded by a failed monsoon—an annual weather event that usually strikes the subcontinent between June and September and is essential to India's agricultural yields—and the resulting drought in 1918, which left millions of malnourished Indians more susceptible to getting sick. India was, and remains, predominantly rural. The pandemic forced many out of the fields and into densely populated cities, where the virus spread more easily. Yet the colonial regime continued to send Indian-grown food to Europe to feed Allied troops. The pandemic, in turn, made food insecurity even direr as agricultural laborers became ill and died. Food prices soared.[43]

Among those stricken by the second wave of the pandemic in the fall of 1918 was Mahatma Gandhi, the man who would lead India's independence movement. Just three years earlier, he had returned to India from South Africa, where he had first employed strategies of nonviolent civil resistance. As Gandhi recovered from the flu, the cascading misery and revealed injustices exposed by the virus helped produce a wave of anticolonial sentiment and momentum for his cause. Local and caste organizations mobilized to provide relief, filling a vacuum left by the British authorities' indifference to the crisis and their inability to handle it. While such organizations had existed before, the pandemic helped unify them across the country around a single cause, ultimately providing Gandhi with the grassroots support he had previously lacked.[44]

To head off the possibility of revolution, the Imperial Legislative Council in Delhi imposed the Rowlatt Act in March 1919, indefinitely extending wide-ranging wartime powers to crack down on the press, detain activists without trial, and arrest individuals suspected of sedition or treason. The act provoked protests, which in turn led to attacks on demonstrators, culminating in the April 13, 1919, Amritsar Massacre in Punjab (which occurred on the same day as the beginning of the Red Summer in America). Even though India would not gain independence until 1947, historians look back at this period of immense popular discontent following the pandemic as the point of no return for British rule.[45]

CRASH AND BURN

Once the U.S. economy recovered from the deep 1920–21 recession, it boomed for the remainder of the Roaring Twenties. Then, as the decade came to a close, the bottom fell out again. On October 29, 1929, Wall Street crashed, setting off a massive international financial crisis. The world had become dependent on the United States to absorb imports and prop up international lending. Consequently, the international economy was in no position to weather the storm unleashed in New York. Across the globe, investments dried up, industrial output fell, and demand cratered. Protectionist impulses deepened in America and elsewhere. Even Britain abandoned its commitment to free trade. Between 1929 and 1932, the value of trade fell by 70 percent worldwide, and (to borrow a contemporary term) the world economy deglobalized. Unemployment skyrocketed to between one-fifth and one-third of the industrial workforce in advanced economies, and rates of poverty and acute food insecurity sharply increased. In the United States, GDP fell by nearly 26 percent from 1929 to 1932, while the total GDP of the world's eleven advanced economies fell by almost 17 percent over the same period.[46]

Economic conditions were now ripe for political and geopolitical upheaval. For years in the wake of the 1917 Russian Revolution, the specter of Bolshevism hung over European affairs, with constant fears that economic conditions would incite communist uprisings. Yet the biggest dangers ended up coming from the right. Escalating economic anxiety mixed with theories of racial supremacy and fears of demographic decline and cultural degeneracy. The result was a toxic brew of right-wing nationalism, populism, anti-Semitism, and xenophobia. Spain descended into civil war as reactionary nationalist forces took on the left-leaning Republic, drawing in foreign powers on each side and culminating in the establishment of Francisco Franco's right-wing dictatorship in 1939. And in Germany, as we saw in Chapter 1, the fragile Weimar Republic gave way to a fascist dictatorship when Adolf Hitler and the Nazi Party seized control in 1933.

Elsewhere, one weak and divided democracy after another fell to dictators and one-party rule during this period. In Europe, only Britain, France, and a handful of northern European democracies survived until the outbreak of World War II. Outside Europe, with the exception of the United States and Britain's settler dominions such as Canada and Australia, free societies were rare. Democracy remained out of reach in British and French colonies, and important powers such as Turkey and China consolidated under new authoritarian rulers. In the Soviet Union, led by Stalin, politics turned increasingly totalitarian. And in Japan, an experiment with parliamentary democracy in the 1920s was overtaken by nationalism and militarism in the 1930s.[47]

Economic calamity, political instability, and democratic backsliding, in turn, translated directly into geopolitical turmoil. The Great Depression seemed to discredit the liberal order represented by Britain, France, and the United States. The distribution of power continued to shift, and challenges grew from revisionist states. The ideological struggle between democracy, communism, and fascism intensified and internationalized. And the foreign policies of the world's most powerful democracies were plagued by indecision and isolationism.

Soon, embittered and opportunistic authoritarian states were on the move. Imperial Japan seized Manchuria in 1931, followed by a more general war in China in 1937. Fascist Italy invaded Ethiopia in 1935 and joined with Nazi Germany to support nationalist forces in the Spanish Civil War. Hitler's Germany reoccupied the Rhineland in 1936, absorbed Austria and portions of Czechoslovakia in 1938, and invaded Poland in

1939. With these gambits, Japan, Italy, and Germany aimed to carve out spheres of influence in the Asia-Pacific, the Mediterranean and North Africa, and Europe, hoping to establish a new international architecture better aligned with their security and economic imperatives and their ideological ambitions. Accompanying these territorial moves was a massive rearmament campaign—and an ensuing great-power arms race in ships, tanks, guns, and aircraft—that further contributed to spiraling international instability.[48]

THE FAILURE OF THE FREE WORLD

In no small measure, the slide toward another world war was a consequence of the failure of democratic nations—what would later be called the "free world"—to stick together. Britain and France remained powerful in the interwar years, but they were incapable of standing shoulder to shoulder until 1939. They were distracted by growing challenges across their empires, and in the aftermath of the Great Depression they faced profound public pressure to focus on the home front. As authoritarian states pressed in Asia, the Mediterranean, North Africa, and eastern and central Europe, Britain and France were overwhelmed by the sheer number of international crises that needed managing. They also had incompatible national goals. France desired firm alliances to restrain Germany, while Britain sought to avoid being entrapped in the kinds of ironclad security commitments thought to have produced World War I. These diametrically opposed strategies ensured a divided front, with each democratic nation trying to deal with the challenge Germany posed through a mix of denial, buck-passing, and appeasement.[49]

Even more important was America's failure to assume a leadership role in the interwar years. At the end of World War I, the United States was the most powerful country in the international system. America had one of the world's largest populations (more than 100 million, compared to 44 million in Britain, 39 million in France, 62 million in Germany, and 138 million in the Soviet Union). The U.S. economy—which combined unparalleled natural resources, agricultural and industrial production, and capital—was triple the size of Britain's, and it had overtaken the onetime liberal hegemon as the hub of global finance and commerce. While America's armed forces had been relatively modest before World War I and shrank in size after the conflict, the war had revealed the immense latent potential of the United States to mobilize and project military might. Moreover, befitting America's status as a global maritime power, the U.S. Navy rivaled Great Britain's Royal Navy during the interwar years. Overall, the disparity between the United States and other great powers was not as wide as it would be at the end of World War II or the end of the Cold War. But America's growing preeminence after World War I meant that only the United States was capable of anchoring a new order.[50] However, it chose not to.

American foreign policy during the early interwar period was not, as often described, strictly isolationist. The United States did indeed pull back—but not completely and not right away. During the 1920s, many U.S. policymakers hoped to continue the international transformation and democratization set in motion by the Paris Peace Conference, but to do so in a manner that minimized foreign entanglements. The United States remained diplomatically engaged in managing great-power relations, taking advantage of America's considerable political clout and growing economic centrality in the interwar years. The country sought diplomatic progress toward disarmament, most notably in the form of the 1922 Washington Naval Treaty. And it worked to reduce economic burdens on Germany and relieve intra-European tensions over reparations payments via the 1924 Dawes Plan and the (never implemented) 1929 Young Plan, using America's privileged position in the world's financial system as leverage.[51]

Yet despite all these efforts, the United States proved unwilling to make the types of firm security guarantees required to actually sustain the international order it had helped birth, instead seeking to maintain what Tooze describes as a "privileged detachment." Republican administrations in the 1920s resisted being pulled into efforts to contain resurgent revisionist states, either through the League of Nations—which America remained apart from following Wilson's failure to secure Senate ratification—or via direct security commitments to France and Great Britain in support of the European Peace Pact signed at Locarno in 1925. Instead, all Washington could muster was the 1928 Kellogg-Briand Pact, a multilateral political commitment to eschew armed aggression that was disconnected from the League and had no enforcement mechanism.[52]

As a consequence of America's half-in, half-out approach, the postwar order did not implode right away, but rather limped along until it was toppled by the Great Depression. The economic shock waves reverberating from New York turned America's privileged financial status into a global liability. Rising U.S. tariffs then set off a spiral of beggar-thy-neighbor policies across the international system. And it was at this point that the United States truly became isolationist.

As the 1930s unfolded, the liberal international order Woodrow Wilson had dreamed of collapsed as one multilateral agreement and institution after another proved impotent. The Washington Naval Treaty failed to constrain Japan's military buildup; the Locarno Treaties could not preserve territorial integrity in Europe against German designs; the Kellogg-Briand Pact failed to outlaw war. Meanwhile, the League of Nations, absent an American commitment, proved incapable of resolving international conflicts or deterring aggression in Manchuria or anywhere else, and by the mid-1930s it essentially stopped functioning altogether.[53]

The net result was the worst of all possible worlds—to invert the phrase coined by Gottfried Wilhelm Leibniz and popularized by Voltaire. The liberal international order had come to represent a threat to revisionist authoritarian powers, encouraging them to challenge and overturn the system. Yet the community of democracies meant to defend this order was too distracted and divided, and too bereft of American leadership, to marshal a coordinated response and the requisite preponderance of power needed to ward off the threat.[54] "World War I had seen the first effort to construct a coalition of liberal powers to manage the vast unwieldy dynamic of the modern world," Tooze writes. Yet that coalition disintegrated. "The failure of the democratic powers opened a strategic window of opportunity in the early 1930s. We know what nightmarish forces would tear through that window."[55]

THE WORLD BECAME TOO SMALL

In his 2004 novel *The Plot Against America*, Philip Roth envisioned an alternative history in which the famed aviator, Medal of Honor recipient, and noted anti-Semite Charles Lindbergh defeated incumbent president Franklin Delano Roosevelt in the 1940 election. In the book, Lindbergh campaigned on an isolationist, antiwar platform, and then, once in office, signed a treaty with Nazi Germany promising not to oppose German ambitions in Europe. The novel's main protagonists are the Roths, an all-American Jewish family in Newark, New Jersey, forced to contend with rising, and increasingly institutionalized, anti-Semitism and violence.[56] The book was made into a critically acclaimed HBO limited series in 2020, where many of its themes of a celebrity-turned-politician winning election on an isolationist, fearmongering, and xenophobic platform took on new resonance: a warning about the types of forces growing in the United States and beyond in the Trump era.

In reality, Lindbergh never became president. But he did leverage his notoriety to become a chief spokesperson for the America First Committee, a prominent anti-interventionist organization formed in 1940. At its height, the America First Committee claimed 800,000 members, including many prominent U.S. politicians and celebrities. Lindbergh was chosen as its face due to his status as a wildly popular hero. He had also garnered considerable public sympathy after the kidnapping and death of his twenty-month-old son Charles in 1932 (known at the time as "The Crime of the Century"). But he was also a deeply problematic figure. Lindbergh was a white supremacist with a record of making anti-Semitic statements. He visited Germany several times and had expressed admiration for what Hitler had achieved in the mid-1930s. Once the war began, he declared that the Nazis would inevitably win.

Nevertheless, Lindbergh's fame made him a prominent figure in the debate about possible American involvement in the war. "Now that we have become one of the world's greatest nations, . . . [s]hall we submerge our future in the endless wars of the old world? Or shall we build our own defenses and leave European war to European countries?" he asked his listeners during an infamous June 1940 radio address. "Shall we continue this suicidal conflict between western nations and white races, or shall we learn from history . . . that a civilization cannot be preserved by conflict among its own peoples, regardless of how different their ideologies may be?"[57] As Lindbergh toured the country for the America First Committee, he portrayed the United States as impregnable from foreign threats so long as the country remained vigilant in defending its hemisphere and stayed out of European affairs. The Axis powers, therefore, did not represent a danger worth risking war over. The United States would remain safe as long as it remained free of foreign involvements. "There is a policy open to this nation that will lead to success—a policy that leaves us free to follow our own way of life, and to develop our own civilization," he argued in an April 1941 address. "It demands faith in an independent American destiny. This is the policy of the America First Committee today."[58]

On the other side of the debate was President Roosevelt, who confided to his treasury secretary, Henry Morgenthau, in June 1940 that he was "absolutely convinced that Lindbergh is a Nazi."[59] In making the case that the United States needed to take on an internationalist role commensurate with its great-power status, however, FDR had to tread lightly. The Great Depression had, understandably, reinforced America's long-held impulse to remain aloof from affairs outside the Western Hemisphere. As FDR sought to rebuild the U.S. economy, he was also hesitant to get involved overseas lest it mobilize the isolationist lobby at home against his New Deal program.[60] He was sensitive to the fact that the majority of Americans wanted to stay out of foreign conflicts. During his 1936 reelection campaign, Roosevelt spoke to this sentiment. As he told an audience in Chautauqua, New York, in August: "We are not isolationists except insofar as we seek to isolate ourselves completely from war." But then he added: "Yet we must remember that so long as war exists on earth there will be some danger that even the nation which most ardently desires peace may be drawn into war."[61]

As the storm clouds gathered in Europe, Roosevelt knew U.S. isolation was unsustainable. Therefore, he pivoted to a renewed effort to internationalize American conceptions of national security. Key to FDR's argument to the American people was the claim that interdependence among nations meant the country's fate was inextricably linked to foreign events. "It is easy for you and for me to shrug our shoulders and to say that conflicts taking place thousands of miles from the continental United States . . . do not seriously affect the Americas—and that all the United States has to do is to ignore them," he said during a September 3, 1939, fireside chat. "Passionately though we may desire detachment, we are forced to realize that every word that comes through the air, every ship that sails the sea, every battle that is fought does affect the American future."[62] On June 10, 1940, shortly after getting word that Mussolini's Italy was set to declare war on France (and four days before Paris would fall to the Nazis), Roosevelt spoke to graduating students at the University of Virginia Law School and gave up any pretense of American neutrality. "Some indeed still hold to the now somewhat obvious delusion that we ... can safely permit the United States to become ... a lone island in a world dominated by the philosophy of force. Such an island may be the dream of those who still talk and vote as isolationists," but it "represents to me and the overwhelming majority of Americans today a helpless nightmare of people without freedom—the nightmare of a people lodged in prison, hungry, and fed through the bars from day to day by the contemptuous unpitying masters of other continents."[63]

When Japanese planes bombed Pearl Harbor on December 7, 1941, it settled the debate. The United States declared war on the Axis powers. The America First Committee was disbanded. The world had demonstrably become too small, and the country—as powerful and seemingly distant as it was—could not wall itself off from the dangers of a collapsing international order beyond its shores.

Primed for Peril

THE MOMENT WHEN a shock hits matters as much as the shock itself. The assassination of Archduke Franz Ferdinand in 1914 set off a global war because Europe was a geopolitical tinderbox. The assassination of John F. Kennedy in 1963 did not, perhaps because the United States and the Soviet Union had already been to the brink and back over the Cuban missile crisis a year earlier. The great crash and banking crisis of 1929–33 occurred at a time when economists and political leaders fundamentally misunderstood financial crises and favored policy responses that made matters worse. In 2008–9, the policymakers at the helm had studied the Great Depression and drawn the right lessons from it. In other words, context is everything.

The Great Influenza occurred at a time when the public was familiar with suffering and brutalized by the mass death of World War I. The misery, hardship, and isolation of the pandemic were widespread and painful, but its effects were often submerged in a world besieged. In America and elsewhere, it became a "forgotten pandemic," as the historian Alfred Crosby described it.[1] Few books about the collapse of world order in the interwar period say much about the Great Influenza, though, as we have argued, it did play a role. The virus may have hastened the defeat of Germany in World War I. And Wilson, sick with the flu at an inopportune moment, failed to deliver completely on his vision for a new liberal international order and struggled to build unified support for it at

home. More generally, the pandemic wounded already battered economies, heightened inequalities across the globe, and contributed to social
unrest. The consequences of these developments, often ignored by historians, reverberated through time, in big and small ways, contributing
to international disorder. That said, the influenza pandemic was not the
principal catalyst for the events that culminated in a second world war.
Other factors were in play. And to the extent that the pandemic played a
distant role, it did so because it occurred in an international context that
was already primed—for so many other reasons—for domestic instability, nationalist rivalry, and military conflict.

The international response to World War I and the last great pandemic failed to create a functioning global order. It took the intersecting
economic, political, and geopolitical crises of the interwar years, culminating in the even more devastating World War II, to finally do so. But
even then, the opportunity to think and act anew had to be seized. It
required big ideas. And it took bold and sustained American leadership,
working in concert with the rest of the free world.

As early as 1941, U.S. president Franklin Delano Roosevelt and British prime minister Winston Churchill signed the Atlantic Charter, which
outlined the creation of a politically and economically open, stable, and
managed postwar international system with the United States and other
liberal democracies at its core. This new order took shape after the defeat
of the Axis powers with the creation of a set of multilateral institutions
and democratic alliances: the United Nations, the World Bank, the International Monetary Fund, the General Agreement on Tariffs and Trade
(which would later become the World Trade Organization), the North
Atlantic Treaty Organization, and the U.S.-Japan alliance. It also involved
ambitious nation-building efforts to reconstruct European economies via
the Marshall Plan and use the occupations of West Germany and Japan to
refashion fascist and imperialist powers into modern democracies. The
nations of Europe initiated a decades-long process of integration, culim-
inating in the European Union. Tucked under an umbrella of American protection, the world's leading democracies transcended centuries
of military rivalry and, as the Cold War unfolded, found common cause
against the Soviet Union.[2]

Nested within this web of multilateral institutions and agreements was a new global public health regime designed to manage and coordinate responses to public health emergencies. This was not a completely novel development. During the mid-nineteenth century, as railways and steamships connected more and more of the world, European countries began holding periodic International Sanitary Conferences. The first treaty on cholera was finalized in 1892, followed by a consolidated treaty covering cholera, plague, and yellow fever in 1903. New organizations were eventually established, most notably the International Sanitary Bureau, which eventually became the Pan-American Health Organization, in 1902, and the Office International d'Hygiène Publique (OIHP) in 1907. After World War I, the League of Nations Health Organization came into being, with the OIHP given an advisory capacity. Yet despite all these efforts, international coordination to combat infectious disease remained limited.

At the United Nations Conference on International Organization held in San Francisco in 1945 to draw up the UN charter, a recommendation was made by China and Brazil to hold additional meetings to set up a new global health entity. It was approved. In April 1948, the League's Health Organization and OIHP were folded into the new World Health Organization as a specialized agency of the UN. Two months later, the first World Health Assembly, the decision-making body of the WHO, was convened in Geneva. In 1951, the WHO combined a dozen existing treaties and conventions from the international sanitary conferences into binding International Sanitary Regulations (renamed the International Health Regulations in 1969), which were strengthened in 1995 and again in 2005. Numerous new global health organizations and initiatives emerged alongside the WHO, including the Joint United Nations Programme on HIV/AIDS (UNAIDS) in 1994, Unitaid (which invests in innovation focused on HIV/AIDS, tuberculosis, and malaria) in 2006, and the Global Health Security Agenda in 2014. Important public-private partnerships were also established, most notably Gavi, the Vaccine Alliance (formerly the Global Alliance for Vaccines and Immunization) in 2000 and the Global Fund to Fight AIDS, Tuberculosis, and Malaria (the Global Fund) in 2002.[3]

In the late 1990s, pressure increased on the WHO to take a more prominent role and to adapt to the rapidly accelerating pace of globalization. The United States in particular urged the agency to place greater emphasis on emerging infectious diseases. This move paid off. In the first two decades

of the twenty-first century, the WHO played an important role in managing the international response to the 2002–4 SARS epidemic, the 2009
H1N1 flu pandemic, and the 2015–16 Zika epidemic, although it largely
failed to effectively deal with the 2014-16 Ebola epidemic.[4] However, as
we'll see in Part II, this preparation fell short when disaster struck in 2020.

ON THE EVE OF COVID-19

By the beginning of May 2021, when we completed writing this book,
152 million people worldwide had been infected by COVID-19 and the
global death toll had risen to at least 3.2 million.[5] As we write these pages,
it is impossible to know how many people will ultimately be sickened or
die from the virus before the pandemic runs its course. Nevertheless,
in all likelihood the grim tally will be much lower in absolute and relative terms than the direct human costs produced by the Great Influenza,
which killed an estimated 50 million people. Yet, paradoxically, the impact of COVID-19 on human and world affairs might prove greater. As
we detail throughout this book, the virus and its aftershocks seem likely
to accelerate and magnify instability within countries—including economic marginalization, state fragility, and democratic backsliding—and
contribute to greater frictions among nations for years to come.

The counterintuitive notion that COVID-19 could be more impact-
ful on international order than the Great Influenza even if it kills fewer
people derives from the specific context in which the current "once-in-
a-century" pandemic occurred. Most people alive in today's Western democracies, for example, have never experienced total war or other great
calamities that kill hundreds of thousands or millions of their fellow citizens. The weight of the dead from the coronavirus pandemic therefore
seems heavier than it did a century ago.[6]

More broadly, four key factors compromised the international community's geopolitical immune system on the eve of COVID-19: hyperglobalization, inequality, the rise of populist nationalism, and growing
U.S.-China rivalry. As a consequence of these trends, the world was especially vulnerable to precisely the type of transnational crisis set in motion
by the pandemic. The novel coronavirus emerged against the backdrop of
a world increasingly in disarray, with the old international order already
teetering on the brink of collapse.[7]

A HYPERGLOBALIZED WORLD

Globalization is a fuzzy concept, but it typically refers to the volume and velocity of cross-border flows of trade, investment, technology, information, and people (workers, migrants, travelers, and tourists). Economically, globalization is not a new phenomenon. In some respects, it can be traced back centuries to the Silk Road, which brought luxury goods from China to customers throughout Eurasia, and later to the spice trade emanating from the Islamic world. It expanded further from the fifteenth to the eighteenth centuries as European states set up supply chains between their imperial homelands and the far-flung colonies they ruthlessly controlled. The first modern wave of globalization, however, is usually linked to the nineteenth century, and in particular the time between 1870 and World War I, when the industrial revolution and British hegemony on the seas significantly expanded global trade. On the eve of the Great War, the "trade openness index" (the sum of world exports and imports divided by GDP) stood at 18 percent. But as a consequence of the economic dislocations from World War I, the influenza pandemic, monetary policy in the 1920s, new immigration restrictions, the Great Depression, spiraling protectionism, and another world war, the international system deglobalized, producing a trade openness index of 10.1 percent in 1945.[8]

In the post–World War II era, from the mid-1940s on, the process of globalization gradually resumed, spurred by the second industrial revolution and America's postwar efforts to champion an open, rule-based international economic system. By 1980, the trade openness index had reached 39.5 percent. The liberalization of China's and India's economies, followed by the end of the Cold War and the collapse of the Soviet Union, then triggered a massive acceleration of globalization. Free markets, free trade, and free flows of information took off like a rocket, increasingly fueled by the internet and other emerging digital technologies. In 2008, the trade openness index stood at 61.1 percent. Then the subprime mortgage crisis hit, and the ensuing global financial crash created the first reversal in globalization in more than seven decades. The ratio of trade flows to global output began to decline, and by the time Donald Trump walked into the Oval Office in 2017, the trade openness index was down to 53.5 percent.[9]

Of course, trade is only one metric of globalization. But other measures tell a similar story. In 2018, three scholars at New York University's Stern School of Business compiled a composite "global connectedness index" derived from 3 million data points on trade, capital, information, and people flows. Taken as a whole, the study found that globalization had reached an all-time high in 2017 (although an update to the study showed a modest reduction the following year).[10]

When it comes to pandemics, globalization contributes to a double-edged vulnerability. Its associated trends—including rapid urbanization in developing countries, wide-scale human encroachment on natural habitats, industrial farming, global wildlife trade, and climate change—have increased the prospects of disease transmission from animals to human populations. Meanwhile, unprecedented interconnectedness means that the potential for contagions to rapidly spread around the globe is now much greater than it was at any previous time in human history. The 1918–20 influenza pandemic spread around a planet with 1.8 billion people on it, largely driven by the immense mobilizations and demobilizations of troops involved in World War I. Today, any one of the planet's 7.8 billion people can board an airplane and fly anywhere on the globe in less than a day (often in just a few hours), and there are more than 1 billion international border crossings each year. For many people, the rise of budget airlines over the past two decades means these flights are cheap and more affordable than ever before. The world has been fundamentally rewired; an intercontinental war is no longer required to accelerate a global contagion.[11]

But the relationship between globalization and pandemics goes in the other direction as well. Due to growing interdependence, pandemics and other major transnational shocks are now much more capable of disrupting the underpinnings of modern economies, societies, and international relations. For that reason, neither COVID-19 nor any future pandemic needs to be as deadly as the Great Influenza to have an outsized effect—a new reality that is both significant and troubling.

This prospect has long been recognized by the U.S. intelligence community. In 1979, the United States government established the National Intelligence Council (NIC) to serve as the intelligence community's center for long-term strategic analysis. Since 1997, the NIC has periodically released reports identifying key trends likely to shape world affairs in the decades ahead. In December 2004, it released a report written by its

2020 Project, which had as its aim "mapping the global future" of the year we just experienced. The project involved extensive consultations with governmental and outside academic experts from the United States and around the world, including conferences on five continents. Among the report's prescient predictions was that China would emerge as a major global power "similar to the advent of a united Germany in the 19th century and a powerful United States in the early 20th century." It also identified globalization "as an overarching 'mega trend,' a force so ubiquitous that it will substantially shape all the other major trends in the world of 2020."[12] The study made clear, however, that progress toward greater international integration was reversible, and that globalization could be made vulnerable. In a section called "What Could Derail Globalization?" the report concluded: "Short of a major global conflict, which we regard as improbable, another large-scale development that we believe could *stop* globalization would be a pandemic."[13] It is notable that the report was written two years after the outbreak of a disease now known as severe acute respiratory syndrome, caused by a novel coronavirus, SARS-CoV, which emerged in and spread from China.

In its next global trends report, published in 2008, the NIC reiterated this warning, noting that a pandemic could cause "economic loss on a global scale."[14] The NIC's 2012 study described "an easily transmissible novel respiratory pathogen" as a potential "black swan" event, warning that a severe pandemic of this sort could be "among the most disruptive events possible" in a globalized world.[15] And the 2017 NIC global trends report, released just as Trump was taking office, envisioned a scenario in which a long period of slow or no global economic growth was set in motion by, among other things, a pandemic that dramatically reduced global trade and productivity, resulting in a more fractured and volatile world.[16]

The NIC was far from an isolated voice. In a speech to the National Institutes of Health (NIH) in November 2005, President George W. Bush warned that a devastating national security threat could arise from a new strain of influenza that spread easily and to which there was little or no natural immunity. Although nothing as deadly was sweeping the globe at the time of the president's remarks, "if we wait for a pandemic to appear," Bush said, "it will be too late to prepare."[17] Bush's successor was similarly concerned. In 2014, during the Ebola outbreak, President Barack Obama said, "We were lucky with [the 2009–10] H1N1 [swine flu]—that it did not prove to be more deadly. We can't say we're lucky with Ebola because obviously it's having a devastating effect in West Africa but it is not airborne in its transmission." He then added: "There may and likely will come a time in which we have both an airborne disease that is deadly."[18] The growing concern even seeped into popular culture, as illustrated by the 2011 Hollywood movie *Contagion*. And prior to COVID-19, Trump administration officials, including the director of national intelligence, the secretary for health and human services, and a senior official on the National Security Council, all spoke publicly about the threat of pandemics.[19] The NIC's analysis, however, highlighted not just the profound potential of a novel virus such as SARS-CoV-2 (which causes the disease COVID-19) to unleash massive human suffering, but also the possibility that such a contagion could break the highly globalized international system.

INEQUALITY

While hyperglobalization made the world more susceptible to mass disruption from a transnational shock, a second trend—the enormous inequality that has arisen alongside globalization—ensured that hundreds of millions of people would be particularly vulnerable if and when the shock arrived.

According to the World Bank, the combined gross domestic product of all countries in the world increased from around $1.4 trillion in 1960 (in current U.S. dollars) to nearly $88 trillion in 2019, far outpacing population growth and contributing to rising average per capita incomes across the planet.[20] But globalization-fueled economic growth also produced clear winners and losers. Among those that have done extremely well are the top 1 percent of earners—the world's wealthy. Additionally, many of the world's poor have benefited, as hundreds of millions of people were lifted out of poverty and into the burgeoning middle classes of large emerging economies such as China, India, Indonesia, Brazil, and Mexico. In 1990, 36 percent of the global population, or 2 billion people, lived in extreme poverty. By 2015, the number of individuals living in extreme poverty had been reduced to 10 percent of the world's people, or 736 million people.[21] For this reason, income inequality between countries has declined somewhat in recent decades.

Nevertheless, all this apparent progress obscured lingering vulnerabilities. Yes, there were tremendous worldwide economic gains. But many around the globe were left behind or continued to live on thin margins prone to disruption. In advanced industrial countries, the economic growth seen in recent decades has not redounded to the benefit of many in the working and middle classes, who have seen their wages stagnate and face the prospect of their children faring even less well than they have. Millions have been left behind as creative destruction (such as incessant product and process innovation), market efficiencies, automation, digitization, and trade accompanying globalization have displaced jobs, disrupted communities, and produced stagnant wages.[22] Meanwhile, in low- and middle-income economies, hundreds of millions of people were still living in extreme poverty on the eve of the coronavirus pandemic. In addition, an estimated 70 percent of workers earned their livelihoods in the informal sector, laboring in agriculture, construction, street vending, and other jobs with low daily wages, no employment protections, and few if any social safety nets. By the nature of these jobs, informal workers are at greater risk of poverty, with little protection against the type of public health and economic shocks unleashed by COVID-19.[23] As a consequence, significant inequality has remained or worsened in many countries despite average incomes increasing in recent decades.[24] Globally, the gap between those at the very top and those at the very bottom was particularly striking—and getting worse—prior to the pandemic.

Every January for the past half century, the world's financial, technological, and political elite have converged at the Alpine village of Davos, Switzerland, for the World Economic Forum. In recent years, the international development charity Oxfam has been shaming them with startling statistics on inequality. During the lead-up to the 2017 Davos session, Oxfam reported that the sixty-one richest people in the world in 2016 had the same net worth as the poorest half of humanity (around 3.7 billion people); in 2017 that number was forty-three people, and in 2018 it was twenty-six.[25] In its final Davos-timed report before the coronavirus spread, Oxfam found that the world's richest 1 percent in 2019 had more than twice as much wealth as the other 6.9 billion people on earth put together; the world's 2,153 billionaires had more wealth than 4.6 billion people (60 percent of the global population); and the twenty-two richest men in the world had more wealth than all the women living on the continent of Africa.[26] As we shall see in Part III of this book, the COVID-19 crisis laid bare all these vulnerabilities and inequalities.

POPULIST NATIONALISM

What do America, Brazil, India, Hungary, Mexico, the Philippines, Poland, Turkey, and the United Kingdom all have in common? Prior to COVID-19, their leaders all exhibited a third important trend: a dramatic growth in populist nationalism around the globe. While each leader was responsive to local conditions, and some became full-blown authoritarians while others remained democrats, populist nationalists all have their own version of Donald Trump's "America First"—the creed that one's own country has lost out due to the machinations of other countries, a global elite, and their domestic fifth columns. In Brazil, President Jair Bolsonaro's creed is "Brazil Above Everything, God Above Everyone"; in the United Kingdom, Brexiteers demanded that their country "Take Back Control"; in Hungary, the ruling party, Fidesz, uses "For Us Hungary Comes First"; and in Poland, the Law and Justice Party has the rather unoriginal "Make Poland Great Again." They prioritize national sovereignty above all. They are highly skeptical of multilateral organizations abroad and established institutions at home (what Trump called the "deep state"). They see the mainstream media as especially nefarious. They claim to speak for the common person and usually oppose immigration and multiculturalism. When in power, the populist nationalists tend to be more interested in the symbolism of governance and hot-button cultural issues than the rather mundane and complex task of delivering public services.

Analysts disagree on the precise cause of resurgent populist nationalism. One explanation is that it is a cultural backlash against modernity—particularly mass migration, multiculturalism, and the spread of progressive values such as same-sex marriage. Political scientists Pippa Norris and Ronald Inglehart have argued that "the orthogonal pull of cultural politics generates tensions and divisions within mainstream parties, as well as allowing new opportunities for populist leaders on the left and right to mobilize electoral support."[27]

A second explanation is economic. For Stanford University's Francis Fukuyama, populist nationalism is a reaction to the capture of democratic political systems by powerful interest groups that worsened inequality and economic stagnation, particularly for the working and middle classes in the United States and other advanced industrial economies.[28] In his book *The Retreat of Western Liberalism*, the *Financial Times* columnist Edward Luce argues that it is a combination of a loss of middle-class incomes and the disdain with which elites can treat those voters who have concerns about the modernization of society.[29] Outside the West, inequality, inadequate service delivery, the perception of widespread corruption, and fragile institutions have also provided openings for populist nationalists on the right and the left.[30]

Cultural and economic forces are not necessarily mutually exclusive explanations. Indeed, both could have contributed to the growth of populist nationalism as a political force in the decade following the 2008–9 global financial crisis. Consider a number of other factors as well. Social media has allowed groups of like-minded people to circumvent traditional gatekeepers to political activity (editors, producers, and political parties) and create their own movements. Meanwhile, some foreign actors—most consequentially Vladimir Putin's Russia—have deliberately stoked preexisting divisions within democracies by undermining the notion that there is a shared objective truth and by spreading disinformation online or through new media outlets.

In the West, the first successful populist political movement of the post–Cold War era occurred in June 2016 when a majority of the British electorate voted to leave the European Union. This was significant in several respects. It represented a rejection of the establishment in both the Conservative and Labour Parties, of the media, and of national institutions—such as the Treasury and the Central Bank—that had warned of the consequences of leaving the EU. When the economic sky did not immediately fall, many Brexit advocates asked why they had been listening to the experts at all. As Michael Gove, then the United Kingdom's justice secretary, memorably put it in 2016: "The people in this country have had enough of experts. . . . People from organizations with acronyms saying that they know what is best and getting it consistently wrong."[31] It also represented a nationalist rejection of the United Kingdom's European partners. The British people decided that Europe was holding their country back. They

had little to learn or gain from the European Union, so they would dis-
engage from it. Britain could be more self-reliant and look to the rest of
the world, including those places where populism was on the rise. Finally,
Brexit was an all-consuming task that would take a generation or more to
fully implement. It needed to have priority over all other issues. Yes, it was
disruptive, but the short-term pain would be worth it, or so the argument
went. These factors were embodied in the rise of Boris Johnson, who became prime minister in July 2019 and won a general election in December
of that year. In his appearance and mannerisms, Johnson bore more than
a passing resemblance to Trump—a comparison he embraced, although
Johnson had more mainstream views on international cooperation and
climate change.[32]

The second shock, of course, was Trump's victory in the November
2016 U.S. presidential election. Even more than Brexit, Trump represented a rejection of the establishment and the mainstream media. He
came to power with a core set of visceral beliefs that amounted to a
grievance that other countries were using American alliances, free trade,
and international agreements to take advantage of the United States. He
would address this by standing up to America's so-called friends and to
"deep state" bureaucrats in Washington. As a consequence, he hollowed
out America's capacity to tackle shared problems (such as a pandemic) at
home and to lead in crisis response overseas. Trump's relentless assault
on the media and expertise, as well as the constant flow of disinformation
emanating from his White House and Twitter feed, brought into question
the very idea that truth itself existed outside the "alternative facts" he himself promoted.[33] The result: his supporters lacked confidence in science
and trust in government at the very moment the country needed both
the most. However, more pointedly, the country itself was submerged in
chaos, as the administration failed to offer the American public clarity on
what was happening or to provide a clear national plan as the COVID-19
crisis unfolded.

Other similar shocks occurred around the world. In 2018, Bolsonaro,
known as the "Trump of the Tropics," became president of Brazil. A former army captain, Bolsonaro lacked the backing of a major party, was an
apologist for the country's history of military dictatorship and torture,
espoused racist views, attacked "gender ideology," and had radical policy
positions, including stopping Brazil's efforts to combat climate change

and liberalizing gun ownership to fight crime.[34] Bolsonaro's political fortunes and populist message benefited from a corruption scandal that engulfed the established parties and a severe recession that saw 13 million people out of work. And he took advantage of the growth of evangelical Christianity and a lingering respect in some quarters for Brazil's days as an authoritarian regime. Bolsonaro routinely clashed with the courts and other domestic institutions. When European governments harshly criticized Bolsonaro over devastating fires burning through the Amazon in 2019, he responded by insulting the French president's wife and rejecting the paltry assistance offered by the G7.[35]

U.S.-CHINA RIVALRY

A fourth key pre-COVID trend was the resurgence of great-power rivalry, particularly between the United States and China. In the 1990s and 2000s, American leaders believed that China and Russia were converging with the West on basic questions of international order. In a seminal speech to the National Committee on U.S.-China Relations in September 2005, deputy secretary of state Robert Zoellick reflected that, "while not yet democratic," China "does not see itself in a twilight conflict against democracy around the globe" and it "does not believe that its future depends on overturning the fundamental order of the international system." Zoellick expressed the hope shared by many in Washington that China would become "a responsible stakeholder" in the international order.[36] Successive administrations understood that both sides would have a far from easy path. But there was optimism that common ground could be found to address shared challenges, while the old-style geopolitical rivalries of the past could be avoided. Over time, integration into the U.S.-led liberal order might even lead to gradual political reform within China and other autocratic countries.[37]

As the past decade has shown, these expectations were shattered by what actually took place. Under Xi Jinping and Vladimir Putin, China and Russia diverged from American and European concepts of international order. China sought territorial revisions in the South China Sea and East China Sea, while Russia intervened in Ukraine, as part of broader efforts to carve out zones of military, political, and economic dominance. Beijing and Moscow also became more vocal and assertive in articulating an alternative order organized around the sovereign right of leaders to act as they wish within their borders and spheres of influence. Yet, even as they were promoting sovereignty for themselves, Beijing and Moscow began to actively intervene in the politics of other nations, albeit in different ways. China tended to be more subtle, illicitly manipulating the politics of democracies to promote policies to its liking and using its economic leverage to coerce political and business leaders. In one case, an Australian member of Parliament had to resign because of his ties to a Hong Kong donor with connections to the Chinese Communist Party. This incident and others saw a major crackdown by the Australian government on Chinese political interference.[38] Russia favored the blunt instruments of hacking and disinformation, culminating in the unprecedented interference in the U.S. presidential election of 2016. Both China and Russia shared the same goal, however, of creating a world safe for authoritarianism.

Meanwhile, Xi's regime became much more repressive at home. He weaponized a campaign against corruption to take out his political opponents within the CCP. Xi also expanded the CCP's tools for social control, marrying millions of security cameras with new technological innovations in the field of facial recognition and artificial intelligence to build a domestic surveillance system of astonishing scope and ambition. Beijing's new methods of digital authoritarianism were used to monitor the Muslim Uighur population in Xinjiang province, where as many as 1 million Uighurs were sent to internment camps (officially dubbed "Vocational Education and Training Centers" by the government). Nationalist rhetoric toward Taiwan was also dialed up, while aggressive steps were taken to gut the freedoms and autonomy underlying the "one country, two systems" model in Hong Kong.[39]

Part of this divergence was driven by Xi and Putin's belief that, left to its own devices, a liberal international order posed an existential threat to their model of authoritarianism. They were not necessarily wrong. Many Western policymakers saw political liberalization as a possible—and desirable—side effect of Chinese and Russian integration into the U.S.-led international system. The free flow of information through social media and other parts of the web, a free press that was highly capable and willing to investigate sensitive stories inside China and Russia, energetic nongovernmental organizations wanting to hold governments to account, and the enduring appeal of democracy all piled pressure on the autocrats.

On top of all this was China's meteoric economic rise, which seemed to position it for eventual superpower status, and Russia's military modernization, which in conjunction with the country's vast energy resources allowed Putin to become more assertive despite Russia's demographic and economic stagnation. Mixing economic, political, and military coercion with more ambiguous "gray zone" tactics, Beijing and Moscow were able to put the United States and its democratic allies under increasing pressure in Asia and Europe. Further afield, China's massive Belt and Road Initiative—which provided hundreds of billions of dollars in (often predatory) loans for infrastructure projects in Asia, the Middle East, Africa, Europe, and Latin America in a bid to make Beijing the center of a vast new economic network—and Russia's interventions in the Middle East added to the heat. Western officials increasingly worried about technological innovations that could upset the military balance, as well as the risks of dependency on Chinese technologies, such as 5G mobile networks in telecommunications.

This was all bubbling to the surface around 2015 and 2016. Had Hillary Clinton been elected president, she too very likely would have taken the United States in a more competitive direction with respect to China. But the rivalry was turbocharged under Trump. He was much closer to a nineteenth-century or interwar nationalist than to America's post–World War II internationalist tradition. Skeptical of alliances and an open global economy, he preferred a mercantilist mindset whereby the United States saw international economics in zero-sum terms and used its power to impose economic terms favorable to itself on other, less powerful nations. Trump saw free trade deals and multilateral financial institutions as constraining America's freedom of action.[40] He obsessed over the trade deficit with China and pursued that grievance relentlessly. Upon taking office, Trump targeted allies and adversaries alike with tariffs, economic threats, and unilateral sanctions.

Very few members of Trump's national security team shared his opposition to America's alliances and global leadership role, but they were worried about China. So they used Trump's worldview as a license to pursue a much tougher line toward Beijing, not just on trade but geopolitically too. In December 2017, national security advisor H. R. McMaster produced a National Security Strategy that made great-power competition the organizing principle of U.S. foreign policy doctrine; the Pentagon followed up with a revised National Defense Strategy in 2018 emphasizing similar themes. The administration deepened relations with Taiwan, sending serving U.S. officials there for the first time since 1979 and organizing a significant arms sale to the Taiwanese military. The United States and China competed over game-changing technologies such as artificial intelligence and biotechnology, as well as in conventional arms and outer space. The Trump administration pushed to "decouple" critical technology sectors from China, particularly on 5G, and pressed U.S. allies to do the same, with the goal of undermining and gaining greater independence from Beijing. It identified Chinese espionage as a major threat and began deporting Chinese officials and civilians who were believed to be involved in covert activities. Ideological competition escalated too. Senior cabinet members, particularly secretary of state Mike Pompeo, began to routinely denounce the Chinese Communist Party and highlight its abuses of the Uighur population in Xinjiang.[41]

There were complications and twists and turns. On a personal level, Trump admired Xi's authoritarianism and showed little concern for abuses in Hong Kong or internment camps in Xinjiang, reportedly even going so far as to tell Xi the camps were the right thing to do.[42] There were lingering doubts about whether he would really stand by U.S. allies in a time of crisis. But on the eve of the coronavirus pandemic, the United States and China were already on the brink of a spiraling confrontation. In many respects, the U.S.-China competition had become a contest of systems: free societies standing against resurgent authoritarianism. And this had profound implications for everything from technology policy and the economy to human rights, global health, the environment, and national security. The COVID-19 pandemic would enter this centrifuge of spinning rivalry at dizzying speed.

It was not just the United States. By the end of 2019, Europe remained committed to a policy of engagement with China, but it was also taking steps to reduce Chinese influence, protect itself against Beijing's economic practices, and to speak with one voice. The EU's 2019 document "The EU and China: A Strategy Outlook" described this shift in approach, stating: "China is, simultaneously, in different policy areas, a cooperation partner with whom the EU has closely aligned objectives, a negotiating partner with whom the EU needs to find a balance of interests, an economic competitor in the pursuit of technological leadership, and a systemic rival promoting alternative models of governance."[43]

ON THE THRESHOLD

As a consequence of all these dynamics, the post–World War II international order was careening toward a cliff, and the COVID-19 pandemic pushed it over the edge. Hyperglobalization meant the interdependent international system as a whole was more susceptible to a major transnational shock than ever before. Profound inequality meant that hundreds of millions of people around the world were extremely vulnerable not only to the virus but to the economic disruptions flowing from it. The rise of populist nationalism sweeping the globe meant that key countries were inclined to downplay the virus, ignore expertise, slow-roll responses, and shun cooperation with other nations. And the worsening U.S.-China rivalry meant that the world's two leading power centers were more intent on jockeying for relative advantage than on finding ways to foster international cooperation.

Unlike in every other major crisis of the post–Cold War period, when the COVID-19 pandemic hit, the United States failed to lead or seek to mobilize global action. With Trump breaking with tradition, a provocative question emerged: would other nations coalesce around a common purpose and self-organize to combat a shared existential threat in the absence of American leadership? For the most part, this did not happen. Instead, the void was filled with an every-nation-for-itself approach that left everyone worse off. As Princeton University's G. John Ikenberry, one of the leading U.S. theorists of the modern international system, observed: "Not since the 1930s has the world been this bereft of even the most rudimentary forms of cooperation."[44]

The 1930s reference is telling. The shadow of the interwar years—the last time the international order collapsed into chaos—hung over the world even before the contagion struck in December 2019.[45] And, as a consequence of COVID-19 and the pandemic politics it unleashed, the gathering storm clouds grew darker still.

But must it be so?

In his famous study *The Twenty Years' Crisis*, the historian E. H. Carr offered a withering critique of the utopian faith in liberal international-ism prominent in some British and American circles during the interwar years. Carr outlined the realist view that "history is a sequence of cause and effect, whose course can be analyzed and understood by intellec-tual effort, but not . . . directed by 'imagination.'"[46] Through this fatalistic lens, the coronavirus pandemic would seem to represent an insurmount-able challenge to international order and an irresistible accelerant to grim historical forces.[47]

Yet Carr was also careful to caution against "pure realism" because it "fails to provide any ground for purposive or meaningful action" and be-cause it "offer[s] nothing but a naked struggle for power which makes any kind of international society impossible."[48] Even with compelling struc-tural conditions pushing in one direction, people retain agency—and moments of profound crisis are precisely the times when opportunities can emerge to change course.[49] We can choose to make a bad situation worse, or we can push against seemingly intractable realities and make things better.

The liberal international order that emerged after the calamities of the interwar years and World War II—of which the global health regime became a part—was always highly imperfect. But it also produced un-precedented levels of economic growth, dramatic reductions in poverty, expanding freedom, declining levels of armed conflict, and transformative improvements in human health.

Yet, as we document throughout this book, the global response to COVID-19 revealed just how much the old order had broken down, how ill-equipped it was to handle the types of crises likely to be with us for the remainder of this century—and just how much work lies ahead to repair it. When the novel coronavirus emerged in Wuhan, the interna-tional community failed to come together, and the institutions created to protect public health were not up to the task. The Chinese Communist Party's lack of transparency hid the initial outbreak from the world, while China's growing influence in the WHO undermined the organization's initial response and credibility. Hyperglobalization ensured the virus would spread rapidly, and enormous inequalities within and between countries meant that responses aimed at containing the virus, and resources available to deal with its knock-on effects, would vary greatly across the international community. The WHO struggled to provide coherent guidance to rich and poor countries alike. Meanwhile, the rise of Trumpism and populist nationalism elsewhere generated a scenario no one had contemplated: the possibility that world leaders would actively attempt to sabotage pandemic response. And the escalating rivalry between Washington and Beijing warped the national responses of the world's two most consequential nations while paralyzing international efforts to collectively address the pandemic and its aftershocks. It is possible that a uniquely talented American president could have defied these trends and fashioned a cooperative response out of the chaos. It is surely true that a normal president would have avoided many of Trump's unforced errors. But it is also the case that the challenge in 2020 was not just Trump, as problematic as he was. All told, a system that was primed for peril failed at the worst possible time.

PART II

· · · · ·

INTERNATIONAL CRISIS, NATIONAL RESPONSES

4

Secrets and Lies

IN JULY 2019, the Chinese Center for Disease Control and Prevention (CCDC) held a training exercise for 8,200 officials. The scenario: a traveler arrives in China with a highly contagious virus. The officials' task: raise the alarm and locate the other passengers before the contagion spreads. It was the largest CCDC operation since the response to the SARS outbreak.

SARS, a disease produced by a novel coronavirus that emerged in southern China in November 2002, is believed to have originated in bats. Its symptoms resemble influenza and include cough, fever, and headache; in some cases, however, the disease can lead to severe respiratory problems.[1] The response to SARS was also a textbook example of how not to respond to a pandemic. The outbreak started in Guangdong province; the authorities knew they had a problem but kept it under wraps, because they did not want to disrupt the tourist season during the Lunar New Year in January 2003. As residents exchanged information by text message, the authorities accused a hundred people of rumormongering. The Chinese media, which back then still existed as a relatively independent entity, was banned from reporting on the outbreak. The *Southern Metropolis Daily*, a newspaper in Guangdong, ignored the censor and blew the whistle.[2]

When the virus arrived in a People's Liberation Army (PLA) base in Beijing, the military offered no public acknowledgment. However, Jiang

Yanyong, a seventy-three-year-old army doctor stationed there, was suspicious of a cover-up and wrote a letter accusing the government of underestimating the number of fatalities from the virus. He sent it first to Chinese media outlets and then to U.S. media, including a young reporter at the *Wall Street Journal* named Matthew Pottinger, who would play a significant role in the American response to the COVID-19 crisis seventeen years later. As the *Journal* was checking its facts, Pottinger was scooped by *Time* magazine. The story was now out worldwide, but China still refused to cooperate with the international community.[3]

At the time, the director of the World Health Organization was a medical doctor and a former prime minister of Norway, Gro Harlem Brundtland. When news of SARS became public, she used her position to very vocally demand that the Chinese government operate more transparently and cooperatively. She had no legal authority to speak out; she just did. Interviewed during the COVID-19 pandemic, Brundtland reflected on that time: "What China did then was, for days and then weeks, to refuse to take my call to the health minister of China. . . . I then spoke out because there was no alternative and I had no response so I had to speak out publicly against China to ask them to answer my calls and then they did."[4] She was willing to push back in other ways as well. In 2018, she told a Taiwanese audience that during SARS "I had the responsibility to work with the health authorities of Taiwan to help prevent spreading in Taiwan or from Taiwan or into Taiwan. In that way," she said, referring to China, "the governments that were most against Taiwan becoming part of the UN system had to shut up."[5]

Brundtland's actions made a difference. After weeks of indecision, Beijing came clean, acknowledging the scale of the problem and beginning to cooperate with the WHO. Before the WHO would declare that the virus was under control in July 2003, SARS would spread internationally, infect 8,098 people, and claim 774 lives. Shortly afterward, China introduced new regulations to promote openness in dealing with viruses. It established the Contagious Disease National Direct Reporting System, which was meant to be independent and protected from political interference. Doctors would report cases directly to a team in Beijing tasked with tackling outbreaks early on, before they could truly wreak havoc.[6] As Dali Yang, a professor at the University of Chicago, later put it: "In a country known for its bureaucratic hierarchy, this information system is designed for attention escalation—and rapid response."[7]

The new system was used with considerable success during the H1N1 influenza outbreak of 2009 and the spike in avian flu cases in 2017. In a speech in 2019, George Gao, the director of the CCDC, who had been trained at Oxford and was persuaded to return to China after SARS to help with the reforms, confidently declared that while infectious diseases can emerge at any time, China was now better prepared. "I am confident to say that there will be no 'SARS incident' [like 2003]," he said. "This is due to the fact that our country's infectious disease surveillance network is very well established. When the virus comes, we can stop it."[8] The improved system was on full display in the July 2019 training exercise.

China has not historically been a particularly big player in global public health, but in the 2010s it began to look for opportunities to make contributions consistent with its expertise. For instance, China became involved in malaria prevention programs because a Chinese scientist, Tu Youyou, received a Nobel Prize in Medicine for developing the drugs artemisinin and dihydroartemisinin to treat the disease. The Ebola outbreak of 2014–15 was the first time China sent a high-powered team (led by George Gao) abroad as part of an international effort. Yet its contribution remained marginal compared to other countries. China was only a small financial contributor to the WHO—ranking sixteenth in 2018, behind several private foundations and countries such as Kuwait and Sweden.[9]

What really seemed to matter, though, was its national system, which appeared highly capable of managing a crisis of this sort. On the surface, China seemed prepared—but there were troubling signs for those who looked closely. A comprehensive health security assessment by Johns Hopkins University, the Nuclear Threat Initiative, and the Economist Intelligence Unit released in 2019 highlighted gaps in China's health emergency response system, especially in the realm of communication between the government and the public, and between public health professionals and hospitals.[10] Moreover, in a crisis, China's national health system was only one part of the puzzle. The provinces and localities play a key role and there was considerable variation between them.

American health experts in Beijing had a long history of cooperation with their Chinese counterparts on wide-ranging topics, from training Chinese public health officials on field epidemiology, to collaborating on cancer research, to establishing protocols for the safety of the food and medical products bound for the United States—but even these previously positive collaborations began to fray in the years leading up to the SARS-CoV-2 outbreak. Adrienne Parrish Fuentes was the health attaché at the U.S. embassy in Beijing. Employed by the U.S. Department of Health and Human Services, she led a team of dozens of CDC, FDA, and NIH officials in China, all based at the U.S. embassy. She had been hired to her position in October 2016, shortly before the U.S. election that elevated Trump to the presidency. Before COVID-19, one of the policy issues she was most focused on was engaging China on sharing samples of a strain of bird flu known as H7N9. Public health experts believed that this form of influenza (or some variant) could be the most likely source of the next global pandemic. One of the tools in place to prevent this from happening was a small network of labs called WHO Collaborating Centers for Influenza (six in total: two in the United States, and one each in the United Kingdom, Australia, Japan, and China) that are responsible for conducting research and sharing samples of influenza strains of concern. Such sharing across national borders is a complex task that involves international agreements and many levels of country-specific bureaucracy. Health ministries typically make commitments to share these viruses "in a timely manner" as a matter of global public health importance, but at the country level the approvals to release these potentially deadly viruses must be executed by multiple government ministries. For the first two years of her tour, at the direction of the National Security Council, Parrish Fuentes was engaged with her Chinese counterparts to share H7N9 samples requested by the WHO Collaborating Center in Atlanta at a faster pace. Officials at the White House and the Biomedical Advanced Research and Development Authority at the U.S. Department of Health and Human Services (HHS) were frustrated with the slow pace of Chinese approvals to share virus strains with the WHO network. Senior U.S. officials raised the issue with their Chinese counterparts multiple times, in Beijing and on the sidelines of the World Health Assembly. The U.S. ambassador to China, Terry Branstad, even went to the research facility housing the strains of flu to make the case personally. U.S. officials did not know if the delay was because of bureaucratic inertia or deliberate secrecy, but whatever the reason, China continued to withhold some of the samples.

In the spring of 2019, the U.S. embassy had hosted an event to mark forty years of U.S.-China relations. One of the key topics highlighted during the commemoration was public health cooperation because it was widely regarded as a success story in a sometimes tumultuous bilateral relationship. The HHS team had planned to have speakers from the CCDC and an NIH grantee at the event. China's National Health Commission (NHC) was also to attend. Trade tensions had also been building, and twenty-four hours before the event all the health counterparts canceled, leaving the team to scramble to bring on other speakers. It was a harbinger of things to come.

THE COVER-UP

The first person who is known to have become sick with COVID-19 developed symptoms in Wuhan, China, on December 1, 2019. We still know very little about the origins of SARS-CoV-2, the novel coronavirus responsible for the respiratory disease COVID-19 that would upend the whole world in short order, but it is believed to have originally come from bats. Early on, the Huanan Seafood Wholesale Market, a "wet market" selling a variety of live animals in Wuhan, was suspected of being the original source of the outbreak because a number of those infected in December had some connection to it. It was not clear how the novel coronavirus had made its way to Wuhan, but many scientists speculated that it may have jumped from bats in southern China to another animal that was then transported to the Huanan market, where it made an additional jump to humans.

Within the U.S. government, however, the suspicions of some national security analysts and officials centered on the Wuhan Institute of Virology (WIV). The WIV studied bat coronaviruses and researchers there were known to have engaged in so-called gain-of-function experiments in which the genome of a virus is deliberately modified to give it new properties, such as enabling it to infect a new species or spread more easily. The goal of such research need not be nefarious; indeed, American universities and institutions had partnered with Chinese counterparts at the WIV on gain-of-function experiments to predict how deadly viruses might evolve in order to develop countermeasures. It was therefore conceivable that SARS-CoV-2 had accidentally "leaked" from the Wuhan lab to the nearby community.[11] The Chinese government and the scientists who worked at the WIV vehemently denied that this laboratory facility was the source of the contagion. Beijing later floated its own theories, including the unfounded notion that the contagion had made its way to China through frozen food imported from abroad.[12] Without a thorough international investigation with full access and cooperation from Chinese authorities, the truth regarding the origins of SARS-CoV-2 would remain impossible to discern.

What is not in dispute is that by mid-December, the novel coronavirus was circulating in Wuhan. Cases began to trickle in, with patients displaying similar symptoms (a persistent cough, shortness of breath, and fatigue), but doctors were slow to notice a pattern. On Christmas Day, medical staff began to fall ill with pneumonia. Doctors at Wuhan Central Hospital took a sample from a patient's lungs and sent it to the private company Vision Medicals, which specializes in pathogenic gene diagnostic services. The report came back on December 26: a short genetic sequence of the virus suggested it was "bat SARS-like coronavirus." The company informed the Wuhan office of the CCDC.[13] Although local government officials began to privately warn of a pneumonia of unknown origin in Wuhan, no one told the headquarters of the CCDC in Beijing, possibly because they did not want to acknowledge to Beijing that they had a problem. CCDC director Gao learned of the outbreak from leaked reports by Wuhan officials on December 30. Stunned, he called them, only to find that the virus had been circulating for almost a month. He had been cut out of the loop. The surveillance system that had been put in place after SARS had failed.[14] By this time, social media was rife with rumors of a new SARS.

December 30 was also the day that a Wuhan doctor named Ai Fen got the results back from a patient's laboratory test: the mysterious disease appeared to be like SARS. She sent a video of the affected patient's lungs to a colleague and informed her bosses. The report ended up with Li Wenliang, a doctor at Wuhan Central, who told a hundred colleagues in a WeChat posting: "7 SARS cases confirmed at Huanan Seafood Market." He later updated his post to say: "Coronavirus confirmed, and type being determined . . . Don't leak it. Tell your family and relatives to take care."[15]

On December 31, the WHO office in Beijing informed the organization's headquarters in Geneva of the Wuhan pneumonia cases, which officially became the moment the world discovered the outbreak. At that point Wuhan health officials issued a statement saying that twenty-seven people had contracted pneumonia connected to the seafood market. The statement went on: "The investigation so far has not found any obvious human-to-human transmission or infection of medical staff. . . . The disease is preventable and controllable."[16] In Taipei, officials from the Taiwan Centers for Disease Control began to receive reports of a SARS-like virus in Wuhan. Alarmed, they sent an email to the WHO warning of an "atypical pneumonia" in the city, a phrase understood to mean human-to-human transmission. But they never received a response.[17] That evening Gao called Ian Lipkin, a professor of epidemiology at Columbia University, and told him that he had identified the virus as a new coronavirus, but it was "not highly transmissible."[18]

The outbreak in Wuhan quickly became the embassy team's top priority; within a week, it was the only thing they were working on. U.S. officials got in touch with their contacts at China's National Health Commission, and the U.S. CDC was in contact with the CCDC, but the information provided was never more than what was in the official reports. The decades-old track record of U.S.-China cooperation on public health seemed to be of little use during this burgeoning crisis. Back channels where more sensitive information could be conveyed did not materialize. In fact, on the Chinese side, all such means of communication went dark. No one was talking. The HHS team pushed their Chinese counterparts to gain access to critical information about human-to-human transmission or cases of infected health care workers or evidence of asymptomatic transmission, but the National Health Commission was adamant through most of January that there was no evidence of human-to-human transmission. Chinese authorities were clearly worried though, as it soon became clear to staff across the U.S. embassy that the entire Chinese government was seized with managing the growing Wuhan crisis. One U.S. embassy official told us they had never seen Chinese officials as "unconfident, terrified, and nervous" as they were during this period.

Dozens of new patients were now arriving in Wuhan's hospitals, all displaying similar symptoms. Samples from six of the original seven patients were sent to the WIV and a number of other Chinese laboratories around January 2. The next day, China's National Health Commission issued a secret order prohibiting the labs from publishing their results. They also required them to destroy or hand over the samples of the virus. Even though the scientists had the full genetic sequence of the virus, they could not do anything with the information. On January 8, the *Wall Street Journal* reported that Chinese scientists had discovered a novel coronavirus, naming it SARS-CoV-2. Two days later, Chinese authorities acknowledged that the *Journal*'s report was correct. Still, they would not release the genetic sequence of the virus.

Zhang Yongzhen was one of the Chinese scientists who mapped the genetic sequence of the virus. He did so in collaboration with an Australia-based virologist, Edward Holmes. Holmes grew increasingly anxious that they were prohibited from sharing this vital information with the world. After the *Wall Street Journal* story and confirmation from the Chinese government, Holmes pressed Zhang again. Zhang was conflicted but agreed: the world needed to know. On January 11, Holmes emailed the information to Virological.org, a website based in Scotland, and he quickly posted a link on Twitter to their story. The next day, January 12, with the cat out of the bag, the Chinese government finally released their own findings on the virus's genome.

The WHO was privately alarmed, according to the Associated Press, whose reporters gained access to a trove of internal documents months after the outbreak had become a pandemic. The week of January 6, Maria Van Kerkhove, an American epidemiologist working for the WHO, said in an internal meeting, "We're going on very minimal information. . . . It's clearly not enough for you to do proper planning." Dr. Gauden Galea, the WHO's top official in China, said in another meeting, "We're currently at the stage where yes, they're giving it to us 15 minutes before it appears on [China Central Television]." There was deep frustration that WHO officials were being denied access to the raw data. "This would not happen in Congo and did not happen in Congo and other places," Michael Ryan, executive director of the WHO Health Emergencies Programme, said, apparently referring to the Ebola outbreak that had emerged in that country in 2018. "We need to see the data. . . . It's absolutely important at this point." WHO officials debated among themselves how to persuade China to release detailed patient data. Ryan argued it was time to "shift gears" and apply more pressure. Reflecting on the WHO's struggles with China during SARS, he told colleagues: "This is exactly the same scenario, endlessly trying to get updates from China about what was going on. . . . WHO barely got out of that one with its neck intact given the

issues that arose around transparency in southern China." He wanted to
be as aggressive as Brundtland had been during SARS and call out Beijing.[19]

WHO officials also believed that Washington was fully aware of their
private deliberations. Approximately two dozen Americans from the U.S.
CDC and NIH were posted inside the WHO, just as other countries had
their own representatives. It was widely assumed that some of these individuals would share information with their home governments and even
the press, as someone did to the Associated Press. As one WHO official
put it to us, "The Americans knew everything we knew."

All these frustrations would remain strictly private. Shortly after Ryan
warned his colleagues about China's secrecy, the WHO's Galea went on
Chinese state television and said:

> It appears that the cases have stopped, new cases have stopped after the
> market was temporarily closed. And we can see that there is no clear
> evidence of sustained human-to-human transmission. The sheer speed
> of the response in China, the quality of the closure of the hospital—the
> market, the extremely rapid investigation, shows the increase in capac-
> ity that China has acquired.[20]

Unlike in 2003, the current director general of the WHO had no intention of calling China out. Tedros Adhanom Ghebreyesus had served
as health minister and subsequently as foreign affairs minister for Ethiopia before being elected WHO's director general in 2017. He believed
that it was only by working constructively with China that its government
could be persuaded to cooperate. They were facing an immense crisis,
and in his view, the international community should show some empa-
thy and patience. Senior WHO officials also believed that Xi Jinping was
a different type of Chinese leader—more dictatorial and less susceptible
to outside pressure than his predecessors. If they tried to call him out, Xi
was likely to shut them out completely and nothing would get done; he
would not tolerate a Brundtland-like strategy. Working with China was
the last, best hope of stopping the virus, they believed, and if that meant
publicly flattering the regime, then that was the price that would have to
be paid. Organization officials saw Tedros as a consummate politician,
in the best sense of that term—someone who was constantly consulting

with stakeholders and adopting a very "organic approach" to a problem, feeling his way through and persuading leaders about why they needed to come on board. Confrontation was not his default stance; conciliation was how he got things done.

Some public health experts also believed that Tedros's personal background shaped his worldview in ways that would have significant implications for his leadership of the WHO. Given their experience of colonialism, many African nations (including Ethiopia, which was not formally colonized but had been occupied for several years after a war with Italy in the 1930s) are more skeptical of Western interventionism than Americans or Europeans. In international organizations, African member states tend to be protective of sovereignty for precisely this reason: to protect against overreach and undue meddling by Western powers. With some of these sensitivities, Tedros was closer to the Chinese view of sovereignty than he was to the Europeans.[21]

The U.S. embassy in Beijing quickly went into crisis mode by mid-January when it began to undertake emergency planning. Ambassador Branstad, a former governor of Iowa who had first met Xi Jinping when Xi visited Iowa on an agricultural study trip in 1985, began holding town hall meetings to brief the community on developments. He made clear that the priority was to find out what was happening in Wuhan and to protect Americans in China. They had to discover how bad the spread really was and where the virus had originated. The United States had a consulate in Wuhan, but there were no HHS officials on the ground there; instead, State Department foreign service officers covered the health portfolio. In daily calls, Parrish Fuentes and the embassy health team, including epidemiologists from the U.S. CDC, gave State Department officials in Wuhan a crash course in epidemiology. They were told what to look for, where to look (including at the Huanan market and at local hospitals), and the right questions to ask. But access to information was very limited. Updates on case numbers, local lockdowns, and circumstances at local hospitals were sent from across the U.S. mission in China back to Washington on a daily basis.

On January 14, the WHO acknowledged there could be "limited human-to-human transmission, potentially among families." The next day, Li Qun, the head of the CCDC's emergency center, claimed: "After careful screening and prudent judgment, we have reached the latest understanding that the risk of human-to-human transmission is low."[22] A health worker at a Wuhan hospital later told PBS that by this time, "everyone knew it was human-to-human transmission. Even a fool would know. So why say there is no human transmission? This made us very confused. Very confused and very angry."[23]

LOCKDOWN

By mid-January, Thailand and Japan were reporting cases of the novel coronavirus—all involving people who had come from Wuhan. The Lunar New Year, one of the busiest travel periods in Asia, was fast approaching, raising fears of further contagion. Not everyone appeared outwardly concerned. Chinese authorities continued to say very little publicly and kept their neighboring states in the dark as well. On January 18, Wuhan held a mass Lunar New Year banquet. And over the course of the holiday, 5 million people would leave the city without screening.[24] Two days later, Chinese state media reported that, for the first time, President Xi had ordered officials to contain the virus. After weeks of silence, secrecy, and misdirection, the Chinese leader had finally publicly recognized the severity of the crisis and personally begun to oversee its management. And yet Xi gave a speech that day that made no mention of human-to-human transmission. His omission was grossly misleading. A few hours later, Zhong Nanshan, an epidemiology expert and head of the task force in Wuhan, confirmed that human-to-human transmission was happening.[25]

In her diary of life in Wuhan during the virus, Fang Fang, an award-winning Chinese author, wrote: "My first reaction was shock, but that turned into anger. This new information was completely at odds with what we had seen and heard earlier. Official media sources had been consistently telling us that this virus was 'Not Contagious Between People; It's Controllable and Preventable.'"[26] Fang had previously sent a message to a WeChat group saying: "The government would never try to conceal something so huge." Later she would write, "We have placed too much faith in the government."[27]

The situation at WHO headquarters in Geneva was not much better. On January 22–23 the WHO Emergency Committee met to discuss whether to declare COVID-19 a public health emergency of international concern (PHEIC), a formal designation of a pandemic that would take the international response to the next level. Revisions to the International Health Regulations (IHR) in 2005 granted the director general the power to declare a PHEIC by relying on information from nonstate actors and over the objections of member states. It was an extraordinary and radical power given to the WHO in the aftermath of SARS at a time of low tension between the major powers. As David Fidler, an expert in international health law at Indiana University and the Council on Foreign Relations, put it,

> A PHEIC declaration is designed to heighten public health and po-
> litical awareness of the need to double-down on core components of
> the IHR—conducting surveillance, notifying cases of serious disease
> events, sharing information on outbreaks and response strategies, co-
> operating with WHO and other countries, strengthening public health
> capacities, and implementing trade and travel measures that help rather
> than hinder response activities.[28]

However, under Tedros's leadership, the WHO had grown skeptical of the benefits of the PHEIC power. In 2019, the Emergency Committee decided on three separate occasions not to declare a PHEIC in response to an Ebola outbreak in the Democratic Republic of the Congo (DRC); each time, Tedros endorsed this decision. This delay sparked considerable controversy among global health experts. An editorial in the medical journal *The Lancet* after the Emergency Committee decided in June 2019, for the third time, not to issue a declaration about the outbreak, which had begun the previous September, observed that the committee had decided "the economic harms associated with a PHEIC declaration would outweigh the benefits." This, the editorial said, was "more political than technical" and "a mistake." It concluded: "The committee seems to have favored local protectionism over global galvanizing."[29] Under considerable pressure, the WHO finally declared a PHEIC a month later, in July 2019, after the Ebola virus spread to Goma, a city in eastern DRC bordering Rwanda, raising fears it would go international. To close observers, though, the message was clear: the WHO was reluctant to use the power it had at its disposal.

In the days leading up to the Emergency Committee meeting on

January 22, 2020, to address the mounting COVID-19 crisis, Chinese officials intensely lobbied the committee members against declaring a PHEIC, and Beijing's ambassador to the organization made it clear that such an action would be seen as a vote of no confidence in China. Their efforts were successful: the committee was split down the middle. The decision was ultimately Tedros's, and, just as in the case of Ebola, he chose to delay the designation. He did not have the cover of full support from the committee, but there is no sign that he was personally more forward-leaning on wanting to make a declaration. He was also weighing the risk of alienating China at a time when he needed their cooperation.

Tedros was focused on getting permission to visit Beijing, where he could press Xi personally to share vital information. Ryan would later tell the press, "The WHO doesn't interact in public debate or criticize our member states in public. What we try to do is work with our member states constructively, pointing out to them when we believe their measures are not adequate, aggressive enough or comprehensive enough."[30] It was a mantra WHO officials would repeat again and again when asked about why they didn't put pressure on the Chinese government.

Senior WHO officials were also of the view that reforms to the IHR in 2005 had removed the discretion that Brundtland previously had been able to exercise during SARS. According to their internal legal analysis, which we have seen, the 2005 reforms prevented the director general from contradicting a member state and from going public when that state was not following the rules. It very clearly laid out a dispute resolution mechanism that should be followed in the case of a disagreement. Their hands were tied, they argued. In essence, the WHO's position was that legally it did not have a choice, but in any event organization officials felt that the stance they were obliged to take was also the wisest one.

This interpretation of the IHR was strongly disputed by U.S. officials and by several experts on international public health we spoke to. Fidler told us: "There is nothing in the IHRs that required the WHO to be obsequious in its response to China during COVID. In fact, the IHRs provide the director general with additional authority—for instance, to declare a PHEIC over the objections of the member state where the outbreak occurred—that Gro Brundtland did not have in 2003." Fidler went on to say that the notion that there were only two options—the Brundtland path and what Tedros chose to do—was a false dichotomy. In reality, there were a myriad of options in between. For one thing, Tedros could simply have remained silent about aspects of China's response, which would, Fidler said, have "spoken volumes." Or the WHO could have focused attention on the risk of human-to-human transmission that Chinese authorities were downplaying despite evidence to the contrary.[31]

The U.S. permanent representative to the WHO, Andrew Bremberg, had previously served in the White House during the Trump administration as director of the Domestic Policy Council. Around the third week in January, as Tedros was trying to get permission to go to Beijing, Bremberg spoke with him. Bremberg told the WHO director general, "The United States has your back 100 percent. If there's ever anything you need, just pick up the phone and call. But please start being careful because you are getting out over your skis and you risk politicizing the virus." Referring to Tedros's praise for the Chinese government in tackling the virus, he went on: "You are saying things we hope are true, but we fear might not be. Please be careful, you are putting your personal and institutional reputation at risk."

To understand why the WHO and the United States clashed over how to handle China, it is helpful to first recognize what they agreed on. They both agreed that the situation in China was dire and could pose a threat to the rest of the world, that the Chinese government was covering up vital information, and that the authoritarian nature of Xi's regime posed a unique challenge when it came to managing the crisis. What they disagreed on was how to proceed. The WHO thought they would simply not be able to function if they alienated Beijing. They looked at the confrontational approach Trump had taken over the past three years and concluded that it had not made Beijing more cooperative. They believed that their approach would get results, albeit slowly—Chinese authorities were cooperating with Galea, the head of the WHO's office in Beijing, and they would soon be allowed to visit. They also had some sympathy for China's predicament and were genuinely impressed with the speed and scale of the response. From the WHO's perspective, they were alone. No one else had an alternative plan to get China to cooperate. As they saw it, there was nothing to stop the United States from rallying other countries to put pressure on China—although they noted that, at the time, Trump was praising Xi—but that was not their job. In this assessment the WHO was not alone; British officials, for example, felt that America's position, that it was a fool's game to try to influence China from within, was not a realistic option for their government to follow. The British embassy in Beijing was frustrated with China's refusal to share information, one British official told us, but felt that they had to engage constructively.

U.S. officials, on the other hand, believed they had seen this movie before. The Chinese government was covering up a crisis to save its own skin, just as it had in 2003. Time was of the essence. Xi was an autocrat, but he cared about China's standing in the world. If the WHO, with its moral authority, was to accurately describe to the world the regime's obstructionism and delaying tactics, as they were doing in internal meetings, it might make the Chinese more cooperative. After all, Beijing had only released their findings on the SARS-CoV-2 genome after independent scientists did so. They always had to be pushed. Moreover, indulging China also meant delaying actions, such as declaring a PHEIC or encouraging travel restrictions, that could have rallied the world to contain the virus. For American national security officials, the WHO's decision not to speak out was not just a matter of coddling China; it also was a conscious decision that meant losing time in the hope of cooperation from Beijing that might never come. Every day spent praising China was effectively a day in which the WHO was complicit in concealing the truth about human-to-human transmission. According to multiple Trump administration sources we spoke to, U.S. officials also felt that as long as Tedros continued to praise China, the Europeans would not risk criticizing Beijing for fear of tarnishing the WHO. There was another reason for Washington's frustration with the WHO, one fraught with irony: U.S. officials could not count on President Trump to put pressure on China because he was still trying to remain on Xi's good side after the January U.S.-China trade deal. So they turned instead to an international multilateral institution—just the kind that the administration typically loved to criticize and accuse of trampling the rights of sovereign states.

Meanwhile, the U.S. embassy in Beijing had formally closed for the Lunar New Year holiday, and many staff had gone on vacation, as was custom. Branstad had gone to New Zealand on January 23, but stayed in daily contact with U.S. deputy chief of mission Bill Klein. The hospitals in Beijing and Shanghai informed the embassy not to send their personnel there if they felt ill. Then Singapore, where U.S. diplomats would be medevaced to in case of an emergency, also sent a message saying do not come. Klein spoke with Branstad: "Holy shit, China is closing down. The uncertainty of what is going on is increasing by the hour. We don't know if it is safe or not." Branstad and Klein were worried that the Chinese system was imploding. Branstad cut his trip short. He knew he would have to make some of the most important decisions of his tenure, including on an emergency evacuation of American diplomats unprecedented in its scale and speed. He returned on January 28.

Those in the embassy quickly learned to assess the situation based on the actions China was taking on the ground rather than on any official messaging from the authorities. What they saw was a massive increase of police on the streets, the army called in, and travel restrictions imposed on Hubei province, where the city of Wuhan is located. This was it, Parrish Fuentes realized: a mass quarantine unlike anything the world had seen in modern history. It was imposed on Thursday, January 23.

Xi ordered a lockdown within, and a cordon around, Wuhan and three other cities—an extraordinary move that quarantined more than 100 million people. The scale and draconian nature of the public health intervention were unprecedented. Xi would go on to declare the fight against the virus to be "a people's war." The use of private vehicles was banned. People were confined to their homes except for permitted trips to the grocery store and hospitals. All of China declared a level 1 emergency response, the highest level possible, transferring responsibility and authority for the response to the State Council in Beijing. In just two weeks, two new infectious disease hospitals were built in Wuhan. Stadiums were converted into temporary hospitals for people with mild symptoms. Nearly 43,000 doctors, nurses, and public health specialists arrived in the city from all over China.[32] The regime would organize a massive effort to produce personal protective equipment (PPE), including masks, gloves, hazmat suits, and respirators, and, when needed, to import supplies from abroad.

Lunar New Year fell on Saturday, January 25, two days after the lockdown was announced. As previously noted, this holiday was traditionally the busiest travel period of the year, comparable to Thanksgiving and Christmas in the United States rolled into one. The U.S. embassy worried that travelers might spread the virus around Asia. Wuhan was now locked down, but infected people might have already have left for Shanghai, Beijing—really anywhere, including abroad. But Beijing allowed flights outside Wuhan to continue as normal. The embassy health team was dismayed that Chinese officials would allow unfettered travel given the high risk of contagion.

Tedros had been pressing Chinese officials for permission to travel to Beijing, and he finally got his visit on January 28. He was accompanied by Ryan and other senior WHO staff. WHO officials told us that the delegation was moved by the gravity of the crisis they witnessed firsthand and genuinely impressed by the steps Beijing was taking to contain the spread of the virus. Their meeting with Xi was very polite, but when they met with the Chinese foreign minister, Wang Yi, Tedros began pushing for additional cooperation, speaking in a low-key but insistent manner. Ryan and others in the room worried this approach would backfire. But Tedros got what he had come for: a promise to allow an international team into China, among other things. He saw this as a vindication of their approach.

With Beijing's commitment in hand, Tedros was happy to shower praise on China's response, saying it showed "China's efficiency and the advantages of China's system." "Xi's personal guidance and deployment," Tedros continued, "show his great leadership capability."[33] At a press conference in Geneva hours after returning from China, Ryan sounded a very different note in public than in the private meetings earlier in January, saying: "We've seen no obvious lack of transparency. . . . I was involved in 2002 and 2003 in SARS and I can tell you from direct operational experience that there is no comparison between the behavior of China then and the behavior of China now."[34]

The public rhetoric, which was so at odds with the regime's secrecy and cover-up as well as with the WHO's private assessments, dismayed U.S. officials. Lost in the personal praise of Xi and the whitewashing of his regime's secrecy was something even more remarkable. In previous disease outbreaks the WHO had always advised against restrictions on travel and trade, largely because of their impact on the world's most vulnerable people. That position was derived from their experience fighting viruses in the developing world. The fact that the WHO would embrace these measures now was a sign of how bad things really were.

The attention of the U.S. embassy in Beijing quickly turned to protecting Americans. They had thousands of personnel and family members in China. There were thirty-five Americans stuck in the consulate in

Wuhan, including diplomats, family members, and construction workers. Wuhan had to be dealt with first but no one knew how. The Chinese
were so distracted by the mounting crisis that they had little interest in
helping, at least at first. The embassy looked at an evacuation by land but
that was too complicated. The State Department offered a plane with 201
seats. China offered a slot between midnight and 4 a.m. on the twenty-
eighth and the thirty-five Americans in the consulate left along with
approximately 160 other Americans in Wuhan. In the days that followed,
the embassy realized they had another 1,000 or so Americans in Hubei
who wanted to get out, including between 100 and 150 infant children
born in the United States who were living with grandparents while their
Chinese-born parents worked in America. The Chinese government was
adamant that non-U.S. passport holders would not be allowed to travel,
meaning the infants would be unaccompanied on the plane. In a chaotic
week, Branstad and Klein negotiated their passage out of the country,
but right until the last moment they were unsure it would work. They
told the grandparents, just turn up at the airport and we will figure it
out. By that point, the Chinese officials, spread across numerous departments, all of which needed to sign off on the travel, wanted to help
foreigners leave as soon as possible—it would be one less problem to
deal with. They agreed to let the grandparents go. It was a small but significant humanitarian victory for the embassy. Five planes left over the
course of the week. But that was just Hubei.

On January 30, Branstad sent a cable to Washington requesting a voluntary evacuation of nonessential personnel, especially family members.
On January 31, they received a response: such an evacuation was to be
mandatory instead of merely voluntary. All family members, personnel
under age twenty-one, and nonessential diplomats were to leave as soon
as practically possible. The embassy was to work toward reducing the
number of diplomats by two-thirds (they ended up with 20 percent of
their personnel in place). In all, over 1,000 Americans left—the largest
emergency evacuation of U.S. diplomats in the history of the State Department. Branstad sought flexibility to have embassy staff return, but the
State Department wanted to reduce the number of staff as much as possible. The embassy believed Washington did not fully appreciate the value
of maintaining a substantial presence in the country, especially once the

public health crisis eased. An embassy is like a nuclear power plant, embassy officials felt—you can't just turn it off; you have to keep it running. There was an additional practical reason for the alarm in Washington. In the realm of espionage, China and the United States were rivals, and precautions on this front were significant. Senior officials in Washington worried that the virus could give China a rationale to isolate senior U.S. diplomats in hospitals and compel them to provide blood samples. This could not be allowed; under no circumstances were U.S. officials to allow the Chinese government to detain them under the guise of treatment. They would have to come home.

In the days after the WHO's trip to China, Bremberg asked Tedros to press Chinese officials for samples from the earliest cases of COVID-19. U.S. scientists desperately needed access to these samples to better understand how the virus might be evolving. Tedros did ask Beijing to share samples, but in a manner that would not ruffle any feathers; in other words, he went about it secretly. Days and then weeks went by with no response from China. Bremberg grew increasingly frustrated. There comes a point, he told Tedros, when you just have to say, "We tried, but they won't cooperate." In addition to their philosophical disagreement with the United States about how to secure cooperation from China, WHO officials felt that the Americans really wanted to criticize China directly, even though this could blow apart any prospect of cooperation with Beijing, because it would serve the larger purpose of bolstering Trump's anti-China efforts. U.S. officials disputed this, saying that they only ever asked the WHO to accurately describe what China was doing or not doing and that he did not ask them to criticize China directly, although undoubtedly others would do so. A WHO expert group, including two Americans, did get permission to visit China in mid-February, but their visit was strictly controlled by Chinese authorities. Only a small subset of the group was permitted to travel to Wuhan, and then only for a day, to visit two hospitals. They were not allowed to go to the market thought to be the first site of the outbreak. Indeed, the group had to agree in advance not to investigate the origins of the virus or China's initial response. The final report of the group praised Xi for having "personally directed and deployed the prevention and control work" on the virus.[35]

Within a month of the lockdown, the virus in Wuhan appeared to be under control. Extraordinary containment measures, it seemed, had worked.[36] Going into the spring, China took other actions unfathomable in the United States or other democracies. It separated families if one member tested positive, a policy that included infants. It succeeded in re-opening universities, but it prohibited students from leaving campus and enforced that edict with facial recognition cameras adjusted to identify individuals even when they wore a face mask. At the same time, given its population density, China struggled to implement social distancing in classrooms or workplaces.[37] The images from Wuhan stunned the Chinese people. On social media, people vented their anger at the government cover-up and repression, calling COVID-19 "China's Chernobyl moment"—drawing comparisons to the Soviet nuclear disaster that exposed the lies and incompetence of the communist regime. But Beijing dug in. By March, Chinese authorities seemed to be gaining the upper hand over the virus. And, having contained one threat, they would soon go after other enemies.

QUASHING DISSENT

Beijing realized if news of its botched initial response leaked out, it could damage the Chinese Communist Party. So Xi was determined to act quickly against any dissenting voices inside China that questioned the official narrative. He would also dramatically ramp up China's propaganda efforts internationally to muddy the waters on what was known about China's role in the COVID-19 crisis. This was very much in keeping with his increasingly authoritarian style of governing. In the years leading up to the pandemic, Xi had cracked down on freedom of speech and even on freedom of thought. For example, professors were monitored in their classrooms as they taught. People were ascribed a social credit score based on their behavior that would partly determine whether they could travel overseas, get into a university, or be hired by the state.

While defeating the contagion was a focus, the CCP also oversaw something they could control more directly: they tried to cut off the flow of information about the disease by cracking down on anyone who tried to raise the alarm. The doctors were first in line. After Dr. Li Wenliang posted his WeChat message of warning, he was reprimanded by hospital

authorities and arrested by the police. He was released only after signing a statement confessing to "illegal acts," and he was told he would be
arrested again if he spoke out further. But Li was not deterred. He went
public with Weibo messages on January 31 and February 1 warning the
world, publishing the letter reprimanding him, and revealing that he had
contracted COVID-19. A week later, on February 7, he died of the disease.[38] On his deathbed he told a reporter, "I think there should be more
than one voice in a healthy society, and I don't approve of using public
power for excessive interference." Within hours of his death, more than 2
million people had shared the hashtag #Iwantfreedomofspeech.[39]

Dr. Ai, who had discovered the virus on December 30, sent a warning to her colleagues on New Year's Day and told her colleagues to wear
masks. She was quickly reprimanded by her superiors, who later told her:

> When we go out to take part in meetings we can't even raise our heads.
> This or that director criticizes us and talks about how our hospital has
> that Ai Fen. As the head of the emergency unit at Wuhan Central Hospital
> you are a professional. How can you go and stir up a rumor like this
> without reason, without any organizational discipline?[40]

In early March, Ai gave an interview to China's *Renwu* magazine and
criticized the regime for lying about the virus. "If I had known what was
to happen," she said, "I would not have cared about the reprimand. I
would have fucking talked about it to whoever, wherever I could." Chinese authorities quickly tried to scrub the interview from the internet,
but users rapidly reposted it, sometimes using Morse code or emojis to
evade the censors.[41] The Australian news show *60 Minutes* would later
report that Ai's friends could not reach her for over two weeks, and she
was presumed missing. After an international outcry, she posted a video
to Weibo saying she was free to move about China—but it was unclear
if the video was staged by the regime.[42] Chinese netizens nicknamed her
the "Whistle-giver."

While the government under Xi operated with secrecy and self-
interest, many average people on the ground did not. The risks for doing
so were immense, but it did not compromise their commitment to spreading the truth by any means necessary. Fang Bin, a clothing salesperson in

Wuhan, began posting videos in mid-January to document the outbreak. On February 1, he posted a forty-minute video that showed eight corpses in body bags piled up beside a minivan outside a hospital. "This is too many," he lamented. The video quickly went viral. That night, Fang's house was raided, and he was taken away by the authorities. He was released days later. On February 13, he posted a thirteen-second video saying, "All people revolt—hand the power of the government back to the people." The police came to his door again, this time claiming to be concerned for his health. He refused them entry, so they broke down the door. He has not been heard from again.[43]

Chen Qiushi, a human rights lawyer who became a citizen journalist, cut his teeth covering the Hong Kong protests. Toward the end of January, he went to Wuhan to visit hospitals and interview patients. He told his 400,000 YouTube subscribers: "I will use my camera to document what is really happening. I promise I won't . . . cover up the truth."[44] On February 7, he went missing. The timing was hardly an accident. In early February, the Politburo Standing Committee met to discuss the outbreak and called for "increased internet control."[45] Later in the spring, authorities would arrest Chinese programmers working for a GitHub project called Terminus2049, which sought to prevent digital records about the early stages of the virus from being erased, including Ai's interview.[46] By the end of March, Chinese authorities acknowledged they had punished 897 people for "spreading rumors" about the virus. The real number was believed to be much higher.[47]

The regime did not stop at Chinese journalists, activists, and programmers. In February, Beijing expelled three *Wall Street Journal* reporters from the country over an opinion piece ("China Is the Real Sick Man of Asia") written by the foreign policy analyst Walter Russell Mead. In response, the United States reduced the number of Chinese citizens who would be allowed to work for the five Chinese state-run news organizations in America. The move provided Beijing with a helpful pretext to ramp up its efforts at controlling the information flow: China's Foreign Ministry spokesperson Hua Chunying tweeted, "Now the US kicked off the game, let's play."[48] China then expelled all reporters from the *New York Times*, *Washington Post*, and *Wall Street Journal*. Ostensibly, the quarrel was only tangentially related to COVID-19, but it served a larger purpose for Beijing.

WOLF WARRIOR DIPLOMACY

As the world began to realize that a disaster was unfolding in China, Beijing—concerned with the potential of being completely cut off—put considerable pressure on other countries to keep travelers moving between them and China. Some countries, such as Vietnam and Australia, ignored the admonition and put bans in place. Other countries, such as South Korea and Italy, allowed travel to continue. Cambodia's sixty-seven-year-old leader, Hun Sen, refused to impose travel restrictions, saying it would destroy his country's ties to China. He even offered to fly to Wuhan in January, when the virus was at its peak. He was apparently returning a favor—China had played an instrumental role in helping Sen consolidate his hold on power.[49]

At the outset of the crisis, the European Union discreetly sent humanitarian assistance to China, a maneuver that was itself important (the discretion was intended to avoid embarrassing Beijing). French president Emmanuel Macron told an aide that the Chinese government would remember this goodwill gesture when the time came.[50] By March, when the pandemic was raging in Europe, China appeared to reciprocate and began to send aid—yet Chinese authorities insisted that its arrival be met with some fanfare and public declarations of support from recipient countries, making the whole thing appear explicitly transactional. It was also frequently unclear whether the shipments of supplies were considered aid or exports. In one case, Italy donated thirty tons of equipment to China, which the Chinese later returned—and then charged the Italian government for it.[51] A study by the German Marshall Fund found that countries that had close and friendly relations with China received more assistance than countries that did not.[52] In other cases, the supplies China provided were defective: Sweden had to return 600,000 Chinese-made masks, and Spain had to discard 50,000 Chinese-produced testing kits.[53] The EU's high representative for foreign affairs and security policy, Josep Borrell, warned: "There is a geo-political component including a struggle for influence through spinning and the 'politics of generosity.'"[54]

China became even more assertive on the global stage in 2020, using its economic and political power in brazen ways that it had previously avoided. This was quickly labeled "wolf warrior diplomacy," after a popular and jingoistic Chinese action movie. In the movie, a brilliant renegade soldier named Leng Feng joins an elite PLA unit that fights mercenary organizations, including Americans. When he joins the unit, his commander asks the soldiers to say why the ceremony is so important. "Because we are so fucking special," they roar. Then he asks, "What is our motto?" "Be humble," they say while grinning.[55]

Wolf warrior diplomacy was particularly acute in Europe. Lu Shaye, China's ambassador to France, tweeted conspiracy theories suggesting that the virus originated in the United States.[56] The Chinese embassy in France published five anonymous articles on its website titled "Observations of a Chinese Diplomat Stationed in Paris." They accused French politicians of racism, propagated the conspiracy theories about the virus originating in America, and blamed nursing home staff in Europe for "abandoning their positions overnight, deserting collectively, and leaving their residents to die of hunger and disease."[57] France's minister of foreign affairs, Jean-Yves Le Drian, summoned Lu on April 14 to reprimand him for these statements.[58]

There were also worrying signs that the European Union might buckle under Chinese pressure. In early May, ambassadors to China from all twenty-seven EU member states published an op-ed in the English-language *China Daily* calling for cooperation between the EU and China. The op-ed was overwhelmingly positive. However, it was soon alleged that the Chinese government had agreed to let the article be published only after it deleted parts of the text that criticized Beijing's handling of COVID-19. The CCP also refused to let the article—already scrubbed of any problematic points of view—be published in Mandarin.

Despite initial hedging, Europeans soon turned against China's actions. They put in place investment controls to prevent Chinese companies or state-backed actors from taking advantage of the pandemic-induced recession to scoop up European assets at low prices. Several governments started to push Huawei, China's telecommunications giant, out of their 5G infrastructure—complying with a U.S. request that had previously been viewed with skepticism. For the first time, European policymakers talked about diversifying their ties internationally to make the EU less dependent on China. They began to speak up more confidently against China's assertiveness, particularly its crackdown on student protesters in Hong Kong and its mass repression of the Muslim Uighur population in Xinjiang.

Reactions were similar on the other side of the globe. When the Australian government called for an international investigation into the origins of COVID-19, the Chinese ambassador in Canberra, Cheng Jingye, said in an interview, "The Chinese public is frustrated, dismayed and disappointed with what you are doing now. In the long term, for example, I think if the mood is going from bad to worse, people would think why we should go to such a country while it's not so friendly to China."[59] He questioned whether they would continue to drink Australian wine and eat Australian beef. Within two weeks, China imposed tariffs on Australian beef and barley. Shortly thereafter, Australia was subjected to a sustained and massive cyberattack on a wide range of political and private-sector organizations that the Australian prime minister attributed to a "state-based actor," widely believed to be China.[60]

None of this came out of the blue. China had targeted Australia for several years prior as a key U.S. ally in the region. Australia's early decision to exclude Huawei from its 5G telecommunications system and its efforts to thwart illicit Chinese interference in its democracy set a template for other democracies to follow, further infuriating Beijing. Australia would not be cowed now and embraced its role as a middle power that punched above its weight. So instead of backing down, Canberra continued to press for an inquiry, and by mid-May the WHO bowed to international pressure and agreed to a "comprehensive evaluation" of the pandemic. However, as we shall see in Chapter 12, Beijing subsequently used a variety of tactics to delay and obstruct the investigation.[61]

China faced a backlash in Africa as well, after five Nigerians tested positive for COVID-19 in early April in Guangzhou and widespread reports emerged of Africans being forcibly evicted from their homes in the city.[62] After managing to suppress the virus, Chinese citizens cast a suspicious eye on foreigners. McDonald's apologized after one of its restaurants in Guangzhou posted an "unauthorized" sign on the door saying: "We've been informed that from now on black people are not allowed to enter the restaurant."[63] A racist cartoon went viral online showing Chinese sanitation workers sorting foreigners into trash and recycling bins depending on their skin color.[64] African ambassadors in China wrote to the foreign minister to say they observed "with consternation the discrimination and stigmatization of Africans" in China, including evictions from hotels and residences, forcible testing without reasonable cause, the confiscation of passports, the separation of families where one member is African and the other Chinese, and persistent harassment by the authorities. They demanded immediate "cessation of forceful testing, quarantine and other inhuman treatments meted out to Africans."[65]

China had invested billions of dollars in Africa over the past decade and saw it as a region where it could increase its influence at the expense of the United States. This included gaining preferential access to natural resources. And though China had previously offered medical assistance to numerous African nations to address endemic health concerns and improve health care, Beijing's response to COVID-19 placed that assistance in jeopardy. China's approach to African debt quickly also became a major bone of contention. China is the world's largest creditor (larger even than the World Bank), and when the pandemic hit, it held approximately 20 percent of the debt of African countries, much higher than the typical figure it held in nations elsewhere on the globe.[66] According to the International Monetary Fund, nineteen African countries were in debt distress or at high risk of it in 2020.[67] Perhaps unsurprisingly, there were numerous calls for China to forgive these loans as a way of spurring a coronavirus recovery in Africa and elsewhere. Yet Chinese officials were very cagey in their response, promising only to forgive a very small part of these financial obligations.[68]

The pandemic did not damage China's reputation and influence in all places. In January and February 2020, it was widely believed that COVID-19 might drive a wedge between Beijing and Moscow, which had become more closely aligned geopolitically over the past decade. The two nations share a 2,500-mile land border, and Russia widely believed that the virus would soon cross over. In anticipation, Russian president Vladimir Putin closed the border in late January, and in mid-February he banned all Chinese citizens from entering the country.[69] Tempers frayed. The Chinese embassy in Moscow published a letter on February 24 criticizing the "ubiquitous monitoring" of Chinese nationals, which, they pointed out, "does not exist in any country, even in the United States and in Western states."[70] Remarkably, however, COVID-19 never really spread from China to Russia. Instead, it came to Russia from the West—from Europe. Ironically, in mid-April it was China that closed the border with Russia due to concern that it was a significant source of coronavirus cases, mainly from returning Chinese citizens.[71]

Yet these restrictions did little to damage Sino-Russian relations. Putin and Xi kept in close contact throughout the winter and spring of 2020 and never criticized each other. The Chinese embassy in Moscow retracted its letter within days of issuing it, claiming that reports of discrimination were false, and it began defending Russian authorities.[72] With relations between the United States and China plummeting, Moscow and Beijing drew closer together. Senior officials on both sides defended the other from attacks by the West. As China lost friends, Russia became an even more valuable partner. And as Russia's economy deteriorated rapidly due to the pandemic and the plunging price of oil, it became more reliant on Chinese imports and investment.[73]

Overall, however, the global consequences of China's initial response to the virus were becoming clear by the early spring. Analysts in China were aware that the country might be overplaying its geopolitical hand. An April 2020 report by the Ministry of State Security (China's premier intelligence agency), for example, warned that global anti-China sentiment was at its highest point since the Tiananmen Square crackdown in 1989. This rising hostility, the report noted, might even tip China and the United States into an outright confrontation.[74] The fact that the virus had originated in China and been covered up was a major reputational blow to the regime. Most people around the world do not pay all that much attention to geopolitics, but in this case their lives were upended because of something that happened in China. Governments across the globe knew that they could not trust the information coming out of Beijing—now or in the future.

SOWING DISINFORMATION

China supplemented its so-called mask diplomacy with a massive global disinformation campaign. The centerpiece of this effort was to raise doubts about the virus's origins. On February 27, Zhong Nanshan, a Chinese infectious disease expert, told a press conference, "The infection was first spotted in China but the virus may not have originated in China."[75] On March 8, China's ambassador to South Africa tweeted:

> Although the epidemic first broke out in China, it did not necessarily mean that the virus is originated from China, let alone "made in China."[76]

Foreign Ministry spokesperson Zhao Lijian, a particularly brash and assertive Chinese diplomat, tweeted out to his 300,000 followers on March 12:

CDC was caught on the spot. When did patient zero begin in US? How many people are infected? What are the names of the hospitals? It might be US army who brought the epidemic to Wuhan. Be transparent! Make public your data! US owe us an explanation![77]

Later that day, he also tweeted an article from a pro-Kremlin website with an endorsement:

This article is very much important to each and every one of us. Please read and retweet it. COVID-19: Further Evidence that the Virus Originated in the US.[78]

In May the *Global Times*, an English-language mouthpiece for the CCP, followed up with an editorial reinforcing Zhao's claims: "New findings have potentially altered the timeline of the coronavirus outbreak in the US, with a large number of COVID-19 cases misclassified as influenza last winter. As a country with the highest number of infections and deaths and more early cases revealed, the US' role in the origin and spread of the coronavirus has become a major concern."[79] Meanwhile, the China Global Television Network made a short video partly in Arabic and targeted at viewers in the Middle East that informed them of "new facts" indicating the U.S. Army might have brought the virus to Wuhan during a sports competition.[80] An investigative report by the Associated Press and the Atlantic Council's Digital Forensic Research Lab found that Chinese diplomats and state media orchestrated a major effort to spread and amplify conspiracy theories that blamed the United States for the virus.[81]

Chinese officials also took direct aim at the American response to the virus. "Aside from the devastation caused by the novel coronavirus, there is also a political virus spreading through the US," China's foreign minister, Wang Yi, said. "This political virus is the use of every opportunity to attack and smear China. Some politicians completely disregard basic facts and have fabricated too many lies targeting China, and plotted too many conspiracies."[82] After President Trump asked at a White House press conference whether disinfectant might usefully be injected as a possible treatment for COVID-19, the chief spokesperson for the CCP in Beijing tweeted:

Mr President is right. Some people do need to be injected with #disinfectant, or at least gargle with it. That way they won't spread the virus, lies and hatred when talking.

Hua, the foreign ministry's spokesperson, tweeted at secretary of state Mike Pompeo to "stop lying through your teeth" in reference to comments he made on Fox News accusing Beijing of wasting "valuable days" and letting "hundreds of thousands" of people leave Wuhan for other countries, including Italy.[83]

Beijing also appears to have sought to sow discontent within the United States. American intelligence agencies believe that in mid-March 2020, China actively pushed out false text messages telling Americans that a friend of a friend or a relative had confided that the federal government was about to shut down the entire country once they had the military ready to enforce it.[84] This prompted a National Security Council tweet in response: "Text message rumors of a national #quarantine are FAKE. There is no national lockdown."[85] Trump, however, seemed unconcerned. When asked on Fox News about China's disinformation campaign, he said, "They do it and we do it and we call them different things. Every country does it."[86]

Laura Rosenberger, who was then leading the Alliance for Securing Democracy Project at the German Marshall Fund, described the disinformation strategy's goals: "to deflect blame from Beijing's own failings and to highlight other governments' missteps, portraying China as both the model and the partner of first resort for other countries." Chinese officials, she wrote, "experimented with tactics drawn from Russia's more nihilistic information operations playbook" designed to undermine public confidence in the notion of objective truth and a shared set of facts.[87] China's online campaign did not come out of the blue. Executives at Twitter, for example, noticed a significant increase in the volume and aggression of Beijing's social media strategy following the 2019 Hong Kong protests. The number of Chinese officials with Twitter accounts increased exponentially, and they all adopted a very combative tone.[88] In June 2020, Twitter took down 23,750 accounts engaged in "a range of manipulative and coordinated activities" and "spreading geopolitical narratives favorable to the Communist Party of China."[89]

The European response to China's disinformation campaign was initially mixed, but over time it got tougher. For example, in April 2020, the EU watered down a report on disinformation, removing explicit references to China and Chinese operations, including those in France, after "heavy pushback" from Beijing. Monika Richter, an analyst working in the EU's External Action Service, wrote in an internal email: "Such appeasement will set a terrible precedent and encourage similar coercion in the future." News of the watering down soon became public, and in the ensuing political uproar, the EU restored its criticism of China by releasing an updated report.[90] Then, in June, an EU report was even blunter in its criticism of Beijing as a peddler of COVID-19 disinformation.[91]

UNDERSTANDING CHINA'S RESPONSE

The question remains: why did China respond in this way, across multiple dimensions? After SARS, the regime admitted it made mistakes and put in place measures to insulate the public health system from political pressure. The new system worked fairly well with H1N1, and China played a constructive role during the international response to Ebola in 2014–16. But in 2020, none of this mattered. Not only did China's history with SARS repeat itself but it did so with a vengeance. The crackdown on doctors, activists, and reporters was worse than before. Dali Yang, a professor at the University of Chicago, offers one explanation, placing the blame on local CCP authorities in Wuhan who were slow to activate the system and who then silenced local journalists and doctors raising the alarm. "The infectious diseases sentinel system," Yang wrote, "only works if the hospitals and local health administrations actively engage with it and contribute to the information. In Wuhan, the system failed, monumentally. The failure has laid bare the inherent tensions of a reporting system that is also beholden to the political imperatives of provincial and municipal Communist Party bosses."[92]

This explanation is not entirely convincing, however. For one thing, reports were swirling on Chinese social media in late December 2019. It is likely Beijing noticed. But more important is that once Xi took control of the situation—first secretly on January 7, and then publicly on January 23—the strategic control of messaging accelerated. If the Chinese president wanted to encourage doctors to speak up, he would have rewarded those who blew the whistle instead of "disappearing" or marginalizing them. Moreover, without an official acknowledgment of error or accountability for what transpired in 2020, no one, in China or around the world, will believe future official messaging, even if the government begins operating in better faith and with greater transparency. Xi's actions sent a clear message that inconvenient truths would not be tolerated. The CCP would decide what would be communicated both domestically and abroad. As the journalist Giles Whittell observed, the regime's actions were "clear evidence of a system more concerned to contain information than the virus."[93]

Some in China appeared to recognize the country's missteps and the inherent dangers of Beijing's failure to reckon honestly with them. One such voice is Yao Yang, an award-winning academic economist at Peking University. He received his PhD from the University of Wisconsin, Madison. In an interview, he predicted that "once the pandemic is over, it is quite likely that the West will have a new viewpoint of China's political system, and it is entirely possible that the West will unite in a fundamental challenge to the Chinese system." That is not an unusual view, but what was particularly striking was what he said next:

> There is still time to pull back from the brink. From China's perspective, we should put together a comprehensive explanation or a White Paper about the Wuhan virus situation, in which we recount straightforwardly what happened between the end of December and January 23, saying what we did and why we made mistakes. We should state clearly that during this period we did indeed drag our feet and weigh the pros and cons, but did not purposefully engage in a cover-up. . . . Explaining the process clearly and admitting our errors and delays will pull the rug out from under the West. If they still don't accept it, then there's no way to convince them.[94]

But this view appears not to be the dominant one. China's leadership clearly hoped, and continues to hope, that its massive—and apparently successful—effort to contain the virus at home will eclipse its early mistakes and cover-ups, especially when contrasted with America's very public failure. In many ways, Trump's loud and disastrous handling of COVID-19 will inevitably shape how all other international responses are viewed. From the perspective of the CCP, the Chinese response provides a concrete example of how its brand of authoritarianism outperforms democracy in general—and, more pointedly, how superior it is to the U.S. model in particular. As we will see in Chapter 6, there is very little correlation between the varied political systems around the world and how each responded to the pandemic. Nevertheless, the performance of the China model is something the Beijing elite clings to, believes in, and promulgates. "The United States is in such deep, deep trouble. It is a failure," a Chinese official told us in June 2020. "Imagine if China had 3 million cases. We forgave Wuhan when we saw New York, it almost caved despite having all the information we did not have at the time. We did not know early on what we were dealing with."[95]

This reality meant that China increasingly strode across the world stage with a sense of triumph. The writings and remarks of China's foreign policy and intellectual elite suggest that this is a widely shared view. Fu Ying holds the rather bureaucratic-sounding title of chairperson of the National People's Congress Foreign Affairs Committee, but she is also one of the very few public intellectuals believed to be in Xi Jinping's wider orbit. She served as ambassador to Australia, the United Kingdom, and the Philippines, where she earned a reputation as a hard-liner and a tough negotiator. In a series of articles during the COVID-19 crisis, she put the pandemic in the context of a longer process of a changing power dynamic defined by China's rise and America's decline. In *The Economist*, she wrote that, unlike after September 11, 2001, or the financial crisis of 2008, the United States "demonstrated neither a commitment to solidarity and co-operation, nor a willingness or capacity for global leadership."[96] In another piece, she wrote that as a result of this U.S. position, "American hegemony has tended to contract, and its 'beacon effects' have started to fade. The Chinese progress and U.S. regression," she argued, "mirror the two countries' evolution in opposite directions within the same global regime."[97]

Echoing these themes, Yuan Peng, a research professor and president of the China Institutes of Contemporary International Relations, outlined his view of the virus in two articles in the summer of 2020, calling it part of a "once in a century" event—the decline of the U.S.-led international order and the rise of something new. This had already been under way before 2020, he acknowledged, but COVID-19 was a catalyst. "The pandemic is as bad as a world war," he wrote. He went on to say:

> The world during and after the pandemic is like the world after WWI. At the time, the British Empire no longer had the means to fulfill its ambitions, and the sun which had once "never set" on the empire was . . . rapidly disappearing beyond the horizon. . . . In the current pandemic, Trump's America not only has not assumed its world leadership responsibility, selfishly hiding its head in the sand, but in addition, because of policy failures, it has become a major disaster center of the world pandemic. . . . This is a blow to America's soft and hard power, and America's international influence has suffered a serious decline.[98]

From Beijing's perspective, what started out as a potentially existential challenge to the regime was quickly turning into an opportunity to consolidate and accelerate China's rise. Whatever mistakes China may or may not have made, the opportunities presented by America's missteps were just too enticing to pass up.

Opportunities Lost

THE FIRST CASES of Ebola emerged in West Africa—Guinea, Sierra Leone, and Liberia—in March 2014. A particularly nasty virus transmitted by bodily fluids, it starts with fevers, aches, pains, and fatigue before progressing to severe diarrhea, vomiting, abdominal pain, bleeding, and often death. By the early summer, it became clear that the disease could quickly spread across a number of other African countries, and then to the rest of the world. The international community, including the United States, was initially slow to respond. The World Health Organization seemed out of its depth. It saw its job as primarily providing advice, not leading a response. Governments around the world, which initially included the Obama administration, wanted medical doctors on the ground to act as first responders and take charge of the problem themselves. The governments of Guinea, Sierra Leona, and Liberia decided to put a lid on what they were seeing. Though their countries were directly affected, they feared scaring off foreign investors, who could be spooked by any official signals of alarm. By August, however, public health experts worried that the virus was "spiraling in to an out of control crisis."[1] The WHO met in early August and did little to change the situation on the ground. But the UN secretary general, Ban Ki-moon, was worried. He had always insisted that he did not want to see another Rwanda on his watch (a reference to the 1994 genocide), and yet here was another massive humanitarian crisis in Africa emerging in slow motion. A week later, under significant public pressure, the WHO finally declared Ebola a "public health emergency of international concern," a crucial designation that signaled to the world that action was required.[2]

But it was simply rhetoric. The WHO still took no action. Ban, growing more anxious by the day, continued to apply pressure. With time running out and a concern for what this would mean for his legacy, he shifted his attention to the UN General Assembly, an annual gathering of world leaders, in mid-September as an opportunity to spur the world into action. In U.S. president Barack Obama, he found a willing actor.

On September 10, 2014, Obama's national security advisor, Susan Rice, convened cabinet members and other senior officials in the White House Situation Room. Although it was the day before the thirteenth anniversary of the 9/11 attacks, they were not there to discuss terrorism. Rather, they had gathered to develop a response to the Ebola crisis, which potentially posed an even graver threat. Tom Frieden, the director of the CDC, presented a "hockey stick" chart projecting a huge increase in potential cases in the coming months. Absent significant intervention, Frieden explained, over a million people in the region and around the world could be infected by January 2015. Hundreds of thousands could die. Rice made it clear that Obama now viewed Ebola as a "tier-one" national security emergency, a designation that made it equivalent to the situation in Iraq and Syria, where ISIS had recently taken over a wide swath of territory.[3] Six days later, Obama traveled to the CDC in Atlanta, Georgia, to outline his administration's strategy: American diplomats would marshal a global coalition to provide medical assistance, and U.S. development and health professionals would go to West Africa to work alongside thousands of American troops to contain the virus. At home, there would be steps taken to improve the screening of travelers to the United States and prepare hospitals in case Ebola reached America's shores. If America did not act aggressively, Obama warned, many thousands would die and entire nations could become destabilized. The consequences would produce ripple effects far beyond the African continent. Ebola "is not just a threat to regional security," Obama emphatically declared. "It's a potential threat to global security."[4]

A week later, Obama, along with Ban and Japanese prime minister Shinzo Abe, made a big push at the UN General Assembly, and created an international coalition to address the crisis, which operated through the UN Mission for Ebola Emergency Response (UNMEER). Countries sent significant numbers of military personnel and health officials to West Africa to tackle the disease. Tony Banbury, who was to become head of UNMEER, told us, "There was very little cooperation before September 2014, but from that point forward it was a model of best practice."[5] It took six months, from the moment the first cases of Ebola were detected in March, to rally the world in 2014, which was the equivalent of December 2019 to May 2020 in the COVID-19 crisis.

Within sixty days, UNMEER had made significant progress in isolating approximately 70 percent of those infected with Ebola in the three countries. By July 2015, it had accomplished its mission of suppressing the virus. The Obama administration learned from Ebola, just as it had learned from the H1N1 influenza outbreak in 2009. It established the Directorate for Global Health Security and Biodefense at the National Security Council (NSC). And the administration even ran a pandemic tabletop exercise in 2017 during the presidential transition, briefing approximately thirty members of the incoming Trump team on a hypothetical scenario of a global influenza that overwhelmed national health care systems and resulted in travel bans.[6]

Once in office, the Trump administration appointed an experienced senior director for global health and biodefense—a retired navy rear admiral named Timothy Ziemer. The son of missionaries, Ziemer grew up in the central highlands of French Indochina, now Vietnam. He would return to Vietnam as a navy pilot during the war. Ziemer left the navy after thirty years of service and went into development, working for World Relief, a faith-based nongovernmental organization working on microfinance, food security, HIV/AIDS and malaria, and other issues. From that point forward, he became committed to global public health. In 2006, in the George W. Bush administration, he became the coordinator of the President's Malaria Initiative, a position he continued to hold in the Obama administration.[7]

Now working for Trump on the NSC, Ziemer would give Lieutenant General H. R. McMaster, Trump's second national security advisor (the first, Michael Flynn, was forced to resign after just twenty-four days), weekly updates on the seasonal flu, Ebola, and other infectious diseases. Ziemer wanted to make sure that public health and the threat of infectious diseases remained a priority item on the list of national security threats. It was not easy. As he saw it, McMaster's view of the world revolved around intentional events—actions by states and nonstate actors—rather than unintentional ones such as pandemics and climate change. But he made progress. Whenever he provided data, McMaster would take out his notebook and write down the numbers. On one occasion Ziemer was asked to participate in a global risk assessment meeting, composed of people from the intelligence community and a couple of his NSC colleagues. The discussion focused on measuring threats by the projected body count. Attention quickly turned to terrorism or a clash with another major power. Ziemer interrupted after twenty minutes to say: "If we are determining risk based on the number of casualties and body count, then I get the blue ribbon. The risk and threat of a pandemic will kill hundreds of thousands of Americans." He felt like the skunk at the picnic, but the argument prevailed.[8] Later, in December 2017, when the NSC released the National Security Strategy, arguing that great-power competition was America's preeminent strategic challenge, global public health was also prominently featured.[9]

Ziemer continued to make his mark. For example, while the Trump administration had opposed Tedros Adhanom Ghebreyesus's candidacy to lead the WHO because they thought he was unlikely to reform the organization, when he was elected to that position in 2017, Ziemer helped secure him an invitation to meet with Trump. U.S. officials told Tedros that they needed three things from the WHO during his tenure: accelerated reform of the organization's bureaucracy, full transparency to comply with the International Health Regulations, and allowing Taiwan to be an observer. Ziemer was not optimistic that the advice would be followed—Tedros had China's backing, and he did not seem like the type of leader who would challenge Beijing.

Ziemer was also involved in another decision that would prove controversial several years later. Since the early 2000s, the CDC had dozens of officials stationed in Beijing to work with the Chinese Center for Disease Control. This presence was funded through the President's Emergency Plan for AIDS Relief (PEPFAR), which was a signature initiative of President George W. Bush and is widely regarded as the most successful global public health initiative in the nation's history. Congress had reduced funding for PEPFAR's operations in China, and as the program was winding down, these individuals were moved to other countries where they were needed more, including places that PEPFAR had prioritized since

the beginning, such as Uganda. Observers would later point to the rede-
ployment as blinding the United States to what was happening in China.
However, when COVID-19 struck Wuhan, there were still between
eleven and thirteen U.S. CDC experts who worked on infectious diseases
stationed in Beijing.

Unfortunately for Ziemer, McMaster's time was limited. Trump
wanted a national security advisor who would do as he was told, but Mc-
Master did not operate that way. Rather, he was inclined to impose a
rigorous decision-making process where alternative points of view were
aired and policies went through a formal interagency review. It frustrated
Trump, though McMaster was not the only one who irritated the president.
Secretary of State Rex Tillerson, Defense Secretary Jim Mattis, and Na-
tional Economic Council head Gary Cohn were all part of the so-called
Axis of Adults, seen as constraining Trump's impulses on the world stage.
Mattis, a highly regarded former Marine general, was untouchable for a
while because he was widely revered among Republicans in Congress.
But the others were not so lucky. By April, McMaster was out, along with
Cohn and Tillerson. Trump then brought in McMaster's replacement:
John Bolton, whom he had frequently seen on Fox News. Bolton had
publicly advocated for preventive attacks on Iran and North Korea, and
was widely known as Washington's uber-hawk. He was even more committed than McMaster to the notion that national security was primarily
about intentional threats. And he wanted to reduce the NSC staff, which
he thought had grown too large over the years. So he abolished the office within the NSC dealing with global health and biodefense, folding
it into the office dealing with counterproliferation and weapons of mass
destruction. Ziemer was pushed out and reassigned to the U.S. Agency
for International Development (USAID), the government's development
arm; he was replaced within the NSC by someone who had a background
in weapons of mass destruction and arms control, although his team kept
their jobs. In his memoir, *The Room Where It Happened*, published in
2020, Bolton argued that he had consolidated the offices to "reduce du-
plication and overlap" since it made "good management sense."[10] Ziemer
did not disagree with the need to streamline the NSC, but he did worry
that there would no longer be a dedicated global health advocate to
pound the table and pester the national security advisor. Other things
began to break down too. McMaster had checked in regularly with Mark

Green, a retired general who ran USAID. That stopped under Bolton and his successor, Robert O'Brien. It was another key channel of communication that went cold.

Still, there was at least one senior NSC official watching for warning signs. Matthew Pottinger, the U.S. deputy national security advisor, had been a journalist with the *Wall Street Journal* in 2003, reporting from China during the SARS pandemic. He wrote stories about Beijing's cover-up and eventually left the country convinced of the nefariousness of the Chinese Communist Party. After 9/11, Pottinger joined the Marine Corps and served in Afghanistan with Flynn. Back in the United States, Pottinger later coauthored an influential report on intelligence gathering in Afghanistan with Flynn, and the two had remained close.[11] When Trump unexpectedly won the presidency in 2016, Flynn tapped Pottinger to head up the Asia team in the White House.

Pottinger had a reputation as a thoughtful hawk on China, and he steered official U.S. policy in the direction of containing Beijing's global ambitions. As he saw it, the CCP was ideologically committed to upending the international order and moving it toward its brand of authoritarianism. Notably, Pottinger's wife, Yen, had worked as a virologist at the CDC, and his brother Paul specialized in infectious disease. All of this meant he was more attuned to the dangers of a pandemic, particularly a coronavirus emanating from China, than your typical national security professional.[12]

By December 2019, Trump was on his fourth national security advisor, Robert O'Brien. There was very little formal process. Trump was subject to mood swings and paid little attention to detail. And yet, despite everything, the Trump administration's national security team would actually be among the very first to understand the gravity of what was happening in China and the global threat it posed. This was primarily because of Pottinger and his efforts, but O'Brien also took an early interest. The Europeans, on the other hand, would be about a month behind.

But the precise reason the administration recognized the threat from the pandemic—its inherent distrust and fear of the CCP—also meant that its international response to COVID-19 would be viewed through, and organized around, the prism of China policy and the perceived dangers of Xi's regime. USAID would be cut out of the loop. A senior Trump administration official told us that Ziemer's departure meant that the government had lost someone of "unimpeachable integrity" on global public health who "had a genius for logistics." And although "Pottinger understood the challenge," the official added, "he had a lot on his plate." A senior foreign official from an allied country who worked closely with the Trump administration echoed this, telling us, "Pottinger was concerned from both points of view—China and global public health—but by that stage the system was so broken that it would be very difficult for him to pull together a whole-of-government approach. They [the U.S. government] focused on the lane they were most comfortable with."

As the administration began to formulate its response to the emerging coronavirus pandemic, those who favored a more comprehensive approach nationally and internationally were excluded or marginalized at crucial moments. The result was that the Trump administration was more focused on holding China responsible and reducing U.S. reliance on Beijing in the future than on the minutiae of global public health policy or the hard work of rallying the world to roll back the pandemic. That would set the United States on a collision course with many of its partners.

THE ALARM BELL

Shortly before midnight on December 30, 2019, Sharon Sanders, a Florida-based blogger on a site called Flu Trackers, staffed 24/7 by volunteers all over the world, read some alarming statements online by public health officials in Hubei province, China. Originally a financial variance analyst, she was trained to "look for things that did not fit" and had been tracking infectious diseases in China for fourteen years. Over the next half a day, Sanders and other commentators would post a dozen messages speculating on a new and mysterious virus that had emerged.[13] Using Flu Trackers, Sanders and her team were the first Americans to notice COVID-19 and bring it to the public's attention.

Early the next morning, on New Year's Eve, scientists at the CDC picked up the same chatter and began to email each other. "Any of your folks know more about the 'unknown pneumonia'?" one asked.[14] Later that day, Chinese authorities informed the WHO's China Office of an unfamiliar case of pneumonia. Anthony Fauci, the head of the U.S. National Institute of Allergy and Infectious Diseases, and Robert Redfield, the head of the CDC, immediately recognized the risk; maybe it was a new SARS. On January 1, the CDC circulated a situational report on a "China pneumonia of unknown etiology," its first daily briefing on what would become known as SARS-CoV-2, the novel coronavirus that causes COVID-19. It stated the basic facts as then understood: the virus had originated near the Huanan Seafood Wholesale Market in Wuhan, SARS was suspected but not confirmed, and to date there were twenty-seven cases.[15]

On January 3, Redfield reached out to his Chinese counterpart, George Gao, with whom he had worked closely over the years, and proposed "working collaboratively with the government of China on pneumonia and respiratory infectious diseases." He offered to send technical experts to assist, but, to his surprise, Gao stonewalled. Subsequent requests were met with the same response. Something had changed. There would be no access.[16] Over the next ten days, Fauci and Redfield noted with alarm the virus spread in China. After Chinese scientists published the virus's genome on January 10, Fauci ordered that work begin on a vaccine. But it was not until January 13, when the first case was reported in Thailand, that they realized Chinese officials had been lying about the virus's transmissibility between people. According to investigative journalist Bob Woodward in his book *Fear*, Fauci's response was: "Holy shit. They haven't been telling us the truth. It really is transmitting efficiently."[17]

What Fauci and Redfield did not know at the time, despite their efforts, was that the novel coronavirus was already in the United States. Epidemiologists would later go back and test thirteen people in Ohio who demonstrated symptoms of COVID-19 in January. The tests showed they had antibodies for the virus, which meant they had been positive at the time. The first case was a woman in her forties who fell sick on January 2. This was just days after U.S. officials even became *aware* of an outbreak in China. Little did they know that it was already moving across borders—indeed, it was already spreading at home. More U.S. cases occurred on January 7 and 13, two more on the fifteenth, and one on the eighteenth.[18] On January 19, a thirty-five-year-old man walked into an urgent care clinic in Snohomish County, Washington, and said he was suffering from a cough and fever. It had been going on for four days, which also happened to be how long it had been since he had returned from a trip to visit family in Wuhan. The next day, he tested positive for COVID-19.[19]

U.S. immigration officials began screening passengers from Wuhan on January 17, but it mattered little; the screening did not include travelers from other parts of China or the rest of the world. In other words, the virus was moving undetected to and within the United States even as American officials thought they knew where to look.

Pottinger's view was that cooperation with the CCDC was irrelevant because the Chinese health agency was completely cut out of the loop. Gao had not even known about COVID-19 until he heard about it on social media on December 30. One of China's leading epidemiologists discovered it the same way as the blogger Sharon Sanders did.[20] Pottinger saw all this as part of a bigger problem. It was tempting, he thought, for U.S. public health experts to assume that China would behave more transparently because it was a signatory to the International Health Regulations, which required them to do so, but there was no means of enforcement, so the commitment was effectively meaningless. Worse, it created the false impression that the United States had a guardrail in place. Pottinger had déjà vu—this felt like SARS all over again. U.S. officials thought that because they were funding the Wuhan Institute of Virology, they had their finger on the pulse. But the CCP would do what the Chinese regime felt it had to do to survive—using the tools of secrecy and control—just as it had in 2003 with SARS.

In mid-January, as the COVID threat grew, the National Security Council began preparing options to keep Americans home from work and, if necessary, to shut down entire cities in response.[21] But it was hard to get anyone's attention in the administration. For the first two weeks of January, Trump was preoccupied with trade negotiations with China. He hoped that 2020 would be the year of his big deal with China. He would negate Democratic attacks on his foreign policy by proving that he was the negotiator in chief, fighting hard for U.S. interests while also cashing in the chips at just the right moment. He hoped to reach agreements with Iran, the Taliban, and possibly Russia, and to try again with North Korea. China would be the jewel in the crown.

The so-called phase one trade deal with Beijing was sealed on January 15. Trump had won the presidency complaining vociferously about China's economic practices and starting during his second year in office he routinely imposed tariffs on it, often threatening even more. So the January agreement was the culmination of years of difficult negotiations with Beijing. The deal did not address most of the underlying sources of U.S.-China trade tensions—including Chinese subsidies and state-owned enterprises—but it did require China to purchase $200 billion of U.S. products, provided greater access to the Chinese market for U.S. agriculture, and included some safeguards to protect corporate secrets.[22] In the weeks that followed, even as his own administration was monitoring and developing strategies around what they were seeing out of Wuhan, Trump was reluctant to issue public statements that would distract from his achievement. Consequently, even as evidence mounted that Beijing was failing to be transparent with the international community about COVID-19, he continued to heap public praise on China's president, Xi Jinping, and expressed confidence in the Chinese response to the outbreak. On February 7, for instance, he tweeted:

> Just had a long and very good conversation by phone with President Xi of China. He is strong, sharp and powerfully focused on leading the counterattack on the Coronavirus. He feels they are doing very well, even building hospitals in a matter of only days. . . . Great discipline is taking place in China, as President Xi strongly leads what will be a very successful operation. We are working closely with China to help![23]

Not until mid-February did White House officials discover that Xi had been chairing emergency meetings on COVID-19 beginning on January 7, a week before the trade deal was signed.[24] Xi had to have known, they concluded, about human-to-human transmission, but when Vice Premier Liu He and other officials traveled to Washington for the signing ceremony on January 15, they said nothing about this.

Trump was first briefed on COVID-19 on January 23, two days after the first confirmed American case. (At that stage, U.S. officials did not realize that the virus had been circulating since early January.) The president's daily brief (PDB), the highly classified daily assessment of world events and threats prepared by the intelligence community, reportedly provided Trump with a warning about the emerging dangers, but Trump did not read written briefs and had no personal knowledge of pandemics. Thus, he was given a verbal presentation of the PDB, which framed the virus as "just like the flu" and unlikely to end up as a global pandemic.[25] (Notably, January 23 was also the day Xi took full control of fighting the virus in China.) O'Brien and Pottinger were furious with the PDB briefer, believing that the intelligence community had grossly understated the danger. But the presentation was all Trump had—and he was not the kind of person to fact-check the presentation against the actual written report. Regardless, it would take something much more dramatic to pique the president's interest, let alone move him to action. On January 28, at another PDB, O'Brien made sure to tell Trump COVID-19 would be "the biggest national security threat you face in your presidency." Pottinger backed him up, saying, "It's going to be 1918," to which Trump replied, "holy fuck." Trump would later deny that moment had occurred, but he did tell Woodward that he first started to "see" the coronavirus "toward the end of January."[26] From the perspective of NSC officials, the U.S. intelligence community had been completely asleep at the switch and had failed to make pandemic disease a priority. That was the case despite the fact that the National Intelligence Council had long warned of the potentially devastating effects of a global contagion, as we saw in Chapter 3. Confronted with competing intelligence requirements, they had passed the buck to the CDC and had no intelligence collection capabilities on global health–related matters inside China. They were even slow to absorb and understand the mounting publicly sourced information showing where the global COVID-19 outbreak was headed.[27]

On January 29, the administration announced the creation of a Coronavirus Task Force with the secretary of health and human services, Alex Azar, as chair. The next day, Trump said, "We're working very closely with China and other countries, and we think it's going to have a very good ending for us."[28] On January 31, Trump met with Fauci, Redfield, O'Brien, Pottinger, and other advisors. Their overwhelming advice was to shut down all travel between China and the United States with one exception: allow Americans to return. Trump agreed. It was a significant step, and one that he would point to repeatedly in the months that followed, although United Airlines, one of the major U.S. carriers, had already announced it was suspending flights out of China.[29] Of the 40,000 U.S. travelers allowed to return from China after that point, none received adequate testing or were placed in quarantine.[30] Four days later, Trump gave the annual State of the Union address, which was more than 6,300 words long. A mere thirty-nine of those words were on COVID-19. "We are coordinating with the Chinese government and working closely together on the coronavirus outbreak in China. My administration will take all necessary steps to safeguard our citizens from this threat," he promised.[31]

THE LOST MONTH

Trump's decision to impose a travel ban on China set the stage for a hugely consequential struggle between two factions in his administration. One group, "the 1918 faction," included Pottinger, O'Brien, and trade advisor Peter Navarro. They believed what they told the president: the United States was headed for a potential repeat of the Great Influenza a century earlier. They wanted to impose travel restrictions on Europe, not a complete ban but rather a "level three" advisory recommending that people not travel, along with targeted cancellations of specific routes. This group also sought massive amounts of funding for medical supplies, therapeutics, vaccines, and diagnostics. In other words, they wanted to prepare for what was coming. A second group, "the wait and see" faction, consisted of Chief of Staff Mick Mulvaney, Treasury Secretary Steve Mnuchin, and Vice President Pence's chief of staff Marc Short. They worried about the economic consequences of further travel restrictions and wanted to give people information but let them make their own decisions. They were not proactively opposed to increased funding for supplies, but they did not push for it either. Throughout February, Trump effectively sided with this second group. He felt he did his bit with the travel ban and he was reluctant to do anything that might disrupt the economy.

On February 6, Trump spoke with President Xi and offered to send technical experts to China. But Xi remained noncommittal. Trump pressed, but to no avail, and so he turned to other topics. There is little evidence that Trump was moved to do much else.[32] It is clear from Trump's conversation with Woodward that the rapidly spreading contagion was not a priority for him for the next couple of weeks, even though the first case of community transmission within the United States was detected on February 15 (an American woman had tested positive even though she had not been to China or been in close contact with anyone who had). "The coronavirus was not yet a focus [for Trump]," Woodward wrote, describing a call he had with the president on February 19. Instead, they spoke about Iran, attorney general Bill Barr, and the political impact of social media.[33] Those in the corridors of power at the White House also remained dismissive. Virtually no one in the West Wing wore a mask, and those staffers at the NSC, which is housed in the Eisenhower Executive Office Building across a narrow alley from the White House, who donned one were ridiculed by the inner circle or told that the boss did not like it.[34] Trump admitted to Woodward on February 7 that the virus was "more deadly than the flu, maybe five times more so," but he continued to publicly play it down (he justified this to Woodward by saying that he didn't want to create a panic).[35] For instance, on February 27 he said publicly, "It's going to disappear. One day—it's like a miracle—it will disappear."[36]

As the virus began to take hold across America, early efforts with testing proved difficult. On February 8, the CDC realized that there was a flaw that contaminated the early COVID-19 test they had developed—in their rush to produce a diagnostic tool they had cut corners and produced materials contaminated with snippets of the virus.[37] One Trump administration official told us this was the real black swan in the U.S. response—a pandemic had been widely predicted by experts for years but no one expected a catastrophic early mistake in producing a reliable test. There were other problems too. The administration tried to send individual states supplies when they had shortages of ventilators and PPE, but what was lacking was "bidirectional learning"—a systematic effort to both provide advice to the states on how to more effectively fight the virus and to take lessons gleaned from their respective experiences that could be passed on to others. The pandemic also revealed inherent weaknesses in America's health infrastructure—for instance, there was no way for public health data systems to interact with the systems that collected data in hospitals and laboratories where infections would be first detected. This broken chain of essential information impaired the federal government's ability to respond and provide advice quickly.[38]

Deborah Birx was the U.S. global AIDS coordinator and the U.S. special representative for global health diplomacy. A career civil servant, she had served in this role since the Obama administration. In February, she was in South Africa as part of her work on HIV/AIDS. Every evening on CNN, she watched briefings of American officials claiming that the virus was under control, and she yelled at the television, "This is going to be a pandemic!" She told Margaret Brennan of CBS News that at the time she was thinking, "This is how the world missed HIV—if you're only looking for sick people you miss a lot of what is happening under the surface." With COVID, community spread was highly likely: "When we were asking people coming into this country about symptoms rather than testing everybody, that's when I started to get really worried." The 1918 faction grew increasingly alarmed as they witnessed the administration's failure to follow up on the travel ban. They were particularly frustrated that the administration had not sought funding from Congress to make the necessary preparations for what was surely coming. The task force was not functioning well. Stephen Hahn, the head of the Food and Drug Administration, was not even a member. According to one senior Trump administration official we spoke to, this was "a catastrophic mistake." The FDA was needed for emergency use authorization, for its expertise on testing, therapeutics, vaccine development, and much more.

Pottinger needed someone in the White House who could do battle with those urging caution and provide expert public health advice. He called Birx repeatedly throughout February, asking her to come on board. They had known each other for many years. Both of them had been in Asia during SARS, and they were aligned in terms of how they saw the COVID-19 threat. Though she said no "about twenty times," she eventually changed her mind once it became apparent the administration was missing important pieces in the response, including testing. Birx then became the only full-time White House official working exclusively on fighting the coronavirus. But it was not easy. Her requests for more staff were denied. Over time, she managed to recruit a number of volunteers from other agencies.[39] By the end of February, some in the 1918 faction felt it was already too late. They had failed to act on the scale required. The die had been cast. As Pottinger had warned Trump a month earlier, it would be 1918 redux.

The politics of COVID-19 inside the White House reached a boiling point on February 26 when Dr. Nancy Messonnier, director of the CDC's National Center for Immunization and Respiratory Diseases, told a press conference: "This new virus represents a tremendous public health threat." She urged parents to pay attention. "I understand this whole situation may seem overwhelming and that disruption to everyday life may be severe," she said, but "these are things that people need to start thinking about now. I had a conversation with my family over breakfast this morning and I told my children that while I didn't think that they were at risk right now, we as a family need to be preparing for significant disruption of our lives."[40] The stock market plummeted in the last week of February as awareness spread that the pandemic was likely to hit the United States.

Trump was in India on his first visit there as president, a thirty-six-hour whirlwind trip that included a rally in front of 100,000 people at the Taj Mahal. On his way back, he grew furious about the drop in the markets and called Azar to complain about Messonnier.[41] The next day, Trump put Vice President Mike Pence in charge of the Coronavirus Task Force. According to Olivia Troye, who worked for Pence at the time, "The reaction in the White House was very much one of 'we have to control the messaging' and that's when you see a complaint and the [vice president] brought in to run the task force."[42] From that point forward, Troye says, Trump shifted to politicizing the task force's work, "which is very detrimental during a pandemic crisis of this magnitude because you now have fundamentally divided the country on a very critical issue where you are going to put lives at risk."[43] The task force would calibrate messages so that they were in line with what Trump was saying, and voices like Messonnier's were silenced. Pence did correct one mistake though: a senior administration official told us that at his first meeting in charge, Pence looked around the room and asked, "Where's the head of the FDA?"[44]

Trump continued to downplay the virus, declaring on Twitter on February 24 that COVID-19 was "very much under control" and then tweeting, "Stock market starting to look very good to me," even as some of his aides were providing private assessments that were much less confident.[45] In the months that followed, the White House and Azar would try to control and manage the CDC's efforts to guide businesses and the American public on how best to contain the outbreak. It sought to edit the CDC's findings and recommendations, which included eliminating social distancing restrictions on religious services, reducing them for bars and restaurants, and delaying an order to ban cruise ships from setting sail. The White House eventually stripped the agency of its lead role in collecting data about the virus from hospitals.[46]

By early March, the situation was becoming increasingly dire, and dramatic action became necessary. The number of known cases on March 1 was sixty-six. Two weeks later, it had increased exponentially to 1,682.[47] During this period, the stock market endured some of the biggest losses in its history, official projections estimated a dramatic spike in cases and deaths, and businesses began to close in New York and Washington State.[48] On March 11, Trump gave a rushed Oval Office address, only the second of his tenure, in which he banned all travel from Europe.[49] The speech was nothing short of a disaster, giving the impression that U.S. citizens would be stranded and that trade would cease. The desperation among Americans was palpable. Throughout the night, families called their loved ones traveling in Europe. Some paid up to $20,000 for a one-way ticket home. A *New York Times* journalist in Paris for the week with his wife described trying to buy a ticket that night as being "like trying to catch a firefly that hovered before you for a moment and then winked out before you could grab it."[50] By the time the White House clarified what they meant—that the ban did not apply to American citizens, green card holders, or trade—the damage was already done: flights and airports were packed to the rafters with travelers returning from Europe. Naturally, this frenetic rush continued to bring the virus to U.S. shores, and the markets plunged again.

On March 15, at the behest of Fauci and Birx, Trump agreed to shut down the country, announcing actions that gave the nation fifteen days to slow the spread. This included asking Americans to stay at home, avoid gatherings of more than ten people, and practice social distancing. Trump's advisors knew it would not be enough, but it was all they could get. They would ask for, and receive, an extension in early April, but within days Trump grew antsy and began agitating for a full reopening by Easter. He would again relent and accept that it would take longer, only to soon thereafter flip-flop once more in favor of reopening.[51] Some of this was moot anyway. The United States is a federal system with considerable power vested in the states. From early March, prior to Trump's national lockdown, states including California, New York, and Washington had taken dramatic action to close schools and nonessential businesses, ban large gatherings, and restrict travel. Other states, such as Arkansas, Iowa, Nebraska, North Dakota, and South Dakota, refused to put in place any stay-at-home orders, on either a statewide or citywide basis.[52] In other words, as Trump politicized the federal government's messaging, the states took the cue to do the same.

From mid-April on, Trump continued to double down, criticizing his medical advisors and state governors, downplaying the virus's dangers, and calling for a return to normal. A faction within the administration agreed: they too wanted to reopen the economy and learn to live with the pandemic. The president's son-in-law and senior advisor, Jared Kushner, treasury secretary Steve Mnuchin, and economic advisor Larry Kudlow, among others, felt that allowing scientists to dictate government action was "like the school nurse trying to tell the principal how to run the school."[53] Meanwhile, Americans continued to get sick, with around 30,000 new cases and 2,000 deaths each day.[54]

Over the next several months, Trump would lose interest in fighting COVID-19. He would repeatedly question his own scientific experts, including Fauci, Redfield, and Birx. To him, this was not a public health crisis so much as a political one, as he became more focused on the risk that a continued economic slowdown posed to his reelection prospects in November. He criticized states that locked down, and he urged governors to open up. He repeatedly declared that the country was getting back to normal and tried to wind down the Coronavirus Task Force in early May, something he had to reverse himself on after an outcry.[55] As we shall see in Chapter 12, he pinned all of his hopes on a vaccine. Trump's outspokenness had a chilling effect. Republicans who spoke out early in favor of a robust national response, such as Senator Tom Cotton, simply stopped talking about the pandemic publicly. Governors who recognized the threat the pandemic posed to their states found themselves attacked by the president on Twitter—in early April he tweeted, "Liberate Michigan" and "Liberate Minnesota."[56] The virus had become a political litmus test, and Trump was too much of a force within Republican politics and among his base to be meddled with.

THE SINGULAR FOCUS

As the Trump administration surveyed the accumulating wreckage, they drew one conclusion above all others: This was not an act of God, like an earthquake or tsunami. It was the act of an enemy, a disaster brought forth by the Chinese government, which had failed to cooperate with the international community. They strongly suspected that the virus originated in a laboratory, not in a wet market. And they accurately saw that Beijing was using the pandemic as an opportunity to press its geopolitical advantage around the world: using mask diplomacy to pressure smaller

countries that needed assistance and bullying those that asked inconvenient questions. Beijing also cracked down on student protesters in
Hong Kong and effectively ended what political autonomy the region had
left. That was not all—it also increased pressure on Taiwan and engaged
in a deadly border clash with India. The Trump administration saw the
international dimensions of COVID-19 as a China problem rather than
a global public health crisis, a framing that would have major consequences for world politics.

When Trump first created the task force, he excluded USAID and
its administrator, Mark Green. It meant that there was initially no one
included who understood the full global scope of the crisis, its implications, and how to properly respond globally. There were contacts between
the CDC and the State Department with lower levels of USAID, but the
highest levels of the task force were missing the top voices of the U.S.
government's lead agency for administering U.S. global health programs
around the world as well as its lead for responding to overseas humanitarian crises. Green was dismayed by the decision. He passionately believed that USAID's capabilities and prior experiences with dealing with
global health emergencies needed to be fully represented. He resigned
from the administration in March. At the time, he said it had nothing to
do with the COVID response, telling a reporter, "They're not related at
all." However, a person familiar with his thinking told us that his exclu-
sion from the task force was an important factor in his decision.[57]

The Trump administration had plenty of China hawks, but they were
divided in terms of how they viewed the issue. This broke down along
similar lines to the divide in February between the 1918-ers who wanted
to mobilize the country for the pandemic and the Wait and See-ers who
wanted to give the public information but avoid costly action, although
there were some additional voices on each side. Although Trump routinely
criticized China, he saw the problem almost entirely through the lens of
trade. Economic officials such as Mnuchin, Kudlow, and the U.S. trade
representative, Bob Lighthizer, wanted to make progress on that front,
but they basically agreed with Trump that a wider strategy of containment was not worth pursuing. Another group, the hard-liners—including
Pompeo, Pottinger, defense secretary Mark Esper, and Navarro—believed
the United States was in a broader long-term competition with China
and sought to reorient U.S. policy in that direction. They saw the nature

of the CCP itself as the threat, wanted a massive military buildup to counter it, and sought to decouple the U.S. economy from its reliance on China for technology, supply chains, and finance.

The president's political calculus on China changed as the virus ravaged the United States, with his preferences shifting toward the hard-liners. The president switched after he realized the enormousness of the crisis and the threat it posed to his administration and his personal political prospects. Reflecting on Trump's shift in thinking, commerce secretary Wilbur Ross, who was not a hard-liner, told the *Wall Street Journal* shortly before the November election, "It's been an evolution. . . . There isn't one sort of big bang." But an unnamed official told the *Journal* that the Chinese foreign ministry's insinuation in mid-March that the U.S. Army brought the virus to Wuhan might have been the tipping point for Trump.[58] Two Trump administration officials who favored continued engagement with China and pushed back against the hard-liners told us that before COVID-19, Trump was something of a moderating force on China policy but he was so upset at how it had jeopardized his reelection prospects that he was willing to endorse everything the hard-liners wanted.

Whatever the immediate cause, the change was real. In an interview, a member of the hard-line group reflected: "There's no question that the pandemic and China's efforts to exploit the pandemic were galvanizing for a unified U.S. response [to China]." The United States, the official said, began to work with its allies "to talk through an agenda that was much more aggressive and directly responding to the pandemic and China's cynical response." The administration started in Asia, deepening cooperation with the other three nations of the so-called Quad (a grouping that includes the United States, Australia, India, and Japan) on diversifying supply chains and countering Chinese disinformation. They soon began replicating this agenda elsewhere, including in Europe, where they found a receptive audience among national security professionals increasingly alienated by Beijing's wolf warrior approach. China had overplayed its hand. Domestically, the administration also went into overdrive on China. It closed the Chinese consulate in Houston against the advice of the U.S. ambassador to China, imposed restrictions on Chinese technology companies such as ByteDance, sent health and human services secretary Azar to Taiwan, agreed to a new Taiwan arms sale, and imposed new sanctions on China over its violation of the "one country, two systems" model in Hong Kong and mass human rights abuses in Xinjiang. As the official told us: "I don't think those things necessarily would have happened without COVID. The list of actions flies off the chart starting in late spring of 2020. More than in the prior three years combined."

Even though they viewed the pandemic through the prism of geopolitical competition with China, Pottinger and O'Brien were concerned about COVID-19 early on and pushed for policies that would tackle it more systematically both at home and abroad, including more testing and contact tracing. Other members of the foreign policy team, however, showed no such interest, preferring to use the crisis as a cudgel to go after Beijing. Pompeo was the most striking example. He had risen rapidly during the Trump era from a member of the House of Representatives to CIA director and then secretary of state. The secret to his success was his ability to manage Trump politically. He never fell out with him, which with Trump was an art unto itself. On one occasion, Trump remarked to a reporter that Pompeo was the only member of his cabinet he never had an argument with. This set Pompeo apart not only from the initial Axis of Adults (McMaster, Mattis, Tillerson, and Trump's second chief of staff, John Kelly) but also from Bolton and Esper, who occasionally pushed back against Trump while in the administration, and then spectacularly so once they left. Two Trump administration officials told us they believe Pompeo turned hard against China after his first official trip there in October 2018. He went hoping to engage but felt very badly treated, including being lectured to. After that point, these officials believe, it became extremely personal for him. Moreover, they said, Pompeo was the most political member of the cabinet and, like Trump, blamed China for the reversal in the administration's political fortunes. Several European officials who worked closely with the Trump administration told us that in contrast to other China hawks like Pottinger and O'Brien, Pompeo displayed no interest in tackling the public health aspects of the pandemic. He repeatedly cast blame on China for the virus, but he did not make a single speech calling for the United States to rally the world to otherwise confront the coronavirus, as America had done during the Ebola epidemic. He drew no attention to the myriad of ways in which the pandemic was unraveling international order. Rather, in Pompeo's view, the Europeans believed, it simply exemplified Chinese malevolence. There is also no evidence that Pompeo saw advancing cooperation on the public health dimension to the crisis as a personal priority, which is a glaring indictment for America's premier diplomat at the time of a grave international crisis.[59]

As we saw in the introduction, on March 26 Pompeo blew up the G7 ministerial meeting over his insistence on using the term "Wuhan virus" in the group's communiqué. It was not the only time he played saboteur. In April, the French tried to pull together a meeting of the five permanent members of the UN Security Council—the United States, China, Russia, France, and the United Kingdom—to discuss COVID-19 and a possible global cease-fire agreement for all conflicts for the duration of the pandemic. It fell apart because of the U.S.-China rivalry. The Trump administration wanted a resolution blaming China, while China wanted a resolution saying it was not responsible. The French in partnership with the Tunisians, who held one of the Security Council's rotating seats, worked for weeks to find a way to break the impasse. On May 7, one day before the seventy-fifth anniversary of the end of World War II in Europe, Nicolas de Rivière, the French ambassador to the United Nations, reached an agreement between all fifteen Security Council member states on the text of a resolution. The United States, which had criticized the WHO for being too close to China, had objected to a reference to the organization's efforts to combat the pandemic in conflict zones; China wanted it in. They compromised on "wishy-washy" words positively referring to "specialized health agencies." De Rivière agreed on the terms with the U.S. ambassador to the UN, Kelly Craft, and put the resolution "under silence" (the diplomatic term of art meaning that the negotiations were settled unless a member state objected within seventy-two hours). The resolution was to come into effect automatically at 2 p.m. on May 8. At 1 p.m., the United States came forward and said, in a statement that most people involved believed was written by or for Pompeo, that it could not support the resolution. Craft had been overruled at the last minute.

According to a senior French official, Paris was incredulous and "pissed off"—but they had leverage. Neither the United States nor China was "comfortable with the idea of blocking a humanitarian truce and wanted to blame the other." France kept pressure on both. In June, they finally agreed on a compromise, essentially using the transitive property: the resolution would not mention the WHO, but it would refer to a General

Assembly resolution that did mention it. It made little sense, but it was the kind of fudge that diplomacy sometimes relies on. Washington and Beijing signed on, and the resolution went into effect. As we will see in Chapter 9, it did not bring about an end to hostilities around the globe, but it did allow the UN to put some pressure on warring parties to allow access to conflict zones for humanitarian missions. Above all, the cease-fire resolution was a reminder of how difficult it had become to get anything done internationally in the context of the escalating U.S.-China rivalry.[60]

The Trump administration also continued to push for a full investigation into the origins of COVID-19 and aired its suspicions that the virus was a Chinese lab experiment gone wrong. U.S. officials pointed to a 2018 cable from the U.S. embassy in Beijing expressing concern about a lack of adequately trained personnel at the Wuhan Institute of Virology.[61] They were not alone. A number of U.S. analysts also had serious doubts about China's official story—that the virus had jumped to humans from an animal in the Huanan wet market in Wuhan. They pointed to an abundance of circumstantial evidence: bats were not sold in the market, so it would have had to come from an animal that ate an infected bat; bat coronaviruses most genetically similar to SARS-CoV-2 are found in bats that live far from Wuhan; the Huanan market is blocks from a laboratory that studies bat coronaviruses; the first known case of COVID-19 in Wuhan was not at the market; and the U.S. embassy had previously expressed concern about safety protocols in the lab. The alternative theory that circulated in Washington was that it was an accident at the WIV lab.[62] Some in the Trump administration were determined to find and leverage classified intelligence that might prove these suspicions true. In early May, for instance, Pompeo told the ABC Sunday show *This Week*, "There's enormous evidence" COVID came from a lab.[63] He would later walk back that assertion after being challenged on it.[64] Trump also told the media that he had "high confidence" that the virus came from the Wuhan Institute of Virology, but when asked to elaborate, he said, "I can't tell you that. I'm not allowed to tell you that."[65] National Security Council officials would acknowledge that they had no definitive proof, only circumstantial evidence; they pointed out that the wet market theory also relied on circumstantial evidence rather than hard proof. As the year dragged on, they felt the balance of circumstantial evidence pointed toward the lab theory. Toward the end of the administration, in late December 2020, Pottinger would tell British lawmakers that he now regarded this as the most credible explanation, something that China's Foreign Ministry hotly contested.[66]

Intelligence analysts who were sympathetic to the lab theory acknowledged that they would never know for sure. As one former intelligence analyst who worked on biosecurity told us: "If it did spread from a wet market, we need to know how, because it doesn't bode well" if it is that easy for a virus to leap from a bat to another animal and then to a person and, within weeks, cause a global pandemic. On the other hand, the analyst said, "if it was a lab accident, that raises a different set of questions and challenges." In some ways, the former analyst said, it might be easier to understand if it was a lab accident, but it is important to know the truth regardless. A senior national security official from a U.S. ally that worked closely and amicably with the Trump administration told us that in their government's view, "The Trump administration did get a bit too far forward on backing a particular horse. The evidence wasn't all in. Pompeo certainly raised important questions but we never felt the evidence for the lab theory got to the point where it became the most likely explanation. We always maintained the position that the jury is still out."

For most of the world, the fight over the origins of the virus was a distraction. The United States seemed to be investing its resources in propagating a fringe theory about SARS-CoV-2's origins instead of combating the reality of COVID-19 and its consequences. There would always be time to answer these questions, but containment was a priority that could not wait. For the Trump administration, however, assigning blame was a more urgent matter. They had little patience for a delayed reckoning, or for anyone who sought to challenge that impulse. This approach gave Beijing cover to dismiss calls for an inquiry as politically motivated.

THE WHO AND THE UNFIRED ARROW

Significant clashes would come over the World Health Organization. In a press conference on April 14, Trump announced he was suspending funding to the WHO (pending a review by his administration) because of its "role in severely mismanaging and covering up the spread of the coronavirus."[67] The Trump administration was furious at the WHO for letting China off the hook. Pottinger believed that the WHO's pressure on China during SARS had shamed Beijing into coming clean and acknowledging what was happening. Yet at the outset of the COVID outbreak, from the White House's perspective, Tedros did the opposite. For many in Trump's national security team, what was happening at the WHO was emblematic of a much broader geopolitical trend: the rising influence of the CCP on the world stage. This, they believed, had to be dealt with immediately.

It is unclear just how much Trump personally bought into the belief in the nefariousness of the CCP as the key driver of the pandemic. He certainly blamed the WHO for its coolness toward his travel ban. China also served as a useful foil to displace responsibility for his own mistakes in downplaying the virus and vouching for Xi. But the combination of the administration's critique of the WHO and the president's own political agenda was a powerful driver of policy. As was often the case with Trump, administration officials were not able to fully control what the president did once he was seized by an impulse. He was prone to sudden and dramatic actions without forewarning or consultation. So it was with the WHO.

The news that America planned to walk away from the WHO shocked European allies, who saw the organization doing the best it could under the circumstances.[68] Yes, Tedros was reluctant to call out China, but he was also in a difficult position. After all, the WHO required the consent of its member states to operate, and China was among its most powerful. It was perfectly reasonable to push for reforms to the WHO, the Europeans believed, but to threaten withdrawal to force the issue in the middle of the worst pandemic in a century was crazy. There would be time to deal with that later. Tedros was relatively unfazed. He approached Andrew Bremberg, the U.S. permanent representative to the WHO, and offered to praise Trump's response to the pandemic and to say publicly that the president had been treated very unfairly by the media. Would that help? asked Tedros. To an astonished Bremberg, it seemingly proved the U.S. case: after denying he was praising Xi Jinping without cause, here Tedros was promising to do the same for Trump. For WHO officials, it showed something different: Tedros was being consistent and would compliment leaders publicly while pushing them privately to secure practical cooperation.

In early May, some progress had been made about a partial restoration of funding whereby the United States would match China's payments. But on May 15, Fox News host Tucker Carlson ran a segment reporting that a draft letter had been prepared for Trump to this effect and advising the president to reject it.[69] Fox Business host and Trump confidant Lou Dobbs followed up with a tweet saying:

> Top WH Advisors are working for whom exactly? Surely not for our historic President or this great nation.[70]

Trump responded to him on Twitter:

> Lou, this is just one of numerous concepts being considered under which we would pay 10% of what we have been paying over many years, matching much lower China payments. Have not made final decision. All funds are frozen. Thanks![71]

A senior Trump administration official told us that the draft letter proposing to match U.S. funding to China's funding was actually dictated by Trump personally. According to the official, senior figures in the Office of Management and Budget, and also Peter Navarro, were strongly opposed to any restoration of funding to the WHO. The letter dictated by the president ended up in Tucker Carlson's hands and, for those seeking to derail funding, it had the desired effect: Trump completely disavowed it. In Geneva, WHO officials noticed how Pompeo, who they believed had orchestrated the proposed deal and seemed fairly pragmatic on the issue, suddenly denounced the proposed restoration of funding and became much more critical of the organization after the Fox News treatment.

On May 18, Trump formalized his original position during the opening of the World Health Assembly with a letter to Tedros. The missive provided further details of Trump's complaints and warned, "If the World Health Organization does not commit to major substantive improvements within the next 30 days, I will make my temporary freeze of United States funding to the World Health Organization permanent and reconsider our membership in the organization."[72] The assembly passed a resolution urging an assessment of what had gone wrong with China and calling for reform to the WHO. Bremberg felt that a resolution was a positive step if it led to action but, so far, the WHO had given no indication that it was willing to make any concessions to keep the Americans in, except for offering to praise Trump. Bremberg was initially reluctant to issue a list of specific demands in case that rendered them too toxic for Tedros to adopt. But as time ticked by he wrote a memo, vetted with a number of like-minded countries, calling for several actions, including initiating an investigation into the organization's performance during the pandemic, having Tedros call on China to share samples of the virus, acknowledging it was wrong to criticize the restriction of travel, and dispatching a team to Taiwan to study their success in containing COVID-19. If he could make progress on these issues, he believed he could convince Trump to make a deal.

On May 29, eleven days into the thirty-day notice, Bremberg was in talks with WHO officials to find a way that they could meet the president's demands, and he passed along the list to them. Yet just hours later, without notifying Bremberg or any of his fellow officials, Trump declared in a speech that he would preempt his own timetable and leave the WHO immediately.[73] At the White House, senior advisors were surprised but not disappointed. It is unclear exactly what happened. The tense phone call in which German chancellor Angela Merkel had infuriated Trump by telling him she would not be attending the G7 at Camp David had taken place the evening before—so perhaps that had soured the president's mood. Multiple officials told us that the speech that day was originally supposed to be about China, but Trump was unhappy with the draft of the speech he was given that morning. One official felt that Trump added the withdrawal from the WHO to give it more juice, but he never intended to actually leave. Afterward, Trump spoke with Bremberg on the phone. "I've given you all the leverage you could possibly want," he said. "Now go and negotiate me a great deal."

Bremberg spoke with Tedros twice that weekend and met with him for four hours the following Saturday, hoping to strike a deal. He was following a template that had succeeded before. In 2018, Trump had announced he was withdrawing from the Universal Postal Union (UPU). The United States had been asking for reform to the sliding scale of charges that favored Chinese companies over American ones but had gotten nowhere. Trump's announced withdrawal spurred other countries into action. Bremberg had played a key role in bringing the UPU issue to

Trump's attention and devising the negotiation strategy. By late 2019, a
coalition proposed reforms very similar to those advocated by the United
States, and the reforms passed unanimously.[74]

But Trump's May 29 announcement to withdraw from the WHO did
not have the same effect as his UPU play. The talks with the WHO dragged
on but never went anywhere. Tedros and the WHO never offered concessions or proposed a pathway forward. Other countries did not intervene
to push for reforms to keep the United States in. Part of the reason was
that other governments, including America's European allies, believed that
Trump really meant it. After all, he had announced it not just once but
twice. And he was caught up in an election campaign where bashing the
WHO and China served his political interests. Bremberg's perspective
was that critics had gotten it wrong. Trump was not intent on leaving;
he was negotiating, just like with the UPU. But the moment for such a
deal had passed. On July 6, with little progress to speak of, the United
States sent a formal letter of intent to withdraw. For WHO officials, it
was absurd to conflate the UPU with the WHO in the middle of a global
pandemic. They felt that the United States was demanding the WHO's
unconditional surrender, with a signing ceremony to boot. They believed
that nothing they offered would ever be enough. Even if they negotiated
in good faith, Trump could very well just blow the whole thing up
at the end. Indeed, European governments believed Trump did exactly
this when he announced he was pulling out of the Iran nuclear deal in
2018 even as his diplomats were close to negotiating a compromise with
the Europeans. So the WHO went through the motions of engaging the
Trump administration even as they basically gave up.

For his part, Bremberg felt a deal was possible but WHO officials
never really tried and gave him nothing to bring to Trump. Bremberg
looked on in frustration three days after the formal notice of America's
intent to withdraw when Tedros met one of the U.S. demands that he had
previously resisted: announcing the formation of an independent panel
for pandemic preparedness and response to evaluate the world's reactions
to the pandemic with a commitment to issue an interim report later in
2020. If the WHO had wanted to negotiate with Trump, they could have
used that announcement as a chip, but WHO officials had already decided that negotiating with Trump was not a game they wanted to play.[75]

Pottinger shared others' misgivings about announcing the U.S. departure in the manner that the president did. But he also felt it forced a necessary issue—the world would have to figure out an alternative to the WHO. And he had something in mind. Pottinger worked with others inside the government to develop an initiative called America's Response to Outbreaks (ARO, pronounced "arrow"). It was modeled on PEPFAR, the widely successful program to combat HIV/AIDS, but with a robust multilateral framework. It would include the G7 countries plus Australia, Brazil, India, South Korea, and Taiwan. The idea, as with PEPFAR, was to deepen surveillance for emerging pathogens and use public health money to incentivize countries to live up to their commitments under the IHR. The coalition could also inflict collective punishment on countries that failed to live up to these commitments. The ARO concept was the subject of intense bureaucratic debate. The White House wanted the State Department to run it, but USAID initially felt the program should be under its authority. The Office of Management and Budget hated it because they thought it created an expensive new bureaucracy. Interagency discussions over ARO continued throughout the year. The NSC felt they were close to reaching agreement after the November election, when they announced a blizzard of other foreign policy initiatives. But Trump had lost all interest and focused instead on overturning the election results.

PURCHASING POWER

As 2020 wore on, Trump allowed his team to pursue tough-on-China policies, but the president's mind was often elsewhere, chasing whichever rabbit happened to appear that particular day. Like much of the rest of the world, the United States and its diplomatic apparatus began to focus on the narrow task of securing crucial medical supplies and drugs that the country needed. The crisis had exposed how much America relied on China for personal protective equipment (PPE)—just under half of all exports of PPE to the United States came from there, something the administration recognized as a strategic vulnerability.[76] In the long term, the nation would perhaps produce PPE at home. In the short term, it would have to hustle to secure supplies around the world. Yet even this effort reflected Trump's personal hunches and whims. In mid-March, he touted the anti-malaria drug hydroxychloroquine as "a game changer" and a "gift from God" in treating COVID-19.[77] Doctors were skeptical. Hydroxychloroquine was unproven as a treatment for the virus and had potentially severe side effects. But Trump was determined. Much of the supply of hydroxychloroquine came from India, the world's largest producer of generic drugs. On March 25, Indian authorities prohibited export of the drug except in humanitarian circumstances or to fulfill earlier orders. They worried that Trump's statements would increase demand internationally and jeopardize the domestic supply.[78] On April 4, they went further, completely prohibiting exports. Trump called Indian prime minister Narendra Modi hours later and urged him to reconsider. The official record of the call released by the Indian Ministry of Affairs made no mention of the spat. Instead, it claimed the two leaders discussed the impact of the pandemic on the global economy and the "significance of practices such as Yoga and Ayurveda . . . for ensuring physical and mental well-being in these difficult times."[79] Two days later Trump told a press conference:

> I don't like that decision [blocking exports of hydroxychloroquine]. . . .
> I would be surprised if [Modi] would, you know, because India does
> very well with the United States. For many years, they've been taking
> advantage of the United States on trade. So, I would be surprised if that
> were his decision . . . I called him. And I said, "We'd appreciate your
> allowing our supply to come out." If he doesn't allow it to come out, that
> would be okay, but, of course, there may be retaliation. Why wouldn't
> there be?[80]

This put intense pressure on India, and days later it reversed the decision. In late April, India shipped 50 million tablets of hydroxychloroquine to the United States, which would amount to India's biggest export of the drug to another country.[81] In response, Trump tweeted:

> Extraordinary times require even closer cooperation between friends.
> Thank you India and the Indian people for the decision on HCQ. Will
> not be forgotten![82]

Several weeks later, Trump donated 200 ventilators to India.[83]

This was illustrative of a broader pattern. Normally in response to an international crisis, whether it was the Indian Ocean tsunami in 2004 or

the Ebola crisis in 2014, the United States provided international assistance and encouraged others to do the same. Yet as Tanisha Fazal, a professor of political science at the University of Minnesota, has observed,
one of the remarkable aspects of America's health diplomacy during
COVID-19 is that it was a *recipient* of foreign assistance from other
countries. This assistance was given not primarily for humanitarian reasons but rather, as Fazal wrote, out of "a desire to shore up relations with
the U.S. and curry the favor of the Trump administration."[84] In late April,
Turkey sent an aircraft to Andrews Air Force base with half a million
masks, face shields, goggles, and disinfectant.[85] Even Beijing was asked to
help out. On March 27, Jared Kushner reached out to Cui Tiankai, China's
ambassador to the United States, as part of his effort to secure mask supplies. He told Cui:

> When we get out of this there's going to be a lot of people very angry
> with China. And how you guys act now with a lot of the materials that
> are made in China is going to be looked at very carefully by the country
> and the world. . . . I'm going to start working to find supply [of masks]
> here and I want to make sure that I'm not going to have any restrictions
> getting out the supply that I'm able to procure in China.[86]

Kushner also made an urgent request to the United Arab Emirates for
testing equipment. Three and a half million of these kits were delivered
in April, but U.S. government labs found them to be "contaminated and
unusable."[87] These bilateral efforts were not particularly successful, owing
perhaps to the ad hoc nature of an effort run by someone with no experience in international procurement. By mid-May the Trump administration had acquired 85 million masks, whereas the French government
had procured 400 million masks for a population one-fifth of America's.[88]

Meanwhile, individual states were left to fend for themselves. The administration offered to help governors acquire needed supplies, but the
offer was widely seen as a political favor. Some governors took matters
into their own hands. Larry Hogan, the Republican governor of Maryland,
was so exasperated with the White House that he negotiated his own
agreement with the government of South Korea, with the help of his wife,
Yumi, who is Korean American. Hogan got the State Department and
Food and Drug Administration to sign off, but he was still so concerned

that the shipment might be seized by the federal government that he sent the Maryland National Guard and police to the runway to protect the cargo—500,000 tests—when it landed. "It was like Fort Knox to us, because it was going to save the lives of thousands of our citizens," Hogan said. "That was so important to us that we wanted to make sure that that plane took off from Korea safely, landed here in America safely, and that we guarded that cargo from whoever might interfere with us getting that to our folks that needed it."[89] Hogan's efforts were in vain though; the tests proved to be flawed and were never used.

DO NOT LOOK TO AMERICA

America's chaotic response to COVID-19 was all the more apparent from an international perspective. Overall, during the first year of the pandemic, the United States consistently accounted for nearly 20 percent of global COVID deaths despite having only 4 percent of the world's population.[90] A Columbia University study found that between 130,000 and 210,000 U.S. deaths could have been avoided if the Trump administration had exercised the measures employed by other advanced democracies.[91] If the United States had dealt with the pandemic as well as Germany, for example, it would have had 40,000 deaths by November instead of over 225,000.[92] As we will see in Chapter 12, this picture began to change in late 2020 and early 2021, when European deaths rose considerably and the United States made progress on the vaccine. But it is undeniable that early stumbles by the Trump administration embedded a negative image of America around the world. There was no U.S. national strategy. Nor was there a consistent message around social distancing or mask wearing. Key agencies, such as the CDC, were micromanaged and muzzled by the White House. Authorities at both the federal and state levels failed to develop adequate programs for testing, contact tracing, and quarantining. George Packer of *The Atlantic* put it starkly in a June 2020 article: "Every morning in the endless month of March," he wrote, "Americans woke up to find themselves citizens of a failed state."[93] The world took note. Writing in *Foreign Affairs*, former Australian prime minister Kevin Rudd said the international community "has seen what 'America First' means in practice: don't look to the United States for help in a genuine global crisis, because it can't even look after itself."[94]

Much of the U.S. failure was Trump's personal failure. Early on, he was dismissive despite warnings from his health advisors and national security aides. In March and April, as Birx noted, Trump came to appreciate the gravity of the situation, but as the pandemic dragged on he just wanted to put it behind him.[95] He continuously downplayed its importance and outsourced responsibilities to contain the virus entirely to the states. Rather than lean on Birx, Fauci, or Redfield, he empowered a set of advisors who fed him alternative data and information suggesting the situation was more favorable than it actually was. Trump also actively promoted disinformation publicly, whether around the virus's origins, its scale and scope, or how to address it. In one particularly infamous example, he suggested injecting disinfectant to prevent infection. He also said the virus would go away on its own. A September study for the Alliance for Science at Cornell University found that for the first five months of 2020, English-language media published more than 1.1 million articles containing disinformation about COVID-19, which was approximately 3 percent of all coverage. Mentions of Trump accounted for 37.9 percent, leading the authors to conclude "that the President of the United States was likely the largest driver of the COVID-19 misinformation 'infodemic'" across the globe.[96]

For much of the world, the U.S. response became synonymous with Trump. While there was no magic formula to effectively fight the virus, and many countries struggled, one thing appeared clear: do not emulate the Americans.

The Good, the Bad, and the Ugly

THE EUROPEANS WERE slower than the Americans to understand the significance of COVID-19 despite receiving similar warnings. Based in Stockholm and created two years after the SARS outbreak, the European Centre for Disease Control and Prevention (ECDC) became aware of the mysterious cases of pneumonia from Wuhan on New Year's Eve, when the World Health Organization informed the world. But whereas senior U.S. officials sounded the alarm and had their cause taken up by the deputy national security advisor, the ECDC was constrained by its lack of authority. As an agency of the European Union, it can offer scientific advice but has no actual power. The European Union was created in 1957 as the European Economic Community, with six members forming a common market; over time it grew to twenty-eight countries (twenty-seven after Brexit), acquired a formal role in almost all aspects of member states' domestic policies, including currencies, competition law, education, and infrastructure, and implemented a regulatory structure that connected its members. The EU increasingly thought of itself as a unified state, with Brussels as its decision-making capital during times of crisis. The members often bitterly disagreed over what should be done—the euro crisis, which began in 2009, almost tore the EU apart over a six-year period—but they were always engaged in intensive discussions with each other.

Health, however, was one of the few issues that remained the exclusive responsibility of individual governments. Each country's government ran the country's hospitals, sourced medical supplies, decided when to declare a public health emergency, and determined what restrictions to put in place. The EU had very little power or authority.[1] In 2020, this blind spot would produce a whole host of problems that reflected both the unique arrangements of the EU as a unified group of member states and the catastrophic effects of the pandemic itself.

On January 17, another EU agency (the European Commission's health security committee) held a conference call to brief the member states on the virus. Less than half (twelve out of twenty-seven) called in. Italy was not one of them; the government didn't consider it a priority. But that soon changed. On January 30, when two Chinese tourists in Rome tested positive, the Italian government swung into action, canceling flights to China and requesting an emergency meeting of EU health ministers. This emergency meeting would not take place until February 13—the Croatian government, which held the rotating presidency of the EU Council, was distracted by a domestic scandal—but no one considered the delay an issue. What was the rush? Furthermore, the EU was focused on more pressing matters (or so it felt at the time). After three and a half years of negotiation and forty-seven years of membership, the United Kingdom was formally leaving the EU on January 31, 2020. A new era was about to begin—though it was not the era they expected.[2]

As the situation in Wuhan worsened, the EU sent fifty tons of protective equipment to China.[3] European officials said little about it, largely out of respect for Chinese authorities. French president Macron reportedly told an aide that Chinese officials would remember Europe's gesture of goodwill and support.[4] Despite the infections in Italy, other European officials still did not see the coronavirus as a major problem. On February 7, Josep Borrell, the EU's high representative for external relations (effectively the EU's foreign minister), visited Washington for the first time in his new role to meet with Secretary of State Mike Pompeo and Jared Kushner. They talked about the Middle East peace plan, Iran, and Africa. Neither he nor his American counterparts brought up COVID-19.[5]

On February 14, China sent a small delegation to the Munich Security Conference, an annual gathering of over 1,000 members of the national security elite from Europe and the United States. The delegation was led by Wang Yi, the Chinese foreign minister, and Fu Ying, the chair of the National People's Congress Foreign Affairs Committee, who also plays a leading role in the regime's interaction with Western policy elites. The Chinese delegation clashed repeatedly with a bipartisan American delegation at the conference on technology and China's Belt and Road Initiative, with Yi and Fu trading barbs with Pompeo and Speaker of the House Nancy Pelosi, respectively. The Europeans were struck by the depth of the U.S.-China divide, which appeared to overshadow everything else. The coronavirus was also not a primary discussion point. It was addressed in specialized sessions on health security hosted in secondary rooms, but not on the main stage. In retrospect, after the March lockdowns were imposed on both sides of the Atlantic, American participants wondered if they had taken too big a risk in attending. The situation was even worse than they knew: days before the conference began, virologists discovered a subtle mutation in the virus between two infected patients that proved that presymptomatic transmission had occurred in late January at an auto plant in Munich.[6] The virus was already there in the city. The organizers worked closely with authorities and the WHO, but sheer luck also played a role in preventing the conference from turning into a superspreader event that infected leaders, defense ministers, and senior parliamentarians from around the world.

The virus soon began to spread throughout Lombardy, Italy's wealthiest region and home to its most advanced health care system. On February 23, after more than 130 cases were discovered, the government used the military and police to seal off eleven towns. Two weeks later, the Italian government locked down the entire country, but the plan leaked to the public prematurely. As a result, tens of thousands of Italians fled from the north, where the infections were concentrated, to the south.[7] Meanwhile, Italians felt that the EU was doing little to assist them in combating the outbreak and contending with the economic fallout. Anger bubbled over after Christine Lagarde, the president of the European Central Bank, said it was not the bank's role to "close spreads," which was seen as a clear signal that it would not address Italy's rising borrowing costs.[8] Italy, Spain, and other southern EU member states had bitter memories of the euro crisis, when Germany and a number of other northern EU member states, including the Baltic states and the Netherlands, imposed strict austerity measures that the governments of the southern states felt were unwarranted and unfair. The euro crisis divided Europe along creditor-debtor lines. Those tensions had eased as growth returned, but they still remained beneath the surface, both in the south and in the north, with each suspicious of the other. After Lagarde's comments, the Italian president, Sergio Mattarella, made a prime-time address to the nation in which he took a moment to offer a warning. Referring to the ECB's reluctance to ease Italy's borrowing costs, he said that the EU should not be putting obstacles in Italy's way. "I hope that everyone fully understands, before it is too late, the seriousness of the threat to Europe."[9]

March proved chaotic across the continent. The EU had a serious shortage of masks, ventilators, and other critical supplies, but its leaders were unaware. Once the penny dropped, it was every nation for itself. Decades earlier, the vast majority of EU member states had abolished all borders between themselves, creating a common travel area, known as the Schengen Area. Now borders began to close again. The German government was one of the first to do so. It also banned the export of medical protective equipment except in rare cases of emergency aid.[10] Berlin then actively blocked the shipment of masks through Germany to Austria and Switzerland. As one senior German official noted to us, the foreign ministry was transformed into "a giant consular operation" as they tried to get their citizens home while negotiating rights of transit for EU citizens in Germany to return to their home countries. It was a throwback to a long-gone nationalist era.

On March 3, Macron announced he was nationalizing "all stocks and the production of protective masks" for distribution to its citizens. But the public was still largely oblivious. In northwest France, the small town of Landerneau hosted an event to break the world record for the largest gathering of Smurfs: 3,500 people arrived in blue body paint and danced in conga lines. The mayor of Landerneau, Patrick Leclerc, told Agence France-Presse, "We must not stop living. It was the chance to say that we are alive." One attendee reportedly said. "There's no risk, we're Smurfs. Yes, we're going to Smurferize the coronavirus."[11] A day later, France banned all gatherings over 1,000 people. By March 14, all nonessential businesses, including restaurants and cafes, would be closed.

The nationalization of mask production was a harbinger of things to come. In March and April, European countries would compete with one another to secure essential equipment and materials. Around 20 percent of all surgical procedures in the EU used protective equipment imported from Asia by the Swedish medical company Mölnlycke. Mölnlycke's distribution center for southern Europe, Belgium, and the Netherlands is based in Lyon, France's second-largest city. Armed with Macron's directive, the French government seized all 6 million masks at the Lyon facility, which were destined for Italy, Spain, Switzerland, Belgium, Portugal, the Netherlands, and France itself. The move infuriated Sweden, which had adopted its own novel approach to the pandemic of avoiding lockdowns or restrictions by seeking herd immunity. Swedish prime minister Stefan Löfven raised the matter directly with Macron. A Swedish official told the *Irish Times*, "The French often evoke solidarity within the EU. The really fundamental principle of free movement of goods within the EU is toppled."[12]

The Swedes were not the only ones to feel aggrieved. As we saw in Chapter 4, China made a concerted effort to use pandemic assistance to increase its influence in Europe, and by comparison, some governments found the EU lacking in this regard. In an emotional press conference, Serbian president Aleksandar Vučić, whose nation is in talks to join the EU, responded to the restrictions by saying: "The only country that can help us is China. . . . By now, you all understood that European solidarity does not exist. That was a fairy tale on paper. I believe in my brother and friend Xi Jinping, and I believe in Chinese help."[13]

Attempting to cope with the first hotspot in Europe, Italy's leaders also felt resentment toward the EU and were positively inclined toward China. In what was perceived as a rebuke of the EU, Italy's foreign minister, Luigi Di Maio, posted a video welcoming a Chinese plane landing with aid.[14] Italy's permanent representative to the European Union wrote in an op-ed: "Italy has already asked to activate the European Union Mechanism of Civil Protection for the supply of medical equipment for individual protection. But, unfortunately, not a single EU country responded to the Commission's call. Only China responded bilaterally. Certainly, this is not a good sign of European solidarity."[15]

To Italians, the EU seemed disinterested in helping Italy as the crisis spread. A Tecnè poll taken in March found that 67 percent of Italians thought that EU membership was a disadvantage, up from 47 percent in 2018.[16] Janez Lenarčič, the European commissioner responsible for crisis management, later told *The Guardian*: "No member state responded to Italy's request and to the commission's call for help. . . . Which meant that not only is Italy not prepared . . . Nobody is prepared . . . The lack of response to the Italian request was not so much a lack of solidarity. It was a lack of equipment."[17]

On March 16, Macron addressed the French public. "We are at war" against an "invisible, elusive enemy," he told them. The French would only be allowed to leave their homes for essential reasons and would need to present a time-stamped and signed form to police if asked. Macron had won the presidency in 2017 by breaking with his party, the Socialists, setting up his own, and running on an unambiguously pro-EU platform. But his two predecessors in the presidency had failed to be reelected, and in February 2020 Macron's personal approval ratings had been hovering in the low 30s.[18] Partly for this reason and partly because he has the confidence and ambition of a young man who has conquered all before him, Macron was imbued with a sense of purpose—that he had the responsibility and historical obligation to convert the EU into a genuine superpower. The COVID-19 pandemic fundamentally threatened that vision. In March, as he looked around in horror, Macron saw EU member after EU member go its own way, without a care in the world for how their decisions impacted others. Even German chancellor Merkel failed to mention the EU in her otherwise moving address to the nation on the challenges the pandemic posed to Germany.[19]

It was not just Italy and France. Europe was generally pummeled in the first two months of the pandemic. In Spain, after a series of mass gatherings in early March, the country saw an explosion in cases; Spain's deaths from the virus exceeded those of Italy by the end of the month.[20]

Yet not all EU member states saw COVID-19 as a serious threat. The Swedish government, following the advice of its public health agency, Folkhälsomyndigheten (FHM), adopted a de facto herd immunity strategy from the get-go. The FHM opposed economic lockdowns and kept bars, nightclubs, restaurants, and gyms open. Swedish public health officials resisted even the feeblest measures to contain virus spread. The country was the world's sole democratic nation that did not mandate even limited use of masks throughout 2020. Meanwhile, the government failed to build out a robust contact tracing or testing regime similar to other wealthy countries. And the experiment seemed to have failed: by mid-August, 20 percent (at most) of the population had antibodies—a far cry from the 70 percent needed to reach herd immunity. By mid-June,

Sweden ranked fifth in the world for deaths as a proportion of the population, with over 5,000 dead.[21] There was also no apparent economic benefit. Sweden's economy declined by 8.7 percent for the second quarter of 2020, the highest drop in its neighborhood (Denmark's fell by 7.4 percent, Norway's by approximately 7 percent, and Finland's by 3.2 percent).[22]

Most of central and eastern Europe—including the Czech Republic, Hungary, Poland, and Slovakia—initially escaped largely unscathed because they moved more quickly than western Europe to close schools and nonessential businesses.[23] However, as we will see in Chapter 12, their luck would not last—some of these countries would be the hardest hit in the second wave six months later.

There was at least one standout success story in the first wave, however: Germany. The most populous country and the largest economy in the EU seemed to have things under control and was able to flatten the curve. The German government put in place a comprehensive tracking and tracing system, building a small army of contact tracers, called containment scouts, by recruiting thousands of people from all walks of life. Anyone who came within six feet of an infected person for more than fifteen minutes was put in state-mandated quarantine and contacted daily by tracers, who would arrange for groceries to be dropped off if needed. A contact-tracing app launched in June was downloaded 16 million times within a month. Germany was an early mover on testing, carrying out far more than other major European countries, although they would catch up later. As a consequence of all these efforts, the country succeeded in flattening the curve. By June, Germany had 10.3 deaths per 100,000 inhabitants, compared with 43 for France, 55.4 for Italy, and 57.9 for the United Kingdom. New infections peaked at 5,595 per day (on a rolling seven-day average) in April and declined to 344 by July.[24]

Elsewhere in Europe, a large part of the problem was that, as we have seen, health care was one of the few policy topics that the EU had little to no role in—it was entirely the responsibility of the national governments. For all their experience in pooling sovereignty and cooperation, EU member states had almost no experience doing so on health. They quickly learned, though. Several weeks into the crisis, Germany realized that the residents of the French region of Alsace were closer to a German hospital than they were to a French one. They offered to treat those ill with COVID-19 in the German states of Rhineland-Palatinate,

Baden-Württemberg, and Saarland. This gesture had real symbolic value. It showed that Europeans could fight this together.[25]

European leaders came to realize that COVID-19 could destroy everything they had worked for since the formation of the EU nearly three decades earlier. EU Commission president Ursula von der Leyen confessed that "we had a glimpse into the abyss."[26] Mario Centeno, the president of the Eurogroup, warned that the eurozone was at risk of breakup. Merkel acknowledged that "the European Union is facing the biggest test since its foundation."[27] The challenge, she said, "will be about showing that we are ready to defend our Europe, to strengthen it."[28] Pedro Sánchez, the prime minister of Spain, warned that if the EU did not meet the coronavirus challenge, "we will fail as a union."[29] "We have reached a critical juncture," he wrote, and "even the most fervently pro-European countries and governments, as is Spain's case, need real proof of commitment."[30] Macron told the *Financial Times*, "We are at a moment of truth, which is to decide whether the European Union is a political project or just a market project. I think it's a political project. . . . We need financial transfers and solidarity, if only so that Europe holds on."[31] It was at this moment in April that France and Germany began work in earnest on a common EU response. Crucially, many Germans who had previously been skeptical understood that Italy, Spain, and other nations badly affected by the pandemic were not at fault—a stark contrast to the financial crisis of 2008–9, when Germans tended to blame the debtor nations for their predicament.[32]

As we shall see in Chapter 7, the European Central Bank played an important role in shoring up the European economy, in a manner similar to the U.S. Federal Reserve, by buying private assets. But in early May, even this strategy was placed in jeopardy, with a hugely significant constitutional court judgment in Germany that effectively placed restrictions on the ability of the Bundesbank (the German central bank)—and by extension the ECB—to buy bonds.[33] The message was clear: Don't count on the ECB to save the day; the politicians would need to act too. In mid-May, Merkel and Macron made a joint appearance to push for a €500 billion recovery fund, which would be raised by the European Commission borrowing in bond markets. This was a true crossing of a Rubicon, the moment when Germans accepted what they had long opposed—the need for the EU to have its own shared debt. It was heralded as a Hamiltonian moment, invoking U.S. treasury secretary Alexander Hamilton (later the subject of a blockbuster musical), who arranged for the new nation to take on the debts of the individual American states in exchange for mutualizing the debt (in other words, he created a national debt)—a hugely consequential act that turned the young United States into a unified country. The Irish finance minister, Paschal Donohoe, described the European action as "a moment of imagination driven by necessity."[34]

The agreement did not quite live up to the billing in every respect. Mutualization would not apply to outstanding debt, and it was intended to be temporary—just for the duration of the crisis. And the EU would not have the power to tax its citizens. Nevertheless, it was a momentous step forward.

France and Germany's efforts to bury their past differences and to move toward that Hamiltonian moment might not have been possible if the United Kingdom had remained a member of the European Union. Britain had vetoed treaties in the past, including in 2011, when then prime minister David Cameron stood alone in opposition to a treaty to save the euro. But with the United Kingdom now out of the picture, new opponents popped up, including a group known as the Frugal Four—the Netherlands, Austria, Denmark, and Sweden—which would accept the recovery fund only if it came in the form of a loan. After a long and difficult negotiation, they were persuaded to accept a compromise that left the core idea—the mutualization of debt—intact.

With the deal struck, the outlook suddenly seemed bright. Continental Europe seemed to be over the worst of the pandemic. Europeans went back to work over the summer, returned to cafes and restaurants, and took vacations. There were still hotspots—a new outbreak in northern Spain and a spike in parts of southeastern Europe (Croatia, Bulgaria, Macedonia, and Serbia)—but these seemed to be the exceptions, not the norm. A travel piece for CNN observed, "Visiting many parts of Greece right now is almost like visiting a country where COVID-19 never happened."[35] The contrast with the United States, where the case count continued to rise, was stark. The Europeans had an explanation. Professor Lothar Wieler, the head of the Robert Koch Institute, Germany's equivalent of the CDC, stated that things had improved "because we stemmed the first wave of the epidemic by many of our citizens changing their behavior."[36] As we'll see in Chapter 12, however, this success would not survive much longer than Europe's summer.

EAST ASIA'S SUCCESS

Taiwan is only 110 miles from China, but it managed to prevent COVID-19 from ever establishing a foothold on the island. Taiwan's foreign minister, Joseph Wu, attributed the country's effective response in 2020 to their experience with SARS in 2003, which resulted in 668 cases and 181 deaths. "We were hit hard and we learned our lesson," he reflected.[37] New institutions were put in place. Taiwan's Centers for Disease Control was the only health agency in the world that monitored rumors on the Chinese internet in December and concluded that the outbreak in Wuhan could be a new pandemic. This was why Taiwan sent an email to the WHO on December 31 warning of "atypical pneumonia." Unfortunately, no one paid any attention to Taipei's warning, including the United States (U.S. officials would later come to regret this).

Even this early, Taiwan's government started to get very nervous. National elections were approaching on January 11, and rallies were planned with tens of thousands of people. But authorities believed they could contain the threat by screening passengers from Wuhan, and Beijing had unintentionally made this easier. In 2019, to increase pressure on Taiwan, China stopped issuing visas for independent tourism by Chinese citizens. The Taiwanese elections went off without a hitch. Taiwan then sent its public health experts, all of whom had been trained by the U.S. CDC, to Wuhan on January 12–15. But they were deeply frustrated by the lack of access on the ground. Even worse, when they tried to relay what they learned to the World Health Organization, the WHO—fearful of offending China—refused to acknowledge or publish these warnings.[38]

By the Lunar New Year, on January 25, Taipei was alarmed. All government departments mobilized for a unified response. The health minister gave a briefing every single day, which fortified an already high degree of public trust. Taiwan quickly created technological tools that would allow it to avoid a full lockdown. The GPS-based Intelligent Electronic Fence System, a collaboration between Taiwan's government and cellphone carriers, triangulated the location of all individuals under quarantine every ten minutes. If a person went outside the quarantine perimeter or could not be located within two consecutive periods (twenty minutes), a notification was automatically sent to the individual, the police, and local government.[39]

As the scale of the crisis in Wuhan became clear, some countries banned travel from Taiwan as well as China, ostensibly to recognize China's sovereignty over Taiwan. Meanwhile, Beijing launched a disinformation campaign alleging mass graves and the burning of bodies in Taiwan and a cover-up by the government. But Taiwan had experienced such tactics before and was able to swat them back. They began to reach out to other nations bilaterally with offers of help and advice, sending more masks overseas than China—and with no strings attached. The Foreign Ministry used the hashtag #TaiwanCanHelp online.[40]

South Korea exemplified another early success story. On January 20, the United States and South Korea both reported their first case of COVID-19. A month later, South Korea had the most confirmed infections outside China, and its president, Moon Jae-in, publicly apologized for the country's mask shortage. While the virus surged around the world, South Korea's pandemic response protocols kicked into gear. South Korea had experience in 2015 with MERS, a zoonotic virus that jumped from camels to humans in the Middle East. South Korea suffered more cases than any nation outside Saudi Arabia and had thirty-six deaths. Consequently, the government rewrote its public health laws and implemented sweeping legislation, embracing a "test, trace, and isolate" mantra to deal with future pandemics. The *Wall Street Journal* would later attribute South Korea's success in containing COVID-19 to "a constant fear of failure."[41]

As the threat from the novel coronavirus grew, South Korea was quick to translate these plans into action. Less than a week after its first case of COVID-19, health officials met with twenty medical and pharmaceutical companies to jump-start the production and approval of test kits. About two weeks later, on February 4, the government approved and distributed test kits capable of producing results in six hours. Barely a month into the crisis, the country began drive-through testing, eventually setting up dozens of facilities. By early March, Korea had tested over 145,000 people across 600 test centers, often using ten-minute rapid tests. Within weeks, the country had the capacity to test 20,000 people per day, making it the most aggressive and successful testing strategy in the world. Seoul also implemented a very aggressive contact tracing program—every person who went to a bar, nightclub, or movie theater had to scan their phone upon entry so the authorities would know how to follow up in the event of an outbreak.[42] Every confirmed patient in South Korea was isolated and treated in a hospital or government dormitory regardless of whether they displayed symptoms. Mask wearing was also nearly universal.

Together, these measures enabled South Korea to effectively halt COVID-19 transmission, avoiding a national lockdown and the accompanying economic fallout. Life began to normalize in Korea throughout the spring and early summer. Many schools reopened. So did public swimming pools, art galleries, and beaches, albeit with pandemic protocols in place. In April, 29 million South Koreans voted in national elections—the highest turnout in thirty years—without a single case of COVID transmission. In November, thousands of fans filled the country's baseball stadiums for playoff games.[43]

The contrast with the American experience is striking. From April to September, South Korea averaged just 77 new cases per day, compared to an average of 38,000 in the United States over the same period; even accounting for the fact that South Korea's population is one-sixth of the U.S. population, the disparity between the two countries, which were hit by the pandemic at the exact same time, is remarkable. In 2020, the U.S. COVID death rate was more than 500 times South Korea's. While the United States experienced a deep recession—the economy contracted by 3.5 percent in 2020—South Korea's economy was expected to contract by less than 1 percent.[44]

While Taiwan and South Korea managed to contain the virus at the outset of the crisis, Japan's early experience with COVID-19 was a global embarrassment. On January 20, the *Diamond Princess*, a British cruise ship with passengers from Japan, Argentina, Australia, Canada, and the United Kingdom, departed the Japanese port of Yokohama. A passenger from Hong Kong who later tested positive for COVID-19 was onboard. His infection precipitated an outbreak—621 passengers and crew (approximately 20 percent of all those aboard) contracted the virus within a period of three weeks—and led to the ship's return to and quarantine at Yokohama. The situation onboard was chaotic. There was no adequate separation between the healthy and sick. After two weeks, Japanese authorities allowed a thousand passengers to leave following a negative test. The problem was the tests were unreliable—the incubation period was at least five days—so passengers could have been infected on the ship but only tested positive well after leaving. Japan's decision was denounced by U.S. and Hong Kong officials.[45]

The *Diamond Princess* was the first of many cruise ships to find itself stranded at sea thanks to a little-known loophole in international law: onboard a ship, passengers are beyond national borders, and governments can refuse entry if they have a contagious disease. Another cruise ship, the *Westerdam*, crisscrossed the South China Sea during this period, having been denied entry to Japan, the Philippines, and Thailand. Eventually it was allowed to dock in Cambodia, where it was personally greeted by the prime minister—a move praised by the WHO as an act of international solidarity (even though masks were not worn as the passengers were welcomed onshore and social distancing was not observed). At least one passenger later traveled to Malaysia, where she developed symptoms and tested positive.

The *Diamond Princess* debacle did have a silver lining for Japan: it ensured high-level attention on the virus at an early stage in the spread, and Japan's experts took advantage of their access to the ship to better understand it. This early proximity paid dividends. Drawing on their study of the *Diamond Princess*, Japan adopted the "Three C's Strategy," urging its public to avoid closed spaces, crowded places, and close-contact settings. This approach, in conjunction with universal mask wearing, the country's voluntary national lockdown on April 7, and a national state of emergency nine days later, helped prevent a severe first wave in Japan.[46]

Japan's initial virus response—and its relative success (setting aside the *Diamond Princess*)—was abnormal. Unlike South Korea, Japan had virtually no testing infrastructure. By May, it had tested a mere 0.185 percent of the population. And unlike China, it was legally difficult for Japan's government to enforce a nationwide lockdown, owing to fears of repression that dated back to the days of the Japanese Empire. As a result, Japan's COVID response was highly normative—people complied because it was the right thing to do and because their neighbors were complying. During the initial months of the pandemic, in-person social interaction dropped 70–80 percent as people strictly followed the government's social distancing recommendations. On May 26, prime minister Shinzo Abe lifted the country's state of emergency and several weeks later triumphantly remarked to *PBS NewsHour* that Japan had "control[led] the spread."[47]

Abe spoke too soon. As life returned to normal, replete with sumo wrestling matches and baseball games, cases began to climb again. The government's poor reopening strategy and specific focus on revitalizing the domestic economy proved costly. Contradictory messaging was also a problem. In early summer, the Japanese government launched its "Go to Travel" campaign, which incentivized domestic travel in an attempt to boost Japan's tourism industry. The program, which would be suspended in December, was linked to increased COVID-19 transmissions. By August, Japan was firmly in the midst of a second wave, albeit less severe than the first, and soon found itself leaderless after the surprise resignation of Abe, who had been Japan's longest-serving prime minister, due to ill health. Shigeru Omi, the head of the expert panel advising Abe on COVID-19, acknowledged to the *Financial Times* in the summer that South Korea and Taiwan responded better than Japan because they had been affected by SARS and MERS and were more alert. Japan, he said, was prepared, but not as well as they were.[48]

There were other success stories in Asia as well. Vietnam, for instance, responded decisively and swiftly in late January, closing schools, suspending flights to China (despite pressure to not do so), and developing an early and effective diagnostic test. These measures, many of which were debated in Vietnam's mid-January COVID strategy meetings, would be adopted by other countries months later. Vietnam also played to its strengths, adopting a preventative approach that emphasized wide-scale contact tracing, strict lockdowns, and quarantine facilities (which housed 200,000 people from late January to May), rather than a more expensive mass testing regime (like South Korea), which would have required infrastructure and expense beyond Vietnam's capacity. For a twenty-two-day period that spanned February and March, Vietnam did not record a single new COVID-19 infection. Despite a population above 95 million and an acute physical proximity to China (with which Vietnam shares an 800-mile border), Vietnam did not register its first death from the virus until July 31, 2020. As with South Korea and Taiwan, previous experience mattered. Hanoi's response was a byproduct of the country's fight against SARS in 2003.[49]

The distant island nation of New Zealand did not record its first COVID-19 case until February 28, 2020, but its government began formulating and implementing a national coronavirus response on February 2, just days after the WHO deemed the virus a global health emergency. New Zealand's government strictly followed WHO recommendations on testing, contact tracing, and isolation. And although its approach was heavy-handed at times—New Zealand instituted a national lockdown in late March, when cases numbered below 100—the country's "go early and go hard" strategy was among the world's most effective. The country, which has a population of 5 million, recorded only twenty-five COVID-19 deaths between February 2020 and January 2021. It was also able to reopen its economy over the summer and went 102 days without a single case. A number of factors accounted for New Zealand's success, starting with its sustained focus on emergency management. Although New Zealand's background in emergency management stems from natural hazards (wildfires and earthquakes) and not diseases, the country has long invested in becoming a "disaster-resilient nation." When the government asked citizens to "unite as a team of five million" to fight COVID, it could draw on a strong tradition of adhering to emergency protocols and taking collective action.[50]

For the most part, nations in Asia and Oceania dealt with the pandemic better than the rest of the world, but they also displayed revealing differences. Remarkably, most managed to contain the pandemic without national lockdowns (New Zealand being an exception), preferring to couple extensive testing with aggressive contact-tracing programs and targeted quarantine efforts to isolate those infected. Virtually all adopted extreme travel policies, closing their countries off from the rest of the world—certainly the infected parts—even when their case count was very low. Above all, previous experience with crises and failure on diseases meant that they had gone through the necessary political process of reform. Where other parts of the world were theoretically ready, the successful countries in Asia, to a varying degree, were psychologically ready.

THE NATIONALISTS

As the world became more nationalist over the past decade, many nationalist leaders tended to get lumped together. To be sure, there were similarities among them: they tended to be skeptical of elites; they jealously protected national sovereignty; many were climate skeptics; and they all had good relations with the Trump administration. But COVID-19 revealed some important differences as well. Nearly all of them struggled, albeit in different ways. Some, such as Brazilian president Jair Bolsonaro, followed

Trump's lead in downplaying the severity of the virus, setting up conditions for slow, inconsistent, and uncoordinated governmental responses. Others, such as India's prime minister, Narendra Modi, acted early and confidently, but without consulting experts or having a coherent plan. In Israel, prime minister Benjamin Netanyahu also acted assertively out of the gate, but then took his foot off the gas too early and badly mismanaged the resulting COVID surge. Like Bolsonaro and Trump, British prime minister Boris Johnson was also initially dismissive of the virus, only shifting to a more activist posture after the abject failure of the country's response and his own brush with COVID-19. And one leader, sometimes grouped in with the nationalists because of his rapport to Trump, Australia's Scott Morrison, actually stepped up to the plate and turned in one of the world's best performances.

Brazil confirmed the first COVID-19 case (a Brazilian man returning from Italy) in Latin America on February 26. Mercifully, the Carnaval celebrations, with millions of partiers thronging the streets and bars, had recently ended. Of all Latin American countries, Brazil seemed uniquely well positioned to deal with a pandemic. It has a universal health care system, including a robust community-based primary health program that also reaches its indigenous communities. Brazilian officials had dealt well with other infectious diseases, particularly Zika, which affected unborn children, and HIV/AIDS. They even had an energetic and highly competent minister of health, Luiz Henrique Mandetta.[51] There was just one problem: Bolsonaro.

The Brazilian president traveled to Florida in early March for a meeting with Donald Trump. Days after, several members of the Brazilian delegation tested positive for COVID, including his press secretary. Bolsonaro called the deadly virus "a fantasy" and a "measly cold" that did not justify an economic shutdown.[52] As was the case in the United States, Brazil's national response was de facto delegated to the country's twenty-seven state governors, regionalizing public health measures. As states issued stay-at-home orders, Bolsonaro excoriated them as "scorched-earth" policies that would crush an economy still recovering from the country's 2015–16 financial crisis. Throughout March and April, Bolsonaro's efforts to undermine the pandemic response were seemingly endless. He issued a (failed) executive order stripping states of the right to restrict freedom of movement. He decapitated the Health Ministry by firing Mandetta for critiquing his lack of response. By late March, people in Brazil's cities began protesting the Bolsonaro administration's inept pandemic response by banging pots outside their window every night around 8:30 p.m. This would last for months as Brazil's death toll soared.[53]

Brazil soon emerged as a regional pandemic epicenter. By May, it had over 100,000 confirmed cases and 10,000 deaths. Yet Bolsonaro continued to encourage his supporters to ignore stay-at-home orders—and they poured into his mass rallies by the busload. Then Bolsonaro himself contracted COVID-19 in mid-July, but it was not enough to shame the president into compliance with WHO guidelines. While infected, Bolsonaro was spotted without a mask, talking to others. By October, Brazil passed the 5-million-case mark with 150,000 deaths, second in the world in deaths only to the United States. Undeterred, Bolsonaro continued to double down, calling on Brazilians to "stop being a country of sissies."[54] After all, "We are all going to die one day," he said.[55]

Despite this, his popularity with the public did not suffer. Bolsonaro ended the year with his highest-ever approval ratings: 37 percent of Brazilians said his performance was excellent or good, 33 percent said it was bad or terrible, and 28 percent said it was "regular." Over half of Brazilians (52 percent) said he was not to blame for COVID-19 deaths. At first blush, Bolsonaro's approval numbers seem puzzling. But as Brian Winter of the Americas Society and Council of the Americas pointed out, Bolsonaro actually took advantage of the crisis by providing half the population with $115 per month, which cut in half the number of citizens living on $2 or less per day. The lax approach to lockdowns also meant that the economic contraction—Brazil's economy shrank by 4.5 percent in 2020, according to the IMF—was milder than in other Latin American countries, like Argentina and Peru. As in the United States, many working-class citizens saw the lockdown as benefiting the privileged, who could work from home.[56]

Halfway around the world, India seemed at first to be relatively unaffected by the pandemic, recording only 500 diagnosed cases (in a country with nearly 1.4 billion people) heading into the last week in March. Then, on March 24, Prime Minister Modi declared one of the world's most stringent national lockdowns—with only four hours' notice to prepare. Chaos ensued. Tens of millions of low-wage migrant workers found themselves stranded in India's cities and unable to get home. Little was provided by way of unemployment benefits or food, so 400 million work-ers found themselves on the brink of poverty. The government lacked the capacity to test or conduct contact tracing. Economic activity effectively ceased, but with little positive impact on public health. Despite a steady rise in COVID cases, Modi announced a premature, phased end to the lockdown on June 1, unleashing an uncontrolled surge in the virus. In June, the case count hovered around 200,000; one month later, it had nearly quadrupled to 720,000 cases. By the end of September, India was second only to the United States in case count—over 6 million Indians had contracted the virus (compared to just under 7 million Americans). Many public health experts argued that due to the Indian health care sys-tem's limited testing capacity, official estimates of COVID-19 represented only a fraction of the actual toll.[57]

India's chaotic response was perfectly in keeping with Modi's highly per-sonalized approach to leadership. All edicts concerned with COVID-19 were announced by Modi personally, rather than by cabinet members or other party officials. The pandemic provided a convenient excuse to cease holding press conferences and parliamentary debates from April to Sep-tember. It left no space to question his handling of the pandemic or pres-ent an alternative narrative. Modi supplemented these tactics by ramping up state-sponsored intimidation and censorship of journalists reporting on the crisis around the country.[58] Simultaneously, Modi attempted to improve his standing with his middle- and upper-class supporters while leaving the most vulnerable Indians to flounder in the ensuing economic downturn. Trumpeting a 10 percent GDP stimulus package—which in reality turned out to be 1–2 percent of GDP—Modi hastened the pri-vatization of public assets by advancing commercial coal mining, raising the foreign direct investment (FDI) limit on defense manufacturing, and auctioning off six airports to public-private partnerships. Meanwhile, in eastern Bihar state, Modi's ruling Bharatiya Janata Party (BJP) promised free COVID-19 vaccines, but only if their party won regional reelection campaigns.[59]

Indian Muslims, who make up 14 percent of the population, were scapegoated for the virus. The vilification of the Muslim community as "superspreaders" began in early April, when a government spokesperson linked the rise in national COVID-19 cases to an 8,000-person gathering of a Muslim missionary organization, Tablighi Jamaat, in mid-March.

Almost immediately, the hashtag "CoronaJihad" went viral on Indian Twitter, as reports that Muslims were intentionally infecting Hindus sky-rocketed. Fake news stories highlighting pictures of Muslims allegedly spitting in food, poisoning water supplies, or licking utensils to spread COVID-19 circulated on Facebook, on Twitter, and in WhatsApp groups. Politicians from Modi's BJP stoked the conspiracy theories, calling the Jamaat event a "Talibani crime." These stories, in turn, led to widespread calls for a social and economic boycott of Muslim-owned businesses. Posters sprang up barring Muslims from entering Hindu neighborhoods, and mosque attacks became commonplace. A video circulated of Muslim men being kicked and humiliated for fishing in the Krishna River, their attackers accusing them of "spreading the disease." Not only did COVID-inspired Islamophobia harm the physical and economic well-being of an already marginalized community within India, it also hampered pandemic containment efforts, as Muslims avoided testing sites for fear of abusive treatment.[60]

In Israel, another overconfident leader struggled to respond effectively. The coronavirus hit Israel during a prolonged period of political instability. The third election in the space of a year took place on March 2 and saw the country still deadlocked between Prime Minister Netanyahu's Likud Party and the opposition Blue and White bloc led by former general Benny Gantz. With fears mounting about the pandemic, Netanyahu seized the moment to show he was in control and that a change in leadership was all but inconceivable. He painted a dire picture, harking back to the "Black Death, cholera, and the Spanish flu." "Our people has withstood fierce storms," he said in a speech in March. "We survived Pharaoh and though the battle will be hard and uncompromising, we will also survive corona." This stance, senior officials believed, tapped into something deep in the country's psyche—Israelis were willing to believe bad things could happen quite suddenly. In responding, Israel had some natural advantages. It is a small country with heavily policed land borders; 95 percent of all travelers come through one airport. The country has an advanced health care system, a logistical system that is second to none, and mandatory national military service.[61]

At the same time, Israelis were not uniformly behind imposing a draconian lockdown. An influential group with connections to the government, including university presidents and CEOs, advocated for a policy of herd immunity and later for an easing of restrictions on economic grounds. But Netanyahu took bold steps at a time when the number of cases was still low relative to other nations—closing the nation's borders and halting international travel, closing nonessential businesses, and imposing a strict stay-at-home order. Flights from the United States posed a thornier problem. The government was under pressure from the Trump administration not to suspend them. As a consequence, 50 percent of Israel's new infections came from America. But within days, those flights were shut down as well. Israel also became the first democratic country to deploy its intelligence services for internal COVID tracing. The program, run by the Shin Bet, drew on counterterrorism technologies and troves of intelligence data warehoused in a top-secret database known as "the Tool."[62]

These early measures were so effective that there was virtually no curve for Israel to flatten.[63] Instead, Israeli COVID case counts remained low. By the end of March, Netanyahu's popularity was at 60 percent, giving him a huge advantage over his rival, Gantz (now the defense minister and, due to a power-sharing agreement, the "alternative" prime minister). Netanyahu's political interests and the national interest seemed aligned at the beginning. They soon diverged, however. The prime minister insisted on running the pandemic response himself. He was used to dealing with the intelligence and military apparatus, which followed his orders promptly and precisely. He was less accustomed to corralling civilian agencies that could not respond as quickly. Experts were shut out or marginalized. For example, relying on the security services' surveillance technology—whereby a text was sent to an individual who had been in close proximity to an infected person—meant that the government did not develop a civilian system of contact tracing that used trained personnel to locally suppress outbreaks when they occurred. As one Israeli health official told us: "The technology piece is only one part of the game. It provides about 30 percent of the notifications you need. You have to have an efficient human contact tracing capability. And you need to be very fast. . . . We wasted three months from March to June and did not develop that capability." Meanwhile, the Israeli government consulted officials from Taiwan, South Korea, and other Asian countries that had handled the pandemic well. But they did not act on that advice.[64]

In late May, Netanyahu celebrated Israel's success, urging citizens to "have a cup of coffee or a beer" and "have a good time."[65] Schools re-opened, and large-scale gatherings were permitted. From June 15 to June 25, more than 2,000 weddings were held across Israel. But the country's fortunes quickly changed. By early July, cases surged and Israel quickly boasted the world's worst daily rate of new cases per capita. Netanyahu admitted that the country reopened too rapidly, saying, "In retrospect, as part of the trial-and-error, it is possible to say that this last stage was too soon." He contemplated a second national lockdown, but it was not instituted until late September. By that point, Israel had hit its peak caseload—over 9,000 new cases per day. *Haaretz* political analyst Anshel Pfeffer wrote in July: "Israel's failure, at this point, is of a magnitude that seems to defy all its perceived advantages in dealing with the crisis."[66]

If you want to understand why some countries led by nationalist leaders fared better than others, the contrast between the United Kingdom and Australia is particularly instructive. Both countries are islands, and thus have more control over their own borders than landlocked nations. British prime minister Boris Johnson and Australian prime minister Scott Morrison are both center-right leaders who cozied up to Donald Trump and were not shy about their nationalist leanings. Johnson, of course, led Britain's exit from the EU and dismissed experts who warned against Brexit as "Project Fear." For his part, Morrison was a climate skeptic and liked to slam "globalists." And yet the two leaders and countries handled the pandemic very differently. The United Kingdom had one of the world's worst performances in terms of case count and fatalities. Australia had one of the very best.

In February, while Johnson was riding high on the back of Brexit, Britain's medical experts were oddly pessimistic about their capacity to defeat the virus and the risks of a gradual approach. British medical experts had been meeting on COVID-19 since January 22, around the time Chinese authorities acknowledged the seriousness of their situation, through the Scientific Advisory Group for Emergencies (SAGE) and a number of related committees. However, they continually rejected the bold actions that were employed in China or even measures that American health officials such as Anthony Fauci and Robert Redfield unsuccessfully pushed for. They worried that a massive effort to prevent the first wave might reduce the country's capacity to deal with a larger second wave. They rejected measures such as banning mass gatherings on the grounds that people would gather in smaller venues. (Oddly, they never considered that those too might be closed.)

Trump administration officials were particularly shocked to see the United Kingdom play down the virus and consider herd immunity as a viable option. One official told us, "We thought they were out of their minds. We told them it would be an absolutely devastating approach to deal with the pandemic. We thought they were nuts and they thought we were nuts. It turns out, in the end, we were a little more right than they were."

Johnson only really engaged in the response to COVID-19 on March 2, and he was reluctant to undertake actions that might impinge on individual freedoms. He had once famously quipped, "The real hero of *Jaws* is the mayor. A gigantic fish is eating all your constituents and he decides to keep the beaches open." And during the pandemic this old quote made the rounds as an insight into his philosophy of life.[67] The upshot was that the United Kingdom was much slower than other European countries to impose restrictions.

By mid-March the British government advised those with symptoms to stay home for a week and the elderly not to go on cruise ships. Otherwise, little changed. From March 10 through 13, 150,000 people attended the Cheltenham race festival, and 3,000 Atlético Madrid soccer fans traveled to Liverpool for a Champions League match. At the time, Madrid was already under a partial lockdown. Both the Cheltenham and Liverpool happenings would later be regarded as superspreader events. At a March 12 press conference, Johnson's chief scientific advisor announced a national "delay" strategy designed to achieve gradual herd immunity; the country's chief medical officer predicted a mortality rate below 1 percent. It only took a weekend for that plan to fall apart. Leading U.K. universities predicted that Johnson's delay approach could cost 250,000 lives and would do little to ease the burden on hospitals. On March 16, Johnson reversed himself, calling for increased testing and for the public to avoid pubs, restaurants, and unnecessary travel. A week later, the United Kingdom entered a national lockdown.[68]

Only four days into the lockdown, Johnson himself tested positive for the virus. He was later hospitalized and spent multiple days in the intensive care unit. Meanwhile, the country's slow-moving response continued. Massive testing shortages placed Britain well behind other developed countries and its European cohort. A Reuters investigation conducted in early April found that the prime minister's chief scientific and medical advisors did not study stringent lockdown models until mid-March, and a review of committee meetings found that "almost no attention was paid to preparing a programme of mass testing."[69]

By late April, Johnson claimed that the United Kingdom was "past the peak" of the virus.[70] The government rolled out phased reopening plans in May, and schools opened in June. Despite fears of a resurgence, Britain's summer reopening was a success. Cases remained flat, and researchers at the University of Oxford made significant progress in developing a COVID-19 vaccine.[71] However, as we will see in Chapter 12, Britain's good fortune, like the EU's, would not last.

Contrast this with Australia. In mid-December 2019, near the height of summer in the Southern Hemisphere, Australian prime minister Morrison took a long-planned holiday to Hawaii. Bushfires were spreading in New South Wales, the country's most-populated state, and had already claimed several lives. Soon, #wheresScotty and #Wherethebloodyhellareyou began trending on Twitter. Australians erupted in anger at the prime minister for being out of the country during a growing crisis. Temperatures hit 107 degrees Fahrenheit (41.9 degrees Celsius), which seemed to discredit, in real time, Morrison's long-standing skepticism about climate change. He returned from Hawaii early, but he was still pilloried for not doing enough. By the end of the crisis, the bushfires had ravaged 46 million acres, destroyed 3,500 homes, and resulted in the deaths of 33 people. Further, an additional 400 people died from respiratory illnesses related to smoke inhalation.[72]

Morrison, who is conservative and religious, was often lumped in with Trump, Johnson, and Bolsonaro. But the searing political pain of the bushfires and the widespread perception in a traumatized country that he was slow to respond would have a transformative effect on how Morrison dealt with COVID-19, which emerged mere weeks after the fires were brought under control. He was determined not to get called out again. The Australian novelist Richard Flanagan called it Morrison's "Damascene moment," after which "things once deemed fantastical became commonplace."[73]

As a former executive in the tourism industry, Morrison was always comfortable with data, so he began to absorb as much of it as he could and, unlike more populist leaders, was willing to be guided by what he saw. On March 13, he brought in opposition parties (which he had previously derided as socialist) to form a national cabinet for the first time since World War II, declaring: "Today is not about ideologies. We checked those at the door." Whereas Johnson and other right-wing leaders flirted with or even embraced the idea of herd immunity, Morrison called it a "death sentence" and trusted the scientists.[74] The Australian government introduced a massive stimulus, provided free childcare for a million families, and doubled unemployment benefits.[75]

There were some missteps early on. On March 19, 2,700 passengers from the cruise ship *Ruby Princess* were allowed to disembark in Sydney with no restrictions even though COVID-19 was on the ship. This was the single largest source of cases and fatalities in Australia in the first wave. But Australia quickly took a tough stance in pursuit of severe suppression of COVID-19. Individual Australian states imposed travel restrictions. Meanwhile, the central government in Canberra launched the COVIDSafe app to help with contact tracing, closed the country to foreigners, and banned Australians from leaving the country unless they received an exemption. They also required Australians returning home from abroad to undertake a mandatory and strictly enforced two-week quarantine at their own expense. Since quarantine spaces were limited, prospective travelers had to apply for a room and make the case on a needs basis. As a result, thousands of Australians were unable to travel home. The results were startling. By June, Australia, a country of 25 million people, had only 20 cases per day, down from a still modest peak of 400 per day in late March. Polls showed 54 percent of Australians said they trusted the federal government (up from 25 percent in 2019) and the Australian public service (up from 38 percent in 2018). Sixty-nine percent of Australians said that Morrison was handling the coronavirus well.[76]

DETERMINANTS OF DIVERGENCE

In 2020, as COVID-19 circulated the globe, nations all went their own way. Some performed well; many others struggled. And, as we will see in Chapter 12, even some that managed to bring the virus under control early had troubles with it during the second wave in the fall and winter.

Taking a step back to look at the wider picture, what accounts for the difference in national performance? Chinese officials would have you believe the key variable was regime type. As soon as the Chinese Communist Party had the virus under control at home, they leaned into the narrative that the "institutional advantages of the Chinese system"—namely, clear top-down direction and an iron grip—were the key to its effectiveness. It was in sharp contrast to the slow and disorderly responses marshaled by the world's leading democracies, especially the United States. But the reality was more complicated. It is true that authoritarian regimes in China, Rwanda, Singapore, Thailand, and Vietnam performed well in suppressing COVID-19, while democracies including Italy, Spain, the United Kingdom, and the United States struggled. But it is also the case that authoritarian states such as Iran, Russia, and Venezuela failed to contain the virus, while democracies including Australia, Canada, Costa Rica, Germany, Japan, New Zealand, South Korea, and Taiwan did well—at least initially. The autocracy-versus-democracy dichotomy thus turns out to not be very helpful.[77]

Several other factors appear to have been more important in explaining cross-national variation. The first is speed. Governments that moved proactively—or very quickly once initial cases were detected—were more effective in containing initial COVID-19 outbreaks. This included implementing testing, tracing, and isolation procedures. It meant encouraging masking and hand hygiene. And it entailed imposing border and travel restrictions, limitations on public gatherings, school and workplace closures, and other social distancing requirements. In contrast, where the pace of public health interventions lagged behind infection rates, governments had difficulty keeping up with the exponential spread of the virus and, in many instances, were forced to rapidly escalate to even more draconian lockdown measures in an effort to "flatten the curve."[78]

The ability of countries to move quickly and effectively was associated with pre-COVID institutional capacity and underlying socioeconomic conditions, but not in a deterministic fashion. In 2005, the International Health Regulations were revised to better address new and reemerging infectious diseases, enhance transparency, and require countries to "strengthen and maintain core public health capacities for surveillance and response" to prevent epidemics and pandemics. Progress on developing these capabilities across the 194 WHO member states was slow, prompting the Obama administration to launch the Global Health Security Agenda in 2014, hoping to improve IHR adherence and provide capacity-building assistance. On the eve of COVID-19, however, no country was fully prepared, and many of those that seemed better prepared reacted poorly anyway. In 2019, Johns Hopkins University, the Nuclear Threat Initiative, and the Economist Intelligence Unit released the Global Health Security Index. The index was based on 140 questions broken into six categories relevant to pandemic preparedness: prevention of the emergence or release of pathogens; detection and reporting for epidemics of potential international concern; rapid response capacity; the sufficiency and robustness of a country's health care system; compliance with international health norms and commitment to address gaps; and a country's overall risk environment and vulnerability to biological threats. The index was impressive, but ultimately it proved not to be a good predictor of whether countries reacted swiftly and seriously at the outset of the crisis. Some of the countries with high index scores—Australia (number 4), Canada (number 5), Thailand (number 6), Denmark (number 8), South Korea (number 9), and Finland (number 10)—responded quickly and well. But others at the top of the list—including the United States (number 1), the United Kingdom (number 2), the Netherlands (number 3), and Sweden (number 7)—did not.[79]

Nevertheless, among those that *did* act early and decisively, the evidence suggests that interventions were most effective in countries with capable government institutions, clear coordination mechanisms between central and local authorities, and sufficient resources to execute their pandemic response and provide relief to quarantined citizens. Countries lacking these advantages had a much harder time. As we will see in Chapter 8, many low- and middle-income countries struggled even when they acted early because their testing and tracing capacity was limited and social distancing and lockdown requirements were often impractical and hard to enforce.[80]

Some scholars contend that cultural differences explain at least part of the variation in outcomes. In particular, the "collectivist" cultures of East Asia may have contributed to more deference to authority—and thus higher degrees of compliance with public health mandates—than was the case in the more "individualistic" Western countries.[81] But this broad generalization proves not as informative as two other factors.

The first is the level of trust in government. Using measures from the World Values Survey, one analysis found that countries with low levels of trust suffered the most COVID-19 deaths during the first wave, controlling for other variables such as population age structure and the size and timing of the pandemic. Another study, using international survey data from twenty-three countries, concluded that those nations with higher levels of trust in government had higher rates of compliance with public health measures including frequent handwashing, avoiding large gatherings, and quarantine requirements. This trust, in turn, was enhanced where governments were seen to be well organized, disseminated clear messages and knowledge on COVID-19, and were perceived to carry out public health measures fairly.[82]

Trust may have been particularly important in countries lacking recent experience with previous contagions. "Government trust assumes an outsize role when the threat is new to a population that does not perceive itself as vulnerable," argue Thomas J. Bollyky and Samantha Kiernan, of the Council on Foreign Relations, and Sawyer Crosby, a data analyst at the University of Washington.[83] In settings without recent experience with epidemics and pandemics, "people are likely to adopt protective behavior, such as wearing face masks or social distancing, only when public health officials and government leaders have increased their awareness of the risk, as well as of the need and efficacy of precautionary measures. Governments must earn and maintain public trust for these efforts to succeed."[84]

Trust could also prove to be a double-edged sword. In the United States, for example, one study of variation across Republican- and Democratic-leaning counties showed compliance with stay-at-home orders was higher in the latter (because Democrats tend to have more faith in experts and bureaucrats) and lower in the former (due to lower levels of trust in expertise and governments among Republicans). Yet high levels of trust were also associated with *low* compliance in circumstances where trusted officials or prevailing community attitudes expressed skepticism about COVID-19 and actually *discouraged* compliance with public health measures.[85] In other words, leadership mattered. In countries where leaders were not trusted or where they abused that trust, the outcomes were worse. And in a number of countries, especially those with populist leaders who refused to take the coronavirus seriously or who rejected scientific advice more broadly, leadership failures proved catastrophic.

Moreover, trust was not enough to guarantee lasting success in containing the virus. Countries such as Israel and Germany enjoyed high levels of trust in government, but they reopened too early and suffered under a second wave. What seems to have distinguished most of the enduring success stories was a recent experience with a national crisis response *failure*, usually with respect to another epidemic or pandemic. Countries and territories, such as Canada, China, Hong Kong, Japan, Singapore, South Korea, Taiwan, Thailand, and Vietnam, that had contended with SARS, H1N1, or MERS developed institutional capacities and social habits that helped them to respond more quickly and seriously in 2020.[86] As we will see in Chapter 11, the same was true of Rwanda, which had experience with HIV/AIDS and Ebola. And in Australia's case, as we have seen, the prime minister had just failed to deal adequately with disastrous bushfires. The experience of failure and fear of a recurrence encouraged these countries to stay the course and not be diverted.

PART III

· · · · ·

NEW WORLD DISORDER

7

The Great Lockdown

WHILE POLITICAL LEADERS and billions of people around the world were laser-focused on the immediate threat to public health and the total disruption of everyday life, tremors from the pandemic rippled outward, laying the conditions for additional crises—financially, in the developing world, in conflict zones, and for the future of democracy and the use of technology. The immediate problem arose in financial markets. The world had last experienced a financial crisis in 2008. At the time, the causes seemed mysterious; while the trigger was the failure of subprime mortgages, it later became clear that vulnerabilities had been building in the markets for a while, thanks to the deregulation of the financial sector, the development of complex financial instruments, and the widespread distribution of risk that was poorly understood. In 2020, the cause was clear—the pandemic and the forced lockdown of the economy—but the effect would still be complex and surprising.

On Wednesday, February 19, 2020, stock exchanges in the United States and Europe reached all-time highs. The markets were certainly aware of the novel coronavirus, which hung overhead like a dark cloud, but Chinese authorities seemed to have contained its spread in Wuhan. As the Dow Jones closed in on 30,000 points for the first time in its history, the *Wall Street Journal* ran a story about fund managers buying vanity license plates saying DOW40K. "Nothing says stock-market bull like a vanity plate on a BMW," the *Journal* reported.[1] The next day, Italian authorities announced quarantines on several towns in northern Italy. Over the weekend, the cloudy sky gave way to a torrential downfall. The Dow plunged 1,000 points on February 24 and another 800 the next day. Eight of the Dow's ten largest point drops in history would take place between February and June 2020. By mid-March, the Cboe Volatility Index, known as Wall Street's "fear gauge," closed at its highest level ever.[2]

With a 3.5 percent drop in worldwide GDP, the pandemic caused the largest and deepest contraction in the global economy in modern history. For much of 2020, the projected contraction appeared to be even worse.[3] The downturn was unique in that it decimated demand and supply simultaneously. "The Great Lockdown," as the IMF put it, shut large sections of the economy and disrupted supply chains, while job losses, wage cuts, and an impending sense of doom impacted consumer spending.[4] The effect resembled the outbreak of war more than a normal economic crisis, though wartime demand usually means that production shifts to weapons, ammunition, and other necessary military goods. It would be the first time since the Great Depression that advanced economies, emerging markets, and developing countries would all be simultaneously thrust into a recession.

The mechanics of the lockdown itself were unprecedented and relatively straightforward. By mid-March, virtually all major economies realized that to protect lives and slow the spread of the virus, they would need to prevent people from congregating in significant numbers. Overnight, large sections of the economy were put on ice—restaurants, entertainment, travel and tourism, retail, and a considerable portion of manufacturing—while other industries, particularly in the services sector, went virtual. Social distancing—the U.S. Centers for Disease Control and Prevention would recommend six feet between individuals to avoid the contagion—was encouraged. Countries would handle the economic dislocations from the Great Lockdown in different ways. The U.S. Congress passed the $2.2 trillion CARES Act, which increased unemployment benefits by $600 per week and distributed $1,200 checks to adults earning less than $75,000 per year.[5] European countries paid employers to keep workers on their books. Some countries would have a light lockdown—in the United States, people were encouraged to stay at home—but others, like France, instituted draconian measures, requiring detailed paperwork for anyone who needed to leave the house.

The pandemic would bring the U.S. financial system close to collapse for the second time in twelve years, necessitating an extraordinary intervention by central bankers—specifically U.S. Fed chair Jerome Powell. Although many hoped for a quick V-shaped recovery, some worried that it could look like a U (with a prolonged downturn), an L (a new depression), or a W (a short recovery followed by a second slump). Ultimately, it would look like a K, in which certain economic sectors and social strata within and among countries thrived or bounced back quickly, while others were devastated and likely to struggle for years just to get back to where they had been at the end of 2019—if that was even possible. After the global economy went comatose, energy demand dried up. Saudi Arabia and Russia would fall out over whether to try to prop up the price of oil, with Moscow hoping to use the crisis to bankrupt the U.S. shale industry. Amid all this chaos, oil prices went negative for the first time. As borders closed and supply chains broke down, *The Economist* asked, "Has COVID-19 killed globalization?"[6]

"THE CORE WAS ABOUT TO BLOW"

The Fed was aware of the novel coronavirus throughout February but saw it largely as a danger to other economies rather than an existential threat to the United States. Toward the end of the month, senior Fed officials attended meetings overseas. Powell attended a gathering of the G20 finance ministers in Riyadh, while Lael Brainard, who served as a Fed governor, joined a meeting of the Financial Stability Board in Amsterdam. Both came back with the same conclusion: this could be a systemic event. Powell's monthly statement on February 28 maintained the language the Fed had used a month earlier—"the coronavirus poses evolving risks to economic activity"—and promised to closely monitor developments, but now the Fed was preparing for the worst. By early March, officials realized that the markets had frozen—they no longer regarded U.S. Treasuries as a safe haven.

U.S. Treasuries are the safest and most liquid asset in the world and the benchmark by which all other securities are priced. Ideally, the stock market and the market for Treasuries are supposed to be inverted—as the price goes up, the yield of Treasuries goes down, and as the price goes down, the yield for Treasuries goes up. At its most basic level, when things look bad, investors shift their market positions and begin buying Treasuries, the safest of all government bonds; when things look good, the opposite happens. In the very early stages of the COVID crisis, investors did the former, engaging in a "Flight to Safety." But this was far from a normal crisis and this tendency did not last long. Soon, the "Dash for Cash" became more common as investors began to avoid financial assets altogether, even if they were low risk, and sought to literally acquire cash. The sell-off of Treasuries started with foreign and central banks because they needed to raise dollars to defend their own currency. Much of the cash they raised was left under the proverbial mattress—it was just sitting in accounts. Domestic institutions were selling at the same time. In a typical crisis they would buy Treasuries as part of a rush to safety, but now they sold in large volumes. One possible reason is that they were required to have a certain balance of products in their portfolios—say, 70 percent in shares and the rest in bonds. As equity prices fell, they had to try to rebalance their portfolios. Meanwhile, the asset management industry—including Wall Street giants such as BlackRock—liquidated their Treasuries to an unprecedented degree. Many hoped these mutual funds could help the system absorb a shock by buying assets when others would not, but instead they joined the panic and were an amplifier of stress. These funds faced a "liquidity gap"— more fund investors than expected wanted their money back, and because the funds could not liquidate their other assets quickly enough, they had to sell the Treasuries in their portfolios. Since many of the positions hedge funds took in the markets became untenable with the enormous daily drops, those entities also unloaded Treasuries to an unprecedented extent.

The Fed has conventional and unconventional ways of responding to an economic crisis like this. The conventional way is the ability to control the costs of borrowing. To do so, the Fed can reduce interest rates to stimulate the economy (or raise them to slow it down). But since 2008 the Fed has used this tool often, and rates have remained relatively low for the past decade. It did, however, have a little bit of room for cuts in early 2020, so it reduced the rate by half a percentage point.[7] Other central banks in New Zealand, Japan, South Korea, and Australia followed suit with actions of their own.[8] But it would not be nearly enough. The central banks would have to get innovative, just as they had twelve years earlier during the financial crisis. With economies grinding to a halt, it was absolutely vital to maintain the flow of credit.

That brings us to the unconventional part of the Fed's crisis authority under Section 13(3) of the Federal Reserve Act, which allows for the
Fed to exercise emergency powers in the name of financial stability to provide credit when credit markets seize up.[9] The Fed can provide financing
directly to banks, businesses, and households, which includes buying
private-sector assets. In March and April, it would take this option in a
massive way, and in the process it would become less like a central bank
and more like a regular commercial bank.

The key moment came on Sunday, March 15. The Fed announced
it was cutting interest rates and would buy $700 billion in bonds. Un-
fortunately, this action spooked the markets, revealing what damage the
pandemic might do to the economy. When markets opened on Monday
morning, there were hardly any buyers. This was the moment when the Fed
realized that the Treasury market and its underlying plumbing—seamless
market liquidity—were at risk. Companies struggled to access the short-
term lending markets they relied on to make payroll. That day, the Dow fell
by 13 percent—the second-largest one-day drop in its history. "There was
a massive financial problem that was not self-correcting. . . . The core was
about to blow," one Fed official told us. "We were staring into the abyss."
The Fed would have to take another route, one far more dramatic.

On March 23, it committed to unlimited purchases of Treasuries.[10] It
would lend directly to American businesses, make massive purchases of
corporate bonds and riskier junk bonds, provide emergency facilities to
bolster credit markets, and work with foreign central banks to maintain
liquidity globally. The Fed had bought large quantities of Treasuries before; what was truly unique in this case was expanding the scope of its
buying to include a much wider array of private asset types. In just six
weeks, from early March to mid-April, the Fed pumped $2 trillion into
the American economy, almost twice as much as in the six weeks after
the fall of Lehman Brothers in 2008.[11] "When it comes to this lending,"
Powell said on March 26, "we're not going to run out of ammunition."[12]
The Fed also undertook a series of actions to make it easier for other
countries to hold Treasuries, which helped stabilize the international financial system.

The writer Sebastian Mallaby pointed out, however, that the response
in 2020 was in many ways an extension of what the Fed did in 2008–9.
We were living in "the age of magic money," Mallaby wrote, in which the

Federal Reserve and a small number of wealthy countries could conjure up whatever ammunition was necessary to save the system. They could do this because the specter of inflation, which had long constrained the ability of central banks to issue new money, had all but disappeared, allowing "central banks to not merely tolerate budget deficits but also facilitate them."[13]

Some felt the Fed's action to save the system had an unintended consequence of reinforcing a two-tier economy. Writing in *Foreign Affairs*, Raphaële Chappe and Mark Blyth observed:

> The United States seems to have stumbled into a monetary policy regime that has untethered the fate of economic elites, who derive most of their income from state-protected financial assets, from that of ordinary people, who rely on low and precarious wages. Such a regime offers permanent protections to those with high incomes from financial assets; everyone else gets little more than temporary help in times of crisis.[14]

Financial Times columnist Edward Luce pointed out that the problem was that the United States was overly reliant on the Federal Reserve as a blunt instrument. This, he wrote, "tightens a doom loop in which the U.S. sovereign must eventually reckon with the ever-widening class of risk it is underwriting."[15] The wealthy asset-owning class and major companies thrive, while families and individuals who do not own stocks and bonds get left behind.

"WE'RE NOT HERE TO COVER SPREADS"

The European Central Bank had been slow to respond to the euro financial crisis, which began in 2009. With the eurozone on the brink in 2012, the president of the ECB at the time, Mario Draghi, promised to do whatever it took. He launched a program called Outright Monetary Transactions, which would have allowed the ECB to purchase assets from countries that had an open line of credit with the bank. The program never had to be used, but it sent a much-needed message. In late February 2020, the ECB, now under the leadership of Christine Lagarde, a former IMF head and finance minister of France, saw another storm brewing. Italy was under siege from the virus as the health care system in Lombardy collapsed. Lagarde pressed Europe's leaders for a fiscal response, but time was of the essence. As the markets plummeted, the ECB decided to act.

On March 12, they announced significant long-term financing, a targeted increase in liquidity, and the purchase of €120 billion in bonds, spread across the eurozone. While they were meeting, their phones lit up with a news notification that the WHO had just declared the coronavirus a pandemic. Though the ECB's actions helped a little, they were virtually meaningless to Italy, which was seeing its cost of borrowing rise, in a worrying echo of the euro crisis. As we saw in Chapter 6, at a briefing to explain the decision, Lagarde said the ECB was "not here to close spreads"—a reference to the difference in borrowing costs between eurozone member states.[16] Lagarde immediately walked back the comment in an interview with CNBC, but to Italians, the message was clear—they were on their own.

That was a Thursday. On Monday, March 16, as U.S. markets plummeted after the Fed's initial announcement, Italy's cost of borrowing began to rise again. It would spike from 1.8 to 2.37 percent over the next two days.[17] That looked like the beginning of something more troubling. European stocks fell by 11 percent. Italian prime minister Giuseppe Conte said the central bank should be "not hindering but facilitating."[18] French president Emmanuel Macron publicly criticized the bank. The situation continued to deteriorate.

In the six days since the ECB's last meeting, European governments had announced lockdowns, the markets were in turmoil, and there was a general sense that the world was facing calamity. On Wednesday, March 18, the ECB held an emergency meeting to reconsider. A senior ECB official told us: "We didn't have the same level of fear about a financial crisis as the U.S. did. With us it was more of a macro issue—there is going to be a gigantic recession, and how do we deal with it?" The reason was that European money markets were about one-tenth of the size of American ones, so the potential collapse in U.S. Treasuries was perceived to be a far greater problem for the United States than for the EU.[19]

Much like the United States, however, the old tools would not be enough. They would have to invent something new. According to Bank of Greece governor Yannis Stournaras, "There was a sense that maybe we should keep some weapons for the future. What we didn't know was that the future would arrive so quickly."[20] The board would unanimously agree to undertake a €750 billion bond purchasing program and to lift the caps on how much debt of each nation it could buy. In a statement shortly before midnight, Lagarde announced there were "no limits" to what the ECB would do. She had come around to Draghi's position after all. The minutes from the meeting revealed that three governors had raised strenuous objections. In an interview with *Le Parisien* a couple of weeks later, Lagarde reflected: "Before March, people said to me, 'The toolbox is empty, you have nothing left, you can't use the monetary weapon'—and then we did!"[21]

Other countries acted too, even if they initially had reservations. In early March, Jon Cunliffe, deputy governor of the Bank of England, said that since the pandemic had resulted in "a pure supply shock there is not much we can do about it."[22] But the Bank of England would soon jump into action, with its "largest and fastest" program of asset purchases, "£200bn of gilts and corporate bonds, equivalent to around a tenth of U.K. GDP."[23] Japan was already on the brink of a recession at the turn of the new year—a new consumption tax had caused a sharp drop in GDP (an annualized decline of 6.3 percent) in the fourth quarter of 2020—and was considering a fiscal stimulus.[24] With little room to cut already low interest rates, the Bank of Japan announced early on that it would pump liquidity into the economy by buying unlimited amounts of government bonds and providing zero-interest-rate financing to banks so they could lend to businesses.[25] However, the pandemic did negatively impact the Bank of Japan's long-term goal of halting deflation—with declining demand, low oil prices, and a government campaign to subsidize travel, prices would fall at their fastest rate in ten years.[26]

All told, the central banks of the G7 economies, including the U.S. Federal Reserve, would increase their assets by $7 trillion in just eight months—over double the increase in their assets in the year following the collapse of Lehman Brothers in 2008. They did this individually and without much coordination between them, unlike in 2008.[27] One reason for this was the fact that the United States was not pressing for a collective response by the G7 or G20. But as a senior ECB official told us, this was less important than it might have been in 2008. "It was so obvious that everyone had to go all in that coordination wasn't really needed," the official noted. "You didn't need to think about the rest of the world, you just had to go to the max anyway" to save your own skin.

Of course, not all countries were able to do what the United States, the eurozone, the United Kingdom, and Japan did, which was simply to add to their balance sheets. As we shall see, poorer nations do not live in the era of "magic money." They will struggle to borrow and will likely face an era of austerity, corporate bankruptcies, and maybe even a sovereign debt crisis in years to come. And even among the lucky few, the United States appeared to be in a league of its own. Yet the fact that central bankers from some of the world's wealthiest countries were able and willing to intervene on so massive and unconventional a scale was a profoundly important event that may have prevented the Great Lockdown from becoming an even more cataclysmic financial crisis. In this respect, while pandemic politics around the globe proved to be a disaster on many fronts, the economic decisions made by key nations did offer some protection and a ray of optimism in the midst of the ongoing crisis.

A TSUNAMI OF DEBT

Emerging markets and the developing economies, however, had none of the advantages of wealthy nations. Their economies were already vulnerable on the eve of the pandemic, thanks to lingering poverty, yawning inequality, large informal economic sectors with few social safety nets, limited health care infrastructure, and reliance on foreign debt. Unlike the financial centers of the G7 countries, if their central banks printed more money their currencies would weaken and negatively impact their country's ability to import and service debt, potentially depleting their reserves. The pandemic piled on the pressure. In March alone, investors withdrew over $83 billion in securities from emerging markets. Some of this was offset by American and European efforts to pump liquidity into their own companies, as it benefited those that were operating in developing countries too. But it was not enough to avert a fiscal squeeze. Governments across the developing world saw their economic models crushed as income from trade, commodity prices, tourism, and remittances all plummeted. In just the first nine months of 2020, global indebtedness increased by $15 trillion. The burden was especially high in emerging markets, where debt ballooned by 26 percent to nearly 250 percent of GDP.

To help combat the resulting "debt tsunami," major international financial institutions—including the World Bank, IMF, and regional development banks—approved around $237 billion in emergency assistance and lines of credit. But only $11.6 billion (5 percent of the total) went to low-income countries.[28]

During the financial crisis of 2008–9, the world acted rapidly through the G20. There was no such response this time around. Saudi Arabia chaired the group in 2020 and had no affirmative agenda at the start of the year. The Saudi crown prince, Mohammed bin Salman (or MbS, as he is commonly known), was widely regarded as a pariah after the brutal murder of *Washington Post* columnist Jamal Khashoggi in 2018. (Khashoggi was assassinated by a group of Saudi agents after being lured to the Saudi consulate in Istanbul, Turkey, an operation that U.S. intelligence concluded MbS had approved.) A G20 virtual summit was convened on March 26, and leaders called for "solidarity" and "a united front against this common threat," but it was more rhetoric than action.[29] In April, the G20 agreed to allow the world's seventy-three poorest countries to suspend repayment of official bilateral loans through the end of the year with the goal of freeing up fiscal headroom to invest in health care, emergency stimulus, and assistance to the poor. But this accounted for less than 10 percent of the new borrowing costs in 2020.[30] Former U.K. prime minister Gordon Brown, who led the group during the international financial crisis in 2009, wrote in June that the G20 had "gone AWOL—absent without lending—with no plan to convene, online or otherwise, at any point in the next six months. This is not just an abdication of responsibility; it is, potentially, a death sentence for the world's poorest people."[31]

By the time the G20 met again (virtually) in November, a few weeks after the U.S. presidential election, six countries had defaulted on their debts—Ecuador, Lebanon, Belize, Suriname, Argentina, and Zambia—although the connection to the pandemic crisis was unclear.[32] President Trump attended the opening session but then skipped much of the rest, including the session focused on pandemic response, to play golf. There was some meaningful progress: the G20 announced that the hardest-hit countries could potentially get an extension on their debt payments through at least mid-2021 and in the most severe cases may be eligible for a debt write-off. But beyond easing short-term obligations from bilateral government loans, it remained unclear how extensively private-sector creditors—who owned close to 20 percent of the debt costs that had to be paid in 2020—would join in. The burden was put on distressed countries to approach private lenders to negotiate better terms, something many countries were reluctant to do for fear of crushing their credit rating. China—the single largest creditor to many developing countries, including through its Belt and Road Initiative—also remained difficult about its participation in debt relief. By the end of 2020, the G20 debt suspension initiative had delivered only about $5.7 billion in relief to forty-six eligible countries. According to analysts at the Brookings Institution, these arrangements were not nearly enough, given the $356 billion in debt service on public and publicly guaranteed debt due in 2021 and another $329 billion due in 2022.[33] In December, Kristalina Georgieva, the IMF's managing director, in reference to emerging markets, warned: "We know we must act quickly to restructure their debts . . . so there is no spillover to the rest of the world."[34] In early 2021, the World Bank assessed that these historically high debt levels made "the global economy particularly vulnerable to financial market stress."[35] Even if an imminent debt crisis failed to materialize, the fiscal overhang from the pandemic in emerging markets and developing countries was likely to be substantial for years to come, constraining their ability to recover.

A TWO-TIER ECONOMY

Billions of people around the world were fully concerned with basic needs: they may have lost their job or seen their wages cut; they may have quit their job to care for their kids; their kids might not be in school or have access to the internet to participate in school remotely. For these people, the Great Lockdown was far worse than the global financial crisis. "This situation is so dire that it deserves to be called a 'depression'—a pandemic depression," the economists Carmen Reinhart and Vincent Reinhart wrote in *Foreign Affairs*. "Unfortunately, the memory of the Great Depression has prevented economists and others from using that word, as the downturn of the 1930s was wrenching in both its depth and its length in a manner not likely to be repeated."[36]

Major democracies saw their economies take an unprecedented hit in 2020. The U.S. economy fell by 31.4 percent in the second quarter, rose by 33.4 percent in the third quarter, and ended the year down by 3.5 percent—its worst annual performance since the Great Depression. The eurozone's economy fell by 6.8 percent in 2020; the United Kingdom's declined by 9.9 percent, the largest drop in annual output since the Great Frost of 1709 (which still holds the record as Europe's coldest winter of the past 500 years); Japan's economy dropped by 4.8 percent; and South Africa's fell by 7 percent. Australia almost avoided a drop thanks to strong growth in the second half of the year, seeing a decline of only 1.1 percent. While these declines were steep, they were also lopsided, with most of the pain coming in the first six months after the pandemic was declared, but with robust growth later on in 2020.[37]

Government actions tried to ease the pain. According to the IMF, fiscal support to address the economic effects of the virus totaled $14 trillion globally in 2020, with global public debt amounting to 98 percent of GDP.[38] About half was extra spending or tax cuts, and the other half came in the form of liquidity support, such as loans, guarantees, and equity purchases by the public sector. In the United States, the $2.2 trillion CARES Act created the Paycheck Protection Program, a program of forgivable loans to help companies survive and keep their employees on their books, in addition to providing direct payments and enhancing unemployment benefits to many Americans. A report by the *New York Times* found that "total employee compensation was down only 0.5 percent for those nine months" from March through November. Part of this was due to some sectors, like grocery stores, faring well even though others collapsed. But it was also because of the CARES payments. Unemployment insurance paid out $499 billion over those nine months, twenty-five times more than in the same period in 2019. However, as the year went on, Washington was slow to follow up on the CARES Act. A second package, long delayed and with direct payments of only $600, would be agreed and passed into law in December.[39]

Across America, after the initial shock, white-collar workers generally did fine—they were able to work from home and in many sectors they actually did better in 2020 than before. These workers often ended up spending less and saving more. They also bought larger and more expensive houses, where they would spend more time because of the pandemic; this drove up home prices. A report by the online real estate brokerage Redfin found that the demand for second homes doubled from the year before, with vacation spots such as Lake Tahoe, Cape Cod, Palm Springs, and the Jersey Shore being especially popular.[40] By contrast, people who worked in restaurants, retail, office maintenance, and manufacturing either could not work because they could not socially distance or saw the need for their work disappear. Approximately 110,000 restaurants in the United States either closed permanently or for the long term, representing one-sixth of the total. High-profile retailers including Brooks Brothers, J. Crew, JCPenney, L'Occitane, and Neiman Marcus filed for bankruptcy.[41]

Lower-income workers in the United States were hit much harder than others. In April 2020, unemployment hit 21.2 percent for workers with less than a high school degree, compared with 17.3 percent for those who graduated from high school and 8.4 percent for those with a bachelor's degree. Nearly half of lower-income workers had trouble paying their bills during the pandemic, while less than a quarter had rainy-day funds sufficient to cover expenses for three months. These metrics were approximately twice as bad as the numbers for middle-income workers. Meanwhile, 59 percent of lower-income parents whose children's schools had switched to remote learning said their children would face digital obstacles such as the lack of internet access or a computer—almost double the number of middle-income parents. A study by researchers at the University of Chicago, the University of Notre Dame, and Zhejiang University found that poverty in the United States rose each month from June to November 2020, even though the unemployment rate fell by 40 percent in the same period. Race was also a factor. Less than one in five Black Americans and one in six Hispanics were able to telework at the beginning of the pandemic, while the unemployment rate at the end of 2020 was 9.9 percent for Blacks and 9.3 percent for Hispanics, compared to 6 percent for whites.[42]

Other wealthy economies also experienced unequal consequences. A study by the McKinsey Global Institute in Europe found that there was a large overlap between jobs vulnerable to COVID-19 in the short term and jobs vulnerable to automation over the longer term, particularly in sectors such as customer service and sales, food services, and building occupations.[43] Even if economies in Europe recovered rapidly, these workers might never regain their jobs, as employers took the opportunity of a reset to accelerate changes that were already under way.

But by the end of 2020, it was also clear that many large corporations had not only avoided collapse but actually thrived. As Nike chief executive John Donahoe put it on a call to talk about his company's strong rebound from the initial shock of a lockdown, "These are times when the strong can get stronger."[44] Wall Street giant Goldman Sachs had its best year in a decade.[45] Starbucks would end 2020 with its shares 20 percent higher than when the year began, largely because it was poised to fill the vacuum left by over 2,000 small coffee shops that had to close permanently because of the pandemic in the United States alone.[46]

In the decade following the 2008–9 financial crisis, the United States and other democracies were roiled by mounting economic inequality and political populism on the right and on the left, fed by the widespread perception that the globalized system is rigged in favor of the elite while ordinary people get left behind. Now the disruptions and disparities produced by COVID-19 and the Great Lockdown threatened to turbocharge these tensions.

THEY COULD NOT GIVE IT AWAY

The view from Long Beach, California, is normally pristine and clear, but in April 2020 the sea off Long Beach was dotted with supertankers anchored in place, carrying a total of 20 million barrels of crude oil. Giant salt caverns along the Gulf Coast, used by the Strategic Petroleum Reserve to store oil, were approaching capacity.[47] On January 2, 2020, the price of a barrel of oil was $61.18. On February 6, it dropped to $50.95. By March 2, it had fallen another 20 percent and seemed destined to plummet further. No one knew where the bottom lay. Analysts identified an unusual problem: if producing nations kept pumping oil into the global economy, pretty soon there would be nowhere to store it.[48]

Cushing, Texas, with a population of 7,800, is the main storage location for the oil that backs West Texas Intermediate crude oil futures, known in the markets as WTI contracts. WTI, along with Brent North Sea crude, also functioned as a global benchmark for the price of oil and was used by financial markets as a reference price for a variety of transactions.[49] A person who buys a WTI future is committing to storing that barrel on a certain date if they cannot find a buyer. On April 20, demand completely dried up. Anyone left holding an oil future that came due the next day either had to pay for storage at Cushing, which was full, or pay someone else to take it off their hands. As a result, the price of a WTI future fell below zero and continued dropping till it was *minus* $37.63 a barrel. In one sense, it was not all that surprising—to avoid being stuck with thousands of barrels of oil with nowhere to store them, traders were willing to pay a premium. But the very notion that oil could be negatively priced stunned the world and was yet another blow to a global economy that was teetering on the brink.

The Great Lockdown meant people simply stopped moving: they no longer made the commute to work, they did not board airplanes for business trips or vacations, and many would not even shop in person, preferring online outlets. This precipitous decline in demand would have significant geopolitical consequences.

For the oil industry, the pandemic came on the heels of a tumultuous decade. Oil traded at around $100 per barrel from 2011 to September 2014, which was about five times the price of the early 2000s. This was very good for the oil-producing nations, like Saudi Arabia, but after 2014 the price began to drop, both because American shale oil came online (as a consequence of fracking) and because of a slowing of demand in Asia. The Organization of Petroleum Exporting Countries (OPEC), the cartel of oil-producing nations, was no longer able to dictate the price the way it used to. In 2012, OPEC had earned $1.2 trillion in revenue; in 2015, it earned less than half that.[50] New energy powerhouses such as Russia and the United States were not members of OPEC, while some countries that were (Venezuela, Libya, and Nigeria) saw their output of oil collapse for a variety of reasons, including domestic unrest and civil war.

To exercise influence, OPEC would need to partner with Russia, then the world's largest producer of oil. But the Russians had no intention of joining forces. The price fell further, to below $30 a barrel in 2016. With all the producers under financial pressure, Russian president Vladimir Putin and Saudi Arabia's Mohammed bin Salman, then the kingdom's deputy crown prince, got together on the fringe of a 2016 G20 meeting in Hangzhou, China, and agreed that something needed to be done. A couple of months later, the ten countries of OPEC would strike a deal with eleven non-OPEC members, led by Russia, to cut oil production. This became known as OPEC+ or the Vienna Alliance, named after the city where the deal was made. It was widely seen as a burgeoning partnership between Riyadh and Moscow—two authoritarian states with ambitious but insecure leaders who worried about the United States and democratic revolutions. The Saudi energy minister, Khalid al-Falih, later hailed the alliance, saying it would last for "decades and generations."[51]

This Saudi-Russian petroalliance would last for just over three years, until the pandemic swept across the world in 2020. As the price of oil plummeted in March, OPEC members grew concerned. Saudi Arabia required a price around $80 a barrel to break even in its annual budget.[52] The OPEC cartel proposed a production cut of 1.5 million barrels a day. But the Russians would not go along.[53] Moscow had its own motives— namely, that low prices would help cripple the U.S. shale industry, which had spurred the United States to become the world's largest producer of crude oil in 2008 and 2009. American production of crude more than doubled between 2010 and 2019, when it peaked at 13 million barrels a day.[54] They were also frustrated at new U.S. sanctions on Russian energy giant Rosneft and on the proposed Nord Stream 2 gas pipeline from Russia to Germany. With a $170 billion national wealth fund to cushion the blow of a price war, Moscow felt it could take a risk.

The Saudis responded by doing a complete U-turn: instead of cutting production, they increased it, effectively launching a price war with Russia. Within minutes of markets opening on March 9, oil plunged by 30 percent. A spokesperson for Rosneft now dismissed the alliance as meaningless, arguing that American shale had simply replaced any cuts in production that were made after 2016.[55] Dmitry Kiselyov, the director of Russia's main state news agency, posted to social media: "Now we have a chance not just to produce and sell as much as we need to, but to throw American shale overboard. Our budget is much more stable than Saudi Arabia's and is ready for low oil prices, unlike the Kingdom's."[56]

President Donald Trump initially welcomed the price war as good for motorists, but he quickly changed his tune when it became clear it would hit the U.S. energy sector in states with a strong Republican voter base, such as North Dakota, Pennsylvania, and Texas.[57] Senator Kevin Cramer of North Dakota, a Republican, summed up the mood in Washington as he fumed about the Saudis: "They've spent over the last month waging war on American oil producers while we are defending theirs. This is not how friends treat friends. Frankly, I think their actions have been inexcusable and they are not going to be easily or quickly forgotten."[58] Trump soon hit the phones, calling Putin and MbS, and emphasizing that the U.S. oil industry was "under siege" from the price war.[59] After several weeks, a deal was struck to cut the global oil supply by almost 10 percent. Trump played a role, leaning at the very end on Mexico's populist president, Andrés Manuel López Obrador, to come on board.[60] Obrador had been obstinate and hoped that a deal would be struck without Mexico having to cut production.[61]

Even after the deal, tensions ran high in OPEC+. The April agreement was seen as favoring Russia and Saudi Arabia, while the UAE, Iraq, and Kuwait were the biggest losers.[62] Russia continuously exceeded its quota, and Riyadh let it slide. But when the UAE overproduced, the Saudis became "furious, and summoned UAE Energy Minister Suhail Al-Mazrouei to Riyadh for a public dressing down."[63] The UAE grew more estranged from its long-standing ally Saudi Arabia on oil production and moved closer to the Russian position.

Oil prices would recover somewhat over the summer as China's economy sprang back to life, Europe's lockdowns eased, and American employment numbers exceeded expectations. But the second wave of the virus would keep the price relatively low throughout the rest of the year.

The consequences for the American oil industry could be profound even if the global economy bounces back. A June 2020 report by the consulting firm Deloitte found that at a price level of $35 a barrel, approximately half of all U.S. shale firms would either become insolvent or have "stressed financials."[64] Indeed, many firms did go bankrupt in the fall of 2020. That allowed ConocoPhillips and Chevron to make major shale investments, consolidating some of the U.S. shale industry's largest players.[65] An industry survey in September suggested that oil prices needed to hit $50 a barrel for shale exploration to resume.[66] OPEC countries need oil at around $60 a barrel to break even—and at that price shale should come back strongly.[67]

By the end of 2020, oil prices shot up to just below $50 per barrel, a nine-month high, and they would rise to $60 per barrel by the end of March 2021. For OPEC+ the challenge was clear: to increase oil prices to generate revenue without allowing prices to get high enough for the American shale industry to recover—and, in the process, to keep its competing factions in check. Throughout the first few months of 2021, they zig-zagged between maintaining limitations on supply and increasing it in anticipation of robust economic growth.[68] However, even if the increase in oil prices to $60 or more was ultimately sustained, it still might not be enough for American shale. Investors may remain wary of putting money into an industry that just suffered an economic hurricane, especially given the volatility in the years before the pandemic, the uncertain prospects about an economic recovery, and OPEC+'s ability and willingness to drive the price down again.

THE END OF GLOBALIZATION AS WE KNOW IT?

On March 2, 2020, President Trump, Vice President Pence, and other senior American officials met with Daniel Menichella, the head of the German medical company CureVac. Headquartered in the German city of Tübingen, with operations in Boston, it was in the early stages of developing a COVID-19 vaccine.[69] Shortly after the meeting, the German newspaper *Die Welt* reported that the Trump administration had offered the company $1 billion for exclusive access to its results.[70] The German public reacted with shock. They expected this type of behavior from China (a Chinese firm, Midea, had controversially purchased the industrial robotics company Kuka in 2016), but not from their closest ally.

The German interior minister, Horst Seehofer, said the proposed deal was "a question of national security." The government, he said, must guarantee the security of "our medical products and our medicines" as well as the country's borders. In the ensuing uproar, Menichella resigned. Shortly after this incident, CureVac announced they would hold an IPO in July. The German government would acquire a 23 percent stake in CureVac to give it financial security. Peter Altmaier, the economics minister, told the press, "For me, and for the federal government, it is elementary from an industrial point of view that we maintain and strengthen key industries in Germany. Germany is not for sale. We do not sell our silverware."[71]

The COVID-19 pandemic was, in many ways, the first truly global moment since the end of the Cold War: a virus emerging from a Chinese city and cascading across the globe, disrupting the lives of billions of people in a matter of months. But it also seemed to mark the end of an era defined by globalization—everyone was forced to shelter in place, hotels shuttered, flights halted, and once-bustling cities fell silent. *The*

Economist warned: "The pandemic will politicize travel and migration and entrench a bias towards self-reliance. This inward-looking lurch will enfeeble the recovery, leave the economy vulnerable and spread geopolitical instability."[72]

The Economist was wrong about one thing, though. Governments were not *choosing* to politicize globalization. They were genuinely fearful. As we saw in Chapter 6, European countries banned exports of medical supplies. The United States was a player too. U.S. buyers intercepted a shipment of masks at a Shanghai airport as it was about to be flown to France and offered three times what the French had paid.[73] In another incident, a shipment of 200,000 masks destined for Germany from a 3M factory in Bangkok ended up going to the United States.[74] Governments worried about being unable to carry out their most basic task—to protect their citizens.

European Commission vice president Věra Jourová said that for Europeans, "this crisis [COVID-19] has revealed our morbid dependency on China and India as regards pharmaceuticals."[75] Macron told the *Financial Times* that the pandemic "will change the nature of globalization, with which we have lived for the past 40 years," and said it is "clear that this kind of globalization was reaching the end of its cycle."[76] Japan launched a special fund of $2.2 billion for companies shifting production facilities out of China.[77] In March, Canada was buying 0.2 percent of its personal protective equipment from domestic sources; by September, that number increased 250-fold, to half of all of its PPE purchases.[78]

The effect of the pandemic was most dramatically felt in the easy movement of people, which in many parts of the globe was assumed to be an immutable fact of modern life. Travel, both domestic and international, suddenly stopped. By mid-April, the average number of commercial flights per day worldwide fell to just over 28,000 from 111,000 a year earlier. The number of international flights plummeted by 66 percent, recovering to a decline of 48 percent year on year by September.[79] Even this vastly underestimated the collapse: many scheduled flights were virtually empty—they were kept on the books so pilots could log the required number of flying hours needed to maintain their licenses. Told another way, each empty flight represented the absence of businesspeople traveling for work, families returning home, vacationers going places, and students returning to school. By mid-May, 70 percent of destinations surveyed by the UN World Tourism Organization had completely closed their borders to tourism.[80]

And yet, as the year progressed, it became clear that the unique nature of the crisis meant that globalization would be subject to ebbs and flows rather than a complete unraveling. By September 2020, global trade was just 2 percent below its pre-coronavirus levels (it would still be down about 9 percent for the year).[81] By November, the number of countries that were closed to foreign nationals had fallen to 27 percent, and 75 percent of countries had eased their restrictions.[82] Meanwhile, work increasingly went virtual, as companies began adopting Zoom and other videoconference platforms wherever possible. The *DHL Global Connectedness Index*, a report by the logistics company DHL and New York University's Stern School of Business, examined the impact of the pandemic across four areas—the movement of people, trade, capital, and information—and found that globalization was unlikely to fall below levels seen during the 2008–9 global financial crisis.[83]

Moreover, globalization declined in some countries more than others. For the most part, advanced industrialized countries were hit hardest. Global foreign direct investment flows declined by 49 percent in the first half of 2020 compared with 2019. The fall was steepest in developed economies, which saw a drop of 75 percent, compared to only 16 percent for developing economies (including China). Remarkably, flows to developing Asia (China, Vietnam, and others) accounted for almost half of all global FDI during this period.[84] The recovery in trade was driven largely by China and Latin America. The enrollment of new international students fell by 43 percent in the United States and 50 percent in Australia but actually increased by 9 percent in the United Kingdom, perhaps because it was easier to get a visa to study in Britain.[85]

The real blow to globalization in 2020 was not the mechanics of how to improve resilience in the event of another pandemic. It was the deteriorating relations and mounting rivalry between the United States and China. As we saw in Chapters 4 and 5, the two were already in the midst of a significant geopolitical clash and were taking steps to disentangle (or "decouple") their economies from each other. As Julian Gerwitz, then of the Council on Foreign Relations, has shown, China's Xi Jinping enlarged the definition of national security to include the risks of dependency on the United States and other democracies.[86] This was under way before Trump became president but accelerated while he was in office, as Beijing faced a U.S. administration that freely used tariffs and sanctions. For example, Chinese banks considered moving away from the SWIFT payments system—used globally to transfer money and communicate between banks—to hedge against the risk of U.S. sanctions.[87] Meanwhile, there was growing concern in Washington about a variety of interdependencies with China, particularly in the realm of technology, where China used access to the American market to make significant advances in strategically important technologies such as artificial intelligence. The pandemic, and the general anger with China that followed, served as a catalyst: the United States launched a blizzard of activity of its own aimed at decoupling America from China.[88]

For over twenty-five years the world has integrated and become more connected whenever it appeared to be economically rational. Companies built complex supply chains. Universities went global. Information was abundant and cheap. Capital flowed to wherever it would secure a return. This was predicated on the assumption that the connections countries built would not be exploited for geopolitical reasons except in very rare cases, and then usually with the support of the wider international community. Now, as great-power competition intensified, the world seemed to increasingly be splitting into two blocs—one largely organized around the United States and one organized around China. These blocs have economic, technological, military, and ideological dimensions, although the dividing lines in some areas—such as 5G technology—are often fuzzy. Unlike in the Cold War, these blocs interact with each other and even overlap. Australia, for example, is a staunch ally of the United States, but it is also, and will remain, economically engaged with China. But in 2020, the lines between the two alternative models became clearer. The world was headed for a very different, more bifurcated type of globalization.

CHINA RISING

The Roaring Twenties followed the pain of the Great Influenza and World War I. Could the same happen again? By the early spring of 2021, the global economy seemed primed for a rebound—but questions remained. Would COVID-19 have a long tail, suppressing travel and putting governments under pressure to cut back spending and raise taxes once the emergency had passed? Would people be frugal—slow to eat out, travel, and consume more entertainment—in which case the restaurant, travel, and entertainment sectors might take years to fully recover, with knock-on effects for employment and inequality? Or would these sectors bounce back quickly, thanks to pent-up demand from enforced savings and a desire to return to normalcy? The truth was that no one knew. Even with a quick recovery, the world would likely be back at 2019 levels only at some point in 2022, which is still well behind where it would have been if the pandemic had never occurred.

The world's major economies may have generally suffered in 2020, but there was one big exception: China. It ended the year with an expected growth rate of 2 percent, low by its standards but still relatively stronger than its competitors. Airline traffic in China ended 2020 8 percent higher than at the end of 2019, while in the United States and Europe it declined by 41 percent and 68 percent, respectively.[89] A study by the Centre for Economics and Business Research found that as a result of COVID-19, China would overtake the United States as the world's largest economy five years earlier than projected, in 2028 instead of 2033.[90] On New Year's Eve 2020, thousands of people partied in the streets, bars, and clubs of Wuhan while Times Square was deserted and silent for the first New Year's Eve since 1907.[91] China would be blamed by much of the world for failing to act to stop the spread of the virus early on. Its assertive foreign policy and its brutal crackdown in Hong Kong would alienate Europeans and harden skeptical views in the United States. But in raw economic terms, China would escape much of the turmoil that affected the rest of the world. In some respects, it may have even gained from it.

Vulnerable States, Vulnerable Peoples

IF YOU OPEN your closet and pull out a T-shirt from the Gap, a blouse from H&M, a pair of Levi's jeans, a dress from Marks & Spencer, or a sweater from Zara, there is a decent chance the tag reads "Made in Bangladesh." The South Asian country is the second-largest exporter of ready-made garments in the world (the first is China), and the industry accounts for a jaw-dropping 80 percent of Bangladesh's export revenue. It employs roughly 4 million Bangladeshis—the majority of whom are women working as seamstresses—who live paycheck-to-paycheck, earn about $110 a month, and support their families on the thinnest of margins. So when COVID-19 upended global trade and supply chains, shuttered retailers, and crippled consumer demand, the worldwide economic wipeout threatened to bring Bangladesh's garment sector and many Bangladeshis down with it.[1] "My family runs on my single income," said Fatema Akther, a garment worker in Dhaka, the nation's capital, after being laid off in March 2020. "I don't know how my family will survive."[2] Fatema's plight was illustrative of a drama that would unfold nationwide as COVID-19 placed both the lives and livelihoods of millions of Bangladeshis at risk.

On the eve of the pandemic, the country's demographic conditions and threadbare health system left it highly susceptible to a novel contagion. Bangladesh is the size of Iowa yet home to 165 million people—more than fifty-two times Iowa's population—with 1,240 people per square kilometer (compared to 455 in India, 275 in Pakistan, 148 in China, and

36 in the United States). As a consequence of overcrowding, measures such as social distancing are nearly impossible to execute. Consider Dhaka: the city itself has more than 10 million residents, and 21.5 million people live in the greater Dhaka area, making it one of the most densely populated cities on the planet. Around 4 million people inhabit more than 5,000 slums scattered around the megacity, with around 75 percent of those households constrained to a single room. In these sprawling shantytowns, sanitation is abysmal and the spread of communicable diseases commonplace—perfect conditions for the rapid spread of a deadly virus.[3]

The country's health care system was also in no position to handle a major outbreak. In 2019, Bangladesh ranked 113th out of 190 countries in the Global Health Security Index. It only had 0.8 hospital beds per 1,000 people (compared to 2.9 in the United States and 4.3 in China), and the country's entire health system had just 1,169 intensive care unit beds (432 in public hospitals and 737 in private ones). Complicating matters further, Bangladesh had the worst doctor-to-patient ratio in South Asia.[4]

These conditions put a premium on Bangladesh's government taking swift action once the threat of COVID-19 emerged. On January 31, 2020, the government sent a plane to collect 341 Bangladeshi citizens stranded in Wuhan, which was already under lockdown. Five weeks later, on March 7, Bangladesh reported its first confirmed case of COVID-19. Beginning on March 17, all schools were ordered closed. Soon Prime Minister Sheikh Hasina's government imposed even more stringent containment measures. International flights to ten countries were suspended (although some flights to China, Hong Kong, Thailand, and the United Kingdom continued). On March 26, the government put in place a national lockdown, closing all private businesses and public offices, with the exception of emergency services. All domestic travel by air, water, and rail was banned. People were asked to stay at home, practice social distancing when in public, and avoid large gatherings. Hundreds of thousands of Bangladeshi migrants who had recently returned from abroad were told to isolate themselves for two weeks. The army was deployed to help enforce restrictions and keep people off the streets. The national lockdown was originally intended to last two weeks, but most of its provisions were extended through the end of May.[5]

From the very beginning, however, Bangladeshi authorities struggled

to enforce public health measures. Within days of the mid-March admonition to avoid crowds, 25,000 people attended a religious gathering
in Raipur town in Lakshimpur district in southern Bangladesh to recite
Khatme Shifa prayers (Quranic verses of healing) in the hopes of ward-
ing off the coronavirus.[6] Throughout the lockdown, large numbers of individuals gathered at kitchen markets and relief distribution centers, and
internal migrants—suddenly out of work—streamed out of Dhaka back
to their villages.[7] Prominent religious figures in the Muslim-majority
nation also continued to encourage congregations at mosques despite
warnings from authorities.[8] On occasion, people flouted lockdown orders en masse. In one notorious example in mid-April, tens of thousands
of Bangladeshis defied stay-at-home instructions to attend the funeral
of Maulana Jubayer Ahmed Ansari, a popular Islamic emir, in the village of Bertola, about sixty-two miles east of Dhaka.[9] The government
seemingly lacked the capacity or the political will to clamp down on such
gatherings.

The structure of Bangladesh's economy also ensured that lockdown
measures would come at a high cost. Over the past several decades,
Bangladesh had become a poster child for the benefits of globalization.
Steady economic progress lifted tens of millions of Bangladeshis out of
poverty. Beginning in the early 2000s, integration into the global apparel
value chain created more than 3 million jobs, and it was widely credited
as a catalyst of both sustained economic growth and significant poverty
reduction. According to the Bangladesh Bureau of Statistics, the national
poverty level was cut from nearly 49 percent in 2000 to approximately 22
percent in 2018. And with an average annual economic growth rate of
6.5 percent between 2010 and 2016, Bangladesh, once one of the world's
poorest countries, was elevated into the ranks of lower-middle-income
nations in 2015 (currently defined by the World Bank as countries with a
per capita income of between $1,036 and $4,045).[10]

This progress was fragile, however, and it masked considerable challenges. Despite economic gains, lingering poverty and a lack of savings
remained features of everyday life for millions of Bangladeshis. Prior to
the pandemic, more than a fifth of the population lived below the poverty line, with around 14.5 percent in extreme poverty (that is, on less than
$1.90 per day). Moreover, around 89 percent of Bangladesh's workforce
was employed in the informal economy, toiling as daily wage laborers,

self-employed persons, piece-rate workers (who get paid per item made regardless of how long it takes), other hired labor, and unpaid family labor. In cities such as Dhaka, the informal economy is characterized by multitudes of rickshaw and cart pullers, head-loaders, construction workers, barbers, cobblers, garbage collectors, waste recyclers, and street vendors of vegetables, fruits, and meats. These jobs rarely come with adequate wages, good working conditions, or social protections. Overall, only 15 percent of the country's population earned more than 500 taka ($5.90) a day. Only 13 percent of the population had access to the internet, and even among those who did, the option to work remotely was hardly commonplace.[11]

As a consequence of these underlying vulnerabilities, the human costs inflicted on Bangladesh by the pandemic-induced global recession and domestic disease control policies were ferocious. Sales of ready-made garments from Bangladesh were crushed by the cancellation or postponement of several billion dollars in orders from major retailers in importing countries.[12] According to the IMF, Bangladesh's overall garment exports fell by 83 percent in April from the previous year.[13] From March to May, garment exports fell by a total of nearly 55 percent.[14]

By early April, 1 million garment workers (one out of every four) had been laid off or furloughed—with 72 percent of furloughed workers sent home without pay.[15] Unable to sustain a shutdown of the economy for too long, the government began allowing hundreds of garment factories in industrial belts in the suburbs of Dhaka to resume operations, to avoid losing more business from American and European brands. "We have to accept coronavirus as part of life," Mohammad Hatem, the vice president of the Bangladesh Knitwear Manufacturers and Exporters Association, argued. "If we don't open factories, there will be economic crisis." Many workers felt they had no choice but to return to work. "The fear of coronavirus is there," Mofazzal Hossain, a factory worker in the Dhaka suburb Ashulia, told Agence France-Presse. "But I am now more worried about losing my job, wages and benefits."[16] Sampa Akter, a Dhaka resident trying to make a living by sewing jeans destined for shopping malls around the world, echoed these sentiments. "I'm very scared and vulnerable," she said. "It's not only me. All my coworkers are in the same position."[17]

Even as factories began to resume operations, the pandemic continued to suppress global demand and big fashion brands kept canceling orders, leading many factories to run at slightly above half capacity.[18] "We are not getting wages for the last three months," Abdur Rahim, a textile worker, complained in May. "We are literally starving."[19] It was not until September that orders really began picking up again, with about 90 percent of canceled orders restored by the end of 2020. But, even then, price cuts by global apparel retailers and the steep discounts they demanded on shipped goods significantly cut into export earnings.[20]

Workers across Bangladesh's immense informal sector also saw jobs and incomes evaporate. "Coronavirus has spread here like anything," Imran Hossain, a daily wage laborer who typically earned 300–500 taka ($3.50–$5.90) a day doing fix-it jobs, said in June. "People are scared and don't call me for any work."[21]

Meanwhile, remittance payments flowing into the country from Bangladeshi migrants living overseas dried up. Before the pandemic, an estimated 10 million Bangladeshis lived and worked abroad.[22] The money they sent back home provided a crucial lifeline for poor households and made up around 6 percent of the country's GDP in 2019.[23] More than 70 percent of Bangladeshi migrant workers living overseas were based in Gulf oil-exporting countries such as Saudi Arabia and the United Arab Emirates. On average, these migrant laborers sent back around $1,100 per year to their families in Bangladesh.[24] But as oil prices abruptly declined and Gulf nations went into lockdown, many migrants lost their jobs and were forced to head home. Remittances fell by 12 percent in March, 23 percent in April, and 13 percent in May, before beginning to rebound thereafter.[25] (By the end of the year, official remittance totals would actually be up due to new government cash incentives for inflows through formal channels and expanded digital banking services. But the apparent increase was also partly an accounting artifact stemming from the shift of remittance transactions from informal networks involving the physical movement of cash across borders to formal banking transfers due to pandemic-related travel restrictions.[26])

To prop up the economy, the government approved billions of dollars in stimulus aimed at affected industries, export-oriented ones in particular. They also allocated hundreds of millions of dollars in cash assistance for low-income workers and impoverished families, and increased efforts to make rice available to the extremely poor at prices below the market rate to stave off growing food insecurity. Yet destitute Bangladeshis struggled to receive much of the assistance because of the government's inability to accurately identify those in need, problems with local relief distribution, and a general climate of corruption.[27]

The net impact of these developments on the poor was devastating. A survey of more than 2,000 randomly selected mothers in rural Rupganj County, on the outskirts of Dhaka, found that during the first eight weeks of stay-at-home orders, median monthly family income fell from $212 to $59 and the number of families experiencing extreme poverty increased from 0.2 percent to 47.3 percent. Before the pandemic, the study found, 5.6 percent experienced moderate food insecurity and another 2.7 percent experienced severe food insecurity; by mid-June, the numbers had increased to 36.5 percent and 15.3 percent, respectively.[28] Nationwide, another study found that the average family income in Bangladesh declined by around 74 percent during the heart of the lockdown, from March to the end of May.[29] As of June 2020, an analysis by the South Asian Network of Economic Modelling, a Dhaka-based research organization, estimated that Bangladesh's national poverty rate had already doubled from 20.5 percent in 2019 to around 41 percent as a result of the pandemic, effectively erasing fifteen years of economic progress.[30] All told, the United Nations estimated that economic growth in Bangladesh plunged to 0.5 percent in 2020, compared to 8.4 percent in 2019. As a result, tens of millions of Bangladeshis were thrown back into poverty.[31]

As economic concerns mounted, the government took additional steps in May to gradually reopen the economy and allow gatherings for prayer services during the Muslim holy month, Ramadan. In late June, Bangladesh resumed international flights.[32] These moves were economically essential and culturally understandable—but they also contributed to a surge in COVID-19 cases. As of May 1, 2020, Bangladesh reported a total of around 8,200 confirmed cases and 170 deaths; a month later, following the easing of restrictions, the total was nearly 50,000 with 672 deaths.[33] By late December, the total confirmed cases exceeded 500,000 with around 7,600 recorded deaths. After India, Bangladesh was the second-most-affected country in South Asia.[34] Given its population density, however, the number of confirmed deaths per 100,000 people appeared surprisingly low, and the case fatality rate (the number of confirmed deaths per confirmed case) hovered around 1.5 percent, far below the rate common in high-income nations.[35] There was speculation that some combination of the general youth of the population (only 5.2 percent of the population was sixty-five or over in 2019), more resilient immune systems accustomed to combating a range of diseases beyond COVID-19, and a weaker strain of coronavirus might explain the discrepancy.[36]

But in truth, the real extent of the devastation was impossible to know: limited testing meant the official count may have significantly underestimated the true infection rate and death toll. This problem was compounded in late June when the government began charging for COVID-19 tests at prices no poor Bangladeshi could afford. As a result, the number of people tested declined from more than 18,000 a day at the end of June to 12,000–15,000 per day by the fall. Testing was even rarer outside the capital. So it is no surprise that discrepancies began to emerge: The lack of nationwide testing contributed to a 12 percent positivity rate by September, significantly higher than the 7–8 percent positivity rate sought by public health officials. Meanwhile, anecdotal evidence from graveyard managers across Dhaka suggested that deaths might be up to four times higher than recorded.[37]

Then, just when it seemed that things could not get any worse, they did. In May, Cyclone Amphan, the most severe weather event Bangladesh had experienced in two decades, smashed into the country, devastating coastal villages and leaving half a million people homeless. This was followed by unusually heavy monsoon rains starting in June, which produced the worst flooding in a decade. By the end of July, an estimated 24 to 37 percent of Bangladesh's landmass was under water, nearly 1 million homes had been inundated, and 4.7 million Bangladeshis had been affected. Monsoon season (usually June to September) always brings torrents of heavy rain; it is essential for South Asia's agriculture. But in recent years, as climate change has accelerated, monsoon season has increasingly brought cyclones and disastrous floods. And while it is difficult to attribute any given storm to human-induced global warming, data clearly shows a link between the mounting global climate crisis and a broader pattern of more severe and frequent river flooding across Bangladesh. So it was in 2020.[38]

Many of the people most exposed to the pandemic's impact suddenly found themselves on the front lines of environmental disaster. It created a vicious cycle: the plight of COVID-19 and the problems of flooding reinforced each other. The latter made it even more challenging to observe public health measures such as social distancing and frequent handwashing, while placing additional socioeconomic pressure on people already pushed to the brink by mounting joblessness and diminished remittances. The pandemic, in turn, made it more difficult for Bangladeshis to cope with the floods. Prior to COVID-19, many rural Bangladeshis adapted to seasonal flooding by working in cities until the water receded. The pandemic and lockdown turned this pattern on its head, forcing many living in urban areas to return home to their flood-prone villages.[39] One of them was twenty-two-year-old Mohammad Sumon. In April, Mohammad and his wife lost their jobs at a garment factory in Dhaka "because the factory said they weren't getting orders due to the coronavirus." So the couple returned to Mohammad's home village, Jamalpur, about 100 miles from the capital, in the hopes that he could support them by working as a part-time mechanic. But that too became impossible, "because the water had risen and I couldn't step out," he said. "I don't know how we will manage."[40]

AN EARLY REPRIEVE?

We normally associate infectious disease outbreaks and pandemics with dangers that emerge from developing nations and spread to more developed ones. Yet at the very outset of the coronavirus crisis, the pandemic seemed to impose a lighter toll on low- and middle-income nations. Why was the global South seemingly spared the initial onslaught afflicting China and the West? Early speculation by some scientists held that warmer and more humid temperatures, as well as younger populations, in tropical and subtropical countries might have been keeping the virus at bay. And during the initial period of the pandemic, the contagion did indeed remain concentrated in temperate-zone countries. The initial centers of gravity for the pandemic were China, then Italy, and then the United States. Far fewer cases were reported in developing countries.[41]

But in the second half of March, the pandemic picked up momentum across the globe. And despite moves by most countries to impose stringent lockdowns and mobility restrictions, by April COVID-19 had finally taken root in many poorer nations. As spring turned to summer, the global South joined the devastation that was enveloping the world.[42] Why?

The initial reprieve appears to have been the consequence of lower degrees of connectivity to the global economic system—best illustrated through flight routes. Countries with a high volume of routes to and from China were affected first. If you have ever looked at a map of international airline routes, then you have seen the multiple destinations where the pandemic took root, traveled, and emanated: moving from more connected destinations to less, from China to Europe and the United States—and then beyond.[43]

Once the virus made landfall in poorer nations, however, conditions were ripe for rapid spread. What proved to be the case in Bangladesh was common elsewhere. Dense cities and poverty-stricken slums in many developing countries made social distancing impractical, as did crowded rural households and communal living conditions. Poor sanitation and inadequate health care systems further complicated containment efforts. Then there was inadequate health infrastructure. In 2017, the World Bank and the World Health Organization estimated that at least half of the world's people lacked access to essential health services.[44] Whether measured by medical personnel, hospital beds, critical medical equipment, or numbers of doctors and nurses, many nations across the global South were ill-prepared for COVID-19. In April, for example, the WHO reported fewer than 2,000 working ventilators to serve hundreds of millions of people in public hospitals across forty-one African countries. Ten countries in Africa lacked a single ventilator.[45]

The lack of widespread testing makes it difficult to quantify with any precision the true impact across the global South. The majority of COVID-19 cases and deaths in poor countries have likely gone uncounted. Nevertheless, available evidence suggests that the number of deaths per 100,000 people in the population was often lower in developing nations than in richer ones. While this could be a byproduct of poor documentation, it seems likely that differences were at least in part a result of much younger populations and lower rates of obesity (a major risk factor for COVID patients) in many developing countries.[46]

ECONOMIC VULNERABILITY

On April 9, Kristalina Georgieva, the managing director of the International Monetary Fund, stated bluntly: "Just as the [COVID-19] health crisis hits vulnerable people hardest, the economic crisis hits vulnerable countries hardest."[47] As the virus cut a wide swath across the planet, whatever advantages some poorer nations may have enjoyed in initially avoiding the worst of the pandemic were massively outweighed by other factors that made them much more vulnerable to catastrophic second- and third-order economic and humanitarian consequences. The overall structure of the labor force was of particular concern. With 70 percent of workers in emerging markets and developing economies earning their livelihoods in the informal sector prior to the pandemic, few households had the economic cushion to weather the COVID storm.[48] As nations moved to lock down their economies, it was impossible for street vendors, seasonal construction workers, agricultural laborers, waste pickers, and domestic help to continue their livelihoods. With no digital or remote alternative available, whole ways of life were quickly eliminated. Sheltering inside meant a loss of income. For those who chose to leave the house to work to support their families, it meant risk of exposure. But what choice did they have?

For the millions of people living on the thinnest margins, the excruciating dilemmas this crisis wrought are difficult to fathom. In 1990, 36 percent of the global population lived in extreme poverty. By 2015 that number had been reduced to 10 percent, or 736 million people.[49] Progress notwithstanding, it still meant that there were hundreds of millions living hand to mouth when COVID-19 arrived. Any disruption—let alone total lockdowns brought about by a once-in-a-lifetime pandemic— amounted to a potential death sentence.

The external shock produced by the global economic crisis was acutely and severely felt across the whole developing world. Trade and supply chain disruptions hit countries such as Mexico, Thailand, Tunisia, and Vietnam. Falling tourism hammered countries such as Ethiopia, the Maldives, Mauritius, Nepal, the Seychelles, Sri Lanka, Thailand, and the small states of the Caribbean. Remittances from migrants who worked in wealthier nations and in normal times sent money back shrank significantly. As these remittances dried up, the impact was felt by families in places as diverse as El Salvador, Gambia, Guatemala, Haiti, Honduras, Lesotho, Nicaragua, Nepal, and Venezuela. Crashing oil prices threatened countries including Angola, Azerbaijan, Bolivia, Gabon, Iraq, Iran, Kazakhstan, Libya, Nigeria, South Sudan, Sudan, and Venezuela. Meanwhile, as global demand plummeted, falling commodity prices slashed the export revenues of countries such as the Democratic Republic of the Congo, Mozambique, and Peru.[50] To add insult to injury, capital actually flowed out of these developing economies as investors, staring at a spiraling calamity, became more skittish and risk averse. As a result, access to financing diminished and the cost of borrowing increased at the exact moment when countries required historically high spending to address the crisis. Many poor countries found themselves in an impossible financial bind.[51]

Internally, the public health measures that had proven effective in buying time to flatten the curve in wealthier nations—stay-at-home orders, business closures, quarantines, and other protocols—had limited impact in many developing ones. Too many governments in low- and middle-income countries lacked the capacity to capitalize on lockdowns to quickly ramp up COVID testing, contact tracing (which requires a large health care labor force), and workable isolation strategies. They were also unable to rapidly build up health care infrastructure and purchase needed equipment.[52] A worldwide scarcity of testing kits and the global scramble for protective equipment meant poorer nations stood last in line to receive essential supplies.[53]

As a result, a particularly cruel process unfolded across the global South whereby initial containment measures proved insufficient to keep the virus in check but inflicted grave damage on vulnerable people and economies already battered from the pandemic-induced worldwide recession. It therefore proved impossible—and untenable—to maintain containment measures. With the livelihoods of millions of people hanging in the balance, it was not feasible, humane, or enforceable to shut down commerce and force people to stay indoors for too long.[54] One South African study on the effects of disrupted health services and incomes in sub-Saharan Africa, published in June, for example, estimated that extended lockdown measures risked killing many more people than the disease itself.[55]

There was also little access to adequate social safety nets, such as stimulus checks issued by the government or extended unemployment benefits. For example, by the fall, G20 countries had put forward stimulus funding packages that averaged 22 percent of GDP to benefit their citizens and hold together parts of the economy. By comparison, the average country in sub-Saharan Africa was able to spend only 3 percent of GDP.

When it came to aid for the poorest citizens, the World Bank estimated that the average advanced economy spent $695 per person, compared to $4 per person in developing countries.[56]

As the WHO attempted to offer guidance, the organization clearly wrestled with the profound public health and economic dilemmas facing the developing world. But its messages were mixed and often incoherent. On January 23, a WHO representative in Beijing described China's lockdown of 11 million people in Wuhan as "a very important indication of the commitment to contain the epidemic," while calling it "unprecedented in public health history" and noting it was "certainly not a recommendation the WHO has made."[57] A month later, an assistant director general of the organization praised China's draconian actions, claiming they had "changed the course of the virus." Other countries were advised to "think about whether they apply something, not necessarily through lockdowns, but the same rigorous approach."[58] On March 11, 2020, the day the WHO declared COVID-19 a pandemic, the organization's director general, Tedros Adhanom Ghebreyesus, called on countries to take "urgent and aggressive action" to suppress and control the virus.[59] Two weeks later, after a meeting between the WHO representative in Dhaka and the Dhaka South City Corporation mayor, Sayeed Khokon, the mayor claimed the WHO had recommended that Bangladesh move into lockdown—an assertion the organization immediately denied, saying it had instead simply "presented several alternatives."[60]

Then, on April 14, the WHO updated its COVID-19 guidance, seeming to caution developing countries against the most stringent measures:

In many countries where community transmission has led to outbreaks with near exponential growth, countries have introduced widespread population-level physical distancing measures and movement restrictions in order to slow spread and set in place other control measures. Physical distancing measures and movement restrictions, often referred to as "shut downs" and "lock downs," can slow COVID-19 transmission by limiting contact between people. However, these measures can have a profound negative impact on individuals, communities, and societies by bringing social and economic life to a near stop. Such measures disproportionately affect disadvantaged groups, including people in poverty, migrants, internally displaced people and refugees, who most often live in overcrowded and under resourced settings, and depend on daily labour for subsistence.[61]

On the very same day, however, the organization's regional director for Southeast Asia lauded India's "tough and timely" nationwide shutdown, saying it "would go a long way in arresting the virus spread."[62] Through late spring and summer, the WHO urged developing countries to be cautious in lifting stay-at-home orders lest it contribute to uncontrolled spread of the coronavirus. Matshidiso Moeti, WHO regional director for Africa, acknowledged in May that "these actions came at great social and economic cost, particularly for the most vulnerable and there is an understandable push to lift the measures as rapidly as they were implemented." But, she added, "WHO urges countries to follow a step by step approach" in opening back up.[63] And as restrictions eased and COVID cases inevitably escalated, the WHO urged governments to consider reimposing intermittent lockdowns to curb the spread.[64]

In other words, the WHO had difficulty reconciling the inherent tension between the emergency public health measures required to contain exponential growth of the virus and the harsh economic realities present throughout much of the developing world. On October 8, 2020, David Nabarro, special envoy on COVID-19 for the WHO, tried to make the guidance crystal clear: "The only time we believe a lockdown is justified is to buy you time to reorganize, regroup, rebalance your resources, protect your health workers who are exhausted, but by and large, we'd rather not do it."[65] The tragic reality was that many poorer nations that imposed strict lockdowns were simply in no position to avail themselves of the time purchased at such great cost.

In January 2021, the World Bank estimated that emerging markets and developing economies contracted by 2.6 percent in 2020, representing the worst economic performance in the developing world since at least 1960 (the earliest year with available aggregate data). Excluding China, the downturn was projected to be a whopping 5 percent. More than 80 percent of emerging markets and developing economies experienced recessions, reflecting a higher share of suffering than was the case during the 2008–9 financial crisis. The pandemic caused per capita incomes to fall in more than 90 percent of emerging markets and developing economies;

in over half of these countries, five or more years of gains were wiped out, and more than a quarter saw at least ten years of per capita gains erased.[66]

Consequently, poverty rates across the developing world increased in 2020 for the first time since 1998.[67] In just the first six months of the crisis alone, the Institute for Health Metrics and Evaluation estimated that extreme poverty across the globe had already increased by 7 percent, swelling the ranks of the world's poorest by 37 million people.[68] All told, the World Bank projected that 110 to 150 million people could be added to the rolls of the extremely impoverished by the end of 2021, representing the largest projected increase since it began tracking data, while the UN Development Programme estimated that the pandemic could increase the current number by 207 million. The UN also assessed that the pandemic could force 490 million people into poverty as defined more broadly to include those losing access to either clean water, adequate food, or shelter.[69] Moreover, even as the world economy continues to bounce back from the Great Lockdown, deepening poverty could linger for years. Homi Kharas, a senior fellow at the Brookings Institution, calculated that half of the expected rise in extreme poverty could become permanent.[70] In the absence of dramatic action, the UN warned that the global poverty rate could still be as high as 7 percent by 2030, compared to the pre-pandemic projection of 3 percent.[71]

The long-term ripple effects on development and inequality stemming from disruptions in childhood education, nutrition, water, sanitation, and access to vaccinations for other diseases could also be profound. A November 2020 report by UNICEF found that the number of children living in "multidimensional poverty"—defined as lacking access to education, health, housing, nutrition, sanitation, or water—had already increased by 15 percent (representing an additional 150 million children) by mid-2020 due to the pandemic. "And there are more hidden impacts," the report continued, including "loss of future employment potential, rising violence, increased poverty, mental health issues and COVID-related long-term morbidity for children who are malnourished or already vulnerable."[72] In December, the UN Office for the Coordination of Humanitarian Affairs estimated that pandemic-related disruptions in essential health services could wipe out twenty years of progress in combating HIV/AIDS, tuberculosis, and malaria, potentially *doubling* annual death tolls from these diseases.[73]

Taken together, the sheer scale of economic misery set in motion by COVID-19 seemed almost unimaginable. Yet the international community did far too little to help those most at risk. Major donors were already becoming increasingly stingy before the pandemic. In 2019, the volume of international humanitarian assistance around the world dropped by $1.6 billion to less than $30 billion—the first such decrease since 2012— even as humanitarian requirements increased.[74] Then, as the pandemic wreaked its havoc, most wealthy countries became fixated on their crises at home. Cooperation aimed at assisting the world's poorest nations and people was scant. In March 2020, the UN announced the COVID-19 Global Humanitarian Response Plan (GHRP), aimed at addressing the short-term needs of five dozen of the world's most vulnerable countries. The initial financial appeal for the plan, which would be implemented by UN agencies in cooperation with international nongovernmental organizations, was for $2 billion; that amount was increased to $6.7 billion in May and $10.3 billion in July.[75] Combined with other humanitarian appeals, in 2020 the UN was asking for the largest-ever donations from member states, a total of $39 billion. But by November only $17 billion had been provided. Meanwhile, the UN anticipated that a record 235 million people would need humanitarian assistance in 2021—a 40 percent increase from the 168 million in need in 2020.[76]

PERU'S POTEMKIN PROGRESS

It was not just the world's poorest countries that were pummeled by the pandemic. Many nations that had been rapidly on the rise fared no better. No country epitomized this more than Peru.

In the decades before COVID-19, Peru was one of Latin America's true success stories—a country that had moved beyond insurgency and dictatorship to become one of the region's most dynamic economies. Propelled by free market reforms, fiscal discipline, and strong mineral and agricultural exports, the country's economy grew by 6.1 percent annually between 2002 and 2013, outpacing most other countries in the region. Peru catapulted into the upper tier of middle-income countries (defined by the World Bank as having per capita incomes of between $4,046 and $12,535). As per capita incomes increased, poverty declined and the middle class swelled.[77]

Peru reported its first COVID case on March 6, when a twenty-five-year-old man who had traveled to Spain, France, and the Czech Republic tested positive.[78] This was typical: initially COVID-19 came to Latin America through wealthier citizens who had recently traveled overseas.[79] But soon the contagion became indiscriminate, with the harshest impacts falling on the poor and marginalized. By May, COVID-19 was so pervasive throughout Latin America that the WHO declared it the new global epicenter of the pandemic.[80]

Unlike regional powers Brazil and Mexico, Peru took the outbreak seriously from the start. The same day the WHO officially declared COVID-19 to be a global pandemic, March 11, Peru canceled all classes in public and private schools. Four days later, when the country had only seventy-one confirmed COVID-19 cases and no deaths, President Martín Vizcarra declared a state of emergency, moving aggressively to seal the country's borders, limit domestic travel, and forbid nonessential businesses' operations. It was one of the earliest and most stringent lockdowns in Latin America. The nation's police and army were mobilized to help enforce containment measures, detaining thousands of people who violated the protocols. Only in July did the government begin gradually reopening the economy. This seemed to put Peru in a good position: early moves to shut down the country bought time to stock up on ventilators and add hundreds of new intensive care beds across the country. The government also tested people at a higher rate per capita than anywhere else in Latin America.[81]

After nearly two decades of impressive economic growth, Peru had resources its neighbors did not, and it quickly rolled out one of the region's biggest economic relief packages. Aid not only aimed to keep businesses afloat and people on official payrolls but also targeted the poor and workers in the informal economy with cash transfers. The government initially provided approximately 7 billion soles (1.1 percent of GDP) in direct transfers to support vulnerable households during the lockdown, and in late July it approved an additional cash transfer of 6.4 billion soles (0.9 percent of GDP).[82]

In other words, Peru seemed to do a lot of things right. And yet it was not enough. By July, when public health restrictions were loosened, the country of 33 million people had more than 288,000 confirmed cases of COVID-19 and 9,860 deaths. Peru rocketed to the second-highest number of cases (after Brazil) in Latin America, and it became one of the globe's worst coronavirus hotspots. In mid-August, as cases spiraled out of control, the government was forced to reimpose some restrictions. By late December, the number of cases had climbed to more than 1 million, with more than 37,000 deaths. At the time, this represented the sixth-highest number of recorded deaths per 100,000 people in the world.[83] Peru's fate seemed similar to that of other middle-income countries in Latin America, including Argentina, Bolivia, Brazil, Colombia, Ecuador, and Mexico, all of which had very high numbers of deaths per capita and case fatality rates. Moreover, analysis of excess deaths in Peru suggests that the real toll was perhaps double the reported figure.[84]

How could this happen? Put simply, Peru's actions to contain the virus were not enough to overcome the deep structural challenges it—like so many other developing nations—faced: densely packed cities, an underresourced health care system, gaping inequality, a large number of informal workers, and grinding poverty. Across Latin America, almost one-fifth of the population lives in situations that make social distancing a pipe dream; in pre-COVID Peru, more than one-third of the urban population resided in crowded slums in the capital, Lima, and other cities. These impoverished neighborhoods—characterized by shacks made of wood, scrap metal, and bricks—also typically lack adequate sanitation and clean water and have limited access to health care.[85] "They asked us to wash our hands," Hugo Ñopo of the Peruvian research group Grade said in June, "but [only] one in three poor households has access to running water."[86]

For decades, Peru also had one of the lowest levels of public investment in health care in Latin America. The result was a run-down system with low capacity, a shortage of essential supplies, and highly unequal access to care. Though the government acted quickly, the systemic vulnerability at the heart of the problem was too deep to overcome.

Economic disparities were another critical factor. In 2018, Peru's Gini coefficient—a common measure of inequality—was 0.43 (the average across Latin America and the Caribbean as a whole was 0.46). A Gini coefficient of zero expresses perfect equality, whereas a coefficient of 1 expresses maximum inequality. By comparison, the average score in high-income countries in 2018 was 0.32. Peru's inequality was emblematic of Latin America's standing as the second-most-unequal region in the world (after sub-Saharan Africa).[87] Consequently, despite years of economic growth, poverty remained a major challenge. In 2018, 16.8 percent of Peruvians still fell below the poverty line, and the proportion of people living in extreme poverty was 3.7 percent.[88] The pandemic "expos[ed] the fact that there are still a lot of people in poverty who we didn't see before," a Peru-based advisor for an international nongovernmental organization advocating for informal workers remarked in June. "They are earning day to day and working in difficult conditions."[89]

Moreover, many Peruvians not technically considered poor still worked in highly precarious circumstances. Across Latin America and the Caribbean, about 54 percent of the labor force works in street sales, small retail shops, part-time construction, domestic work, and other jobs in the informal economy. In Peru prior to the pandemic, that number was nearly 70 percent.[90] "The government's [lockdown] strategy works for the 30 percent of Peru that is employed in the formal sector, that's been growing economically," Iván Hidalgo Romero, academic director at the Institute of Government and Public Management in Lima, observes. "But there's another 70 percent of Peru, which is informal, that doesn't have access to basic services of health, education, nutrition, or to pensions and financial safety nets."[91] This combination meant that millions of Peruvians had little to no cushion against the twin shocks of the pandemic and lockdown. The veneer of meteoric economic progress had obscured these underlying realities—but COVID-19 revealed them.

Economic assistance from the government helped, but the sheer scale of the crisis overwhelmed these efforts. The lack of adequate, up-to-date information on impoverished households frustrated government attempts to assist those most in need. This became harder still as tens of thousands of Peruvians fled the cities for their home villages, which complicated disbursement of the economic relief that so many of them needed. The fact that only 43 percent of Peruvians had a bank account made cash transfers difficult to execute. And local corruption further weakened the impact of assistance programs; by June, anticorruption prosecutors had opened more than 500 inquiries looking into reports that officials diverted assistance for the poor into their own pockets.[92]

Socioeconomic conditions also aggravated design flaws in the government's pandemic containment strategy. "When the option is to die of hunger or hope that this illness doesn't get you," Luis David Arias Gutiérrez, a street vendor in Lima, said in June, "of course you break quarantine to try and feed your family."[93] The stringency of the lockdown led to crowds clustering at markets and banks at particular times, helping spread the virus. Because over 40 percent of Peruvian homes lack refrigerators, daily trips to the market are a part of life. This was always going to make it difficult for many Peruvians to stay home. But by limiting times and days available for people to shop for food, and by prohibiting delivery services and closing restaurants even for takeout, government restrictions produced massive crowds desperate to get to stores during operating hours. Thus the country's markets became "the main sources of contagion," President Vizcarra acknowledged. "We had markets with 40, 50, 80 percent of sellers infected. . . . You would buy, you would get infected, you would go home with the virus, and you would spread it to the whole family," he told the BBC.[94] Similarly, the widespread lack of bank accounts created swelling crowds outside banks as desperate people waited to receive physical cash payments that would help them weather the crisis.[95]

As the virus seeped through these cracks, the Peruvian economy was effectively crushed. Total economic activity fell by more than 40 percent in April, the first full month of the lockdown, and then contracted by a record 72 percent in the second quarter. In October, the IMF estimated that Peru's economy would decline by 13.9 percent in 2020. In December, the International Labour Organization estimated 2020 job losses in Peru to total 1.5 million.[96] This mirrored the calamity throughout Latin America and the Caribbean, with the IMF calculating that the economic contraction spawned by the pandemic was 7.4 percent in 2020, amounting to the region's worst downturn on record.[97]

All of this threatened to throw Peru's success story out the window. The number of Peruvians living in poverty was estimated to have increased to 25.8 percent by the end of 2020, jumping around 9 percentage points from the previous year, while the ranks of the extremely poor were forecast to more than double, from 3.7 percent to 7.6 percent.[98] "Here we are congratulating ourselves in Peru for starting to be a middle-class country," Pablo Lavado, an economist at Lima's Pacific University, told the *New York Times* in June. "But it turns out our middle class is very vulnerable, very fragile."[99] The same proved true across Latin America. As Luis Alberto Moreno, the president of the Inter-American Development Bank from 2005 to 2020, observed:

Latin America's COVID-19 crisis is, above all, a crisis of inequality. All over the world, the virus has fallen hardest on vulnerable racial and socioeconomic groups, revealing vast inequalities in access to education, health care, and other resources. . . . This is a crisis that has been decades in the making, one that therapeutics or a vaccine will not solve.[100]

WORSE THAN THE CONTAGION

"It has been clear for some time that it is not the virus itself doing most harm in vulnerable countries," Mark Lowcock, the UN's undersecretary general for humanitarian affairs and emergency relief coordinator, wrote in December 2020. "It is the secondary impacts of the subsequent lockdowns and global recession." Moreover, while the coronavirus "has been devastating . . . for many countries," Lowcock observed, "it was yet another layer of hardship on top of protracted conflicts, the effects of climate change, and the worst locust plague for a generation."[101]

Consider the case of Kenya. In early 2020, hundreds of millions of desert locusts descended across East Africa. The crop-eating pests devoured everything in their path. It was the worst infestation in seventy years, exacerbated by abnormally heavy rainfalls the previous fall caused by the Indian Ocean dipole, a phenomenon made worse by the warming of the Indian Ocean due to climate change. Troublingly, this accelerated the locusts' breeding capacity. "They are up and down, they are everywhere," Mwikali Nzoka said as she observed her eight-acre farm in Maseki, a town in eastern Kenya, in February. "It was so green here. It might become a desert soon."[102]

In the five years preceding COVID-19, Kenya's economy grew by an average of 5.7 percent per year, making it one of the fastest-growing countries in sub-Saharan Africa.[103] Yet more than a third of the country's 46 million people still experienced extreme poverty, and 14.5 million experienced some level of food insecurity. In a country where three-quarters of the population earn all or part of their income from agriculture, the locusts and the effects of climate change were already posing an enormous challenge. Then the pandemic struck.[104]

By the end of March, with relatively few COVID-19 cases reported, President Uhuru Kenyatta's government moved to suspend most air travel, tighten border controls, close schools and churches and mosques, restrict public gatherings, severely limit movements within the country, and impose curfews in urban areas.[105] But given that only 23 percent of Kenyan households have an internet connection and nearly 84 percent of the workforce are informal laborers, such measures were of limited value. Just as we saw with Bangladesh and Peru, for the significant number of Kenyans living in urban slums—in this case, in Nairobi, Mombasa, and elsewhere—social distancing was simply a fantasy. People left their homes to eke out a living. On several occasions, Kenyan police were accused of using excessive force to enforce lockdowns, shooting and beating people found shopping at markets or out on the street returning from work, prompting protests and further clashes.[106]

As in so many other countries, the global economic crisis pushed Kenya to the edge of disaster. The country's exports, tourism revenue, and remittance flows suffered, and personal incomes fell. Kenya's finance minister estimated that COVID-19 would cause Kenya's once-impressive economic growth to fall to around 0.6 percent in 2020—not nearly enough to keep pace with the country's rapidly growing population.[107]

As economic marginalization deepened, a battle developed for something many in wealthier countries take for granted: food. Lockdown disruptions contributed to short-term spikes in prices for maize and beans in Nairobi and other localities as demand grew and cross-border trade was disrupted.[108] In April, thousands of hungry people, desperate for help, stampeded food aid deliveries in the Kibera neighborhood of Nairobi, the country's largest slum. Many were injured and two people were killed. Men with sticks beat people back, and the police fired tear gas.[109] That same month, a video went viral of a widow in Mombasa who once washed laundry but now struggled to find work. The clip showed her cooking stones for her eight children in the hope that they would fall asleep before realizing there was no food to eat.[110]

Abundant rains helped keep Kenya's agricultural production high. But falling incomes meant that many Kenyans' ability to afford the available food was declining. In a June survey conducted by the International Committee of the Red Cross in the Lamu area, for example, 85 percent of respondents reported that food prices at local markets had increased, while 82 percent said the pandemic had reduced their incomes and thus their ability to buy food.[111] All told, outside of active conflict zones in Africa, Kenya was listed among the nations on the continent projected to be in the greatest need of humanitarian relief, with 3.6 million facing hunger.[112] The situation in many of Kenya's neighbors—including Ethiopia, South Sudan, Sudan, and Somalia—was even worse.

Mounting distress forced a gradual reopening of Kenya's economy at the end of April, and in early July many other restrictions were scrapped. The rollback of containment measures occurred despite rising infection rates: cases increased from a total of around 6,700 (with 149 confirmed deaths) at the beginning of July to 34,000 (with 577 confirmed deaths) by September and approximately 96,000 (with 1,670 confirmed deaths) by the end of the year. Yet, interestingly, case fatality rates appeared exceedingly low (around 1.7 percent as of December, far below the global average), perhaps a result of the youthful composition of the population in Nairobi and Mombasa, where COVID-19 was most prevalent.[113] Kenya was not unique in this regard. In September, the WHO observed that deaths from the virus remained relatively low across sub-Saharan Africa. In fact, despite a second wave of cases in the fall and winter, by December almost every one of the fifty-four countries on the continent registered fewer total deaths than the United States suffered each day.[114] In a cruel twist, in Africa as a whole, economic marginalization and food insecurity unleashed by the pandemic and the measures to contain it loomed much larger than the disease itself.

A PANDEMIC OF HUNGER

Globally, from 1990 to 2015, the number of people facing chronic hunger dropped by roughly a quarter. But by 2020, that number had risen from 796 million to 821 million, with those experiencing acute hunger increasing by 70 percent to 135 million.[115] Hunger plagued even agriculture-rich regions, such as Latin America. A 2019 report by the UN Food and Agriculture Organization (FAO) found that despite Latin America and the Caribbean producing 23 percent of global agricultural and fisheries exports, one in three people in the region experienced food insecurity.[116] Worldwide, the biggest factors driving these trends were ongoing armed conflicts, climate change, and existing economic vulnerabilities. The pandemic intersected with these existing trends and magnified their impact. Food insecurity worsened in Afghanistan, Burkina Faso, Central African Republic, Chad, Democratic Republic of the Congo, Ethiopia,

Guatemala, Haiti, Honduras, Kenya, Lebanon, Lesotho, Myanmar, Niger, Palestine, Pakistan, Somalia, South Sudan, Sudan, Uganda, Yemen, and elsewhere.

There were fears at the outset of the COVID crisis that it might trigger reductions in the aggregate worldwide food supply. In the United Kingdom, for example, nonprofits warned that farmers would be forced to throw out a third of their harvests in the case of a coronavirus-induced shortage in the migrant workforce.[117] In some developing countries, pastoral communities were unable to move animals to seasonal sources of food and water, harming the animals' health and reducing the sales value of their livestock.[118] Globally, however, production levels for rice, wheat, and maize—the three most widely consumed staple crops—managed to remain at or near all-time highs despite the pandemic.[119]

Disruptions in the global food trade caused by COVID-19 were also less than initially feared. By late April 2020, seventeen countries had announced or introduced temporary export restrictions on foodstuffs, including Russia, the world's largest exporter of wheat.[120] At their height, total export restrictions represented about 5 percent of the caloric value of globally traded food.[121] This created particular risks for sub-Saharan Africa, which relies heavily on imports of cereals to compensate for shortages in local food production.[122] But most of these restrictions proved short-lived (as of September, only Kyrgyzstan had such a ban still in place), and generally speaking, the global food trade proved more resilient than overall trade.[123]

It is important to note, however, that hunger crises rarely originate from problems with aggregate supply. Rather, they stem from disruptions in supply chains that prevent food from getting to those who need it. Hunger is also impacted by sudden changes in economic circumstances— such as spikes in food prices or declines in income—that limit the poor's access to food. And it was here where the impact of the pandemic on food insecurity was most acute.

By December 2020, the FAO had reported seven consecutive months of rising world food prices, producing an almost six-year high in the index of cereals, oilseeds, dairy products, meat, and sugar; a separate estimate by the World Bank found that food prices increased by 14 percent across the globe in 2020 even as income losses made it harder for many to afford to eat.[124] Price hikes were even more pronounced in certain locales.

In Syria, monthly food costs surged 240 percent, and in Sudan, the price of staple food crops doubled.[125] In large part, local fluctuations were the consequence of restrictions put in place to contain the pandemic. Farmers, traders, and workers involved in agricultural and food supply chains were typically exempt from lockdowns and mobility restrictions. But curfews limited the work of farmers and traders bringing food to the markets. Some street and open-air markets were closed. And with broader restrictions on travel, the local cost of food soared. Simply put, at a time when incomes were falling and prices were rising, millions of people across the developing world could not access the essential food items they required.[126] Meanwhile, falling commodity export prices, declining tourism, and other sources of economic distress robbed developing countries of the cash required to address mounting humanitarian needs. And as international donor countries suffered their own economic crises and turned inward, the revenue and political will to provide necessary aid failed to materialize.

In August 2020, the United States Department of Agriculture predicted that the income shock from COVID-19 would add 83.5 million people in low- and middle-income countries to the global ranks of the chronically hungry.[127] Meanwhile, the UN World Food Programme (WFP) estimated that in countries where it operated, approximately 272 million people were acutely food insecure or at risk of being so due to COVID-19, doubling the 2019 total. Absent concerted international action, the UN agency concluded, the pandemic might eventually produce famines in as many as thirty-five countries.[128] The humanitarian organization Oxfam echoed those concerns, noting that COVID-19 had "combined with the impacts of conflict, spiraling inequality, and an escalating climate crisis to shake an already broken global food system to its foundations, leaving millions more on the brink of starvation."[129]

On October 9, 2020, the WFP was awarded the Nobel Peace Prize for its efforts to combat surging global hunger in the midst of the pandemic. While the committee noted the WFP's efforts to ramp up assistance, the award seemed to be driven primarily by a desire to call attention to the escalating food crisis unleashed by COVID-19. Immediately following the announcement, David Beasley, the executive director of the WFP, issued an urgent plea to the international community—and to the world's many billionaires in particular—to step up to provide $5 billion in additional aid. In the absence of more resources, Beasley predicted, there were "a dozen or two dozen places around the world that, if we don't get the support that they need, . . . you are going to have famine . . . of biblical proportions." He also warned that food crises sparked by the pandemic could fuel further destabilization, conflict, and mass displacement, contributing to a vicious cycle that threatened to immiserate millions more people around the world.[130] In December, Beasley predicted that 2021 was likely to be "the worst humanitarian crisis year since the beginning of the United Nations" more than seven decades ago.[131]

9

Conflict and Contagion

On February 24, 2020, Ali Rabiei, a government spokesperson for the Islamic Republic of Iran, stepped to the podium. His objective was simple: reassure the Iranian people that the regime had COVID-19 contained. Standing next to him was Iraj Harirchi, Iran's deputy health minister and the official in charge of battling the outbreak. Both men offered confident and comforting words, but the video of the press conference told a different story. Throughout the briefing, Harirchi coughed, wiped his face and eyes, and sweated profusely. A day later, the public learned that Harirchi had contracted COVID-19, which showed that the contagion was not, in fact, under control.[1] Not only was the virus spreading throughout Iran, but it had penetrated the inner sanctum of the Iranian government.

The virus seems to have traveled to Iran via Chinese students or workers visiting seminaries in the holy city of Qom. Though the Iranian government had reported the first confirmed fatalities from the disease on February 19, COVID-19 had been circulating unchecked in the holy city for weeks. Because Qom is the spiritual center of Iran's clerical establishment, with a steady stream of religious pilgrims and official visitors, the outbreak in the city helped radiate the virus outward to other population centers and facilitated its spread within elite circles. It soon became impossible to mask the growing crisis. A video widely shared on social media revealed body bags piling up at a Qom cemetery, and satellite images surfaced showing mass graves being dug in the city.[2] By mid-March, tens of thousands of Iranians were infected, including dozens of government officials and prominent religious figures. At the time, the World Health Organization estimated that the mounting Iranian death toll, officially numbered in the thousands, might be off by a factor of five.[3]

The refusal to level with the Iranian people about what was happening in Qom was indicative of the regime's bungled response. Early on, as the epidemic raged in Wuhan, Iran's government hesitated to cut off travel to China out of concern about alienating its largest trading partner and the only remaining buyer of the country's oil. Early suspicious cases were dismissed, and the regime failed to prepare the nation's health care system.[4] Then, when Tehran finally announced a ban on flights from China in early February, Mahan Air—a private airline operated by the regime's praetorians, the Islamic Revolutionary Guard Corps (IRGC)—continued to covertly fly routes to and from Chinese cities.[5] To further maintain the appearance of normalcy, Iranian officials encouraged mass demonstrations to celebrate the forty-first anniversary of the Iranian revolution on February 11 and went ahead with the scheduled February 21 parliamentary elections—decisions that undoubtedly facilitated the spread of the virus.

Even as the Revolutionary Guard was circumventing official efforts to contain COVID-19, it sought to politicize the pandemic, casting blame on Iran's enemies and positioning the IRGC as national heroes. Guard officials described the virus as an "American biological invasion" and a "Zionist biological terrorist attack." A professor at the IRGC-run Baqiyatallah University of Medical Sciences declared on Iranian state TV that the contagion was a "biological ethnic weapon" specifically created by both the Americans and Israelis to target Iranian DNA. The country's supreme leader, Ayatollah Ali Khamenei, echoed these conspiracy theories.[6] Meanwhile, the Guard presented itself as the nation's health savior, ready to help beleaguered doctors and nurses. In early March, Iranian authorities announced that 300,000 troops from the IRGC and its Basij militia would deploy across the country to help sanitize public places, direct traffic, and test and treat sickened individuals.[7]

As COVID-19 spread, the country found itself caught in an economic maelstrom. In 2015, Iran had reached an agreement with the Obama administration, along with China, France, Germany, Russia, and the United Kingdom, to constrain its nuclear activities in exchange for sanctions relief. But regime corruption and mismanagement had prevented Iran from reaping the full economic benefits. Then, in May 2018, President Trump walked away from the nuclear accord—which he had described as a "disaster" and "the worst deal ever negotiated" during the 2016 presidential campaign—and reimposed sweeping economic penalties on Tehran. American sanctions cut Iran off from the global financial system and crippled its ability to sell oil. In doing so, Trump promised that his "maximum pressure" campaign would force the regime to capitulate to a tougher nuclear agreement and tame Iran's support for terrorism and militancy across the Middle East. The opposite happened. Iran resumed nuclear activities prohibited under the nuclear pact and ramped up its regional provocations: targeting shipping in the Persian Gulf, launching drone and missile strikes against Saudi oil infrastructure, and authorizing Iranian-backed Shia militia to launch rockets against U.S. forces in Iraq. Nevertheless, Trump's sanctions *did* succeed in decimating the Iranian economy. Oil exports—which made up a substantial portion of Iran's overall economic activity and, especially, government revenue prior to the reimposition of sanctions—plummeted from around 2.5 million barrels per day in 2018 to a few hundred thousand barrels a day in early 2020. Inflation skyrocketed, Iran's currency sank, and unemployment swelled. Iran's economy declined by more than 7 percent in 2019, and the country was poised for a dismal 2020 even before the pandemic.[8] Sanctions also complicated Iran's ability to manage the coronavirus. Although there were technical exemptions for humanitarian and medical assistance, the sweeping nature of Trump's maximum pressure campaign made foreign entities skittish about providing such aid during the pandemic—a problem made all the worse when the United States completely blacklisted Iran's entire banking system in October 2020.[9]

Already on economic life support, Iran was further battered as COVID-19 destroyed global demand for oil and Russia and Saudi Arabia refused to cut production. The resulting steep decline in oil prices hit all oil producers hard—but Iran suffered disproportionately because sanctions forced it to sell its oil below market prices.[10] Moreover, while the regime never imposed a complete lockdown, the steps it took to curtail the spread of COVID-19—including incrementally ratcheting up restrictions on public and religious gatherings, schools, and businesses from late February to mid-March—further compounded its already abysmal economic situation. Millions of Iranians lost jobs or had their wages and hours cut. Declining tax revenues due to business closures and ongoing sanctions robbed the regime of the financial wherewithal to provide an adequate safety net.[11] All told, the International Monetary Fund estimated that Iran's economy declined by another 5 percent in 2020.[12]

As Iran sought to pull itself out of its economic death spiral, it increasingly turned to China. Trade relations between the two nations had already deepened in the wake of Trump's reimposition of sanctions. During an August 2019 visit by Iranian foreign minister Javad Zarif to Beijing, China's foreign minister, Wang Yi, had described the two countries as "comprehensive strategic partners." The pandemic provided an incentive to make this a reality. In July, a leaked document suggested that Iran and China were edging toward a twenty-five-year strategic agreement to deepen trade, political, cultural, and military ties. The deal was signed in March 2021, potentially paving the way for as much as $400 billion in Chinese investment in Iranian infrastructure over the course of twenty-five years and the integration of the Islamic Republic into China's Belt and Road Initiative. In exchange, Beijing would reportedly gain preferential access to Iranian oil.[13]

Iran's president, Hassan Rouhani, was also forced to ease up on restrictions at home in a desperate attempt to salvage the economy. In the months before the pandemic, economic conditions and grievances against the regime had driven widespread demonstrations across the country. In November 2019, an estimated 200,000 Iranians in more than 100 cities and towns had taken to the streets. The demonstrations had prompted mass arrests, and the IRGC and other security forces had gunned down hundreds of people. It was the deadliest response to political unrest since the revolution, outstripping even the violence deployed by the regime during the 2009 Green Movement protests.[14] Then, as COVID-19 entered the mix, the regime was confronted by new existential challenges. By early April 2020, conditions had become so dire that fifty economists sent a letter to Rouhani warning that the pandemic and associated economic situation could spark escalating social upheaval. Shortly thereafter, Rouhani eased businesses and government entities back online, declaring it "a necessity for the country."[15]

The decision to loosen restrictions before the virus was under control predictably contributed to a second devastating wave of infections.

When the lockdown was lifted in April, Iran had officially reported around 70,000 COVID-19 cases and 4,400 deaths. By July, the numbers skyrocketed to nearly 230,000 confirmed cases and almost 11,000 deaths—by far the highest tally in the Middle East. And this was only officially released data; the actual numbers were likely much higher.[16] Rouhani had let slip that serological testing suggested that as many as 25 million Iranians (out of a total population of 83 million) might have been exposed.[17] Beginning in October, the regime had no choice but to reimpose some of the containment measures it had eased months earlier in Tehran and other cities, shutting public spaces, canceling events, and closing schools, mosques, movie theaters, museums, wedding venues, beauty salons, gyms, cafes, zoos, and swimming pools.[18] By the end of the year, Iran recorded more than 1.2 million COVID-19 cases and 55,000 deaths (representing 426 percent and 404 percent increases, respectively, in just six months). As eye popping as these numbers were, health officials acknowledged that the real number of cases was probably twice as high, and a senior member of Iran's Supreme Medical Council said that deaths were likely three or four times higher than the official number.[19]

SPILLOVER

In the weeks following the initial outbreak in Iran, more than 130,000 Afghans who had sought refuge and work in their neighboring nation returned to Afghanistan. The two countries share a 500-mile border, and many Afghans had made the journey to Iran years earlier to escape war, drug trafficking, and economic deprivation. Now they were reversing course. "The situation [in Iran] was getting worse every day," one young Afghan laborer at a camp in Herat province, on the Iranian border, told *The Guardian*. "Because of the quarantine I couldn't work anymore," and "I was afraid of the coronavirus."[20] As the mass exodus ensued, returnees encountered few border controls and no medical screenings—so they came back to Afghanistan carrying the virus unchecked and unmonitored. On February 25, Afghanistan reported its first case of COVID-19 in Herat, which would become the Afghan epicenter of the pandemic.[21] The Iranian outbreak was spreading beyond its borders.

Soon the Afghan government jumped into action to contain the virus, closing schools and banning large gatherings and celebrations. By late

March, government offices and all nonessential businesses in Kabul and other provincial capitals were ordered closed, domestic airlines were grounded, and road travel was restricted. The imperative to do so was clear: given the inadequacy and fragility of Afghanistan's health care system, there was no prospect of the country handling the full brunt of COVID-19. Months after the contagion reached the country, there were still only a few hundred ventilators available nationwide for 35 million Afghans.

As was the case in many low-income nations, the fact that the majority of Afghans worked in the informal sector and fell below the poverty line meant that social distancing was neither feasible nor enforceable, especially given the limited capacity and reach of the government. Low health literacy, a paucity of masks, and limited awareness of handwashing techniques further complicated the situation. So too did religious beliefs—including gathering in mosques—and a degree of cultural fatalism built up over decades of disaster after disaster assailing the Afghan people. Add porous borders and an ongoing war, and the difficulties of containing COVID-19 proved insurmountable. Given this, most early containment measures were abandoned by June.[22] By the end of the year, official public health advisories were the butt of jokes, and many Afghans shunned masks and social distancing. "There's no coronavirus," a young seller of secondhand shoes in Kabul told the New York Times. "It's a lie told by the government."[23]

Given Afghanistan's limited testing capacity, it is impossible to know with any precision how hard the country had been hit. Between March and December, only 180,000 tests were conducted throughout the country.[24] In April, the Ministry of Public Health estimated that 25 million Afghans would eventually be infected with the coronavirus, and 110,000 would die—surpassing the total number of civilians killed in Afghanistan since the U.S. invasion in 2001.[25] Four months later, based on antibody tests conducted on approximately 9,500 people across Afghanistan by the WHO and Johns Hopkins University, Afghanistan's health minister estimated that 31.5 percent of the country's population, and 53 percent of Kabul's nearly 5 million residents, had already been infected. Though the official tally at the time stood at only 37,000 cases and around 1,300 deaths, it seems likely that the actual numbers were significantly higher. Overrun by endless disease and conflict, the health care system struggled to differentiate between deaths caused by COVID-19 and those resulting from other causes.[26]

The pandemic also placed additional stress on Afghanistan's brittle economy. "The war has been an economic blow, but trade continues despite fighting," Abdul Qayum Rahimi, the governor of Herat province from January 2019 to early April 2020, told the *New York Times*. In contrast, "the virus, it stops everything."[27] In July, the World Bank reported that Afghanistan's economy, which grew by 2.9 percent in 2019, sharply contracted in the first half of 2020. It also estimated that the poverty rate would rise to between 61 and 72 percent (up from 55 percent in 2017, the last time it was measured) due to disruptions in shopkeeping, street and market sales, and daily labor in construction, agriculture, and personal services.[28] And, in a country already accustomed to acute food shortages, pandemic-related spikes in food prices further threatened vulnerable segments of the population. The Integrated Food Security Phase Classification initiative estimated that the number of Afghans hit by severe food insecurity had increased from 12 million at the beginning of 2020 to 13.15 million by November, with an additional 10.56 million people on the edge. Altogether, over half the country's population was in need of livelihood support or food aid.[29]

The COVID-19 outbreak came at a particularly fraught time for a country trying to extricate itself from decades of war. A week after the country's first confirmed cases, the Trump administration and Taliban militants reached a fragile peace deal in Doha, Qatar. The accord called for the withdrawal of U.S. forces over the course of fourteen months in exchange for the Taliban severing ties with Al Qaeda, ensuring Afghanistan would not be a safe harbor for other international terrorists, and entering talks with the Afghan government. But the ensuing peace talks, originally planned for March, were delayed until September, as the two sides bickered over the release of prisoners. Meanwhile, violence against Afghan security forces raged throughout the spring and summer even as the number of American troops in the country declined from 13,000 to 8,600. By November, the Trump administration announced that the number would fall further, to 2,500 military personnel by January 2021.[30] As the American presence dwindled, the virus hit the Afghan security forces hard. In June, security officials from the heavily contested Nangahar, Ghazni, Logar, and Kunduz provinces told the *Washington Post* that between 60 and 90 percent of their forces had been infected with COVID-19. Fearing further spread, American and NATO troops advising Afghan forces suspended most in-person training throughout the country.[31]

This convergence of challenges—some due to the pandemic, some simply a reality of a country long afflicted by war—gifted the Taliban with an opportunity to strengthen their bargaining position.[32] The Taliban also sought to play up their willingness to help contain the virus, filling a perceived void left by the Afghan government. In March, the Taliban's spokesperson tweeted that the group "via its Health Commission assures all international health organizations and WHO of its readiness to cooperate and coordinate with them in combating the coronavirus."[33] In reality, however, the group appeared to take few steps to implement public health measures in the areas they occupied.[34] Reports also surfaced of serious illness and COVID-related deaths among the senior ranks of the Taliban, including unconfirmed reports that the group's supreme leader had been infected, creating additional uncertainty about the balance of power between factions supporting peace talks and those taking a harder line.[35]

AN OPENING FOR ISIS

Iraq, neighboring Iran to the west, initially had better luck. The country reported its first case the day before Afghanistan did, and its initial outbreak was similarly linked to arrivals from Iran. Iraq's high degree of social, religious, and economic interconnectedness with Iran seemed to put the country in a particularly precarious spot. Cognizant of these vulnerabilities, and knowing the country's dilapidated health care system could easily be overwhelmed, Iraqi authorities moved quickly to impose a twenty-four-hour curfew, restrict domestic travel, cancel religious festivals, and close borders, airports, schools, and businesses. These measures kept the virus in check throughout the early spring. But movement restrictions were loosened for Ramadan in late April. And as public protests over COVID-related measures grew and the price of oil—which accounts for 90 percent of the Iraqi government's revenue— plummeted, authorities were forced to loosen economic restrictions and border controls. Social distancing, proper hygiene, and the use of masks were encouraged, but many Iraqis—including those who could simply no longer afford to stay home—ignored the guidance.[36]

An explosion of cases ensued just as a new Iraqi government, led by Prime Minister Mustafa al-Kadhimi, came to power. At the beginning of May, there were just over 2,100 confirmed cases and fewer than 100 deaths. By June, there were approximately 6,900 confirmed cases and 215 deaths. The numbers increased to more than 51,000 and 2,050 by July and nearly doubled month after month. By the end of the year, Iraq had reported nearly 600,000 cases and 13,000 deaths.[37] The health care system—badly strained by years of war and economic distress—was overrun. The UN envoy to Iraq estimated in August that the pandemic had increased poverty in Iraq by 10 percent, noting that one-third of the country's population now fell below the poverty line and that 3 million Iraqis (out of a population of 40 million) could not afford to buy food.[38]

The pandemic also distracted from the campaign to keep pressure on the Islamic State in Iraq and Syria (ISIS). Iraqi security forces had to contend with the possibility of contagion within their own ranks, and they were diverted away from counterterrorism missions to support government responses to COVID-19, including curfews and restrictions on vehicle movements.[39] As they did, U.S. troops and other coalition forces supporting Iraqi military operations also pulled back. American forces had already been consolidating onto fewer bases due to escalating tensions with Iran. These tensions got worse in the aftermath of Trump's decision to authorize a drone strike on Iranian general Qasem Soleimani, the head of the IRGC–Quds Force (Iran's elite covert action wing), on January 3. The strike, which was in retaliation for rocket attacks by Iranian-backed militia against bases hosting U.S. troops and the siege of the American embassy in Baghdad by pro-militia groups, was aimed at "restoring deterrence."[40] It did not. Although COVID-19 and associated movement restrictions complicated Iranian logistical and financial support for proxy militia forces in Iraq, the Iranian regime sensed potential American weakness and tried to exploit it. At the same time, playing up the threat from the "Great Satan" served as a convenient way for the Iranian regime to divert attention from its own mishandling of the virus.[41] Consequently, Tehran greenlit an increase in militia rocket and roadside bomb attacks against American troops and contractor convoys, and in response, the U.S. military shrank its footprint across Iraq to protect its forces.[42]

As the COVID-19 outbreak worsened, several countries in the counter-ISIS coalition—including Canada, the Czech Republic, France, New Zealand, Portugal, Spain, and the United Kingdom—also withdrew forces as a precaution. American operations against ISIS fighters continued, but interactions with Iraqi forces were substantially curtailed, with physical engagements, advising, and training shifting online.[43] In late August, the Trump administration and the Kadhimi government—pressured to limit the American presence due to rising tensions with Iran—reached an agreement to reduce U.S. troop levels in Iraq by about one-third, from 5,200 to about 3,000. Following the agreement, the Trump administration announced additional withdrawals, promising to reduce the force to 2,500. And then, in September, Secretary of State Pompeo threatened to close the U.S. embassy in Baghdad unless the Kadhimi government took steps to end escalating attacks by Iranian-backed militia.[44]

Although Trump declared victory against the Islamic State in 2018, the reality was that ISIS was diminished but not destroyed—and it suddenly saw a chance to make a comeback. By the end of 2017, after more than three years of brutal fighting, ISIS had lost most of the territory under its control in Iraq and Syria. But as American forces were increasingly diverted to protect themselves against Iranian proxies, there was a substantial upswing in the number and complexity of ISIS attacks beginning in mid-2019.[45] Further U.S. retrenchment forced by the pandemic accelerated these trends.

"What you are witnessing these days are only signs of big changes in the region that'll offer greater opportunities than we had previously in the past decade," ISIS leader Abu Ibrahim al-Qurashi posted online in May.[46] The Islamic State called for supporters to spread the coronavirus and step up attacks.[47] Across the summer of 2020, American military commanders noted a surge in ISIS activity, attributing the increase in attacks to "opportunistic exploitation of a confluence of factors," including the Iraqi security forces' "preoccupation" with measures to contain COVID-19.[48] The Islamic State also sought to take advantage of fresh opportunities online. As social media platforms shifted attention away from cracking down on jihadist content toward combating misinformation associated with the pandemic, ISIS increased propaganda and recruiting efforts in cyberspace. The group even sought to exploit the crisis to raise cash, creating a website to sell fake "FDA-approved" N95 masks and other personal protective equipment for hospitals, nursing homes, and fire departments.[49]

THE FURY OF THE VIRUS AND THE FOLLY OF WAR

"Our world faces a common enemy: COVID-19," United Nations secretary-general António Guterres said on March 23. Noting that vulnerable populations in conflict zones—including women and children, people with disabilities, the marginalized, the internally displaced, and refugees—were also at greatest risk from the pandemic, Guterres called for an immediate global cease-fire. "The fury of the virus illustrates the folly of war," Guterres declared. "End the sickness of war and fight the disease that is ravaging our world."[50] Six days later, Pope Francis reinforced the secretary-general's plea. It was imperative "to follow it up by ceasing all forms of hostilities, encouraging the creation of corridors for humanitarian aid, openness to diplomacy, and attention to those who find themselves in situations of vulnerability," Francis declared during his weekly blessing, delivered from the Vatican Apostolic Library instead of St. Peter's Square because of the lockdown in Italy. "May our joint fight against the pandemic . . . inspire a renewed commitment to overcome rivalries among leaders of nations and those parties involved."[51]

These calls came relatively early in the pandemic—when COVID-19 was still largely concentrated in China and the West—in anticipation of the potentially devastating impacts the pandemic could have once it inevitably took hold in war-torn societies with large, vulnerable populations and ruined health care systems. Yet the appeal to a common humanity in the face of a shared external foe failed. A number of warring parties around the world acknowledged openness to the idea. But in none of the four countries listed by the World Bank in 2020 as engaged in "high-intensity" conflict (Afghanistan, Libya, Somalia, and Syria) nor in any of the thirteen nations described by the Bank as "medium-intensity" conflicts (Burkina Faso, Cameroon, Central African Republic, Chad, Democratic Republic of the Congo, Iraq, Mali, Mozambique, Myanmar, Niger, Nigeria, South Sudan, and Yemen) did conflict cease.[52] Fighting also continued in other countries experiencing some level of insurgency, separatism, or organized extremist and criminal violence (including Bangladesh, Colombia, Egypt, Ethiopia,

India, Mexico, Pakistan, the Philippines, Sudan, Thailand, Turkey, Ukraine, and Venezuela).

Even in conflict zones where one party supported humanitarian de-escalation, other combatants demurred and fighting resumed in full force. In Colombia, for example, left-wing National Liberation Army (ELN) rebels announced a unilateral cease-fire in April, only to see the government in Bogotà balk.[53] Likewise, in Cameroon, the Southern Cameroons Defense Forces (a prominent Anglophone separatist group) endorsed the global cease-fire for two weeks to allow medical assistance to enter areas under its control, but the Ambazonia Defense Forces (the largest Anglophone rebel organization) declined to stand down, and the Francophone-dominated government also refused to declare a truce. As hostilities continued, all sides targeted aid workers, disrupting humanitarian assistance shipments at a time when Cameroon was experiencing one of the highest rates of COVID-19 infection in Africa.[54]

Elsewhere, violence actually escalated in the immediate aftermath of the UN's call for global cease-fire. By June, according to the Armed Conflict Location and Event Data Project, political violence had increased in forty-three countries and remained constant in another forty-five since the start of the pandemic.[55]

In Libya, for example, the UN-backed Government of National Accord (GNA) and its adversary, the Libyan National Army (LNA), both claimed to support a humanitarian stand-down to address COVID-19 prior to the UN call. Yet both sides later rejected a formal cease-fire. Instead, the flow of weapons from external backers (from Turkey and Qatar to the GNA and from the United Arab Emirates, Egypt, France, and Russia to the LNA) increased, as did the shelling of neighborhoods in Libya's capital, Tripoli, where civilians were ordered to shelter in place and attacks continued on hospitals essential to dealing with the pandemic. In September, Stephanie Williams, the top UN official for Libya, warned that conditions had reached a "decisive turning point" because of the compounding hardship produced by the war and COVID-19, observing that the situation appeared to be "spiraling out of control."[56] The pandemic created challenges for those seeking to broker and sustain a deescalation, forcing UN-organized meetings to be held under tight public health restrictions or virtually. As one Western diplomat told Frederic Wehrey of the Carnegie Endowment for International Peace: "You just can't do real political dialogue over Zoom."[57] Nevertheless, in late October, stalemate on the battlefield enabled a formal UN-brokered truce, signed in Geneva, that calmed the situation somewhat. The GNA and LNA promised to forge a political road map and hold elections. And in February 2021, negotiations produced a new national unity government.[58]

Conflict also worsened in war-torn Yemen. The Saudi-led coalition increased airstrikes by 30 percent in the weeks after the UN cease-fire plea, while the coalition's Iranian-backed Houthi opponents—in control of the capital, Sanaa, and much of northern Yemen—launched a major assault on the oil-rich Marib province in central Yemen. In early April, the Saudis declared a two-week unilateral cease-fire that was then extended through Ramadan, ostensibly to focus on the virus. But the fighting continued, with both sides blaming the other for breaches. And as Saudi Arabia and the United Arab Emirates increasingly turned inward to confront the virus at home and deal with the economic fallout from plunging oil prices (and, for the Saudis, the forced cancellation of the lucrative annual hajj, the pilgrimage of millions of Muslims to Mecca), the alliance of Yemeni factions they backed on the ground to oppose the Houthis blew apart. Southern separatists backed by the UAE displaced the Saudi-backed (and internationally recognized) government of Abdrabbuh Mansur Hadi in the port city of Aden, creating a new "war-within-a-war." Warring parties exploited COVID-19 public health measures, such as restrictions on freedom of movement, to vie for territorial control and block the delivery of humanitarian aid.[59]

As Yemen's war raged on, the country reported its first confirmed COVID-19 case in April, although the lack of testing made it impossible to know how far the virus had—or eventually would—spread. In Houthi-controlled areas of the country, medical teams were also pressured to suppress information about the extent of the outbreak.[60] But it was clear that, in a country already suffering from the worst human-made humanitarian emergency in the world, the consequences were potentially dire. Lise Grande, the head of the UN's Office for the Coordination of Humanitarian Affairs, warned at the time that 16 million (out of 28 million) Yemenis were vulnerable to eventual infection—in a country with a war-ravaged health system and only 700 intensive care unit beds, including 60 for children, and 500 ventilators for the entire country.[61] By July, at least ninety-seven Yemeni health care workers had already succumbed to the coronavirus, increasing the strain on remaining medical personnel battling a host of crises beyond COVID-19, from malnutrition to diphtheria and dengue fever.[62] "The worst-case scenario—which is the one we're facing now—means that the death toll from the virus could exceed the toll of war, disease, and hunger over the last five years [in Yemen]," Grande observed in June.[63] "For us, death is normal," Amal Mansoor, a twenty-eight-year-old freelance journalist living in Sanaa, said that same month. "But I'm still afraid of the coronavirus."[64] In September, the United Nations announced that it was forced to cut critical aid to 300 health centers across Yemen because the international community failed to provide sufficient funding. By the end of the year, funding cuts from the Trump administration, Saudi Arabia, and the UAE left 4 million Yemenis without much-needed humanitarian aid, sending the country teetering back toward famine.[65]

Zooming out to see the broader picture, there are several reasons that the global call for combatants to put down arms to jointly fight the virus went unheeded. First, nearly all the underlying conditions that have historically driven internal armed conflicts were exacerbated by COVID-19.[66] Political scientists argue that internal wars typically result from the intersection of state failure—that is, the inability of governments to provide essential services and security—and some combination of economic, social, and political grievances or predation by opportunistic rebel groups and government elites. Research has consistently identified several indicators associated with higher levels of state fragility and civil strife, including poor health, low per capita income, economic vulnerability produced by dependence on oil and other natural resources, low levels of international trade, government discrimination, democratic backsliding, and instability in neighboring countries—and all of these were exacerbated by the pandemic. In July, for example, a group of conflict researchers at the University of Denver's Korbel School of International Studies updated a statistical model of internal war to include the possible effects of COVID-19. Prior to the pandemic, their statistical simulation—which incorporated a wide array of human and social development indicators—predicted that the number of armed conflicts around the world would plateau or even decline starting in 2020 and continue on that path through the remainder of the decade. However, when they updated their model to account for possible effects of COVID-19 and associated disruptions, using economic projections from the International Monetary Fund and making certain assumptions about the pandemic's prevalence and mortality, their analysis produced a very different result. Instead of predicting a gradual decline in violence, the model now forecasted that thirteen *additional* countries would be at risk of descending into internal war by 2022, potentially producing the highest level of instability in more than three decades.[67]

Second, it is clear that many warring parties across the globe either distrusted calls for a pandemic cease-fire or, more cynically, saw opportunities to seize on the crisis to shift circumstances in their favor. In some countries, insurgents and terrorists exploited the diversion of security services and the pullback of international forces, as the Taliban in Afghanistan and ISIS in Iraq did. Similarly, in Mexico, drug cartels exploited the vacuum created by sickened police officers, the diversion of security forces to guard medical centers, and the need to convert military barracks into COVID-19 clinics.[68]

In other conflict zones, the government sought to use the virus to tilt dynamics on the ground in its favor. In Syria, COVID-19 struck at a time when President Bashar al-Assad's government believed it was on the cusp of victory in the country's brutal nine-year-old conflict. The outbreak hit the capital, Damascus, and other regime-controlled areas hard, despite official government statistics claiming the country had relatively few cases.[69] Iran's economic difficulties also curtailed financial support for Afghan and Pakistani fighters supporting Assad's regime, while the pandemic prompted other Iranian-backed militia to return home to Iraq and Lebanon. This might have created breathing room for the remaining armed opposition groups, which were clustered in Syria's northwestern Idlib province, home to 4 million Syrians and a bombed-out health care infrastructure. In the context of a fragile pause in fighting aimed to ease human suffering, Russia and China, both backers of Assad, worked at the UN Security Council in July to restrict the number of authorized border crossings into Syria to just one (through Turkey) and to ensure that all humanitarian assistance across internal lines go through the regime. The Assad regime, in turn, curtailed humanitarian aid to Idlib in an effort to ensure that COVID-19 would hit the last remaining rebel stronghold the hardest. From the late summer through the winter, cases surged in Idlib, where hundreds of thousands of displaced Syrians resided in camps, unable to social distance and without access to proper sanitation.[70]

Finally, even in places where a cease-fire might have proved possible, there was no international support system in place to enforce such arrangements. Travel and movement restrictions put in place to contain COVID-19 limited the ability of international mediators to engage with combatants and made it difficult to bring warring parties together.[71] The pandemic undermined UN peacekeeping missions, freezing troop rotations and minimizing interactions with local populations.[72] And squabbling on the UN Security Council dealt a further blow to peace efforts. The United States and Russia tied up initial efforts to back the call for a global cease-fire by insisting that they be allowed to continue counterterrorism operations. Washington and Beijing then clashed on whether to include an endorsement of the World Health Organization's efforts to combat the pandemic, with the Trump administration blocking a resolution in May that was supported by fourteen other members of the Security Council because it included a small, indirect reference to the WHO.[73] The French realized it would be difficult to get a resolution, but they hoped that the permanent members of the Security Council could nevertheless engage in a dialogue that would clarify the rules of the road. France's efforts failed, and Paris cast blame on the United States, China, and Russia for having little interest in it.[74] The Security Council finally endorsed a global cease-fire on July 1—more than three months after Guterres's urgent plea—but it had little effect.

In at least one instance, the international discord and distraction produced by the pandemic seemed to provide an opening for a long-dormant armed conflict to reemerge. On September 27, Azerbaijani forces launched an offensive into the breakaway region of Nagorno-Karabakh, an Armenian ethnic-majority territory that, while internationally recognized to be part of Azerbaijan, has long operated as a de facto independent state. In the early 1990s, Azerbaijan and Armenia clashed over the status of the region in a war that killed thousands. Ever since, the Organization for Security and Cooperation in Europe (OSCE) Minsk Group (chaired by France, Russia, and the United States) had sought to sustain a cease-fire. Yet the co-chairs had been unable to convene face-to-face with Armenia and Azerbaijan's foreign ministers since January 2020, and in April the OSCE Minsk Group was forced by the pandemic to suspend

on-the-ground monitoring of the cease-fire across the line of control sep-
arating Armenian and Azerbaijani forces. The international community
also failed to bring the parties together after clashes between the two sides'
forces left dozens of people dead in July. Just two days prior to launching
the September offensive, Azerbaijani president Ilham Aliyev complained
to the UN General Assembly about the lack of progress in resolving the
dispute. And, in the face of a stalled negotiating process and distracted
world powers, Aliyev appeared to calculate that he had an opportunity to
win by force what he had not achieved at the bargaining table.[75]

The result was a dramatic military escalation with Armenia and the
prospect of a wider interstate conflict. Turkey, which shares ethnic and
cultural ties with Azerbaijan, backed Aliyev, seeing the conflict as an opportunity to expand Ankara's influence. Meanwhile, Russia attempted to
broker a deescalation but leaned toward Armenia, with which Moscow
has a collective security arrangement. The pandemic made any international effort to stop the fighting harder. "In the past," *The Economist*
notes, "the ground would have been thick with negotiators from an al-
phabet soup of peacemaking outfits and concerned nations, all trying
to build local and regional confidence." Yet COVID-19 "makes that sort
of diplomacy much harder in conflict zones all around the world."[76]
As the fighting escalated, thousands were killed. Then, in November,
the downing of a Russian helicopter by Azerbaijani forces prompted a
threat of direct military intervention by Moscow. Under intense pressure, the sides finally agreed to end the bloodshed and accept Russian
peacekeepers.[77]

STRANDED

The Greek island of Lesbos resides just off the coast of Turkey, and for
years it has been a staging point for refugees attempting to make their
way from war zones in Central Asia and the Middle East to Europe. On
September 2, authorities reported the first confirmed case of COVID-19
at the island's Moria camp. Moria was built to house 3,000 refugees, but it
was home to some 13,000 displaced people from Afghanistan, Iraq, Syria,
and elsewhere, making it the largest such facility in Europe. Residents
at the camp lived cramped together in tents, with limited access to toi-
lets, showers, or health care services. To prevent the virus from reaching

Moria, strict movement restrictions had been instated by Greek authorities in February, and all new arrivals were tested and quarantined if they tested positive. Such measures kept COVID-19 out of the camp for months. But starting in mid-August, the number of cases increased in the island's capital, Mytilene, not far from the camp, and the virus managed to slip through the cracks.[78] Fearing conditions were ripe for the rapid spread of the contagion, authorities clamped down.

On September 8, camp residents protested new quarantines put in place after at least thirty-five refugees tested positive for COVID-19. Some desperate and furious individuals set fires—triggering a fast-moving blaze that quickly consumed most of the camp.[79] Suddenly, people already displaced by war and economic hardship found themselves displaced yet again, forced to sleep along roadsides or in nearby supermarket parking lots, gas stations, and cemeteries. Meanwhile, the thirty-five camp residents who had tested positive had gone missing, sparking fears among the island's citizens that the refugees would spread the virus across Lesbos. The now homeless refugees demanded that they be allowed to leave the island to make their way to Europe, but Konstantinos Kostakos, the director of the Greek migration minister's office, made it clear that "the Greek government will not be blackmailed. What happened—this 'burn and go' tactic—will not be tolerated."[80] New protests erupted, and riot police responded with tear gas. The refugees and migrants were relocated to Kara Tepe, a hastily constructed camp nearby that was even more squalid and uninhabitable than Moria.[81]

According to the United Nations, from 2000 to 2019, the number of international migrants worldwide increased from 174 million to 272 million.[82] Many of these migrants left their homes in search of greater economic opportunity elsewhere, while others fled civil war, collapsing states, horrific levels of criminal violence, persecution, and environmental disaster. At the beginning of 2020, the UN High Commissioner for Refugees estimated that there were almost 80 million displaced people around the globe, including nearly 46 million internally displaced individuals, approximately 30 million refugees, and around 4 million people awaiting the outcome of asylum requests. This startling statistic—more than 1 percent of the world's population—represented the highest level of displacement since World War II. About two-thirds came from just five countries: Syria, Venezuela, Afghanistan, South Sudan, and Myanmar.

And around 85 percent of refugees were hosted in developing nations, typically a country neighboring the one they fled.[83]

As COVID-19 spread throughout the developing world, the international community braced for a brutal outcome. Most anticipated the contagion would be impossible to contain once it found a foothold inside refugee camps. After all, the majority of low- and middle-income nations that held refugees struggled to provide basic services even during normal times. Moreover, a huge proportion of refugees live in crowded camps with limited sanitation and little access to soap or clean water—conditions ripe for disaster.[84] In April, David Miliband, the CEO and president of the International Rescue Committee, predicted "death on an absolutely appalling scale."[85]

By the fall of 2020, the virus had been detected in dozens of camps for refugees and internally displaced people across the world, including camps in Cox's Bazar in Bangladesh housing 745,000 Rohingya refugees from Myanmar as well as camps in Greece, Iraq, Jordan, Kenya, Lebanon, the Palestinian territories, Syria, and elsewhere. Yet the reported number of confirmed cases and deaths from the disease remained modest through the autumn and winter. None of the world's largest refugee camps reported widespread COVID-19 outbreaks, likely due to the isolation of these camps.[86] Some speculated that the low numbers were due to a lack of testing and that it was only a matter of time before the unseen virus picked up momentum. "There is consensus that there is community transmission going on, but we don't know the extent to which people are getting infected," Mercy Laker, a deputy country director for Care in South Sudan, said in September. "So it's definitely a time bomb."[87] Regardless, for the moment, the absence of major outbreaks seemed to represent a sliver of good news in an otherwise bleak landscape.

That did not mean displaced people were spared—far from it. Living conditions for refugees, already precarious, deteriorated, and many asylum seekers had their petitions denied. At the height of the pandemic, 168 countries closed borders, and 90 of those countries refused to make exceptions for those seeking asylum.[88] As they responded to the pandemic and the economic fallout, host nations often excluded refugees from assistance programs aimed at protecting vulnerable populations. Jobs and incomes for refugees evaporated as well. In places where refugees manage to find work, they typically do so in the informal sector.

As we saw in the previous chapter, these were precisely the type of jobs most threatened by the COVID-19 crisis, with one study estimating that refugees were 60 percent more likely than others to work in jobs highly impacted by the pandemic and the economic downturn.[89] In September, a Norwegian Refugee Council survey of internally displaced people and refugees in fourteen countries found that 77 percent had lost a job or income since March 2020, 71 percent had difficulty affording rent or housing, and 70 percent had been forced to reduce the number of meals in their households.[90] In Turkey, for example, economic difficulties caused many Syrian refugees to lose their jobs and meager incomes, while forcing others to accept jobs others refused to do because of the higher risks of catching COVID-19.[91] Regionwide, the UN estimated that the rate of extreme poverty for Syrian refugees increased from a pre-pandemic level of 55 percent to 75 percent by September.[92]

As the pressure on fragile states and at-risk populations grew, efforts by UN agencies, nongovernmental organizations, and their partners to ramp up assistance to vulnerable refugee populations faced significant challenges. Travel restrictions and lockdowns prompted by the pandemic disrupted aid shipments to refugee camps.[93] And some nongovernmental organizations were forced to decrease the number of staff going into camps in order to reduce the risk of bringing the virus with them.[94] Humanitarian staffing in Rohingya camps in Bangladesh, for example, was reduced by 80 percent to help control the spread of COVID-19—a trade-off that essentially removed the support such personnel provided.[95] While reported cases inside the camps remained low, the fear of what might happen if the contagion picked up speed inside their overcrowded confines was substantial. "The combination of the size of the camps and a pandemic is something completely new. Both aid agencies and the state are facing challenges," Pablo Percelsi, the head of the International Committee of the Red Cross delegation in Bangladesh, said in September. "If something goes wrong, it could lead to very bad consequences."[96]

Furthermore, travel restrictions and border closures temporarily froze migration across much of the globe, leaving many would-be migrants stranded.[97] For the same reason, asylum-seekers found themselves increasingly stuck as countries shut their doors and the UN suspended all travel for refugee resettlement. In the 1990s, on average 1.5 million refugees were able to return to their country of origin each year. Over the past decade, that number has declined to around 385,000. With Trump in office, the United States moved to significantly curtail the number of asylum cases it would consider, setting a restrictionist example for other nations to follow. The pandemic made this increasingly bleak situation even worse.[98]

These problems are not likely to abate anytime soon. As the virus lingers in many conflict zones and poorer nations, and the economic hangover produces higher rates of unemployment across the globe, there will be considerable political pressure to continue keeping migrants and refugees out. As a consequence, it may be difficult, if not impossible, for many migrants and refugees fleeing hardship and violence to find safe harbor for years to come.

Demagogues and Democracy

WHEN THE NOVEL coronavirus made landfall in the mountainous South American nation of Bolivia in March 2020, the country was in the midst of a political transition. Or so it seemed.

In November 2019, Bolivia's socialist president, Evo Morales, fled the country after fourteen years in office. During his long tenure, Morales—a charismatic left-wing populist and the country's first indigenous president—gained widespread acclaim for his focus on Bolivia's deep inequalities and injustices. His policies helped cut the number of Bolivians living in extreme poverty by more than half, improving the lives of millions, including many indigenous Bolivians who had long been marginalized by the country's white elite.[1] But Morales was also a deeply polarizing figure, both at home and across Latin America's intense left-right ideological divide. And the longer he remained in office, the more allegations of corruption and abuses of power—including the persecution of opponents, harassment of journalists, and the erosion of judicial independence—surrounded him.

Weeks before he went into exile, Morales had declared a narrow victory that would have given him an unprecedented (and constitutionally questionable) fourth term. Observers from the Organization of American States (OAS), however, concluded the elections were riddled with irregularities and fraud, raising the prospect that he may have manipulated computer databases used to tally votes to stay in power.[2] Protests erupted across the country, triggering strikes and disruptive roadblocks in Bolivia's biggest cities, and pro- and anti-Morales demonstrators clashed violently in the streets. Mutinies among the country's security services ensued: police officers joined the protests, and commanders of the Bolivian military and national police stepped in to "suggest" that the president resign. On November 10, Morales resigned and, fearing for his life, sought refuge in his rural stronghold in the central coca-growing region of Chapare. The next day he fled to Mexico on a private jet sent by Mexican president and left-leaning populist Andrés Manuel López Obrador. In December, Morales was granted asylum in Argentina.

In a country with a history of 190 revolutions and military coups, Morales's supporters saw his removal as yet one more military usurpation of democracy. To his critics, however, it represented liberation from a creeping socialist autocracy.[3] The country seemed to be at an inflection point—but the future remained highly uncertain.

With Morales gone, the next three officials in the line of succession—all members of Morales's Movement Toward Socialism (MAS) party—resigned, making Jeanine Áñez, the second vice president of the Senate, the country's interim president. A little-known far-right senator, Áñez promised to run a caretaker government, unify the country, and respect the prospect of a new free and fair election scheduled for May 2020. She also pledged not to run herself and to step aside once a new leader was selected.

Nevertheless, Áñez immediately began maneuvering to stay in power, weaponizing the state apparatus to attack her MAS opponents. She greenlit a violent crackdown on pro-Morales protesters, granting security forces free rein to reestablish order. They did so with impunity, allegedly killing twenty-three indigenous anti-government demonstrators.[4] Inside the administration, Áñez stacked her cabinet with conservative ministers and, though Bolivia's constitution defines the country as a secular state, quickly infused Catholicism into the trappings of government. The move rallied Bolivia's conservative religious groups to her side while creating considerable anxiety among the nation's majority indigenous population.[5] As she strode into the presidential palace for the first time, in front of right-wing allies and the media, Áñez brazenly hoisted a large leather-bound Bible over her head and declared, "The Bible has returned to the palace."[6]

Other swift actions were taken to overturn Morales's left-wing geo-political alignment in the region. Seven hundred Cuban doctors providing public health care across Bolivia were expelled, full diplomatic relations with the United States and Israel were restored, and the government swung behind the Trump administration's efforts to pressure the Nicolás Maduro regime in Venezuela. Morales's legacy was purged at every turn.

On January 24, 2020, barely two months after assuming the role of interim president, Áñez reversed her earlier commitment, announcing her candidacy in the upcoming election. Then COVID-19 emerged, creating a convenient opportunity for Áñez to continue her power play.[7] On March 17, shortly after Bolivia confirmed its first two cases, she implemented a strict national quarantine, suspending public transportation and imposing stay-at-home orders (only one person from each household was permitted to leave their home once a week). A week later, citing the pandemic as a reason, she announced that the May election would be indefinitely postponed. She then issued Supreme Decree 4200, imposing criminal charges (including up to ten years in jail) for any "individuals who incite non-compliance" or "misinform or cause uncertainty to the population," again under the guise of pandemic response.[8] The criminalization of "disinformation" was later expanded to allow charges against anyone who published information the government deemed to generate uncertainty or put public health at risk in any medium, including print, online, and through artistic expression.[9]

As the coronavirus crept across the country, the government seemed more focused on targeting opponents than grappling with the outbreak. Within a month of Supreme Decree 4200's implementation, sixty-seven "political actors" were arrested.[10] In late April, police in riot gear raided the home of a MAS Senate candidate, arresting her and several others for violating quarantine orders.[11] Meanwhile, government prosecutors were pressured to target more than 100 former MAS officials and supporters with corruption, sedition, and terrorism charges. The MAS-majority parliament was also intimidated by senior military officials to get in line and bend to the will of the interim president.[12]

On April 30, the Bolivian parliament passed a law requiring that the presidential election occur within ninety days. Áñez immediately accused the MAS opposition of putting the lives of Bolivians at risk in an

attempt to regain control of the country.[13] And despite the legislative action, the interim president managed to keep the election further at bay.

Yet, ironically, while Áñez sought to seize on COVID-19 to solidify
her grip, the government's inept response to the worsening outbreak
threatened it. During lockdown, little had been done to assist the millions of Bolivians laboring in the country's informal sector with no economic safety net, estimated to make up around 83 percent of the country's
workforce.[14] This not only undermined support for her government but
also ensured that many struggling Bolivians would ignore stay-at-home
orders to scrape out a living. By the beginning of May, the number of
recorded COVID-19 cases in Bolivia had increased to around 1,200 with
66 confirmed deaths. In June, to lessen the severe economic strain, the
government was forced to relax some public health restrictions. Predictably, infections spiked. Prior to the easing of restrictions, the country
had recorded more than 10,500 cases and 343 deaths. A month after they
were lifted, the numbers jumped to 34,000 and 1,200, respectively.

As the virus spun out of control, rumors of miracle cures circulated.
Politicians and popular public figures promoted the notion that drinking
chlorine dioxide—a disinfectant normally used to clean swimming pools
and floors—could keep the virus at bay. Desperate Bolivians with little
access to hospitals lined up to buy the elixir.[15] By August, COVID-19
infections had skyrocketed to nearly 79,000 cases and more than 3,000
deaths. In a country of only 11.5 million people, this toll represented one
of the highest death rates per capita in the world. As Bolivia's under-
funded and beleaguered health system was swamped and funeral homes
and cemeteries were inundated, the actual numbers were difficult to verify. An analysis of excess deaths between March and August by the New
York Times suggested the real death toll might be nearly five times higher
than the official figures.[16] The economic impact was also brutal, with the
World Bank estimating that the Bolivian economy declined by 7.3 percent in 2020, while poverty increased by almost nine percentage points
(from 22 to 31 percent).[17]

Áñez's machinations were widely seen as undermining Bolivia's effort to forge a coherent response to the outbreak. "She is not recognized
as a legitimate leader," Santiago Anria, a professor of political science
and Latin American studies at Dickinson College in Pennsylvania, told
the New York Times, "which makes it extremely difficult to coordinate a

complex response that the pandemic requires."[18] Corruption further gutted the government's credibility. In May, Áñez's health minister Marcelo Navajas was arrested on charges that he had used money from international donors to buy hospital ventilators for twice as much as they were worth.[19]

As was the case with a number of other world leaders, in early July Áñez tested positive for COVID-19, along with half of her cabinet, including the new health minister, María Eidy Roca. The contagion's advance into the corridors of power contributed to the nationwide sense that Bolivia had simply been overwhelmed by the pandemic.[20] Áñez recovered from the coronavirus, but her political prospects continued to sink.

That same month, in a move seen as yet another attempt by Áñez to consolidate power, Bolivia's electoral court again delayed elections from September 6 to October 18.[21] The reaction was immediate and fierce. Nearly 150,000 labor unionists, miners, coca leaf farmers, indigenous activists, and other MAS supporters took to the streets. They used sandbags, piles of wood, and burning tires to set up dozens of roadblocks across the mountainous country, paralyzing Bolivia's already weakened economy. The disruptions also blocked ambulances, cutting off some patients from critical medical supplies—as a result, at least thirty patients died from shortages of oxygen and other equipment.[22]

The demonstrators saw all of this as necessary. "We are in a dictatorship, and we are in the streets because we want a return to democracy," Segundina Orellana, executive director of the group of coca leaf farmers, told the *Washington Post*. Áñez "has used the pandemic as a pretext to cling to power. We want immediate elections," she continued. "We are the majority in this country, and we will not allow them to treat us like this."[23]

Back in April, Áñez had been leading in a field of eight candidates, with 69 percent of Bolivians approving of her management of the COVID crisis. But as the deaths piled up, her lead diminished.[24] Once the protests began, Áñez was polling significantly behind conservative front-runner Carlos Mesa and MAS candidate Luis Arce, a finance minister for former president Morales.[25] On September 17, when it became clear her presence was splitting the conservative vote, Áñez withdrew from the race.[26]

On October 18, 2020, almost a year to the day of Morales's escape into exile, Luis Arce won in a landslide. Promising a return to stability while eschewing the antidemocratic excesses that had come to define the

Morales period, Arce's platform resonated with the Bolivian people.[27] The OAS, which had criticized the 2019 vote, described the 2020 election as "exemplary."[28] And with the nation moving on and MAS back in power, the threat of prosecution for Morales abated, and the former president returned to the country shortly thereafter.

"I think the crisis of the last year did a lot of damage to Bolivian democracy, part of an accumulative process," Fernanda Wanderley, director of the socioeconomic institute at the Universidad Católica Boliviana, observed after the October election. "But in the end, Bolivia found a path to overcome that crisis, and was able to conduct a clean, legitimate election in which the winner was decided by the popular vote." In short, "democracy won in Bolivia," she said.[29]

As we shall see in this chapter and in Chapter 11, in numerous countries across the globe, illiberal leaders sought to capitalize on the pandemic to strengthen their authority, target opponents, erode civil liberties, and manipulate elections. Yet people pushed back, even under significant duress, suggesting the enduring hope for greater freedom and democracy held by millions of average people around the world.

THE GLOBAL DEMOCRATIC RECESSION

In 1991, the late Harvard University political scientist Samuel Huntington coined the phrase "the third wave" to describe a surge of political liberalization and democratic governance across the globe that started in the 1970s and 1980s and accelerated after the fall of the Berlin Wall in 1989 and the demise of the Soviet Union two years later. According to Huntington, the first wave involved the gradual spread of democracy in the nineteenth century, and the second occurred in the decades after World War II. Each wave was followed by reversals, with some countries slipping back into autocracy. Yet even if it felt like a two-steps-forward-one-step-back development, the aggregate number of democracies worldwide increased.[30] Then, as the Cold War ended, former Soviet republics and communist nations in eastern Europe moved toward greater political freedom. The end of superpower patronage also forced many military regimes and one-party dictatorships in the developing world to transition toward democracy. As a result, the third wave accelerated.

Using data from the organization Freedom House—which annually scores countries based on ten measures of political rights and fifteen measures of civil liberties—and other sources, Stanford University's Larry Diamond estimates that by 1993, the majority of countries with a minimum of 1 million people (seventy-seven in total) were democratic. According to Diamond, the number of democracies peaked in 2006 at eighty-six.[31] Another analysis, by the Varieties of Democracy Institute (V-Dem), based on an even more robust database of political indicators from 1789 to the present, found that the number of democracies reached its height at ninety-eight in 2010.[32]

Then things took a turn. During the 2010s, a "third wave of autocratization" took hold.[33] Trends were particularly bleak in the years immediately preceding the pandemic. According to Freedom House, twenty-two of the forty-one countries consistently rated "free" from 1985 to 2005 registered a net reduction in freedom in the five years before COVID-19 emerged.[34] V-Dem found that democracy declined in twenty-six countries in 2019 alone. For the first time since 2001, the majority of countries (ninety-two) were autocracies, and for the first time since the end of the Cold War, the majority of the world's people (54 percent) did not live in a democracy. All the trends seemed to be going in the wrong direction: 35 percent of the global population lived in countries undergoing autocratization, while only 8 percent lived in countries that were becoming more democratic.[35]

Some democracies in this period fell from uprisings and coups. For example, in 2013, Egypt's military rode popular unrest to overthrow the democratically elected government of Mohamed Morsi. In Thailand in 2014, a coup replaced a fragile democracy with a military junta. But more often, democratic backsliding emerged from illiberal leaders duly elected—such as Vladimir Putin in Russia, Hugo Chávez in Venezuela, Viktor Orbán in Hungary, Recep Tayyip Erdogan in Turkey, Sheikh Hasina in Bangladesh, Narendra Modi in India, Jaroslaw Kaczyński and Andrzej Duda in Poland, Rodrigo Duterte in the Philippines, Jair Bolsonaro in Brazil—who then chipped away at the institutional checks and balances, norms, and civil liberties that undergird free societies. These leaders seized on highly polarized political contexts, exploited economic and cultural anxieties, and deployed nationalist, antiestablishment, populist, and xenophobic appeals to win elections.[36] Once in office, they followed an illiberal "playbook" of sorts: extending executive power; limiting legislative oversight; compromising the independence of the judiciary, the military, and other government institutions; cracking down on political opposition, civil society, and the media; and controlling information while propagating disinformation.[37] And, as we will see, this playbook was tailor-made to take advantage of national crises such as a deadly pandemic.

The trend toward democratic backsliding has been further compounded by the shift in the global balance of power, with the United States and other advanced industrialized democracies increasingly challenged by a more assertive Russia and a rising China. The two authoritarian states differ in important ways: Russia has used its still considerable strategic assets to reassert itself despite long-term decline, while China is a rapidly rising superpower. Yet both have pursued similar goals: seeking to carve out military, political, and economic spheres of influence in their respective regions; undermining human rights and democratic norms that might otherwise endanger their regime's hold on the country; and aiming to end the American supremacy that emerged after the Cold War.[38]

Putin's Russia has pursued regional dominance by illegally annexing Crimea and supporting separatists in eastern Ukraine in an attempt to undermine its nascent democracy and prevent Kyiv's alignment with the West. The Kremlin has also used cyberattacks, covert and overt disinformation campaigns, and financial support to populist movements on the right and left to sow division within and between Western democracies. Putin has sought to influence referendums and elections in the United Kingdom, the United States, France, and elsewhere, with the aim of empowering movements and leaders skeptical of the transatlantic alliance. And Russia's vast oil and gas resources have been leveraged to coerce governments and buy influence in both eastern and western Europe.[39]

Under Xi Jinping, China has sought to become the preeminent power in Asia—flexing its muscles in the South China Sea, in the East China Sea, and across the Taiwan Strait—at the expense of the United States and its regional allies. China's Belt and Road Initiative (which involves seventy countries), new international economic institutions such as the Asian Infrastructure Investment Bank, and new multilateral agreements such as the fifteen-nation Regional Comprehensive Economic Partnership are all illustrative of Beijing's assertive pursuit of global influence.

It has made massive investments in emerging technologies such as 5G and artificial intelligence at home and then aggressively exported these technologies abroad. In doing so, Beijing has sought to influence global norms—consistent with its own regulatory and governing principles—that determine how these technologies are managed and used. As Xi has consolidated power and taken steps to increase the repressive apparatus of the Chinese Communist Party, he has held up China's blend of state-run capitalism and digital authoritarianism as a model superior to liberal democracy—an effort greatly aided by the economic and political struggles across the West in the aftermath of the 2008–9 global financial crisis.[40]

Meanwhile, America's ability to credibly push back against revisionist authoritarian powers has eroded. For decades, the United States saw itself as the leader of the so-called free world. After the Cold War, successive U.S. administrations sought to marry unrivaled military strength, economic power, and idealism in an effort to more expansively promote human rights and democracy. The democratic project was never simple, and America's performance at home and abroad has been far from perfect. Nonetheless, the democratic wave of the 1990s was very much the work of U.S. activism on the world stage. After 9/11, however, the nation-building fiascos in Afghanistan and, most critically, in Iraq greatly tarnished the perceived effectiveness and legitimacy of American democracy-promotion efforts.[41]

In the years before COVID-19, however, the biggest challenges to America's ability to stand up for democracy around the world—and serve as a "shining city on a hill," as Ronald Reagan liked to say—were much closer to home. Even before Donald Trump became president, hyperpartisanship, polarization, growing inequality, and the outsized role of money in politics had made the nation increasingly unrepresentative and dysfunctional. Trump's win in 2016 made this all the more apparent. Tragically, his own illiberal playbook mirrored the actions of autocrats abroad: winning the White House on the back of populism and nativism, fanning the flames of xenophobia and racism, ignoring congressional oversight, attacking the independence of courts, and compromising the apolitical nature of law enforcement, intelligence agencies, and the military. He flagrantly ignored the rule of law, denigrated the free press, and actively spread disinformation. With Trump, the United States abandoned its long-standing tradition of championing human rights and democracy around the world. America's closest democratic alliances in Europe and Asia were treated as transactional protection rackets instead of ironclad security commitments. Meanwhile, the world's autocrats and strongmen, including Putin, Xi, Erdogan, Orbán, Duterte, Bolsonaro, Kim Jong-un (North Korea), Mohammed bin Salman (Saudi Arabia), and Abdel Fattah al-Sisi (Egypt) found a supplicating American president eager to embrace their brand of leadership.[42]

PANDEMIC BACKSLIDING

Like so many of the global trends explored in this book, COVID-19 accentuated already precarious democratic conditions around the world. While the emergency measures adopted in most established democracies did not fundamentally undermine liberal democratic principles, the pandemic was seen as an opportunity to consolidate power by illiberal leaders in several countries with weaker democratic institutions. Jeanine Áñez attempted to run this play in Bolivia but failed. Others had more success.[43]

In the Philippines, President Rodrigo Duterte—who had spent years eroding the country's democratic institutions and attacking civil liberties—exploited the pandemic to get Congress to pass legislation in mid-March that gave him sweeping unilateral powers to both respond to the crisis and crack down on those who spread "false information" (that is, anyone who disagreed with official messaging). As Duterte touted his new authority to "move, decide, and act freely for the best interest of the Filipino people during this health crisis," prominent Philippine human rights groups described his actions as "tantamount to autocracy."[44] These executive authorities were extended in August and then again in September (for a year), prompting fears that Duterte intended to impose a permanent state of emergency on the fragile democratic nation.[45]

In India, Prime Minister Narendra Modi—backed by his Hindu-nationalist Bharatiya Janata Party—also used emergency responses to the pandemic to consolidate his grip. Government measures disempowered India's states and marginalized parliamentary opposition. Critics of Modi's lockdown, including journalists and activists, were commonly harassed. And BJP officials scapegoated the country's large Muslim-minority population, accusing them of being superspreaders. All of this exacerbated the backsliding evident in the world's largest democracy since Modi and the BJP came to power in 2014.[46]

In neighboring Sri Lanka, a similar story played out, but with two power-hungry brothers at the center of it. In November 2019, just months before the pandemic arrived in the country, Gotabaya Rajapaksa was elected as Sri Lanka's new president. He had been the nation's defense minister from 2005 to 2015 and had overseen the defeat of the Tamil Tiger separatists in 2009 after twenty-six brutal years of suicide bombings and war. He owed his position to his brother, Mahinda Rajapaksa, who was president at the time. Mahinda Rajapaksa's decade of rule was notable for his efforts to enhance executive powers at the expense of Parliament, compromise the independence of the judiciary, and undermine the rule of law. When the brothers lost power in 2015, it looked like Sri Lanka was turning the page and moving toward more democratic and accountable governance.[47]

Four years later, however, a series of bombings on Easter Sunday by Islamic State militants created an opportunity for Gotabaya Rajapaksa to leverage his reputation for fighting terrorists to return the family to power.[48] This time it was Gotabaya as president, with Mahinda appointed as prime minister. There was just one problem: the Rajapaksa brothers lacked a working majority in the legislature. So in early March, Gotabaya Rajapaksa dissolved Parliament, with the aim of holding new elections on April 25 to win a two-thirds majority for his Sri Lanka Podujana Peramuna (SLPP) party.

Just as the Rajapaksa brothers were working to re-create their past dominance of Sri Lankan politics, the pandemic offered them a golden opportunity to use emergency powers to do so. The country confirmed its first case of COVID-19 on January 27 after a Chinese tourist visiting the country fell ill, and by March the contagion began spreading within its borders. Soon thereafter, the government imposed a monthslong nationwide curfew.[49] In the weeks following the dissolution of the legislature in March, as the outbreak worsened, the country's National Elections Commission decided to indefinitely delay the April parliamentary elections because of the threat from the disease. This hurtled the country into uncharted territory. Because Sri Lanka's constitution specifies that Parliament can remain dissolved for no more than three months before an election must be held, the country entered political limbo. For the first time in its modern history, the president would be able to rule without legislative oversight.[50]

President Rajapaksa moved swiftly to exploit the political vacuum, appointing former military officials to key ministry posts. Meanwhile, he used lockdown orders—which proved relatively effective in containing the virus—to crack down on journalists, lawyers, human rights activists, and others opposing the government.[51] Anyone who criticized or contradicted the official line on the coronavirus became vulnerable to arrest. And, as was the case in India, Sri Lanka's Muslim minority population was accused of spreading COVID-19, with some members of government blaming Muslims for the inability of other Sri Lankan communities to celebrate the Sinhala and Tamil New Year.[52]

Parliamentary elections were finally held in August, with Mahinda Rajapaksa serving as the face of the SLPP campaign. The party won in a landslide, securing enough seats (in combination with allied parties) for a two-thirds majority. The outcome set the Rajapaksa family up to once again push the country in a more autocratic direction.[53] Within two months, the Parliament passed the twentieth amendment to the Sri Lankan constitution, weakening the powers of the prime minister and Parliament and granting virtually unfettered authority to the presidency. In an odd addition, the amendment also specified that Sri Lankans of dual nationality could now serve in Parliament or as president, opening the way for yet another brother, Basil Rajapaksa, to enter the legislature and cement the family's dynastic future.[54]

Halfway around the world, Hungary offers perhaps the starkest example of a would-be autocrat taking advantage of the pandemic. The country was a vibrant liberal democracy at the turn of the century. But in the decade before COVID-19, Prime Minister Viktor Orbán and his populist-nationalist Fidesz party changed laws and regulations, amended the country's constitution, and took other steps to systematically dismantle Hungary's democratic norms and institutions. Executive powers were enhanced, the judiciary and key state institutions lost their political independence, and measures were taken to coerce and censor independent journalists and news organizations. All the while, Orbán called for the defense of Christian civilization against foreign influence and the supposed onslaught of immigrants and refugees (especially from Muslim nations). Orbán took pride in transforming his country into what he described as an "illiberal democracy."[55]

By 2020, however, the democracy part of Orbán's formulation was very much in doubt. When COVID-19 arrived, Hungary was already on the cusp of becoming the first authoritarian regime in the European Union.[56] Then, on March 30, when the country had around sixty confirmed cases, Orbán was granted vast powers under the guise of combating the virus. This included the authority to suspend existing laws, indefinitely rule by decree, and punish anyone "disseminating false information."[57] According to R. Daniel Kelemen, a professor of political science and law at Rutgers University, Hungary became the world's first "coronavirus autocracy."[58] On June 18, Parliament voted to end these emergency powers. But the seeming rollback was a mirage. The new law permitted the government to reintroduce rule by decree whenever it declared a state of public health emergency, without need for a parliamentary vote. In other words, it did not eliminate emergency powers so much as normalize them. "There is no place to step back from here," Zoltán Fleck, a law professor and director at the Károly Eötvös Institute, a pro-democracy organization in Budapest, told the *New York Times*. "They have worked very successfully to make permanent the essence of such emergency situations."[59] In November, as the second wave of the pandemic swept across Europe, the state of emergency was reinstated. "We have to put aside political debates, fast action and measures brought in time are needed," Orbán said, citing the prospect of surging coronavirus cases to once again reassert rule by decree.[60]

ELECTION GAMES

Holding an election in the midst of a pandemic is, to say the least, a fraught affair. But the first country to attempt a nationwide election during the COVID crisis, South Korea, was actually a success story. As we saw in Chapter 6, the country's effective early response to the virus was one of the few bright spots in the world. Its election, held in April 2020, was no different. The South Korean government did not make voters choose between voting and protecting their health. It took proactive steps to ensure voting could be conducted safely. Voting by mail and early in-person voting were expanded to reduce crowd sizes on election day. More than half a million government workers and volunteers were mobilized to disinfect 14,000 polling places. Separate polling stations were also set up in hospitals so COVID-19 patients could vote. Voters were required to wear masks and were given hand sanitizer and gloves upon their arrival at the polls. Every voter was subject to a temperature check, and if a voter's temperature was too high, they were directed to a special voting place. Lines were marked to ensure each voter was appropriately spaced from the others, and the floors were covered with paper to ensure the facilities were not contaminated. The voting places were repeatedly cleaned throughout the day. As a result, the election was conducted safely and credibly, and it produced the highest voter turnout in nearly three decades.[61]

Elsewhere, however, many governments seemed less interested in conducting elections safely than in using COVID-19 to manipulate the timing and conduct of elections in their favor. In Burundi, for example, after fifteen years of autocratic rule by President Pierre Nkurunziza, a forthcoming election held promise of a potential democratic turnaround. Yet in the spring of 2020, the government used the pandemic to stack the deck in favor of Nkurunziza's hand-picked successor, Évariste Ndayishimiye. In the lead-up to the May 20 vote, the government downplayed the risk of the coronavirus. It expelled the country's WHO representative for raising concerns about holding large election rallies. And it took few precautions to protect people going to the polls. Then, on election day, the government imposed a complete social media blackout and used COVID-19 quarantine requirements to justify blocking regional election observers from confirming the fairness of the process. Despite allegations of massive fraud, Ndayishimiye was declared the winner.[62]

That same month, in Poland, incumbent president Andrzej Duda—backed by the nationalist Law and Justice Party (PiS)—also hoped to move forward with elections. Duda sought to exploit the fact that lockdown orders essentially prevented the opposition from campaigning. Meanwhile, he remained free to hold public events and benefit from favorable coverage by state-controlled media.[63] To address COVID concerns, PiS hastily organized an all mail-in ballot system. But, under pressure from the opposition, the election was delayed to late June to accommodate the possibility of safely voting in person. It did not make much of a difference. While in the ensuing weeks Poland's strict lockdown was loosened, the government maintained its ban on large public gatherings. Duda thus retained his significant advantage in holding campaign events. In a field of eleven candidates, Duda—whose campaign was notable for its anti-LGBTQ and xenophobic rhetoric—ultimately received 44 percent of the vote, compared to the 30 percent secured by his chief rival, Rafał Trzaskowski, the liberal mayor of Warsaw. Duda then narrowly defeated Trzaskowski 51 to 49 percent in a runoff two weeks later, further entrenching Poland's slide toward illiberal populism.[64]

These were not isolated examples. All told, from late February 2020 through March 2021, the International Institute for Democracy and Electoral Assistance found that at least forty-one countries and territories postponed national elections or referendums due to COVID-19.[65] In many instances, these decisions were temporary and justifiable based on public health concerns. In September 2020, for example, New Zealand delayed its election for fear of a renewed spike in COVID-19 cases. A month later, the vote went forward without incident, with Prime Minister Jacinda Ardern and her Labour Party decisively winning reelection, in part due to Ardern's admirable handling of the pandemic.[66] But postponements in a number of other countries seemed to be motivated at least in part by the desire of leaders to cling to power.

That appeared to be the case in Ethiopia—and the implications proved disastrous. In the spring of 2018, a wave of popular protests brought the reformist prime minister Abiy Ahmed to power. Abiy moved quickly to make peace with Eritrea (for which he won the Nobel Peace Prize in 2019) and to push for democratic reforms. This included dismantling the Ethiopian People's Revolutionary Democratic Front (EPRDF)—a coalition of four main political parties, largely divided along ethnic and geographic lines—that had ruled the country since 1991. The effort represented a particular affront to Ethiopia's Tigrayan ethnic minority. Tigray, the northernmost region of Ethiopia, is home to only 6 percent of the country's 110 million people, but the Tigray People's Liberation Front (TPLF) had long dominated the EPRDF coalition. The TPLF, infuriated by the purging of Tigrayan officials from the government and the arrest of numerous TPLF associates on corruption and other charges, refused to join Abiy's new Prosperity Party. As a consequence, in 2019, frictions mounted between the Tigray region and the Abiy government.[67]

In a country with a long history of repression and questionable elections, Abiy promised to hold Ethiopia's first truly free and fair elections in fifteen years in August 2020. But in March, elections were postponed due to concerns about COVID-19, though at the time Ethiopia only had twenty-five confirmed cases.[68] Then, in June, Abiy's government announced that elections would be indefinitely delayed, saying the vote would be held nine to twelve months after health officials deemed the pandemic under control. The decision effectively extended the terms of Ethiopia's current federal and regional governments (due to expire in early October) beyond their five-year constitutional mandate. This was all presented as a prudent response to emergency conditions. But to the TPLF and other critics, it appeared as if Abiy was maneuvering to unconstitutionally extend his power.[69]

In defiance, in September the Tigray region went forward with an election of its own, but Abiy's government refused to acknowledge it. Tigray, in return, declared it would not recognize the Abiy administration beyond the expiration of its original term on October 5 (the term Abiy had unilaterally extended). The federal government responded by suspending funding and cutting ties with Tigray, a move the region described as "tantamount to a declaration of war." Rhetoric then turned to action. On November 4, the government launched a bombing campaign and ground offensive against the region after accusing the TPLF of attacking a federal military base in west Tigray.[70] Two weeks later, in a bizarre twist, the Ethiopian army chief of staff used a television address to accuse WHO director general Tedros Adhanom Ghebreyesus, a former member of the TPLF who had previously served as the country's health minister, of helping provide arms to Tigrayan fighters.[71] As the country seemed to tip into civil war, thousands were killed and as many as 2 million people (about one-third of the Tigrayan population) were displaced, including tens of thousands who fled into neighboring Sudan. At the end of November, the Ethiopian army eventually seized the Tigrayan capital, Mekele, declaring victory. But the TPLF retreated to the mountains and pledged to fight on, raising the prospect that Ethiopia could face a long and costly insurgency.[72]

Rights, Robots, and Resistance

THE SMALL, LANDLOCKED nation of Rwanda had big reasons to worry about COVID-19. With 13 million people in a country roughly the size of Massachusetts, Rwanda had the second-highest population density on the African continent (after Mauritius), making it vulnerable to rapid transmission. And, despite providing nearly universal health care to its citizens, the low-income nation had limited resources, with only one doctor per 10,000 citizens and very few intensive care units. All of this put a premium on early containment.[1] So President Paul Kagame's government had to act fast.

In January, a few months before it reported its first case, the Rwandan government deployed fever scanners and handwashing stations to all border posts and stationed medical staff at Kigali International Airport to screen travelers for the coronavirus. As the threat grew, the government moved swiftly to impose some of the most stringent measures deployed anywhere in the world. In early March, it banned gatherings at places of worship, schools, weddings, and sporting events. Nonessential businesses were shuttered, and social distancing and hygiene requirements were imposed across the country, with special protective measures implemented for those parts of the economy—such as agricultural collection centers—that were allowed to stay open. Borders were closed, flights into the country were banned, and domestic travel between cities and districts was suspended. The government also encouraged the use of mobile money apps and online banking to limit physical interactions. On March 21, the government imposed a nationwide stay-at-home order. In late April, the lockdown was loosened, but the government put in place a mask mandate for all public places and multifamily compounds. A night-time curfew was also maintained, and places of worship and schools remained closed.[2]

As was the case in many other countries that acted quickly, recent experience contending with infectious diseases appeared to play a role in shaping the Rwandan government's actions. In particular, Rwanda's history of combating HIV/AIDS and its success in preventing the 2019 Ebola epidemic in the Democratic Republic of the Congo from crossing its border clearly contributed to the rapidity and seriousness of its response to COVID-19.

Kagame's government also employed a number of innovations to keep the virus at bay. To account for limited COVID-19 testing capacity, the government used a rapid "pool testing" approach that evaluated batches of samples from groups of people and then tested them individually only if a certain batch came back positive. Rwandan mathematicians designed a special algorithm to help lab technicians decide how many samples to pool and how many individuals from the pool to test if there were positive results. As of the end of September, Rwanda had conducted 37,000 tests per million people, ranking it third in Africa. Those who tested positive were mandated to stay in a government-run COVID-19 clinic and their contacts were required to quarantine.[3]

Rwanda's approach to surveillance and enforcement combined a mix of low- and high-tech strategies. The country's security services were authorized to ensure compliance with lockdown orders and movement restrictions, and health care workers, police, and even college students were mobilized as contact tracers. Meanwhile, the government used cutting-edge technologies, including human-sized robots in COVID-19 clinics to take patients' temperatures, deliver medicines, and detect if patients were not wearing masks. Above the skies of Rwanda's capital, Kigali, drones were used by police to identify those violating prohibitions against large gatherings and other infractions. Drones were also deployed to spread public health messages (complementing government-sponsored TV and radio awareness campaigns) and to transport protective equipment, test samples, and medical supplies between cities and distant rural areas.[4]

From a public health perspective, the country's aggressive strategy appeared to pay significant dividends. Compliance rates were high, with cellphone data suggesting that Rwanda was second only to South Africa on the African continent in terms of physical distancing.[5] By the end of 2020, Rwanda had recorded only 8,383 COVID-19 cases and 92 deaths. As was the case in many other countries, Rwanda was hit by a significant second wave of the pandemic in the new year. Despite a renewed lockdown, cases surged to nearly 22,000 by the end of March 2021. Nevertheless, with only 307 confirmed fatalities by that point, Rwanda's deaths per capita still remained among the lowest in the world.[6]

There was a more troubling side to the Rwandan government's response, however—one consistent with a long-standing pattern of repressive governance under Kagame and his Rwandan Patriotic Front (RPF) party. Together, they rose to power in 1994 after ousting the Hutu extremists responsible for the mass killing of 800,000 ethnic Tutsis and moderate Hutus during the Rwandan genocide. Kagame formally became president in 2000, and the country's 2003 constitution granted him expansive executive powers and the ability to remain president until 2034. Two decades later, Kagame's government had overseen an extended period of stability and economic development, leading to significant reductions in poverty, improvements in health and education, and women's empowerment. But the regime's rule was also grounded in widespread surveillance and the near-complete suppression of political dissent.[7]

Emergency measures during the pandemic played into these authoritarian tendencies. By the late summer of 2020, more than 70,000 people had been arrested for violating COVID-related restrictions, such as curfews and mask mandates. Detained individuals were often taken to sports stadiums where they could be questioned and forced to listen, under armed guard, to all-night lectures about the dangers of the coronavirus. Those violating mask requirements more than twice could be jailed for up to a year. The government also arrested journalists and human rights activists for reporting on abuses by police enforcing government restrictions. Meanwhile, Rwandan police signaled that they intended to use the surveillance technologies deployed to enforce public health measures to help maintain order and security even after the pandemic was over.[8] "Policing is more efficient with technology," a police spokesperson told the *Wall Street Journal* in September. "We are in a much better control of the situation than before."[9]

CIVIL LIBERTIES UNDER EMERGENCY

The Rwandan case is emblematic of a fundamental dilemma posed by pandemics. By their very nature, significant public health emergencies require decisive government action. As we discussed in Part II of this book, governments that moved swiftly to deploy measures to encourage social distancing, impose stay-at-home orders where necessary, restrict movement, provide widespread testing and contact tracing, and isolate ill individuals were generally better positioned to slow the spread of COVID-19. But aggressive action and strict enforcement of public health measures can easily bleed into abuses of civil liberties. The threat of a deadly contagion and the nature of containment measures can provide an all-too-tempting rationale and toolkit for leaders to crack down on dissent. While most consolidated democracies kept emergency measures largely within the constraints of their respective constitutions during the COVID-19 crisis, this was not the case in many countries where commitments to basic freedoms and the rule of law were already fragile.[10]

Across the world, the pandemic was used to accelerate the assault on civil liberties. Governments in Bangladesh, Ghana, India, Nigeria, the Philippines, Russia, Serbia, Tanzania, Turkey, Zimbabwe, and elsewhere used COVID-19 as a rationale to fine, harass, arrest, and drive journalists into hiding for spreading "fake news"—that is, any information at odds with the government's public line about the pandemic.[11] All told, by the fall of 2020, 47 percent of countries in the world had imposed some restrictions on the media as part of their response to the coronavirus, and 38 percent had imposed pandemic-related restrictions on free speech and criticism of the government.[12]

In several countries, health care workers attempting to provide warnings and truthful information about COVID-19 outbreaks were targeted. As we saw in Chapter 4, Chinese officials cracked down on doctors seeking to warn their colleagues about the novel coronavirus early in the outbreak. Similar steps were taken by governments in Egypt, Kyrgyzstan, Russia, and Venezuela to silence and arrest health workers accused of disseminating information at odds with the regime's public line on the pandemic.[13] In one extreme example, three front-line doctors in Russia who had been critical of their government's response to the crisis mysteriously fell from hospital windows; two of them died and the third was sent to the hospital in critical condition.[14]

Broadly, public health measures were seized upon to crack down on regime critics, civil society leaders, and political opposition figures in Azerbaijan, Bangladesh, the Balkans, Cambodia, Thailand, Venezuela, Zimbabwe, and elsewhere.[15] Large-scale arbitrary arrests, excessive force, and other abuses by police and military forces enforcing lockdowns were reported in El Salvador, Kenya, Liberia, Nigeria, the Philippines, South Africa, Uganda, and numerous other countries.[16] By October, Freedom House had documented detentions and arrests linked to the pandemic response in at least sixty-six countries and found evidence of police violence against civilians in at least fifty-nine countries. These abuses were most common in authoritarian countries and partial democracies.[17]

BRAVE NEW WORLD

As governments sought to monitor and slow the spread of COVID-19, many turned to new high-tech tools. Some seemed both sensible and relatively benign, such as the use of medical robots in a handful of countries to minimize the exposure of front-line health workers to COVID-19. In early March, for example, China constructed a "smart field hospital" in Wuhan completely run by medical robots and other Internet of Things devices.[18]

More troubling was the deployment of robotic surveillance tools. China repurposed and reprogrammed drones to spray disinfectant, deliver medical samples, chastise people for being out of their homes and for not wearing masks, check for fevers at a distance using thermal imaging, and otherwise monitor and enforce the world's biggest quarantine.[19] In India, authorities in Delhi and across the country used drones to sanitize large areas, monitor traffic, and identify lockdown violators.[20] Spanish police used drones to blast warning messages telling people in Madrid to vacate public parks and stay inside during the country's declaration of an emergency in March.[21] That same month, in the French city of Nice, drones were used to monitor compliance with travel restrictions and social distancing; two months later, the Conseil d'État (one of

France's supreme courts) banned the use of drones for COVID-related surveillance on privacy grounds.[22]

Even more pervasive was the proliferation of mobile smartphone apps designed to disseminate public health alerts, assess personal health status, facilitate contact tracing, and enforce the isolation of infected individuals. In Poland, for example, those required to quarantine were given a choice between having police periodically check in to verify compliance and downloading an app requiring the individual to take selfies at randomly assigned times to verify their whereabouts.[23] By the fall of 2020, one survey documented 120 COVID apps in seventy-one countries.[24]

These digital tools—which typically leveraged a smartphone's Bluetooth or Global Positioning System (GPS) technology—proved indispensable to containing the pandemic. But they also raised long-term questions about enhanced state surveillance. The data typically collected by these apps—including where people live, with whom they reside and come into contact, their movements and daily routines, and their health conditions—was both sensitive and highly susceptible to abuse by governments and criminals. Developers in some countries, such as Estonia and the United States, appeared to emphasize privacy safeguards. But elsewhere, whether by design or due to the urgent conditions under which these digital tools were developed, the imperative to act often overrode any principled stand to protect data privacy.[25]

Critics warned that autocracies such as Bahrain, China, Russia, Saudi Arabia, and Turkey could exploit the data collected by COVID-19 apps to further tighten social control.[26] But red flags were also raised in some democracies. In South Korea, for example, researchers identified several vulnerabilities in a widely used app for tracking the real-time location of people under quarantine, potentially allowing hackers access to a wide array of personal information. When made aware of the security vulnerabilities, South Korean authorities said they had put a priority on the speed of app development over security in order "to save lives." (Later, they addressed the issue.)[27]

In India, even more serious concerns were raised over the Aarogya Setu app. The mobile app collected the user's name, phone number, age, gender, profession, and other personal details, and evaluated their risk of infection based on geolocation, self-reported symptoms, medical history, and travel records. The phone's Bluetooth and GPS were used to track the user's location every fifteen minutes and to trace their contacts. The data was automatically shared with the government. The app also alerted users if they had come into contact with an infected person and allowed other users to see regional concentrations of the outbreak within a range of 6 miles from their device. In April, India became the first democracy in the world to make downloading the app mandatory for millions of its citizens. Initially food delivery workers, other service providers, and all federal government employees were required to download it. Then, in May, the mandate was extended to all public and private sector employees, all train travelers, and others living in areas deemed high risk. One Delhi suburb threatened fines and jail time for people who failed to install it. As a result, by late August, Aarogya Setu had been downloaded 152 million times, making it the world's most popular COVID-19 app. India promised to take steps to improve transparency and data security. But in the absence of a national privacy law, concerns lingered over Aarogya Setu and dozens of other similar apps employed throughout the country.[28]

The pandemic also allowed authorities around the world to justify gaining greater access to existing troves of telecommunications information. An October 2020 study by Freedom House found that at least thirty of the sixty-five countries surveyed had sought expanded access to cellphone location data.[29] The justifications seemed reasonable: the access would enable governments to better conduct contact tracing and enforce social distancing and quarantine measures. It would also facilitate the use of Big Data analytics to understand and predict broad patterns of people's movements and behaviors, helping to assess the effectiveness of public health interventions and more efficiently allocate resources. But human rights organizations noted considerable risk of abuse given the lack of transparency, proportionality, and privacy protections associated with many of these arrangements—and the prospect that enhanced state surveillance capacity would long outlive the COVID emergency.[30]

Brazil provides one example of this dynamic. In the months before the pandemic, the Bolsonaro government had already moved to compel all federal bodies to share citizen data on everything from health records to facial profiles, fingerprints, and other biometric information for the purposes of creating a vast consolidated database. The stated goal was to improve government efficiency and service delivery. But it raised questions about whether the government could be trusted with the data. Then COVID-19 arrived. While Bolsonaro consistently downplayed the pandemic (even after contracting COVID-19 himself), his administration continued using the crisis to further centralize mass data collection. This included a mandate that the country's telecom companies hand over data on 226 million Brazilians as a monitoring measure.[31]

Elsewhere, governments justified redirecting technologies and telecommunications data previously used for narrow national security purposes to fight COVID-19. Pakistan, for example, retooled a system used to track jihadists—originally designed by the country's spy agency, Inter-Services Intelligence—to trace coronavirus cases.[32] Similarly, Israeli prime minister Benjamin Netanyahu employed emergency powers to authorize the domestic intelligence agency Shin Bet to repurpose a program used to hunt terrorists to instead track (without their consent) the cellphones of Israelis suspected or confirmed of having COVID-19.[33]

Perhaps most ominous was the prospect that—under the guise of pandemic response strategies—these tactics would eventually be integrated into a wider ecosystem of ubiquitous sensors, facial recognition and other biometric technologies, and artificial intelligence (AI) algorithms. In Paris, for example, authorities employed CCTV cameras, facial recognition programs, and AI to measure aggregate compliance with mask mandates in the city's metro system; by the summer, New York City was contemplating doing the same (although the system was never implemented).[34]

China—the world's pacesetter and lead exporter of digital authoritarianism—appeared to be especially poised to exploit the pandemic to speed up the arrival of this dystopian future. Beijing's efforts to contain the COVID-19 outbreak took advantage of the country's massive preexisting digital surveillance program, including a nationwide network of millions of security cameras, facial recognition technologies and other biometrics, telecommunications tracing, digital passenger information, and internet, chat, and social media monitoring. The pandemic augmented this panoptic system by providing an excuse to expand the deployment of security cameras beyond public spaces to citizens' front doors (or even inside their homes) to enforce quarantines, and to deploy thermal scanners and facial recognition technology at transportation hubs and other public places. Meanwhile, an enormous amount of additional information began flowing to the central government and to local authorities from intrusive new mobile phone apps and other COVID-related collection efforts—all integrated into AI-enabled Big Data analytics aimed at giving authorities a much clearer picture of social behavior.[35] The near-term purpose of these actions was to stop the spread of the contagion. But they also served the CCP's more enduring objective of ensuring stability via social control.[36] As Lydia Khalil of the Lowy Institute, a prominent Australian think tank, argues, the pandemic "provided a proof of concept, demonstrating to the CCP that its technology with 'Chinese characteristics' works, and that surveillance on this scale and in an emergency is feasible and effective."[37]

The potential implications expanded far beyond China's shores. Although Beijing was active in exporting its surveillance systems and methods prior to COVID-19, its success in leveraging these technologies to roll back the virus at home seemed likely to further expand the appeal of its digital authoritarian toolkit abroad. Existing authoritarian regimes were not the only potential customers. In Ecuador, for example, Chinese-engineered surveillance systems integrating thousands of cameras with geolocation technologies—already in use by Ecuadorean police—were quickly augmented with data from COVID-19 tracking apps and redirected to combat the pandemic.[38]

CRACKDOWNS

The growth of high-tech surveillance was not the only opportunity for social control presented by the global health crisis. States also exploited the chance to get millions of people demanding greater freedom and better governance around the world off the streets. The decade before COVID-19 saw more mass protests around the world than at any time since World War II. The number of pro-democracy protests reached an all-time high in 2019, with the organization V-Dem estimating that 44 percent of countries experienced substantial pro-democracy demonstrations (up from 27 percent a decade before).[39] That year—in places as diverse as Algeria, Chile, France, Hong Kong, India, Iraq, and Lebanon—millions of demonstrators railed against rising inequality, the high cost of living, inadequate services, corruption, government repression, and police abuse. Yet as nations banned large gatherings and issued stay-at-home orders in response to the pandemic, many protest movements were forced to stand down. The effect was to relieve political pressure on a number of governments under siege. "The virus is just what the government needed,"

Antonio Cueto, a volunteer rescue worker who assisted protesters in Chile, told the *Washington Post*. "It's saved them for a bit."[40] Similarly, in India, Prime Minister Narendra Modi's imposition of a nationwide lockdown effectively ended widespread criticism and protests of his anti-Muslim citizenship policies.[41] Modi also employed antiterror laws to charge hundreds of journalists, political activists, and members of civil society who opposed him, including several organizers of antigovernment peaceful protests from early 2020.[42]

In other locales, the pandemic seemed to provide a window for leaders to attempt to crush pro-democracy movements altogether. In Algeria, the government capitalized on the COVID-induced lull in demonstrations to launch a massive campaign of arrests aimed at ending a yearlong protest movement challenging the regime.[43] In the Philippines, President Rodrigo Duterte carried out mass arrests, while issuing "shoot-to-kill" orders to security services to deal with "troublemakers" violating or protesting lockdown orders. "Do not challenge the government," Duterte threatened would-be demonstrators in April. "You will lose."[44]

Hong Kong, the site of some of the world's largest and most dramatic pre-pandemic protests, provides yet another illustration. Starting in March 2019 and continuing for nearly a year, pro-democracy demonstrators streamed into the streets of the semiautonomous city-state to demand protection of their basic rights. Over the course of 2019, as many as 2 million Hong Kongers—out of a population of 7.5 million—joined the protests. The proximate cause was outrage over a law permitting the extradition of Hong Kong residents to mainland China and Taiwan. But the deeper issue was growing concern over the Hong Kong government's collusion with the CCP in Beijing to destroy the principle of "one country, two systems." The freedoms and political autonomy enshrined in the territory's Basic Law, agreed to as part of the 1997 transfer of Hong Kong from British colonial rule to China, were promised to endure until 2047—and now they seemed to be in existential jeopardy.[45]

Hong Kong's free press played a vital role in making the world aware of COVID-19 in the first place, calling attention to the efforts by Chinese officials to cover up the virus and silence health workers such as Li Wenliang. Meanwhile, given Hong Kong's proximity to the mainland, the territory's government proactively enacted measures to detect and minimize the possible spread of the coronavirus on January 3, nearly three weeks before the first two confirmed cases on January 22.[46] In late January, it closed ten of thirteen border checkpoints and shut down schools.[47] The city also put in place extensive testing, contact tracing, and surveillance of travelers, and it provided residents an interactive online map to track confirmed cases, including the dates and times of movement of individuals who tested positive. Then, in late March, having recorded 411 cases and four deaths, Hong Kong closed its borders completely and required all visitors to quarantine. Indoor and outdoor public gatherings of more than four people were banned (in July, the government lowered the cap to two), and government offices, video game arcades, movie theaters, gyms, karaoke bars, nightclubs, mah-jongg parlors, and other leisure venues were closed. Having lived through the 2003 SARS outbreak, Hong Kongers took the risk of infection seriously. Mask wearing was nearly universal and compliance with social distancing regulations was high.[48]

With government actions and public concern over COVID-19 discouraging crowds, the scale of pro-democracy demonstrations dwindled starting in January. Social distancing regulations were used disproportionately to target pro-democracy activists, breaking up even small, dispersed gatherings. "They are using this law politically to suppress the freedom of assembly in Hong Kong," Roy Tam, a pro-democracy district councilor, noted.[49] With the virus deterring people from congregating, Hong Kong police targeted opposition figures without fear of sparking mass protests. "Hong Kong people are very alert to the concern of infection, so [the authorities] are using the chance of the pandemic," Lee Cheuk Yan, a veteran politician and activist arrested in April, told *The Guardian*. "This is a golden opportunity for them."[50]

Roundups of activists began in April with the arrest of fifteen high-profile advocates and former pro-democracy legislators and continued throughout the year, resulting in hundreds of politically motivated arrests.[51] As one analyst with close ties to the CCP admitted at the time, Beijing was eager to take advantage of the lull "to end the chaos in Hong Kong once and for all."[52] Three days after his arrest on April 18, Martin Lee, the founder of Hong Kong's Democratic Party, penned an op-ed with a stark warning. "Hong Kong people now face two plagues from China: the coronavirus and attacks on our most basic human rights," he wrote. "We can all hope a vaccine is soon developed for the coronavirus.

But once Hong Kong's human rights and rule of law are rolled back, the fatal virus of authoritarian rule will be here to stay."[53]

In June, as the world's attention remained focused on the pandemic and the global economic crisis, authorities in Beijing pounced, imposing a draconian new National Security Law on Hong Kong aimed at strangling the opposition before the protest movement could rematerialize. The law established a vast security apparatus in the territory and granted the CCP broad powers to oversee and manage schools, social organizations, the media, and the internet in Hong Kong and crack down on political dissent under the cover of combating "secession," "subversion," "terrorism," and "collusion with foreign forces." Almost immediately, the law was used to crack down on press freedoms, pro-democracy slogans, social media, and other forms of peaceful expression, and to arrest a number of high-profile activists and politicians.[54]

Then, in late July, Hong Kong's chief executive, Carrie Lam, cited the pandemic as a justification for postponing Legislative Council elections (due to take place in September) for a year, blocking another pathway for the pro-democracy movement to make gains. While the virus was used as a rationale, the territory had recorded only 3,000 cases and two dozen deaths from COVID-19 at the time.[55] This was followed in August with a ban on twelve pro-democracy candidates who had planned to run in the elections. In November, the entirety of Hong Kong's elected pro-democracy opposition resigned from the city's Legislative Council in protest of Beijing's use of the security law to force the expulsion of four fellow lawmakers.[56] By the end of the year, the prospect of rescuing any semblance of democracy and autonomy in Hong Kong seemed more remote than ever.

RESISTANCE

Yet, despite clear setbacks, protest movements around the globe did not die. Instead, they adapted. Some shifted toward organizing community responses to COVID outbreaks and other economic and social consequences of the pandemic, such as surging gender-based violence under lockdown. Others turned to methods such as car caravans, collectively banging pots and pans inside homes, and walkouts from "essential" but unsafe workplaces.[57]

And even as governments were deploying new digital tools to police lockdowns, activists were also utilizing this domain in creative ways. In Russia, activists "tagged" themselves in digital space in front of government buildings. In Chile, thousands shared a virtual mural on social media demanding more stringent actions to stem the pandemic, while others projected images of past demonstrations and victims of state repression onto buildings throughout the capital, Santiago. Some activists in Hong Kong used the popular video game *Animal Crossing*—in which players build their own island and invite others to visit—to design and share pro-democracy images and hold virtual protests, prompting the removal of the game from Chinese online stores.[58]

Traditional protest movements also reemerged, driven back into the streets by perceived state corruption and mishandling of the pandemic, by outrage at government attempts to exploit COVID-19 to curtail civil liberties and manipulate elections, and by the heightened inequalities resulting from the crisis. In Sudan, for example, the Million Man March movement decried the slow transition to democracy. In Kyrgyzstan, protesters brought down President Sooronbay Jeenbekov amid allegations of vote-rigging and corruption. As we saw in the previous chapter, demonstrators in Bolivia were outraged over the perception that their government was exploiting the pandemic for political gain. Similar protests broke out in Israel, Serbia, and Uganda.[59]

Meanwhile, in Belarus, mass protests erupted after President Alexander Lukashenko declared victory in the country's August election, claiming he had secured a sixth term in office with 80 percent of the vote. As with previous plebiscites in Europe's most authoritarian country, the election was marred by extensive repression and allegations of widespread fraud. But the background conditions this time around were different. Lukashenko's failure to take COVID-19 seriously had breathed new life into a once-marginalized opposition. In March, as countries around the world were imposing strict public health measures, Lukashenko refused to follow suit, fearing it would further damage an economy already battered by Russia's decision in February to reduce energy subsidies and the worldwide plunge in oil prices.[60] Lukashenko characterized lockdown measures as an act of "frenzy and psychosis," and instead encouraged Belarussians to drink vodka, visit saunas, and drive tractors to ward off the virus.[61] Even after Lukashenko himself contracted COVID-19 in July, the government took no meaningful action, leaving it to local officials and civil society to self-organize to combat the pandemic. As a result, coronavirus cases surged, reaching at least 68,000 by the time of the election. As early as April, Ryhor Astapenia, a Belarus analyst at the British think tank Chatham House, observed that Lukashenko was "playing a dangerous game with not only public health, but [his] own political role."[62] Public disillusionment with the regime grew, even among segments of the establishment.[63] "In the runup to the election," Lucan Ahmad Way, a political science professor at the University of Toronto observed, "there was a palpable sense that people had had enough."[64]

Demonstrations began the day after the rigged election. As August progressed, more than 100,000 Belarussians turned out in the capital, Minsk, each weekend to demand new, free, and fair elections.[65] Mass pro-democracy protests persisted for months in the face of a brutal regime response—including mass arrests, excessive use of force by security services, and torture—and threats by Russian president Vladimir Putin to intervene on Lukashenko's behalf.[66]

Around the world, COVID-19 heaped new grievances upon old ones. In some places, protesters railed against their governments for not taking the virus seriously enough. But elsewhere, demonstrators fumed at their governments for doing too much rather than too little. Across the United States in the spring and summer of 2020, for example, demonstrators took aim at state and local officials enforcing lockdown orders. In an eerie prologue to the January 6, 2021, riotous siege of the U.S. Capitol in Washington, DC—which threatened the very heart of American democracy—armed protesters stormed the Michigan state capitol building on April 30, 2020. The demonstration occurred with the encouragement of President Trump, who just days before the demonstration had told his supporters to "Liberate Michigan" on Twitter. The swarm of protesters, some wearing military fatigues and carrying assault rifles, demanded entry into the state House of Representatives' chamber, chanting "Let us in." In October, the FBI disrupted a plot to overthrow the Michigan government, including a plan to kidnap the state's governor, Gretchen Whitmer, and bomb the state capitol. A number of the plotters had participated in anti-lockdown protests in April, May, and June.[67]

By the end of 2020, according to Benjamin Press and Thomas Carothers of the Carnegie Endowment for International Peace, anti-lockdown demonstrations had emerged in at least twenty-six countries. Besides the United States, protests against curfews and stay-at-home orders occurred in countries as diverse as Australia, Germany, Mexico, and Nigeria.[68]

In other locales, the coronavirus triggered renewed demonstrations by exacerbating pre-pandemic demands for more responsive governance. Lebanon provides a case in point. Even before COVID-19, the small Middle Eastern nation was experiencing acute fiscal, banking, and exchange rate challenges, all amounting to the worst economic crisis in the country's history.[69] Rising poverty, the lack of government services, widespread corruption, and a dysfunctional sectarian political system sparked a mass protest movement in the fall of 2019, forcing the resignation of Prime Minister Saad Hariri.[70] In mid-March, as the government locked the country down to contain the coronavirus, protests necessarily dissipated. Swift government action helped keep COVID-19 infection rates on par with success stories such as Australia, New Zealand, and South Korea.[71] Yet while public health restrictions successfully tamped down the spread of the virus, they also dealt another devastating blow to the economy. Business closures, job losses, currency depreciation, soaring inflation, and inadequate government support crushed livelihoods, worsening extreme poverty and producing widespread hunger.[72] As a staggered reopening concluded in June, protesters returned to the streets.[73]

It was an increasingly explosive situation. And then, on August 4, a literal explosion rocked the country when 2,750 tons of ammonium nitrate improperly stored in a warehouse at the Beirut port detonated. The massive blast caused destruction over a six-mile radius and was heard more than 150 miles away. At least 180 people died, more than 6,500 were injured, 300,000 people were displaced, and 70,000 were left unemployed. Blaming government negligence and corruption for the carnage, tens of thousands of demonstrators flooded Beirut. Clashes with security forces left hundreds injured.[74] In response to mounting public vitriol, Prime Minister Hassan Diab and his entire cabinet resigned; in October, Saad Hariri (who had stepped down a year earlier) was tasked with forming yet another government.[75]

In the midst of Lebanon's political chaos, efforts to control the pandemic collapsed. Protests in the streets, mounting homelessness, large numbers of volunteers assisting with clearing debris and providing humanitarian relief, overwhelmed hospitals, and widespread mistrust of the government all made social distancing measures moot. Coronavirus cases skyrocketed, with infections increasing from around 5,000 on the day of the port explosion to nearly 45,000 just two months later. By the end of the year, Lebanon, a country of just 6.8 million people, had more than 160,000 cases, effectively nullifying the early progress it had made in containing the virus.[76]

Western democracies were not immune to demands for greater justice and accountability. In the United States, the pandemic highlighted and accentuated profound inequalities, contributing to a historic wave of racial justice protests nationwide during the summer of 2020. The impacts of the virus fell hardest on Black, Latinx, and Native American populations. People of color were at much greater risk of contracting the coronavirus due to higher rates of work in essential service sectors that remained open during lockdowns. Black Americans and other minorities were more likely to hold jobs that could not be done remotely, less likely to have paid leave, more likely to lack an economic cushion, and less likely to live in households with multiple earners than whites. Exposure risks were further magnified by the fact that people of color were more likely to live in densely populated urban areas and to be more reliant on public transportation.[77] And, once infected, Black and Latinx Americans were 4.7 times more likely to be hospitalized and twice as likely to die of COVID-19 compared to whites, largely due to a higher prevalence of other preexisting health conditions and less access to health care—themselves byproducts of systemic racial inequalities.[78]

Pre-pandemic inequality—including lower levels of income and wealth, higher rates of unemployment, lower savings, and greater food and housing insecurity—also left Black Americans much more susceptible to the massive economic disruptions produced by the pandemic. In April 2020, the unemployment rate for Black Americans was 16.7 percent, compared with 14.2 percent for whites; in May, the Black unemployment rate increased to 16.8 percent, while the white unemployment rate fell to 12.4 percent.[79]

As the dual health and economic crises highlighted and exacerbated centuries-old racial disparities in the United States, the horrific killing of George Floyd—a Black man arrested for allegedly using a counterfeit $20 bill—at the hands of Minneapolis police on May 25 lit a spark. Floyd had tested positive for COVID-19 in April, and an autopsy would later reveal that traces of the disease lingered in his body from the previous infection. But the cause of death was another human being, not the coronavirus.[80] A bystander video of the deadly arrest showed Floyd struggling and declaring "I can't breathe" as officer Derek Chauvin kneeled on his neck. The clip was broadcast in an endless loop on cable news and social media to millions of Americans cooped up at home.

Large-scale protests demanding police reform and racial justice immediately erupted in Minneapolis and then quickly spread across the United States and around the world. Black Americans, fed up with living in underresourced and overpoliced communities, were joined by a multiracial, multigenerational coalition. Widespread outrage at injustice was the driving force, but growing frustration with stay-at-home requirements and the disproportionate impact of the economic downturn on young people of all races also seemed to play a role in the movement's momentum.[81] Over the coming weeks, demonstrations swept through 140 U.S. cities. At the movement's peak, on June 6, half a million people protested in 550 locations. Four polls conducted in June and July suggested that the number of Americans who had attended a Black Lives Matter or police brutality demonstration totaled between 15 million and 26 million, making it the largest protest movement in U.S. history.[82] By late August, one study found, there had been over 7,750 protests across more than 2,440 locations in all fifty U.S. states and Washington, DC. And while President Trump and conservative media in the United States attempted to portray the movement as anarchic and violent, the same study concluded that more than 93 percent of the protests had been peaceful.[83]

Moreover, in a poignant reminder that the world remained invested in the fate of American democracy, protests in solidarity with the Black Lives Matter movement were held in Berlin, Brussels, Copenhagen, Johannesburg, London, Mexico City, Nairobi, Rio de Janeiro, Paris, Seoul, Sydney, and dozens of other cities and locales around the globe. Demonstrators, ranging from a few hundred to tens of thousands, braved the pandemic to voice outrage at the police brutality on display in George Floyd's killing—often linking the incident to local struggles for racial justice—and to demand that the United States live up to its stated ideals.[84] As one common slogan held aloft at a mid-June rally attended by thousands in Tokyo declared: "Racism *is* a pandemic."[85]

All told, by October, Freedom House estimated that there had been significant protests in at least ninety countries, in every region of the world, since the onset of the pandemic (despite 158 countries putting in place new COVID-related restrictions on such gatherings). Approximately 39 percent of democracies, 60 percent of partial democracies, and 43 percent of autocracies experienced demonstrations.[86]

Consequently, as 2020 came to a close, the contest between the forces of authoritarianism and democracy remained fully engaged, although the side that would ultimately win out remained highly uncertain. New emergency powers, disruptions to legislative processes and elections, widespread threats to civil liberties, abuses by security services, dystopian technologies, and attacks on critics and activists associated with government responses to the pandemic had combined to weaken political freedoms in eighty countries.[87] But the desire for greater freedom and more accountable and representative government was equally evident. People in many nations stood up, often at great risk, to keep hope for a more just future alive.

PART IV

TOWARD A
POST-COVID WORLD

Variants and Vaccines

THE TECHNICAL NAME for the virus that produces the COVID-19 disease is SARS-CoV-2. But to epidemiologists, SARS-CoV-2 is broad enough to encompass a series of variants that emerge naturally as the original coronavirus spreads and evolves. As a result, the waves of the pandemic are not waves of exactly the same thing. The emergence of new variants, sometimes very early on, adds layers of complication and danger. The genome of SARS-CoV-2 has approximately 30,000 letters of ribonucleic acid (RNA) that force the human body to assemble up to twenty-nine types of protein to spread the virus and infect the body. As the virus replicates, small copying errors sometimes occur. These are mutations. And when a virus is widely circulating and causing many infections, the likelihood of mutations increases. A virus with one or more distinctive mutations, in turn, is known as a variant. A new variant may not meaningfully change the ability of the original virus to infect and kill people. But some do.[1]

The first variant of SARS-CoV-2 was a single mutation labeled 614G. It was discovered in eastern China in January 2020, very early in the pandemic. Scientists suspect that this 614G variant was more contagious than the original Wuhan variant and it was this one that made its way to Italy and then on to New York and the rest of the United States.[2]

In late November 2020, scientists identified a new variant, known as B.1.1.7, in the United Kingdom, thought to be 30 to 50 percent more contagious than other versions of the virus, and increasingly linked to a higher risk of death.[3] The first known case of B.1.1.7 was traced back to September 20, and by the middle of November, it accounted for roughly one-quarter of cases in London.[4] It reached the United States in late December, and by early February 2021 it was doubling there every ten days.[5] As of late March, it had been detected in over ninety countries. Despite growing evidence that B.1.1.7 was both more contagious and deadlier, emerging vaccines—including those produced by Pfizer-BioNTech, Moderna, and AstraZeneca in late 2020 and by Johnson & Johnson in early 2021—still seemed effective in combating it. Testing conducted in Israel in early February 2021 revealed that although the variant was present in close to 80 percent of samples, widespread vaccination was damping its effect.[6]

Around the same time, two other concerning variants were also discovered: P.1 in Brazil and B.1.351 in South Africa. Both shared a number of similar mutations and appeared to be more transmissable. Most disturbingly, unlike the U.K. variant, available vaccines seemed somewhat less effective against P.1 and significantly less effective against B.1.351. Initial studies suggested that the AstraZeneca vaccine, in particular, was 86 times less effective against the South African variant.[7] By late March 2021, the P.1 variant had spread to at least twenty-five countries and the B.1.351 variant had spread to forty-eight countries.[8]

The trio of dangerous variants came to light against the backdrop of surging COVID-19 infections across the globe. By the beginning of September 2020, the world had recorded 25.77 million COVID-19 cases; by the end of the year, that number had reached more than 83.56 million. That represented a 224 percent increase in worldwide cases in just four months. The biggest increases during this period were in Europe (549 percent, with a 699 percent increase in the European Union), North America (219 percent, with a 231 percent increase in the United States), and Asia (187 percent; 189 percent excluding China, which saw only a 7 percent reported increase). The increase was significant but less profound in Africa (119 percent) and South America (107 percent), and it was very slight in Oceania (just 12 percent).[9]

As 2020 came to a close, therefore, a race was on between emerging variants and surging cases, on the one hand, and new hope for an end to the pandemic raised by a growing number of vaccines, on the other.

THOSE SUMMER DAYS

By early summer 2020, many governments assumed that patterns of COVID-19 infection were no longer likely to increase exponentially. They thought they understood how the novel coronavirus spread and how contagious it was. They believed early containment measures had worked and they would have plenty of warning of a second wave before it hit. So they had some breathing space to relax public health measures. In many countries, this proved to be a dangerous miscalculation.

This was certainly the case in Europe, where Europeans thought they had put the worst of the pandemic behind them. After strict spring lock-downs, the curve had fully flattened. Whereas at its peak around April 1, the EU had seen almost 30,000 new COVID-19 cases per day, the daily case rate was around 4,000 by June 1, and it remained steady until mid-July.[10] Unsurprisingly, then, European leaders were eager to lift corona-virus restrictions by the summer. August especially beckoned, a month that Europeans like to take off.[11] As early as April 18, European Commission president Ursula von der Leyen declared, "We will find smart solutions to have some vacation."[12] Likewise, the German interior minister, Horst Seehofer, told reporters on May 13, "The clear objective is that we want free travel in Europe again as of mid-June."[13]

Sure enough, a month later, the European Commission recommended that internal EU borders be reopened by June 15 and that restrictions on nonessential travel into the EU gradually be lifted after June 30.[14] They knew that the virus had not disappeared, and that it would stage a comeback in their own backyards in the fall and winter. But at the time, Europeans were convinced that the harshness of their spring lockdowns would allow them to reap lasting benefits.

The contrast with the approach taken in Asia and Oceania was stark. On July 26, China reported sixty-one new coronavirus cases. While tiny compared to infections elsewhere, it was still China's highest number since early March. Around the same time, Vietnam had its first cases of community infection (passed from one person to another) since April, in tourist hotspot Danang. New Zealand, for its part, reported its first new cases of COVID-19 in 102 days on August 11. The response in each country to these small increases in absolute terms was overwhelming—local lockdowns and isolation of those exposed to the virus, testing and contact tracing, and a draconian travel policy, effectively closing the country to outside visitors.[15]

Europeans were determined not to follow suit. After suffering a 99 percent drop in international tourism between April and June 2020, Spain received over 4 million visitors in July and August.[16] Nightlife and beaches drew throngs of people, with clubs and discos staying open until the early morning hours to compensate for the spring's economic catastrophe.[17] At one now-infamous beach club outside the Spanish city of Málaga, a DJ was filmed spitting at his audience on a crowded dance floor.[18] The Greek islands also reopened to select countries, welcoming tourists from most of Europe, Israel, Japan, Australia, and New Zealand.[19]

Although Greece subjected tourists from some higher-risk European countries to mandatory testing at the airport, in other places, testing and quarantine measures were rarely enforced. By late July, it became clear that the virus was spreading again. With the notable exception of Italy, lower compliance with pandemic-related hygiene measures was observed across the continent.[20] Jean-François Delfraissy, who had been tapped in March to lead the French government's Scientific Council on COVID-19, lamented that "the French have lost the notion of social distancing and caution."[21]

In many cases, younger people were driving the virus spread. In late July, Spanish minister of finance and government spokesperson María Jesús Montero expressly sought to caution "people who are younger, because some of the outbreaks are linked to the behavior in nightlife venues or places where a large number of people gather."[22] By mid-August, even the WHO agreed: at a virtual briefing, Regional Director for the Western Pacific Takeshi Kasai said, "People in their 20s, 30s and 40s are increasingly driving the spread."[23] Increases in cases were also substantial in central and eastern European countries such as Serbia, Romania, and Poland, which had mostly escaped western Europe's deadly first wave.[24]

Nevertheless, by summer's end, EU leaders still believed they could handle the expected second wave. On September 1, the daily new case rate was still lower than it had been during the spring peak (slightly over 20,000 new COVID-19 cases per day on September 1 compared to almost 30,000 on April 1), and the pace of increase was far less dramatic than it had been in late March.[25] Meanwhile, compared to the peak daily death rate of almost 3,000 in early to mid-April, from the end of June to mid-September the daily deaths did not exceed 200.[26] Europeans remained convinced that they had learned the lessons from the spring. The scramble for precious medical supplies was behind them. They would coordinate more closely at the EU level. The situation looked to be under control.

Above all, leaders wanted to keep internal borders within the EU open. Freedom of movement is a cornerstone of the single European market. In early September, a confidential EU briefing paper observed that while "it remains the responsibility of each member state to enact the measures it sees fit . . . a coherent response is critical to avoid a fragmented approach as seen earlier in the year as well as to preserve the integrity of the Schengen area."[27] Throughout the next few months, even as the EU reeled from a second wave, borders remained open. Reflecting on this in early December, von der Leyen told the *Financial Times*, "One of the biggest achievements of the EU is the open single market and the Schengen principles for passport-free travel. Border closures due to coronavirus cut these freedoms—and then nothing was functioning anymore."[28]

What Europeans did not understand as they entered the fall was that they would not just be forced to deal with a return of the virus. They would also have to contend with new variants that would prove more contagious and undo their best-laid plans.

AN UNQUIET CHRISTMAS

On December 20, with the United Kingdom and the EU deadlocked in talks on a post-Brexit trade agreement, France closed its borders to passengers and vehicles from the United Kingdom, causing massive backups of trucks in the British port town of Dover, which sits on the narrowest part of the English Channel. Some British officials wondered whether it was a ploy to give them a sense of the turmoil a no-deal Brexit would cause, but French officials claimed it was solely because of fear of the new B.1.1.7 variant that had emerged in Britain. After forty-eight hours, British ministers announced that border restrictions would be lifted the following day for all visitors (including truck drivers), who would need to test negative for COVID-19. But the restrictions were just a sign of things to come.[29]

Meanwhile, after completing a six-week lockdown in mid-December, Ireland had one of the lowest case counts in Europe, with just 10 new cases each day per 100,000 people. By January 11, however, Ireland had the highest number of new daily cases per 100,000 people in the world, with 132. The B.1.1.7 variant had coincided with Christmas travel from the United Kingdom. More Irish people were infected (46,000) in a seven-day period in early January 2021 than during March to October 2020.[30] The Irish government was stunned and quickly reimposed a strict lockdown that would last for months. What happened in Ireland was a warning to the rest of the EU: the new variants combined with any relaxation of social distancing rules could lead to a rapid and catastrophic reversal in fortune.

In January 2021, Germany, France, and many other European countries followed suit and went into lockdown. The Netherlands experienced what its police association called the most violent protests in forty years as thousands of mostly young men took to the streets in multiple cities to object to the country's first curfew since World War II. The protesters looted shops, attacked police officers, and destroyed property, including a coronavirus testing center.[31] Borders began to close again. Germany placed restrictions on its frontier with the Czech Republic and Austria, resulting in long delays for truckers. France required a negative COVID test for visitors from other EU member states, while also closing the country to nonessential travel from almost all non-EU countries.[32]

Europe's political leaders exchanged barbs on the restrictions, which critics saw as yet another blow to European integration caused by COVID-19, jeopardizing the future of Europe's borderless Schengen Area. Ursula von der Leyen told the media, "Last spring we had 17 different member states that had introduced border measures and the lessons we learned at the time is that it did not stop the virus but it disrupted incredibly the single market and caused enormous problems." She was blunt in her assessment: "The virus taught us that closing borders does not stop it." But the commission president's remarks angered Germany's interior minister, Horst Seehofer, who told the German tabloid *Bild*, "We are fighting the mutated virus on the border with the Czech Republic and Austria." The European Commission "should support us and not put a monkey wrench in the works with cheap advice," he said.[33]

A MOONSHOT AT WARP SPEED

Unlike Europe, the United States never had a lull. Once the pandemic seemed to be under control in the Northeast and on the West Coast, it spiked in the South and the Midwest. Nationally, the picture was grim throughout the summer and fall of 2020. The seven-day case average peaked at 75,687 per day on July 16 before declining to approximately 35,000 per day in early September. From that point forward, however, it began to rise again, crossing the threshold of 100,000 daily cases on November 4 and reaching an astonishing 300,669 on January 8, 2021, the highest yet, with a seven-day average for daily deaths over 3,300.[34] In the dark winter of 2020–21, each and every day more Americans were dying from COVID-19 than had been killed on 9/11. Yet, unlike the terrorist attacks two decades earlier, the pain and suffering caused by the pandemic did not unify the country. Instead, it became a point of partisan strife.

The Trump administration continued to delegate most COVID-related decisions to the states, contributing to an incoherent patchwork of interventions. The aggregate availability of testing increased markedly, but it remained uneven across the country.[35] States and localities also varied wildly in terms of mask mandates, social distancing requirements, stay-at-home orders, and business and school closures. For his part, President Trump appeared to lose all interest in containing the virus and instead tried to project that everything was returning to normal. The White House pressured the CDC to make its guidance for reopening the economy vaguer, to play down the risk of children returning to school, and to discourage testing of people without COVID-19 symptoms.[36] Meanwhile, some prominent Trump advisors seemed to favor a "herd immunity" approach that would prioritize reopening the economy while allowing COVID-19 to spread through most of the population.[37] But there was one area where the Trump administration saw the federal government playing a critical role: vaccine development.

Pharmaceutical companies around the world began work on a vaccine immediately after scientists Zhang Yong-Zhen and Edward Holmes released the genetic sequence of COVID-19 to the world on January 11, 2020.[38] However, few believed they would develop a safe and effective vaccine as quickly as they did. Speaking to the U.S. Senate on March 3, 2020, Anthony Fauci said that even if vaccine development was incredibly fast, "the entire process . . . would take a year to a year and a half" before it was available to the public.[39] In his book about the coronavirus, *Apollo's Arrow*, published in October 2020, Nicholas Christakis, director of Yale's Human Nature Lab, noted that traditionally vaccines do not arrive until herd immunity has already been achieved and that a COVID-19 vaccine was unlikely before 2022.[40] Against any historical metric, 2022 would have constituted an incredible success. Until COVID-19, the record for developing a vaccine was for mumps—and that took four years.[41] Most had taken a decade or more, while some, like a vaccine for HIV/AIDS, still do not exist.

Once a vaccine candidate is developed, several types of testing take place: laboratory testing, animal studies, and human clinical trials in three phases to determine whether individuals suffer any negative effects from the jab. Phase 1 involves a small group of adults (typically 20–80), phase 2 involves several hundred, including some who may be at higher risk, and phase 3 is when the vaccine is given to thousands of people.[42] Most vaccine candidates do not survive trials. It often takes at least a year to even recruit the right pool of people for phase 3 alone. In the United States, if these trials are successful, the vaccine candidate is then submitted to the Food and Drug Administration, which goes through its own exhaustive review process. The FDA stated in advance that a COVID-19 vaccine would have to be proven to be at least 50 percent effective before being authorized for use.[43] On top of all that, building the manufacturing capacity to produce it in large quantities is extremely expensive and time-consuming. Thus, investors will only put significant money into manufacturing once a vaccine has been rigorously vetted and determined to be successful.

The United States has a long reputation for inventing its way out of national security crises and conflicts. The most famous example is, of course, the Manhattan Project and the creation of the atomic bomb during World War II. The invention of the microchip in 1959 helped give the United States a decisive technological competitive advantage over the Soviet Union. In 1969, at the height of the Cold War, America became the first nation to put a human being on the moon—and the term "moonshot" is now employed for any endeavor in which the government engages in a monumental effort to leap forward in science and technology. Even following the disastrous invasion of Iraq, U.S.

development of drone technology transformed the conflict and the global war on terrorism. The same dynamic was evident in coping with the global pandemic. The United States may have struggled mightily in the face of COVID-19—but it also ended up pumping much more money into vaccine development than any other nation and harnessed an advanced industrial base that was second to none.

On May 15, 2020, President Trump announced the formation of Operation Warp Speed (OWS), an ambitious public-private partnership that aimed to get more companies involved in vaccine development at a massive scale.[44] The OWS program was largely financed by emergency COVID-19 funding passed by Congress as part of the April stimulus package. The congressional appropriations had not provided money specifically for vaccines, but several accounts contained funds that were available for vaccine-related activities carried out by the Department of Health and Human Services and the Department of Defense. The Trump administration then shifted billions of dollars from other public health projects, such as replenishing the national stockpile of protective medical gear and ventilators, to OWS. By mid-October, OWS had announced contract awards in support of six vaccines, with obligations totaling at least $10 billion and an estimated value of $18 billion.[45] The idea behind OWS was simple: remove the financial risk for companies associated with the rapid development and testing of vaccines and cut through the red tape associated with approving and distributing them. The government paid companies to build manufacturing plants and produce millions of doses before the vaccines were proven effective. If one of them succeeded, it would be worth it.[46]

Trump chose a man named Moncef Slaoui to head the initiative. Slaoui was born in Morocco. As a child, his younger sister died of whooping cough—a tragedy that led Slaoui to develop an interest in medicine. When he was seventeen, he enrolled in college at the Free University of Brussels, where he studied molecular biology and immunology. He moved to the United States to pursue postdoctoral studies at Harvard University and Tufts University. He subsequently joined the vaccine department of pharmaceutical giant GlaxoSmithKline (GSK), where he rose to be chairman of research and development, and eventually chairman of global vaccines in 2009. In 2017, after thirty years, he left GSK and joined the board of Moderna.[47]

Operation Warp Speed directly funded vaccine work by Oxford University-AstraZeneca, Moderna, Johnson & Johnson, and several others. Another major player, Pfizer (in collaboration with the German company BioNTech) operated independently and put its own money at risk because it worried about political influence. However, Pfizer did receive a $1.9 billion advance purchase agreement in July 2020. The OWS initiative received some criticism domestically because it tapped senior pharmaceutical executives, including Slaoui, and then funneled enormous amounts of money to these firms. Senator Elizabeth Warren called on Slaoui to resign or be fired because he held millions of dollars in GSK stock, which she said was a conflict of interest. There were controversial decisions too. One Maryland company, Novavax, was on its last legs in 2019. It had existed for thirty-three years without once producing a successful vaccine (it had come close on a number of occasions). At a time when it was facing delisting from the Nasdaq and the financial short-sellers were circling, OWS injected $1.6 billion into the company in May.[48]

Astonishingly, by mid-November 2020, less than a year into the pandemic, the first COVID-19 vaccines that had successfully completed all the necessary testing began to come online.[49] The vaccine developed by Pfizer-BioNTech demonstrated a stunning effectiveness rate of 95 percent, while a similar vaccine produced by Moderna was shown to be 94 percent effective. In mid-December, the U.S. FDA issued emergency use authorizations for both. Beyond their remarkable efficacy, the Pfizer-BioNTech and Moderna vaccines were notable in a second respect: they relied on a revolutionary technology developed over the past decade that utilized messenger RNA (mRNA). As Dr. Philip Dormitzer, the chief scientific officer for viral vaccines at Pfizer, described it, with a gene-based vaccine such as mRNA, "you don't inject . . . a piece of the virus . . . [Y]ou simply inject an instruction set that teaches your body how to make a piece of the virus, and then your body learns to recognize the piece that it has made and make it a target for the antibodies to kill the virus."[50] This method focused on the "spike protein" found on the surface of the virus. In one of the most common artist-generated images of SARS-CoV-2 that has circulated widely in the media, the spike protein is the distinctive red spike with a crown that sits on the blue virus surface.[51]

In an interesting twist, Pfizer's choice to hold off on participating in

OWS may have had a catalytic effect on the development of the Moderna vaccine. A senior Trump administration official told us that Pfizer's decision to go it alone was seen as a sign that they were supremely confident that their mRNA method would work. Prior to that, influential figures working on OWS were skeptical that the technology behind the Moderna vaccine would pan out, but it was the same type that Pfizer was using. "That's when we realized we have a real horse race here" between the pharmaceutical companies, the official said.

Meanwhile, a third vaccine, produced by a partnership between Oxford University and the British-Swedish company AstraZeneca, was developed using an adenovirus-based technique whereby the scientists added the gene for the coronavirus spike protein to another virus like the common cold or flu. In this case, the Oxford-AstraZeneca team used a modified version of a chimpanzee adenovirus.[52] This vaccine also reported test results in November, showing a respectable efficacy rate of 63 percent. (The vaccine was approved for use by the European Medicines Agency in January 2021, but further U.S.-based trials delayed judgment by the FDA, and as of the end of March, the AstraZeneca vaccine had not yet been issued emergency use authorization in the United States.[53]) Then, in February 2021, another adenovirus-based vaccine, developed by Johnson & Johnson, demonstrated a 72 percent overall efficacy rate in the United States (and 64 percent in trials held in South Africa) and received FDA emergency use authorization. The vaccine raised hopes for more rapid immunizations since, unlike the two-dose Pfizer-BioNTech, Moderna, and AstraZeneca vaccines, the Johnson & Johnson vaccine only required one shot.

The OWS bet on Novavax seemed to pay off. In March 2021, Novavax announced it had produced a vaccine that was 96.4 percent effective against the original COVID-19 virus, even higher than Pfizer and Moderna (although it appeared to be less effective against the British and South African variants, with 86 and 49 percent efficacy, respectively).[54]

One question that arises is whether Trump deserves credit for the development of the vaccine. And, if so, does that compensate for his other failings? Other writers—those more expert in immunology, industrial policy, and logistics—will be better placed than us to pass definitive judgment on this question. But it is possible to draw a few provisional conclusions.

The first thing to acknowledge is that OWS did not occur in a vacuum.

Some of the preliminary research informing the rapid development of COVID-19 vaccines had already been done with work on the spike proteins in HIV, as well as in SARS and MERS (which are also coronaviruses). This prior work helped scientists quickly identify the spike protein of SARS-CoV-2 and understand that it was the right target for a vaccine. Moreover, incredible advances had been made on mRNA technology over the previous decade. This was not targeted at coronaviruses, but, as Slaoui put it,

> it is 100 percent the same product in terms of chemical composition whether you have a vaccine against COVID, flu, herpes, or hepatitis. All of the work on that platform over the last 10 years to understand the toxicology, the clinical expectation of safety, and the manufacturing strategy was all relevant to the COVID-19 vaccine because it involves the same processes.[55]

At the same time, it is clear that OWS did help significantly. The Trump administration poured vast sums of money into vaccine development. By contrast, the EU, with a far larger population, spent just $2.7 billion. The administration essentially gave the pharmaceutical industry a blank check and trusted its executives, which others may not have been inclined to do. In an interview with *Science*, Slaoui gave his opinion on Trump:

> I completely disagree with the values that he projects, as a person, in terms of respect, in terms of capacity to listen, accepting diversity. Many of the policy decisions that ended up politicizing this pandemic were wrong, particularly around wearing the mask. But at the same time, I do think that Warp Speed was absolutely visionary to put together science, government, the military, and the private sector and just give us full empowerment.[56]

Ultimately, the rapid development of vaccines demonstrated some of America's core strengths as a superpower: an unrivaled high-end technological industrial base, the potential for public-private partnership, and a willingness to make enormous investments without any guarantee of success. Yet the tremendous accomplishment would also create new problems, challenges, and geopolitical developments. Some countries handled the vaccine rollout better than others, and the major powers would use the distribution of life-saving inoculations to advance their foreign policy goals, raising significant global equity concerns.

EUROPE'S VACCINE WOES

In the spring of 2020, the Europeans helped lead the way—working alongside the WHO, other world leaders, the Bill & Melinda Gates Foundation, CEPI, Gavi, The Global Fund, Unitaid, and other international organizations—in creating the Access to COVID-19 Tools (ACT) Accelerator. The multilateral framework sought to provide billions of dollars to support the development and equitable global distribution of COVID-19 tests, treatments, and vaccines, and to strengthen health care systems buckling under the pandemic. The vaccine pillar of the ACT-Accelerator, called COVAX (shorthand for COVID-19 Vaccines Global Access), was co-managed by CEPI, Gavi, and the WHO. The aim of the initiative was to speed up vaccine research and development and to provide incentives to quickly scale up production by making up-front investments in a wide portfolio of vaccine candidates, including some that might not pan out. Then, all nations participating in COVAX would gain access to the vaccines developed on an equal basis regardless of their income. Funding to poorer nations would provide a critical lifeline for inoculations they might not otherwise be able to afford, while COVAX also enabled wealthier self-financing countries to gain access to vaccines in the event they lacked sufficient bilateral deals with pharmaceutical companies. An ambitious target of making 2 billion doses available worldwide by the end of 2021 was set.[57]

"Past experience has taught us that even when tools are available, they have not been equally available to all," WHO Director General Tedros Adhanom Ghebreyesus declared during the virtual launch event for the ACT-Accelerator and COVAX in April. "We are facing a common threat, which we can only defeat with a common approach."[58] German chancellor Angela Merkel concurred: "This concerns a global public good, to produce this vaccine and to distribute it in all parts of the world." But in this global endeavor, two critical players were conspicuous by their absence: China and the United States. A spokesman for the U.S. mission to the WHO in Geneva justified the Trump administration's decision to stay away by saying, "We remain deeply concerned about the WHO's effectiveness, given that its gross failures fuel the current pandemic." French president Emmanuel Macron, however, thought it would eventually be possible to bring Beijing and Washington into the fold. "I hope we'll manage to reconcile around this joint initiative both China and the U.S.," he said, "because this is about saying 'the fight against COVID-19 is a common human good and there should be no division in order to win this battle.'"[59] But it took months for Macron's aspirations to materialize. By late August, 172 nations had expressed interest in participating in COVAX (including 92 low- and middle-income countries and 80 potential self-financing countries), but China did not do so until October, and America did not commit to COVAX until February 2021, once Trump had exited the scene.[60] Even then, as nations provided funding to COVAX, it had no pathway to actually procure vaccines in the quantities required to carry out its mission.

While the Europeans were attempting to fill the vacuum in global leadership left by the U.S. and China, within the European Union itself the approach to vaccine development was chaotic. For a while, it looked like the larger countries might go their own way. France and Germany initiated joint negotiations to buy vaccines, and they were soon joined by the Netherlands and Italy in a coalition that became known as the Inclusive Vaccine Alliance. On June 13, 2020, the alliance announced it had reached a deal with AstraZeneca. Other European governments were alarmed. If every country took care of itself, huge disparities would arise among the twenty-seven member states. Some large and competent countries might do quite well, but smaller countries and those lacking adequate expertise would suffer. The euro crisis had already split the EU between creditor and debtor countries and brought it to the brink of collapse. EU leaders were determined to avoid a repeat of a two-tier Europe on vaccinations.[61]

There were advantages to a collective approach. The EU is the world's largest economic bloc—by negotiating collectively, it can leverage its size and secure a better deal. European leaders also worried that if they did not work together on the vaccine, they would be dependent upon Trump's America—which had already tried to acquire a stake in a European biotechnology company called CureVac. Faced with resistance, the quartet of countries agreed to merge their efforts into an EU-wide initiative led by von der Leyen's European Commission. On June 17, with a budget of $2.7 billion, the Emergency Support Instrument was launched with a mandate to procure vaccines for the member states and Norway.[62]

The EU had no experience with major procurement projects, particularly in health care, so it fell back on what it was good at. One of the EU's top trade negotiators, an Italian named Sandra Gallina, was put in charge. She approached it like a trade negotiation. She wanted a good price, access to several vaccines, and for the companies to remain liable for anything that went wrong. This dragged out the negotiations. At a European Parliament hearing in September, speaker after speaker called on Gallina to ensure that the pharmaceutical companies would be held liable for anything that went wrong with the vaccine. They also spoke about the risk of transferring billions of euros to companies without adequate scrutiny or transparency. Gallina replied:

> The negotiations have been very difficult because we started with the idea that we wanted to uphold the status quo so . . . all the rights of European citizens are totally unchanged. . . . I was very strict at the beginning that our status quo has to remain. We have two elements in our status quo: liability and indemnification. As regards both we did not change an iota . . . [on liability]. It is the system we know. We would not be so mad as to change such a system.[63]

Unlike the United States, the European Commission had no ability to absorb the costs of such liabilities unless the member states each agreed to do so individually, which they did not.[64]

This legalistic approach might have made sense for a trade deal, but it was gravely out of step with what other countries were doing in the middle of a global pandemic when pharmaceutical firms were faced with many different buyers. The United States threw money at the problem and also granted liability waivers on the basis that the vaccines would be approved by the regulator, so the companies would be off the hook. After all, they were adhering to a rapid timeline at the request of governments. Israeli prime minister Benjamin Netanyahu called the CEO of Pfizer thirty times, imploring him to use Israel as an opportunity to collect data on the effectiveness of the vaccine, paying more than other countries were offering, and waiving all liability. The United Kingdom hired a vaccine team that included a venture capitalist who specialized in investing in pharmaceutical companies, former executives from pharmaceutical firms, soldiers from its army's 101st Logistic Brigade, and a civil servant from the Submarine Delivery Agency. They focused on supply chain issues, including sourcing key components for production and the location of the factories, instead of price and liability.[65] The head of the U.K. effort frequently held biweekly meetings with Slaoui, the OWS chief, to discuss strategy while the EU chose to go its own way.[66]

In the end, the EU did secure a lower price than the United States. The EU paid less than $2 and $15 per dose to AstraZeneca and Pfizer, respectively, whereas the United States paid $4 and $20. Israel, meanwhile, paid $28 for each Pfizer dose. But there was a downside: the EU's agreements took longer to finalize and were vaguer on questions of supply.[67] This left much less time to iron out problems in production and distribution. The EU was also heavily invested in the Oxford-AstraZeneca vaccine. Confidential EU documents obtained by a German media outlet also revealed that over half of EU member states wanted more "traditional" vaccines and were "very little interested" in the new mRNA vaccines developed by Pfizer-BioNTech and Moderna, mainly because they required subzero temperatures for storage and were more expensive.[68]

Unfortunately for the EU, AstraZeneca was beset by production problems. On January 22, 2021, the company informed the EU that it would only be able to deliver a third of the vaccines it had promised by March due to construction problems, generating a firestorm of criticism. Controversially, AstraZeneca would continue to fulfill its contractual obligations to the United Kingdom in full. There was plenty of blame to go around. The German finance minister, Olaf Scholz, erupted at a cabinet meeting, calling the European Commission's management of the vaccine "a total shitshow." EU leaders accused AstraZeneca of giving preference to the British government, which was continuing to receive its orders in full and was making rapid progress on vaccinating its public. The contrast with a successful and rapid vaccination program in the United Kingdom was particularly difficult to take after Brexit. In Germany, the tabloid *Bild* ran a front-page headline that read, "Dear Britain We Envy You," while the weekly *Die Zeit* said that the European Commission had unintentionally offered "the best advertisement for Brexit: it is acting slowly, bureaucratically and in a protectionist manner. And if something goes wrong, it's everyone else's fault."[69]

But the drama surrounding AstraZeneca was only beginning. On January 28, Commission president von der Leyen, who had been keeping a low profile on the question of vaccine procurement but took personal control of the portfolio from Gallina after the controversy broke, announced that the EU would enact a temporary mechanism to prevent the export of vaccines produced within the bloc.[70] Amid criticism that Britain was receiving special treatment from the company, the mechanism was clearly targeting AstraZeneca. Ironically, the AstraZeneca vaccine had not yet even received approval for use in the European Union; that would only come the following day. The commission president's announcement immediately provoked an uproar, especially since it included unilaterally triggering an emergency brake procedure in the U.K.-EU Brexit agreement, effectively reinstating a hard border between Northern Ireland and the Republic of Ireland. Realizing the gravity of its mistake, and under pressure from the Irish government, the European Commission rolled back its decision within hours.

Meanwhile, AstraZeneca's effectiveness was being called into question. On the same day von der Leyen announced vaccine export controls, Germany's vaccination advisory committee warned against administering the AstraZeneca vaccine to those 65 and older.[71] The next day, Macron chimed in, calling it "quasi-ineffective" on people over 65.[72] Just hours later, the vaccine was authorized for use by the European Medicines Agency (EMA), with the caveat, "There are not yet enough results in older participants (over 55 years old) to provide a figure for how well the vaccine will work in this group," adding that they expected it to be effective based on experience with other vaccines and evidence of immunity in this age group.[73]

By the end of February 2021, Europeans were fed up with their slow vaccine rollout and the controversy surrounding AstraZeneca, in which the EU, along with the United Kingdom, had been so heavily invested. While 14 percent of Americans, 27 percent of Britons, and a whopping 53 percent of Israelis had received at least one dose of a coronavirus vaccine by that time, only 5 percent of EU citizens had. Several EU member states began looking for ways to go beyond the bloc's joint approach to cut their own side deals on vaccines, thus moving full circle back to the "go it alone"

approach that had seemed to tempt France and Germany back in the previous spring.[74] According to an investigation by the European Anti-Fraud
Office seen by the *New York Times*, several EU member states turned to the
black or gray market for vaccines, either negotiating with manufacturers
directly or even doing vaccine exchanges among themselves.[75]

These troubles notwithstanding, AstraZeneca was becoming the
backbone of the COVAX initiative because, unlike Pfizer and Moderna,
it did not need to be shipped and stored at ultralow temperatures. Yet
trust in the vaccine within Europe was so low that in mid-March, after
reports surfaced of a small number of patients (37 out of 17 million) who
developed blood clots after receiving an AstraZeneca shot, France, Germany, Italy, and others temporarily suspended its use.[76] It seemed that
the sluggish rollout could not get any worse. The EMA quickly confirmed
the safety of the vaccine, leading the European nations to reverse their
suspensions almost as quickly as they had issued them, but not before
the episode had further tarnished public trust in the vaccine.[77]

Several officials from France and Germany told us that despite all the
shortcomings they did not regret the joint EU approach to vaccines. The
alternative, they said, could have torn the EU apart if some countries
suffered while others powered ahead. That may well be true, but there
are still lessons to be learned. The fundamental problem is that the European Union was too cautious, risk averse, and resource starved when
it came to vaccine development. There was no European version of Operation Warp Speed. After all, the Europeans' first agreement on vaccine
procurement—with AstraZeneca—was not secured until August, months
after the Americans had gotten a head start with OWS. The European
Commission has no ability to raise revenue on its own. It can only spend
what the member states give it. They allocated $2.7 billion for vaccine
development, a fraction of what the United States spent, even though the
EU has a larger population. The member states did not trust the commission and wanted to keep it on a tight leash. Von der Leyen noted in an
interview with the *Financial Times* that "the U.S. has a strong advantage
by having BARDA," referring to the massive National Institutes of Health
research project on vaccines, which formed the basis of OWS. "This," she
said, "is an infrastructure Europe did not have."[78] Gallina, who had led
the EU's negotiating team on vaccine procurement, insisted that she was
not jealous of the U.S. experience because, she believed, "the situation

here in Europe is, may I say, better." But von der Leyen herself was more willing to admit the advantages of the American model and, in early February, the commission president hired Slaoui as a consultant after he stepped down as head of OWS.[79] The following month Slaoui gave the *New York Times* his bottom line assessment: the EU shopped for vaccines like a customer while the United States basically went into business with the drugmakers. Later in the spring of 2021, von der Leyen took a lead from Netanyahu's playbook and dealt personally with the CEO of Pfizer, Albert Bourla, to secure additional vaccines from the European Union.[80]

RUSSIA AND CHINA SKIP THE LINE

Despite all the attention given to vaccines developed by the Americans and Europeans, the world's first COVID-19 vaccines emerged elsewhere. On August 11, 2020, Russia granted regulatory approval to Sputnik V. The name was an allusion to the Cold War–era space race, when, in 1957, the Soviet Union launched Sputnik I, the first artificial satellite put into orbit. The approval of Russia's vaccine came a mere ten days after the completion of phase 1 and phase 2 clinical trials, and the vaccine candidate, developed by the state-run Gamaleya Research Institute of Epidemiology and Microbiology, had been tested on only seventy-six people. The Ministry of Health nonetheless issued a registration certificate for Sputnik V, allowing it to be administered to select medical staff and individuals at high risk for COVID-19. The Kremlin's early approval of Sputnik V before phase 3 trials sparked criticism and worry around the world, from scientists and commentators alike. But President Putin endorsed it, saying at a cabinet meeting that it "works effectively enough" and that his daughter had already received it. Per the certificate, however, the vaccine was not to be used widely until January 1, 2021, by which time larger clinical trials would be completed. An interim analysis of phase 3 clinical trials of Sputnik V released on February 2, 2021, said its efficacy rate was 92 percent— which seemed comparable to Pfizer-BioNTech and Moderna—although the data had not yet been scrutinized by Western regulatory agencies.[81]

China also developed several vaccines that it approved for either emergency or public use in the country, with two preferred by the Chinese government: Sinovac's CoronaVac and Sinopharm's BBIBP-CorV. After running successful phase 1 and phase 2 trials in China in spring

2020, phase 3 trials for CoronaVac were launched in Brazil, Indonesia, and Turkey in July. That same month, the Chinese government approved the vaccine candidate for domestic emergency use, and the vaccine was approved for general public use in December. Results from the Brazilian and Turkish trials yielded differing effectiveness rates—50.38 percent and 83.5 percent, respectively—which were generally lower than those for Western vaccines. Sinopharm's BBIBP-CorV vaccine had a similar trajectory. It was authorized for emergency use in the summer as phase 3 trials started in the United Arab Emirates, Morocco, and Peru, and then approved for general use in China at the end of the year.[82]

As the global race for the vaccine ensued, U.S. officials believed that Russia and China were making significant efforts to steal secrets from Western pharmaceutical firms. In July 2020, for instance, the Department of Justice indicted Li Xiaoyu and Dong Jiazhi, two Chinese hackers, for exploiting "research vulnerabilities" in biotech companies, among other crimes. On several occasions, the cyber intrusions occurred the day after the company announced it was working on a coronavirus vaccine. At the press conference announcing the indictment, FBI deputy director David Bowdich said the scale and scope of Chinese government-directed hacking are "unlike any other threat we're facing today."[83] Microsoft and a number of major pharmaceutical companies let it be known that they were experiencing vaccine-related hacking from Chinese, Russian, North Korean, and Iranian sources.[84]

Russia and China also sought to exploit their national vaccine efforts for geopolitical advantage. Despite struggling to administer the vaccine at home, Russia was eager to distribute it abroad. Throughout late 2020, Kremlin-supported outlets had been touting the virtues of Sputnik V while disseminating disinformation about vaccines developed in the West, calling them unsafe and stressing the potentially harmful side effects. Much of the propaganda was aimed at central and eastern European countries, and by the time Sputnik V became available for distribution, it was clear that the Kremlin's efforts had paid off. On January 20, 2021, Hungary took advantage of a 2001 loophole in EU law to issue a six-month authorization for Sputnik V without approval from the EMA. Three weeks later, it became the first EU member state to administer the Russian jab. As of mid-February 2021, more than fifty countries had ordered doses of Sputnik V.[85]

Following the same playbook as the Russians, state-run media in China sought to undermine Western vaccines, while Beijing used its own vaccine diplomacy to advance its political and economic interests. To make inoculations widely available in low- and middle-income countries, China made a $1 billion loan to governments across Latin America and the Caribbean. In early March 2021, the foreign ministry announced that China would provide free vaccines to sixty-nine countries and commercially export them to an additional twenty-eight countries. It remained unclear whether China would be able to meet its promises. But having received a black eye in some countries for its heavy-handed and overly transactional approach to providing medical assistance in 2020, Beijing clearly saw an opportunity to change the narrative once again by pledging huge quantities of cheap vaccines to the developing world.[86] Yet there were signs that Beijing's vaccine diplomacy, like its previous mask diplomacy, came with strings attached. One notable example was Paraguay, whose foreign ministry released a statement in late March suggesting that offers of vaccines manufactured in China made to the country had been conditional on breaking ties with Taiwan. (The Paraguayan statement was careful to state that the proposal had been made by individuals "whose legitimacy and ties to the government of the People's Republic of China are not proven.")[87]

The jockeying among the great powers was perhaps most evident in Brazil, where the impact of COVID-19 proved unrelenting. Despite the fact that Brazil had recorded 2.83 million new coronavirus cases and more than 50,000 deaths in the final three months of 2020, President Jair Bolsonaro had declared that the country had reached "the tail end" of the pandemic by December. He was wrong. In late 2020, the P.1 variant was discovered in the Amazon region and it quickly gained a foothold throughout the country, with twenty-one of twenty-six Brazilian states reporting cases of the P.1 variant by the end of February. The new strain seemed not only to be more contagious but, some initial studies suggested, capable of reinfecting some people who had already recovered from COVID-19. In the first three months of 2021, Brazil recorded a whopping 5 million additional coronavirus cases and more than 126,000 new deaths. With nearly 12.75 million total cases and over 321,000 deaths since the beginning of the pandemic, Brazil now ranked as the second-hardest hit country on Earth (behind the United States), and in late March it surpassed the United States in new daily cases and deaths. The health system was crumbling and 125 Brazilians were dying of COVID-19 every hour.[88]

In the fall of 2020, Brazilian officials had announced plans to buy 46 million doses of China's CoronaVac—which was undergoing clinical trials in the country—as part of the national immunization program (along with plans to purchase and manufacture the AstraZeneca vaccine). But Bolsonaro, a populist ally of Donald Trump, reversed course, denigrating the Chinese vaccine and writing on social media on October 21: "The Brazilian people will not be anyone's guinea pig."[89] Meanwhile, the Trump administration had worked to discourage Brazil from acquiring Russia's Sputnik V. In a report published by the U.S. Department of Health and Human Services, Russia and other nations were accused of "working to increase their influence in the region to the detriment of U.S. safety and security," prompting the department's global affairs office and other American agencies "to dissuade countries in the region from accepting aid from these ill-intentioned states."[90]

By late January, the Brazilian government had begun inoculating elderly individuals and health care workers—but the country of 213 million people faced an acute shortage of vaccines. With COVID-19 surging and the United States and other wealthy nations seen as hoarding vaccine supplies for domestic use, Bolsonaro's government did another U-turn, asking China to expedite the shipment of tens of millions of CoronaVac doses and to provide the ingredients to mass-produce the vaccine in Brazil. In the absence of alternatives, they were willing to turn to Beijing even though Brazilian trials had shown the vaccine to be just over 50 percent effective.[91] By March, Brazil had secured contracts for 200 million vaccine doses, half of which were CoronaVac and the other half AstraZeneca. That same month, Brazil reached a deal to acquire 10 million doses of Sputnik V, even though the Russian-made vaccine had not yet been approved by the country's health agency.[92]

"COVID, COVID, COVID, COVID"

Even though vaccine developments had been progressing at an incredible pace, there was no scenario in which they would be ready to mitigate the spread of the virus by the time of the U.S. presidential election in November 2020. Of course, Trump had a personal political stake in how the pandemic was perceived. Behind in the polls, partly because of the virus, he was desperate to get back to campaigning and speak to Americans who were tired of restrictions on their daily lives.

Trump had held two indoor rallies in June 2020, including one on June 20 in Tulsa, Oklahoma, that Herman Cain, a former presidential candidate, attended. Ten days after the rally, Cain fell ill with COVID-19. He would die from it on July 30. By that point Trump had briefly suspended his rallies as the country reached its second peak of cases. But he restarted them in mid-August, appearing at several large events each week. On August 27, Trump accepted the Republican nomination at a crowded in-person event held on the White House South Lawn.[93] Few attendees wore masks or socially distanced. As September progressed, Trump hosted more and more events in person. When he introduced Amy Coney Barrett on September 26 as his nominee to replace the recently deceased Ruth Bader Ginsburg on the Supreme Court, he held the announcement ceremony in a packed Rose Garden, along with an indoor reception where masks were scarce. Within a week, eleven people who attended the event would be diagnosed with COVID-19; the number would grow to thirty-seven after twelve days. They included Senators Thom Tillis and Mike Lee, former New Jersey governor Chris Christie, and the president himself.[94]

On September 29, Trump participated in his first presidential debate with Joe Biden in Cleveland, Ohio. The two men, separated by more than a dozen feet, repeatedly shouted at each other across the stage, sparring in what was widely panned as the most contentious and disorderly presidential debate in history.[95] Asked about his views on masks, Trump said they were "OK," but that he only wore them when he felt he needed to. "Tonight is an example. Everyone has had a test and you've had social distancing and all of the things you have to," Trump declared, before proceeding to mock Biden for always wearing a mask.[96] Trump was right that everyone in attendance had committed to taking COVID-19 tests, administered by the Cleveland Clinic. But the president and his entourage had arrived too late for them to be given the tests.[97]

Just three days later, on October 2, Trump tweeted that he and the first lady had tested positive for COVID-19. White House chief of staff Mark Meadows told reporters Trump's condition was "very concerning," and the president was rushed to Walter Reed National Military Medical

Center for treatment. Trump was much sicker than the doctors acknowledged to the public, with "extremely depressed blood oxygen levels at one
point and a lung problem associated with pneumonia caused by the coronavirus," according to a *New York Times* report several months later. Officials believed he would need to be put on a ventilator. At Walter Reed, he
was given access to experimental therapeutics unavailable to the general
public. Within days, Trump recovered.[98]

Unlike Woodrow Wilson, whose bout with influenza a century earlier appeared to alter his decision-making, Trump's brush with the coronavirus did not seem to fundamentally change his behavior. If anything,
Trump emerged defiant. He doubled down, portraying himself as an in-
vulnerable superman. Despite the death of nearly 210,000 Americans by
that point, Trump described his quick recovery as evidence that the pandemic was nothing to worry about. "Don't be afraid of COVID. Don't let
it dominate your life," he tweeted as he prepared to leave Walter Reed on
October 5. "I feel better than I did 20 years ago!"[99]

Trump then took his message on the road, continuing to dismiss public health concerns around mass gatherings even as U.S. coronavirus cases
mounted. He moved forward with dozens of largely mask-free, potentially
superspreading political rallies across the country aimed at propelling him
to a second term. At one event in Omaha, Nebraska, a week before the
election, Trump complained, "With the fake news, everything is COVID,
COVID, COVID, COVID," before adding: "I had it. Here I am, right?"[100]

Trump was keenly aware that the pandemic could cost him the election. He was the most unpopular president in modern U.S. history.[101]
In early 2020, as an incumbent riding a strong economy, he appeared
to stand a decent chance of winning a second term. That was before
COVID-19 changed everything. In late October, he told a large crowd
in Erie, Pennsylvania—a key swing state—that he had never expected to
have to campaign for their votes in person. "Before the plague came in, I
had it made. I wasn't coming to Erie. I mean, I have to be honest, there's
no way I was coming," Trump declared. "I didn't have to. I would've called
you and said, 'Hey, Erie. You know, if you have a chance, get out and vote.'
We had this thing won."[102]

"If he loses, it's going to be because of COVID," Republican National
Committee chair Ronna McDaniel said in the days leading up to the election.[103] And, indeed, available evidence shows that the pandemic played

a central role in the election, although not in a straightforward or one-sided fashion.

Concerns over the safety of in-person voting at the polls contributed to a massive increase in mail-in ballots across the United States. The ease of casting mail-in ballots and intense partisan feelings for or against Trump, in turn, combined to produce record turnout. In the lead-up to November 3, polls consistently showed a majority of Americans disapproved of Trump's handling of the COVID-19 crisis. The fact that Trump and many of his inner circle became infected seemed to symbolize his administration's unserious, mismanaged approach. Meanwhile, Trump's best argument for reelection—the strength of the U.S. economy—was undermined by the skyrocketing joblessness and waves of collapsing businesses unleashed by the pandemic.

Yet on election day itself, the impact of the virus was complicated. The pandemic clearly shaped the views of those who voted against Trump. A postmortem prepared by his chief pollster after the election concluded that Trump's mishandling of the COVID-19 response had hurt him badly, especially in states he had won in 2016 but which flipped to Biden in 2020.[104] Survey data collected by the Associated Press VoteCast—which included interviews with more than 110,000 likely voters, conducted over several days before the November 3 election and until polls closed that day—showed that 41 percent of voters viewed COVID-19 as the most important issue facing the country (no other issue came close). Of those, 73 percent voted for Biden, compared to 25 percent for Trump. Of the 50 percent of respondents who said the pandemic was "not at all under control," 83 percent pulled the lever for Biden, compared to 15 percent for Trump.[105]

At the same time, the pandemic appears to have influenced the record number of people who voted *for* Trump. A CNN exit poll found that of the 61 percent of Americans who said the preelection rise of coronavirus cases was "important" to their presidential vote, 52 percent voted for Biden, but of the 79 percent who said the rise in cases was "a factor" in their vote, 56 percent voted for Trump.[106] In a deeply polarized political ecosystem, many Republicans seemed to agree with Trump's narrative of downplaying the dangers of the pandemic. They also tended to subscribe to Trump's claim that containment measures implemented by state and local officials rather than his administration's incompetence were responsible for the economic downturn. And many Republicans seemed concerned that Biden's proposals for getting COVID-19 under control would shutter schools and businesses and prevent the reopening of the economy.[107] In the AP VoteCast survey, of the 28 percent of respondents who said the economy and jobs were their top concern, 82 percent voted for Trump (compared to just 16 percent for Biden). When asked "Which should be the federal government's highest priority?" only 39 percent said "limiting additional damage to the economy even if it increases the spread of the coronavirus"—but of those, 86 percent voted for Trump.[108] The CNN exit poll found similar results.[109]

In the end, Joe Biden received 81 million votes to Trump's 74 million—a huge differential of 7 million votes. The tally in the Electoral College was 306 for Biden and 232 for Trump, which happened to be exactly the margin Trump won by in 2016. Yet despite Biden's impressive win, the unprecedented number of mail-in votes slowed the count, delaying final results for days. That delay and the narrow margin of Biden's victory in a number of key swing states provided plenty of space for Trump and his supporters to peddle disinformation (what would later be described as "The Big Lie"), falsely claiming that Biden had somehow "stolen" the election. The charge was nonsense, rejected by state election officials (including Republicans), by the U.S. Supreme Court, and in more than sixty lawsuits the Trump campaign unsuccessfully brought in courts around the country.[110] But polls showed that a majority of Republican voters believed it.[111] Bucking the long-standing American tradition of peacefully transferring power, Trump's refusal to concede defeat led to the rockiest presidential transition in memory, capped by the violent siege of the U.S. Capitol—egged on by Trump himself—on January 6, 2021. But America's democratic institutions ultimately held, and Biden was inaugurated on January 20.

THE WHO AND CHINA, ACT II

On Tuesday, January 5, 2021, at the WHO's first press conference of the new year, director general Tedros Adhanom Ghebreyesus told reporters that members of the international scientific team investigating the origins of COVID-19 had begun traveling from their home countries to China. He continued:

We learned that Chinese officials have not yet finalized the necessary permissions for the team's arrival in China. I'm very disappointed with this news given that two members had already begun their journeys and others were not able to travel at the last minute. But I have been in contact with senior Chinese officials and I have once again made it clear that the mission is a priority for WHO and the international team. I have been assured that China is speeding up the internal procedure for the earliest possible deployment.[112]

It was a stunning statement. For the past year, Tedros had steadfastly refused to say anything that could be interpreted as criticism of the Chinese government's management of the pandemic. Tedros had not called out Beijing for denying his organization the access it needed to critical samples or data on the virus even though his own team privately said the WHO should do so. This infuriated U.S. officials—not least then-president Trump, who called the WHO a "puppet of China."[113] By early 2021, however, as the Trump administration receded in the rearview mirror, the director general changed his tune. A senior Trump administration official told us, "It was literally what we were begging him to do last year." The results were immediate. On January 14, the WHO international investigative team arrived in Wuhan.[114]

The international scientific investigation had been a long time in the making. As we saw in Chapter 4, the Australian government, which has been at the forefront of the global effort to confront China in recent years, had joined the United States in calling for an investigation of Beijing's pandemic response as early as April 2020.[115] Furious, the Chinese government said this effort "[hurt] the feelings of the Chinese people."[116] In retaliation, Beijing imposed tariffs on Australian barley, beef, coal, cotton, and wine, costing up to $19 billion per year.[117] At the World Health Assembly in May, Chinese president Xi finally agreed to an independent investigation after the pandemic was contained.[118] But China's reversal came with no small number of obstacles, including tactics to delay and obstruct the investigation.

In July 2020 (the same month Trump announced the U.S. withdrawal from the WHO), China permitted two WHO officials to travel to the country, but they were placed in a fourteen-day quarantine upon arrival.[119] The Chinese government had promised them high-level virtual meetings, but all they got were a slow pace of low-level sessions. The WHO officials were pessimistic about the fate of the mission. Tedros called the Chinese foreign minister and complained: the meetings were terrible, he argued, and the team could not do its job. The situation improved, but when the experts exited quarantine, they were barred from visiting Wuhan.[120] Although the Chinese government and the WHO designed a plan during the July visit to further investigate how the novel coronavirus had spread to humans—which involved Chinese scientists examining hospital records and samples of sewage and blood donations, interviewing victims, and mapping products and individuals who had made contact with the Wuhan wet market—Beijing delayed the follow-on WHO visit for months.[121]

The WHO scientific investigative team was finally allowed into China on January 14, 2021. Two days before their arrival, the *Global Times*, the state-run tabloid that has been described as "China's Fox News," ran a piece citing "experts" arguing that the upcoming WHO visit "shows the country has always been dedicated to making its contribution to the global fight against the pandemic with a transparent, responsible attitude and a spirit of respect for science."[122] The WHO team was forced to spend the first two weeks of their visit in quarantine before finally moving to a lakeside hotel in Wuhan. Their goal was to visit labs, markets, and hospitals in the area to finally get more definitive answers on the pandemic's origins. The investigative team managed to get access to some new information, especially aggregated data, which was helpful in their inquiry. However, other information was held back, including raw data on early COVID-19 cases that could help ascertain how and when the virus originally spread in China.[123]

Chinese officials, meanwhile, were frustrated with the team's questions and requests for data and stipulated that Chinese scientists should oversee parts of the investigation.[124] They encouraged the WHO to accept explanations pushed by Chinese state media and certain government officials, including the possibility that the virus may have originated outside of China.[125] Thea Kølsen Fischer, a Danish epidemiologist and member of the team, told the *New York Times*, "It was my take on the entire mission that it was highly geopolitical. Everybody knows how much pressure there is on China to be open to an investigation and also how much blame there might be associated with this."[126]

After four weeks on the ground (including the two in quarantine) the WHO unveiled its preliminary findings at a press conference in Wuhan on February 9.[127] Peter Ben Embarek, the WHO's food safety and animal disease specialist and chair of the investigation team, said the theory that SARS-CoV-2 escaped from a lab was "extremely unlikely" and "isn't a hypothesis we suggest implies further study." He explained that the virus had likely jumped from one animal species to another before being transmitted to humans. This seemed consistent with the most widely held hypothesis about COVID's origins, while seemingly dismissing the claims made by some Trump administration officials about a possible link to the Wuhan Institute of Virology. At the same time, in what was seen as a public relations victory for Beijing, the investigative team also held open two other explanations pushed by the Chinese government: that the coronavirus might have been imported into China via frozen food and that a first outbreak could have occurred outside of Wuhan, even outside of China.[128] One member of the WHO team, Peter Daszak, president of EcoHealth Alliance, even told reporters that the investigation might turn to examine other countries, particularly in Southeast Asia, from which the infected animal or animal products sold at the Wuhan market might have originated.[129]

When Embarek seemed to publicly rule out the lab theory, officials in WHO headquarters in Geneva were stunned. "We fell off our chairs," one told us. Geneva felt the experts did not have sufficient access or the underlying data needed to make an assessment on the lab theory one way or the other. When the investigative team came back, Tedros told them they did not have enough information to make any judgment. The investigative team was defensive. They felt that even getting a reference to the lab was a victory. Their Chinese counterparts had not wanted to include it at all, so they believed that saying it was "extremely unlikely," not impossible, was a win. Tedros, who had previously worked in a lab himself, would have none of it. He told them they should not have compromised on the language.

The reaction from the United States, now led by Joe Biden, to the WHO team's public statements was swift and skeptical. President Biden's national security advisor, Jake Sullivan, issued a statement on February 13 referencing China's refusal to share data on early COVID-19 cases. "We have deep concerns about the way in which the early findings of the

COVID-19 investigation were communicated and questions about the process used to reach them," Sullivan said. "It is imperative that this report be independent, with expert findings free from intervention or alteration by the Chinese government." This all seemed to suggest that, while the new U.S. administration had rescinded Trump's notice of withdrawal from the WHO and was committed to reengaging with the organization, it would refuse to simply accept the status quo. In Sullivan's words, "Reengaging the WHO also means holding it to the highest standards. And at this critical moment, protecting the WHO's credibility is a paramount priority."[130]

On March 30, six weeks after the completion of their investigation, the WHO team finally released its report. The lab claim was still there, with the report stating: "introduction through a laboratory incident was considered to be an extremely unlikely pathway."[131] Tedros was frustrated—he believed the report was excellent in many ways but, as he had told them, the team should not have drawn this conclusion. He had made clear at a press conference the day before that "all hypotheses [regarding the origins of SARS-CoV-2] are open" and merited continued investigation.[132] Now, as the report was rolled out, he highlighted the inadequacy of Beijing's cooperation and the limitations of the team's report. "In my discussion with the team," he said, "they expressed the difficulties they encountered in accessing raw data. I expect future collaborative studies to include more timely and comprehensive data sharing." In discussing the report's dismissal of the possibility that the novel coronavirus may have leaked from a lab, he pointedly added:

> I do not believe that this assessment was extensive enough. Further data and studies will be needed to reach more robust conclusions. Although the team has concluded that a laboratory leak is the least likely hypothesis, this requires further investigation, potentially with additional missions involving specialist experts, which I am ready to deploy.[133]

Meanwhile, the new U.S. secretary of state, Antony Blinken, questioned the report's methodology and process, "including the fact that the government in Beijing apparently helped write it."[134] A joint statement issued on March 30 by the United States, Australia, Canada, the Czech Republic, Denmark, Estonia, Israel, Japan, Latvia, Lithuania, Norway,

Slovenia, South Korea, and the United Kingdom noted their "shared concerns that the international expert study [convened by the WHO] on the sources of the SARS-CoV-2 virus was significantly delayed and lacked access to complete, original data and samples."[135] A similar statement by the European Union followed.[136]

The Chinese were not happy with all the criticism. Tedros talked to the Chinese ambassador to the WHO in Geneva to clear the air. Tedros explained that in 2020 he had restrained himself from criticizing China, even as others were accusing the WHO of complicity with Beijing's cover up, because he had lacked firsthand information. Now he was going to tell the truth about the report even if China did not like it.[137]

One senior Trump administration official told us that Biden's election may have stripped away some of the cover Tedros had previously enjoyed. As long as Trump was playing the pantomime villain, bashing the WHO and displacing blame at every opportunity, other countries would stand by the director general, even if they had concerns of their own. But with Trump out of the way, Tedros was more exposed to broader criticism for appearing to bend to China's preferences. Sensing this, the official continued, Tedros had begun to change tack—hence his growing willingness to call Beijing out for obstruction beginning in January. Officials at the WHO dispute this, arguing that the contrast between Tedros's approach in early 2020 compared to early 2021 was explained by the different phases of the pandemic and the urgency of securing Chinese cooperation at the outset. In the beginning, a WHO official told us, Tedros desperately needed China to work with the organization to contain the contagion before it spread around the globe, so he was keen to avoid any public criticism of Beijing. In contrast, by 2021, the pandemic had reached a different stage, and Tedros was now more willing to diplomatically push back. He had also exhausted all other options—he had given China time and space and yet it had continued to drag its heels.

Fighting for a Better Future

THE LEADERS OF the G7—the grouping of the world's seven wealthiest democracies—were due to convene for their forty-seventh annual summit in Cornwall, United Kingdom, in June 2021. But the United Kingdom, which held the group's presidency, could not wait. It called for an emergency virtual summit to be held four months early, on February 19. There was much to discuss. The COVID-19 pandemic was still raging, with headlines about revolutionary vaccines competing with news of mutant strains rampaging across Britain and other nations. However, Downing Street's sense of urgency was also driven by another factor: the arrival of a new administration in Washington.

British prime minister Boris Johnson had spent considerable time cultivating a good relationship with Donald Trump, a fellow populist. At the same time, the two differed on key issues, such as climate change and the importance of multilateral institutions including the World Health Organization and the COVAX initiative. Moreover, unlike Trump or Brazil's leader, Jair Bolsonaro, Johnson's personal bout of COVID-19 triggered a real shift in his approach to the virus—he took it seriously. But Johnson was also anxious about Joe Biden, the new occupant of the White House. Johnson was aware that Democrats viewed him as a Trump ally. Furthermore, Johnson's government had clashed with candidate Biden in the run-up to the election over the prime minister's approach to exiting the European Union. The Americans worried that the split with the EU would create a hard border between Ireland (which would remain in the EU) and Northern Ireland (which would exit with the United Kingdom), jeopardizing the 1998 Good Friday Agreement that had brought an end to about thirty years of conflict known as the Troubles. In September 2020, Biden had issued a warning on Twitter, which he knew Johnson would take seriously given the United Kingdom's need to chart a viable economic path outside the EU.

> We can't allow the Good Friday Agreement that brought peace to Northern Ireland to become a casualty of Brexit. Any [future] trade deal between the U.S. and U.K. must be contingent upon respect for the Agreement and preventing the return of a hard border. Period.[1]

Months later, with Britain's G7 presidency, Johnson thought he had an ace in the hole. He had the power to hold a meeting a month into the Biden administration and forge a personal bond with the new U.S. president. He hoped to take advantage of Biden's commitment to reengage America's closest democratic allies and turn the page on the turbulence of the Trump era. There seemed to be a renewed opportunity to find common cause—to combat the pandemic, address the economic fallout, and grapple with other shared threats. "The solutions to the challenges we face—from the colossal mission to get vaccines to every single country, to the fight to reverse the damage to our ecosystems and lead a sustainable recovery from coronavirus—lie in the discussions we have with our friends and partners around the world," Johnson said ahead of the online meeting.[2]

The Biden team also saw an upside to an early summit. There was some internal deliberation about whether to focus attention on the G7 or the larger G20 in the early months of the administration. The latter could prove vital for navigating issues such as mounting emerging-market debt. But the G20 is also a collective in which China and Russia play a more prominent, and potentially unhelpful, role. Given the escalating geopolitical rivalry, aggravated by the pandemic, Johnson's proposed meeting seemed like a way for the new administration to cement the support of the world's leading democracies immediately and more seamlessly. "It was a chance for us to be on offense rather than play defense," one White House official told us.

This was significant. After the financial crisis of 2008–9, the Obama administration made a conscious effort to work with the G20 because of a belief that it was necessary to bring rising powers into the international order. When asked at the G20 press conference in 2009 if U.S. influence had diminished, Obama replied, "If there's just Roosevelt and Churchill sitting in a room with a brandy, that's an easier negotiation. But that's not the world we live in, and it shouldn't be the world that we live in."[3] But twelve years later, the Biden administration recognized that the idea of a more inclusive order would not get you very far unless the United States first built consensus within its democratic core.

Johnson's gambit seemed to work. In March 2020, G7 foreign ministers could not agree on a common approach to fighting the pandemic, due in part to the Trump administration's insistence that COVID-19 be called the "Wuhan virus." As we saw in the introduction, plans to hold a G7 leaders' summit in the United States that summer also collapsed over intramural, and often deeply personal, disputes. This time around, however, the G7 leaders went out of their way to emphasize solidarity. "Drawing on our strengths and values as democratic, open economies and societies," their February 19 joint statement declared, "we will work together and with others to make 2021 a turning point for multilateralism and to shape a recovery that promotes the health and prosperity of our people and planet." The leaders agreed to "intensify cooperation" on the pandemic and economic recovery measures, "accelerate global vaccine development and deployment," and strengthen the World Health Organization.[4]

A major issue was unequal access to lifesaving vaccines. "Just 10 countries have administered 75 per cent of all COVID-19 vaccines," UN secretary-general António Guterres said two days before the G7 convened. "Meanwhile, more than 130 countries have not received a single dose."[5] WHO officials echoed these concerns. "I need to be blunt," Tedros Adhanom Ghebreyesus told the WHO Executive Board in January. "The world is on the brink of a catastrophic moral failure—and the price of this failure will be paid with lives and livelihoods in the world's poorest countries."[6] The issue was top of mind at the summit, where the assembled leaders promised additional funding for COVAX to bolster the purchase and distribution of vaccines to poorer countries. This included $4 billion in new funds from the United States for COVAX, a program the Trump administration had refused to participate in. (The money was approved by the U.S. Congress in December 2020.) The American contribution was meaningful. The U.S. funds, $2.5 billion of which were made immediately available, brought the total funding for COVAX to $8.6 billion. That still left a projected funding shortfall of $3.1 billion required for global vaccines, but the remaining $1.5 billion disbursement of U.S. cash would help close that gap across 2021 and 2022.[7]

Yet money was not the only, or most pressing, problem. Rather, as Kate Elder, senior vaccines policy advisor for Médecins Sans Frontières (Doctors Without Borders), observed, the real challenge was that advance purchase arrangements negotiated by wealthy countries like the United States and the United Kingdom to inoculate their national populations had "sucked up the supply" available for distribution to poorer countries. Consequently, COVAX simply had "very few tangible doses ready to distribute to the multitude of countries that are relying upon it."[8]

European leaders at the G7 shared that view. French president Emmanuel Macron was emphatic that funding alone was not sufficient to ensure equitable distribution so long as there was not enough vaccine made available for purchase. Macron called on members to allocate up to 5 percent of current vaccine supplies to developing countries. "We are allowing the idea to take hold that hundreds of millions of vaccines are being given to rich countries and that we are not starting in poor countries," Macron told the *Financial Times*. "It's an unprecedented acceleration of global inequality and it's politically unsustainable too because it's paving the way for a war of influence over vaccines." Warning that Beijing and Moscow could make additional geopolitical inroads by providing vaccines to developing countries if the G7 failed to deliver, Macron added: "You can see the Chinese strategy, and the Russian strategy too."[9]

The U.S. position, however, remained that all Americans who wanted to be inoculated should receive a shot before any of its vaccine supplies were sent overseas. Biden administration officials felt constrained by domestic politics, knowing that there would be an outcry if the vaccine was exported while it was still needed to address the dire situation at home. The best thing they could do, they thought, was to produce so much of the vaccine and distribute it so quickly that America would be in a position to share it with the world as soon as possible.[10] The U.S. position irritated EU officials, who, as we saw in Chapter 12, were struggling to vaccinate their own populations yet still exported 34 million doses to thirty-one countries.

As a practical matter, however, differences between Washington and its allies seemed mild compared to what they had been under Trump. German chancellor Angela Merkel explained the shift in her characteristically straightforward way: "The change in the United States of America [since Biden's election], in particular, has strengthened multilateralism."[11]

Almost as if to prove Merkel's point, the White House followed up the G7 leaders meeting with a virtual summit of the so-called Quad on March 12, where Biden was joined by Australian prime minister Scott Morrison, Indian prime minister Narendra Modi, and Japanese prime minister Yoshihide Suga. Among the commitments made, the four democratic nations agreed to invest in expanded global vaccine manufacturing capacity, including U.S. financial support for the Indian manufacturer Biological E, with the goal of addressing vaccine shortages in Southeast Asia and elsewhere.[12] Then, a week later, responding to criticism that it was sitting on a large stockpile of AstraZeneca vaccine not yet approved for emergency use in the United States, the Biden administration agreed to "loan" millions of doses to Canada and Mexico. Those governments would provide an equivalent number of doses later to the United States when their supplies of vaccines increased.

Matters seemed to come to a head in April when the world experienced its worst-ever weeks of the pandemic. Despite news that the excess mortality rate from COVID-19 for Americans had surpassed that of the Great Influenza, the public health situation in the United States had markedly improved thanks to a rapid and successful vaccination program. But it deteriorated rapidly elsewhere. In South America, Argentina, Brazil, Colombia, Peru, and Uruguay all experienced record death rates. In India, a horrific surge fueled by political and religious superspreader events and a double mutation of the virus produced hundreds of thousands of new cases day after day, bringing the country's health system to the brink of collapse. These events seemed to confirm the reality that, despite the promise of vaccines, the pandemic was far from over and humanity was not likely to enter the post-COVID world anytime soon. Indeed, it seemed increasingly likely that the planet might never fully put COVID-19 in the rearview mirror. With worldwide vaccine distribution falling short and so many places for the virus to go, circulate, and mutate, the prospects mounted of the disease becoming endemic in many corners of the globe.[13]

In the spring of 2021, the most urgent task facing the Biden administration and all governments was to engage in a monumental, multinational effort to contain COVID-19 globally and mitigate its effects. A two-tier world was rapidly emerging, divided between the largely vaccinated and the unvaccinated. Such an outcome risked profound human tragedy, compounding existing inequalities and incentivizing reduced connections between the vaccinated and unvaccinated blocs, with less travel, less investment, and less trade. By the end of April, and under intense pressure, the Biden administration agreed to export crucial raw materials for vaccines to India, and it also promised to export its stockpile of AstraZeneca vaccines. In early May, the Biden administration announced it would support the waiver of intellectual property rights pertaining to the vaccine. These steps appeared to lay the foundation for a global effort to fight the pandemic.[14]

These moves seemed to show that Donald Trump's defeat had opened a window of opportunity for America to change course even if there were a few bumps in the road. The U.S. government would now take the pandemic more seriously—not just domestically but as a multidimensional challenge to global security. But even if the United States successfully pivots from "America First" to "America is back," as Biden liked to say, the old international order will not be restored. It was increasingly brittle before COVID-19 and, as we have described throughout this book, the international reaction to the pandemic seemed to push it past the breaking point. Nationalist pressures, aggravated by COVID-19, will not disappear. The era of unquestioned U.S. primacy has passed, and the global distribution of power has shifted. Doubts about America's commitment to sustained multilateral engagement will linger despite Trump's departure from the Oval Office. And the difficulty of cooperating with an ascendant and more assertive China, even on shared problems such as pandemics, is manifest. To be sure, the United States still retains considerable capacity to shape world affairs, especially if it works alongside other leading democracies. But America cannot simply go back to the way things were. And that applies to the world writ large. If the United States hopes to lead once again, it will have to chart a new path forward—one that accounts for new realities and constraints.

That starts with understanding the wreckage caused by COVID-19 and the pandemic politics it unleashed.

THE ENDURING RELEVANCE OF 2020

The COVID-19 pandemic was not the first global crisis of the twenty-first century. During the 2008–9 international financial crisis, the world experienced bigger drops in the stock market, global trade, and economic growth than in the first few years of the Great Depression. Yet policy-makers managed to avert a second depression because the major powers cooperated with each other and made enlightened decisions at home—stimulating the economy, avoiding protectionism, and protecting financial institutions. As Daniel Drezner, a professor of international politics at Tufts University, documented in his book on the subject, "the system worked."[15] This was no accident. Geopolitically, the world was a benign place in 2008. Yes, there was a war in Iraq, and Russia had invaded part of Georgia, but relations between the major powers were generally good, with a near consensus on the global economy. The United States still saw China as being on a pathway to becoming a responsible stakeholder in the international order. Populist nationalism was a thing of the past, or so it seemed.

Then, in 2020, the system failed. In the face of a once-in-a-century pandemic and a historic global economic catastrophe, there was hardly any international cooperation. Nations looked after themselves and governments went in different directions domestically. A tiny few succeeded. Some of the most powerful, like the United States, failed catastrophically. While this was shocking, in retrospect it is not surprising. In the decade before COVID-19, the international order's deterioration was hiding in plain sight. Failing states, yawning inequality, and mounting anxieties produced by globalization left hundreds of millions of people vulnerable, displaced, and dissatisfied. Democracies around the world suddenly found themselves on the back foot, besieged by forces from within and without. Nationalists and populists came to power in Turkey, Hungary, Brazil, and even the United States, while illiberal voices became louder in numerous other countries. China's authoritarian system hardened, while its regional and global ambitions greatly expanded. Russia grew bolder, invading more of its neighbors, interfering in democratic elections across the West, and pioneering new strategies of disinformation. After Trump was elected, the United States pulled back from international cooperation and its traditional leadership role, shredding one multilateral

commitment after another, berating traditional allies, embracing dictatorships, and launching trade wars against multiple countries. Meanwhile,
societies across the globe became increasingly polarized, with plummeting trust in authority of any form—whether governments, the media, corporations, or scientific expertise. As we discussed in Chapter 3,
when the COVID crisis hit, the international community's collective
immune system was already deeply compromised.

Even if the world pursues a more cooperative response to the pandemic in 2021 and beyond, the year 2020 will forever stand as an example
of what happens when the planet confronts a major crisis in the absence
of international leadership and a collective response. Not all the results
were negative, however. Some things still managed to function. For instance, in the face of the Great Lockdown, the world's central banks kept
liquidity flowing and governments sought to stimulate the economy, at
least initially, even though the G20 finance ministers did very little to
facilitate it. It was a form of mutually reinforcing unilateralism without
extensive, formal cooperation—and it did much to keep the global economy afloat. Government officials in several G7 countries would say this
was "correlation without coordination."

Throughout 2020, experts warned that vaccine nationalism would
undermine the multilateral cooperation needed to develop and deploy
the vaccines equitably. Initially, the United States and China both stayed
out of COVAX, exacerbating these concerns. But vaccine competition
proved to have mixed consequences. There is no question that the unprecedented national race for the vaccine, particularly in the United
States, accelerated development, providing the world with larger quantities of viable vaccines at a much earlier stage than anticipated. Could
this have been accomplished multilaterally with sufficient political will
by world leaders? Almost certainly yes. There is no reason why America's
Operation Warp Speed would be inherently incompatible with participation in COVAX and a commitment to share the vaccine with front-line
health care workers and vulnerable people around the world. The Trump
administration could have pursued this route. Instead, America and other
key states decided to go it alone. Ultimately, it is hard to argue that great-
power competition and rivalry impaired the *development* of vaccines. But
it did raise serious questions about how the United States, China, and
Russia would ultimately *distribute* vaccines, and what role geopolitical

considerations—rather than public health or equity concerns—would ultimately play in their calculations.

It is also important to acknowledge that, even as governments competed, the development of vaccines was actually made possible by a remarkable process of collaboration among scientists and the business community that could only take place in an open and interconnected world, pandemic politics notwithstanding. For example, Pfizer, the company that developed the first highly effective vaccine, was led by Albert Bourla, a Greek immigrant who became an American citizen. Pfizer partnered with a German company, BioNTech, founded by Turkish immigrants. The Pfizer-BioNTech partnership thrived even though Merkel and Trump were hardly speaking and the U.S. administration sought to acquire another German pharmaceutical firm. If the open and collaborative world of science breaks down into rival blocs that see innovation as zero-sum, the negative consequences for global public health will be profound. Fortunately, that did not occur in 2020.

If monetary policy and vaccine development were qualified successes, in most other areas the system short-circuited. Borders were closed in a chaotic way that left tens of millions stranded throughout the crisis. This could have been avoided if best practices had been shared more transparently. Governments competed for critical medical supplies, outbidding each other on runways and seizing shipments if given the opportunity. The United Nations Security Council was paralyzed by disputes between the United States and China, preventing the major powers from cooperating to ease violent conflicts and provide humanitarian relief. New foreign policy crises popped up with frequency—whether it was China's move on Hong Kong, the deadly China-India border clash, renewed warfare between Azerbaijan and Armenia, or violent conflict in Ethiopia. All of these took place in 2020. There would be no G7 summits with a single message to calm a volatile global situation, let alone a common course of action. Initial economic stimulus efforts proved insufficient to prevent nations from drifting back into a severe recession or worse. Escalating poverty and food insecurity threatened to immiserate tens of millions in low- and middle-income countries, reversing decades of progress in development and creating growing prospects of mass displacement. As the Bill & Melinda Gates Foundation put it in September 2020, development was set back "about 25 years in about 25 weeks."[16] And there was scant international action to provide vulnerable states and people with the debt relief or humanitarian assistance they so desperately needed. Meanwhile, democracy and civil liberties around the world, already under siege for years before COVID-19, took another body blow, with digital technologies turbocharged by the pandemic creating new threats to personal freedom that could persist for years to come.

None of this will stay in the past. The aftershocks from the pandemic will linger for many years. In December 2020, during a virtual United Nations General Assembly summit on COVID-19, UN chief Guterres was stark in this regard:

> Nearly a year into the pandemic, we face a human tragedy, and a public health, humanitarian and development emergency. For the first time since 1945, the entire world is confronted by a common threat, regardless of nationality, ethnicity or faith. But while COVID-19 does not discriminate, our efforts to prevent and contain it do.
>
> ... And when countries go in their own direction, the virus goes in every direction. The social and economic impact of the pandemic is enormous, and growing. Thanks to the hard work and dedication of scientists and researchers from around the world, ... vaccines may become available within the next weeks and months. But let's not fool ourselves. A vaccine cannot undo damage that will stretch across years, even decades to come.[17]

Geopolitically, the COVID-19 crisis also offered the world a glimpse of what an ascendant China that neither effectively leads nor cooperates with other nations on shared problems looks like. In many respects, this was a natural extension of dynamics already in motion before the pandemic. After Xi Jinping became general secretary of the Chinese Communist Party in 2012, and then president in 2013, China became more dictatorial and repressive. He consolidated his power over the CCP, and the party, in turn, tightened its grip on Chinese society. The Chinese government has engaged in massive human rights abuses in Xinjiang and cracked down on freedoms in Hong Kong. China has become more assertive and revisionist abroad—in the South China Sea, in the East China Sea, and vis-à-vis Taiwan; through its Belt and Road Initiative investments in Asia, the Middle East, Africa, Europe, and Latin America; through

Beijing's efforts to use trade, investment, and technology to gain influence in Asia and Europe; and through its campaign to establish new economic institutions and shape global norms consistent with the interests and values of the CCP.

But as the world's most populous country and second-largest economy, China was also widely seen as an indispensable (if difficult) partner on transnational challenges such as climate change, global public health, nonproliferation, and the management of financial crises. Pre-COVID, many governments believed that in a new crisis China would cooperate with other nations as it did in 2008–9. In the early days of the financial crisis, for example, the Russians approached the Chinese with a plan to short the stocks of the massive American mortgage companies Freddie Mac and Fannie Mae in order to further destabilize the American economy (both companies were taken over by the federal government in 2008 to soften the shock of their collapse). The Russians were marginal players in the global economy and may have seen an opportunity to bring other powers down to their level. Instead, Beijing rejected the offer, promptly informed U.S. treasury secretary Hank Paulson of the scheme, and worked *with* the Americans in the months that followed.[18]

The United States, other democracies, and private institutions had invested considerable resources in scientific exchanges with China in the years before COVID-19, with the expectation that it would be more transparent and effective in dealing with a future pandemic than it had been during the 2003 SARS outbreak. Even if progress had been made, COVID-19 shattered it. All the systems China had put in place to improve its pandemic response initially failed. Local authorities tried to silence doctors who alerted the Chinese people about the virus. When Beijing took control, it doubled down on secrecy and repression. Cooperation with the WHO was minimal. The only silver lining was that some of China's scientists shared information with their international counterparts on their own, perhaps a positive consequence of investments made in peer-to-peer cooperation over the preceding decade. China eventually succeeded in controlling its domestic outbreak. But it then embarked on a massive global disinformation campaign and used its economic power and dominance of key supply chains to coerce critics of its response at home and abroad, employing transactional mask diplomacy and sharp-elbowed wolf warrior tactics to advance its geopolitical interests. It also took advantage of the world's focus on the pandemic to essentially end Hong Kong's autonomy.

The deterioration in relations between Washington and Beijing during the COVID-19 pandemic cannot be dismissed as purely Trump's fault; China also experienced a rapid deterioration in its relations with the European Union, Australia, African nations, and others. This dynamic was particularly pronounced in advanced industrial democracies. An October 2020 survey of opinion in twelve democracies by Pew found that majorities in each of the countries polled had a negative view of China. This number soared to 86 percent in Japan, 85 percent in Sweden, 81 percent in Australia, 75 percent in South Korea, 74 percent in the United Kingdom, 73 percent in the Netherlands, Canada, and the United States, 71 percent in Germany, 70 percent in France, 63 percent in Spain, and 62 percent in Italy. The survey also showed that most had little trust in Xi's actions on the global stage (notably, however, even fewer had confidence in Trump), and a majority believed China had done a poor job handling COVID-19 (though still better than the United States).[19]

The Chinese government appeared relatively unperturbed by its early stumbles in the COVID-19 crisis. Senior officials repeatedly pointed to China's massive lockdown as evidence that it responded more decisively and effectively than Western countries, particularly the United States. The Chinese economy also recovered faster and on a steeper curve than any other major economy, likely leapfrogging a few years in closing the economic gap with America (although much will depend on the scale of U.S. investments to improve its competitiveness in the coming years).[20] The lesson for Beijing appears to be that the crisis clearly demonstrated the superiority of the Chinese system. And if international cooperation means greater transparency, then why bother?

The fact remains, though, that since the virus emanated from China (as SARS did seventeen years before), what happens inside China matters to the rest of the world. It cannot be ignored, however much Beijing may say it is none of anyone else's business. The regime's early mishandling of the pandemic directly and negatively affected billions of people around the world, and the world will remember that. Its wolf warrior diplomacy and other provocations weakened the constituencies in the West that favored cooperation and engagement. This was especially true in Europe, which might have worked more closely with China to offset the Trump administration's unilateralism had Beijing behaved more responsibly—and with a lighter touch—throughout.

For the same reason, China's actions *should* have provided a geopolitical opportunity for the United States in 2020. But while America remained a superpower, it did not act like one. Not only did the Trump administration fail to contain the pandemic at home, it failed so spectacularly and shambolically that it left an indelible stain on Washington's global standing. Prior to COVID, the United States had been the indispensable power in every international crisis for the past thirty years. Only the United States had the will and capacity to rally the world to resolve shared challenges. It was the United States that drove the response to the financial crisis in 2008–9. In 2014, it was the United States that created the international coalition that would successfully contain the spread of the Ebola virus in West Africa, and it was Washington that mobilized more than five dozen nations to combat the rise of ISIS. In problems large and small, for better or worse, the United States was always present and engaged. No other country had the same standing to convene other nations or set the international agenda.

Yet the signs of an impending retrenchment were also present. Public exhaustion with the "forever wars" in Afghanistan and Iraq and the hangover from the financial crisis left many Americans yearning to turn inward. President Trump seized on this sentiment, winning in 2016 on a neo-isolationist "America First" platform. He rejected the notion that the United States should try to lead the international community, and believed other countries were ripping the American people off. Whereas his predecessors saw the post–World War II alliances and international institutions Washington had created as an integral part of American power, Trump saw the so-called liberal world order as rigged against the United States. He pulled out of international agreements, including the Paris Agreement on climate change, the Iran nuclear deal, and the Trans-Pacific Partnership trade agreement. He levied tariffs on America's closest allies while treating U.S. treaty commitments to NATO and South Korea like protection rackets. He withdrew troops and abandoned local allies in Syria by tweet, and repeatedly threatened to do the same in South Korea. He yanked GIs out of Germany because of a personal grudge with Merkel. He curtailed support for the United Nations while regaling UN audiences once a year at General Assembly meetings with speeches elevating nationalism over multilateralism. In the absence of a real global crisis, the spectacle of it all was often more pronounced than the substance. The muscle memory of the Pentagon, the State Department, the Treasury Department, and other U.S. agencies meant that much of America's traditional role remained in place—however precariously—despite the president's machinations.

But when the novel coronavirus hit, the consequences of Trump's behavior were revealed. America sat on the sidelines as the world fell apart. No attempt was made to coordinate the G7 or the G20 to mount a collective response. Instead, the administration torpedoed efforts to craft a common G7 response over petty disagreements about what to call the virus. It also refused to accept a UN Security Council resolution on global conflicts because of a passing favorable reference to the WHO. Never has such a great power seemed so small. There was no attempt to mobilize a common approach to the development and distribution of a vaccine or rally a response to the global humanitarian calamity set in motion by the pandemic. This could have easily been done alongside Operation Warp Speed—indeed, America's remarkable investments in vaccine development would have given the Trump administration a unique platform for international collaboration and assistance. Instead, America's inward turn seemed complete. And as the year progressed, the president of the United States became bored with the pandemic and stopped dealing with it altogether at home or abroad.

The November 2020 election provided an emergency reset button, but this correction may prove insufficient to mitigate the long-term strategic cost for America's failure to confront COVID-19 in 2020. The fact that the failure occurred at all—and that Trump did well enough to win more than 74 million votes (to Biden's 81 million) and maintain considerable influence over the Republican Party—will likely impact global perceptions of the United States for years. Given the deeply polarized and partisan nature of U.S. politics, many countries will continue to have doubts regarding Washington's ability and staying power to successfully reengage the world, even if the Biden administration's efforts to contain the virus prove successful and reengagement with the world returns as a priority. America's closest democratic allies in Europe and Asia welcome the end of the Trump era, but their ability to rely on the United States has been compromised by the experience of 2020. Better international cooperation across a range of critical issues is possible—but the days of Washington calling the shots are probably over.

There are already signs of greater self-reliance. After COVID-19 struck, many Europeans realized that they were squeezed between an aggressive China and a nationalistic United States. Even with Biden as president, Europeans see the need to take care of themselves, protect their own interests, and become more self-sufficient in the arena of public health. As one German official told us, "It is not possible to retreat behind national borders, but maybe it is possible to retreat behind European borders." It was no surprise, therefore, when French president Macron continued to emphasize the importance of Europe moving toward greater "strategic autonomy" even after Biden won the U.S. election.[21]

PREPARING FOR THE NEXT PANDEMIC

Each year, between two and five new zoonotic viruses are discovered that have jumped from animals to humans.[22] As the world grows more urban, as deforestation further displaces animals from their natural habitat, and with meat very much a part of global supply chains, the chances of another major pandemic will only accelerate.[23] In the years ahead, shifting climatic zones will also force animals out of their habitats and into greater contact with people (thus increasing the risk of zoonotic diseases) and expand the range of mosquitoes and other sources of vector-borne infectious diseases. Meanwhile, regardless of what the true origin of SARS-CoV-2 and the ensuing COVID-19 pandemic was (and our view is that there is simply not enough evidence as of this writing to conclude one way or the other), the risk of future lab accidents is real and must also be addressed. As all these risks accumulate, we can demand—but we cannot expect—full transparency and cooperation from China and others. And even with sufficient political will, many poorer countries will lack the resources and capacity to identify and contain viruses early, requiring substantial assistance from wealthier countries.

The COVID-19 pandemic has been devastating, but the next virus could easily be worse. The world produced a number of viable COVID vaccines in record time. But even with continued scientific advances, what will happen if a vaccine takes years to develop—or remains completely out of reach—next time? Writing in the *London Review of Books*, Rupert Beale of the Francis Crick Institute put it succinctly:

> To have several highly effective vaccines for this horrible virus after less than a year is a quite astonishing achievement, among the greatest things that we—by which I mean both humanity in general and molecular biologists in particular—have ever accomplished. We've been skillful, but we have also been lucky. A SARS-CoV-2 vaccine turns out to be relatively easy to develop. The virus that causes the next pandemic may not be so forgiving.[24]

Countries with experience with SARS, MERS, H1N1, and other infectious diseases tended to perform better during the COVID-19 crisis. The question we must now confront as a global community is: what did we collectively learn from this shared calamity? The answer is not simple or obvious. After all, the world had plans to deal with a potential pandemic prior to 2020. Governments invested in global public health. Dozens of warnings were issued about this type of threat over the years. Before COVID-19, the United States was ranked the world's most-prepared country, and the United Kingdom was number two. China had made important reforms after SARS and seemed to be cooperating with other countries. When put to the test, none of this bore out. How can we be assured that the efforts we make over the next decade will not result in a similarly disastrous outcome?

To begin with, the world must engage in a painful and rigorous post-mortem exercise that spares no one. There are easy villains, including Xi and Trump, but there is plenty of blame to go around. Trump, for example, was not the only one ignoring the initial warnings or downplaying the virus throughout. Other populist leaders such as Brazil's Bolsonaro and Hungary's Orbán did so as well. Europe's leaders, meanwhile, did almost nothing to prepare, even as the virus spread through Italy. Prior to the pandemic, Western governments assumed most contagions would spread outward from—and could therefore be contained—in the developing world. But COVID-19 circulated among the world's most interconnected and advanced economies first, hitting the ski slopes in the Alps long before it made landfall in the global South. When the contagion first emerged in China, the WHO and many national security experts were wrong to dismiss the importance of imposing rapid travel bans, bowing to Beijing's will. It was also shortsighted to encourage many low-income nations to impose nationwide lockdowns when they were in no position to ensure individual compliance on social distancing, build up sufficient health care capacity, or provide adequate safety nets for idle workers. A rigorous process of self-criticism will be essential for identifying necessary reforms and preparing for future pandemics.

Americans also must find a consensus on facts and science. In November 2020, Laurie Garrett, the veteran American global public health expert who had warned of a global pandemic since the mid-1990s, observed that throughout her career she had made one catastrophic analytical mistake. In all of the scenario planning exercises she designed and took part in, she never once considered the possibility that the White House would be the primary source of obstruction and disinformation. She understood that they might be ill-prepared and slow to respond, as Ronald Reagan was during the AIDS epidemic, but not that the president would be an active saboteur.[25]

Trump's denialism and public statements full of disinformation convinced tens of millions of Americans that COVID-19 was not a serious disease, even as the infection rate and death toll spiraled to record highs. He even crowded out and silenced voices in the Republican Party who understood the threat and advocated for a strong response. Since Trump remains the most powerful force in Republican politics, the question is whether half the country will continue to portray the coronavirus as a "hoax," paint public health precautions such as masks as partisan attacks on personal freedom, and dismiss government experts as deep-state traitors. If so, large swaths of the U.S. population will resist thinking seriously about future biological threats. Will Republicans in Congress or a future Republican president make it a priority? As we have shown, there were senior officials within the Trump administration who grasped the significance of the crisis early on. Some Republican senators and members of Congress did too. The problem is they lost the argument to Trump and others who were complacent. Creating a unified national response centered on science, trust, and careful preparation will be an enormous challenge for U.S. political leaders—but it is absolutely necessary.

Within days of taking office, the Biden administration released a 200-page *National Strategy for the COVID-19 Response and Pandemic*

Preparedness. The strategy sought to reestablish trust with the American public. It aimed to scale up testing, accelerate vaccine distribution, encourage masking, ramp up production of PPE, and secure supply chains. It sought to bolster emergency relief, implement measures to safely reopen schools and businesses and promote safe travel, and take other steps to roll back the pandemic and address its economic fallout, including for disproportionately affected minority communities. It also called on the United States to restore global leadership in combating COVID-19 by remaining in the WHO and pressing for reforms, joining the COVAX initiative, and seeking to strengthen other multilateral initiatives, including the Coalition for Epidemic Preparedness Innovations, the Global Fund to Fight AIDS, Tuberculosis, and Malaria, and Gavi, the Vaccine Alliance. It elevated support for the Obama-era Global Health Security Agenda and other multilateral efforts aimed at building health infrastructure and pandemic preparedness, and it committed to humanitarian assistance to countries hit hard by the virus and the consequences of increased poverty and food insecurity. Meanwhile, the administration moved quickly to reconstitute the White House National Security Council Directorate for Global Health Security and Biodefense (established in the wake of the Ebola epidemic, but dismantled by the Trump administration) and other administration-wide infrastructure for monitoring and responding to biological threats. And the administration sought funding to establish a new National Center for Epidemic Forecasting and Outbreak Analytics to modernize global early warning and response to emerging biological risks.[26]

All of these commitments are vital correctives and are long overdue. But there are a number of other urgent policies the United States should pursue to enhance global pandemic preparedness and resilience to transnational threats.

First, the United States must build a bipartisan consensus at home on the threat posed by pandemics, how to respond, and the need to invest accordingly. America's greatest weakness in the face of a pandemic is that it is divided on fundamental matters. Extreme polarization, media echo chambers, and disinformation have all contributed to high levels of distrust on public health issues. An objectively devastating pandemic was dismissed; commonsense safety measures became partisan political cudgels. If the United States remains divided on these basic questions and on the very idea that a pandemic poses an existential threat, it will be impossible to prepare adequately to deal with it. And if Trump continues to play a leading role in American politics and pushes the line that his administration did everything right and the vaccine was enough, the task will be that much more difficult.

Faith in government and expertise cannot be fixed overnight. But a competent federal response by the Biden administration to the tail end of the COVID-19 crisis—including truthful and consistent communication from the White House and other government officials, better intra- and intergovernmental cooperation, and effective handling of the distribution of COVID-19 vaccines in the United States and overseas—could start to rebuild the underlying faith in public health measures that will inevitably be required to more effectively contain the next global contagion.[27]

Second, as the Biden administration pushes for reforms at the World Health Organization, it should seek to address the core shortcomings revealed by the COVID-19 crisis. As we saw in Chapters 4 and 5, the WHO was overly deferential to China for much of the pandemic. Its advice on lockdowns and travel restrictions left much to be desired. Having said that, it is also clear the WHO felt trapped between two rival superpowers and still worked tirelessly under very difficult circumstances. The WHO is the only organization that has near global membership, has an unlimited health mandate, and is perceived as internationally legitimate. The organization has adopted reforms before, most recently in response to the West Africa Ebola outbreak in 2014. After shortcomings in the WHO's initial response were exposed, some progress was made, including the creation of the Emergency Program and the Contingency Fund for Emergencies, which aimed at improving the organization's ability to respond and deploy quickly in the face of a crisis.[28] These changes appeared to pay dividends, contributing to the WHO's more effective response to the 2018–20 Ebola outbreak in the Democratic Republic of the Congo.[29]

The Biden administration is right to emphasize the importance of the United States working from inside the WHO to enact additional reforms, rather than attempting to defund and tear the organization down, as Trump did. Leaving, threatening to leave, or reducing levels of support will not result in the WHO's collapse and the creation of a more palatable alternative; it would simply empower other nations to push their own agendas at the WHO, including those, like China, with less of an interest in transparency.

But what reforms should the United States seek to ensure that the WHO is more independent and effective?[30] It is critical for the WHO to be free from political interference during future health emergencies, and it must require all members to commit to higher levels of transparency and cooperation, based on the lessons of COVID-19. This requires additional measures—including the threat of sanctions—to ensure immediate and unfettered access for WHO officials in "a public health emergency of international concern" to both the source of the disease and to samples of it. To further reduce the WHO's dependence on voluntary contributions from member states to carry out its functions, the organization will also need a significant and sustained increase in its funding.

In addition, the WHO should update its own advice on travel to and from affected countries, as travel restrictions did play a useful role in slowing the spread of the virus. And Taiwan should be admitted as an observer state. From 2009 to 2015 it was an observer at the World Health Assembly, but Beijing changed its position in 2016 because it was unhappy with the outcome of the Taiwanese election.[31] Taiwan played an important role in containing COVID-19 and in global public health more generally, and it should not be excluded for political reasons.

While pressing for such reforms, we must also recognize that geopolitical constraints will make wholesale implementation difficult in the near or even medium term. For instance, several investigations into the WHO's performance during previous health emergencies recommended sanctions in the event of noncompliance by a member state—including by the IHR Review Committee in 2011 and the Ebola Interim Assessment Panel in 2015—but they never happened.[32] Margaret Chan, the former director general of the WHO, looked into ways that the WHO might reprimand countries that disobey IHR.[33] The problem is that it is nearly impossible to imagine all governments agreeing to a universally applicable mechanism for sanctions or the enforcement of IHR. Even in the case of the International Atomic Energy Association (IAEA), which monitors obligations and reports violations under the Nuclear Non-Proliferation Treaty, sanctions need to be voted upon by the UN Security Council—which means consent is required from China, France, Russia, the United Kingdom, and the United States. Xi Jinping is very unlikely to make a credible commitment to greater transparency, while the shadow of Trump's "America First" agenda within the Republican Party may contribute to lingering doubts about the United States' long-term commitment to the WHO. Nevertheless, it is important to publicly make the case for WHO reform in the hope that at some point in the future the political constraints will loosen.

President Biden should also regularly and firmly raise global public health cooperation with President Xi, reevaluating cooperation as it existed prior to COVID-19 and reinstating and reforming it where necessary. Improved coordination, where possible, has to take place at the leader level for reforms to have any prospect of success and longevity. But we should not expect such reforms to be easy. The harsh reality is that the WHO is likely to continue to be a battleground between the United States, other democratic nations, and China for many years to come. Democratic countries are unlikely to secure all the reforms they deem necessary in the wake of the COVID-19 pandemic. And even in the unlikely case that those reforms appear adequate, there may be no predictable means of enforcing them. When the next crisis hits, there can be no guarantee that major powers will comply with their obligations. Therefore, the United States can, and should, create and participate in parallel global public health arrangements if it deems it necessary, even as it remains fully engaged in the WHO.

That brings us to our third recommendation: it will be necessary to create new international arrangements and coalitions of like-minded states to supplement the WHO's work. The United States can lead this effort. The George W. Bush administration strengthened the global fight against HIV/AIDS through the President's Emergency Plan for AIDS Relief program launched in 2003. In response to the 2009 H1N1 influenza pandemic and the 2014 Ebola epidemic, the Obama administration sought to improve international cooperation and biopreparedness through the Global Health Security Agenda. The Trump administration's nationalist approach to COVID-19 gravely undermined this tradition— but the Biden administration has an opportunity to resuscitate it.

Some countries have proposed a new international treaty on pandemics. This idea was welcomed by the United States, China, and the WHO.[34] It is worth pursuing, but the negotiations will be prolonged, difficult, and inevitably subject to the pressures of resurgent geopolitical rivalries. Devoting all of the international community's energy toward developing a new treaty could divert diplomatic resources from the immediate steps required to improve global preparedness. The hard reality is this: for years to come, existing international public health arrangements will likely prove insufficient due to inadequate national capabilities and the refusal by some countries to cooperate in the event of an outbreak.

For that reason, the United States should consider creating a new Global Alliance for Pandemic Preparedness (GAPP): a "coalition of the willing" of like-minded states, regularly convening at the head-of-state level, working alongside nongovernmental and philanthropic organizations and private-sector actors. Any nation should be able to join the GAPP—contingent on accepting the conditions for membership. However, those conditions should be strict: among members, there would be a commitment to transparency beyond what is called for in the IHR, including greater inspections access for the WHO, not dissimilar to the powers enjoyed by the IAEA in the nuclear arena. Crucially, when the WHO declares an international public health emergency, GAPP members would coordinate on travel and trade restrictions, as well as public messaging and financial penalties and sanctions. The latter would be aimed at non-GAPP countries that fail to provide sufficient access or fail to fully cooperate with the WHO.[35] The GAPP would work to support, not supplant, the WHO and IHR. Among the goals of this new coalition would be to rewire medical supply chains to make them more resilient to shocks and protectionism; establish enduring mechanisms for encouraging better scientific and technical collaboration to combat emerging infectious diseases; and develop mechanisms for the rapid development and equitable distribution of diagnostics, therapeutics, and vaccines in future pandemics (building off the example of the ACT-Accelerator/COVAX).

The GAPP would also build upon and greatly expand the Global Health Security Agenda, with the aim of helping developing nations build greater capacity for pandemic preparedness and response. Coordinated foreign assistance should aim to help countries comply with IHR requirements by building comprehensive early-warning systems for infectious disease and boosting contact-tracing capabilities. Assistance should strengthen health surveillance at airports, ports, and border crossings, build laboratory capacity for testing, and provide the training and critical equipment necessary for front-line health care workers to respond to emergencies. It should also design coordination and communications systems—and appropriate legal infrastructures—to enable central governments to work with local authorities and communities to rapidly contain outbreaks.[36] These efforts should leverage new technologies whenever possible, while doing so in a manner consistent with human rights concerns. To make investments sustainable, the United States and other GAPP members should consider creating an international health security financing mechanism. And to incentivize the responsible use of funds, recipient countries that demonstrate a track record over time of effectively using assistance to build pandemic preparedness should be eligible for additional aid and concessional loans.[37]

For those Americans skeptical of foreign assistance, it may be helpful to view this as enlightened self-interest, not charity. As COVID-19 vividly demonstrates, in today's hyperglobalized world, a biological incident anywhere can quickly become a catastrophe everywhere.[38]

Lastly, beyond improving pandemic preparedness, there will continue to be an urgent need for bilateral and multilateral assistance to help developing nations recover from the developmental and humanitarian catastrophes set in motion by the coronavirus and the Great Lockdown. Decades of poverty alleviation have been reversed. We have a moral obligation and a strategic interest to recover what has been lost and put development on a more resilient footing. The United States should press for global debt relief programs that include bilateral creditors, multilateral creditors, and the private sector, with the aim of freeing up resources for low- and middle-income countries to strengthen social safety nets for the growing ranks of the poor and those working precariously in the informal economy.[39] The international community must also recognize that efforts to respond to COVID-19 have set back decades of progress in improving public health across the developing world by diverting scarce resources away from routine immunizations, improving child and maternal health, and fighting diseases such as tuberculosis, malaria, and HIV/AIDS. This places an imperative on increasing investments in public health infrastructure more broadly.

There is also the opportunity to restructure economies around the world in ways that would reduce risks associated with *other* existential transnational threats—especially, climate change. The global economic downturn produced by the pandemic created a brief reduction in carbon dioxide emissions, but despite the landmark 2015 Paris climate accord, emissions of carbon dioxide and other heat-trapping gases continue to increase. According to the Intergovernmental Panel on Climate Change, the international body of thousands of experts that represents the scientific consensus on climate, the world is on track to warm by around 3 degrees Celsius by the end of the century—a rate and magnitude of change that scientists warn could be cataclysmic. If humanity is to head off the worst potential consequences of climate change by limiting warming to 1.5 to 2 degrees Celsius, the international community has only a few decades to aggressively reduce carbon emissions, and it must achieve carbon neutrality by midcentury.[40] Absent such drastic, cooperative action, the world will see more droughts crippling food supplies and worsening water scarcity; more intense hurricanes, storms, and flooding; more frequent and devastating wildfires; expanding zones for vectors of infectious disease; the inundation of many coastal areas and low-lying nations by sea-level rise, displacing hundreds of millions of people; and the devastation of ocean and terrestrial ecosystems already pushed to the brink by other human activities.

Trillions of dollars will be spent in the coming decades to dig out of the economic hole left by COVID-19. Stimulus and recovery funding can either reinforce the dangerous climate status quo or provide the United States and other nations enormous opportunities to lean into a "green recovery." Investing in renewable energy such as solar and wind power; technology and infrastructure for low- and zero-emission vehicles, aviation, trains, and ships; the promotion of "circular economy" models that drastically reduce resource use and eliminate waste; low-carbon retrofitting and construction; urban redesign; new programs for forest conservation, ecosystem restoration, and sustainable agriculture; and projects to enhance the climate resilience of vulnerable communities—all of this is a potential win-win. A green recovery from COVID-19 could create good jobs in both the near and long terms and unleash enormous innovations in cutting-edge technological fields while reducing the greenhouse gas emissions that imperil the planet. It will also enable countries and communities to better adapt to and ride out the inevitable shocks from climate change.[41] At the February 2021 G7 summit, the United States and its allies pledged to "put our global ambitions on climate change and the reversal of biodiversity loss at the center of our plans" to "build back better" from the pandemic.[42] In the years ahead, that new sense of collective purpose must become a reality.

A STRATEGIC FRAMEWORK FOR THE POST-COVID ERA

Grappling with the broader implications of COVID-19 and its after-shocks for American foreign policy, the geopolitical landscape, and the future of international order will also be essential. When the Cold War ended, American foreign policy was dominated by aspirations to spread the benefits of economic globalization and political liberalism, integrate important powers such as China and Russia into the U.S.-led international order, and manage the challenge posed by humanitarian disasters and rogue states.[43] Then the 9/11 attacks reoriented U.S. foreign policy around the so-called global war on terrorism. The result was a tremendous overinvestment in the greater Middle East at the expense of other regions and priorities. In recent years, a new consensus has taken shape, arguing for a shift in America's primary strategic focus toward great-power competition.[44] This view recognizes that a stable and open international system is founded on healthy regional orders in Asia and Europe. If those regional orders fall apart, so too will the international order. China's rapid rise has caused it to seek an enhanced sphere of influence in the Pacific and to push back U.S. influence. Globally, it uses state-backed enterprises to gain a technological edge in artificial intelligence, facial recognition, and 5G. It also actively promotes illiberal values in international institutions and uses its economic power to coerce middle-sized and small countries. Meanwhile, Russia has invaded its neighbors, interfered in democratic elections (including in the United States), and intervened militarily in Syria. The shift in U.S. strategic thinking toward greater emphasis on great-power competition has been motivated by the necessity to push back against these revisionist authoritarian forces in order to protect and preserve classically liberal values and interests at home and abroad.

Others, however, have argued that the greatest threats facing humanity are not powerful state actors but transnational dangers such as pandemics and climate change.[45] As every human being on the planet experienced in 2020, transnational threats do not respect national boundaries. And because the fates of people, economies, and nations have become so intertwined after decades of globalization, the consequences of transnational shocks can quickly ripple across the international system. Given the devastation wrought by the COVID-19 pandemic, the dangers are now self-evident. Other transnational threats such as climate change could be even graver. We are already seeing the impact of the unfolding climate crisis and, in the not too distant future, the profound disruptions of unchecked global warming on human health, societies, economies, and international security in an interconnected world could be truly apocalyptic.[46]

Like the end of the Cold War and the attacks on 9/11, we are now embarking on a new period: the "post-COVID" era. But the fact that we are entering the post-COVID era does not, in and of itself, tell us very much about the fundamental dynamics likely to define it or how U.S. foreign policy should adjust to new realities. The story of the global response to the pandemic in 2020, however, provides some fundamental insights.

The irony of COVID-19 is that the world of 2020 included a huge number of institutions that did not exist in 1918-20, and yet governments still went their own way, largely because of strategic rivalries and nationalist impulses. In this way, the coronavirus crisis illustrates the negative synergy between great-power competition and transnational threats—one that fundamentally changes both for the worse. This geopolitical dimension to pandemic response is a new phenomenon that policymakers must now grapple with. As David Fidler of the Council on Foreign Relations observes:

> Global health benefitted from the absence of balance-of-power politics in the post–Cold War era and U.S. willingness to catalyze unprecedented developments, including funding increases for HIV/AIDS, the adoption of the IHR (2005), and the emergency response for the Ebola outbreak in West Africa. However, concerns increased during the 2010s that the distribution of power in the international system was, indeed, changing because Chinese and Russian efforts to challenge the United States gained momentum. . . . The shifting geopolitical terrain raised questions about how the re-emergence of the balance of power might affect global health and U.S. leadership in this area.[47]

The pandemic answered those questions. Great-power rivalry made the pandemic both more likely and harder to contain. The Chinese government was obsessed with regime survival at home and capitalizing on the pandemic to expand its influence abroad. Meanwhile, the Trump administration's decision to frame the international dimensions of its COVID policy almost exclusively through a competitive geopolitical lens with China eviscerated the prospects for a multilateral response. Every other nation, meanwhile, had to helplessly watch the superpower scrum while largely fending for themselves.

Relations between Washington and Beijing are likely to continue to deteriorate. The Chinese and American visions for the world are simply incompatible with each other, and this conflict will not change until one side abandons its vision or accepts that it cannot be implemented. Each side creates negative externalities that affect the other, even if unintentionally. For instance, America's press freedom reveals secrets, corruption, and wrongdoing that are destabilizing for the Chinese Communist Party. Meanwhile, Beijing's technological advances can be exported abroad and used to make democracies dependent upon a system that is fundamentally illiberal, potentially compromising freedoms in the United States and elsewhere. Even with diplomacy, friction will be endemic to the Sino-U.S. relationship and impact the broader international order for the foreseeable future. If cooler heads prevail, outright confrontation can be avoided—but strategic competition cannot.

The dilemma is clear: we live at a time when mounting transnational threats require more international cooperation than ever before, and yet a changing distribution of power and escalating rivalry among the world's major powers make the very collaboration we so desperately need more difficult to achieve. The uncomfortable truth is that there is no longer any reason to expect that nations are converging on a single unified purpose or model of global governance. The aspirations of the old international order have fallen by the wayside. The challenge will be for world leaders to find ways to work together when their interests align even in the midst of accelerating competition.

In the debate over whether it is great-power competition or transnational threats that define the current strategic environment, the answer is clearly *both*. The United States therefore needs an approach to defending its interests and addressing transnational challenges that will work *even if* relations between the major powers remain contentious.

In Washington, that means seizing on the lessons of 2020 to build a new bipartisan consensus around the need for critical domestic investments and renewed support for American global leadership. The pandemic laid waste to large swaths of the U.S. economy. And America's failed response has accelerated China's ascendance. Those twin realities should provide bipartisan impetus to make key investments that not only fuel near-term recovery but do so in a manner that spurs the innovation needed to outcompete China *and* build greater resiliency against transnational threats. That means making significant investments in health care, education (especially STEM), worker retraining and upskilling, and digital and clean energy infrastructure. It also includes significantly expanding federal research and development in the technological domains that will dominate the remainder of this century.

Meanwhile, COVID-19 and the horrendous humanitarian and development consequences associated with it will likely be with us for a long time. Variants will continue to emerge and become a global threat if the world is not fully vaccinated. Although the pandemic temporarily halted immigration and refugee flows, the accumulating immiseration of millions of people across developing countries will eventually create an unstoppable movement of desperate people. Many, especially in Latin America and the Caribbean, will set out for the United States. Enlightened self-interest should drive U.S. policymakers to address these challenges *before* they result in mass displacement that crashes upon America's shores. The imperative to check China's malign influence abroad also provides a powerful rationale for America to provide humanitarian and development assistance and, more broadly, to embrace its closest allies and recommit to deep international engagement. If Washington fails to lead in shaping the institutions, rules, norms, and multilateral arrangements around critical issues such as cyber, artificial intelligence and other emerging technologies, trade, development, the environment, and human rights, Beijing will—and it will do so in a manner that is increasingly incompatible with the security, prosperity, and way of life of the United States and other free societies.

RALLYING THE FREE WORLD

The interwar period of the 1920s and '30s—which followed World War I and the last great pandemic—was a time of massive economic, social, and political upheaval. Rising nationalism and the revisionist ambitions of authoritarian powers collided with fragile international institutions incapable of managing great-power rivalry. The United States turned inward, the community of democracies fell apart, and the world was once again plunged into darkness. The disturbing parallels between that chaotic and conflict-prone era and our own were already emerging before COVID-19—and today's pandemic has provided another eerie and unnerving parallel. We cannot afford to let history repeat itself.

Avoiding that outcome requires more than just a return to internationalism—it requires an active effort by the United States to reinvigorate the "free world." This is not a call for American missionary zeal or the type of militarized liberal crusades witnessed after 9/11. Rather, it is a recognition that the existing community of democracies is increasingly at risk from within and without and must be defended. It is also the simple recognition that the United States will be most effective in advancing its interests and in addressing collective challenges when it works alongside its democratic allies—principally in Europe and Asia—and builds international cooperation outward from this core of states.

That means more than just teaming up with democracies to deter and defend against traditional military aggression by revisionist authoritarian powers like Russia and China. It means developing a common free-world agenda on cybersecurity, countering disinformation and authoritarian interference in democratic institutions, checking the spread of digital authoritarianism, and defending human rights. It means countering weaponized corruption, combating infrastructure and energy coercion, regulating emerging technologies, and securing vital technology supply chains. And in those areas, such as public health, climate change, nuclear nonproliferation, and international economics, where coordination with China and other authoritarian powers may be essential, it means coming to a common understanding among democracies first, which can then be leveraged to approach negotiations with Beijing and other authoritarian states from a position of combined strength. The advanced liberal democracies of North America, Europe, and Asia together represent the strongest military alliances in history and more than half of global GDP. That is real power—both "hard" (coercive) and "soft" (attractive)—and therefore real possibility to collectively shape a better future.

The COVID-19 pandemic will not be the last global contagion to emerge in our lifetimes nor, as climate change and other transnational dangers grow, will it be the last major shock to our interconnected world.

Democratic nations will either address these common threats together, pool their strength, and press other countries to follow suit—or they will each go their own way and the ability to head off the next calamity, when it inevitably strikes, will be diminished.

Despite all the carnage wrought by COVID-19, in an odd way, the world may have actually been lucky that the first global pandemic to really test our collective defenses and preparedness was not as lethal as it could have been. It exposed our shortcomings—political, economic, and geopolitical—while still providing an opportunity to prepare for the even graver challenges ahead. But this only matters if we heed this timely warning, learn the right lessons, and stand together to fight for a better future.

ACKNOWLEDGMENTS

This book had its origins in the early stages of the pandemic when we both wrote speculative articles about its impact on the international order—Colin in *War on the Rocks* and Tom in *The Atlantic*. As we talked over Zoom in April 2020 about those pieces, we realized that there was a story to be told about how governments, international organizations, and peoples around the world were responding to, and being impacted by, COVID-19—and what it all meant for world order. It would be important, however, that it be empirically rooted in what transpired over the course of the year. At the time, we had no idea what a monumental endeavor we were embarking upon.

This book would not have been possible without the cooperation and support of a great number of people. In the first instance, we would like to thank the editors of the outlets in which our initial articles appeared: Ryan Evans at *War on the Rocks*, and Jeffrey Goldberg, Yoni Appelbaum, and Whitney Dangerfield at *The Atlantic*, where Tom is a contributing writer. We both had coauthors for some of those earlier articles on the pandemic; Colin would like to thank Ariana Berengaut and Tom would like to thank Kurt Campbell for their crucial insights, without which this project would never have gotten off the ground.

The pandemic has been the top story in the world since March 2020. Journalists from around the globe have written incredible investigative articles on every aspect of the pandemic. We have greatly benefited from this work and would never have been able to put the pieces of the global puzzle together on our own. We strongly encourage our readers to make good use of the endnotes—there are countless gems in there.

We are also indebted to all of the officials and former officials who were sources for this book, a few of whom are named but most of whom are not. These interviews enabled us to tell key parts of the story of the past year. We recognize that as critics of the Trump administration, Trump administration officials took a leap of faith in talking with us and we are grateful for that. We hope that they find the book fair even if they do not agree with everything in it.

We have both been blessed to work at wonderful national institutions that encourage rigorous scholarship and debate while providing the time and space to take on a project of this magnitude. Colin is grateful to his many colleagues at Stanford University's Freeman Spogli Institute for International Studies and the Center for International Security and Co-operation. In particular, he would like to thank Michael McFaul, Rod Ewing, Harold Trinkunas, and Andrea Gray for their tremendous leadership, support, and encouragement.

Tom would like to thank all of his colleagues at The Brookings Institution: President John R. Allen, Vice President and Director for Foreign Policy Suzanne Maloney, his colleagues at Brookings' Center for the United States and Europe (Pavel Baev, Carlo Bastasin, Celia Belin, Natalie Britton, Giovanna DeMaio, James Goldgeier, Fiona Hill, James Kirchick, Kemal Kirisci, Caroline Klaff, Gibbs McKinley, Molly Montgomery, Jérôme Nicolaï, Steve Pifer, Lucy Seavey, Amanda Sloat, Constanze Stelzenmueller, Chloe Suzman, and Torrey Taussig), as well as Madiha Afzal, William Burke-White, Tarun Chhabra, Rush Doshi, Leah Dreyfuss, Vanda Felbab-Brown, Jeff Feltman, Samantha Gross, Ryan Hass, Robert Kagan, Emilie Kimball, Tanvi Madan, Chris Meserole, Andrew Moffatt, Anna Newby, Victoria Nuland, Ted Reinert, Bruce Riedel, Frank Rose, Natan Sachs, Suzanne Schaefer, Kevin Scott, Mireya Solis, Angela Stent, Jonathan Stromseth, Strobe Talbott, and Tamara Wittes.

Tom is also grateful to the Robert Bosch Foundation, the Carnegie Corporation of New York, and the members of the Foreign Policy Leadership Council for their ongoing support to the Brookings Institution, which, in part, made this book possible. Brookings is committed to quality, independence, and impact in all of its work. Activities supported by its donors reflect this commitment and the analysis and recommendations are solely determined by the scholars. The views expressed are solely the responsibility of the authors.

We were extremely fortunate to have a stellar team of research assistants from Stanford University and Brookings over the course of the project: Agneska Bloch, Elena Crespo, Samuel Denney, Dakota Foster, Jonah Glick-Unterman, Heajune Lee, and Filippos Letsas. They drafted informational memos on every aspect of the pandemic, sourced articles from all over the world (often in foreign languages), and edited and fact-checked the manuscript multiple times. We also greatly benefited from their insights, advice, and good humor during our weekly research meetings. They were extraordinary and we are very grateful.

Several scholars offered advice and provided helpful comments on the manuscript or parts of it: Josh Busby, Larry Diamond, Frank Gavin, Bruce Jones, Jeremy Konyndyk, Stewart Patrick, Doug Rediker, Jeremy Shapiro, and David Victor. We benefited from conversations and collaborations on the geopolitical impact of the pandemic with: Robert Blackwill, Hal Brands, Michael Fullilove, David Gordon, Niamh King, Edward Luce, Evan Medeiros, David Miliband, Yascha Mounk, and Kori Schake. We would like to offer a special word of thanks to Michael O'Hanlon, who read the entire manuscript, offered sage advice, and organized the peer review process at Brookings on a very compressed timeline. The constructive comments and suggestions provided from three anonymous peer reviewers helped refine and strengthen the final product.

There is one other key person (not a source) who helped us on portions of our research, but we cannot recognize them by name because they would potentially face consequences from their home government for working with us. You know who you are—thank you!

It is no exaggeration to say that two people were indispensable in this book being published. Our brilliant agent, Bridget Matzie, skillfully guided us through the entire project from the concept and proposal through to publication. Pronoy Sarkar, our editor at St. Martin's Press (until the end of March 2021, when he left for another job in publishing), believed in the book from the very beginning. He was an indefatigable champion for it, often boosted our spirits when the task seemed impossible, and encouraged us to be as comprehensive and ambitious as possible in what we hoped to accomplish. After Pronoy left, we were very lucky to get another exceptional editor, Tim Bartlett, who masterfully guided us through the endgame. We would like to thank Alan Bradshaw for his

ACKNOWLEDGMENTS

meticulous work on editing and finalizing the manuscript, Rebecca Lang who handled publicity, Martin Quinn on marketing, the jacket designer, Ervin Serrano, and associate editor Alice Pfeifer.

Last but not least, we are forever grateful to our families. Colin dedicates this book to his loving wife, Rebecca, his daughter, Nora, and his son, Rylan. He could not have made it through the stress of writing the manuscript while managing the dislocations produced by the pandemic, successfully battling cancer, and assisting in a grueling presidential election and transition without their unfailing support. Likewise, Tom would like to thank his parents, Bernard and Gay, and his siblings, Peter, Bernard, John, and Cathy, their spouses and partners, Ingrid, Pam, and Gib, and his in-laws, Kathleen, Niamh, Irene, Shane, James, and Katie. A particularly difficult part of the pandemic has been not being able to see you all for so long. None of this would have been possible without the love, support, and infinite patience of his wife, Karen, and son, Senan, to whom this book is dedicated.

NOTES

INTRODUCTION

1. Michael Crowley, "Trump Says He Is 'Considering' Hosting G7 Summit at Camp David," *New York Times*, May 20, 2020, https://www.nytimes.com/2020/05/20/us/politics/trump-g7-coronavirus.html.
2. These observations about Angela Merkel are derived from interviews with multiple German and French officials. Angela Merkel, "Commencement Address," Harvard University, May 30, 2019, https://www.americanrhetoric.com/speeches/angela merkelharvardcommencementenglish.htm.
3. Jane C. Timm, "Trump Says He Is Postponing G7 Summit," NBC News, May 30, 2020, https://www.nbcnews.com/politics/donald-trump/trump-says-he-postponing -g7-summit-n1219896.
4. Johns Hopkins University & Medicine, Coronavirus Research Center, https://coronavirus .jhu.edu/; International Monetary Fund, "Transcript of the World Economic Outlook Press Briefing," January 26, 2021, https://www.imf.org/en/News/Articles/2021/01/28 /tr012621-transcript-of-the-world-economic-outlook-update-press-briefing.
5. "United States: Cumulative Confirmed Deaths: How Do They Compare to Other Countries?" Our World in Data, accessed March 30, 2021, https://ourworldindata .org/coronavirus/country/united-states.
6. Colin H. Kahl, *States, Scarcity, and Civil Strife in the Developing World* (Princeton, NJ: Princeton University Press, 2006).
7. Thomas Wright, *All Measures Short of War: The Contest for the 21st Century and the Future of American Power* (New Haven, CT: Yale University Press, 2017).
8. Thomas Wright, "Stretching the International Order to Its Breaking Point," *The Atlantic*, April 4, 2020, https://www.theatlantic.com/ideas/archive/2020/04/pandemic -lasts-18-months-will-change-geopolitics-good/609445/; Colin Kahl and Ariana Berengaut, "Aftershocks: The Coronavirus Pandemic and the New World Disorder," *War on the Rocks*, April 10, 2020, https://warontherocks.com/2020/04/aftershocks -the-coronavirus-pandemic-and-the-new-world-disorder/.

CHAPTER 1: THE GREAT WAR, THE GREAT INFLUENZA, AND GREAT AMBITIONS FOR WORLD ORDER

1. Quoted in John M. Barry, *The Great Influenza: The Story of the Deadliest Pandemic in History* (New York: Penguin Books, 2004), 385. See also Alfred W. Crosby, *America's*

Forgotten Pandemic: The Influenza of 1918, 2nd ed. (New York: Cambridge University Press 2003), 192–95.

2. Quoted in David Petriello, *Bacteria and Bayonets: The Impact of Disease in American Military History* (Havertown, PA: Casemate, 2015), 197. See also Barry, *The Great Influenza*, 383–88.

3. Raymond Poincaré, "Welcoming Address at the Paris Peace Conference," January 18, 1919, https://www.firstworldwar.com/source/parispeaceconf_poincare.htm.

4. Harold Nicolson, *Peacemaking 1919* (London: Faber and Faber, 1933), 25.

5. Quoted in Carol R. Byerly, *Fever of War: The Influenza Epidemic in the U.S. Army During World War I* (New York: New York University Press, 2005), 120.

6. Crosby, *America's Forgotten Pandemic*, 172.

7. Quoted in Crosby, *America's Forgotten Pandemic*, 181.

8. For the best recent account of the origins of World War I, see Christopher Clark, *The Sleepwalkers: How Europe Went to War in 1914* (New York: Harper Perennial, 2014).

9. Adam Tooze, *The Deluge: The Great War, America, and the Remaking of Global Order, 1916–1931* (New York: Penguin Books, 2014), 16, 53.

10. Quoted in Tooze, *The Deluge*, 54.

11. Woodrow Wilson, "Address to Congress Requesting a Declaration of War Against Germany," April 2, 1918, https://millercenter.org/the-presidency/presidential-speeches /april-2-1917-address-congress-requesting-declaration-war.

12. "President Woodrow Wilson's Fourteen Points," January 8, 1918, https://avalon.law .yale.edu/20th_century/wilson14.asp; Woodrow Wilson, "Address of the President of the United States Delivered at a Joint Session of the Two Houses of Congress," February 11, 1918, https://history.state.gov/historicaldocuments/frus1918Supp01v01/d59; Woodrow Wilson, "Address Delivered at Mount Vernon," July 4, 1918, https://history .state.gov/historicaldocuments/frus1918Supp01v01/d206; Woodrow Wilson, "Address Opening the Campaign for the Fourth Liberty Loan, Delivered at the Metropolitian Opera House in New York City," September 27, 1918, https://history.state .gov/historicaldocuments/frus1918Supp01v01/d258.

13. G. John Ikenberry, *After Victory: Institutions, Strategic Restraint, and the Rebuilding of International Order After Major Wars* (Princeton, NJ: Princeton University Press, 2001), chap. 5.

14. Tooze, *The Deluge*, 67.

15. Hew Strachan, "Counting the Cost of the 1918–19 Pandemic," *Engelsberg Ideas*, June 24, 2020, https://engelsbergideas.com/essays/counting-the-cost-of-the-1918-19 -pandemic/.

16. Barry, *The Great Influenza*, chaps. 1–4; Laura Spinney, *Pale Rider: The Spanish Flu of 1918 and How It Changed the World* (New York: PublicAffairs, 2017), chap.11.

17. Barry, *The Great Influenza*, 130–31, 169–75.

18. Spinney, *Pale Rider*, chap. 3.

19. "History of 1918 Flu Pandemic," Centers for Disease Control and Prevention, accessed July 28, 2020, https://www.cdc.gov/flu/pandemic-resources/1918-commemoration /1918-pandemic-history.htm; Byerly, *Fever of War*, 4–5.

20. Howard Phillips, "Influenza Pandemic," *International Encyclopedia of the First World War*, October 8, 2014, https://encyclopedia.1914–1918-online.net/article/influenza _pandemic.

21. John M. Barry, "1918 Revisited: Lessons and Suggestions for Further Inquiry," in *The Threat of Pandemic Influenza: Are We Ready? Workshop Summary* (Washington, DC: National Academies Press, 2005), 58–68, https://www.ncbi.nlm.nih.gov/books /NBK22148/.

22. "History of 1918 Flu Pandemic"; Byerly, *Fever of War*, 5.

23. Eliza McGraw, "Everyone Wore Masks During the 1918 Flu Pandemic. They Were Useless," *Washington Post*, April 2, 2020, https://www.washingtonpost.com/history/2020/04/02/everyone-wore-masks-during-1918-flu-pandemic-they-were-useless/.

24. Martin C. J. Bootsma and Neil M. Ferguson, "The Effect of Public Health Measures on the 1918 Influenza Pandemic in U.S. Cities," *Proceedings of the National Academy of Sciences* 104, no. 18 (April 2007): 7588–93.

25. Barry, *The Great Influenza*, 302.

26. Andrew T. Price-Smith, *Contagion and Chaos: Disease, Ecology, and National Security in the Age of Globalization* (Cambridge, MA: MIT Press, 2009), 63–64.

27. Quoted in Faith Karimi, "Before Trump, Another US President Downplayed a Pandemic and Was Infected," CNN, October 3, 2020, https://www.cnn.com/2020/10/03/us/woodrow-wilson-coronavirus-trnd/index.html.

28. Price-Smith, *Contagion and Chaos*, 64–65.

29. Michael B. A. Oldstone, *Viruses, Plagues, and History* (Oxford: Oxford University Press, 2010), 305. For a detailed discussion, see David T. Zabecki, *The German 1918 Offensives: A Case Study in the Operational Level of War* (London: Routledge, 2006).

30. Erich von Ludendorff, *Ludendorff's Own Story, August 1914–November 1918* (New York: Harper & Brothers, 1919), 2:326, 332–33.

31. Norman Stone, *World War One: A Short History* (New York: Basic Books, 2007), 172–73.

32. Ludendorff, *Ludendorff's Own Story*, 2:277, 282, 317.

33. Crosby, *America's Forgotten Pandemic*, 323.

34. Zabecki, *The German 1918 Offensives*, 237. See also J. H. Johnson, *1918: The Unexpected Victory* (London: Arms and Armour, 1997), 192.

35. Price-Smith, *Contagion and Chaos*, 68–69.

36. Oldstone, *Viruses, Plagues, and History*, 306; Zabecki, *The German 1918 Offensives*, 275.

37. Richard Bessel, *Germany After the First World War* (New York: Oxford University Press, 1993), 46.

38. Bessel, *Germany After the First World War*, 46–47; Byerly, *Fever of War*, 99; Price-Smith, *Contagion and Chaos*, 69.

39. Crosby, *America's Forgotten Pandemic*, 27; Price-Smith, *Contagion and Chaos*, 61.

40. Bessel, *Germany After the First World War*, 224.

41. Price-Smith, *Contagion and Chaos*, 74–76.

42. Byerly, *Fever of War*, 8–9, 99.

43. Crosby, *America's Forgotten Pandemic*, 49.

44. Price-Smith, *Contagion and Chaos*, 64–69.

45. Phillips, "Influenza Pandemic."

46. Quoted in Ikenberry, *After Victory*, 135.

47. Strachan, "Counting the Cost of the 1918–19 Pandemic."

48. Quoted in Margaret MacMillan, *Paris 1919: Six Months That Changed the World* (New York: Random House, 2001), 189.

49. Arthur S. Link, ed., *The Papers of Woodrow Wilson* (Princeton, NJ: Princeton University Press, 1966–1994), 56:312.

50. For an excellent discussion of this period in the negotiations, see MacMillan, *Paris 1919*, chaps. 14–16.

51. Link, ed., *The Papers of Woodrow Wilson*, 56:543. Also quoted in Barry, *The Great Influenza*, 383.

52. Barry, *The Great Influenza*, 382–83; Crosby, *America's Forgotten Pandemic*, 176–81.

53. Crosby, *America's Forgotten Pandemic*, 184–85.

54. MacMillan, *Paris 1919*, 201.

55. Link, ed., *The Papers of Woodrow Wilson*, 57:50–51.

56. Barry, *The Great Influenza*, 384–85; Crosby, *America's Forgotten Pandemic*, 189–92.

57. Treaty of Versailles, Article 231, June 28, 1919, https://www.loc.gov/law/help/us -treaties/bevans/m-ust000002-0043.pdf.

58. Quoted in MacMillan, *Paris 1919*, 467.

59. John Maynard Keynes, *The Economic Consequences of the Peace* (Brentwood, CA: Olive Garden Books, 2013) [originally published in 1919].

60. Barry, *The Great Influenza*, 385.

61. Link, ed., *The Papers of Woodrow Wilson*, 59:233.

62. Quoted in MacMillan, *Paris 1919*, 276.

63. Quoted in Barry, *The Great Influenza*, 386.

64. Quoted in Crosby, *America's Forgotten Pandemic*, 191.

65. Nicolson, *Peacemaking 1919*, 161.

66. MacMillan, *Paris 1919*, 465; see also 461–66.

67. Crosby, *America's Forgotten Pandemic*, 192.

68. MacMillan, *Paris 1919*, 481–83.

69. Nicolson, *Peacemaking 1919*, 153–54.

70. Ian Kershaw, *Hitler: 1889–1939: Hubris* (New York: W. W. Norton, 1998), 97; Joseph Maiolo, *Cry Havoc: How the Arms Race Drove the World to War, 1931–1941* (New York; Basic Books, 2010), 41.

71. Adolf Hitler, *Hitler's Words*, edited by Gordon William Prange (Washington, DC: American Council on Public Affairs, 1944), 117.

72. Kershaw, *Hitler*, 104.

73. Kershaw, *Hitler*, 136–37.

74. Norman A. Graebner and Edward M. Bennett, *The Versailles Treaty and Its Legacy: The Failure of the Wilsonian Vision* (New York: Cambridge University Press, 2011), 109.

75. Office of the United States Chief of Counsel for Prosecution of Axis Criminality, *Nazi Conspiracy and Aggression* (Washington, DC: United States Government Printing Office, 1946), 1:185.

76. *The Speeches of Adolf Hitler, April 1922–August 1939*, edited by Norman Hepburn Baynes, vol. 2, part 1 (Oxford: Oxford University Press, 1994), 1041.

77. Office of the United States Chief of Counsel for Prosecution of Axis Criminality, *Nazi Conspiracy and Aggression*, 1:185.

78. Kershaw, *Hitler*, 426.

CHAPTER 2: RIPPLES THROUGH TIME

1. Quoted in John Milton Cooper Jr., *Breaking the Heart of the World: Woodrow Wilson and the Fight for the League of Nations* (New York: Cambridge University Press, 2001), 119; see also 117–18.

2. Adam Tooze, *The Deluge: The Great War, America, and the Remaking of Global Order, 1916–1931* (New York: Penguin Books, 2014), 333.

3. Cooper, *Breaking the Heart of the World*, 88.

4. Margaret MacMillan, *Paris 1919: Six Months That Changed the World* (New York: Random House, 2001), chaps. 23–24.

5. Norman A. Graebner and Edward M. Bennett, *The Versailles Treaty and Its Legacy: The Failure of the Wilsonian Vision* (New York: Cambridge University Press, 2011), 61–62.

6. Cooper, *Breaking the Heart of the World*, 156–57.

7. Arthur S. Link, ed., *The Papers of Woodrow Wilson* (Princeton, NJ: Princeton University Press, 1966–1994), 63:111.

8. Quoted in Cooper, *Breaking the Heart of the World*, 188–89; see also chap. 4 for a discussion of Wilson's health on the trip.

9. Laura Spinney, *Pale Rider: The Spanish Flu of 1918 and How It Changed the World* (New York: PublicAffairs, 2017), 251.

10. MacMillan, *Paris 1919*, 491. See also Cooper, *Breaking the Heart of the World*, 200.

11. Cooper, *Breaking the Heart of the World*, chap. 6.

12. Warren G. Harding, "Americanism," address delivered before the Ohio Society of New York, January 20, 1920, https://millercenter.org/the-presidency/presidential-speeches/january-20-1920-americanism.

13. Harding, "Americanism," 2. See also MacMillan, *Paris 1919*, 489; Tooze, *The Deluge*, 334–36.

14. Cooper, *Breaking the Heart of the World*, 422; see also 288–89, 316–20, 420–23.

15. Robert J. Barro, José F. Ursua, and Joanna Wang, "The Coronavirus and the Great Influenza Epidemic: Lessons from the 'Spanish Flu' for the Coronavirus's Potential Effects on Mortality and Economic Activity," CESifo Working Paper No. 8166, March 2020, 12–13, https://www.cesifo.org/en/publikationen/2020/working-paper/coronavirus-and-great-influenza-epidemic-lessons-spanish-flu. See also François R. Velde, "What Happened to the US Economy During the 1918 Influenza Pandemic? A View Through High-Frequency Data," Federal Reserve Bank of Chicago, Working Paper No. 2020–11, July 7, 2020, https://www.chicagofed.org/publications/working-papers/2020/2020-11.

16. Greg Ip, Danny Dougherty, and Anthony DeBarros, "Lessons for the Coronavirus Crisis from Six Other Disasters," *Wall Street Journal*, March 20, 2020, https://www.wsj.com/articles/lessons-for-the-coronavirus-crisis-from-six-other-disasters-11584719497; Walter Scheidel, "The Spanish Flu Didn't Wreck the Global Economy," *Foreign Affairs*, May 28, 2020, https://www.foreignaffairs.com/articles/united-states/2020-05-28/spanish-flu-didnt-wreck-global-economy.

17. Sergio Correia, Stephan Luck, and Emil Verner, "Pandemics Depress the Economy, Public Health Interventions Do Not: Evidence from the 1918 Flu," Social Science Research Network, June 5, 2020, https://papers.ssrn.com/sol3/papers.cfm?abstract_id=3561560.

18. Steven J. Diner, *A Very Different Age: Americans of the Progressive Era* (New York: Hill and Wang, 1998), 241; David J. Goldberg, *Discontented America: The United States in the 1920s* (Baltimore: Johns Hopkins University Press, 1999), 66–71.

19. See, for example, the discussion of Chicago in Cameron McWhirter, *Red Summer: The Summer of 1919 and the Awakening of Black America* (New York: St. Martin's Griffin, 2012), chap. 12.

20. Alfred W. Crosby, *America's Forgotten Pandemic: The Influenza of 1918*, 2nd ed. (New York: Cambridge University Press 2003), 228–29; Helene Økland and Svenn-Erik Mamelund, "Race and 1918 Influenza Pandemic in the United States: A Review of the Literature," *International Journal of Environmental Research and Public Health* 16, no. 14 (July 2019): 2487, https://www.ncbi.nlm.nih.gov/pmc/articles/PMC6678782/.

21. Vanessa Northington Gamble, "'There Wasn't a Lot of Comfort in Those Days': African Americans, Public Health, and the 1918 Influenza Epidemic," *Public Health Reports* 125, no. 3 (April 1, 2010): 113–22, https://www.ncbi.nlm.nih.gov/pmc/articles/PMC2862340/.

22. Elizabeth Schlabach, "The Influenza Epidemic and Jim Crow Public Health Policies and Practices in Chicago, 1917–1921," *Journal of African American History*, Winter 2019, 42.

23. McWhirter, *Red Summer*; Christina Maxouris, "100 Years Ago, White Mobs Across the Country Attacked Black People. And They Fought Back," CNN, July 27, 2019, https://www.cnn.com/2019/07/27/us/red-summer-1919-racial-violence/index.html.
24. McWhirter, *Red Summer*, 150–51.
25. W. E. B. Du Bois, "Returning Soldiers," *The Crisis*, May 1919, 13, https://glc.yale.edu/returning-soldiers.
26. Quoted in McWhirter, *Red Summer*, 106.
27. Bruce Bartlett, "Woodrow Wilson Was Even More Racist Than You Thought," *New Republic*, July 6, 2020, https://newrepublic.com/article/158356/woodrow-wilson-racism-princeton-university.
28. Link, ed., *The Papers of Woodrow Wilson*, 63:196.
29. McWhirter, *Red Summer*, 56.
30. W. E. B. Du Bois, *Darkwater: Voices from the Veil* (New York: Harcourt, Brace, and Howe, 1920), 36.
31. Graebner and Bennett, *The Versailles Treaty and Its Legacy*, 68.
32. Douglas A. Irwin, "The Pandemic Adds Momentum to the Deglobalization Trend," Peterson Institute for International Economics, April 23, 2020, https://www.piie.com/blogs/realtime-economic-issues-watch/pandemic-adds-momentum-deglobalization-trend#_ftnref2.
33. Barro, Ursua, and Wang, "The Coronavirus and the Great Influenza Epidemic."
34. Richard Overy, *The Inter-Wars Crisis*, 3rd ed. (London: Routledge, 2017), 54–55.
35. Overy, *The Inter-Wars Crisis*, chap. 3.
36. Spinney, *Pale Rider*, 253.
37. Spinney, *Pale Rider*, 253.
38. Spinney, *Pale Rider*, 203, 254.
39. Overy, *The Inter-War Crisis*, 90–93.
40. Christopher S. Rose, "The 'Spanish Flu' in Egypt," blog post, April 10, 2020, https://christophersrose.com/2020/04/10/the-spanish-flu-in-egypt/; Christopher S. Rose, "Implications of the Spanish Influenza Pandemic (1918–1920) for the History of Early 20th Century Egypt," *Journal of World History* 32, no. 2 (March 2021); Spinney, *Pale Rider*, 254.
41. Ida Milne, *Stacking the Coffins: Influenza, War and Revolution in Ireland, 1918–19* (Manchester: Manchester University Press, 2018), 14.
42. David Arnold, "Death and the Modern Empire: The 1918–19 Influenza Epidemic in India," *Transactions of the Royal Historical Society* 29 (2019): 191–95; John M. Barry, *The Great Influenza: The Story of the Deadliest Pandemic in History* (New York: Penguin Books, 2004), 364.
43. Arnold, "Death and the Modern Empire," 192; Spinney, *Pale Rider*, 255–56.
44. Arnold, "Death and the Modern Empire," 198–99; Soutik Biswas, "Coronavirus: What India Can Learn from the Deadly 1918 Flu," BBC News, March 18, 2020, https://www.bbc.com/news/world-asia-india-51904019; Amit Kapoor, "An Unwanted Shipment: The Indian Experience of the 1918 Spanish Flu," *Economic Times*, April 3, 2020, https://economictimes.indiatimes.com/news/politics-and-nation/an-unwanted-shipment-the-indian-experience-of-the-1918-spanish-flu/articleshow/74963051.cms; Spinney, *Pale Rider*, 256–60.
45. A. J. P. Taylor, *English History 1914–1945* (Oxford: Oxford University Press, 1965), 112–13, 152–53.
46. Nicholas Crafts and Peter Fearon, "Lessons from the 1930s Great Depression," *Oxford Review of Economic Policy* 26, no. 3 (Autumn 2010): 285–317; Overy, *The Inter-War Crisis*, chap. 5.
47. Overy, *The Inter-War Crisis*, chap. 6.

48. See Joseph Maiolo, *Cry Havoc: How the Arms Race Drove the World to War, 1931–1941* (New York; Basic Books, 2010); Richard Overy, *The Origins of the Second World War*, 2nd ed. (London: Longman, 1998), chaps. 2, 4; Tooze, *The Deluge*, 512–13.

49. Overy, *The Inter-War Crisis*, 90–93; Overy, *The Origins of the Second World War*, 17.

50. G. John Ikenberry, *After Victory: Institutions, Strategic Restraint, and the Rebuilding of Order After Major Wars* (Princeton, NJ: Princeton University Press, 2001), chap. 5; Tooze, *The Deluge*.

51. Tooze, *The Deluge*, chaps. 21 and 24.

52. Tooze, *The Deluge*, chap. 25.

53. Overy, *The Inter-War Crisis*, chap. 7; Tooze, *The Deluge*, 515–16.

54. Graebner and Bennett, *The Versailles Treaty and Its Legacy*, 59–60.

55. Tooze, *The Deluge*, 511.

56. Philip Roth, *The Plot Against America* (New York: Houghton Mifflin Harcourt, 2004).

57. Quoted in Frank Rich, "Trump's Appeasers," *New York Magazine*, October 31, 2016, https://nymag.com/intelligencer/2016/11/charles-lindbergh-is-a-cautionary-tale -for-republicans.html.

58. Charles A. Lindbergh, "We Cannot Win This War for England," April 23, 1941, http://www.ibiblio.org/pha/policy/1941/1941-04-23a.html.

59. Quoted in Susan Dunn, "The Debate Behind U.S. Intervention in World War II," *The Atlantic*, July 8, 2013, https://www.theatlantic.com/national/archive/2013/07/the -debate-behind-us-intervention-in-world-war-ii/277572/.

60. Overy, *The Origins of the Second World War*, 22.

61. United States Department of State, *Peace and War: United States Foreign Policy, 1931–1941* (Washington, DC: United States Government Printing Office, 1943), 326.

62. Franklin D. Roosevelt, "Fireside Chat 14: On the European War," September 3, 1939, https://millercenter.org/the-presidency/presidential-speeches/september-3-1939 -fireside-chat-14-european-war.

63. Franklin D. Roosevelt, "Stab in the Back" speech, June 10, 1940, https://millercenter .org/the-presidency/presidential-speeches/june-10-1940-stab-back-speech.

CHAPTER 3: PRIMED FOR PERIL

1. Alfred W. Crosby, *America's Forgotten Pandemic: The Influenza of 1918*, 2nd ed. (New York: Cambridge University Press, 2003).

2. G. John Ikenberry, *After Victory: Institutions, Strategic Restraint, and the Rebuilding of Order After Major Wars* (Princeton, NJ: Princeton University Press, 2000), chap. 6; G. John Ikenberry, *Liberal Leviathan: The Origins, Crisis, and Transformation of the American World Order* (Princeton, NJ: Princeton University Press, 2011), chap. 5; Walter A. McDougall, *Promised Land, Crusader State: The American Encounter with the World Since 1776* (Boston: Houghton Mifflin, 1997), chaps. 7–8; Henry R. Nau, *At Home Abroad: Identity and Power in American Foreign Policy* (Ithaca, NY: Cornell University Press, 2002), 75–76; Tony Smith, *Why Wilson Matters: The Origin of American Liberal Internationalism and Its Crisis Today* (Princeton, NJ: Princeton University Press, 2017), chap. 5.

3. For an excellent discussion of the origins of the WHO and the associated global health regime, see Charles Clift, *The Role of the World Health Organization in the International System* (London: Chatham House, 2013), https://www.chathamhouse.org/sites /default/files/publications/research/2013-02-01-role-world-health-organization -international-system-clift.pdf.

4. Stewart Patrick, "When the System Fails," *Foreign Affairs*, July/August 2020, 42, https://www.foreignaffairs.com/articles/world/2020-06-09/when-system-fails.

5. COVID-19 Dashboard, Center for Systems Science and Engineering, Johns Hopkins University & Medicine, Coronavirus Resource Center, https://coronavirus.jhu.edu /map.html, accessed May 5, 2021.

6. Walter Scheidel, "The Spanish Flu Didn't Wreck the Global Economy," *Foreign Affairs*, May 28, 2020, https://www.foreignaffairs.com/articles/united-states/2020-05-28 /spanish-flu-didnt-wreck-global-economy.

7. Richard N. Haass, *A World in Disarray: American Foreign Policy and the Crisis of the Old Order* (New York: Penguin Books, 2018).

8. Douglas Irwin, "The Pandemic Adds Momentum to the Deglobalisation Trend," VoxEU, May 5, 2020, https://voxeu.org/article/pandemic-adds-momentum-deglobalisation -trend.

9. Esteban Ortiz-Ospina and Diana Beltekian, "Trade and Globalization," Our World in Data, revised October 2018, https://ourworldindata.org/trade-and-globalization.

10. Steven A. Altman, Pankaj Ghemawat, and Phillip Bastian, *DHL Global Connectedness Index 2018: The State of Globalization in a Fragile World* (Bonn: Deutsche Post DHL Group, 2019), https://www.dhl.com/content/dam/dhl/global/core/documents /pdf/glo-core-gci-2018-full-study.pdf; Steven A. Altman and Phillip Bastian, *DHL Global Interconnectedness Index: Mapping the Current State of Global Flows—2019 Update* (Bonn: Deutsche Post DHL Group, 2019), https://www.dhl.com/content/dam /dhl/global/core/documents/pdf/g0-en-gci-2019-update-complete-study.pdf.

11. Michael T. Osterholm and Mark Olshaker, "Chronicle of a Pandemic Foretold," *Foreign Affairs*, July/August 2020, 19, https://www.foreignaffairs.com/articles/united -states/2020-05-21/coronavirus-chronicle-pandemic-foretold.

12. *Mapping the Global Future: Report of the National Intelligence Council's 2020 Project* (Washington, DC: National Intelligence Council, 2004), 9–10, https://www.dni .gov/files/documents/Global%20Trends_Mapping%20the%20Global%20Future %202020%20Project.pdf.

13. *Mapping the Global Future*, 27, 30, emphasis in the original.

14. *Global Trends 2025: A Transformed World* (Washington, DC: National Intelligence Council, 2008), 75, https://www.dni.gov/files/documents/Newsroom/Reports %20and%20Pubs/2025_Global_Trends_Final_Report.pdf.

15. *Global Trends 2030: Alternative Worlds* (Washington, DC: National Intelligence Council, 2012), xi, https://www.dni.gov/files/documents/GlobalTrends_2030.pdf.

16. *Global Trends: The Paradox of Progress* (Washington, DC: National Intelligence Council, 2017), 51, https://www.dni.gov/files/documents/nic/GT-Full-Report.pdf. For further discussion of intelligence estimates over this period, see Paul Miller, "How the Intelligence Community Predicted COVID-19," *The Dispatch*, March 26, 2020, https://thedispatch.com/p/how-the-intelligence-community-predicted.

17. George W. Bush, "President Outlines Pandemic Influenza Preparations and Response," White House, November 1, 2005, https://georgewbush-whitehouse.archives.gov/news /releases/2005/11/20051101-1.html.

18. Barack Obama, "Remarks by the President on Research for Potential Ebola Vaccines," White House, December 2, 2014, https://obamawhitehouse.archives.gov/the-press -office/2014/12/02/remarks-president-research-potential-ebola-vaccines.

19. Daniel R. Coats, "Worldwide Threat Assessment of the U.S. Intelligence Community," Statement for the Record to the Senate Select Committee on Intelligence, January 29, 2019, 21, https://www.dni.gov/files/ODNI/documents/2019-ATA -SFR---SSCI.pdf; Andrew Kaczynski and Em Steck, "Top Administration Officials Said

Last Year Threat of Pandemic Kept Them Up at Night," CNN, April 3, 2020, https://
www.cnn.com/2020/04/03/politics/kfile-officials-worried-over-pandemic-last-year
/index.html.

20. "GDP (Current US$)," World Bank Data, accessed July 10, 2020, https://data.worldbank
.org/indicator/NY.GDP.MKTP.CD.

21. *Poverty and Shared Prosperity 2018: Piecing Together the Poverty Puzzle* (Washington,
DC: World Bank, 2018), 1, https://openknowledge.worldbank.org/bitstream/handle
/10986/30418/9781464813306.pdf.

22. National Intelligence Council, *Global Trends: The Paradox of Progress*, 4.

23. *Global Economic Prospects* (Washington, DC: World Bank, 2020), 143, https://
openknowledge.worldbank.org/handle/10986/33748.

24. Christoph Lakner, "A Global View of Inequality," presentation, World Bank, September 16, 2019, http://pubdocs.worldbank.org/en/792141568662759167/World
-Bank-Sep-2019-Lakner-2-public.pdf; *Poverty and Shared Prosperity 2016: Taking
on Inequality* (Washington, DC: World Bank, 2016), https://www.worldbank.org/en
/publication/poverty-and-shared-prosperity-2016.

25. Larry Elliott, "World's 26 Richest People Own as Much as Poorest 50%, Says Oxfam,"
The Guardian, January 20, 2019, https://www.theguardian.com/business/2019/jan
/21/world-26-richest-people-own-as-much-as-poorest-50-per-cent-oxfam-report.

26. *Time to Care: Unpaid and Underpaid Care Work and the Global Inequality Crisis* (Oxford:
Oxfam, 2020), https://oxfamilibrary.openrepository.com/bitstream/handle/10546
/620928/bp-time-to-care-inequality-200120-en.pdf.

27. Ronald Inglehart and Pippa Norris, "Trump, Brexit, and the Rise of Populism: Economic Have-Nots and Cultural Backlash," HKS Working Paper No. RWP16–026,
Kennedy School, Harvard University, July 2016, http://dx.doi.org/10.2139/ssrn
.2818659.

28. Francis Fukuyama, "American Political Decay or Renewal?," *Foreign Affairs*, July/Au-
gust 2016, https://www.foreignaffairs.com/articles/united-states/2016-06-13/american
-political-decay-or-renewal.

29. Edward Luce, *The Retreat of Western Liberalism* (London: Little, Brown, 2017), 12.

30. Bruce Jones and Torrey Taussig, *Democracy and Disorder: The Struggle for Influence
in the New Geopolitics* (Washington, DC: Brookings Institution, 2019), 18–21, https://
www.brookings.edu/wp-content/uploads/2019/02/FP_20190226_democracy
_report_WEB.pdf.

31. "Gove: Britons 'Have Had Enough of Experts,'" interview with Faisal Islam, Sky
News, June 3, 2016, https://www.youtube.com/watch?v=GGgiGtJk7MA.

32. For an account of Brexit, see Tim Shipman, *All Out War: The Full Story of How Brexit
Sank Britain's Political Class* (London: William Collins, 2016); Tim Shipman, *Fall
Out: A Year of Political Mayhem* (London: William Collins, 2018).

33. The literature on Trump is vast, but these characteristics are carefully and vividly laid
out in Philip Rucker and Carol D. Leonnig, *A Very Stable Genius: Donald J. Trump's
Testing of America* (New York: Penguin Press, 2020), and Bob Woodward, *Rage* (New
York: Simon and Schuster, 2020).

34. Bruno Carazza, "Will Brazil's Next President Be a Far Right Nationalist?," *Foreign
Affairs*, July 12, 2018, https://www.foreignaffairs.com/articles/brazil/2018-07-12/will
-brazils-next-president-be-far-right-nationalist.

35. Aurelien Breeden and Megan Specia, "Dispute over Amazon Gets Personal for Bolsonaro and Macron," *New York Times*, August 26, 2019, https://www.nytimes.com
/2019/08/26/world/europe/bolsonaro-macron-g7.html.

36. Robert Zoellick, "Whither China: From Membership to Responsibility," speech,

National Committee on U.S.-China Relations, September 21, 2005, https://www.ncuscr
.org/sites/default/files/migration/Zoellick_remarks_notes06_winter_spring.pdf.

37. Thomas Wright, *All Measures Short of War: The Contest for the Twenty-First Century and the Future of American Power* (New Haven, CT: Yale University Press, 2017).

38. John Garnaut, "How China Interferes in Australia," *Foreign Affairs*, March 9, 2018, https://www.foreignaffairs.com/articles/china/2018-03-09/how-china-interferes -australia.

39. Javier C. Hernández, "Harsh Penalties, Vaguely Defined Crimes: Hong Kong's Security Law Explained," *New York Times*, June 30, 2020, https://www.nytimes.com/2020 /06/30/world/asia/hong-kong-security-law-explain.html.

40. Thomas Wright, "Trump's 19th Century Foreign Policy," Politico, January 20, 2016, https://www.politico.com/magazine/story/2016/01/donald-trump-foreign-policy -213546/.

41. *National Security Strategy of the United States* (Washington, DC: White House, 2017), https://www.hsdl.org/?view&did=806478; *Summary of the National Defense Strategy of the United States of America* (Washington, DC: United States Department of Defense, 2018), https://dod.defense.gov/Portals/1/Documents/pubs/2018-National -Defense-Strategy-Summary.pdf. For a discussion of debates within the Trump administration on China, see Josh Rogin, *Chaos Under Heaven: Trump, Xi, and the Battle for the 21st Century* (Boston: Houghton Mifflin Harcourt, 2021).

42. John Bolton, *The Room Where It Happened: A White House Memoir* (New York: Simon and Schuster, 2020), 312.

43. *EU-China: A Strategic Outlook* (Strasbourg: European Commission and High Representative of the European Union for Foreign Affairs and Security Policy, 2019), https://ec .europa.eu/info/sites/info/files/communication-eu-china-a-strategic-outlook.pdf.

44. G. John Ikenberry, "The Next Liberal Order: The Age of Contagion Demands More Internationalism, Not Less," *Foreign Affairs*, July/August 2020, 133, https://www .foreignaffairs.com/articles/united-states/2020-06-09/next-liberal-order.

45. Robert Kagan, *The Jungle Grows Back: America and Our Imperiled World* (New York: Alfred A. Knopf, 2018).

46. Edward Hallett Carr, *The Twenty Years' Crisis, 1919–1939: An Introduction to the Study of International Relations* (New York: Harper & Row, 1939), 63.

47. Richard Haass, "The Pandemic Will Accelerate History Rather Than Reshape It," *Foreign Affairs*, April 7, 2020, https://www.foreignaffairs.com/articles/united-states /2020-04-07/pandemic-will-accelerate-history-rather-reshape-it.

48. Carr, *The Twenty Years' Crisis, 1919-1939*, 92-93.

49. Sheri Berman, "Crises Only Sometimes Lead to Change. Here's Why," *Foreign Policy*, July 4, 2020, https://foreignpolicy.com/2020/07/04/coronavirus-crisis-turning-point -change/; Jeffrey W. Legro, *Rethinking the World: Great Power Strategies and International Order* (Ithaca, NY: Cornell University Press, 2005).

CHAPTER 4: SECRETS AND LIES

1. "Severe Acute Respiratory Syndrome (SARS)," World Health Organization, https:// www.who.int/ith/diseases/sars/en/, accessed March 30, 2021.

2. John Pomfret, "Following the SARS Playbook, China Keeps a Dangerous Tight Leash on Coronavirus Information," *Washington Post*, January 23, 2020, https://www .washingtonpost.com/opinions/2020/01/23/following-sars-playbook-china-keeps -dangerous-tight-leash-coronavirus-information/.

3. Yanzhong Huang, "The SARS Epidemic and Its Aftermath in China: A Political Perspective," in *Learning from SARS: Preparing for the Next Disease Outbreak:*

Workshop Summary, edited by Stacey Knobler et al. (Washington, DC: National Academies Press, 2004), https://www.ncbi.nlm.nih.gov/books/NBK92479/. Jiang was initially lauded as a hero, although a year later he was forced to go to reeducation camp after he wrote to the government asking for the 1989 Tiananmen Square protesters to be treated as a patriotic movement. He was subsequently confined to house arrest at the age of eighty-eight, mere months before the outbreak of COVID-19.

4. "Politics and Perils of Running the WHO," *The Rachman Review* (podcast), April 23, 2020. She did go on to say that she felt the situation during COVID-19 was different since the Chinese government was communicating with the WHO.

5. "Brundtland Tells of Fight with China During Sars," *Taipei Times*, April 4, 2018, http://taipeitimes.com/News/taiwan/archives/2018/04/04/2003690647.

6. Stephen Lee Myers, "China Created a Fail-Safe System to Track Infections. It Failed," *New York Times*, April 17, 2020, https://www.nytimes.com/2020/03/29/world/asia/coronavirus-china.html.

7. Dali Yang, "China's Early Warning System Didn't Work on Covid-19. Here's the Story," *Washington Post*, February 24, 2020, https://www.washingtonpost.com/politics/2020/02/24/chinas-early-warning-system-didnt-work-covid-19-heres-story/.

8. [Gao Fu, director of the Chinese Center for Disease Control and Prevention: Should not lose confidence in China's vaccines], *China News*, March 5, 2019, http://www.chinanews.com/gn/2019/03–05/8771355.shtml.

9. Josephine Moulds, "How Is the World Health Organization Funded?," World Economic Forum, April 15, 2020, https://www.weforum.org/agenda/2020/04/who-funds-world-health-organization-un-coronavirus-pandemic-covid-trump/.

10. *Global Health Security Index*, Johns Hopkins University, October 2019, https://www.ghsindex.org/wp-content/uploads/2020/04/2019-Global-Health-Security-Index.pdf.

11. Josh Rogin, *Chaos Under Heaven: Trump, Xi, and the Battle for the 21st Century* (Boston: Houghton Mifflin Harcourt, 2021), 267–81.

12. "China's Disputed Virus Theory Has Shoppers Shunning Foreign Food," Bloomberg, January 21, 2021, https://www.bloomberg.com/news/articles/2021-01-21/china-s-disputed-virus-theory-has-shoppers-shunning-foreign-food.

13. "China's COVID Secrets," *Frontline*, PBS, February 2, 2021.

14. Jeremy Page and Lingling Wei, "China's CDC, Built to Stop Pandemics Like COVID, Stumbled When It Mattered Most," *Wall Street Journal*, August 17, 2020, https://www.wsj.com/articles/chinas-cdc-built-to-stop-pandemics-stumbled-when-it-mattered-most-11597675108.

15. Jeremy Page, Wenxin Fan, and Natasha Khan, "How It All Started: China's Early Coronavirus Missteps," *Wall Street Journal*, March 6, 2020, https://www.wsj.com/articles/how-it-all-started-chinas-early-coronavirus-missteps-11583508932.

16. Page, Fan, and Khan, "How It All Started."

17. For the text of the email see: MOHW of Taiwan (@MOHW_Taiwan), "The facts regarding Taiwan's email to alert WHO to possible danger of #COVID19 #email 内容 #TaiwanCanHelp #TaiwanIsHelping @WHO 英文新聞稿: http://at.cdc.tw/23iq82," Twitter, April 11, 2020, 6:05 a.m., https://twitter.com/MOHW_Taiwan/status/1248915057188024320. For analysis, see Zoe Didili, "Taiwan Releases December Email to WHO Showing Unheeded Warning About Coronavirus," NewEurope, April 15, 2020, https://www.neweurope.eu/article/taiwan-releases-december-email-to-who-showing-unheeded-warning-about-coronavirus/.

18. Conversation with George Gao as recounted by Ian Lipkin in "China's COVID Secrets."

19. "China Delayed Releasing Coronavirus Info, Frustrating WHO," Associated Press, June 3, 2020, https://apnews.com/3c061794970661042b18d5aeaaed9fae.
20. "China's COVID Secrets."
21. Interview with David Fidler, March 8, 2021.
22. Page, Fan, and Khan, "How It All Started."
23. "China's COVID Secrets."
24. Page, Fan, and Khan, "How It All Started."
25. Page, Fan, and Khan, "How It All Started."
26. Fang Fang, *Wuhan Diary*, trans. Michael Berry (New York: HarperVia, 2020), 3.
27. Fang, *Wuhan Diary*, 6.
28. David Fidler, "To Declare or Not to Declare: The Controversy over Declaring a Public Health Emergency of International Concern for the Ebola Outbreak in the Democratic Republic of Congo," *Asian Journal of WTO and International Health Law and Policy* 14, no. 2 (September 2019): 292.
29. "The Politics of the PHEIC," *The Lancet*, June 18, 2019, https://www.thelancet.com/journals/lancet/article/PIIS0140-6736(19)31406-0/fulltext.
30. World Health Organization, transcript, "Virtual Press Conference on COVID-19," March 11, 2020, 14, https://www.who.int/docs/default-source/coronaviruse/transcripts/who-audio-emergencies-coronavirus-press-conference-full-and-final-11mar2020.pdf?sfvrsn=cb432bb3_2.
31. Interview with David Fidler, March 8, 2021.
32. Xiaolin Wei, "China's Response to the Coronavirus Pandemic," *Cambridge Core Blog*, April 11, 2020, https://www.cambridge.org/core/blog/2020/04/11/chinas-response-to-the-coronavirus-pandemic/.
33. Ministry of Foreign Affairs of the People's Republic of China, "Xi Jinping Meets with Visiting World Health Organization (WHO) Director-General Tedros Adhanom Ghebreyesus," press release, January 29, 2020, https://www.fmprc.gov.cn/mfa_eng/zxxx_662805/t1737014.shtml.
34. World Health Organization press conference, Geneva, January 29, 2020, https://www.who.int/docs/default-source/coronaviruse/transcripts/who-audio-script-ncov-rresser-unog-29jan2020.pdf?sfvrsn=a7158807_4.
35. Selam Gebrekidan, Matt Apuzzo, Amy Qin, and Javier Hernandez, "In Hunt for Virus Source, WHO Let China Take Charge," *New York Times*, November 2, 2020, https://www.nytimes.com/2020/11/02/world/who-china-coronavirus.html.
36. Benjamin F. Maier and Dirk Brockmann, "Effective Containment Explains Sub-exponential Growth in Recent Confirmed COVID-19 Cases in China," *Science* 368, no. 6492 (May 15, 2020), https://science.sciencemag.org/content/368/6492/742.
37. Peter Hessler, "How China Controlled the Coronavirus," *New Yorker*, August 10, 2020, https://www.newyorker.com/magazine/2020/08/17/how-china-controlled-the-coronavirus.
38. Alex Hannaford, "The Last Days of Dr Li Wenliang, the Chinese Coronavirus Whistleblower," *GQ*, March 16, 2020, https://www.gq-magazine.co.uk/politics/article/dr-li-wenliang-death.
39. Qin Jianhang and Timmy Shen, "Whistleblower Li Wenliang: There Should Be More Than One Voice in a Heathy Society," Caixin, February 6, 2020, https://www.caixinglobal.com/2020-02-06/after-being-punished-by-local-police-coronavirus-whistleblower-vindicated-by-top-court-101509986.html; Giles Whittell, "The Disappeared," *Tortoise*, July 20, 2020, https://members.tortoisemedia.com/2020/07/20/the-disappeared-china/content.html.
40. Page, Fan, and Khan, "How It All Started."
41. Lily Kuo, "Coronavirus: Wuhan Doctor Speaks Out Against Authorities," *The Guard-*

ian, March 11, 2020, https://www.theguardian.com/world/2020/mar/11/coronavirus
-wuhan-doctor-ai-fen-speaks-out-against-authorities.

42. "Whistleblowing Doctor Missing After Criticizing Beijing's Coronavirus Censorship,"
Reporters Without Borders, April 14, 2020, https://rsf.org/en/news/whistleblowing
-doctor-missing-after-criticizing-beijings-coronavirus-censorship; video at https://
www.weibo.com/tv/show/1034:4493260899680260?from=old_pc_videoshow; David
Bandurski, "Whistling Against Deception," China Media Project, March 11, 2020,
http://chinamediaproject.org/2020/03/11/whistling-against-deception/.

43. Whittell, "The Disappeared."

44. "Coronavirus: Why Have Two Reporters in Wuhan Disappeared?," BBC, February
14, 2020, https://www.bbc.com/news/world-asia-china-51486106.

45. Bill Bishop, "Another Standing Committee Meeting on the Outbreak; Economic
Impact," *Sinocism*, February 3, 2020, https://sinocism.com/p/another-standing
-committee-meeting.

46. Jane Li, "Chinese Internet Users Who Uploaded Coronavirus Memories to GitHub
Have Been Arrested," *Quartz*, April 27, 2020, https://qz.com/1846277/china-arrests
-users-behind-github-coronavirus-memories-page/.

47. "China: Protect Human Rights While Combatting Coronavirus Outbreak," Chinese
Human Rights Defenders, January 31, 2020, https://www.nchrd.org/2020/01/china
-protect-human-rights-while-combatting-coronavirus-outbreak/.

48. Hua Chunying 华春莹 (@SpokespersonCHN), "Reciprocity? 29 US media agencies in
China VS 9 Chinese ones in the US. Multiple-entry to China VS Single-entry to the US.
21 Chinese journalists denied visas since last year. Now the US kicked off the game, let's
play," Twitter, March 3, 2020, 1:55 a.m., https://twitter.com/SpokespersonCHN/status
/1234734030907555840.

49. Shibani Mahtani, "'One China' Dispute Means One Big Headache for Taiwan in
Coronavirus Crisis," *Washington Post*, February 4, 2020, https://www.washingtonpost
.com/world/asia_pacific/one-china-dispute-means-one-big-headache-for-taiwan-in
-coronavirus-crisis/2020/02/04/eda3b898–462c-11ea-91ab-ce439aa5c7c1_story.html.

50. Rym Momtaz, "Inside Macron's Coronavirus War," Politico, April 12, 2020, https://
www.politico.eu/interactive/inside-emmanuel-macron-coronavirus-war/.

51. Keoni Everington, "Italy Forced to Buy Back Medical Supplies It Had Donated to
China," *Taiwan News*, April 8, 2020, https://www.taiwannews.com.tw/en/news/3912335.

52. Etienne Soula, Franziska Luettge, Melissa Ladner, and Manisha Reuter, "Masks Off:
Chinese Coronavirus Assistance in Europe," policy paper, German Marshall Fund of
the United States, July 2020, https://www.gmfus.org/sites/default/files/publications
/pdf/ASD-ASIA%20-%20EU%20China%20Coronavirus%20-%20final.pdf.

53. Charlie Campbell, "China's 'Mask Diplomacy' Is Faltering. But the U.S. Isn't Doing
Any Better," *Time*, April 3, 2020, https://time.com/5814940/china-mask-diplomacy
-falters/.

54. Josep Borrell, "The Coronavirus Pandemic and the New World It Is Creating," Delegation of the European Union to China, March 24, 2020, https://eeas.europa.eu
/delegations/china/76401/eu-hrvp-josep-borrell-coronavirus-pandemic-and-new
-world-it-creating_en.

55. Wu Jing, *Wolf Warrior* (film in Chinese), released April 2, 2015.

56. Ambassade de Chine en France (@AmbassadeChine), "Après la fermeture de la Base
Fort Detrick, la grippe N1H1 s'est éclatée aux Etats-Unis. octobre 2019, les organes
américains ont organisé un exercice codé « Event 201 » aux cas de pandémie mon-
diale. 2 mois plus tard, le premier cas de COVID 19 a été confirmé à Wuhan, en
Chine," Twitter, March 23, 2020, 4:53 a.m., https://twitter.com/AmbassadeChine
/status/1242011628608118786.

57. European Think-Tank Network on China, "Covid-19 in Europe-China Relations: A Country-Level Analysis," 2020, 23, https://www.ifri.org/sites/default/files/atoms/files /etnc_special_report_covid-19_china_europe_2020.pdf.

58. Elisa Braun, "Chinese Envoy to France Defends Country's 'Goodwill' amid Coronavirus Diplomatic Row," Politico, April 16, 2020, https://www.politico.eu/article/lu-shaye -chinese-envoy-to-france-defends-country-goodwill-after-coronavirus-diplomatic -row.

59. "Transcript of Chinese Ambassador CHENG Jingye's Interview with Australian Financial Review Political Correspondent Andrew Tillett," Embassy of the People's Republic of China in the Commonwealth of Australia, April 27, 2020, http://au.china -embassy.org/eng/sghdxwfb_1/t1773741.htm.

60. Daniel Hurst, "Cyber-Attack Australia: Sophisticated Attack from State-Based Actor, PM Says," The Guardian, June 19, 2020, https://www.theguardian.com/australia -news/2020/jun/19/australia-cyber-attack-attacks-hack-state-based-actor-says -australian-prime-minister-scott-morrison.

61. Rod McGuirk, "Australia Welcomes Virus Inquiry but Condemns China Tariff," Associated Press, May 18, 2020, https://apnews.com/96294f874151a77ecb9f5ccca4 efe2af.

62. Vivian Wang and Amy Qin, "As Coronavirus Fades in China, Nationalism and Xenophobia Flare," New York Times, May 11, 2020, https://www.nytimes.com/2020/04/16 /world/asia/coronavirus-china-nationalism.html.

63. Matthew Brown, "Fact Check: Black People Being Targeted in Guangzhou, China, over COVID-19 Fears," USA Today, April 16, 2020, https://www.usatoday.com/story/news /factcheck/2020/04/16/fact-check-guangzhou-china-mcdonalds-confirms-incident -targeting-blacks/5139470002/.

64. Keoni Everington, "Photo of the Day: Xenophopia [sic] Made in China," Taiwan News, April 7, 2020, https://www.taiwannews.com.tw/en/news/3911782.

65. "Protest Letter of African Ambassadors in Beijing," Front Page Africa, April 13, 2020, https://frontpageafricaonline.com/opinion/letters-comments/protest-letter-of -african-ambassadors-in-beijing/.

66. Sebastian Horn, Carmen Reinhardt, and Christoph Trebesch, "How Much Money Does the World Owe China?," Harvard Business Review, February 26, 2020, https:// hbr.org/2020/02/how-much-money-does-the-world-owe-china; "Africa's Growing Debt Crisis: Who Is the Debt Owed to?," Jubilee Debt Campaign, 2018, https:// jubileedebt.org.uk/wp/wp-content/uploads/2018/09/Briefing_09.18.pdf.

67. "List of LIC DSAs for PRGT-Eligible Countries as of November 25, 2020," International Monetary Fund, November 25, 2020, https://www.imf.org/external/Pubs/ft /dsa/DSAlist.pdf.

68. Jevans Nyabiage, "China to Forgive Interest-Free Loans That Are Coming Due Xi Jinping Says," South China Morning Post, June 18, 2020, https://www.scmp.com /news/world/africa/article/3089492/china-forgive-interest-free-loans-africa-are -coming-due-xi; Kevin Acker, Deborah Brautigam, and Yufan Huang, "Debt Relief with Chinese Characteristics," China Africa Research Initiative Working Paper No. 39, Johns Hopkins University, June 2020, https://static1.squarespace.com/static /5652847de4b033f56d2bdc29/t/60353345259d4448e01a37d8/1614099270470/WP+39+ -+Acker%2C+Brautigam%2C+Huang+-+Debt+Relief.pdf.

69. For a timeline of the various closures and actions between Russia and China during COVID-19, see Ivan Zuenko, "The Coronavirus Pandemic and the Russo-Chinese Border," ASAN Forum, May 9, 2020, http://www.theasanforum.org/the-coronavirus -pandemic-and-the-russo-chinese-border/.

70. Gabrielle Tétrault-Farber, "China to Russia: End Discriminatory Coronavirus Mea-

sures Against Chinese," Reuters, February 26, 2020, https://www.reuters.com/article
/us-china-health-moscow-letter/china-to-russia-end-discriminatory-coronavirus
-measures-against-chinese-idUSKCN20K1HU.

71. Tommy Yang, "Unease at the Border: Russia and China Seek to Downplay Covid-19
Outbreak in Suifenhe," *The Guardian*, April 18, 2020, https://www.theguardian.com
/world/2020/apr/18/unease-at-the-border-russia-and-china-seek-to-downplay
-covid-19-outbreak-in-suifenhe.

72. Zhuang Pinghui, "Coronavirus: China Embassy U-Turns on Claim Russian Police
Singled Out Chinese," *South China Morning Post*, March 2, 2020, https://www.scmp
.com/news/china/diplomacy/article/3064582/coronavirus-china-embassy-u-turns
-claim-russian-police-singled.

73. Richard Weitz, "The COVID-19 Pandemic Boosts Sino-Russian Cooperation,"
Jamestown Foundation, June 24, 2020, https://jamestown.org/program/the-covid-19
-pandemic-boosts-sino-russian-cooperation/.

74. "Exclusive: Internal Chinese Report Warns Beijing Faces Tiananmen-Like Global
Backlash over Virus—Sources," Reuters, May 4, 2020, https://uk.reuters.com
/article/uk-health-coronavirus-china-sentiment-ex/exclusive-internal-chinese
-report-warns-beijing-faces-tiananmen-like-global-backlash-over-virus-sources
-idUKKBN22G198.

75. China Global Television Network, "Zhong Nanshan: Virus May Not Have Originated
in China," YouTube video, 2:02, posted February 27, 2020, https://www.youtube.com
/watch?v=UILmnQNeDuE.

76. AmbCHENXiaodong (@AmbCHENXiaodong), "Although the epidemic first broke
out in China, it did not necessarily mean that the virus is originated from China,
let alone 'made in China,'" Twitter, March 7, 2020, 11:07 a.m., https://twitter.com
/AmbCHENXiaodong/status/1236322524281044993.

77. Lijian Zhao 赵立坚 (@zlj517), "2/2 CDC was caught on the spot. When did patient zero
begin in US? How many people are infected? What are the names of the hospitals? It
might be US army who brought the epidemic to Wuhan. Be transparent! Make public
your data! US owe us an explanation!," Twitter, March 12, 2020, 10:37 a.m., https://
twitter.com/zlj517/status/1238111898828066823.

78. Lijian Zhao 赵立坚 (@zlj517), "This article is very much important to each and every
one of us. Please read and retweet it. COVID-19: Further Evidence that the Virus
Originated in the US," Twitter, March 12, 2020, 9:02 p.m., https://twitter.com/zlj517
/status/1238269193427906560.

79. "It's US That Fears Probe on Virus Origin: Global Times Editorial," *Global Times*,
May 18, 2020, https://www.globaltimes.cn/content/1188739.shtml.

80. China Global Television Network Arabic, "فله‌ڨيروسكوروناالجديدمنصعنايايالولاتامللاتحدةا
أمريكية؟" YouTube Video, 6:27, posted March 17, 2020, https://www.youtube.com
/watch?v=dlGj1RdUHUM&feature=emb_title; Edward Wong, Matthew Rosenberg,
and Julian E. Barnes, "Chinese Agents Helped Spread Messages That Sowed Virus
Panic in U.S., Officials Say," *New York Times*, August 23, 2020, https://www.nytimes
.com/2020/04/22/us/politics/coronavirus-china-disinformation.html.

81. Erika Kinetz, "Anatomy of a Conspiracy: With Covid, China Took a Leading Role,"
Associated Press, February 15, 2021, https://apnews.com/article/pandemics-beijing
-only-on-ap-epidemics-media-122b73e134b780919cc1808f3f6f16e8.

82. "Coronavirus: China Accuses US of Spreading 'Conspiracies,'" BBC, May 24, 2020,
https://www.bbc.com/news/world-asia-china-52790634.

83. Hua Chunying 华春莹 (@SpokespersonCHN), "#Pompeo said to Fox News 'China
has allowed hundreds of thousands of people to leave Wuhan to go to places like Italy
that's now suffering so badly'. Stop lying through your teeth! As WHO experts said,

China's efforts averted hundreds of thousands of infection cases." Twitter, March 20, 2020, 9:36 a.m., https://twitter.com/SpokespersonCHN/status/1240995658904944640; "Coronavirus: China Says Pompeo 'Lying' in New Clash over Pandemic," *Straits Times*, March 20, 2020, https://www.straitstimes.com/asia/east-asia/coronavirus-china-says -pompeo-lying-in-new-clash-over-bug.

84. Six intelligence community officials told the *New York Times* that the intelligence community had assessed that Chinese operatives helped push these messages across platforms, although they did not necessarily create them. Wong, Rosenberg, and Barnes, "Chinese Agents Helped Spread Messages."

85. NSC (@WHNSC), "Text message rumors of a national #quarantine are FAKE. There is no national lockdown. @CDCgov has and will continue to post the latest guidance on #COVID19. #coronavirus," Twitter, March 15, 2020, 11:48 p.m., https://twitter.com /WHNSC/status/1239398218292748292.

86. Wong, Rosenberg, and Barnes, "Chinese Agents Helped Spread Messages."

87. Laura Rosenberger, "China's Coronavirus Information Offensive," *Foreign Affairs*, April 22, 2020, https://www.foreignaffairs.com/articles/china/2020-04-22/chinas -coronavirus-information-offensive.

88. Interview on background with Twitter executive, August 2020.

89. "Disclosing Networks of State-Linked Information Operations We've Removed," Twitter Safety, June 12, 2020, https://blog.twitter.com/en_us/topics/company/2020 /information-operations-june-2020.html.

90. Matt Apuzzo, "Pressured by China, E.U. Softens Report on Covid-19 Disinforma- tion," *New York Times*, April 24, 2020, https://www.nytimes.com/2020/04/24/world /europe/disinformation-china-eu-coronavirus.html.

91. Mark Scott, Laura Kayali, and Laurens Cerulus, "European Commission Accuses China of Peddling Disinformation," Politico, June 10, 2020, https://www.politico.eu /article/european-commission-disinformation-china-coronavirus/.

92. Yang, "China's Early Warning System."

93. Whittell, "The Disappeared."

94. Yao Yang, "Is a New Cold War Coming?," interview with *Beijing Cultural Review*, April 28, 2020, translation by David Ownby at Reading the China Dream, https:// www.readingthechinadream.com/yao-yang-the-new-cold-war.html.

95. Not-for-attribution small group conversation by Zoom, July 16, 2020.

96. Fu Ying, "Fu Ying on Why China and America Must Co-operate to Defeat Covid-19," *The Economist*, April 29, 2020, https://www.economist.com/by-invitation/2020/04 /29/fu-ying-on-why-china-and-america-must-co-operate-to-defeat-covid-19.

97. Fu Ying, "After the Pandemic, Then What?," China-US Focus, June 28, 2020, https:// www.chinausfocus.com/foreign-policy/after-the-pandemic-then-what.

98. Yuan Peng, "The Coronavirus Pandemic and a Once-in-a-Century Change," June 17, 2020, translation by David Ownby at Reading the China Dream, https://www .readingthechinadream.com/yuan-peng-coronavirus-pandemic.html.

CHAPTER 5: OPPORTUNITIES LOST

1. Interview with Tony Banbury, August 8, 2020.

2. Interview with Tony Banbury, August 8, 2020.

3. Memo from Christopher M. Kirchhoff to Susan E. Rice, July 11, 2016, 19–21, available at https://int.nyt.com/data/documenthelper/6823-national-security-counci-ebola /05bd797500ea55be0724/optimized/full.pdf#page=1.

4. President Barack H. Obama, "Remarks by the President on the Ebola Outbreak at the Centers for Disease Control and Prevention," The White House, September 16,

2014, https://obamawhitehouse.archives.gov/the-press-office/2014/09/16/remarks
-president-ebola-outbreak.

5. Interview with Tony Banbury, January 28, 2021.

6. Nahal Toosi, Daniel Lippmann, and Dan Diamond, "Before Trump's Inauguration, a Warning: The Worst Global Influenza Since 1918," Politico, March 16, 2020, https://www .politico.com/news/2020/03/16/trump-inauguration-warning-scenario-pandemic -132797; James Fallows, "The Three Weeks That Changed Everything," The Atlantic, June 29, 2020, https://www.theatlantic.com/politics/archive/2020/06/how-white -house-coronavirus-response-went-wrong/613591/.

7. Donald G. McNeill Jr., "The Malaria Fighter," New York Times, October 20, 2014, https://www.nytimes.com/2014/10/21/science/a-quiet-approach-to-bringing-down -malaria.html.

8. Author interview with Timothy Ziemer, October 13, 2020.

9. National Security Strategy of the United States, 2017.

10. John Bolton, The Room Where It Happened (New York: Simon and Schuster, 2020), 315–17.

11. Matt Pottinger, Michael Flynn, and Paul Batchelor, "Fixing Intel: A Blueprint for Making Intelligence Relevant in Afghanistan," January 4, 2010, https://www.cnas.org /publications/reports/fixing-intel-a-blueprint-for-making-intelligence-relevant.

12. For more details on Pottinger's role in the administration, including during the pandemic, see Lawrence Wright, "The Plague Year," New Yorker, December 28, 2020, https://www.newyorker.com/magazine/2021/01/04/the-plague-year.

13. Author email correspondence with Sharon Sanders, January 26, 2021; Paul Farhi, "How a Blogger in Florida Put Out an Early Warning About the Coronavirus Crisis," Washington Post, March 14, 2020, https://www.washingtonpost.com/lifestyle /media/the-first-reporter-in-the-western-world-to-spot-the-coronavirus-crisis-was-a -blogger-in-florida/2020/03/13/244f39e6-6476-11ea-acca-80c22bbee96f_story.html; "China—Original 2019-nCov News Thread: Weeks 1–4 (December 30, 2019–January 25, 2020)," Flu Trackers, accessed May 9, 2021, https://flutrackers.com/forum/forum /-2019-ncov-new-coronavirus/china-2019-ncov/821830-china-original-2019-ncov -news-thread-weeks-1-4-december-30-2019-january-25-2020.

14. James Bandler et al., "Inside the Fall of the CDC," ProPublica, October 15, 2020, https://www.propublica.org/article/inside-the-fall-of-the-cdc.

15. Bob Woodward, Rage (New York: Simon & Schuster, 2020), 213–14.

16. Bandler et al., "Inside the Fall of the CDC"; Woodward, Rage, 216.

17. Woodward, Rage, 220. In this book, quotes are not placed in quotation marks. We have included those here to designate where the quote begins and ends.

18. Rich Exner, "Ohio Health Department Identifies 13 Coronavirus Cases in 8 Counties from January," Cleveland.com, May 29, 2020, https://www.cleveland.com /coronavirus/2020/05/ohio-health-department-identifies-13-coronavirus-cases-in -8-counties-from-january.html.

19. Michelle L. Holshue et al., "First Case of 2019 Novel Coronavirus in the United States," New England Journal of Medicine 382, no. 10 (2020): 929–36, https://www .nejm.org/doi/full/10.1056/NEJMoa2001191.

20. Jeremy Page and Lingling Wei, "China's CDC, Built to Stop Pandemics Like COVID, Stumbled When It Mattered Most," Wall Street Journal, August 17, 2020, https://www .wsj.com/articles/chinas-cdc-built-to-stop-pandemics-stumbled-when-it-mattered -most-11597675108.

21. Maggie Haberman, "Trade Adviser Warned White House in January of Risks of a Pandemic," New York Times, April 6, 2020, https://www.nytimes.com/2020/04/06/us /politics/navarro-warning-trump-coronavirus.html.

22. Ana Swanson and Alan Rappeport, "Trump Signs China Trade Deal, Putting Economic Conflict on Pause," *New York Times*, January 15, 2020, https://www.nytimes.com/2020 /01/15/business/economy/china-trade-deal.html.

23. Donald J. Trump (@realDonaldTrump), Twitter, February 7, 2020, https://twitter .com/realDonaldTrump/status/1225728755248828416 (no longer available).

24. Amy Qin, "China's Leader, Under Fire, Says He Led the Coronavirus Fight Early On," *New York Times*, February 15, 2020, https://www.nytimes.com/2020/02/15/world/asia /xi-china-coronavirus.html.

25. Greg Miller and Ellen Nakashima, "President's Intelligence Briefing Book Repeatedly Cited Virus Threat," *Washington Post*, April 27, 2020, https://www.washingtonpost .com/national-security/presidents-intelligence-briefing-book-repeatedly-cited-virus -threat/2020/04/27/ca66949a-8885-11ea-ac8a-fe9b8088e101_story.html; Woodward, *Rage*, 230.

26. The report that O'Brien uttered this warning is in Woodward, *Rage*, xiii. Pottinger's remark and Trump's reply is in Josh Rogin, *Chaos Under Heaven: Trump, Xi, and the Battle for the 21st Century* (Boston: Houghton Mifflin Harcourt, 2021), 216. Trump's denial that O'Brien warned him was made in an NBC town hall on October 15, 2020. Trump's acknowledgment that he first recognized the danger at the end of January is in Woodward, *Rage*, 324.

27. Interview on background with Trump administration official, December 2020.

28. Caitlyn Oprysko, "Trump: Coronavirus Will Have 'A Very Good Ending for Us,'" Politico, January 30, 2020, https://www.politico.com/news/2020/01/30/trump-close -cooperation-china-coronavirus-109701.

29. Sean O'Kane, "United Airlines Suspends Some Flights After Coronavirus Out-break," The Verge, January 28, 2020, https://www.theverge.com/2020/1/28/21112204 /coronavirus-outbreak-united-airlines-china-flights-canceled.

30. Steve Eder, Henry Fountain, Michael H. Keller, Muyi Xiao, and Alexandra Stevenson, "430,000 People Have Traveled from China to U.S. Since Coronavirus Surfaced," *New York Times*, April 4, 2020, https://www.nytimes.com/2020/04/04/us/coronavirus -china-travel-restrictions.html.

31. "Remarks by President Trump in the State of the Union Address," The White House, issued February 4, 2020, https://www.whitehouse.gov/briefings-statements/remarks -president-trump-state-union-address-3/.

32. Woodward, *Rage*, 241–42.

33. Woodward, *Rage*, 246.

34. Lydia Khalil and Olivia Troye, "COVIDcast: Olivia Troye Inside the White House Coronavirus Task Force," in *COVIDcast* (podcast), produced by the Lowy Institute, October 21, 2020, https://www.lowyinstitute.org/publications/covidcast-olivia-troye -inside-white-house-coronavirus-task-force; Annie Karni and Maggie Haberman, "A White House Long in Denial Confronts Reality," *New York Times*, October 6, 2020, https://www.nytimes.com/2020/10/03/us/politics/white-house-coronavirus.html.

35. Woodward, *Rage*, xviii.

36. "Remarks by President Trump in Meeting with African American Leaders," The White House, issued February 28, 2020, https://www.whitehouse.gov/briefings -statements/remarks-president-trump-meeting-african-american-leaders/.

37. Bandler et al., "Inside the Fall of the CDC."

38. Dr. Deborah Birx interview with Margaret Brennan, *Face the Nation*, January 24, 2021, https://www.youtube.com/watch?v=nW41YylWipM.

39. Birx interview with Brennan, *Face the Nation*.

40. "Transcript for the CDC Telebriefing Update on COVID-19," Centers for Disease

Control and Prevention, accessed March 16, 2021, https://www.cdc.gov/media
/releases/2020/t0225-cdc-telebriefing-covid-19.html.

41. Shane Harris, Greg Miller, Josh Dawsey, and Helen Nakashima, "U.S. Intelligence Reports from January and February Warned About a Likely Pandemic," *Washington Post*,
March 20, 2020, https://www.washingtonpost.com/national-security/us-intelligence
-reports-from-january-and-february-warned-about-a-likely-pandemic/2020/03/20
/299d8cda-6ad5-11ea-b5f1-a5a804158597_story.html; Joanna Slater, "Trump's First
Day in India: A Massive Rally with Modi and a Tour of the 'Truly Incredible' Taj Mahal," *Washington Post*, February 24, 2020, https://www.washingtonpost.com/world
/2020/02/24/trump-india-live-updates/.

42. Khalil and Troye, *COVIDcast*.

43. Khalil and Troye, *COVIDcast*.

44. Interview on background with Trump administration official, April 2021.

45. Kate Kelly and Mark Mazzetti, "As Virus Spread, Reports of Trump Administration's Private Briefings Fueled Sell-Off," *New York Times*, October 14, 2020, https://
www.nytimes.com/2020/10/14/us/politics/stock-market-coronavirus-trump.html.

46. Rebecca Ballhaus, Stephanie Armour, and Betsy McKay, "A Demoralized CDC Deals
with White House Meddling and Its Own Mistakes," *Wall Street Journal*, October 15,
2020, .https://www.wsj.com/articles/a-demoralized-cdc-grapples-with-white-house
-meddling-and-its-own-mistakes-11602776561?mod=searchresults&page=1&pos
=1; Bandler et al., "Inside the Fall of the CDC."

47. "Number of Cumulative Cases of Coronavirus (COVID-19) in the United States
from January 20 to November 12, 2020, by Day," Statista, accessed November 13,
2020, https://www.statista.com/statistics/1103185/cumulative-coronavirus-covid19
-cases-number-us-by-day/.

48. For instance, see William Wan et al., "Coronavirus Will Radically Alter the U.S.,"
Washington Post, March 19, 2020, https://www.washingtonpost.com/health/2020/03
/19/coronavirus-projections-us/.

49. "Remarks by President Trump in Address to the Nation," The White House, issued
March 11, 2020, https://www.whitehouse.gov/briefings-statements/remarks-president
-trump-address-nation/.

50. Mike McIntire, "The Tickets Home Were $5,000; They Paid It," *New York Times*,
March 12, 2020, https://www.nytimes.com/2020/03/12/travel/coronavirus-travel-ban
-paris.html.

51. Woodward, *Rage*, 296, 312, 318–19.

52. Sarah Mervosh and Jack Healy, "Holdout States Resist Calls for Stay at Home Orders:
'What Are You Waiting For?,'" *New York Times*, April 3, 2020, https://www.nytimes
.com/2020/04/03/us/coronavirus-states-without-stay-home.html.

53. Philip Rucker et al., "34 Days of Pandemic: Inside Trump's Desperate Attempts
to Reopen America," *Washington Post*, May 2, 2020, https://www.washingtonpost
.com/politics/34-days-of-pandemic-inside-trumps-desperate-attempts-to-reopen
-america/2020/05/02/e99911f4-8b54-11ea-9dfd-990f9dcc71fc_story.html.

54. The Covid Tracking Project, accessed March 16, 2021, https://covidtracking.com
/data/national/.

55. Brian Bennett, "President Trump Is Trying to Get America Back to Normal. His First
Big Trip Was Anything But," *Time*, May 6, 2020, https://time.com/5832623/donald
-trump-coronavirus-normal-arizona/.

56. Michael Shear and Sarah Mervosh, "Trump Encourages Protest Against Governors
Who Encouraged Virus Restrictions," *New York Times*, April 17, 2020.

57. For Green's explanation at the time, see https://www.washingtonpost.com/national

-security/usaid-head-to-resign-amid-coronavirus-pandemic/2020/03/16/9da2af60 -677a-11ea-b5f1-a5a804158597_story.html.

58. Bob David, Kate O'Keefe, and Lingling Wei, "U.S.'s China Hawks Drive Hard Line Policies After Trump Turns on Beijing," *Wall Street Journal*, October 16, 2020, https://www.wsj.com/articles/u-s-s-china-hawks-drive-hard-line-policies-after -trump-turns-on-beijing-11602867030?mod=e2twe.

59. Olivia Nuzzi, "My Private Oval Office Press Conference with Donald Trump, Mike Pence, John Kelly, and Mike Pompeo," *New York*, Intelligencer, October 10, 2018, https://nymag.com/intelligencer/2018/10/my-private-oval-office-press-conference -with-donald-trump.html. For a list of Pompeo's major speeches in 2020, none of which were on the pandemic, see https://2017–2021.state.gov/speeches-secretary -pompeo//index.html.

60. This section is based on an interview on background with a French official and on Giles Whittell, "Trump First," *Tortoise Media*, June 8, 2020, https://members .tortoisemedia.com/2020/06/08/trump-first-goodbye-america/content.html.

61. John Hudson and Nate Jones, "State Department Releases Cable That Launched Claims That Coronavirus Escaped from Chinese Lab," *Washington Post*, July 20, 2020, https://www.washingtonpost.com/national-security/state-department-releases -cable-that-launched-claims-that-coronavirus-escaped-from-chinese-lab/2020/07 /17/63deae58-c861-11ea-a9d3–74640f25b953_story.html.

62. See Rogin, *Chaos Under Heaven*, 267–81.

63. David Sanger, "Pompeo Ties Coronavirus to Chinese Lab Despite U.S. Spy Agencies' Uncertainty," *New York Times*, May 7, 2020, https://www.nytimes.com/2020/05/03 /us/politics/coronavirus-pompeo-wuhan-china-lab.html.

64. Jennifer Hansler and Devan Cole, "Pompeo Backs Away from Theory He and Trump Were Pushing That Coronavirus Originated in a Wuhan Lab," CNN, May 17, 2020, https://www.cnn.com/2020/05/17/politics/mike-pompeo-coronavirus-wuhan-lab /index.html.

65. "Coronavirus: Trump Stands by China Lab Origin Theory for Virus," BBC, May 1, 2020, https://www.bbc.com/news/world-us-canada-52496098.

66. Abul Taher, "China Lab Leak Is the 'Most Credible' Source of the Coronavirus Outbreak, Says Top US Government Official, amid Bombshell Claims Wuhan Scientist Has Turned Whistleblower," *Daily Mail*, January 2, 2021, https://www .dailymail.co.uk/news/article-9106951/Lab-leak-credible-source-coronavirus -outbreak-says-government-official.html; "China Demands Evidence from US Following Adviser's Hype on 'Wuhan Lab Coronavirus Leak' Conspiracy Theory," *Global Times*, January 4, 2021, https://www.globaltimes.cn/page/202101/1211768 .shtml.

67. "Remarks by President Trump in Press Briefing," The White House, issued April 14, 2020, https://www.whitehouse.gov/briefings-statements/remarks-president-trump -press-briefing/.

68. Interviews with several European officials.

69. Victor Garcia and Samuel Chamberlain, "Trump Set to Restore Partial Funding to WHO After Pause to Investigate Coronavirus Response," *Fox News*, May 16, 2020, https://www.foxnews.com/media/exclusive-white-house-set-restore-partial-who -funding.

70. Lou Dobbs "Top WH Advisors are working for whom exactly?," Twitter, May 15, 2020, https://twitter.com/LouDobbs/status/1261485149235163138.

71. Adam Shaw, "Trump Says No Decision Yet on WHO Funding as He Mulls Plan to Match China's Payments," *Fox News*, May 16, 2020, https://www.foxnews.com /politics/trump-says-no-decision-yet-on-who-funding.

72. Donald J. Trump to Tedros Adhanom Ghebreyesus, May 18, 2020, The White House, https://www.whitehouse.gov/wp-content/uploads/2020/05/Tedros-Letter.pdf.
73. Matt Apuzzo, Noah Weiland, and Selam Gebrekidan, "Trump Gave W.H.O. a List of Demands. Hours Later, He Walked Away," *New York Times*, November 22, 2020, https://www.nytimes.com/2020/11/27/world/europe/trump-who-tedros-china-virus.html.
74. Nick Cumming-Bruce, "U.S. Will Remain in Postal Treaty After Emergency Talks," *New York Times*, September 25, 2019, https://www.nytimes.com/2019/09/25/business/universal-postal-union-withdraw.html.
75. Bremberg kept talking with WHO officials and allies to get the talks moving throughout the summer and fall in the hopes of striking a deal he could bring to Trump but no progress was made. "Independent Evaluation of Global COVID-19 Response Announced," World Health Organization, July 9, 2021, https://www.who.int/news/item/09-07-2020-independent-evaluation-of-global-covid-19-response-announced; Pien Huang, "Trump Sets Date to End WHO Membership over Its Handling of Virus," NPR, July 7, 2020, https://www.npr.org/sections/goatsandsoda/2020/07/07/888186158/trump-sets-date-to-end-who-membership-over-its-handling-of-virus.
76. "Politics Aside: U.S. Relies on China Supplies to Fight Coronavirus," *Japan Times*, April 3, 2020, https://www.japantimes.co.jp/news/2020/04/03/asia-pacific/us-relies-on-china-supplies-to-fight-coronavirus/.
77. "Man Dies, Wife Critical After Ingesting Additive to Prevent COVID-19, Doctor Says," ABC 7 News, March 25, 2020, https://abc7news.com/coronavirus-covid-19-chloroquine-hydroxycholoroquine/6045150/.
78. "Govt Bans Export of Anti-Malarial Drug Hydroxychloroquine," *The Hindu*, March 25, 2020, https://www.thehindu.com/news/national/govt-bans-export-of-anti-malarial-drug-hydroxycloroquine/article31158160.ece.
79. Ministry of External Affairs, Government of India, "Telephone Conversation Between Prime Minister and President of USA," press release, June 2, 2020, https://mea.gov.in/press-releases.htm?dtl/32719/Telephone_conversation_between_Prime_Minister_and_President_of_USA.
80. "Remarks by President Trump, Vice President Pence, and Members of the Coronavirus Task Force in a Press Briefing," The White House, April 6, 2020, https://www.whitehouse.gov/briefings-statements/remarks-president-trump-vice-president-pence-members-coronavirus-task-force-press-briefing-21/.
81. Neha Arora and Sumit Khanna, "India Exports 50 Million Hydroxychloroquine Tablets to U.S. for COVID-19 Fight: Source," Reuters, April 30, 2020, https://www.reuters.com/article/us-health-coronavirus-india-hydroxychlor/india-exports-50-million-hydroxychloroquine-tablets-to-u-s-for-covid-19-fight-source-idUSKBN22C2LN.
82. Donald J. Trump (@realDonaldTrump), Twitter, April 8, 2020, https://twitter.com/realDonaldTrump/status/1247950299408498693 (no longer available).
83. Shishir Gupta, "Trump's 200 Ventilators for India Cost $2.6 Million, Reaching in 3 Weeks," *Hindustan Times*, May 19, 2020, https://www.hindustantimes.com/india-news/trump-s-200-ventilators-for-india-cost-2-6-million-reaching-in-3-weeks/story-bO7s9Ng4thj6HuvkcA6DGM.html.
84. Tanisha M. Fazal, "Health Diplomacy in Pandemical Times," *International Organization* 74, no. 51 (2020): 13, https://doi.org/10.1017/S0020818320000326.
85. Jennifer Hansler, Priscilla Alvarez, and Gul Tuysuz, "Personal Protective Equipment Donated from Turkey Arrives in the US," CNN, April 28, 2020, https://edition.cnn.com/us/live-news/us-coronavirus-update-04-28-20/h_c39ec5b84b713f2ef78f1f4517106ea1.
86. Woodward, *Rage*, 292–93.

87. Katherine Eban, "How Jared Kushner's Secret Testing Plan 'Went Poof into Thin Air,'" *Vanity Fair,* July 30, 2002, https://www.vanityfair.com/news/2020/07/how-jared-kushners-secret-testing-plan-went-poof-into-thin-air.

88. Jeremy Konyndyk, "Exceptionalism Is Killing Americans," *Foreign Affairs,* June 8, 2020, https://www.foreignaffairs.com/articles/united-states/2020-06-08/exceptionalism-killing-americans.

89. Paul LeBlanc, "Hogan: Maryland Protected Coronavirus Tests It Secured from South Korea 'Like Fort Knox,'" CNN, April 30, 2020, https://edition.cnn.com/2020/04/30/politics/larry-hogan-coronavirus-masks-national-guard/index.html; Steve Thompson, "Hogan's First Batch of Coronavirus Tests from South Korea Were Flawed, Never Used," *Washington Post,* November 20 2020, https://www.washingtonpost.com/local/md-politics/hogan-korea-coronavirus-tests/2020/11/20/f048c1c8-251b-11eb-a688-5298ad5d580a_story.html.

90. "Coronavirus Resource Center," Johns Hopkins University & Medicine, https://coronavirus.jhu.edu/, accessed April 2 2021.

91. Irwin Redlener et al., *130,000–210,000 Avoidable COVID-19 Deaths—and Counting—in the U.S.* (New York: Columbia University Earth Institute National Center for Disaster Preparedness, 2020), https://ncdp.columbia.edu/custom-content/uploads/2020/10/Avoidable-COVID-19-Deaths-US-NCDP.pdf.

92. The U.S. death rate per 100,000 was 69 and Germany's was 12.17. See Coronavirus Research Center, Johns Hopkins University, https://coronavirus.jhu.edu/data/mortality, accessed October 27, 2020.

93. George Packer, "We Are Living in a Failed State," *The Atlantic,* June 2020, https://www.theatlantic.com/magazine/archive/2020/06/underlying-conditions/610261/.

94. Kevin Rudd, "The Coming Post-COVID Anarchy," *Foreign Affairs,* May 6, 2020, https://www.foreignaffairs.com/articles/united-states/2020-05-06/coming-post-covid-anarchy.

95. Dr. Deborah Birx interview with Margaret Brennan, *Face the Nation,* January 24, 2021, https://www.youtube.com/watch?v=nW41YylWipM.

96. Elizabeth E. Cameron et al., *Global Health Security Index: Building Collective Action and Accountability* (Washington, DC: Nuclear Threat Initiative and Center for Health Security, Johns Hopkins Bloomberg School of Public Health, 2020), https://www.ghsindex.org/wp-content/uploads/2019/10/2019-Global-Health-Security-Index.pdf.

CHAPTER 6: THE GOOD, THE BAD, AND THE UGLY

1. Daniel Boffey, Celine Schoen, Ben Stockton, and Laura Margottini, "Revealed: Italy's Call for Urgent Help Was Ignored as Coronavirus Swept Through Europe," *The Guardian,* July 15, 2020, https://www.theguardian.com/world/2020/jul/15/revealed-the-inside-story-of-europes-divided-coronavirus-response?CMP=share_btn_tw.

2. Boffey et al., "Revealed."

3. Ursula von der Leyen, "President Ursula von der Leyen on Her Phone Call with the Prime Minister of China Li Keqiang," European Commission video, 1:22, March 18, 2020, https://audiovisual.ec.europa.eu/en/topnews/M-004589.

4. Rym Momtaz, "Inside Macron's Coronavirus War," Politico, April 12, 2020, https://www.politico.eu/interactive/inside-emmanuel-macron-coronavirus-war/.

5. Off-the-record conversation with a senior European official, February 2020.

6. Matt Apuzzo, Selam Gebrekidan, and David D. Kirkpatrick, "How the World Missed Covid-19's Silent Spread," *New York Times,* June 27, 2021, https://www.nytimes.com/2020/06/27/world/europe/coronavirus-spread-asymptomatic.html.

7. Angela Giuffrida and Lorenzo Tondo, "Leaked Coronavirus Plan to Quarantine 16m Sparks Chaos in Italy," *The Guardian,* March 8, 2020, https://www.theguardian.com /world/2020/mar/08/leaked-coronavirus-plan-to-quarantine-16m-sparks-chaos-in -italy.

8. See Chapter 7 for more details.

9. "Europe Needs New Measures to Tackle Coronavirus Threat: Italian President," Reuters, March 27, 2020, https://www.reuters.com/article/us-health-coronavirus-eu -italy/europe-needs-new-measures-to-tackle-coronavirus-threat-italian-president -idUSKBN21E36G.

10. "Germany Bans Export of Medical Protection Gear Due to Coronavirus," Reuters, March 4, 2020, https://www.reuters.com/article/health-coronavirus-germany -exports/germany-bans-export-of-medical-protection-gear-due-to-coronavirus -idUSL8N2AX3D9.

11. "French Mayor Defends Smurf Rally After Outcry over Virus," France 24, March 10, 2020, https://www.france24.com/en/20200310-french-mayor-defends-smurf-rally -after-outcry-over-virus; Antonia Noori Farzan, "'We Must Not Stop Living': French Mayor Defends Smurf Rally That Drew Thousands amid Coronavirus Fears," *Washington Post,* March 11, 2020, https://www.washingtonpost.com/nation/2020/03/11 /smurf-coronavirus-france/.

12. Laura Marlowe, "Coronavirus: European Solidarity Sidelined as French Interests Take Priority," *Irish Times,* March 30, 2020, https://www.irishtimes.com/news/world/europe /coronavirus-european-solidarity-sidelined-as-french-interests-take-priority-1 .4216184.

13. Rush Doshi (@RushDoshi), "Serbian President: The only country that can help us is China," Twitter, March 16, 2020, 4:09 p.m., https://twitter.com/RushDoshi/status /1239645067066978311.

14. Jacopo Barigazzi, "Italy's Foreign Minister Hails China's Coronavirus Aid," Politico, March 13, 2020, https://www.politico.eu/article/italys-foreign-minister-hails -chinese-caronavirus-aid/; Andrew Small, "The Meaning of Systemic Rivalry: Europe and China Beyond the Pandemic," European Council on Foreign Relations, May 13, 2020, https://www.ecfr.eu/publications/summary/the_meaning_of _systemic_rivalry_europe_and_china_beyond_the_pandemic.

15. Maurizio Massari, "Italian Ambassador to the EU: Italy Needs Europe's Help," Politico, March 10, 2020, https://www.politico.eu/article/coronavirus-italy-needs-europe -help/.

16. Europe Elects (@EuropeElects), "Italy: Tecnè poll," Twitter, April 11, 2020, 5:00 p.m., https://twitter.com/europeelects/status/1249079936629039110?lang=en.

17. Boffey et al., "Revealed."

18. Emmanuel Macron, "Adresse aux Français, 16 mars 2020," Élysée, March 16, 2020, https://www.elysee.fr/emmanuel-macron/2020/03/16/adresse-aux-francais-covid19; "France—President Emmanuel Macron's Approval Rating," Poll of Polls, Politico, https://www.politico.eu/europe-poll-of-polls/france/.

19. Angela Merkel, "An Address to the Nation by Federal Chancellor Merkel," German Federal Government, March 18, 2020, https://www.bundesregierung.de/breg-en /issues/statement-chancellor-1732296.

20. Giles Tremlett, "How Did Spain Get Its Coronavirus Response So Wrong?," *The Guardian,* March 26, 2020, https://www.theguardian.com/world/2020/mar/26/spain -coronavirus-response-analysis.

21. Mariam Claeson and Stefan Hanson, "COVID-19 and the Swedish Enigma," *Lancet* 397, no. 10271 (January 2021): 259–61, https://www.thelancet.com/journals/lancet /article/PIIS0140-6736(20)32750-1/fulltext; Kelly Bjorklund, "The Inside Story of

How Sweden Botched Its Coronavirus Response," *Foreign Policy*, December 22, 2020, https://foreignpolicy.com/2020/12/22/sweden-coronavirus-covid-response/; Kelly Bjorklund and Andrew Ewing, "The Swedish COVID-19 Response Is a Disaster. It Shouldn't Be a Model for the Rest of the World," *Time*, October 14, 2020, https://time .com/5899432/sweden-coronovirus-disaster/; Eric Orlowski and David Goldsmith, "Four Months into the COVID-19 Pandemic, Sweden's Prized *Herd Immunity* Is Nowhere in Sight," *Journal of the Royal Society of Medicine* 113, no. 8 (August 2020): 292–98, https://doi.org/10.1177/0141076820945282; Bojan Pancevski, "Coronavirus Is Taking a High Toll on Sweden's Elderly. Families Blame the Government," *Wall Street Journal*, June 18, 2020, https://www.wsj.com/articles/coronavirus-is-taking-a -high-toll-on-swedens-elderly-families-blame-the-government-11592479430?mod =article_inline.

22. Norway's numbers were for a slightly different three-month period—March to May instead of April to June. Sinéad Baker, "Sweden's GDP Slumped 8.6% in Q2, More Sharply Than Its Neighbors Despite Its No-Lockdown Policy," *Business Insider*, August 14, 2020, https://www.businessinsider.com/coronavirus-sweden-gdp-falls-8pc -in-q2-worse-nordic-neighbors-2020-8.

23. Drew Hinshaw and Natalia Ojewska, "Covid-19 Rips Through European Countries Spared in the Spring, Straining Hospitals," *Wall Street Journal*, October 16, 2020, https://www.wsj.com/articles/covid-rips-through-european-countries-spared-in -the-spring-straining-hospitals-11602865379?page=2.

24. Guy Chazan, "How Germany Got Coronavirus Right," *Financial Times*, June 4, 2020, https://www.ft.com/content/cc1f650a-91c0-4e1f-b990-ee8ceb5339ea; Chris Morris, "Coronavirus: What Can the UK Learn from Germany on Testing?," BBC News, April 10, 2020, https://www.bbc.com/news/health-52234061; Margherita Stancati and Bojan Pancevski, "How Europe Kept Coronavirus Cases Low Even After Reopening," *Wall Street Journal*, July 20, 2020, https://www.wsj.com/articles/how-europe-slowed -its-coronavirus-cases-from-a-torrent-to-a-trickle-11595240731.

25. Ludwig Burger and John Miller, "Update 1—German, Swiss Hospitals to Treat Coronavirus Patients from Eastern France," Reuters, March 22, 2020, https://www.reuters .com/article/health-coronavirus-germany-france/update-1-german-swiss-hospitals -to-treat-coronavirus-patients-from-eastern-france-idUSL8N2BF0J8.

26. Ursula von der Leyen, quoted in Verena Schmitt-Roschmann, "After Glimpsing 'Abyss,' von der Leyen Determined EU Will Survive," DPA International, March 28, 2020, https://www.dpa-international.com/topic/glimpsing-abyss-von-der-leyen -determined-eu-will-survive-urn%3Anewsml%3Adpa.com%3A20090101%3A2003 28-99-509470.

27. Viktoria Dendrinou, "Euro-Area Finance Chiefs Told to Guard Against Breakup Risks," Bloomberg, March 30, 2020, https://www.bloomberg.com/news/articles/2020-03-30 /euro-area-finance-chiefs-told-to-guard-against-break-up-threat?sref=bxQtWDnd; Angela Merkel, quoted in Andreas Rinke and Markus Wacket, "Coronavirus Pandemic Is Historical Test for EU, Merkel Says," Reuters, April 6, 2020, https://www .reuters.com/article/uk-health-coronavirus-germany-idUKKBN21O175.

28. Rinke and Wacket, "Coronavirus Pandemic Is Historical Test."

29. Pedro Sánchez, "Europe's Future Is at Stake in This War Against Coronavirus," *The Guardian*, April 5, 2020, https://www.theguardian.com/world/commentisfree/2020 /apr/05/europes-future-is-at-stake-in-this-war-against-coronavirus.

30. Sánchez, "Europe's Future Is at Stake."

31. Emmanuel Macron, quoted in Victor Mallet and Roula Khalaf, "FT Interview: Emmanuel Macron Says It Is Time to Think the Unthinkable," *Financial Times*, April 16, 2020, https://www.ft.com/content/3ea8d790-7fd1-11ea-8fdb-7ec06edeef84.

32. Schmitt-Roschmann, "After Glimpsing 'Abyss'"; Rinke and Wacket, "Coronavirus Pandemic Is Historical Test"; Sánchez, "Europe's Future Is at Stake"; Mallet and Khalaf, "FT Interview: Emmanuel Macron."

33. Martin Wolf, "German Court Decides to Take Back Control with ECB Ruling," *Financial Times*, May 12, 2020, https://www.ft.com/content/37825304-9428-11ea-af4b-499244625ac4.

34. "Rebuilding the Trans-Atlantic Relationship After COVID-19," webinar, Brookings Institution, Washington, DC, June 16, 2020, https://www.brookings.edu/wp-content/uploads/2020/06/fp_20200616_transatlantic_covid_transcript.pdf.

35. Barry Neild, "Why Greece Could Be Europe's Best Holiday Ticket Right Now," CNN, August 1, 2020, https://www.cnn.com/travel/article/greece-vacation-right-now-covid-19-intl/index.html.

36. Stancati and Pancevski, "How Europe Kept Coronavirus Cases Low."

37. Patrick M. Cronin, Seth Cropsey, and Robert Spalding, "Transcript: Taiwan's Strong COVID-19 Response: Remarks by Foreign Minister Joseph Wu," Hudson Institute, April 10, 2020, https://www.hudson.org/research/15919-transcript-taiwan-s-strong-covid-19-response-remarks-by-foreign-minister-joseph-wu.

38. Kow-Tong Chen et al., "SARS in Taiwan: An Overview and Lessons Learned," *International Journal of Infectious Diseases* 9, no. 2 (2005), https://pubmed.ncbi.nlm.nih.gov/15708322/; interview with senior Taiwan government official.

39. Yimou Lee, "Taiwan's New 'Electronic Fence' for Quarantines Leads Wave of Virus Monitoring," Reuters, March 20, 2020, https://www.reuters.com/article/us-health-coronavirus-taiwan-surveillanc/taiwans-new-electronic-fence-for-quarantines-leads-wave-of-virus-monitoring-idUSKBN2170SK; interviews with government officials of Taiwan.

40. "Taiwan Can Help, and Taiwan Is Helping!," press release, Ministry of Foreign Affairs, Republic of China (Taiwan), https://en.mofa.gov.tw/cp.aspx?n=AF70B0F54FFB164B.

41. Wudan Yan and Ann Babe, "What Should the U.S. Learn from South Korea's Covid-19 Success?," Undark, October 5, 2020, https://undark.org/2020/10/05/south-korea-covid-19-success/; "Moon Apologizes for Mask Shortage," *Korea Herald*, March 3, 2020, http://www.koreaherald.com/view.php?ud=20200303000718; Brian Kim, "Lessons for America: How South Korean Authorities Used Law to Fight the Coronavirus," *Lawfare*, March 16, 2020, https://www.lawfareblog.com/lessons-america-how-south-korean-authorities-used-law-fight-coronavirus; Derek Thompson, "What's Behind South Korea's COVID-19 Exceptionalism?," *The Atlantic*, May 6, 2020, https://www.theatlantic.com/ideas/archive/2020/05/whats-south-koreas-secret/611215/; Timothy W. Martin and Dasl Yoon, "How South Korea Successfully Managed Coronavirus," *Wall Street Journal*, September 25, 2020, https://www.wsj.com/articles/lessons-from-south-korea-on-how-to-manage-covid-11601044329.

42. Victor Cha, "South Korea Offers a Lesson in Best Practices," *Foreign Affairs*, April 10, 2020, https://www.foreignaffairs.com/articles/united-states/2020-04-10/south-korea-offers-lesson-best-practices; Yan and Babe, "What Should the U.S. Learn"; Dasl Yoon and Timothy W. Martin, "How South Korea Put into Place the World's Most Aggressive Coronavirus Test Program," *Wall Street Journal*, March 16, 2020, https://www.wsj.com/articles/how-south-korea-put-into-place-the-worlds-most-aggressive-coronavirus-testing-11584377217?mod=article_inline; Thompson, "What's Behind South Korea's COVID-19 Exceptionalism?"

43. Yoon and Martin, "How South Korea Put Into Place"; Victor Cha and Dana Kim, "A Timeline of South Korea's Response to COVID-19," CSIS, March 27, 2020, https://www.csis.org/analysis/timeline-south-koreas-response-covid-19; "Covid-19: South

Korea Closes Seoul Schools amid Rise in Cases," BBC, August 25, 2020, https://www
.bbc.com/news/world-asia-53901707; Sangmi Cha, "South Korea: No New Domestic
Coronavirus Cases, No Transmission from Election," Reuters, April 29, 2020, https://
www.reuters.com/article/us-health-coronavirus-southkorea/south-korea-no-new
-domestic-coronavirus-cases-no-transmission-from-election-idUSKBN22C05U;
Matthew Campbell and Heesu Lee, "There's Still Time to Beat Covid Without Lockdowns," Bloomberg, December 10, 2020, https://www.bloomberg.com/features/2020
-south-korea-covid-strategy/.

44. Yoon and Martin, "How South Korea Put into Place"; Philip Bump, "The Difference
     in How the Pandemic Has Affected the U.S. and South Korea Remains Staggering,"
     Washington Post, December 4, 2020, https://www.washingtonpost.com/politics/2020
     /12/04/difference-how-pandemic-has-affected-us-south-korea-remains-staggering/;
     Bhaskar Chakravorti, Ajay Bhalla, and Ravi Shankar Chaturvedi, "Which Economies
     Showed the Most Digital Progress in 2020?," *Harvard Business Review*, December
     18, 2020, https://hbr.org/2020/12/which-economies-showed-the-most-digital
     -progress-in-2020; Edward White and Song Jung-a, "Vaccine Rollout and Tech
     Exports Boost S Korea Growth Expectations," *Financial Times*, January 25, 2021,
     https://www.ft.com/content/e7019c31-e46c-400e-820c-4f19a2788fa2.

45. Eisuke Nakazawa, Hiroyasu Ino, and Akira Akabayashi, "Chronology of COVID-19
     Cases on the *Diamond Princess* Cruise Ship and Ethical Considerations: A Report
     from Japan," *Disaster Medicine and Public Health Preparedness* 14, no. 4 (2020),
     https://www.ncbi.nlm.nih.gov/pmc/articles/PMC7156812/; Kenji Mizumoto, Katsu-
     shi Kagaya, and Alexander Zarebski, "Estimating the Asymptomatic Proportion of
     Coronavirus Disease 2019 (COVID-19) Cases on Board the *Diamond Princess* Cruise
     Ship, Yokohama, Japan, 2020," *Eurosurveillance* 25, no. 10 (March 2020), https://www
     .eurosurveillance.org/content/10.2807/1560-7917.ES.2020.25.10.2000180; Robin
     Harding, Nicolle Liu, and John Reed, "How a Cruise Ship Holiday Turned into a
     Coronavirus Nightmare," *Financial Times*, February 21, 2020, https://www.ft.com
     /content/1a6dd424-546c-11ea-8841-482eed0038b1.

46. Hiromi Murakami, "Resolved: Japan's Response to Covid-19 Is Prudent," CSIS,
     May 20, 2020, https://www.csis.org/analysis/resolved-japans-response-covid-19
     -prudent; "Avoid the Three Cs," Prime Minister's Office of Japan, https://www.mhlw
     .go.jp/content/10900000/000619576.pdf; Motoko Rich, Hisako Ueno, and Makiko
     Inoue, "Japan Declared a Coronavirus Emergency. Is It Too Late?," *New York Times*,
     April 16, 2020, https://www.nytimes.com/2020/04/07/world/asia/japan-coronavirus
     -emergency.html.

47. William Sposato, "Japan's Halfhearted Coronavirus Measures Are Working Anyway," *For-
     eign Policy*, May 14, 2020, https://foreignpolicy.com/2020/05/14/japan-coronavirus
     -pandemic-lockdown-testing/; Lawrence Repeta, "The Coronavirus and Japan's
     Constitution," *Japan Times*, April 14, 2020, https://www.japantimes.co.jp/opinion
     /2020/04/14/commentary/japan-commentary/coronavirus-japans-constitution/;
     Mari Yamaguchi, "Japan's State of Emergency Is No Lockdown. What's in It?," As-
     sociated Press, April 7, 2020, https://apnews.com/article/eb73f1170268ec2cdcf03e6
     97365acb2; Grace Lee, "Is Japan's Pandemic Response a Disaster or a Success?," *PBS
     NewsHour*, June 7, 2020, https://www.pbs.org/newshour/show/is-japans-pandemic
     -response-a-disaster-or-a-success; "Coronavirus: State of Emergency Lifted in Most
     of Japan," BBC, May 14, 2020, https://www.bbc.com/news/world-asia-52658551.

48. Thisanka Siripala, "Japan's Campaign to Revive Virus-Hit Tourism Sector Postponed
     amid Cost Controversy," The Diplomat, June 16, 2020, https://thediplomat.com
     /2020/06/japans-campaign-to-revive-virus-hit-tourism-sector-postponed-amid
     -cost-controversy/; Rocky Swift, "Study Links Japan's Domestic Travel Campaign to

Increased COVID-19 Symptoms," Reuters, December 8, 2020, https://www.reuters
.com/article/health-coronavirus-japan-travel/study-links-japans-domestic-travel
-campaign-to-increased-covid-19-symptoms-idUSKBN28I17C; Sho Saito, Yusuke
Asai, and Nobuaki Matsunaga, "First and Second COVID-19 Waves in Japan: A
Comparison of Disease Severity and Characteristics," *Journal of Infection*, November
2020, https://www.ncbi.nlm.nih.gov/pmc/articles/PMC7605825/; Robin Harding,
"The 'Japan Model' That Tackled the Coronavirus," *Financial Times*, June 2, 2020,
https://www.ft.com/content/7a4ce8b5-20a3-40ab-abaf-1de213a66403.

49. "Deputy PM Orders Ministries to Prevent Acute Pneumonia Spread into Việt
Nam," Viet Nam News, January 17, 2020, https://vietnamnews.vn/society/571291
/deputy-pm-orders-ministries-to-prevent-acute-pneumonia-spread-into-viet-nam
.html; Anna Jones, "Coronavirus: How 'Overreaction' Made Vietnam a Virus Success," BBC, May 15, 2020, https://www.bbc.com/news/world-asia-52628283; Minh
Vu and Bich T. Tran, "The Secret to Vietnam's COVID-19 Response Success," The
Diplomat, April 18, 2020, https://thediplomat.com/2020/04/the-secret-to-vietnams
-covid-19-response-success/; "Vietnam Records First COVID-19 Death After Virus
Re-Emerges: State Media," Reuters, July 31, 2020, https://www.reuters.com/article
/us-health-coronavirus-vietnam-death/vietnam-records-first-covid-19-death-after
-virus-re-emerges-state-media-idUSKCN24W0XS; "Emerging COVID-19 Success
Story: Vietnam's Commitment to Containment," Our World in Data, June 30, 2020,
https://ourworldindata.org/covid-exemplar-vietnam.

50. Paul Dyer, "Policy and Institutional Responses to COVID-19: New Zealand," Brookings Institution, January 24, 2021, https://www.brookings.edu/research/policy-and
-institutional-responses-to-covid-19-new-zealand/; "New Zealand Takes Early
and Hard Action to Tackle COVID-19," World Health Organization, July 15, 2020,
https://www.who.int/westernpacific/news/feature-stories/detail/new-zealand-takes
-early-and-hard-action-to-tackle-covid-19; Nick Perry, "Coronavirus Breaks Out
Again in New Zealand After 102 Days," The Diplomat, August 12, 2020, https://
thediplomat.com/2020/08/coronavirus-breaks-out-again-in-new-zealand-after
-102-days/; Philip Dandolov, "Unearthing the Secret to COVID-19 Successes in
New Zealand and Taiwan," Geopolitical Monitor, December 8, 2020, https://www
.geopoliticalmonitor.com/unearthing-the-secret-to-covid-19-successes-in-new
-zealand-and-taiwan/.

51. Marcia Castro, "Lack of Federal Leadership Hinders Brazil's COVID-19 Response,"
Harvard T. H. Chan School of Public Health, June 25, 2020, https://www.hsph
.harvard.edu/news/features/brazil-covid-marcia-castro/; "Brazil Highlights Treatment for All People with HIV," World Health Organization, November 30, 2018,
https://www.who.int/hiv/mediacentre/news/brazil-hiv-treatment-all-plhiv/en/.

52. Vanessa Barbara, "'We Will All Die One Day,' My President Said," *New York Times*,
April 14, 2020, https://www.nytimes.com/2020/04/14/opinion/coronavirus-bolsonaro
-brazil.html.

53. Simone Preissler Iglesias and Samy Adghirni, "Brazil's State Governors Defy Bolsonaro in Coronavirus Fight," Bloomberg, March 25, 2020, https://www.bloomberg
.com/news/articles/2020-03-25/brazilian-state-governors-defy-bolsonaro-in
-coronavirus-fight; Hu Yiwei, "Graphics: What's Gone Wrong for Brazil's COVID-19
Response?," CGTN, June 16, 2020, https://news.cgtn.com/news/2020–06–16
/Graphics-What-s-gone-wrong-for-Brazil-s-COVID-19-response—Rn0ZueKCMo
/index.html; Fábio Amato, "Coronavírus: MP concentra no governo federal poder
para restringir circulação de pessoas" [Coronavirus: MP concentrates power in the
federal government to restrict the movement of people], Globo.com, March 21, 2020,
https://g1.globo.com/politica/noticia/2020/03/21/coronavirus-mp-concentra

-no-governo-federal-poder-para-restringir-circulacao-de-pessoas.ghtml; Editorial, "COVID-19 in Brazil: 'So What?,'" *Lancet* 395, no. 10235 (May 2020): 1461, https://www.thelancet.com/journals/lancet/article/PIIS0140-6736(20)31095-3/fulltext; Bloomberg Quicktake (@Quicktake), "WATCH: Thousands of people in Brazil banged pots from their balconies in protest against President Bolsonaro's handling of the #coronavirus pandemic," Twitter, March 19, 2020, 10:00 p.m., https://twitter.com/QuickTake/status/1240820403435700226?s=20.

54. Antonia Noori Farzan and Miriam Berger, "Bolsonaro Says Brazilians Must Not Be 'Sissies' About Coronavirus, as 'All of Us Are Going to Die One Day,'" *Washington Post*, November 11, 2020, https://www.washingtonpost.com/world/2020/11/11/bolsonaro-coronavirus-brazil-quotes/.

55. Ernesto Londoño, Manuela Andreoni, and Letícia Casado, "Brazil, Once a Leader, Struggles to Contain Virus Amid Political Turmoil," *New York Times*, May 16, 2020, https://www.nytimes.com/2020/05/16/world/americas/virus-brazil-deaths.html; Ricardo Della Coletta, "Com Covid-19, Bolsonaro passeia de moto e conversa sem máscara com garis no Alvorada" [With Covid-19, Bolsonaro rides a motorcycle and talks unmasked to garbage men at Alvorada], *Folha de S. Paulo*, July 23, 2020, https://www1.folha.uol.com.br/poder/2020/07/com-covid-19-bolsonaro-passeia-de-moto-e-conversa-sem-mascara-com-garis-no-alvorada.shtml; Manuela Andreoni, "Coronavirus in Brazil: What You Need to Know," *New York Times*, January 10, 2021, https://www.nytimes.com/article/brazil-coronavirus-cases.html; "Covid: Brazil's Coronavirus Death Toll Passes 150,000," BBC, October 11, 2020, https://www.bbc.com/news/world-latin-america-54496354; Edmund Ruge, "Brazil's President Says His Country Is Being a Bunch of 'Sissies' About COVID," Vice, November 11, 2020, https://www.vice.com/en/article/v7mea3/brazils-president-says-his-country-is-being-a-bunch-of-sissies-about-covid.

56. Igor Gielow and Thiago Amâncio, "Bolsonaro Maintains Approval Rating, and Majority Don't Blame Him for Covid-19 Deaths, Says Datafolha," *Folha de S. Paulo*, December 14, 2020, https://www1.folha.uol.com.br/internacional/en/brazil/2020/12/bolsonaro-maintains-approval-rating-and-majority-dont-blame-him-for-covid-19-deaths-says-datafolha.shtml; Brian Winter, "A Moment of Truth for Bolsonaro," Think Global Health, January 20, 2021, https://www.thinkglobalhealth.org/article/moment-truth-bolsonaro; *World Economic Outlook Update, January 2021: Policy Support and Vaccines Expected to Lift Activity* (Washington, DC: International Monetary Fund, 2020), 4, https://www.imf.org/en/Publications/WEO/Issues/2021/01/26/2021-world-economic-outlook-update.

57. Amy Kazmin, "Modi Stumbles: India's Deepening Coronavirus Crisis," *Financial Times*, July 27, 2020, https://www.ft.com/content/53d946cf-d4c2-4cc4-9411-1d5bb3566e83; "Coronavirus Government Response Tracker," Blavatnik School of Government, University of Oxford, accessed December 31, 2020, https://www.bsg.ox.ac.uk/research/research-projects/coronavirus-government-response-tracker; "India Coronavirus Map and Case Count," *New York Times*, accessed December 31, 2020, https://www.nytimes.com/interactive/2020/world/asia/india-coronavirus-cases.html; Soutik Biswas, "India Coronavirus: How a Group of Volunteers 'Exposed' Hidden Covid-19 Deaths," BBC, November 20, 2020, https://www.bbc.com/news/world-asia-india-54985981; Aniruddha Ghosal and Sheikh Saaliq, "As India's Virus Cases Rise, So Do Questions over Death Toll," Associated Press, September 17, 2020, https://apnews.com/article/virus-outbreak-international-news-india-1f90b42d999a4c918e550ef36164d3be; Bill Chappell, "Enormous and Tragic: U.S. Has Lost More Than 200,000 People to COVID-19," NPR, September 22, 2020, https://www.npr.org/sections

/coronavirus-live-updates/2020/09/22/911934489/enormous-and-tragic-u-s-has
-lost-more-than-200–000-people-to-covid-19.

58. "Journalists Detained, Assaulted in India During COVID-19 Lockdown," Committee to Protect Journalists, April 28, 2020, https://cpj.org/2020/04/journalists-detained -assaulted-in-india-during-cov/.

59. Christophe Jaffrelot and Jean Thomas Martelli, "Current Crisis Consolidates Populist Rapport Between a Leader and a Fictional Representation of People," *Indian Express*, April 29, 2020, https://indianexpress.com/article/opinion/columns/india-covid-19 -coronavirus-lockdown-narendra-modi-6383721/; Aparna Sundar and Alf Gunvald Nilsen, "COVID-19 in Narendra Modi's India: Virulent Politics and Mass Desperation," *The Wire*, August 1, 2020, https://thewire.in/health/covid-19-in-narendra -modis-india-virulent-politics-and-mass-desperation; Prem Shankar Jha, "Modi's 'Stimulus Package' Is a Gigantic Confidence Trick Played on the People of India," *The Wire*, May 18, 2020, https://thewire.in/political-economy/modis-stimulus-package -is-a-gigantic-confidence-trick-played-on-the-people-of-india; Subrata Nagchoudhury and Shilpa Jamkhandikar, "BJP, Courting Votes in Bihar State, Promises Free COVID-19 Vaccines," Reuters, October 22, 2020, https://www.reuters.com/article/health -coronavius-india-cases-idUSKBN2770EL.

60. Anna MM Vetticad, "Indian Media Accused of Islamophobia for Its Coronavirus Coverage," Al Jazeera, May 15, 2020, https://www.aljazeera.com/news/2020/5/15 /indian-media-accused-of-islamophobia-for-its-coronavirus-coverage; Hannah Ellis-Petersen and Shaikh Azizur Rahman, "Coronavirus Conspiracy Theories Targeting Muslims Spread in India," *The Guardian*, April 13, 2020, https://www.theguardian .com/world/2020/apr/13/coronavirus-conspiracy-theories-targeting-muslims-spread -in-india; Alexandre Capron, "'CoronaJihad': Fake News in India Accuses Muslims of Deliberately Spreading Covid-19," France 24, May 13, 2020, https://observers.france24 .com/en/20200513-india-coronajihad-fake-news-muslims-spreading-covid-19; Vasudha Venugopal, "Tablighi Jamaat Is a Talibani Crime, Not Negligence: Mukhtar Abbas Naqvi," *Economic Times*, April 2, 2020, https://economictimes.indiatimes .com/news/politics-and-nation/tablighi-jamaat-is-a-talibani-crime-not-negligence -mukhtar-abbas-naqvi/articleshow/74940835.cms; "'Do Not Buy from Muslims': BJP Leader in India Calls for Boycott," Al Jazeera, April 29, 2020, https://www .aljazeera.com/news/2020/4/29/do-not-buy-from-muslims-bjp-leader-in-india-calls -for-boycott; Harsh Mander, "The Coronavirus Has Morphed into an Anti-Muslim Virus," *The Wire*, April 13, 2020, https://thewire.in/communalism/coronavirus-anti -muslim-propaganda-india; Soumya Chatterjee and Theja Ram, "COVID-19: Muslims and Muslim Volunteers Heckled, Harassed in Karnataka," *News Minute*, April 6, 2020, https://www.thenewsminute.com/article/covid-19-muslims-amd-muslim-volunteers -heckled-harassed-karnataka-121977; Yasmine El-Geressi, "Blamed, Attacked, Denied Treatment: Coronavirus Fans Islamophobia in India," *Majalla*, May 15, 2020, https:// eng.majalla.com/node/88791/blamed-attacked-denied-treatment-coronavirus-fans -islamophobia-in-india%C2%A0; Meenakshi Ganguly, "India Has Taken Notable Steps to Contain Covid-19—but Failed to Curb Surging Anti-Muslim Rhetoric," Scroll .in, April 18, 2020, https://scroll.in/article/959496/india-has-taken-notable-steps-to -contain-covid-19-but-failed-to-curb-surging-anti-muslim-rhetoric.

61. Benjamin Netanyahu, "PM Netanyahu's Statement to the Media on the Coronavirus," Israeli Government, March 25, 2020, https://www.gov.il/en/departments/news/event _statement250320; Joshua Mitnick, "Israel's Cautionary Coronavirus Tale," *Foreign Policy*, July 22, 2020, https://foreignpolicy.com/2020/07/22/israel-coronavirus -second-wave-netanyahu/.

62. Israeli Office of the Prime Minister and the Ministry of Health, "The Government Approved Emergency Regulations to Restrict Activities in Order to Curb the Spread of Coronavirus in Israel," press release, March 25, 2020, https://www.gov.il/en/departments/news/25032020_01; "Israel Considers Broadening Entry Restrictions for Coronavirus," Reuters, March 8, 2020, https://www.reuters.com/article/us-health-coronavirus-israel-usa-idUSKBN20V0R6; Dov Lieber, "Israel Halts Controversial Coronavirus Surveillance," *Wall Street Journal*, June 9, 2020, https://www.wsj.com/articles/israel-halts-controversial-coronavirus-surveillance-11591734875; David M. Halbfinger, Isabel Kershner, and Ronen Bergman, "To Track Coronavirus, Israel Moves to Tap Secret Trove of Cellphone Data," *New York Times*, March 16, 2020, https://www.nytimes.com/2020/03/16/world/middleeast/israel-coronavirus-cellphone-tracking.html; Tehilla Shwartz Altshuler and Rachel Aridor Hershkowitz, "How Israel's COVID-19 Mass Surveillance Operation Works," *Tech Stream*, July 6, 2020, https://www.brookings.edu/techstream/how-israels-covid-19-mass-surveillance-operation-works/; author interview with an Israeli health official, July 2020.

63. Mark Last, "The First Wave of COVID-19 in Israel—Initial Analysis of Publicly Available Data," *PLoS ONE* 15, no. 10 (October 2020), https://doi.org/10.1371/journal.pone.0240393.

64. Author interview with Israeli health official, July 2020.

65. "Netanyahu to Israelis: Have Fun, We're Easing Coronavirus Restrictions," *Jerusalem Post*, May 26, 2020, https://www.jpost.com/israel-news/netanyahu-to-israelis-have-fun-were-easing-coronavirus-restrictions-629366.

66. Mitnick, "Israel's Cautionary Coronavirus Tale"; Steve Hendrix, "Why Israel Is Seeing a Coronavirus Spike After Initially Crushing the Outbreak," *Washington Post*, July 7, 2020, https://www.washingtonpost.com/world/middlle_east/why-israel-is-seeing-a-coronavirus-spike-after-initially-crushing-the-outbreak/2020/07/07/dd141158-bfbc-11ea-8908-68a2b9eae9e0_story.html; "Netanyahu Admits Israel's Economy Reopened 'Too Soon,'" Jewish Telegraphic Agency, July 10, 2020, https://www.jta.org/quick-reads/netanyahu-admits-israels-economy-reopened-too-soon; Ariel Oseran, "Israel Considers a Second Lockdown as Coronavirus Cases Surge," *The World*, July 17, 2020, https://www.pri.org/stories/2020–070–17/israel-considers-second-lockdown-coronavirus-cases-surge; Anshel Pfeffer, "Why Netanyahu Failed the Coronavirus Stress Test," *Haaretz*, July 10, 2020, https://www.haaretz.com/israel-news/.premium-why-netanyahu-failed-the-coronavirus-stress-test-1.8984398.

67. Graeme Wilson and George Jones, "Boris Johnson Inspired by Jaws Mayor," *Telegraph*, July 18, 2007, https://www.telegraph.co.uk/news/uknews/1557765/Boris-Johnson-inspired-by-Jaws-mayor.html.

68. Hayley Mortimer, "Coronavirus: Cheltenham Festival 'May Have Accelerated' Spread," BBC, April 30, 2020, https://www.bbc.com/news/uk-england-gloucestershire-52485584; Dan Roan, "Liverpool v Atletico Madrid: Mayor Calls for Inquiry amid Coronavirus Concerns," BBC, April 23, 2020, https://www.bbc.com/sport/football/52399569; Anthony Costello, "The United Kingdom Is Flying Blind on Covid-19," *New Statesman*, March 20, 2020, https://www.newstatesman.com/politics/staggers/2020/03/uk-response-coronavirus-pandemic-distancing-medical-advice; Neel Patel, "The UK Is Scrambling to Correct Its Coronavirus Strategy," *MIT Technology Review*, March 16, 2020, https://www.technologyreview.com/2020/03/16/905285/uk-dropping-coronavirus-herd-immunity-strategy-250000-dead/; Andrew Sparrow, "Boris Johnson Warns Britons to Avoid Non-Essential Contact as Covid-19 Death Toll Rises—As It Happened," *The Guardian*, March 16, 2020, https://www.theguardian.com/politics/live/2020/mar/16/boris-johnson-press-conference-coronavirus-live-firms-could-soon-be-allowed-to-run-reduced-services-because-of-coronavirus

-shapps-suggests-politics-live; Amanda Sloat, "Reopening the World: Britain Bungled Its Lockdown and Garbled Its Reopening," Brookings Institution, June 16, 2020, https://www.brookings.edu/blog/order-frsom-chaos/2020/06/16/reopening-the-world-britain-bungled-its-lockdown-and-garbled-its-reopening/.

69. "Coronavirus: Prime Minister Boris Johnson Tests Positive," BBC, March 27, 2020, https://www.bbc.com/news/uk-52060791; "What's Gone Wrong with Covid-19 Testing in Britain," *The Economist*, April 4, 2020, https://www.economist.com/britain/2020/04/04/whats-gone-wrong-with-covid-19-testing-in-britain; Andrew MacAskill, "UK Defends Coronavirus Response After Reuters Investigation," Reuters, April 9, 2020, https://www.reuters.com/article/us-health-coronavirus-britain-modelling/uk-defends-coronavirus-response-after-reuters-investigation-idUSKCN21R33D.

70. Colin Dwyer, "Boris Johnson: U.K. Is 'Past the Peak' of Its Coronavirus Outbreak," NPR, April 30, 2020, https://www.npr.org/sections/coronavirus-live-updates/2020/04/30/848496099/boris-johnson-u-k-is-past-the-peak-of-its-coronavirus-outbreak.

71. "Coronavirus: Boris Johnson Says UK Is Past the Peak of Outbreak," BBC, April 30, 2020, https://www.bbc.com/news/uk-52493500; "In England, Reopening Has Not Been the Disaster Many Feared," *The Economist*, September 3, 2020, https://www.economist.com/britain/2020/09/03/in-england-reopening-has-not-been-the-disaster-many-feared; James Gallagher, "Coronavirus: Oxford Vaccine Triggers Immune Response," BBC, July 20, 2020, https://www.bbc.com/news/uk-53469839; Alistair Smout, "First Human Trial of Oxford Coronavirus Vaccine Shows Promise," Reuters, July 20, 2020, https://www.reuters.com/article/us-health-coronavirus-oxford-vaccine/first-human-trial-of-oxford-coronavirus-vaccine-shows-promise-idUSKCN24L1MP.

72. John Pickrell, "Smoke from Australia's Bushfires Killed Far More People Than the Fires Did, Study Says," *The Guardian*, March 20, 2020, https://www.theguardian.com/australia-news/2020/mar/21/smoke-from-australias-bushfires-killed-far-more-people-than-the-fires-did-study-says.

73. Richard Flanagan, "Did the Coronavirus Kill Ideology in Australia?," *New York Times*, May 18, 2020, https://www.nytimes.com/2020/05/18/opinion/coronavirus-australia.html.

74. Dylan Donnelly, "Australian Prime Minister Lashes Out at UK's 'Death Sentence' Coronavirus Handling," *Daily Express*, May 6, 2020, https://www.express.co.uk/news/world/1278337/Australia-coronavirus-herd-immunity-Scott-Morrison-UK-US-covid-19.

75. Scott Morrison, "Ministerial Statement—Australian Parliament House, ACT," Prime Minister of Australia, April 8, 2020, https://www.pm.gov.au/media/ministerial-statement-australian-parliament-house-act-080420; Samantha Maiden, "ScoMo: Herd Immunity Is a 'Death Sentence,'" *Sunshine Coast Daily*, May 6, 2020, https://www.sunshinecoastdaily.com.au/news/death-sentence-scomos-blunt-response/4009775/.

76. Stephen Duckett and Anika Stobart, "Australia's Coronavirus Response: Four Successes and Failures," *Canberra Times*, June 4, 2020, https://www.canberratimes.com.au/story/6780878/four-ways-australias-coronavirus-response-was-a-triumph-and-four-ways-it-fell-short/; Mark Evans, "Australians Highly Confident of Government's Handling of Coronavirus and Economic Recovery: New Research," *The Conversation*, July 20, 2020, https://theconversation.com/australians-highly-confident-of-governments-handling-of-coronavirus-and-economic-recovery-new-research-142904.

77. Vanessa Molter, "Virality Project (China): Pandemics & Propaganda," Stanford Cyber Policy Center, March 19, 2020, https://cyber.fsi.stanford.edu/news/chinese-state-media-shapes-coronavirus-convo; Rachel Kleinfeld, "Do Authoritarian or Democratic

Countries Handle Pandemics Better?," Carnegie Endowment for International Peace, March 31, 2020, https://carnegieendowment.org/2020/03/31/do-authoritarian-or -democratic-countries-handle-pandemics-better-pub-81404.

78. Theologos Dergiades, Costas Milas, Elias Mossialos, and Theodore Panagiotidis, "Effectiveness of Government Policies in Response to the COVID-19 Outbreak," SSRN, May 15, 2020, https://papers.ssrn.com/sol3/papers.cfm?abstract_id=3602004; Andrea Riccardo Migone, "The Influence of National Policy Characteristics on COVID-19 Containment Policies: A Comparative Analysis," *Policy Design and Practice* 3, no. 3 (2020), https://www.tandfonline.com/doi/full/10.1080/25741292.2020.1804660; Ben Balmford et al., "Cross-Country Comparisons of Covid-19: Policy, Politics and the Price of Life," *Environmental and Resource Economics* 76 (2020), https://link.springer .com/article/10.1007/s10640-020-00466-5; Reinhold Stockenhuber, "Did We Respond Quickly Enough? How Policy-Implementation Speed in Response to COVID-19 Affects the Number of Fatal Cases in Europe," *World Medical and Health Policy* 12, no. 4 (December 2020), https://onlinelibrary.wiley.com/doi/10.1002/wmh3.374.

79. "Frequently Asked Questions About the International Health Regulations," World Health Organization, 2, https://www.who.int/ihr/about/FAQ2009.pdf; "Country Preparedness and COVID-19," Prevent Epidemics, May 5, 2020, https://preventepidemics .org/covid19/science/insights/country-preparedness-and-covid-19/; *Global Health Security Index: Building Collective Action and Accountability* (Washington, DC: Nuclear Threat Initiative and Johns Hopkins Center for Health Security, 2019), https:// www.ghsindex.org/wp-content/uploads/2020/04/2019-Global-Health-Security -Index.pdf; Antonio Timoner, "Policy Responsiveness to Coronavirus: An Autopsy," *Agenda Publica*, June 8, 2020, http://agendapublica.elpais.com/policy-responsiveness -to-coronavirus-an-autopsy/; Thomas J. Bollyky, Sawyer Crosby, and Samantha Kiernan, "Fighting a Pandemic Requires Trust," *Foreign Affairs*, October 23, 2020, https:// www.foreignaffairs.com/articles/united-states/2020-10-23/coronavirus-fighting -requires-trust.

80. Migone, "The Influence of National Policy Characteristics"; "The Politics of Pandemics: Why Some Countries Respond Better Than Others," Knowledge@Wharton, May 26, 2020, https://knowledge.wharton.upenn.edu/article/politics-pandemics-countries -respond-better-others/; Pragyan Deb, Davide Furceri, Jonathan David Ostry, and Nour Tawk, "The Effect of Containment Measures on the COVID-19 Pandemic," working paper, International Monetary Fund, August 7, 2020, https://www.imf.org/ -/media/Files/Publications/WP/2020/English/wpiea2020159-print-pdf.ashx.

81. Andrew Salmon, "Why East Beat West on Covid-19," *Asia Times*, May 15, 2020, https://asiatimes.com/2020/05/why-east-beat-west-on-covid-19/; Carl Benedikt Frey, Chinchih Chen, and Giorgio Presidente, "Democracy, Culure, and Contagion: Political Regimes and Countries' Responsiveness to Covid-19," Oxford University, May 13, 2020, https://www.oxfordmartin.ox.ac.uk/downloads/academic/Democracy -Culture-and-Contagion_May13.pdf; Alberto Ibanez and Gyanendra Singh Sisodia, "The Role of Culture on 2020 SARS-CoV-2 Country Deaths: A Pandemic Management Based on Cultural Dimensions," *GeoJournal*, September 30, 2020, https://www .ncbi.nlm.nih.gov/pmc/articles/PMC7527153/.

82. Bollyky, Crosby, and Kiernan, "Fighting a Pandemic Requires Trust"; Qing Han et al., "Trust in Government and Its Associations with Health Behaviour and Prosocial Behaviour During the COVID-19 Pandemic," PsyArXiv, June 29, 2020, https://psyarxiv .com/p5gns/.

83. Bollyky, Crosby, and Kiernan, "Fighting a Pandemic Requires Trust."

84. Bollyky, Crosby, and Kiernan, "Fighting a Pandemic Requires Trust." For a discussion of the relevant literature, see Daniel Devine, Jennifer Gaskell, Will Jennings, and Gerry

Stoker, "Trust and the Coronavirus Pandemic: What Are the Consequences of and for Trust? An Early Review of the Literature," *Political Studies Review*, August 11, 2020, https://journals.sagepub.com/doi/full/10.1177/1478929920948684.

85. Daniel A. N. Goldstein and Johannes Wiedemann, "Who Do You Trust? The Consequences of Political and Social Trust for Public Responsiveness to COVID-19 Orders," SSRN, April 19, 2020, https://papers.ssrn.com/sol3/papers.cfm?abstract_id=3580547.

86. Migone, "The Influence of National Policy Characteristics"; Junjie Huang, Jeremy Yuen-Chun Teoh, Sunny H. Wong, and Martin C. S. Wong, "The Potential Impact of Previous Exposure to SARS or MERS on Control of the COVID-19 Pandemic," *European Journal of Epidemiology* 35, August 10, 2020, https://www.ncbi.nlm.nih.gov/pmc/articles/PMC7415407/; Ramon Pacheco Pardo et al., "Preventing the Next Pandemic: Lessons from East Asia," King's College London, 2020, https://www.kcl.ac.uk/eis/assets/kdefsresearchreport2020-a4-proof2-singlepage.pdf.

CHAPTER 7: THE GREAT LOCKDOWN

1. Amrith Ramkumar, "Forget Dow 30K. It's Already Hit 40K on License Plates," *Wall Street Journal*, February 18, 2020, https://www.wsj.com/articles/forget-dow-30k-its-already-hit-40k-on-license-plates-11582041560?page=1.

2. Justin Baer, "The Day Coronavirus Nearly Broke the Financial Markets," *Wall Street Journal*, May 20, 2020, https://www.wsj.com/articles/the-day-coronavirus-nearly-broke-the-financial-markets-11589982288.

3. International Monetary Fund, *World Economic Outlook Update, January 2021: Policy Support and Vaccines Expected to Lift Activity* (Washington, DC: International Monetary Fund, 2020), https://www.imf.org/en/Publications/WEO/Issues/2021/01/26/2021-world-economic-outlook-update.

4. *World Economic Outlook, April 2020: The Great Lockdown* (Washington, DC: International Monetary Fund, 2020), https://www.imf.org/en/Publications/WEO/Issues/2020/04/14/weo-april-2020.

5. James Politi and Lauren Fedor, "US Senate Approves $2tn Stimulus Deal to Fight Coronavirus Fallout," *Financial Times*, March 26, 2020, https://www.ft.com/content/9575e856-6ed3-11ea-9bca-bf503995cd6f.

6. "Has Covid-19 Killed Globalisation?," *The Economist*, May 14, 2020, https://www.economist.com/leaders/2020/05/14/has-covid-19-killed-globalisation.

7. Carmen Reinicke, "The Fed Announced an Unexpected Interest Rate Cut on Tuesday. Here's a Timeline of the Last 7 Emergency Rate Cuts," *Markets Insider*, March 4, 2020, https://markets.businessinsider.com/news/stocks/emergency-rate-cuts-events-caused-past-fed-coronavirus-timeline-when-2020-3-1028964493#.

8. Swati Pandey, "Global Central Banks Pull Out All Stops as Coronavirus Paralyzes Economies," Reuters, March 16, 2020, https://www.reuters.com/article/us-health-coronavirus-central-banks-glob/global-central-banks-pull-out-all-stops-as-coronavirus-paralyzes-economies-idUSKBN2130KR.

9. The Federal Reserve, "Section 13: Power of Federal Reserve Banks," https://www.federalreserve.gov/aboutthefed/section13.htm.

10. James Politi, Brendan Greeley, Colby Smith, and Joe Rennison, "Federal Reserve Unleashes Unlimited Treasury Purchase Plan," *Financial Times*, https://www.ft.com/content/b71f0c32-6cfb-11ea-89df-41bea055720b.

11. Sebastian Mallaby, "The Age of Magic Money," *Foreign Affairs* 99, no. 4 (July/August 2020): 65–77, https://www.foreignaffairs.com/articles/united-states/2020-05-29/pandemic-financial-crisis.

12. Christopher Condon, Steve Matthews, Matthew Boesler, and Rich Miller, "Fed Is Not Going to 'Run Out of Ammunition,' Powell Vows," Bloomberg, March 26, 2020, https://www.bloomberg.com/news/articles/2020-03-26/powell-says-fed-will-keep -credit-flowing-as-virus-hits-economy?sref=bxQtWDnd.

13. Mallaby, "The Age of Magic Money."

14. Raphaële Chappe, Mark Blyth, and Sebastian Mallaby, "Hocus-Pocus?," *Foreign Affairs* 99, no. 6 (November/December 2020): 161–66, https://www.foreignaffairs.com /articles/2020-10-13/hocus-pocus.

15. Edward Luce, "America's Dangerous Reliance on the Fed," *Financial Times*, January 3, 2021, https://www.ft.com/content/bcb8d4d9-ca6d-45b7-aafc-9e9ecf672a5b.

16. Martin Arnold and Tommy Stubbington, "Lagarde Triggers Investor Jitters as ECB Launches Virus Response," *Financial Times*, March 12, 2020, https://www.ft.com /content/11ab8f84-6452-11ea-b3f3-fe4680ea68b5.

17. "Italy 10 Year Government Bond," MarketWatch, accessed February 15, 2021, https:// www.marketwatch.com/investing/bond/tmbmkit-10y?countrycode=bx.

18. Jana Randow and Piotr Skolimowski, "Christine Lagarde's $810 Billion Coronavirus U-Turn Came in Just Four Weeks," Bloomberg, April 6, 2020, https://www.bloomberg .com/news/features/2020-04-06/coronavirus-lagarde-s-810-billion-u-turn-came-in -just-4-weeks?srnd=premium&sref=bxQtWDnd.

19. Author interview with three European Central Bank officials, February 12, 2021.

20. Randow and Skolimowski, "Christine Lagarde's $810 Billion Coronavirus U-Turn."

21. "Interview with Christine Lagarde, President of the ECB, Conducted by Matthieu Pelloli and Published on 9 April 2020," European Central Bank, April 8, 2020, https://www.ecb.europa.eu/press/inter/date/2020/html/ecb.in200408~2e7bcefbe5 .en.html.

22. Chris Giles, Robin Harding, Brendan Greeley, and Martin Arnold, "Calls for Policymakers to Act to Prevent Coronavirus 'Doom Loop,'" *Financial Times*, March 1, 2020, https://www.ft.com/content/58410fea-5a30-11ea-a528-dd0f971febbc.

23. Jon Cunliffe, "The Impact of Leveraged Investors on Market Liquidity and Financial Stability," Bank of England, November 12, 2020, https://www.bankofengland.co .uk/-/media/boe/files/speech/2020/the-impact-of-leveraged-investors-on-market -liquidity-and-financial-stability-speech-by-jon-cunliffe.pdf.

24. Robin Harding, "Abenomics on Trial as Japan Teeters on Brink of Recession," *Financial Times*, February 18, 2020, https://www.ft.com/content/f1320946-5208-11ea -8841-482eed0038b1.

25. Robin Harding, "Bank of Japan Steps Up Coronavirus Stimulus with Bond-Buying Pledge," *Financial Times*, April 27, 2020, https://www.ft.com/content/7ba5c507-df9e -4107-87eb-73afa2c13e91.

26. Robin Harding, "Bank of Japan Trims Growth Forecasts but Predicts Stronger Rebound in 2021," *Financial Times*, October 29, 2020, https://www.ft.com/content /6d01dee6-7de4-48bb-8d27-50d3d4e11d16; Yoshiaki Nohara, "Japan Prices Fall at Fastest Pace in a Decade as BOJ Meets," Bloomberg, December 17, 2020, https://www .bloomberg.com/news/articles/2020-12-17/japan-s-consumer-prices-fall-at-fastest -pace-in-a-decade?sref=bxQtWDnd.

27. Interview with Federal Reserve official, January 2021.

28. Jonathan Wheatley, "Pandemic Fuels Global 'Debt Tsunami,'" *Financial Times*, November 18, 2020, https://www.ft.com/content/18527e0c-6f02-4c70-93cb-c26c3680c8ad; Stephanie Segal, Dylan Gerstel, and Joshua Henderson, "International Financial Institutions' COVID-19 Approvals Approach $240 Billion for 2020," Center for Strategic and International Studies, January 25, 2021, https://www.csis.org/analysis /international-financial-institutions-covid-19-approvals-approach-240-billion-2020.

29. "Extraordinary G20 Leaders' Summit: Statement on COVID-19," G20 Saudi Arabia 2020, March 26, 2020, http://www.g20.utoronto.ca/2020/2020-g20-statement-0326 .html.

30. Jonathan Wheatley, "Debt Dilemma: How to Avoid a Crisis in Emerging Nations," *Financial Times*, December 20, 2020, https://www.ft.com/content/de43248e-e8eb -4381-9d2f-a539d1f1662c.

31. Gordon Brown, "The G20 Should Be Leading the World out of the Coronavirus Crisis—but It's Gone Awol," *The Guardian*, June 2, 2020, https://www.theguardian .com/commentisfree/2020/jun/02/g20-leading-world-out-of-coronavirus-crisis -gordon-brown.

32. Robin Wigglesworth, "Zambia's Debt Crisis Casts a Long, Global Shadow," *Financial Times*, November 16, 2020, https://www.ft.com/content/35c58b5f-f890-4390-967a -28c0a0a1fb50.

33. Isabel Debre, "G-20 Agrees on Framework for More Debt Relief amid COVID-19," Associated Press, November 13, 2020, https://apnews.com/article/dubai-united-arab -emirates-coronavirus-pandemic-g-20-summit-6729d0caf1bc639039447f07f3938a0b; Clemence Landers, "A Plan to Address the COVID-19 Debt Crises in Poor Countries and Build a Better Sovereign Debt System," Center for Global Development, December 3, 2020, https://www.cgdev.org/publication/plan-address-covid-19-debt-crises-poor -countries-and-build-better-sovereign-debt-system; "COVID-19: Debt Service Suspension Initiative," World Bank, https://www.worldbank.org/en/topic/debt/brief /covid-19-debt-service-suspension-initiative, accessed January 12, 2021; Homi Kharas and Meagan Dooley, "COVID-19's Legacy of Debt and Debt Service in Developing Countries," Brookings Institution, December 2020, 3, https://www.brookings .edu/wp-content/uploads/2020/12/COVID-19-legacy-of-debt_final.pdf.

34. Wheatley, "Debt Dilemma."

35. *Global Economic Prospects* (Washington, DC: World Bank, January 2021), xvii, https:// openknowledge.worldbank.org/bitstream/handle/10986/34710/9781464816123.pdf.

36. Carmen Reinhart and Vincent Reinhart, "The Pandemic Depression," *Foreign Affairs*, September/October 2020, https://www.foreignaffairs.com/articles/united-states /2020-08-06/coronavirus-depression-global-economy.

37. Martin Crutsinger, "U.S. Economy Shrank by 3.5% in 2020 After Growing by 4% in Last Quarter," Associated Press, January 28, 2021, https://apnews.com/article/us -economy-shrink-in-2020-b59f9be06dcf1da924f64afde2ce094c; Ben Dooley and Makiko Inoue, "Japan's Growth Rebounds but Virus-Related Weakness Looms," *New York Times*, February 14, 2021, https://www.nytimes.com/2021/02/14/business/japan -gdp-economy-coronavirus.html; Martin Arnold and Valentina Romei, "Eurozone Economy Drops into Double Digit Contraction," *Financial Times*, February 2, 2021, https://www.ft.com/content/f8efe708-3c22-493b-88bd-855ec6d98522; Danica Kirka, "UK Economy Suffers Biggest Drop Since 1709," Associated Press, February 12, 2021, https://apnews.com/article/coronavirus-pandemic-economy-4f0b6285a5 7c8b2929e2aceb864e7675; Prinesha Naidoo, "S. Africa Virus-Hit Economy Shrank Most in 100 Years in 2020," Bloomberg, March 9, 2021, https://www.bloomberg.com /news/articles/2021-03-09/south-african-virus-hit-economy-shrank-most-in-100 -years-in-2020?sref=bxQtWDnd; Gareth Hutchens, Stephanie Chalmers, and Michael Janda, "GDP Figures Show Economy Shrank in 2020 but Grew 3.1% in December Quarter," ABC, March 3, 2021, https://www.abc.net.au/news/2021-03-03/gdp -december-quarter-2021/13210412.

38. International Monetary Fund, "Fiscal Monitor Update," January 2021, https://www .imf.org/en/Publications/FM/Issues/2021/01/20/fiscal-monitor-update-january -2021.

39. Jeff Stein and Mike DeBonis, "Senate Majority Leader Announces Approximately $900 Billion Deal on Emergency Relief Package," *Washington Post*, December 20, 2020, https://www.washingtonpost.com/us-policy/2020/12/20/stimulus-congress/.

40. Nicole Friedman, "Pandemic Boosts Upper End of Housing Market Coast to Coast," *Wall Street Journal*, November 11, 2020, https://www.wsj.com/articles/pandemic-boosts-upper-end-of-housing-market-coast-to-coast-11605106801; Lily Katz, "Demand for Second Homes Surges Year over Year in October," Redfin, November 19, 2020, https://www.redfin.com/news/second-home-purchases-soar-coronavirus-pandemic/.

41. Carolina Gonzalez, "Restaurant Closings Top 110,000 with Industry in 'Free Fall,'" Bloomberg, December 7, 2020, https://www.bloomberg.com/news/articles/2020-12-07/over-110-000-restaurants-have-closed-with-sector-in-free-fall; Emily Pandise, "From Brooks Brothers to L'Occitane, Main Street Bankruptcies Continue," NBC News, May 15, 2020, https://www.nbcnews.com/business/consumer/which-major-retail-companies-have-filed-bankruptcy-coronavirus-pandemic-hit-n1207866.

42. Heather Long and Andrew Van Dam, "U.S. Employment Rate Soars to 14.7%, the Worst Since the Great Depression," *Washington Post*, May 8, 2020, https://www.washingtonpost.com/business/2020/05/08/april-2020-jobs-report/; Kim Parker, Rachel Minkin, and Jesse Bennett, "Economic Fallout from COVID-19 Continues to Hit Lowest Income Americans the Hardest," Pew Research Center, September 24, 2020, https://www.pewresearch.org/social-trends/2020/09/24/economic-fallout-from-covid-19-continues-to-hit-lower-income-americans-the-hardest/; Kim Parker, Juliana Menasce Horowitz, and Anna Brown, "About Half of Lower Income Americans Report Household Job or Wage Loss Due to COVID-19," Pew Research Center, April 21, 2020, https://www.pewresearch.org/social-trends/2020/04/21/about-half-of-lower-income-americans-report-household-job-or-wage-loss-due-to-covid-19/; Emily Vogels, "59% of U.S. Parents with Lower Incomes Say Their Child May Face Digital Obstacles in Schoolwork," Pew Research Center Fact Tank, September 10, 2020, https://www.pewresearch.org/fact-tank/2020/09/10/59-of-u-s-parents-with-lower-incomes-say-their-child-may-face-digital-obstacles-in-schoolwork/; Jeehoon Han, Bruce Meyer, and James Sullivan, "Real-Time Poverty Estimates During the COVID-19 Pandemic Through November 2020," University of Chicago Harris School for Public Policy, December 15, 2020, https://harris.uchicago.edu/files/monthly_poverty_rates_updated_thru_november_2020_final.pdf; Elise Gould and Heidi Shierholz, "Not Everybody Can Work from Home," Economic Policy Institute, March 19, 2020, https://www.epi.org/blog/black-and-hispanic-workers-are-much-less-likely-to-be-able-to-work-from-home/; U.S. Bureau of Labor Statistics, "Labor Force Statistics from the Current Population Survey," December 2020, https://www.bls.gov/web/empsit/cpseea04.htm; "COVID-19 Is Affecting Black, Indigenous, Latinx, and Other People of Color the Most," COVID-19 Racial Data Tracker, https://covidtracking.com/race, accessed March 13, 2021.

43. Sven Smit et al., "The Future of Work in Europe: Automation, Workforce Transitions, and the Shifting Geography of Employment," McKinsey Global Institute, 2020, https://www.mckinsey.com/~/media/McKinsey/Featured%20Insights/Future%20of%20Organizations/The%20future%20of%20work%20in%20Europe/MGI-The-future-of-work-in-Europe-discussion-paper.pdf.

44. Khadeeja Safdar, "Nike's Sales Bounce Back from Coronavirus Slide," *Wall Street Journal*, September 22, 2020, https://www.wsj.com/articles/nikes-sales-bounce-back-from-coronavirus-slide-11600809973.

45. "Goldman Sachs: The K Factor," *Financial Times*, October 14, 2020, https://www.ft.com/content/0a1af28c-4e37-40ef-94f9-34d8c6cf1f29.

46. Andrew Edgecliffe-Johnson and Alistair Gray, "Starbucks Chief Bullish as Crisis Engulfs Smaller Coffee Shops," *Financial Times*, December 9, 2020, https://www.ft.com/content/ab959c91-7ef2-44d7-bf8c-d03718ae5393; "Starbucks Corporation (SBUX) Stock Price," Nasdaq, https://www.marketwatch.com/investing/stock/sbux, accessed February 19, 2021.

47. Benji Jones, "13 Stunning Photos of Supertankers and Storage Tanks Reveal the Global Oil Glut in Epic Proportions," *Business Insider*, April 27, 2020, https://www.businessinsider.com/13-photos-reveal-the-epic-oil-glut-in-new-proportions-2020-4; Sam Meredith, "Oil Producers Scramble to find 'Creative' Storage Options After Historic Price Crash," CNBC, April 30, 2020, https://www.cnbc.com/2020/04/30/oil-and-coronavirus-producers-trying-to-find-creative-storage-options.html.

48. Antoine Halff, "Saudi-Russia Oil War Is a Game Theory Masterstroke," *Financial Times*, April 1, 2020, https://www.ft.com/content/1da60fa2-3d63-439e-abd4-1391a2047972..

49. Commodity Futures Trading Commission, "CFTC Staff Publishes Interim Report on NYMEX WTI Crude Contract Trading on and Around April 20, 2020," press release no. 8315–28, November 23, 2020, https://www.cftc.gov/PressRoom/PressReleases/8315-20.

50. "OPEC Members' Net Oil Export Revenue in 2020 Expected to Drop to Lowest Level Since 2002," U.S. Energy Information Administration, November 3, 2020, https://www.eia.gov/todayinenergy/detail.php?id=45736#.X9ty3586EMI.

51. Anjli Raval, "Saudi-Russian Oil Alliance Will Last for 'Decades and Generations'—al Falih," *Financial Times*, January 23, 2018, https://www.ft.com/content/d3e966da-0044-11e8-9650-9c0ad2d7c5b5.

52. Bill Farren-Price, "The Oil Market Just Entered Uncharted Waters," *Financial Times*, March 9, 2020, https://www.ft.com/content/fe6ad16e-620d-11ea-b3f3-fe4680ea68b5.

53. David Sheppard, Anjli Raval, and Derek Brower, "Oil Plunges as Opec Output Cut Talks with Russia Collapse," *Financial Times*, March 6, 2020, https://www.ft.com/content/10f3e9d2-5f94-11ea-8033-fa40a0d65a98.

54. Derek Brower and Myles McCormick, "The US Shale Industry's Top Priority: Win Back Wall Street," *Financial Times*, October 27, 2020, https://www.ft.com/content/fcda3560-7f17-4d90-900f-08abe072899c.

55. Anjli Raval, David Sheppard, and Derek Brower, "Saudi Arabia Launches Oil Price War After Russia Deal Collapse," *Financial Times*, March 8, 2020, https://www.ft.com/content/d700b71a-6122-11ea-b3f3-fe4680ea68b5.

56. Max Seddon, "Russia Says It Can Deal with Pain of a Saudi Oil Price War," *Financial Times*, March 9, 2020, https://www.ft.com/content/4009472c-620e-11ea-b3f3-fe4680ea68b5.

57. David Sheppard, Derek Brower, and Katrina Manson, "US Puts Pressure on Saudi Arabia to End Oil Price War," *Financial Times*, March 25, 2020, https://www.ft.com/content/47c212ee-0212-4cd8-9c30-73391498d346.

58. Jon Gambrell and Ellen Knickmeyer, "OPEC, Oil Nations Agree to nearly 10M Barrel Cut amid Virus," *PBS NewsHour*, April 12, 2020, https://www.pbs.org/newshour/economy/opec-oil-nations-agree-to-nearly-10m-barrel-cut-amid-virus.

59. Donald J. Trump (@realDonaldTrump), Twitter, https://twitter.com/realDonaldTrump/status/1243313399284498434 SUSPENDED TWEET (no longer available).

60. "Oil Accord Highlights the New World Disorder," *Financial Times*, April 13, 2020, https://www.ft.com/content/ac409f96-7cc9-11ea-82f6-150830b3b99a.

61. Jude Webber, "Why Is Mexico Holding Up a Global Oil Deal?," *Financial Times*, April 12, 2020, https://www.ft.com/content/e5cb4029-f96b-432a-8fa3-f8ff5f70554e.

62. Neil Quilliam, "Russia and Saudi Arabia Power Risks OPEC+ Break-Up," Chatham House, November 24, 2020, https://www.chathamhouse.org/2020/11/russia-and-saudi-arabia-power-risks-opec-break.

63. Grant Smith, Javier Blas, and Salma El Wardany, "OPEC+ Works Silently to Repair Crack at Oil Coalition's Core," Bloomberg, December 1, 2020, https://www.bloomberg .com/news/articles/2020-12-01/opec-splits-at-its-core-risking-deal-that-underpins -oil-price.

64. Pippa Stevens, "Shale Industry Will Be Rocked by $300 Billion in Losses and a Wave of Bankruptcies, Deloitte Says," CNBC, June 22, 2020, https://www.cnbc.com /2020/06/22/shale-industry-will-be-rocked-by-300-billion-in-losses-and-a-wave-of -bankruptcies-deloitte-says.html.

65. Rebecca Elliot, "ConocoPhillips to Buy Shale Rival Concho for $9.7 Billion," Wall Street Journal, October 19, 2020, https://www.wsj.com/articles/conocophillips-to -buy-concho-resources-in-9-7-billion-stock-deal-11603107949; Paul Takahashi, "Chevron Completes $13B Acquisition of Noble Energy," Houston Chronicle, October 5, 2020, https://www.houstonchronicle.com/business/energy/article/Chevron-13-billion -acquisition-Noble-Houston-Texas-15621496.php.

66. David Fickling, "Reports of Shale's Death Were Greatly Exaggerated," Bloomberg Quint, October 21, 2020, https://www.bloombergquint.com/gadfly/conoco-concho -deal-shows-shale-oil-s-death-was-exaggerated.

67. Fickling, "Reports of Shale's Death Were Greatly Exaggerated."

68. Alex Longley and Javier Blas, "Oil Rises from the Ashes as the Big Coronavirus Recovery Trade," Bloomberg, December 12, 2020, https://www.bloomberg.com/news /articles/2020-12-13/oil-rises-from-the-ashes-as-the-big-coronavirus-recovery -trade; Summer Said and Benoit Faucon, "OPEC, Allies Agree to Boost Demand, Betting on Demand Rebound," Wall Street Journal, April 2 2021, https://www.wsj .com/articles/opec-agree-to-gradually-boost-oil-output-over-next-three-months -11617293942?page=1.

69. Katrin Bennhold and David Sanger, "US Offered 'Large Sum' to German Company for Access to Coronavirus Vaccine Research, German Officials Say," New York Times, March 15, 2020, https://www.nytimes.com/2020/03/15/world/europe/cornonavirus -vaccine-us-germany.html.

70. Jan Dams, "Diese Erfahrung wird Europa so Schnell Nicht Vergessen," Die Welt, March 15, 2020, https://www.welt.de/wirtschaft/plus206563595/Trump-will-deutsche -Impfstoff-Firma-CureVac-Traumatische-Erfahrung.html.

71. Joe Miller and Clive Cookson, "Berlin to Buy Stake in Covid-19 Vaccine Player CureVac," Financial Times, June 15, 2020, https://www.ft.com/content/bddf086e-b810-4628-aab3 -e2b43d64486e.

72. "Has Covid-19 Killed Globalisation?," The Economist.

73. Kim Willsher, Oliver Holmes, Bethan McKernan, and Lorenzo Tondo, "US Hijacking Mask Shipments in Rush for Coronavirus Protection," The Guardian, April 3, 2020, https://www.theguardian.com/world/2020/apr/02/global-battle-coronavirus -equipment-masks-tests.

74. Bojan Pancevski, "Germany Cries Foul over Berlin-Bound Masks Diverted to U.S.," Wall Street Journal, April 3, 2020, https://www.wsj.com/articles/germany-cries-foul -over-berlin-bound-masks-diverted-to-u-s-11585943440.

75. Joanna Kenner, "The Imperative to Diversify Value Chains Post-Covid-19," Institut Montaigne, June 23, 2020, https://www.institutmontaigne.org/en/blog/imperative -diversify-value-chains-post-covid-19.

76. Emmanuel Macron, "Emmanuel Macron Says It Is Time to Think the Unthinkable," interview by Victor Mallet and Roula Khalaf, Financial Times, April 16, 2020, https:// www.ft.com/content/3ea8d790-7fd1-11ea-8fdb-7ec06edeef84.

77. Isabel Reynolds and Emi Urabe, "Japan to Fund Firms to Shift Production out of

China," Bloomberg, April 8, 2020, https://www.bloomberg.com/news/articles /2020-04-08/japan-to-fund-firms-to-shift-production-out-of-china.

78. Andy Blachford, "Bains: Domestic Industry Now Supplying Half of Canada's PPE Needs," Politico, September 30, 2020, https://www.politico.com/news/2020/09/30 /navdeep-bains-canada-ppe-424029.

79. "Flight Tracking Statistics," FlightRadar24, https://www.flightradar24.com/data /statistics, accessed February 14, 2021; "Coronavirus: How and When Will Aviation Recover from Covid-19," Official Aviation Guide, https://www.oag.com/coronavirus -airline-schedules-data, accessed February 14, 2021.

80. Dirk Glasser et al., "COVID-19 Related Travel Restrictions: A Global Review for Tourism," UN World Tourism Organization, December 2, 2020, https://webunwto .s3.eu-west-1.amazonaws.com/s3fs-public/2020-12/201202-Travel-Restrictions .pdf.

81. CPB Netherlands Bureau for Economic Policy Analysis, "World Trade Recovery Slowed Down in September," press release, November 25, 2020, https://www.cpb.nl /en/world-trade-recovery-slowed-down-in-september.

82. Glasser et al., "COVID-19 Related Travel Restrictions."

83. Deutsche Post DHL Group, "DHL Global Connectedness Index 2020 Signals Recovery of Globalization from COVID-19 Setback," press release, December 3, 2020, https:// www.dpdhl.com/en/media-relations/press-releases/2020/dhl-global-connectedness -index-signals-recovery-globalization-covid-19-setback.html.

84. UN Conference on Trade and Development, "Investment Trends Monitor," no. 36, October 2020, 1–2, https://unctad.org/system/files/official-document/diaeiainf2020d4 _en.pdf.

85. Julie Baer and Mirka Martel, "Fall 2020: International Student Enrollment Snapshot," Institute of International Education, November 2020, https://www.iie.org/Research -and-Insights/Open-Doors/Fall-International-Enrollments-Snapshot-Reports; Peter Hurley, "Coronavirus and International Students," Mitchell Institute at Victoria University, October 2020, https://www.vu.edu.au/sites/default/files/international -student-update-2020-mitchell-institute.pdf; Richard Adams, "UK Universities Recruit Record Numbers of International Students," *The Guardian*, September 24, 2020, https://www.theguardian.com/education/2020/sep/24/uk-universities-recruit-record -numbers-of-international-students.

86. Julian Gewirtz, "The Chinese Reassessment of Interdependence," China Leadership Monitor, June 1, 2020, https://www.prcleader.org/gewirtz.

87. "Chinese Banks Urged to Switch Away from SWIFT as U.S. Sanctions Loom," Reuters, July 29, 2020, https://www.reuters.com/article/us-china-banks-usa-sanctions/chinese -banks-urged-to-switch-away-from-swift-as-u-s-sanctions-loom-idUSKCN24U0SN.

88. Described in Chapter 5.

89. Jon Sindreu, "After Covid, Plane Makers Are Even More Dependent on China," *Wall Street Journal*, December 31, 2020, https://www.wsj.com/articles/after-covid-plane -makers-are-even-more-dependent-on-china-11609429997.

90. Centre for Economics and Business Research, *World Economic League Table 2021* (London: CEBR, 2020), https://cebr.com/wp-content/uploads/2020/12/WELT-2021 -final-29.12.pdf.

91. Julian Kossoff and Kieran Corcoran, "Thousands Packed the Streets to Celebrate New Year's Eve in Wuhan, Where the Coronavirus First Emerged, as Other Cities Worldwide Were Deserted," *Business Insider,* January 1, 2021, https://www .businessinsider.com/china-wuhan-celebrates-new-year-in-style-covid-19 -outbreak-2021-1.

CHAPTER 8: VULNERABLE STATES, VULNERABLE PEOPLES

1. Andreas Becker, "Coronavirus Disruptions Deal Severe Blow to Bangladesh's Garment Industry," Deutsche Welle, June 23, 2020, https://www.dw.com/en/coronavirus-disruptions-deal-severe-blow-to-bangladeshs-garment-industry/a-53895339.

2. Quoted in Rebecca Wright and Salman Saeed, "Bangladeshi Garment Workers Face Ruin as Global Brands Ditch Clothing Contracts amid Coronavirus Pandemic," CNN Business, April 22, 2020, https://www.cnn.com/2020/04/22/business/bangladesh-garment-factories/index.html.

3. "Dhaka, Bangladesh Population," Population Stat, https://populationstat.com/bangladesh/dhaka, accessed March 5, 2021; Bruce Vaugh, "Bangladesh," Congressional Research Service, updated February 2, 2021, https://www.justice.gov/eoir/page/file/1366046/download; "Population, Total," World Bank Open Data, https://data.worldbank.org/indicator/SP.POP.TOTL, accessed December 15, 2020; "The World's Most Densely Populated Cities," World Atlas, October 4, 2020, https://www.worldatlas.com/articles/the-world-s-most-densely-populated-cities.html; "Children in Cities: Bangladesh Among 10 Nations That Top the List for Rapid Urbanization," UNICEF, https://www.unicef.org/bangladesh/en/children-cities%C2%A0, accessed September 18, 2020.

4. Elizabeth Cameron, Jennifer Nuzzo, and Jessica Bell, *Global Health Security Index: Building Collective Action and Accountability* (Washington, DC: Nuclear Threat Initiative and Johns Hopkins Bloomberg School of Public Health, 2019), 130, https://www.ghsindex.org/wp-content/uploads/2019/10/2019-Global-Health-Security-Index.pdf; "Hospital Beds (per 1,000 People)," World Bank Data, https://data.worldbank.org/indicator/SH.MED.BEDS.ZS, accessed September 15, 2020; Mamun Abdullah, "Number of ICU Beds Insufficient to Combat Covid-19 Pandemic," *Dhaka Tribune*, March 21, 2020, https://www.dhakatribune.com/bangladesh/2020/03/21/number-of-icu-beds-insufficient-to-combat-covid-19-pandemic.

5. Shahidul Islam Chowdhury and Manzur H. Maswood, "Government Sends Plane Today to Fly Back Citizens," *New Age Bangladesh*, January 31, 2020, https://www.newagebd.net/article/98179/government-sends-plane-today-to-fly-back-citizens; "Bangladesh Suspends All Passenger Flights with 10 Countries," *United News of Bangladesh*, March 21, 2020, https://unb.com.bd/category/bangladesh/bangladesh-suspends-all-passenger-flights-with-10-countries/47580; Muktadir Rashid, "Flights from All Countries but China, HK, UK, Thailand Suspended," *New Age Bangladesh*, March 22, 2020, https://www.newagebd.net/article/102928/flights-from-all-countries-but-china-hk-uk-thailand-suspended; Faisal Mahmud, "Coronavirus: In Dense Bangladesh, Social Distancing a Tough Task," Al Jazeera, March 20, 2020, https://www.aljazeera.com/news/2020/3/20/coronavirus-in-dense-bangladesh-social-distancing-a-tough-task; Julhas Alam, "Bangladesh's Leader Urges All Citizens to Stay at Home," Associated Press, March 25, 2020, https://apnews.com/article/a6cced0c1975a8859d2d227cf5d79700; Md. Kamruzzaman and SM Najmus Sakib, "Bangladesh Imposes Total Lockdown over COVID-19," Anadolu Agency, March 25, 2020, https://www.aa.com.tr/en/asia-pacific/bangladesh-imposes-total-lockdown-over-covid-19/1778272; Julhas Alam, "Soldiers Enforce 10-Day Shutdown in Bangladesh to Slow Virus," Associated Press, March 26, 2020, https://apnews.com/article/0e6b79ee96d3e1f30b67c1878db34927; Md. Kamruzzaman, "COVID-19: Bangladesh Extends Lockdown Until May 30," Anadolu Agency, May 14, 2020, https://www.aa.com.tr/en/asia-pacific/covid-19-bangladesh-extends-lockdown-until-may-30/1840126.

6. Saiful Islam Swapan, "25,000 Perform 'Khatme Shifa' to Fight Coronavirus in Lakshmipur," *Dhaka Tribune*, March 18, 2020, https://www.dhakatribune.com/bangladesh/nation/2020/03/18/25000-muslims-perform-khatme-shifa-to-fight-coronavirus-in

-lakshmipur; Kate Ng, "Coronavirus: Mass Prayer Gathering Is Held in Bangladesh to Read 'Healing Verses' Against Covid-19," *Independent*, March 19, 2020, https://www.independent.co.uk/news/world/asia/coronavirus-pandemic-bangladesh-india-muslim-prayer-gathering-healing-verses-a9410476.html.

7. Iqbal Mahmud and Muktadir Rashid, "Infection Keeps Rising in Bangladesh as People Defy Lockdown Rules," *New Age Bangladesh*, April 25, 2020, https://www.newagebd.net/article/105144/infection-keeps-rising-in-bangladesh-as-people-defy-lockdown-rules; Sumon Mahmud, "Shoppers Keep Crowding Dhaka Kitchen Markets to Spark Major Concerns amid Lockdown," BD News 24, April 20, 2020, https://bdnews24.com/bangladesh/2020/04/20/shoppers-keep-crowding-dhaka-kitchen-markets-to-spark-major-concerns-amid-lockdown; Rashad Ahamad, "People Keep Leaving Dhaka," *New Age Bangladesh*, August 12, 2020, https://www.newagebd.net/article/113269/people-keep-leaving-dhaka.

8. Ruma Paul, "Bangladesh Shuts Down Villages After Tens of Thousands Attend Cleric's Funeral," Reuters, April 20, 2020, https://www.reuters.com/article/us-health-coronavirus-bangladesh/bangladesh-shuts-down-villages-after-tens-of-thousands-attend-clerics-funeral-idUSKBN2220PA.

9. Kamran Reza Chowdhury, "COVID-19 Cases Soar in Bangladesh; Thousands Defy Lockdown to Attend Imam's Funeral," *Benar News*, April 20, 2020, https://www.benarnews.org/english/news/bengali/cases-climb-04202020173834.html.

10. Thomas Farole, "Making Global Value Chains Work for Workers," World Bank Blogs, December 19, 2019, https://blogs.worldbank.org/jobs/making-global-value-chains-work-workers; *Bangladesh Poverty Assessment: Facing Old and New Frontiers in Poverty Reduction* (Washington, DC: World Bank, 2019), 11, https://www.developmentaid.org/api/frontend/cms/file/2019/10/Bangladesh-PA_-Volume-1.pdf; "Poverty Rate Comes Down at 21.8pc in 2018: BBS," *Daily Star*, May 13, 2019, https://www.thedailystar.net/country/news/poverty-rate-comes-down-218pc-2018-bbs-1742953; "The World Bank in Bangladesh," World Bank, https://www.worldbank.org/en/country/bangladesh/overview, accessed September 15, 2020; "World Bank Country and Lending Groups," World Bank, https://datahelpdesk.worldbank.org/knowledgebase/articles/906519-world-bank-country-and-lending-groups, accessed March 13, 2021.

11. "Poverty Headcount Ratio at National Poverty Lines (% of Population)—Bangladesh," World Bank Data, https://data.worldbank.org/indicator/SI.POV.NAHC?locations=BD, accessed March 13, 2021; "Poverty Headcount Ratio at $1.90 a Day (2011 PPP) (% of Population)—Bangladesh," World Bank Data, https://data.worldbank.org/indicator/SI.POV.DDAY?locations=BD, accessed March 13, 2021; "Poverty Rate Comes Down at 21.8pc in 2018"; *Women and Men in the Informal Economy: A Statistical Picture* (Geneva: ILO, 2018), 88, https://www.ilo.org/global/publications/books/WCMS_626831/lang—en/index.htm; Asif Saleh, "In Bangladesh, COVID-19 Threatens to Cause a Humanitarian Crisis," World Economic Forum, April 6, 2020, https://www.weforum.org/agenda/2020/04/in-bangladesh-covid-19-could-cause-a-humanitarian-crisis/; "Individuals Using the Internet (% of population)—Bangladesh, India," World Bank Data, https://data.worldbank.org/indicator/IT.NET.USER.ZS?locations=BD-IN, accessed September 20, 2020.

12. Ruma Paul, "Garment Exporter Bangladesh Faces $6 Billion Hit as Top Retailers Cancel," Reuters, March 31, 2020, https://www.reuters.com/article/health-coronavirus-bangladesh-exports/garment-exporter-bangladesh-faces-6-billion-hit-as-top-retailers-cancel-idUKKBN21I2R9.

13. "Helping Bangladesh Recover from COVID-19," International Monetary Fund, June 12, 2020, https://www.imf.org/en/News/Articles/2020/06/11/na-06122020-helping-bangladesh-recover-from-covid-19.

14. "COVID-19 Impact on Bangladesh Economy," LankaBangla Asset Management Co. Ltd., Dhaka, 2020, https://www.arx.cfa/en/research/2020/06/soc290620-covid-19-impact-on-bangladesh-economy.

15. Lauren Frayer, "1 Million Bangladeshi Garment Workers Lose Jobs amid COVID-19 Economic Fallout," NPR, April 3, 2020, https://www.npr.org/sections/coronavirus -live-updates/2020/04/03/826617334/1-million-bangladeshi-garment-workers-lose -jobs-amid-covid-19-economic-fallout.

16. Quoted in "Bangladesh Garment Factories Reopen, Defying Virus Lockdown," *Barron's*, April 26, 2020, https://www.barrons.com/news/bangladesh-garment-factories -reopen-defying-virus-lockdown-01587898510.

17. Lauren Frayer, "For Bangladesh's Struggling Garment Workers, Hunger Is a Bigger Worry Than Pandemic," NPR, June 5, 2020, https://www.npr.org/2020/06/05/869486297/for -bangladeshs-struggling-garment-workers-hunger-is-a-bigger-worry-than-pandemi.

18. Zobaer Ahmed, "Coronavirus: Economy Down, Poverty Up in Bangladesh," Deutsche Welle, June 10, 2020, https://www.dw.com/en/coronavirus-economy-down-poverty -up-in-bangladesh/a-53759686; Frayer, "For Bangladesh's Struggling Garment Workers, Hunger Is a Bigger Worry Than Pandemic."

19. Ruma Paul, "Bangladesh Eases Some Restrictions, Extends Lockdown to May 16," Reuters, May 4, 2020, https://www.usnews.com/news/world/articles/2020-05-04 /bangladesh-coronavirus-cases-above-10-000-health-ministry.

20. Ibrahim Hossain Ovi, "2020 Was Possibly the Worst Year for Garment Exporters," *Dhaka Tribune*, December 28, 2020, https://www.dhakatribune.com/business/2020 /12/28/2020-was-possibly-the-worst-year-for-garment-exporters.

21. Ahmed, "Coronavirus: Economy Down, Poverty Up in Bangladesh."

22. Jason Beaubien, "They Pump $15 Billion a Year INTO Bangladesh's Economy—But at What Cost?," NPR, June 3, 2019, https://www.npr.org/sections/goatsandsoda/2019 /06/03/722085193/they-pump-15-billion-a-year-into-bangladeshs-economy-but-at -what-cost.

23. "Personal Remittances, Received (% of GDP)—Bangladesh," World Bank, accessed March 13, 2021, https://data.worldbank.org/indicator/BX.TRF.PWKR.DT.GD.ZS ?locations=BD.

24. International Organization for Migration, "Migration Remittances and Assets in Bangladesh: Considerations About Their Intersection and Development Policy Recommendations," 2010, 1, https://bangladesh.iom.int/sites/default/files/publication /Migration-Remittances-and-assets-in-Bangladesh.pdf.

25. Peter Goodman, "They Crossed Oceans to Lift Their Families out of Poverty. Now, They Need Help," *New York Times*, July 27, 2020, https://www.nytimes.com/2020/07 /27/business/global-remittances-coronavirus.html; Dilip Ratha et al., "COVID-19 Crisis Through a Migration Lens," Migration and Development Brief 32, World Bank, April 2020, 26, https://openknowledge.worldbank.org/bitstream/handle /10986/33634/COVID-19-Crisis-Through-a-Migration-Lens.pdf.

26. Mehedi Hasan, "Remittance Hits a Record in 2020," *Dhaka Tribune*, January 4, 2021, https://www.dhakatribune.com/business/2021/01/04/remittance-hits-a-record-in -2020.

27. Ali Riaz, "Bangladesh's COVID-19 Stimulus: Leaving the Most Vulnerable Behind," Atlantic Council, April 8, 2020, https://www.atlanticcouncil.org/blogs/new -atlanticist/bangladeshs-covid-19-stimulus-leaving-the-most-vulnerable-behind/; Sadiqur Rahman, "The Failure to Deliver Stimulus Aid to the Poor," *Business Standard*, July 3, 2020, https://tbsnews.net/feature/panorama/failure-deliver-stimulus -aid-poor-101188.

28. Jena Derakhshani Hamadani et al., "Immediate Impact of Stay-at-Home Orders to

Control COVID-19 Transmission on Socioeconomic Conditions, Food Insecurity, Mental Health, and Intimate Partner Violence in Bangladeshi Women and Their Families: An Interrupted Time Series," *Lancet* 8, no. 11 (August 2020): 1380–89, https://www.thelancet.com/journals/langlo/article/PIIS2214-109X(20)30366-1/fulltext.

29. "COVID-19 Pandemic Hit Earnings of 74pc Families as Average Income Fell by 74pc: Study," BD News 24, June 2, 2020, https://bdnews24.com/economy/2020/06/02/covid-19-pandemic-hit-earnings-of-74pc-families-as-average-income-fell-by-74pc-study.

30. Selim Raihan, "COVID-19's Effect on Poverty and Policy Response in Bangladesh," *Thinking Aloud* 7, no. 1 (June 2020), https://sanemnet.org//wp-content/uploads/2020/07/Thinking-Aloud_V7_N1-.pdf.

31. United Nations, *World Economic Situation and Prospects 2021* (New York: United Nations, 2021), 106, https://www.un.org/development/desa/dpad/wp-content/uploads/sites/45/WESP2021_FullReport.pdf.

32. Paul, "Bangladesh Eases Some Restrictions"; Md. Kamruzzaman, "Bangladesh: Thousands Gather at Mosques amid Pandemic," Anadolu Agency, May 8, 2020, https://www.aa.com.tr/en/asia-pacific/bangladesh-thousands-gather-at-mosques-amid-pandemic/1833947; Mamun Abdullah, "Bangladesh to Resume International Flights on June 16," *Dhaka Tribune*, June 11, 2020, https://www.dhakatribune.com/bangladesh/2020/06/11/bangladesh-to-resume-international-flights-on-june-16.

33. COVID-19 Dashboard, Center for Systems Science and Engineering, Johns Hopkins University & Medicine, Coronavirus Resource Center, https://coronavirus.jhu.edu/map.html, accessed December 26, 2020.

34. Shaina Ahluwalia and Anurag Maan, "South Asia Reached 10 Million COVID-19 Cases—Reuters Tally," Reuters, November 19, 2020, https://www.reuters.com/article/health-coronavirus-south-asia-cases/south-asia-reaches-10-million-covid-19-cases-reuters-tally-idUSKBN27Z0FV.

35. "Mortality Analyses," Johns Hopkins University & Medicine, Coronavirus Resource Center, https://coronavirus.jhu.edu/data/mortality, accessed December 26, 2020.

36. *World Population Ageing 2019: Highlights* (New York: United Nations Department of Economic and Social Affairs, 2019), 34, https://www.un.org/en/development/desa/population/publications/pdf/ageing/WorldPopulationAgeing2019-Highlights.pdf; "Bangladesh Still Experiences Low Covid Death Rate; Experts Wonder Why!," *United News of Bangladesh*, August 20, 2020, https://www.unb.com.bd/amp/category/Special/bangladesh-still-experiences-low-covid-death-rate-experts-wonder-why/56246.

37. Arafatul Islam, "Why Bangladeshis No Longer Fear the Coronavirus," Deutsche Welle, September 29, 2020, https://www.dw.com/en/bangladesh-coronavirus-no-fear/a-55091050; Sophie Cousins, "Bangladesh's COVID-19 Testing Criticized," *Lancet* 396, no. 10251 (August 2020): 591, https://www.thelancet.com/journals/lancet/article/PIIS0140-6736(20)31819-5/fulltext; Farooq Sobhan, "Bangladesh's Response to the Covid-19 Pandemic," *Round Table* 109, no. 4 (2020): 462, https://www.tandfonline.com/doi/full/10.1080/00358533.2020.1790775?src=recsys.

38. Kendrea Liew, "Bangladesh Faces Twin Crises as Coronavirus Deals New Blow to Flood-Battered Nation," CNBC, September 14, 2020, https://www.cnbc.com/2020/09/14/bangladesh-faces-twin-crises-as-coronavirus-deals-new-blow-to-flood-battered-nation.html; Somini Sengupta and Julfikar Ali Manik, "A Quarter of Bangladesh Is Flooded. Millions Have Lost Everything," *New York Times*, July 30, 2020, https://www.nytimes.com/2020/07/30/climate/bangladesh-floods.html.

39. Liew, "Bangladesh Faces Twin Crises."

40. Naimul Karim, "Update 1—Pandemic Job Losses and Flooding Spark Fears of Hard Times in Bangladesh," Reuters, July 31, 2020, https://www.reuters.com/article /bangladesh-climatechange-floods/update-1-pandemic-job-losses-and-flooding -spark-fears-of-hard-times-in-bangladesh-idUSL5N2F24SA.

41. Hannah Beech, Alissa Rubin, Anatoly Kurmanaev, and Ruth Maclean, "The Covid-19 Riddle: Why Does the Virus Wallop Some Places and Spare Others?," *New York Times*, May 3, 2020, https://www.nytimes.com/2020/05/03/world/asia/coronavirus -spread-where-why.html.

42. "Animated Maps," Johns Hopkins University & Medicine, Coronavirus Resource Center, https://coronavirus.jhu.edu/data/animated-world-map, accessed September 20, 2020.

43. David Hunter, "Coronavirus: There Is No Global South Exceptionalism," The Conversation, May 11, 2020, https://theconversation.com/coronavirus-there-is-no-global -south-exceptionalism-137806; Yasufumi Saito, Andrew James, and Rosa de Acosta, "High-Speed Trains, International Flights: How the Coronavirus Spread," *Wall Street Journal*, March 5, 2020, https://www.wsj.com/graphics/how-the-coronavirus -spread/; Pinelopi Koujianou Goldberg and Tristan Reed, "The Effects of the Coronavirus Pandemic in Emerging Markets and Developing Economies: An Optimistic Preliminary Account," Brookings Institution, 2020, 6, https://www.brookings.edu /wp-content/uploads/2020/06/Goldberg-Reed-conference-draft.pdf.

44. *Tracking Universal Health Coverage: 2017 Global Monitoring Report* (Geneva: World Health Organization and World Bank Group, 2017), v, https://apps.who.int/iris /bitstream/handle/10665/259817/9789241513555-eng.pdf;jsessionid=0D1AE648E7 552E987F30D425CBE26A9D?sequence=1.

45. Ruth Maclean and Simon Marks, "10 African Countries Have No Ventilators. That's Only Part of the Problem," *New York Times*, April 18, 2020, https://www.nytimes.com /2020/04/18/world/africa/africa-coronavirus-ventilators.html.

46. Goldberg and Reed, "The Effects of the Coronavirus Pandemic."

47. Kristalina Georgieva, "Confronting the Covid-19 Crisis," International Monetary Fund podcast, April 9, 2020, https://www.imf.org/en/News/Podcasts/All-Podcasts /2020/04/09/md-curtain-raiser-2020-sms.

48. *Global Economic Prospects, January 2019* (Washington, DC: World Bank Group, 2019), 129, http://pubdocs.worldbank.org/en/196001542819699601/Global-Economic -Prospects-Jan-2019-Topical-Issue-informality.pdf.

49. *Piecing Together the Poverty Puzzle: Poverty and Shared Prosperity* (Washington, DC: World Bank Group, 2017), 1, https://openknowledge.worldbank.org/bitstream /handle/10986/30418/9781464813306.pdf.

50. Raoul Leering and Timme Spakman, "Countries Hit Most by the Coronavirus Value Chain Shock," ING Think, April 2, 2020, https://think.ing.com/articles/countries -hurt-most-by-covid-19-global-value-chain-shock; *Global Economic Prospects, June 2020* (Washington, DC: World Bank Group, 2020), https://openknowledge.worldbank .org/handle/10986/33748.

51. World Bank Group, *Global Economic Prospects, June 2020*, 137, 141; Goldberg and Reed, "The Effects of the Coronavirus Pandemic," 25.

52. See, for example, Nicoli Nattrass and Jeremy Seekings, "Covid vs. Democracy: South Africa's Lockdown Misfire," *Journal of Democracy* 31, no. 4 (October 2020): 106–21, https://www.journalofdemocracy.org/articles/covid-vs-democracy-south-africas -lockdown-misfire/.

53. Gerald Imray and Joseph Krauss, "Worst Virus Fears Are Realized in Poor or War-Torn Countries," Associated Press, June 28, 2020, https://apnews.com/911c9cdb10a 0319fb5f36dc5ddff9d40.

54. Amanda Glassman, Kalipso Chalkidou, and Richard Sullivan, "Does One Size Fit All? Realistic Alternatives for COVID-19 Response in Low-Income Countries," Center for Global Development, April 2, 2020, https://www.cgdev.org/blog/does -one-size-fit-all-realistic-alternatives-covid-19-response-low-income-countries; Zubaida Bai and Nina Rawal, "Why Lockdowns Aren't the Best Way Forward for the Global South," World Economic Forum, August 17, 2020, https://www .weforum.org/agenda/2020/08/why-lockdowns-dont-work-in-lower-income -countries/.

55. S. A. Madhi et al., "COVID-19 Lockdowns in Low- and Middle-Income Countries: Success Against COVID-19 at the Price of Greater Costs," *South African Medical Journal* 110, no. 8 (June 2020): 724–26, http://www.samj.org.za/index.php/samj/article /view/12992.

56. Bill Gates and Melinda Gates, "2020 Goalkeepers Report: COVID-19 a Global Perspective," Bill & Melinda Gates Foundation, September 2020, https://www .gatesfoundation.org/goalkeepers/report/2020-report/#GlobalPerspective; "The Pandemic Is Plunging Millions Back into Extreme Poverty," *The Economist*, September 26, 2020, https://www.economist.com/international/2020/09/26/the-pandemic-is -plunging-millions-back-into-extreme-poverty.

57. "Wuhan Lockdown 'Unprecedented,' Shows Commitment to Contain Virus: WHO Representative in China," Reuters, January 23, 2020, https://www.reuters.com/article /us-china-health-who/wuhan-lockdown-unprecedented-shows-commitment-to -contain-virus-who-representative-in-china-idUSKBN1ZM1G9.

58. Sharon Chen and Claire Che, "WHO Says China Actions Blunted Virus Spread, Leading to Drop," Bloomberg, February 24, 2020, https://www.bloomberg.com/news /articles/2020-02-24/who-says-china-lockdown-blunted-new-epidemic-leading-to -decline.

59. "Coronavirus Confirmed as Pandemic by World Health Organization," BBC News, March 11, 2020, https://www.bbc.com/news/world-51839944.

60. "WHO Bins DSCC Mayor's Claim over Lockdown in Bangladesh," *Dhaka Tribune*, March 21, 2020, https://www.dhakatribune.com/bangladesh/2020/03/21/who -declare-emergency-if-necessary.

61. World Health Organization, "COVID-19 Strategy Update: April 14, 2020," 3, https:// www.who.int/publications/i/item/covid-19-strategy-update—14-april-2020.

62. "WHO Lauds India's 'Tough and Timely' Actions Against Coronavirus," *The Hindu*, April 14, 2020, https://www.thehindu.com/news/national/who-lauds-indias-tough -and-timely-actions-against-coronavirus/article31338150.ece.

63. "WHO Urges Caution as Countries in Africa Ease Lockdowns," World Health Organization Africa, May 28, 2020, https://www.afro.who.int/news/who-urges-caution -countries-africa-ease-lockdowns.

64. "WHO Recommends Pakistan Reimpose Intermittent Lockdowns as COVID-19 Cases Rise Sharply," Reuters, June 9, 2020, https://www.reuters.com/article/us-health -coronavirus-pakistan-who/who-recommends-pakistan-reimpose-intermittent -lockdowns-as-covid-19-cases-rise-sharply-idUSKBN23G2ZJ; "World Health Organization (WHO) Coronavirus Press Conference July 10," Rev, July 10, 2020, https:// www.rev.com/blog/transcripts/world-health-organization-who-coronavirus-press -conference-july-10.

65. Bruce Y. Lee, "WHO Warning About Covid-19 Coronavirus Lockdowns Is Taken out of Context," *Forbes*, October 13, 2020, https://www.forbes.com/sites/brucelee /2020/10/13/who-warning-about-covid-19-coronavirus-lockdowns-is-taken-out-of -context/?sh=23a7578158c4.

66. World Bank, *Global Economic Prospects, January 2021* (Washington, DC: World Bank

Group, January 2021), 6, 21, 25, https://www.worldbank.org/en/publication/global
-economic-prospects.

67. International Monetary Fund, *World Economic Outlook, October 2020*, 36.

68. Gates and Gates, "2020 Goalkeepers Report."

69. *Reversals of Fortune: Poverty and Shared Prosperity* (Washington, DC: World Bank Group, 2020), xi, https://openknowledge.worldbank.org/bitstream/handle/10986/34496/9781464816024.pdf; "COVID-19 Could Push the Number of People Living in Extreme Poverty to over 1 Billion by 2030, Says UNDP Study," United Nations Development Programme, press release, December 3, 2020, https://www.undp.org/content/undp/en/home/news-centre/news/2020/COVID-19_could_push_extreme_poverty_over_1_billion_people_2030.html; Lisa Kurbiel, "Investing in the SDGs in a Post COVID world," *United Nations Action 2030* (blog), January 26, 2021, https://unsdg.un.org/zh-hans/node/53339.

70. Homi Kharas, "The Impact of COVID-19 on Global Extreme Poverty," Brookings Institution, October 21, 2020, https://www.brookings.edu/blog/future-development/2020/10/21/the-impact-of-covid-19-on-global-extreme-poverty/.

71. United Nations Office for the Coordinator of Humanitarian Affairs, *Global Humanitarian Overview 2021* (Geneva: OCHA, 2020), 20, https://reliefweb.int/sites/reliefweb.int/files/resources/GHO2021_EN.pdf.

72. "Averting a Lost COVID Generation: A Six-Point Plan to Respond, Recover and Reimagine a Post-Pandemic World for Every Child," UNICEF, November 20, 2020, 2, https://www.unicef.org/media/86881/file/Averting-a-lost-covid-generation-world-childrens-day-data-and-advocacy-brief-2020.pdf.

73. United Nations Office for the Coordinator of Humanitarian Affairs, *Global Humanitarian Overview 2021*, 8.

74. *Global Humanitarian Assistance Report 2020* (Wilmington, DE: Development Initiatives, 2020), 13, https://devinit.org/resources/global-humanitarian-assistance-report-2020/crisis-financing-covid-19-pandemic-response/#downloads.

75. Edith M. Lederer, "UN Appeals for $6.7 Billion to Fight Virus in Poor Countries," Associated Press, May 7, 2020, https://apnews.com/article/2d4caf7ac7d1d66cccf72b05bf8b9046; "Global Humanitarian Response Plan: July Update," WHO Health Cluster, https://www.who.int/health-cluster/news-and-events/news/GHRP-revision-july-2020/en/, accessed September 5, 2020.

76. United Nations Office for the Coordinator of Humanitarian Affairs, *Global Humanitarian Overview 2021*, 66.

77. "The World Bank in Peru," World Bank, https://www.worldbank.org/en/country/peru/overview, accessed September 5, 2020; World Bank, "World Bank Country and Lending Groups."

78. "Peru Records First Confirmed Case of Coronavirus, President Vizcarra Says," Reuters, March 6, 2020, https://www.reuters.com/article/us-health-coronavirus-peru/peru-records-first-confirmed-case-of-coronavirus-president-vizcarra-says-idUSKBN20T1S9.

79. Linnea Sandin, "Covid-19 Exposes Latin America's Inequality," Center for Strategic and International Studies, April 6, 2020, https://www.csis.org/analysis/covid-19-exposes-latin-americas-inequality.

80. Will Feuer, "South America Is a 'New Epicenter' of the Coronavirus Pandemic, WHO Says," CNBC, May 22, 2020, https://www.cnbc.com/2020/05/22/south-america-is-a-new-epicenter-of-the-coronavirus-pandemic-who-says.html.

81. Ryan Dube, "Coronavirus Hits Peru Hard Despite Strict Lockdown," *Wall Street Journal*, June 14, 2020, https://www.wsj.com/articles/coronavirus-hits-peru-hard-despite-strict-lockdown-11592146800; Diego Quispe, "Decretan estado de emergencia para

frenar el coronavirus" [State of emergency declared to stop the coronavirus], *La República*, March 16, 2020, https://larepublica.pe/sociedad/2020/03/16/coronavirus -en-peru-decretan-estado-de-emergencia-para-frenar-la-epidemia/; Marco Aquino, "Peru Calls Up 10,000 Army Reserves to Enforce Quarantine," Reuters, April 1, 2020, https://www.reuters.com/article/us-health-coronavirus-peru-army/peru-calls -up-10000-army-reserves-to-enforce-quarantine-idUSKBN21J69A; Reuters Staff, "Peru Looks to Restart Economy After Months-Long Lockdown," Reuters, July 1, 2020, https://www.reuters.com/article/us-health-coronavirus-peru/peru-looks-to-restart -economy-after-months-long-lockdown-idUSKBN2427CP.

82. Whitney Eulich, "'We're Invisible': Peru's Moment of Reckoning on Informal Workers," *Christian Science Monitor*, June 30, 2020, https://www.csmonitor.com/World /Americas/2020/0630/We-re-invisible-Peru-s-moment-of-reckoning-on-informal -workers; "Peru," Policy Responses to COVID-19, International Monetary Fund, last modified December 4, 2020, https://www.imf.org/en/Topics/imf-and-covid19 /Policy-Responses-to-COVID-19#N.

83. COVID-19 Dashboard, Johns Hopkins University & Medicine; "Mortality Analyses," Johns Hopkins University & Medicine.

84. Jin Wu et al., "412,000 Missing Deaths: Tracking the True Toll of the Coronavirus Outbreak," *New York Times*, last modified November 27, 2020, https://www.nytimes .com/interactive/2020/04/21/world/coronavirus-missing-deaths.html.

85. Oscar Lopez and Anastasia Moloney, "Analysis—Coronavirus Chases the Slum Dwellers of Latin America," Reuters, March 18, 2020, https://www.reuters.com/article /health-coronavirus-latam/analysis-coronavirus-chases-the-slum-dwellers-of-latin -america-idUSL8N2BA8G5; Azam Ahmed, Anatoly Kurmanaev, Daniel Politi, and Ernesto Londoño, "Virus Gains Steam Across Latin America," *New York Times*, June 23, 2020, https://www.nytimes.com/2020/06/23/world/americas/coronavirus-brazil -mexico-peru-chile-uruguay.html?referringSource=articleShare; "Population Living in Slums (% of Urban Population)—Peru," World Bank Data, https://data.worldbank .org/indicator/EN.POP.SLUM.UR.ZS?locations=PE, accessed September 20, 2020.

86. Quoted in Mitra Taj and Anatoly Kurmanaev, "Virus Exposes Weak Links in Peru's Success Story," *New York Times*, June 12, 2020, https://www.nytimes.com/2020/06/12 /world/americas/coronavirus-peru-inequality-corruption.html.

87. Matías Busso and Julián Messina, *The Inequality Crisis: Latin America and the Caribbean at the Crossroads* (Washington, DC: Inter-American Development Bank, 2020), 3, 17, 46, https://publications.iadb.org/publications/english/document/The -Inequality-Crisis-Latin-America-and-the-Caribbean-at-the-Crossroads.pdf.

88. Laís Abramo et al., *Social Panorama of Latin America* (Santiago: Economic Commission for Latin America and the Caribbean, 2019), 96, https://repositorio.cepal.org/bitstream /handle/11362/44989/1/S1901132_en.pdf. These numbers reflect ECLAC's own estimates. Official Peruvian government estimates were 20.5 percent and 2.8 percent.

89. Quoted in Eulich, "'We're Invisible.'"

90. Florence Bonnet, Joann Vanek, and Martha Chen, *Women and Men in the Informal Economy: A Statistical Brief* (Manchester: International Labour Office, 2019), 10, 87.

91. Ciara Nugent, "Peru Locked Down Hard and Early. Why Is Its Coronavirus Outbreak So Bad?," *Time*, May 29, 2020, https://time.com/5844768/peru-coronavirus/.

92. Taj and Kurmanaev, "Virus Exposes Weak Links in Peru's Success Story"; Teresa Welsh, "Inequality and Corruption: Why Peru Is Losing Its COVID-19 Battle," DevEx, July 1, 2020, https://www.devex.com/news/inequality-and-corruption-why -peru-is-losing-its-covid-19-battle-97604; Yen Nian Mooi, "Banking on Progress in Peru," *Diálogo a Fondo* (IMF blog), December 4, 2018, https://www.imf.org/external /np/blog/dialogo/120418.pdf.

93. Quoted in Eulich, "'We're Invisible.'"
94. Quoted in Pierina Pighi Bel and Jake Horton, "Coronavirus: What's Happening in Peru," BBC News, July 9, 2020, https://www.bbc.com/news/world-latin-america-53150808.
95. Dube, "Coronavirus Hits Peru Hard Despite Strict Lockdown."
96. "Coronavirus: Peru Economy Sinks 40% in April amid Lockdown," BBC, June 16, 2020, https://www.bbc.com/news/world-latin-america-53051157; Joaquín Cottani, "The Effects of Covid-19 on Latin America's Economy," Center for Strategic and International Studies, November 18, 2020, https://www.csis.org/analysis/effects-covid-19-latin-americas-economy; International Monetary Fund, *World Economic Outlook: A Long and Difficult Ascent*, 57; "UNICEF Peru COVID-19 Situation Report No. 9," ReliefWeb, December 4, 2020, https://reliefweb.int/report/peru/unicef-peru-covid-19-situation-report-no-9-2-december-2020.
97. International Monetary Fund, *World Economic Outlook Update, January 2021: Policy Support and Vaccines Expected to Lift Activity* (Washington, DC: International Monetary Fund, 2021), 4, https://www.imf.org/en/Publications/WEO/%20Issues/2021/01/26/2021-world-economic-outlook-update.
98. Claudia Viale, "Peru: Updated Assessment of the Impact of the Coronavirus Pandemic on the Extractive Sector and Resource Governance," Natural Resource Governance Institute, December 18, 2020, https://resourcegovernance.org/analysis-tools/publications/peru-updated-assessment-impact-coronavirus-extractive.
99. Quoted in Taj and Kurmanaev, "Virus Exposes Weak Links in Peru's Success Story."
100. Luis Alberto Moreno, "Latin America's Lost Decades," *Foreign Affairs*, January/February 2021, https://www.foreignaffairs.com/articles/south-america/2020-12-08/latin-americas-lost-decades.
101. United Nations Office for the Coordinator of Humanitarian Affairs, *Global Humanitarian Overview 2021*, 6.
102. Abdi Latif Dahir, "'Like an Umbrella Had Covered the Sky': Locust Swarms Despoil Kenya," *New York Times,* February 21, 2020, https://www.nytimes.com/2020/02/21/world/africa/locusts-kenya-east-africa.html.
103. "The World Bank in Kenya," World Bank, https://www.worldbank.org/en/country/kenya/overview, accessed September 10, 2020.
104. Eunice Njogu, "Millions of Kenyans Go Hungry Every Day. Why, and What Can Be Done," ReliefWeb, March 23, 2020, https://reliefweb.int/report/kenya/millions-kenyans-go-hungry-every-day-why-and-what-can-be-done; "Kenya," United Nations World Food Programme, https://www.wfp.org/countries/kenya, accessed September 20, 2020.
105. William Bellamy, "Kenya's Case of Covid-19," Center for Strategic and International Studies, June 16, 2020, https://www.csis.org/analysis/kenyas-case-covid-19.
106. "Individuals Using the Internet (% of Population)—Kenya," World Bank Data, https://data.worldbank.org/indicator/IT.NET.USER.ZS?locations=KE, accessed September 20, 2020; Louise Donovan and April Zhu, "Kenya's Labor Market Wasn't Made for a Pandemic," *Foreign Policy*, April 10, 2020, https://foreignpolicy.com/2020/04/10/kenya-labor-coronavirus-pandemic-informal-workers-economic-crisis/; "Kenya: Police Brutality During Curfew," Human Rights Watch, April 22, 2020, https://www.hrw.org/news/2020/04/22/kenya-police-brutality-during-curfew; "Kenyan Police 'Killed 15' Since Start of Coronavirus Curfew," Al Jazeera, June 5, 2020, https://www.aljazeera.com/news/2020/06/kenyan-police-killed-15-start-coronavirus-curfew-200605184324568.html.
107. World Bank, "The World Bank in Kenya"; "Kenya's Finance Minister Lowers 2020

Economic Growth Projection," Reuters, November 24, 2020, https://www.reuters.com /article/kenya-economy/kenyas-finance-minister-lowers-2020-economic-growth -projection-idUSN6N2F000M.

108. "Kenya Food Security Outlook Update, June 2020 to January 2021," Famine Early Warning System, July 11, 2020, https://reliefweb.int/report/kenya/kenya-food-security -outlook-update-june-2020-january-2021.

109. Tom Odula and Idi Ali Juma, "Stampede in Kenya as Slum Residents Surge for Food Aid," Associated Press, April 10, 2020, https://apnews.com/article/49ddf9d37f72387 30c16e7b61bfe3de9.

110. "Coronavirus: Kenyans Moved by Widow Cooking Stones for Children," BBC News, April 30, 2020, https://www.bbc.com/news/world-africa-52494404.

111. Email correspondence with the International Committee of the Red Cross, October 30, 2020.

112. Amanda Thomas and Angus Urquhart, *Global Humanitarian Assistance Report 2020* (Bristol: Development Initiatives, 2020), 22–23, https://devinit.org/resources/global -humanitarian-assistance-report-2020/#downloads.

113. COVID-19 Dashboard, Johns Hopkins University & Medicine; "Mortality Analyses," Johns Hopkins University & Medicine; Linda Nordling, "The Pandemic Appears to Have Spared Africa So Far. Scientists Are Struggling to Explain Why," *Science Magazine*, August 11, 2020, https://www.sciencemag.org/news/2020/08/pandemic -appears-have-spared-africa-so-far-scientists-are-struggling-explain-why.

114. "Social, Environmental Factors Seen Behind Africa's Low COVID-19 Cases," World Health Organization Africa, September 24, 2020, https://www.afro.who.int/news /social-environmental-factors-seen-behind-africas-low-covid-19-cases; Max Bearak and Danielle Paquette, "The Coronavirus Is Ravaging the World. But Life Looks Almost Normal in Much of Africa," *Washington Post*, December 11, 2020, https://www .washingtonpost.com/world/africa/africa-coronavirus-low-cases-deaths/2020/12/10 /e907a1c2-3899-11eb-aad9-8959227280c4_story.html.

115. Davis Beasley, "The Looming Hunger Pandemic," *Foreign Affairs*, June 16, 2020, https:// www.foreignaffairs.com/articles/world/2020-06-16/looming-hunger-pandemic.

116. Jason Beaubien, "Latin America Is Facing a Hunger Pandemic," NPR, December 9, 2020, https://www.npr.org/sections/goatsandsoda/2020/12/09/943906342/latin -america-is-facing-a-hunger-pandemic.

117. Gian Volpicelli, "Brexit Hit Farms Hard. Coronavirus May Leave Food Rotting in the Fields," *Wired*, March 31, 2020, https://www.wired.co.uk/article/coronavirus-farms -uk-brexit.

118. "The Hunger Virus: How COVID-19 Is Fuelling Hunger in a Hungry World," Oxfam Media Briefing, July 9, 2020, 4, https://oxfamilibrary.openrepository.com/bitstream /handle/10546/621023/mb-the-hunger-virus-090720-en.pdf.

119. "World Food Situation: FAO Cereal Supply and Demand Brief," Food and Agriculture Organization of the United Nations, http://www.fao.org/worldfoodsituation /csdb/en/, accessed December 26, 2020.

120. David Laborde, Will Martin, Johan Swinnen, and Rob Vos, "COVID-19 Risks to Global Food Security," *Science* 369, no. 6503 (July 2020): 500–502, https://science .sciencemag.org/content/369/6503/500; "Russia Cuts Off Wheat, Other Grain Exports," RFERL, April 26, 2020, https://www.rferl.org/a/russia-cuts-off-wheat-other -grain-exports/30577633.html.

121. David Laborde, Abdullah Mamun, and Marie Parent, "COVID-19 Food Trade Policy Tracker," International Food Policy Research Institute, last modified November 24, 2020, https://www.ifpri.org/project/covid-19-food-trade-policy-tracker.

122. Beasley, "The Looming Hunger Pandemic."

123. Laborde et al., "COVID-19 Risks to Global Food Security."

124. "World Food Index Rises for Seventh Month Running in Dec—FAO," Reuters, January 7, 2021, https://www.reuters.com/article/us-global-economy-food/world-food-price-index-rises-for-seventh-month-running-in-dec-fao-idUSKBN29C12N; David Malpass, "COVID Crisis Is Fueling Food Price Rises for World's Poorest," World Bank Blogs, February 1, 2021, https://blogs.worldbank.org/voices/covid-crisis-fuel-ing-food-price-rises-worlds-poorest.

125. Rachel Scott and Gregory Connor, "Understanding What Data Tell Us About COVID-19's Socio-Economic Impact," United Nations Development Programme, December 2, 2020, https://www.undp.org/content/undp/en/home/blog/2020/understanding-what-data-tell-us-about-covid-19s-socio-economic-i.html.

126. Flore de Preneuf, "Food Security and COVID-19," World Bank, February 5, 2021, https://www.worldbank.org/en/topic/agriculture/brief/food-security-and-covid-19; "Food Crises and COVID-19: Emerging Evidence and Implications," Global Network Against Food Crises, 2020, https://reliefweb.int/sites/reliefweb.int/files/resources/GlobalNetwork_Technical_Note_Covid19_Food_Crises_Sept_2020.pdf; Peter Goodman, Abdi Latif Dahir, and Karan Deep Singh, "The Other Way Covid Will Kill: Hunger," *New York Times*, September 11, 2020, https://www.nytimes.com/2020/09/11/business/covid-hunger-food-insecurity.html.

127. Felix Baquedano, Cheryl Christensen, Kayode Ajewole, and Jayson Beckman, *International Food Security Assessment, 2020–30* (Washington, DC: U.S. Department of Agriculture, Economic Research Service, 2020), 1, https://www.ers.usda.gov/webdocs/outlooks/99088/gfa-31.pdf?v=7588.

128. "COVID-19 External Situation Report #17," World Food Programme, December 2, 2020, 1, https://docs.wfp.org/api/documents/bb06a3493e85496587739785abfe5b28/download/?_ga=2.91035352.331409304.1608577915–248201135.1607796929; Beasley, "The Looming Hunger Pandemic."

129. "The Hunger Virus," 1.

130. Berit Reiss-Andersen, "Prize Announcement," Nobel Prize, October 9, 2020, https://www.nobelprize.org/prizes/peace/2020/prize-announcement/; David Beasley, "Leader of Nobel Peace Prize–Winning World Food Programme on Global Starvation Crisis," interviewed by Amna Nawaz, *PBS NewsHour*, October 9, 2020, https://www.pbs.org/newshour/show/leader-of-nobel-peace-prize-winning-world-food-programme-on-global-starvation-crisis.

131. Michelle Nichols, "U.N. Warns 2021 Shaping Up to Be a Humanitarian Catastrophe," Reuters, December 4, 2020, https://www.reuters.com/article/us-health-coronavirus-un/u-n-warns-2021-shaping-up-to-be-a-humanitarian-catastrophe-idUSKBN28E2R9.

CHAPTER 9: CONFLICT AND CONTAGION

1. "Coronavirus: Iran's Deputy Health Minister Tests Positive as Outbreak Worsens," BBC News, February 25, 2020, https://www.bbc.com/news/world-middle-east-51628484.

2. Erin Cunningham and Dalton Bennett, "Coronavirus Burial Pits So Vast They're Visible from Space," *Washington Post*, March 12, 2020, https://www.washingtonpost.com/graphics/2020/world/iran-coronavirus-outbreak-graves/.

3. "WHO Official Says Iran Death Toll Potentially Five Times Higher," Radio Farda, March 17, 2020, https://en.radiofarda.com/a/who-official-says-iran-death-toll-potentially-five-times-higher/30492491.html.

4. "Flattening the Curve of U.S.-Iran Tensions," International Crisis Group, Middle East & North Africa Briefing Number 76, April 2, 2020, https://www.crisisgroup.org/middle-east-north-africa/gulf-and-arabian-peninsula/iran/b76-flattening-curve-us-iran-tensions.

5. Tara Kangarlou and Joseph Hincks, "'People Are Dying Left and Right': Inside Iran's Struggle to Contain Its Coronavirus Outbreak," *Time*, March 17, 2020, https://time.com/5804706/iran-coronavirus/.

6. Kasra Aarabi, "Iran Knows Who to Blame for the Virus: America and Israel," *Foreign Policy*, March 19, 2020, https://foreignpolicy.com/2020/03/19/iran-irgc-coronavirus-propaganda-blames-america-israel/; "Flattening the Curve of U.S.-Iran Tensions," International Crisis Group.

7. "Iran Mobilizes Military to Fight Coronavirus," Iran Primer, last modified April 27, 2020, https://iranprimer.usip.org/blog/2020/mar/04/iran-mobilizes-military-fight-coronavirus.

8. Dalga Khatinoglu, "Iran Crude Oil Exports Drop to Less Than 250,000 Bpd in February," Radio Farda, March 2, 2020, https://en.radiofarda.com/a/iran-crude-oil-exports-drop-to-less-than-250–000-bpd-in-february/30464729.html; "IMF Says Iran's GDP Will Decline by Six Percent in 2020," Radio Farda, April 14, 2020, https://en.radiofarda.com/a/imf-says-iran-s-gdp-will-decline-by-six-percent-in-2020/30553143.html.

9. "Iran Sanctions: US Moves to Isolate 'Major' Banks," BBC News, October 9, 2020, https://www.bbc.com/news/world-middle-east-54476894; Editorial Board, "Iran's Covid-19 Death Toll Is Rising. Show Mercy, Mr. Trump," *New York Times*, October 13, 2020, https://www.nytimes.com/2020/10/13/opinion/iran-trump-sanctions-covid.html.

10. Garrett Nada, "Iran's Oil Price Plummets," Iran Primer, April 22, 2020, https://iranprimer.usip.org/blog/2020/apr/22/iran's-oil-prices-plummet.

11. Saheb Sadeghi, "Why Hassan Rouhani Ended Iran's Lockdown," *Foreign Policy*, May 5, 2020, https://foreignpolicy.com/2020/05/05/why-hassan-rouhani-ended-irans-lockdown/.

12. International Monetary Fund, *World Economic Outlook, October 2020: A Long and Difficult Ascent* (Washington, DC: International Monetary Fund, 2020), 58, https://www.imf.org/en/Publications/WEO/Issues/2020/09/30/world-economic-outlook-october-2020.

13. Alex Yacoubian, "Iran's Increasing Reliance on China," Iran Primer, October 13, 2020, https://iranprimer.usip.org/blog/2019/sep/11/irans-increasing-reliance-china; Farnaz Fassihi and Steven Lee Myers, "Defying U.S., China and Iran Near Trade and Military Partnership," *New York Times*, last modified November 30, 2020, https://www.nytimes.com/2020/07/11/world/asia/china-iran-trade-military-deal.html; Alam Saleh and Zakiyeh Yazdanshenas, "Iran's Pact with China Is Bad News for the West," *Foreign Policy*, August 9, 2020, https://foreignpolicy.com/2020/08/09/irans-pact-with-china-is-bad-news-for-the-west/; Farnaz Fassihi and Steven Lee Myers, "China, with $400 Billion Iran Deal, Could Deepen Influence in Mideast," *New York Times*, last modified March 29, 2021, https://www.nytimes.com/2021/03/27/world/middleeast/china-iran-deal.html?referringSource=articleShare.

14. "Iran: Thousands Arbitrarily Detained and at Risk of Torture in Chilling Post-Protest Crackdown," Amnesty International, December 16, 2019, https://www.amnesty.org/en/latest/news/2019/12/iran-thousands-arbitrarily-detained-and-at-risk-of-torture-in-chilling-post-protest-crackdown/; Farnaz Fassihi and Rick Gladstone, "With Brutal Crackdown, Iran Is Convulsed by Worst Unrest in 40 Years," *New York Times*, last modified December 3, 2019, https://www.nytimes.com/2019/12/01/world/middleeast/iran-protests-deaths.html.

15. Sadeghi, "Why Hassan Rouhani Ended Iran's Lockdown."
16. "COVID-19 Dashboard by the Center for Systems Science and Engineering," Johns Hopkins University & Medicine, Coronavirus Resource Center, accessed January 1, 2021, https://coronavirus.jhu.edu/map.html.
17. Nasser Karimi, "Iran Surpasses 20,000 Confirmed Deaths from the Coronavirus," Associated Press, August 19, 2020, https://apnews.com/63eea48e390cbd55effcad562 def89d9; Reuters Staff, "Rouhani Says 25 Million Iranians May Have Been Infected with Coronavirus," Reuters, July 18, 2020, https://www.reuters.com/article/us-health -coronavirus-iran/rouhani-says-25-million-iranians-may-have-been-infected -with-coronavirus-idUSKBN24J07V.
18. "Iran Reimposes Restrictive Virus Measures in Tehran," France 24, October 3, 2020, https://amp.france24.com/en/20201003-iran-reimposes-restrictive-virus-measures-in -tehran; "Iran Expands Anti-Virus Measures as Calls for Lockdown Grow," Jordan Times, November 1, 2020, http://www.jordantimes.com/news/region/iran%C2%A0expands -anti-virus-measures-calls-lockdown-grow.
19. Johns Hopkins University & Medicine, "COVID-19 Dashboard"; "Iran Official: Coronavirus Deaths Could Double if Guidelines Not Followed," Al-Monitor, October 15, 2020, https://www.al-monitor.com/pulse/originals/2020/10/iran-official-iraj -haririchi-coronavirus-death-toll.html; Dan De Luce and Leila Gharagozlou, "Iran's Covid Death Toll May Be Four Times the Government's Official Tally, Says Top Doctor," NBC News, October 28, 2020, https://www.nbcnews.com/health/health-news /iran-s-covid-death-toll-may-be-four-times-government-n1245028; "Parliament Speaker Tests Positive on Iran's Deadliest Virus Day," Al-Monitor, October 28, 2020, https://www.al-monitor.com/pulse/originals/2020/10/iran-parliament-speaker -ghalibaf-coronavirus-covid19-test.html.
20. Akhtar Mohammad Makoii and Peter Beaumont, "Afghanistan Braces for Coronavirus Surge as Migrants Pour Back from Iran," The Guardian, April 1, 2020, https:// www.theguardian.com/global-development/2020/apr/01/afghanistan-braces-for -coronavirus-surge-as-migrants-pour-back-from-iran.
21. Mujib Mashal, "Afghanistan's Next War," New York Times Magazine, last modified April 23, 2020, https://www.nytimes.com/interactive/2020/04/22/magazine/afghanistan -coronavirus.html; Sayed H. Mousavi et al., "The First COVID-19 Case in Afghanistan Acquired from Iran," The Lancet 20, no. 6 (June 1, 2020), https://www.thelancet .com/journals/laninf/article/PIIS1473-3099(20)30231-0/fulltext.
22. Andrew Quilty, "Afghanistan's Unseen Covid Crisis," Interpreter, Lowy Institute, August 12, 2020, https://www.lowyinstitute.org/the-interpreter/afghanistan-s-unseen -covid-crisis.
23. Quoted in David Zucchino and Fahim Abed, "'Covid Can't Compete.' In a Place Mired in War, the Virus Is an Afterthought," New York Times, December 20, 2020, https://www.nytimes.com/2020/12/20/world/asia/covid-afghanistan-coronavirus .html.
24. Zucchino and Abed, "'Covid Can't Compete.'"
25. Ezzatullah Mehrdad, Lindsey Kennedy, and Nathan Paul Southern, "In Afghanistan, the Coronavirus Could Be Deadlier Than War," Foreign Policy, April 17, 2020, https:// foreignpolicy.com/2020/04/17/in-afghanistan-coronavirus-could-be-deadlier-than -war/.
26. Ayaz Gul, "10 Million Afghans Likely Infected and Recovered from COVID-19: Survey," Voice of America, August 5, 2020, https://www.voanews.com/south-central -asia/10-million-afghans-likely-infected-and-recovered-covid-19-survey; Zucchino and Abed, "'Covid Can't Compete.'"
27. Quoted in Mashal, "Afghanistan's Next War."

28. *Surviving the Storm: Afghanistan Development Update July 2020* (Washington: World Bank Group, 2020), https://openknowledge.worldbank.org/bitstream/handle/10986 /34092/Afghanistan-Development-Update-Surviving-the-Storm.pdf?sequence =4&isAllowed=y.

29. Ben Farmer and Akhtar Makoii, "Food Shortages in Afghanistan as Coronavirus Worsens Country's Humanitarian Crisis," *Telegraph*, October 13, 2020, https://www .telegraph.co.uk/global-health/science-and-disease/food-shortages-afghanistan -coronavirus-worsens-countrys-humanitarian/; "Afghanistan: COVID-19 Impacts, High Food Prices, Reduced Income and Conflict Are Key Drivers of Food Insecurity," Integrated Food Security Phase Classification, November 2020, https://www .humanitarianresponse.info/sites/www.humanitarianresponse.info/files/documents /files/ipc_afghanistan_acutefoodinsec_2020aug2021march_report.pdf.

30. Robert Burns and Zeke Miller, "US Withdrawing Thousands of Troops from Iraq and Afghanistan," Associated Press, September 9, 2020, https://apnews.com/a6d9550ea12d 041436dda09f30873f55; Julian Borger, "Trump Reportedly Plans to Withdraw Nearly Half of US Troops in Afghanistan," *The Guardian*, November 17, 2020, https://www .theguardian.com/world/2020/nov/16/trump-plans-us-troops-withdrawal-afghanistan.

31. Susannah George, Aziz Tassal, and Sharif Hassan, "Coronavirus Sweeps Through Afghanistan's Security Forces," *Washington Post*, June 25, 2020, https://www .washingtonpost.com/world/asia_pacific/afghanistan-coronavirus-security-forces -military/2020/06/24/0063c828-b4e2-11ea-9a1d-d3db1cbe07ce_story.html.

32. Jarrett Blanc, "The Pandemic Further Complicates Afghanistan's Path to Peace," in *Conflict Zones in the Time of Coronavirus: War and War by Other Means*, edited by Jarrett Blanc, Frances Z. Brown, and Benjamin Press (New York: Carnegie Endowment for International Peace, 2020), https://carnegieendowment.org/2020/12/17 /pandemic-further-complicates-afghanistan-s-path-to-peace-pub-83464.

33. Abdul Qadir Sediqi and Orooj Hakimi, "Coronavirus Makes Taliban Realise They Need Health Workers Alive Not Dead," Reuters, March 18, 2020, https://www.reuters .com/article/health-coronavirus-taliban/coronavirus-makes-taliban-realise-they -need-health-workers-alive-not-dead-idUSL4N2BB2E3.

34. Andrew Watkins, "COVID-19 in Afghanistan: Compounding Crises," International Crisis Group, May 6, 2020, https://www.crisisgroup.org/asia/south-asia/afghanistan /covid-19-afghanistan-compounding-crises.

35. Lynne O'Donnell and Mirwais Khan, "Leader of Afghan Taliban Said to Be Gravely Ill with the Coronavirus," *Foreign Policy*, June 1, 2020, https://foreignpolicy.com/2020/06 /01/afghan-taliban-coronavirus-pandemic-akhunzada/; Jared Schwartz and Yelena Biberman, "A Divided Taliban Could Unleash a New Proxy War in Afghanistan," Atlantic Council, June 29, 2020, https://www.atlanticcouncil.org/blogs/new-atlanticist/a -divided-taliban-could-unleash-a-new-proxy-war-in-afghanistan/.

36. *Operation Inherent Resolve Lead Inspector General Report to the United States Congress* (Washington, DC: Department of Defense, 2020), 15–16, https://media.defense .gov/2020/Aug/04/2002469838/-1/-1/1/LEAD%20INSPECTOR%20GENERAL%20 FOR%20OPERATION%20INHERENT%20RESOLVE%20APRIL%201,%202020%20 -%20JUNE%2030,%202020.PDF.PDF; John Hannah, "Update: COVID-19 in Iraq," Foundation for Defense of Democracies, July 6, 2020, https://www.fdd.org/analysis /2020/07/06/update-covid-19-in-iraq/.

37. Johns Hopkins University & Medicine, "COVID-19 Dashboard."

38. Edith Lederer, "UN Envoy: Pandemic Increased Poverty in Iraq by over 10%," *Washington Post*, August 26, 2020, https://www.washingtonpost.com/world/middle _east/un-envoy-pandemic-increased-poverty-in-iraq-by-over-10percent/2020/08 /26/a19d9528-e7e8-11ea-bf44-0d31c85838a5_story.html; "Facing Pandemic, Eco-

nomic and Political Challenges, Iraq Government 'Operating in the Eyes of Multiple Storms at Once,'" news release, United Nations, August 26, 2020, https://news.un.org/en/story/2020/08/1071102.

39. Department of Defense, *Operation Inherent Resolve*, 16.
40. Humeyra Pamuk and Jonathan Landay, "Pompeo Says Soleimani Killing Part of New Strategy to Deter U.S. Foes," Reuters, January 13, 2020, https://www.reuters.com/article/us-iraq-security-pompeo-soleimani/pompeo-says-soleimani-killing-part-of-new-strategy-to-deter-u-s-foes-idUSKBN1ZC2I3.
41. "Coronavirus and Sanctions Hit Iran's Support of Proxies in Iraq," Reuters, July 2, 2020, https://www.reuters.com/article/us-iran-iraq-proxies-insight-idUSKBN2432EY; Colin Clarke and Ariane Tabatabai, "Why Iran Is Still Attacking American Troops During the Pandemic," Vox, April 22, 2020, https://www.vox.com/world/2020/4/22/21229509/coronavirus-iran-covid-19-attacks-us-troops-iraq.
42. Michael Knights, "Reacting Smartly to Harassing Tactics by Iraqi Militias," Washington Institute for Near East Policy, July 29, 2020, https://www.washingtoninstitute.org/policy-analysis/view/reacting-smartly-to-harassing-tactics-by-iraqi-militias; Katie Bo Williams, "Iran Is Our Top Priority, Says Senior US Commander in Middle East," Defense One, August 12, 2020, https://www.defenseone.com/threats/2020/08/iran-our-top-priority-says-senior-us-commander-middle-east/167651/.
43. Department of Defense, *Operation Inherent Resolve*, 5, 15–16, 33.
44. Gordon Lubold and Michael Gordon, "U.S. to Cut Troop Presence in Iraq by About One-Third, Officials Say," *Wall Street Journal*, August 28, 2020, https://www.wsj.com/articles/u-s-to-cut-troop-presence-in-iraq-by-about-one-third-officials-say-11598625823?st=y7nfogqhwcg80r2&reflink=article_email_share; Lara Seligman, "General Announces Iraq, Afghanistan Troop Drawdowns as Trump Looks to Fulfill Campaign Pledge," Politico, September 9, 2020, https://www.politico.com/news/2020/09/09/iraq-troop-withdrawl-410723; "IntelBrief: Iran Gaining in Battle for Iraq," Soufan Center, October 20, 2020, https://thesoufancenter.org/intelbrief-iran-gaining-in-battle-for-iraq/; Barbara Starr, Ryan Browne, and Zachary Cohen, "US Announces Further Drawdown of Troops in Afghanistan and Iraq Before Biden Takes Office," CNN, November 17, 2020, https://www.cnn.com/2020/11/17/politics/afghanistan-iraq-withdrawal-pentagon/index.html.
45. Michael Knights and Alex Almeida, "Remaining and Expanding: The Recovery of Islamic State Operations in Iraq in 2019–2020," *CTC Sentinel* 13, no. 5 (May 2020), https://www.washingtoninstitute.org/uploads/Documents/opeds/Knights20200526-CTCSentinel.pdf.
46. Quoted in Gayle Tzemach Lemmon, "ISIS Is Using Coronavirus to Rebuild Its Terrorism Network in Iraq and Syria," NBC News, May 28, 2020, https://www.nbcnews.com/think/opinion/isis-using-coronavirus-rebuild-its-terrorism-network-iraq-syria-ncna1215941.
47. Brian Glyn Williams, "Islamic State Calls for Followers to Spread Coronavirus, Exploit Pandemic and Protests," The Conversation, June 23, 2020, https://theconversation.com/islamic-state-calls-for-followers-to-spread-coronavirus-exploit-pandemic-and-protests-136224.
48. Department of Defense, *Operation Inherent Resolve*, 18; Hollie McKay, "ISIS Launched More Than 100 Attacks in Iraq in August, a Sharp Uptick from Previous Month," Fox News, September 3, 2020, https://www.foxnews.com/world/isis-launches-more-than-100-attacks-in-iraq-throughout-august-a-sharp-uptick-from-previous-month.
49. "Amid COVID-19, ISIS Supporters Step Up Efforts to Reestablish Presence on Social Media," Memri, May 15, 2020, https://www.memri.org/jttm/amid-covid-19-isis-supporters-step-efforts-reestablish-presence-social-media; Hollie McKay, "How

ISIS Is Exploiting the Coronavirus Pandemic," Fox News, May 20, 2020, https://www
.foxnews.com/world/how-isis-is-exploiting-the-coronavirus-pandemic; David Choi,
"Fake N95 Face Masks Were Being Sold on This ISIS-Linked Website—and It Shows
How Terror Groups Are Using COVID-19 as a Propaganda Tool," *Business Insider*, August 29, 2020, https://www.businessinsider.com/fake-face-mask-website-isis-2020-8.

50. United Nations Secretary-General, "Secretary-General's Appeal for Global Cease-
fire," statement, March 23, 2020, https://www.un.org/sg/en/content/sg/statement
/2020-03-23/secretary-generals-appeal-for-global-ceasefire.

51. "Pope Francis Calls for Immediate Global Ceasefire," CDE News, March 29, 2020,
https://cde.news/pope-francis-calls-for-immediate-global-ceasefire/.

52. "Classification of Fragile and Conflict-Affected Situations," World Bank, last modified July 9, 2020, https://www.worldbank.org/en/topic/fragilityconflictviolence/brief
/harmonized-list-of-fragile-situations.

53. "Colombia's ELN Rebels Scrap Ceasefire," France 24, April 27, 2020, https://www
.france24.com/en/20200427-colombia-s-eln-rebels-scrap-ceasefire.

54. Daniel Finnan, "Mixed Reception to Call for Covid-19 Ceasefire in Cameroon's Anglophone Regions," Radio France Internationale, March 27, 2020, https://www.rfi.fr/en
/africa/20200327-mixed-reception-to-call-for-coronavirus-ceasefire-in-cameroon-s
-anglophone-regions; Ngala Killian Chimtom, "Cameroon's Deadly Mix of War and
Coronavirus," BBC, May 10, 2020, https://www.bbc.com/news/world-africa-52551848;
Ewelina Ochab, "Is the Cameroon Ceasefire Talk Nearing amid Covid-19 Pandemic?,"
Forbes, July 5, 2020, https://www.forbes.com/sites/ewelinaochab/2020/07/05/is-the
-cameroon-ceasefire-talk-nearing-amid-covid-19-pandemic/#739a93b75255; Ilaria
Allegrozzi, "Renewed Attacks on Aid Workers in Cameroon," Human Rights Watch,
June 4, 2020, https://www.hrw.org/news/2020/06/04/renewed-attacks-aid-workers
-cameroon.

55. "Covid-19 Raises the Risks of Violent Conflict," *The Economist*, June 18, 2020, https://
www.economist.com/international/2020/06/18/covid-19-raises-the-risks-of-violent
-conflict.

56. Edith Lederer, "UN: Libya at 'Turning Point,' COVID Heading 'Out of Control,'"
ABC News, September 2, 2020, https://abcnews.go.com/US/wireStory/libya-turning
-point-covid-heading-control-72781541; "'Which Death Is Going to Be Worse?'
Coronavirus Invades a Conflict Zone," *New York Times*, April 13, 2020, video, 7:43,
https://www.nytimes.com/video/world/africa/100000007058303/coronavirus-libya
-war.html?playlistId=video/latest-video; Hanan Salah, "Despite Covid-19, Libya
War Rages, with Civilians at Risk," Human Rights Watch, May 7, 2020, https://www
.hrw.org/news/2020/05/07/despite-covid-19-libya-war-rages-civilians-risk.

57. Quoted in Frederic Wehrey, "The Pandemic's Ripple Effects Are Among Libya's Many
Miseries," in *Conflict Zones in the Time of Coronavirus*, ed. Blanc, Brown, and Press.

58. Nick Cumming-Bruce and Declan Walsh, "Libya Cease-Fire Raises Hopes for Full
Peace Deal," *New York Times*, October 23, 2020, https://www.nytimes.com/2020/10
/23/world/middleeast/libya-ceasefire.html; Vivian Yee and Mohammed Abdusamee,
"After a Decade of Chaos, Can a Splintered Libya Be Made Whole?," *New York Times*,
February 16, 2021, https://www.nytimes.com/2021/02/16/world/middleeast/libya
-government-qaddafi.html.

59. Declan Walsh, "As Fighting Surges, Yemen Is Hit with 1st Cluster of Covid-19 Infections," *New York Times*, April 29, 2020, https://www.nytimes.com/2020/04/29/world
/middleeast/yemen-saudi-coronavirus-cholera.html; Ben Hubbard and Saeed
Al-Batati, "Saudi Arabia Declares Cease-Fire in Yemen, Citing Fears of Coronavirus," *New York Times*, April 8, 2020, https://www.nytimes.com/2020/04/08/world
/middleeast/saudi-yemen-ceasefire-coronavirus.html; Declan Walsh, "War Within

War: As Saudi Prince Edges Away from Yemen, His Allies Feud," *New York Times*, April 28, 2020, https://www.nytimes.com/2020/04/28/world/middleeast/yemen -separatists-saudi-arabia.html; "Deadly Consequences: Obstruction of Aid in Yemen During Covid-19," Human Rights Watch, September 14, 2020, https://www.hrw.org /report/2020/09/14/deadly-consequences/obstruction-aid-yemen-during-covid-19.

60. Ahmed Nagi, "Yemen's Devastating War Continues Despite an Unchecked Pandemic," in *Conflict Zones in the Time of Coronavirus*, ed. Blanc, Brown, and Press.

61. Comments by Lisa Grande at "Online Event: Crisis and Survival Amidst COVID-19 in Yemen," Center for Strategic and International Studies, April 29, 2020, https:// www.csis.org/analysis/online-event-crisis-and-survival-amidst-covid-19-yemen; Jane Arraf, "Yemen, Already Facing a Health Crisis, Confirms Its 1st Coronavirus Case," NPR, April 10, 2020, https://health.wusf.usf.edu/npr-health/2020–04–10 /yemen-already-facing-a-health-crisis-confirms-its-1st-coronavirus-case#stream/0.

62. Bethan McKernan, "Yemen: In a Country Stalked by Disease, Covid Barely Registers," *The Guardian*, November 27, 2020, https://www.theguardian.com/global -development/2020/nov/27/yemen-disease-covid-war.

63. Sam Kiley, "Yemen Coronavirus: Experts Fear Nation Could Suffer One of the World's Worst Outbreaks," CNN, June 5, 2020, https://www.msn.com/en-us/news/world /yemen-coronavirus-experts-fear-nation-could-suffer-one-of-the-worlds-worst -outbreaks/ar-BB152Re0.

64. Diana Hodali, "Coronavirus in Yemen: A Country on the Brink," Deutsche Welle, June 2, 2020, https://www.dw.com/en/coronavirus-in-yemen-a-country-on-the-brink /a-53651670.

65. "UN Slashes Health Care in Yemen Due to Lack of Funding," *Al-Monitor*, September 23, 2020, https://www.al-monitor.com/pulse/contents/afp/2020/09/yemen-conflict -un-aid.html; Edith Lederer, "UN Aid Chief: Funding Shortage Cuts Aid to 4 Million Yemenis," Associated Press, October 15, 2020, https://apnews.com/article/famine -yemen-saudi-arabia-united-nations-united-arab-emirates-8a1c512273b8d0aafe4f9 a6130c67a80.

66. United Nations Secretary-General, "As COVID-19 Fuels Conflict, Threatens International Security, Global Unity to Fight Terrorism Needed More Than Ever, Secretary-General Tells Aqaba Process Meeting," press release, September 2, 2020, https://www .un.org/press/en/2020/sgsm20227.doc.htm.

67. Jonathan Moyer and Oliver Kaplan, "Will the Coronavirus Fuel Conflict?," *Foreign Policy*, July 6, 2020, https://foreignpolicy.com/2020/07/06/coronavirus-pandemic -fuel-conflict-fragile-states-economy-food-prices/; Barry Hughes, Devin Joshi, Jonathan Moyer, Timothy Sisk, and José Solórzano, *Strengthening Governance Globally: Patterns of Potential Human Progress* (Boulder, CO: Frederick S. Pardee Center for International Futures, University of Denver, 2014), https://pardee.du.edu/sites/default /files/PPHP5_Full_Volume.pdf.

68. Drazen Jorgic and Uriel Sanchez, "As Mexico Focuses on Coronavirus, Drug Gang Violence Rises," Reuters, June 18, 2020, https://www.reuters.com/article/us-health -coronavirus-mexico-cartels/as-mexico-focuses-on-coronavirus-drug-gang-violence -rises-idUSKBN23P1VO.

69. Nick Schifrin and Layla Quran, "Despite Spiraling Coronavirus Crisis, Syria's 'Government Is Not Concerned at All,'" PBS, September 14, 2020, https://www.pbs.org /newshour/show/despite-spiraling-coronavirus-crisis-syrias-government-is-not -concerned-at-all; George Baghdadi, "Syria May Only Be Counting 1.25% of Its Actual Coronavirus Deaths, Study Says," CBS News, September 15, 2020, https://www .cbsnews.com/news/coronavirus-in-syria-deaths-under-counted-amid-civil-war -bashar-assad-regime-blames-sanctions/.

70. Muriel Asseburg, Hamidreza Azizi, Galip Dalay, and Moritz Pieper, "The Covid-19 Pandemic and Conflict Dynamics in Syria: Neither a Turning Point Nor an Overall Determinant," German Institute for International and Security Affairs, May 2020, https://www.swp-berlin.org/10.18449/2020C21/; Will Todman, "Assad Attempts to Weaponize COVID-19 in Syria," *The Hill,* May 27, 2020, https://thehill.com/opinion /international/498943-assad-attempts-to-weaponize-covid-19-in-syria; Jen Kirby, "Syria's Idlib Was Already a Humanitarian Nightmare. Now the Coronavirus Has Arrived," Vox, July 16, 2020, https://www.vox.com/2020/7/16/21322665/syria-idlib -coronavirus-humanitarian-nightmare; Margaret Besheer, "UN Struggles to Meet Humanitarian Needs in Northern Syria," Voice of America, August 27, 2020, https:// www.voanews.com/middle-east/un-struggles-meet-humanitarian-needs-northern -syria; Sultan al-Kanj, "Humanitarian Disaster Looms over Syria's Idlib amid COVID-19 Surge," *Al-Monitor,* November 26, 2020, https://www.al-monitor.com /pulse/originals/2020/11/syria-idlib-hospitals-surge-coronavirus-cases.html.

71. Richard Gowan, "What's Happened to the UN Secretary-General's COVID-19 Ceasefire Call?," International Crisis Group, June 16, 2020, https://www.crisisgroup .org/global/whats-happened-un-secretary-generals-covid-19-ceasefire-call.

72. Richard Gowan and Louise Riis Andersen, "Peacekeeping in the Shadow of Covid-19 Era," ReliefWeb, June 12, 2020, https://reliefweb.int/report/world/peacekeeping -shadow-covid-19-era.

73. Julian Borger, "US Blocks Vote on UN's Bid for Global Ceasefire over Reference to WHO," *The Guardian,* May 8, 2020, https://www.theguardian.com/world/2020/may /08/un-ceasefire-resolution-us-blocks-who.

74. Interview with a French official, August 2020.

75. "De-escalating the New Nagorno-Karabakh War," International Crisis Group, October 2, 2020, https://www.crisisgroup.org/europe-central-asia/caucasus/nagorno -karabakh-conflict/containing-violence-south-caucasus.

76. "Why 'America First' Makes Wars in Other Places More Likely," *The Economist,* October 8, 2020, https://www.economist.com/leaders/2020/10/10/why-america-first -makes-wars-in-other-places-more-likely.

77. Anton Troianovski and Carlotta Gall, "In Nagorno-Karabakh Peace Deal, Putin Applied a Deft New Touch," *New York Times,* December 1, 2020, https://www.nytimes .com/2020/12/01/world/europe/nagorno-karabakh-putin-armenia-azerbaijan.html ?referringSource=articleShare.

78. "Greece Reports First Coronavirus Case in Moria Migrant Camp on Lesbos," Reuters, September 2, 2020, https://www.reuters.com/article/us-health-coronavirus -greece-migrants/greece-reports-first-coronavirus-case-in-moria-camp-on-lesbos -idUSKBN25T1CA; Miriam Berger, "Refugee Camps Have Avoided the Worst of the Pandemic. That Could Be About to Change," *Washington Post,* September 2, 2020, https://www.washingtonpost.com/world/2020/09/01/refugee-camps-have-avoided -worst-pandemic-that-could-be-about-change/.

79. Patrick Kingsley, "Fire Destroys Most of Europe's Largest Refugee Camp, on Greek Island of Lesbos," *New York Times,* September 9, 2020, https://www.nytimes.com /2020/09/09/world/europe/fire-refugee-camp-lesbos-moria.html.

80. Melissa Bell, Elinda Labropoulou, and Chris Liakos, "Riot Police Deployed to New Lesbos Refugee Camp After Fire," CNN, September 11, 2020, https://www.cnn.com /2020/09/11/europe/lesbos-fire-migants-moria-camp-intl/index.html.

81. Helena Smith, "Greek Riot Police Fire Teargas at Refugees Campaigning to Leave Lesbos," *The Guardian,* September 12, 2020, https://www.theguardian.com/world/2020 /sep/12/greek-riot-police-fire-teargas-at-refugees-campaigning-to-leave-lesbos; Sofia Barbarani, "After Moria Fire, Refugees Decry Conditions in New Camp on Lesbos,"

Al Jazeera, September 18, 2020, https://www.aljazeera.com/news/2020/09/moria-fire
-refugees-decry-conditions-camp-lesbos-200918125444995.html.

82. "The Number of International Migrants Reaches 272 Million, Continuing an Upward
Trend in All World Regions, Says UN," United Nations Department of Economic and
Social Affairs, September 17, 2019, https://www.un.org/development/desa/en/news
/population/international-migrant-stock-2019.html.

83. *Global Trends: Forced Displacement in 2019* (Geneva: United Nations High Commissioner for Refugees, 2020), https://www.unhcr.org/5ee200e37.pdf.

84. Hannah Beech and Ben Hubbard, "Unprepared for the Worst: World's Most Vulnerable Brace for Virus," *New York Times*, March 26, 2020, https://www.nytimes
.com/2020/03/26/world/asia/coronavirus-refugees-camps-bangladesh.html
?searchResultPosition=19; Audrey Wilson, "The Coronavirus Threatens Some More
Than Others," *Foreign Policy*, April 14, 2020, https://foreignpolicy.com/2020/04
/14/coronavirus-pandemic-humanitarian-crisis-world-most-vulnerable-refugees
-migrant-workers-global-poor/.

85. Anna Bruce-Lockhart, "'Death on an Appalling Scale'—David Miliband on the
Threat of COVID-19 to Refugees," World Economic Forum, April 9, 2020, https://
www.weforum.org/agenda/2020/04/coronavirus-david-miliband-covid-refugees/.

86. Berger, "Refugee Camps Have Avoided the Worst of the Pandemic"; "COVID-19
Brief: Impact on Refugees," U.S. Global Leadership Coalition, last modified December 8, 2020, https://www.usglc.org/coronavirus/refugees/.

87. Quoted in Berger, "Refugee Camps Have Avoided the Worst of the Pandemic."

88. "COVID-19 Brief: Impact on Refugees."

89. Helen Dempster et al., "Locked Down and Left Behind: The Impact of COVID-19
on Refugees' Economic Inclusion," Refugees International, July 8, 2020, https://
www.refugeesinternational.org/reports/2020/7/6/locked-down-and-left-behind-the
-impact-of-covid-19-on-refugees-economic-inclusion.

90. Daniel Gorevan, *Downward Spiral: The Economic Impact of Covid-19 on Refugees
and Displaced People* (Oslo: Norwegian Refugee Council, 2020), https://www.nrc.no
/globalassets/pdf/reports/nrc_downward-spiral_covid-19_report.pdf.

91. Kemal Kirişci and M. Murat Erdogan, "Turkey and COVID-19: Don't Forget Refugees," Brookings Institution, April 20, 2020, https://www.brookings.edu/blog/order
-from-chaos/2020/04/20/turkey-and-covid-19-dont-forget-refugees/.

92. Bel Trew, "Coronavirus Cases Surge Among Refugees in Middle East as Pandemic
Pushes Most Vulnerable Deeper into Poverty," *Independent*, September 20, 2020,
https://www.independent.co.uk/independentpremium/world/coronavirus-cases
-surge-among-refugees-middle-east-pandemic-pushes-most-vulnerable-deeper
-poverty-b506833.html.

93. Dempster et al., "Locked Down and Left Behind."

94. Nidhi Subbaraman, "'Distancing Is Impossible': Refugee Camps Race to Avert
Coronavirus Catastrophe," *Nature*, April 24, 2020, https://www.nature.com/articles
/d41586-020-01219-6.

95. Berger, "Refugee Camps Have Avoided the Worst of the Pandemic."

96. Quoted in Raquel Carvalho, "Rohingya Refugees in Bangladesh Struggle with Fear
and Stigma amid Coronavirus," *South China Morning Post*, September 13, 2020,
https://www.scmp.com/week-asia/health-environment/article/3101271/rohingya
-refugees-bangladesh-struggle-fear-and-stigma.

97. *Cross-Border Human Mobility amid and After COVID-19* (Geneva: International
Organization for Migration, 2020), https://www.iom.int/sites/default/files/defaul/pp
_cross-border_human_mobility_amid_and_after_covid-19_policy.pdf.

98. Rebecca Root, "Around the World, Migrants and Refugees Are Stranded Between

Closed Borders," DevEx, April 29, 2020, https://www.devex.com/news/around-the
-world-migrants-and-refugees-are-stranded-between-closed-borders-97089; "1 Per
Cent of Humanity Displaced: UNHCR Global Trends Report," United Nations High
Commissioner for Refugees, June 18, 2020, https://www.unhcr.org/en-us/news/press
/2020/6/5ee9db2e4/1-cent-humanity-displaced-unhcr-global-trends-report.html;
"How to Save the U.S. Refugee Admissions Program," International Crisis Group, September 12, 2018, https://www.crisisgroup.org/united-states/002-how-save-us-refugee
-admissions-program; "U.S. Annual Refugee Resettlement Ceilings and Number of
Refugees Admitted, 1980–Present," Migration Policy Institute, last modified September 30, 2020, https://www.migrationpolicy.org/programs/data-hub/charts/us-annual
-refugee-resettlement-ceilings-and-number-refugees-admitted-united; "COVID-19
Brief: Impact on Refugees."

CHAPTER 10: DEMAGOGUES AND DEMOCRACY

1. Isabella Gomez Sarmiento, "How Evo Morales Made Bolivia a Better Place . . . Before He Fled the Country," NPR, November 26, 2019, https://www.npr.org/sections
/goatsandsoda/2019/11/26/781199250/how-evo-morales-made-bolivia-a-better
-place-before-he-was-forced-to-flee.
2. Organization of American States, "Final Report of the Audit of the Elections in Bolivia: Intentional Manipulation and Serious Irregularities Made It Impossible to Val-
idate the Results," press release, December 4, 2019, https://www.oas.org/en/media
_center/press_release.asp?sCodigo=E-109/19; Laurel Wamsley and Barbara Campbell, "In Bolivia, a Power Vacuum and Chaos After Morales Resigns as President and
Departs," NPR, November 11, 2019, https://www.npr.org/2019/11/11/778291867/in
-bolivia-a-power-vacuum-and-chaos-after-morales-resigns-as-president.
3. Jon Lee Anderson, "The Fall of Evo Morales," *New Yorker*, March 16, 2020, https://
www.newyorker.com/magazine/2020/03/23/the-fall-of-evo-morales.
4. Philip Reeves, "Bolivia Twice Delays Elections, Citing Pandemic," NPR, August 9,
2020, https://www.npr.org/2020/08/09/900703256/bolivia-twice-delays-elections
-citing-pandemic.
5. "Bolivia: Interim Government Adopts Abusive Measures," Human Rights Watch, November 19, 2019, https://www.hrw.org/news/2019/11/19/bolivia-interim-government
-adopts-abusive-measures; Anatoly Kurmanaev, "In Bolivia, Interim Leader Sets
Conservative, Religious Tone," *New York Times*, November 16, 2019, https://www
.nytimes.com/2019/11/16/world/americas/bolivia-anez-morales.html; Mac Margo-
lis, "Bolivia's Acting President Has Toxic Ambitions," Bloomberg, February 5, 2020,
https://www.bloomberg.com/opinion/articles/2020-02-05/bolivia-s-acting-president
-has-toxic-ambitions.
6. Morales had removed the Bible from official government ceremonies in favor of acts hon-
oring an Andean earth deity. Stephen Sorace, "Bolivia Interim President Declares 'Bible
Has Returned to the Palace' amid Growing Uncertainty," Fox News, November 13, 2019,
https://www.foxnews.com/world/bolivia-interim-president-bible-palace-elections.
7. Christopher Sabatini, "Democracy Delayed: COVID-19's Effect on Latin America's
Politics," Chatham House, May 19, 2020, https://www.chathamhouse.org/2020/05
/democracy-delayed-covid-19s-effect-latin-americas-politics.
8. "Bolivia Needs an Election, but Covid-19 Makes That Hard," *The Economist*, May
16, 2020, https://www.economist.com/the-americas/2020/05/16/bolivia-needs-an
-election-but-covid-19-makes-that-hard; Jihan Abdalla, "Bolivia's Parliament Passes
Law Calling for Elections in 90 Days," Al Jazeera, May 1, 2020, https://www.aljazeera
.com/news/2020/5/1/bolivias-parliament-passes-law-calling-for-elections-in-90-days.

9. Freedom House, "Bolivia: Supreme Decree Threatens Freedom of Expression," press release, May 14, 2020, https://freedomhouse.org/article/bolivia-supreme-decree-threatens-freedom-expression.

10. "Free Speech Under Threat in Bolivia During COVID-19 Pandemic," CIVICUS, June 5, 2020, https://monitor.civicus.org/updates/2020/05/06/free-speech-under-threat-bolivia-during-covid-19-pandemic/.

11. "Bolivia Needs an Election, but Covid-19 Makes That Hard."

12. Laurence Blair and Cindy Jiménez Bercerra, "Is Bolivia's 'Interim' President Using the Pandemic to Outstay Her Welcome?," *The Guardian,* June 1, 2020, https://www.theguardian.com/global-development/2020/jun/01/bolivia-president-jeanine-anez-coronavirus-elections; César Muñoz Acebes, *Justice as a Weapon: Political Persecution in Bolivia* (Washington, DC: Human Rights Watch, 2020), https://www.hrw.org/report/2020/09/11/justice-weapon/political-persecution-bolivia#.

13. Abdalla, "Bolivia's Parliament Passes Law Calling for Elections in 90 Days."

14. *Women and Men in the Informal Economy: A Statistical Picture* (Geneva: International Labour Office, 2018), 87, https://www.ilo.org/global/publications/books/WCMS_626831/lang—en/index.htm.

15. María Silvia Trigo, Anatoly Kurmanaev, and José María León Cabrera, "With Officials' Backing, Dubious Virus Remedies Surge in Latin America," *New York Times,* July 23, 2020, https://www.nytimes.com/2020/07/23/world/americas/chlorine-coronavirus-bolivia-latin-america.html. Other data on COVID-19 cases and deaths is derived from COVID-19 Dashboard, Center for Systems Science and Engineering, Johns Hopkins University & Medicine, Coronavirus Resource Center, accessed November 27, 2020, https://coronavirus.jhu.edu/map.html; "Mortality Analyses," Johns Hopkins University & Medicine, Coronavirus Resource Center, accessed November 27, 2020, https://coronavirus.jhu.edu/data/mortality.

16. Jin Wu et al., "412,000 Missing Deaths: Tracking the True Toll of the Coronavirus Outbreak," *New York Times,* last modified November 27, 2020, https://www.nytimes.com/interactive/2020/04/21/world/coronavirus-missing-deaths.html.

17. John Otis and Kejal Vyas, "In Bolivia Election, Voters Embrace Another Socialist After Ouster of Evo Morales," *Wall Street Journal,* October 20, 2020, https://www.wsj.com/articles/in-bolivia-election-voters-embrace-another-socialist-after-ouster-of-evo-morales-11603210468; Anastasia Moloney and Wara Vargas, "Bolivians Forced to Get Creative as COVID-19 Hits Cash-in-Hand Workers," Reuters, March 22, 2021, https://www.reuters.com/article/us-livelihoods-coronavirus-bolivia/bolivians-forced-to-get-creative-as-covid-19-hits-cash-in-hand-workers-idUSKBN2BF0D8.

18. María Silvia Trigo, Anatoly Kurmanaev, and Allison McCann, "As Politicians Clashed, Bolivia's Pandemic Death Rate Soared," *New York Times,* August 22, 2020, https://www.nytimes.com/2020/08/22/world/americas/virus-bolivia.html.

19. Trigo, Kurmanaev, and McCann, "As Politicians Clashed, Bolivia's Pandemic Death Rate Soared."

20. "Bolivia President Jeanine Anez Tests Positive for Coronavirus," NDTV, July 10, 2020, https://www.ndtv.com/world-news/bolivia-president-jeanine-anez-tests-positive-for-coronavirus-2260181.

21. Gideon Long, "Bolivia Delays Presidential Election Again over Pandemic," *Financial Times,* July 23, 2020, https://www.ft.com/content/de1fbf40–87a3–4247-a569-c15a27beb68d.

22. María Silvia Trigo and Anatoly Kurmanaev, "Bolivia Under Blockade as Protesters Choke Access to Cities," *New York Times,* August 7, 2020, https://www.nytimes.com/2020/08/07/world/americas/bolivia-roadblock-blockade.html; Trigo, Kurmanaev, and McCann, "As Politicians Clashed, Bolivia's Pandemic Death Rate Soared."

23. Anthony Faiola and Ana Vanessa Herrero, "Protesters Paralyze Bolivia over Elec-

tion Delays, Threaten Escalation," *Washington Post*, August 12, 2020, https://www
.washingtonpost.com/world/the_americas/bolivia-protest-blockade-anez-evo
-coronavirus/2020/08/11/7ffceb50-db48-11ea-809e-b8be57ba616e_story.html.

24. Trigo, Kurmanaev, and McCann, "As Politicians Clashed, Bolivia's Pandemic Death
Rate Soared."

25. Andre Pagliarini, "Bolivia's Covid-19 Election Nightmare Is a Warning," *New Republic*, July 30, 2020, https://newrepublic.com/article/158666/bolivias-covid-19-election
-nightmare-warning; "Bolivia Needs an Election, but Covid-19 Makes That Hard."

26. Ryan Dube, "Bolivia's Interim Leader Exits Election Race to Prevent Morales Party
Victory," *Wall Street Journal*, September 18, 2020, https://www.wsj.com/articles
/bolivias-interim-leader-exits-election-race-to-prevent-morales-party-victory
-11600441630.

27. Brendan O'Boyle, "The Lesson from Bolivia for Latin American Politics," *New York
Times*, October 27, 2020, https://www.nytimes.com/2020/10/27/opinion/bolivia
-election-arce-morales.html.

28. Julie Turkewitz, "How Bolivia Overcame a Crisis and Held a Clean Election," *New
York Times*, October 23, 2020, https://www.nytimes.com/2020/10/23/world/americas
/boliva-election-result.html.

29. Quoted in Turkewitz, "How Bolivia Overcame a Crisis and Held a Clean Election."

30. Samuel P. Huntington, *The Third Wave: Democratization in the Late Twentieth Century* (Norman: University of Oklahoma Press, 1991); Stephan Haggard and Robert
Kaufman, "Democratization During the Third Wave," *Annual Review of Political
Science* 19 (May 2016): 125–41, https://www.annualreviews.org/doi/full/10.1146
/annurev-polisci-042114-015137.

31. Larry Diamond, "The Global Crisis of Democracy," *Wall Street Journal*, May 17,
2019, https://www.wsj.com/articles/the-global-crisis-of-democracy-11558105463.

32. Anna Lührmann et al., *Autocratization Surges—Resistance Grows: Democracy Report
2020* (Gothenburg: V-Dem Institute, 2020), 10, https://www.v-dem.net/media/filer
_public/de/39/de39af54-0bc5-4421-89ae-fb20dcc53dba/democracy_report.pdf.

33. Anna Lührmann and Staffan Lindberg, "A Third Wave of Autocratization Is Here:
What Is New About It?," *Democratization* 26, no. 7 (January 2019): 1095–113,
https://www.tandfonline.com/doi/full/10.1080/13510347.2019.1582029?scroll
=top&needAccess=true.

34. Christopher Brandt et al., *Freedom in the World 2019: Democracy in Retreat* (Washington, DC: Freedom House, 2019), https://freedomhouse.org/report/freedom
-world/2019/democracy-retreat.

35. Lührmann et al., *Autocratization Surges—Resistance Grows*, 9, 13–14; Larry Diamond, "Democratic Regression in Comparative Perspective: Scope, Methods, and
Causes," *Democratization*, September 15, 2020, https://www.tandfonline.com/doi
/full/10.1080/13510347.2020.1807517?src=.

36. Bruce Jones and Torrey Taussig, *Democracy & Disorder: The Struggle for Influence in
the New Geopolitics* (Washington, DC: Brookings Institution, 2019), 22–23, https://
www.brookings.edu/wp-content/uploads/2019/02/FP_20190226_democracy
_report_WEB.pdf; According to V-Dem's data, eighteen of twenty-four countries that
"autocratized" between 2008 and 2018 had societies that were highly polarized and/or
had a populist holding the office of president or prime minister. See Lührmann et al.,
Autocratization Surges—Resistance Grows, 21.

37. Larry Diamond, *Ill Winds: Saving Democracy from Russian Rage, Chinese Ambition, and
American Complacency* (New York: Penguin Press, 2019), chap. 3; Jones and Taussig,
Democracy & Disorder, 23–26; Lührmann et al., *Autocratization Surges—Resistance
Grows*, 16–17.

38. Jones and Taussig, *Democracy & Disorder,* 10.

39. Diamond, *Ill Winds,* chap. 6; Philip Zelikow, Eric Edelman, Kristofer Harrison, and Celeste Ward Gventer, "The Rise of Strategic Corruption: How States Weaponize Graft," *Foreign Affairs,* July/August 2020, https://www.foreignaffairs.com/articles/united-states /2020-06-09/rise-strategic-corruption.

40. Diamond, *Ill Winds,* chap. 7; Jones and Taussig, *Democracy & Disorder,* 28–30.

41. Jones and Taussig, *Democracy & Disorder,* 13.

42. Diamond, *Ill Winds,* chap. 5; David Montgomery, "The Abnormal Presidency," *Washington Post,* November 10, 2020, https://www.washingtonpost.com/graphics/2020 /lifestyle/magazine/trump-presidential-norm-breaking-list/?itid=hp-banner-main.

43. Amanda Edgell et al., "An Update on Pandemic Backsliding: Democracy Four Months After the Beginning of the Covid-19 Pandemic," V-Dem Institute, June 30, 2020, https://www.v-dem.net/media/filer_public/b9/2e/b92e59da-2a06–4d2e -82a1-b0a8dece4af7/v-dem_policybrief-24_update-pandemic-backsliding_200702 .pdf; "Pandemic Backsliding: Democracy During COVID-19 (March to September 2020)," V-Dem Institute, last modified September 2020, https://www.v-dem.net/en /analysis/PanDem/.

44. Lian Buan, "Duterte's Special Powers Bill Punishes Fake News by Jail Time, up to P1-M Fine," Rappler, March 24, 2020, https://www.rappler.com/nation/duterte-special -powers-bill-coronavirus-fines-fake-news; Julie McCarthy, "Concerns in Philippines After Duterte Given Emergency Powers to Fight COVID-19 Spread," NPR, March 24, 2020, https://www.npr.org/sections/coronavirus-live-updates/2020/03/24/820906636 /concerns-in-philippines-after-duterte-given-emergency-powers-to-fight-covid-19 -s; Manuel Mogato and Vince Nonato, "Human Rights Groups: COVID-19 Crisis Not an Excuse to Stifle Dissent, Criticism," One News, March 26, 2020, https://www .onenews.ph/human-rights-groups-covid-19-crisis-not-an-excuse-to-stifle-dissent -criticism; Selam Gebrekidan, "For Autocrats, and Others, Coronavirus Is a Chance to Grab Even More Power," *New York Times,* March 30, 2020, https://www.nytimes .com/2020/03/30/world/europe/coronavirus-governments-power.html.

45. Jason Castaneda, "Why Duterte Wants to Extend His Covid-19 Emergency," *Asia Times,* June 9, 2020, https://asiatimes.com/2020/06/why-duterte-wants-to-extend -his-covid-19-emergency/; "Philippines Lawmakers Extend Duterte's Emergency Powers During Pandemic," *La Prensa Latina Media,* August 24, 2020, https://www .laprensalatina.com/philippines-lawmakers-extend-dutertes-emergency-powers -during-pandmic/; "Asia Today: Duterte Extends Virus Calamity Status by a Year," Associated Press, September 21, 2020, https://apnews.com/article/virus-outbreak -leni-robredo-philippines-asia-east-asia-28b530198c4f86cd7e40675285d2f3a5.

46. Rahul Mukherji, "Covid vs. Democracy: India's Illiberal Remedy," *Journal of Democracy* 31, no. 4 (October 2020): 91–105, https://www.journalofdemocracy.org/articles /covid-vs-democracy-indias-illiberal-remedy/.

47. Neil Devotta, "A Win for Democracy in Sri Lanka," *Journal of Democracy* 27, no. 1 (January 2016) 152–66, https://muse.jhu.edu/article/607624; "Sri Lanka's President Is Amassing Personal Power," *The Economist,* October 31, 2020, https://www .economist.com/asia/2020/10/31/sri-lankas-president-is-amassing-personal-power.

48. Dharisha Bastians and Kai Schultz, "Gotabaya Rajapaksa Wins Sri Lanka Presidential Election," *New York Times,* November 17, 2019, https://www.nytimes.com/2019/11 /17/world/asia/sri-lanka-Gotabaya-Rajapaksa-election.html.

49. "Sri Lanka Confirms First Case of Coronavirus: Health Official," Reuters, January 27, 2020, https://www.reuters.com/article/us-health-china-sri-lanka/sri-lanka-confirms-first-case -of-coronavirus-health-official-idUSKBN1ZQ1WF; "Coronavirus: Sri Lanka Reports Second Case," *The Hindu,* March 12, 2020, https://www.thehindu.com/news/international

/coronavirus-sri-lanka-reports-second-case/article31052303.ece; Ashkar Thasleem, "Sri Lanka Extends Nationwide Curfew to Fight Coronavirus Pandemic," Al Jazeera, March 23, 2020, https://www.aljazeera.com/news/2020/3/23/sri-lanka-extends-nationwide -curfew-to-fight-coronavirus-pandemic; "Asia Today: Sri Lanka Lifts Coronavirus Curfew," Associated Press, June 28, 2020, https://apnews.com/article/438fc5072f35ea28252d b7a1da3f9018.

50. Alan Keenan, "Sri Lanka's Other COVID-19 Crisis: Is Parliamentary Democracy at Risk?," International Crisis Group, May 29, 2020, https://www.crisisgroup.org/asia /south-asia/sri-lanka/sri-lankas-other-covid-19-crisis-parliamentary-democracy -risk.

51. "Sri Lanka: Human Rights Under Attack," Human Rights Watch, July 29, 2020, https://www.hrw.org/news/2020/07/29/sri-lanka-human-rights-under-attack; "Sri Lanka: Increasing Suppression of Dissent," Human Rights Watch, August 8, 2020, https://www.hrw.org/news/2020/08/08/sri-lanka-increasing-suppression-dissent.

52. Seerat Chabba, "Coronavirus Keeps Sri Lanka Without a Functioning Parliament," Deutsche Welle, May 29, 2020, https://www.dw.com/en/coronavirus-keeps-sri-lanka -without-a-functioning-parliament/a-53615108; Sarah Repucci and Amy Slipowitz, *Democracy Under Lockdown: The Impact of COVID-19 on the Global Struggle for Freedom* (Washington, DC: Freedom House, 2020), 5, https://freedomhouse.org /sites/default/files/2020–10/COVID-19_Special_Report_Final_.pdf.

53. Arjuna Ranawana, "Sri Lanka President, Brother Tighten Grip with Big Election Win," Reuters, August 6, 2020, https://www.reuters.com/article/us-sri-lanka-election-result /sri-lanka-president-brother-tighten-grip-with-big-election-win-idUSKCN25308L; Sudha Ramachandran, "Sri Lanka: The Rajapaksas Rise Again," *The Diplomat*, August 7, 2020, https://thediplomat.com/2020/08/sri-lanka-the-rajapaksas-rise-again-2/; Alan Keenan, "Sri Lanka: Landslide Win for the Rajapaksa Puts Democracy and Pluralism at Risk," International Crisis Group, August 12, 2020, https://www.crisisgroup .org/asia/south-asia/sri-lanka/sri-lanka-landslide-win-rajapaksa-puts-democracy-and -pluralism-risk.

54. Krishan Francis, "Sri Lanka Parliament Votes to Strengthen Presidential Power," Associated Press, October 22, 2020, https://apnews.com/article/sri-lanka-constitutions -constitutional-amendments-c984676aac7e6005cd7d81395ba8cb78; "Sri Lanka's President Is Amassing Personal Power."

55. Diamond, *Ill Winds*, 59–62.

56. Anna Lührmann et al., *Democracy Facing Global Challenges: V-Dem Annual Democracy Report 2019* (Gothenburg: V-Dem Institute, 2019), 22, https://www.v-dem.net/media /filer_public/99/de/99dedd73-f8bc-484c-8b91–44ba601b6e6b/v-dem_democracy _report_2019.pdf; Lührmann et al., *Autocratization Surges—Resistance Grows*, 13.

57. Zselyke Csaky, "Hungary's Troubling Coronavirus Response," Freedom House, April 6, 2020, https://freedomhouse.org/article/hungarys-troubling-coronavirus-response.

58. R. Daniel Kelemen, "Hungary Just Became a Coronavirus Autocracy," *Washington Post*, April 2, 2020, https://www.washingtonpost.com/politics/2020/04/02/hungary -just-became-coronavirus-autocracy/.

59. Benjamin Novak, "Hungary Moves to End Rule by Decree, but Orban's Powers May Stay," *New York Times*, June 16, 2020, https://www.nytimes.com/2020/06/16/world /europe/hungary-coronavirus-orban.html; Orsolya Lehotai, "Hungary's Democracy Is Still Under Threat," *Foreign Policy*, July 17, 2020, https://foreignpolicy.com/2020/07 /17/hungary-democracy-still-under-threat-orban-state-public-health-emergency -decree/.

60. "Hungary Reintroduces State of Emergency as Virus Surges," *Barron's*, November 3, 2020, https://www.barrons.com/news/hungary-reintroduces-state-of-emergency

-as-virus-surges-01604432403; "Hungary Declares State of Emergency, Announces COVID-19 Restrictions," Radio Free Europe/Radio Liberty, November 4, 2020, https://www.rferl.org/a/hungary-declares-state-of-emergency-announces-coronavirus-restrictions/30929220.html.

61. Do Kyung Ryuk, JeongHyeon Oh, and Yewon Sung, "Elections During a Pandemic: South Korea Shows How to Safely Hold a National Election During the COVID-19 Crisis," Wilson Center, May 19, 2020, https://www.wilsoncenter.org/blog-post/elections-during-pandemic-south-korea-shows-how-safely-hold-national-election-during.

62. Max Bearak, "Burundi Votes Wednesday in Presidential Election Despite Coronavirus Outbreak," *Washington Post*, May 19, 2020, https://www.washingtonpost.com/world/africa/burundi-votes-wednesday-in-presidential-election-despite-coronavirus-outbreak/2020/05/19/ae2619c6-9952-11ea-ad79-eef7cd734641_story.html; Cristina Krippahl, "Burundians Vote Despite Coronavirus Outbreak," Deutsche Welle, May 20, 2020, https://www.dw.com/en/burundians-vote-despite-coronavirus-outbreak/a-53479621; Hamza Mohamed, "Burundi Election Results: What Next?," Al Jazeera, May 26, 2020, https://www.aljazeera.com/news/2020/5/26/burundi-election-results-what-next.

63. Timothy McLaughlin, "Where the Pandemic Is Cover for Authoritarianism," *The Atlantic*, August 25, 2020, https://www.theatlantic.com/international/archive/2020/08/pandemic-protest-double-standard-authoritarianism/615622/.

64. Joanna Berendt and Marc Santora, "Pandemic Forces Poland to Delay Presidential Election," *New York Times*, May 7, 2020, https://www.nytimes.com/2020/05/07/world/europe/poland-presidential-election-coronavirus.html; "Poland Presidential Election Heads for Second Round," BBC News, June 29, 2020, https://www.bbc.com/news/world-europe-53215106; Loveday Morris, Rick Noack, and Dariusz Kalan, "Polish President Duda Narrowly Wins Reelection, Enabling the Continuation of a Far-Right Agenda," *Washington Post*, July 13, 2020, https://www.washingtonpost.com/world/europe/polish-president-duda-squeaks-a-second-term-electoral-commission-says/2020/07/13/838d4770-c486-11ea-a99f-3bbdffb1af38_story.html.

65. Elections were eventually held in twenty-four of these countries and territories. "Global Overview of COVID-19: Impact on Elections," International IDEA, accessed April 3, 2021, https://www.idea.int/news-media/multimedia-reports/global-overview-covid-19-impact-elections.

66. Praveen Menon, "New Zealand's Ardern Wins 'Historic' Re-Election for Crushing COVID-19," Reuters, October 16, 2020, https://www.reuters.com/article/uk-newzealand-election/new-zealands-ardern-wins-historic-re-election-for-crushing-covid-19-idUSKBN2712ZI.

67. "Powerful Ethiopian Party Accuses Government of Ethnic Crackdown," Reuters, November 20, 2018, https://www.reuters.com/article/us-ethiopia-politics/powerful-ethiopian-party-accuses-government-of-ethnic-crackdown-idUSKCN1NP1JN; Abdi Latif Dahir and Declan Walsh, "Why Is Ethiopia at War with Itself?," *New York Times*, November 5, 2020, https://www.nytimes.com/2020/11/05/world/africa/ethiopia-tigray-conflict-explained.html.

68. Dawit Endeshaw, "Ethiopia Postpones August Election Due to Coronavirus," Reuters, March 31, 2020, https://www.reuters.com/article/us-ethiopia-election/ethiopia-postpones-august-election-due-to-coronavirus-idUSKBN21I2QU.

69. "Steering Ethiopia's Tigray Crisis Away from Conflict," International Crisis Group, October 30, 2020, https://www.crisisgroup.org/africa/horn-africa/ethiopia/b162-steering-ethiopias-tigray-crisis-away-conflict.

70. Dino Mahtani and William Davison, "Ethiopia: Not Too Late to Stop Tigray Conflict from Unravelling Country," Africa Report, November 10, 2020, https://www

.theafricareport.com/49887/ethiopia-not-too-late-to-stop-tplf-conflict-from
-unravelling-country/.

71. Paul Schemm, "Ethiopia's Military Chief Calls WHO Head Tedros a Criminal
Supporting a Rebel Region," *Washington Post*, November 19, 2020, https://www
.washingtonpost.com/world/2020/11/19/ethiopia-who-tedros-criminal-military
-tigray/.

72. Cara Anna, "Ethiopia Declares Victory as Military Takes Tigray Capital," Associated Press, November 28, 2020, https://apnews.com/article/ethiopia-abiy-ahmed
-kenya-0fb8647516d9be83d45fee2f1e4d13ae; Teferi Mergo, "The War in Tigray Is a
Fight over Ethiopia's Past—and Future," *Foreign Policy*, December 18, 2020, https://
foreignpolicy.com/2020/12/18/the-war-in-tigray-is-a-fight-over-ethiopias-past-and
-future/; "Over 2 Million People Displaced by Conflict in Ethiopia's Tigray Region—
Local Official," Reuters, January 6, 2021, https://www.reuters.com/article/ethiopia
-conflict-idINKBN29B1KE.

CHAPTER 11: RIGHTS, ROBOTS, AND RESISTANCE

1. Arafat Mugabo, "Covid-19 Puts Hospitals on Alert, but Where Are Tools?," Rwanda
Today, March 13, 2020, https://rwandatoday.africa/news/Covid-19-puts-hospitals-
on-alert/4383214-5490102-9ne2b4/index.html; Osei Baffour Frimpong, Rigobert
Minani Bihuzo, and Richmond Commodore, *The COVID-19 Pandemic in Africa: Impact, Responses, and Lessons from Ghana, the Democratic Republic of the Congo, and
Rwanda* (Washington, DC: Wilson Center Africa Program, 2020), 3, https://www
.wilsoncenter.org/sites/default/files/media/uploads/documents/The%20COVID
-19%20Pandemic%20in%20Africa%20-%20Impact%20Responses%20and%20
Lessons.pdf.

2. Neil Edwards, "Rwanda's Successes and Challenges in Response to COVID-19," Atlantic Council, March 24, 2020, https://www.atlanticcouncil.org/blogs/africasource
/rwandas-successes-and-challenges-in-response-to-covid-19/; Jonathan Bower, Derek
Apell, Anna Twum, and Umulisa Adia, "Rwanda's Response to COVID-19 and Future
Challenges," International Growth Centre, May 19, 2020, https://www.theigc.org/blog
/rwandas-response-to-covid-19-and-future-challenges/.

3. Ignatius Ssuuna, "Limited COVID-19 Testing? Researchers in Rwanda Have an
Idea," *Washington Post*, August 13, 2020, https://www.washingtonpost.com/world
/africa/limited-covid-19-testing-researchers-in-rwanda-have-an-idea/2020/08/13
/288adc4a-dd34-11ea-b4f1-25b762cdbbf4_story.html; "Rwanda Turns to Mathe-
matical Approach to Enhance Coronavirus Testing," Voice of America, August 13,
2020, https://www.voanews.com/covid-19-pandemic/rwanda-turns-mathematical
-approach-enhance-coronavirus-testing; Leon Mutesa et al., "A Pooled Testing Strategy for Identifying SARS-CoV-2 at Low Prevalence," *Nature*, October 2020, https://
www.nature.com/articles/s41586-020-2885–5; Nicholas Bariyo, "Rwanda's Aggressive
Approach to Covid Wins Plaudits—and Warnings," *Wall Street Journal*, September 29,
2020, https://www.wsj.com/articles/rwandas-aggressive-approach-to-covid-wins
-plauditsand-warnings-11601372482?mod=hp_listb_pos1.

4. Clement Uwiringiyimana, "Rwanda Uses Drones to Help Catch Lockdown Trans-
gressors," *U.S. News & World Report*, April 17, 2020, https://www.usnews.com
/news/world/articles/2020-04-17/rwanda-uses-drones-to-help-catch-lockdown
-transgressors; Jason Beaubien, "Why Rwanda Is Doing Better Than Ohio When
It Comes to Controlling COVID-19," NPR, July 15, 2020, https://www.npr.org
/sections/goatsandsoda/2020/07/15/889802561/a-covid-19-success-story-in-rwanda
-free-testing-robot-caregivers; "COVID-19 Response in Rwanda: Use of Drones

in Community Awareness," World Health Organization Rwanda, July 20, 2020, https://www.afro.who.int/news/covid-19-response-rwanda-use-drones-community -awareness; Bariyo, "Rwanda's Aggressive Approach to Covid Wins Plaudits—and Warnings"; "Rwandan Drones Take to air with COVID-19 Messages," *ADF Magazine*, September 30, 2020, https://adf-magazine.com/2020/09/rwandan-drones-take-to-air -with-covid-19-messages/.

5. Beaubien, "Why Rwanda Is Doing Better Than Ohio."

6. "Rwanda Re-Imposes Strict Lockdown in Capital After COVID-19 Cases Surge," Reuters, January 19, 2021, https://www.reuters.com/article/uk-health-coronavirus -rwanda/rwanda-re-imposes-strict-lockdown-in-capital-after-covid-19-cases-surge -idUSKBN29O0WT; "COVID-19 Dashboard by the Center for Systems Science and Engineering," Johns Hopkins University & Medicine, Coronavirus Resource Center, accessed April 3, 2021, https://coronavirus.jhu.edu/map.html; "Mortality Analyses," Johns Hopkins University & Medicine, Coronavirus Resource Center, accessed April 3, 2021, https://coronavirus.jhu.edu/data/mortality.

7. "Rwanda," Freedom in the World 2020, Freedom House, accessed November 24, 2020, https://freedomhouse.org/country/rwanda/freedom-world/2020; Rodney Muhu- muza, "25 Years After Genocide, Rwanda's Kagame Is Praised, Feared," Associated Press, April 9, 2019, https://apnews.com/article/a97d40a146284383a717aa2ec42eb39b.

8. "Rwanda: Lockdown Arrests, Abuses Surge," Human Rights Watch, April 24, 2020, https://www.hrw.org/news/2020/04/24/rwanda-lockdown-arrests-abuses-surge#; "Rwandans Sent to Late-Night Lectures for Breaking COVID Rules," *Barron's*, Au- gust 7, 2020, https://www.barrons.com/news/rwandans-sent-to-late-night-lectures -for-breaking-covid-rules-01596775807.

9. Quoted in Bariyo, "Rwanda's Aggressive Approach to Covid Wins Plaudits—and Warnings."

10. Richard Youngs and Elene Panchulidze, "Global Democracy & COVID-19: Upgrad- ing International Support," Carnegie Endowment for International Peace, 2020, 9, http://carnegieendowment.org/files/Global_democracy_covid-19_report_FINAL _WEB.pdf; "Pandemic Backsliding: Democracy During COVID-19 (March to Sep- tember 2020)," V-Dem Institute, last modified September 2020, https://www.v-dem .net/en/analysis/PanDem/.

11. Youngs and Panchulidze, "Global Democracy & COVID-19," 12; Travis Waldron and Nick Robins-Early, "Many Countries See the Pandemic as a Crisis. Authoritarians Spot an Opportunity," *Huffington Post*, August 5, 2020, https://www.huffpost.com/entry /authoritarians-coronavirus-pandemic-venezuela_n_5f297afac5b68fbfc8883f0c; Roudabeh Kishi, "How the Coronavirus Crisis Is Silencing Dissent and Sparking Repression," *Foreign Policy*, July 21, 2020, https://foreignpolicy.com/2020/07/21/how -the-coronavirus-crisis-is-silencing-dissent-and-sparking-repression/.

12. Sarah Repucci and Amy Slipowitz, *Democracy Under Lockdown: The Impact of COVID-19 on the Global Struggle for Freedom* (Washington: Freedom House, 2020), 7– 8, https://freedomhouse.org/sites/default/files/2020–10/COVID-19_Special_Report _Final_.pdf.

13. Waldron and Robins-Early, "Many Countries See the Pandemic as a Crisis"; Repucci and Slipowitz, *Democracy Under Lockdown*, 8.

14. Mary Ilyushina, "Three Russian Doctors Fall from Hospital Windows, Raising Ques- tions amid Coronavirus Pandemic," CNN, May 7, 2020, https://edition.cnn.com /2020/05/04/europe/russia-medical-workers-windows-intl/index.html; Damelya Aitkhozhina, "Russia Should Support Health Workers, Not Silence Them," Human Rights Watch, November 2, 2020, https://www.hrw.org/news/2020/11/02/russia -should-support-health-workers-not-silence-them.

15. Youngs and Panchulidze, "Global Democracy & COVID-19," 11; Repucci and Slipowitz, *Democracy Under Lockdown*, 4.

16. "UN Raises Alarm About Police Brutality in COVID-19 Lockdowns," Al Jazeera, April 28, 2020, https://www.aljazeera.com/news/2020/4/28/un-raises-alarm-about-police -brutality-in-covid-19-lockdowns; Mary Beth Sheridan and Anna-Catherine Brigida, "Photos Show El Salvador's Crackdown on Imprisoned Gang Members," *Washington Post*, April 28, 2020, https://www.washingtonpost.com/world/the_americas/el -salvador-prison-crackdown-nayib-bukele/2020/04/27/5d3cea4c-88c9-11ea-80df -d24b35a568ae_story.html; Isaac Mugabi, "COVID-19: Security Forces in Africa Brutalizing Civilians Under Lockdown," Deutsche Welle, April 20, 2020, https:// www.dw.com/en/covid-19-security-forces-in-africa-brutalizing-civilians-under -lockdown/a-53192163.

17. Repucci and Slipowitz, *Democracy Under Lockdown*, 3.

18. Tim Hornyak, "What America Can Learn from China's Use of Robots and Tele- medicine to Combat the Coronavirus," CNBC, March 18, 2020, https://www.cnbc .com/2020/03/18/how-china-is-using-robots-and-telemedicine-to-combat-the -coronavirus.html; Sarah O'Meara, "Coronavirus: Hospital Ward Staffed Entirely by Robots Opens in China," *New Scientist*, March 9, 2020, https://www.newscientist .com/article/2236777-coronavirus-hospital-ward-staffed-entirely-by-robots-opens -in-china/.

19. Mark Hanrahan, "Coronavirus: China Deploys Drones with Cameras, Loudhailers to Chastise People for Unsafe Behavior," ABC News, February 4, 2020, https://abcnews .go.com/International/coronavirus-china-deploys-drones-cameras-loudhailers -chastise-people/story?id=68746989; Yujing Liu, "China Adapts Surveying, Map- ping, Delivery Drones to Enforce World's Biggest Quarantine and Contain Coro- navirus Outbreak," *South China Morning Post*, March 5, 2020, https://www.scmp .com/business/china-business/article/3064986/china-adapts-surveying-mapping -delivery-drones-task.

20. Shreya Chandola, "Drones Emerge as Go-To Technology Partners to Combat COVID-19 in India," *Geospatial World*, April 13, 2020, https://www.geospatialworld .net/blogs/drones-emerging-as-the-go-to-technology-partners-to-combat-covid-19 -in-india/.

21. Charlie Wood, "Spain's Police Are Flying Drones with Speakers Around Public Places to Warn Citizens on Coronavirus Lockdown to Get Inside," *Business Insider*, March 16, 2020, https://www.businessinsider.com/spanish-police-using-drones-to -ask-people-stay-at-home-2020-3.

22. Megan Bourdon and Qayyah Moynihan, "One of the Largest Cities in France Is Us- ing Drones to Enforce the Country's Lockdown After the Mayor Worried Residents Weren't Taking Containment Measures Seriously," *Business Insider*, March 20, 2020, https://www.businessinsider.com/coronavirus-drones-france-covid-19-epidemic -pandemic-outbreak-virus-containment-2020-3; Helene Fouquet and Gaspard Se- bag, "French Covid-19 Drones Grounded After Privacy Complaint," Bloomberg, May 18, 2020, https://www.bloomberg.com/news/articles/2020-05-18/paris-police -drones-banned-from-spying-on-virus-violators.

23. "COVID-19: The Surveillance Pandemic," International Center for Not-for-Profit Law, accessed November 24, 2020, https://www.icnl.org/post/analysis/covid-19-the -surveillance-pandemic.

24. Samuel Woodhams, "COVID-19 Digital Rights Tracker," last modified March 25, 2021, https://www.top10vpn.com/research/investigations/covid-19-digital-rights -tracker/.

25. Adrian Shahbaz and Allie Funk, *Freedom on the Net 2020: The Pandemic's Digital*

Shadow (Washington, DC: Freedom House, 2020), 15, https://freedomhouse.org
/sites/default/files/2020–10/10122020_FOTN2020_Complete_Report_FINAL.pdf.

26. Shahbaz and Funk, *Freedom on the Net 2020*, 16.

27. Choe Sang-Hun, Aaron Krolik, Raymond Zhong, and Natasha Singer, "Major Security Flaws Found in South Korea Quarantine App," *New York Times*, July 21, 2020, https://www.nytimes.com/2020/07/21/technology/korea-coronavirus-app-security.html.

28. Patrick Howell O'Neill, "India Is Forcing People to Use Its Covid App, Unlike Any Other Democracy," *MIT Technology Review*, May 7, 2020, https://www.technologyreview.com/2020/05/07/1001360/india-aarogya-setu-covid-app-mandatory/; Arshad Zargar, "Privacy, Security Concerns as India Forces Virus-Tracing App on Millions," CBS News, May 27, 2020, https://www.cbsnews.com/news/coronavirus-india-contact-tracing-app-privacy-data-security-concerns-aarogya-setu-forced-on-millions/; Woodhams, "COVID-19 Digital Rights Tracker"; Anuradha Nagaraj, "'Black Holes': India's Coronavirus Apps Raise Privacy Fears," Reuters, August 26, 2020, https://in.reuters.com/article/us-health-coronavirus-india-tech-feature-idUSKBN25M1KE.

29. Shahbaz and Funk, *Freedom on the Net 2020*, 18.

30. "Mobile Location Data and Covid-19: Q&A," Human Rights Watch, May 13, 2020, https://www.hrw.org/news/2020/05/13/mobile-location-data-and-covid-19-qa; Shahbaz and Funk, *Freedom on the Net 2020*, 14.

31. Richard Kemeny, "Brazil Is Sliding into Techno-Authoritarianism," *MIT Technology Review*, August 19, 2020, https://www.technologyreview.com/2020/08/19/1007094/brazil-bolsonaro-data-privacy-cadastro-base/.

32. Press Trust of India, "Pakistan Govt Using ISI's System to Track Suspected Covid-19 Cases, Says PM Imran Khan," *India Today*, April 24, 2020, https://www.indiatoday.in/world/story/pakistan-government-isi-system-track-suspected-covid-19-cases-pm-imran-khan-1670378-2020-04-24.

33. Oliver Holmes, "Israel to Track Mobile Phones of Suspected Coronavirus Cases," *The Guardian*, March 17, 2020, https://www.theguardian.com/world/2020/mar/17/israel-to-track-mobile-phones-of-suspected-coronavirus-cases; "Knesset Passes Law Authorizing Shin Bet Tracking of Virus Carriers Until January," *Times of Israel*, July 21, 2020, https://www.timesofisrael.com/knesset-approves-law-authorizing-shin-bet-tracking-of-virus-carriers/.

34. Helene Fouquet, "Paris Tests Face-Mask Recognition Software on Metro Riders," Bloomberg, May 7, 2020, https://www.bloomberg.com/news/articles/2020-05-07/paris-tests-face-mask-recognition-software-on-metro-riders; Elizabeth Kim, "MTA Explores Use of Artificial Intelligence to Measure Mask Compliance on Subways," *Gothamist*, June 24, 2020, https://gothamist.com/news/mta-explores-use-artificial-intelligence-measure-mask-compliance-subways.

35. Emily Weinstein, *China's Use of AI in Its COVID-19 Response* (Washington, DC: Center for Security and Emerging Technology, 2020), https://cset.georgetown.edu/research/chinas-use-of-ai-in-its-covid-19-response/; Shahbaz and Funk, *Freedom on the Net 2020*, 20–21.

36. Ross Andersen, "The Panopticon Is Already Here," *The Atlantic*, September 2020, https://www.theatlantic.com/magazine/archive/2020/09/china-ai-surveillance/614197/.

37. Lydia Khalil, "Digital Authoritarianism, China and Covid," Lowy Institute, November 2, 2020, https://www.lowyinstitute.org/publications/digital-authoritarianism-china-and-covid.

38. Paul Mozur, Jonah M. Kessel, and Melissa Chan, "Made in China, Exported to the World: The Surveillance State," *New York Times*, April 24, 2019, https://www.nytimes

.com/2019/04/24/technology/ecuador-surveillance-cameras-police-government
.html; "Chinese Tech Supports Ecuador's Response to COVID-19," Xinhua Net, May
30, 2020, http://www.xinhuanet.com/english/2020–05/30/c_139100735.htm; Aidan
Powers-Riggs, "Covid-19 Is Proving a Boon for Digital Authoritarianism," Center for
Strategic & International Studies, August 17, 2020, https://www.csis.org/blogs/new
-perspectives-asia/covid-19-proving-boon-digital-authoritarianism.

39. Erica Chenoweth et al., "The Global Pandemic Has Spawned New Forms of Activism—
and They're Flourishing," *The Guardian*, April 20, 2020, https://www.theguardian
.com/commentisfree/2020/apr/20/the-global-pandemic-has-spawned-new-forms-of
-activism-and-theyre-flourishing; Anna Lührmann et al., *Autocratization Surges—
Resistance Grows: Democracy Report 2020* (Gothenburg: V-Dem Institute, 2020),
21, https://www.v-dem.net/media/filer_public/de/39/de39af54–0bc5–4421–89ae
-fb20dcc53dba/democracy_report.pdf.

40. Quoted in Anthony Faiola, Lindzi Wessel, and Shibani Mahtani, "Coronavirus Chills
Protests from Chile to Hong Kong to Iraq, Forcing Activists to Innovate," *Washington Post*, April 4, 2020, https://www.washingtonpost.com/world/the_americas
/coronavirus-protest-chile-hong-kong-iraq-lebanon-india-venezuela/2020/04/03
/c7f5e012-6d50-11ea-a156-0048b62cdb51_story.html.

41. Kenneth Roth, "How Authoritarians Are Exploiting the COVID-19 Crisis to Grab
Power," Human Rights Watch, April 3, 2020, https://www.hrw.org/news/2020/04/03
/how-authoritarians-are-exploiting-covid-19-crisis-grab-power.

42. Roth, "How Authoritarians Are Exploiting the COVID-19 Crisis to Grab Power"; Sreeni-
vasan Jain and Sukriti Dwivedi, "Arrests of 2 More Students in Delhi Riots Case Raise
Questions," NDTV, May 27, 2020, https://www.ndtv.com/india-news/delhi-violence
-arrests-of-2-more-students-in-delhi-riots-case-raise-questions-2235640; Anubhav
Gupta, "In Modi's India, Rights and Freedoms Erode Further amid COVID-19," *World
Politics Review*, June 24, 2020, https://www.worldpoliticsreview.com/articles/28863/in
-modi-s-india-rights-and-freedoms-erode-further-amid-covid-19.

43. "Algeria Cracks Down on Activists in Bid to Break Protest Movement," Arab News,
June 19, 2020, https://www.arabnews.com/node/1692336/middle-east; Timothy Mc-
Laughlin, "Where the Pandemic Is Cover for Authoritarianism," *The Atlantic*, August 25, 2020, https://www.theatlantic.com/international/archive/2020/08/pandemic
-protest-double-standard-authoritarianism/615622/.

44. Quoted in McLaughlin, "Where the Pandemic Is Cover for Authoritarianism"; "Philippines: President Duterte Gives 'Shoot to Kill' Order amid Pandemic Response,"
Amnesty International, April 2, 2020, https://www.amnesty.org/en/latest/news/2020
/04/philippines-president-duterte-shoot-to-kill-order-pandemic/.

45. Victoria Tin-bor Hui, "Crackdown: Hong Kong Faces Tiananmen 2.0," *Journal of
Democracy* 31, no. 4 (October 2020): 122–37, https://www.journalofdemocracy.org
/articles/crackdown-hong-kong-faces-tiananmen-2-0/.

46. Elizabeth Cheung, "Hong Kong Activates 'Serious Response Level' for Infectious
Diseases as Wuhan Pneumonia Outbreak Escalates," *South China Morning Post*, January 4, 2020, https://www.scmp.com/news/hong-kong/health-environment/article
/3044654/hong-kong-activates-serious-response-level; Elizabeth Cheung, "China
Coronavirus: Death Toll Almost Doubles in One Day as Hong Kong Reports Its First
Two Cases," *South China Morning Post*, January 22, 2020, https://www.scmp.com
/news/hong-kong/health-environment/article/3047193/china-coronavirus-first-case
-confirmed-hong-kong.

47. Nicole Liu, Alice Woodhouse, and Naomi Rovnick, "Hong Kong Closes Most Crossings to China as Coronavirus Spreads," *Financial Times*, February 3, 2020, https://
www.ft.com/content/0d0ebf76-4668-11ea-aee2-9ddbdc86190d.

48. Samuel Wong, Kin On Kwok, and Francis Chan, "What Can Countries Learn from Hong Kong's Response to the COVID-19 Pandemic," *Canadian Medical Association Journal* 192, no. 19 (May 2020): 511–15, https://www.ncbi.nlm.nih.gov/pmc/articles /PMC7234274/; "How Hong Kong Beat Coronavirus and Avoided Lockdown," CNBC, July 2, 2020, https://www.cnbc.com/2020/07/03/how-hong-kong-beat -coronavirus-and-avoided-lockdown.html.

49. McLaughlin, "Where the Pandemic Is Cover for Authoritarianism."

50. Quoted in Helen Davidson, "Hong Kong Using Covid-19 Crisis as 'Golden Opportunity' for Crackdown, Says Arrested Leader," *The Guardian*, April 20, 2020, https://www .theguardian.com/world/2020/apr/20/hong-kong-using-covid-19-crisis-as-golden -opportunity-for-crackdown-says-arrested-leader.

51. Vanesse Chan, Bex Wright, Ivan Watson, and Jadyn Sham, "Nearly 300 Arrested in Hong Kong Protests over Postponed Local Elections," CNN, September 6, 2020, https://www.cnn.com/2020/09/06/asia/hong-kong-protests-elections-arrest-intl /index.html; Jessie Pang and James Pomfret, "Hong Kong's Veteran Pro-Democracy Activists Defiant as They Hear Charges in Court," Reuters, May 18, 2020, https:// www.reuters.com/article/us-hongkong-protests-court/hong-kongs-veteran-pro -democracy-activists-defiant-as-they-hear-charges-in-court-idUSKBN22U1BD.

52. Quoted in Austin Ramzy and Elaine Yu, "Under Cover of Coronavirus, Hong Kong Cracks Down on Protest Movement," *New York Times*, April 21, 2020, https://www .nytimes.com/2020/04/21/world/asia/coronavirus-hong-kong-protests.html.

53. Martin Lee, "I Was Arrested in Hong Kong. It's Part of China's Larger Plan," *Washington Post*, April 21, 2020, https://www.washingtonpost.com/opinions/2020/04/21/i -was-arrested-hong-kong-its-part-chinas-larger-plan/.

54. "Hong Kong's National Security Law: 10 Things You Need to Know," Amnesty International, July 17, 2020, https://www.amnesty.org/en/latest/news/2020/07/hong-kong -national-security-law-10-things-you-need-to-know/; Tin-bor Hui, "Crackdown: Hong Kong Faces Tiananmen 2.0."

55. Shibani Mahtani, "Hong Kong Leader Postpones Elections, Further Eroding Political Freedoms," *Washington Post*, July 31, 2020, https://www.washingtonpost.com /world/asia_pacific/hong-kong-leader-postpones-elections-further-eroding-political -freedoms/2020/07/31/79dbf694-d2fb-11ea-826b-cc394d824e35_story.html.

56. Natasha Khan, "Hong Kong Opposition Resigns from Legislature over Latest Beijing Crackdown," *Wall Street Journal*, November 11, 2020, https://www.wsj.com/articles /beijing-ousts-four-opposition-lawmakers-in-hong-kong-11605080352; Repucci and Slipowitz, *Democracy Under Lockdown*, 10.

57. Faiola, Wessel, and Mahtani, "Coronavirus Chills Protests"; Chenoweth et al., "The Global Pandemic Has Spawned New Forms of Activism—and They're Flourishing."

58. Charis McGowan, "How Quarantined Chileans Are Keeping Their Protest Movement Alive," Al Jazeera, April 14, 2020, https://www.aljazeera.com/features/2020/04/14/how -quarantined-chileans-are-keeping-their-protest-movement-alive/; David Gilbert, "Hong Kong Gamers Protested Inside 'Animal Crossing.' Now China Wants to Ban It," Vice, April 10, 2020, https://www.vice.com/en/article/epg3qp/hong-kong-gamers -protested-inside-animal-crossing-now-china-wants-to-ban-it; Thomas Carothers and David Wong, "The Coronavirus Pandemic Is Reshaping Global Protests," Carnegie Endowment for International Peace, May 4, 2020, https://carnegieendowment.org /2020/05/04/coronavirus-pandemic-is-reshaping-global-protests-pub-81629; Youngs and Panchulidze, "Global Democracy & COVID-19," 20.

59. Benjamin Press and Thomas Carothers, "Worldwide Protests in 2020: A Year in Review," Carnegie Endowment for International Peace, December 21, 2020, https://

carnegieendowment.org/2020/12/21/worldwide-protests-in-2020-year-in-review
-pub-83445.

60. Russian subsidies provide access to cheap gas and enable Belarus to import crude oil at below-market prices and then refine it for export.

61. Sam Meredith, "Belarus' President Dismisses Coronavirus Risk, Encourages Citizens to Drink Vodka and Visit Saunas," CNBC, March 31, 2020, https://www.cnbc.com/2020 /03/31/coronavirus-belarus-urges-citizens-to-drink-vodka-visit-saunas.html; Tatsiana Kulakevich, "The Belarus Government Is Largely Ignoring the Pandemic. Here's Why," *Washington Post*, April 21, 2020, https://www.washingtonpost.com/politics /2020/04/21/belarus-government-is-largely-ignoring-pandemic-heres-why/; Casey Michel, "Alexander Lukashenko's Belarusian Dictatorship Is Going Down in Flames," *New Republic*, August 10, 2020, https://newrepublic.com/article/158867/alexander -lukashenkos-belarus-vote-rigging.

62. Quoted in Orlando Crowcroft, "'We Look Like Clowns': Belarus Carries On as Rest of Europe Locks Down," Euronews, April 1, 2020, https://www.euronews.com/2020 /04/01/we-look-like-clowns-belarus-carries-on-as-rest-of-europe-locks-down.

63. Andrey Vozyanov, "Inside Belarus: People Defy Belarusian Authorities to Resist Covid-19 Pandemic," LRT English, May 20, 2020, https://www.lrt.lt/en/news-in -english/19/1178978/inside-belarus-people-defy-belarusian-authorities-to-resist -covid-19-Pandemic; Joerg Forbrig, "Lukashenko's Coronavirus Election," Politico, July 2, 2020, https://www.politico.eu/article/aleksander-lukashenko-belarus -coronavirus-covid19-pandemic-election/; Andrei Makhovsky, "'Game Without Rules': In Belarus Loyalists Turn on President Before Election," Reuters, July 3, 2020, https://www.reuters.com/article/us-belarus-election/game-without-rules-in-belarus -loyalists-turn-on-president-before-election-idUSKBN2441JB; Anton Troianovski, "'Something Broke Inside Belarusians': Why an Apolitical People Rose Up," *New York Times*, August 29, 2020, https://www.nytimes.com/2020/08/29/world/europe /belarus-protest.html; Repucci and Slipowitz, *Democracy Under Lockdown*, 9, 13–14.

64. Lucan Ahmad Way, "Belarus Uprising: How a Dictator Became Vulnerable," *Journal of Democracy* 31, no. 4 (October 2020): 21, https://www.journalofdemocracy.org /articles/belarus-uprising-how-a-dictator-became-vulnerable/.

65. Shaun Walker, "Tens of Thousands Gather in Minsk for Biggest Protest in Belarus History," *The Guardian*, August 16, 2020, https://www.theguardian.com/world/2020 /aug/16/belarus-prepares-for-biggest-protest-yet-after-week-of-anger.

66. Isabelle Khurshudyan, "Russia's Putin Ready to Send Forces to Belarus if Unrest 'Gets out of Control,'" *Washington Post*, August 27, 2020, https://www.washingtonpost .com/world/europe/russia-belarus-forces-putin-protests/2020/08/27/77a6a23c -e856-11ea-bf44-0d31c85838a5_story.html; "Belarus: Systematic Beatings, Torture of Protesters," Human Rights Watch, September 15, 2020, https://www.hrw.org/news /2020/09/15/belarus-systematic-beatings-torture-protesters; Sławomir Sierakowski, "Belarus Uprising: The Making of a Revolution," *Journal of Democracy* 31, no. 4 (October 2020): 5–16, https://www.journalofdemocracy.org/articles/belarus-uprising -the-making-of-a-revolution/.

67. Aaron C. Davis, Dalton Bennett, Sarah Cahlan, and Meg Kelly, "Alleged Michigan Plotters Attended Multiple Anti-Lockdown Protests, Photos and Videos Show," *Washington Post*, November 1, 2020, https://www.washingtonpost.com/investigations/2020/11 /01/michigan-kidnapping-plot-coronavirus-lockdown-whitmer/?arc404=true&itid =hp-more-top-stories; Kathleen Gray, "In Michigan, a Dress Rehearsal for the Chaos at the Capitol on Wednesday," *New York Times*, January 9, 2021, https://www.nytimes .com/2021/01/09/us/politics/michigan-state-capitol.html; Steve Neavling, "Whitmer

Says Armed Protest in Lansing Was Prelude to Violent Capitol Siege," *Detroit Metro Times*, January 18, 2021, https://www.metrotimes.com/news-hits/archives/2021/01/18/whitmer-says-armed-protest-in-lansing-was-prelude-to-violent-us-capitol-siege.

68. Press and Carothers, "Worldwide Protests in 2020."

69. Firas Abi Nassif et al., "Lebanon's Economic Crisis: A Ten Point Action Plan for Avoiding a Lost Decade," Carnegie Middle East Center, January 6, 2020, https://carnegie-mec.org/2020/01/06/lebanon-s-economic-crisis-ten-point-action-plan-for-avoiding-lost-decade-pub-80704.

70. Ben Hubbard and Hwaida Saad, "Lebanon, Mired in Crises, Turns to a Professor as Prime Minister," *New York Times*, December 19, 2019, https://www.nytimes.com/2019/12/19/world/middleeast/lebanon-prime-minister-hassan-diab.html.

71. Petra Khoury, Eid Azar, and Eveline Hitti, "COVID-19 Response in Lebanon: Current Experience and Challenges in a Low-Resource Setting," *Journal of the American Medical Association* 324, no. 6 (August 2020): 548–49, https://jamanetwork.com/journals/jama/fullarticle/2768892.

72. Martin Patience, "Coronavirus: Lebanon's Woes Worsen as Country Pushed to the Brink," BBC News, May 27, 2020, https://www.bbc.com/news/world-middle-east-52756418; "Economic Crisis Combined with COVID-19 Is Pushing Lebanon Towards a Hunger Crisis," Save the Children, accessed November 15, 2020, https://www.savethechildren.org/us/charity-stories/lebanon-economic-hunger-crisis; Lina Mounzer, "In Lebanon, a Pandemic of Hunger," *New York Times*, May 6, 2020, https://www.nytimes.com/2020/05/06/opinion/lebanon-protests-coronavirus.html.

73. "Tense Anti-Government Protests Resume in Lebanon After Covid-19 Lockdown Lifted," France 24, June 6, 2020, https://www.france24.com/en/20200606-tense-anti-government-protests-resume-in-lebanon-after-covid-19-lockdown-lifted; "Lebanon Protests: Hundreds Take to Streets for Second Night," BBC News, June 13, 2020, https://www.bbc.com/news/world-middle-east-53031683.

74. Ben Hubbard and Mona El-Naggar, "Clashes Erupt in Beirut at Blast Protest as Lebanon's Anger Boils Over," *New York Times*, August 8, 2020, https://www.nytimes.com/2020/08/08/world/middleeast/Beirut-explosion-protests-lebanon.html; "Lebanon: Lethal Force Used Against Protesters," Human Rights Watch, August 26, 2020, https://www.hrw.org/news/2020/08/26/lebanon-lethal-force-used-against-protesters.

75. Tamara Qiblawi, "Protesters Wanted Change but Lebanon's Elite Picks Veteran Saad Hariri to Lead Crisis-Wracked Country," CNN, October 22, 2020, https://www.cnn.com/2020/10/22/middleeast/saad-hariri-prime-minister-lebanon-intl/index.html.

76. Ruth Sherlock, "After Beirut Explosion, Lebanon Sees a Spike in Coronavirus Infections," NPR, September 2, 2020, https://www.npr.org/sections/coronavirus-live-updates/2020/09/02/908726243/after-beirut-explosion-lebanon-sees-a-spike-in-coronavirus-infections; Timour Azhari, "Lebanon's COVID-19 Surge: What Went Wrong?," Al Jazeera, October 8, 2020, https://www.aljazeera.com/news/2020/10/8/lebanons-covid-surge-what-went-wrong-and-what-to-do; COVID-19 Dashboard, Center for Systems Science and Engineering, Johns Hopkins University & Medicine, Coronavirus Resource Center, accessed November 24, 2020, https://coronavirus.jhu.edu/map.html.

77. Kim Parker et al., "What Unites and Divides Urban, Suburban, and Rural Communities," Pew Research Center Social & Demographic Trends, May 22, 2018, https://www.pewsocialtrends.org/2018/05/22/demographic-and-economic-trends-in-urban-suburban-and-rural-communities/; Elise Gould and Valerie Wilson, "Black Workers Face Two of the Most Lethal Preexisting Conditions for Coronavirus—Racism and Economic Inequality," Economic Policy Institute, 2020, https://www.epi.org/publication/black-workers-covid/; Emily Benfer and Lindsay Wiley, "Health Jus-

tice Strategies to Combat COVID-19: Protecting Vulnerable Communities During a Pandemic," *Health Affairs*, March 19, 2020, https://www.healthaffairs.org/do/10.1377 /hblog20200319.757883/full/; L. Ebony Boulware, "Race Disparities in the COVID-19 Pandemic—Solutions Lie in Policy, Not Biology," *JAMA Network Open* 3, no. 8 (August 2020), https://jamanetwork.com/journals/jamanetworkopen/fullarticle/2769381.

78. Claudia Wallis, "Why Racism, Not Race, Is a Risk Factor for Dying of COVID-19," *Scientific American*, June 12, 2020, https://www.scientificamerican.com/article/why -racism-not-race-is-a-risk-factor-for-dying-of-covid-191/; William F. Marshall III, "Coronavirus Infection by Race: What's Behind the Health Disparities," Mayo Clinic, August 13, 2020, https://www.mayoclinic.org/coronavirus-infection-by-race/expert -answers/faq-20488802.

79. Gould and Wilson, "Black Workers"; Nate Rattner and Tucker Higgins, "As New Data Shows Early Signs of Economic Recovery, Black Workers Are Being Left Out," CNBC, June 5, 2020, https://www.cnbc.com/2020/06/05/coronavirus-recovery-black-workers -are-being-left-out-data-shows.html.

80. Faith Karimi and Maggie Fox, "George Floyd Tested Positive for Coronavirus, but It Had Nothing to Do with His Death, Autopsy Shows," CNN, June 4, 2020, https:// www.cnn.com/2020/06/04/health/george-floyd-coronavirus-autopsy/index.html.

81. Eliott McLaughlin, "How George Floyd's Death Ignited a Racial Reckoning That Shows No Signs of Slowing Down," CNN, August 9, 2020, https://www.cnn.com /2020/08/09/us/george-floyd-protests-different-why/index.html.

82. Audra Burch et al., "How Black Lives Matter Reached Every Corner of America," *New York Times*, June 13, 2020, https://www.nytimes.com/interactive/2020/06/13 /us/george-floyd-protests-cities-photos.html; Larry Buchanan, Quoctrung Bui, and Jugal K. Patel, "Black Lives Matter May Be the Largest Movement in U.S. History," *New York Times*, July 3, 2020, https://www.nytimes.com/interactive/2020/07/03/us /george-floyd-protests-crowd-size.html.

83. Roudabeh Kishi and Sam Jones, "Demonstrations & Political Violence in America: New Data for Summer 2020," Armed Conflict Location & Event Data Project, 2020, https:// acleddata.com/acleddatanew/wp-content/uploads/2020/09/ACLED_USDataReview _Sum2020_SeptWebPDF_HiRes.pdf.

84. "Protests Worldwide Embrace Black Lives Matter Movement," Reuters, June 6, 2020, https://www.reuters.com/article/us-minneapolis-police-protests-global/protests -worldwide-embrace-black-lives-matter-movement-idUSKBN23D0BO; Jen Kirby, "'Black Lives Matter' Has Become a Global Rallying Cry Against Racism and Police Brutality," Vox, June 12, 2020, https://www.vox.com/2020/6/12/21285244/black-lives -matter-global-protests-george-floyd-uk-belgium; Anne-Christine Poujoulat, "Protests Across the Globe After George Floyd's Death," CNN, June 13, 2020, https://www .cnn.com/2020/06/06/world/gallery/intl-george-floyd-protests/index.html.

85. Kim Kyung Hoon, "Black Lives Matter Protesters March Through Tokyo," Reuters, June 14, 2020, https://www.reuters.com/article/us-minneapolis-police-protests-japan /black-lives-matter-protesters-march-through-tokyo-idUSKBN23L0FZ.

86. Repucci and Slipowitz, *Democracy Under Lockdown*, 13.

87. Repucci and Slipowitz, *Democracy Under Lockdown*, 1.

CHAPTER 12: VARIANTS AND VACCINES

1. Jonathan Corum and Carl Zimmer, "Bad News Wrapped in Protein: Inside the Coronavirus Genome," *New York Times*, April 3, 2020, https://www.nytimes.com /interactive/2020/04/03/science/coronavirus-genome-bad-news-wrapped-in -protein.html; Jonathan Corum and Carl Zimmer, "Coronavirus Variants and

Mutations," *New York Times*, last modified March 22, 2021, https://www.nytimes .com/interactive/2021/health/coronavirus-variant-tracker.html.

2. James Glanz, Benedict Carey, and Hannah Beech, "Evidence Builds That an Early Mutation Made the Pandemic Harder to Stop," *New York Times*, November 24, 2020, https://www.nytimes.com/2020/11/24/world/covid-mutation.html.

3. Benjamin Mueller and Carl Zimmer, "U.K. Virus Variant Is Probably Deadlier, Scientists Say," *New York Times*, February 13, 2021, https://www.nytimes.com/2021/02 /13/world/europe/covid-uk-variant-deadlier.html.

4. Maya Wei-Haas, "Why New Coronavirus Variants 'Suddenly Arose' in the U.K. and South Africa," *National Geographic*, December 23, 2020, https://www.nationalgeographic .com/science/article/why-new-coronavirus-variants-suddenly-arose-in-uk-and-south -africa.

5. "Emerging SARS-CoV-2 Variants," Centers for Disease Control and Prevention, accessed February 17, 2021, https://www.cdc.gov/coronavirus/2019-ncov/more /science-and-research/scientific-brief-emerging-variants.html; Benjamin Mueller, "How British Scientists Found the More Infectious Coronavirus Variant," *New York Times*, January 16, 2021, https://www.nytimes.com/2021/01/16/world/europe/uk -coronavirus-variant.html.

6. Isabel Kerchner and Carl Zimmer, "Israel's Vaccination Results Point a Way Out of Virus Pandemic," *New York Times*, February 5, 2021, https://www.nytimes.com/2021 /02/05/world/middleeast/israel-virus-vaccination.html.

7. Benjamin Mueller, Rebecca Robbins, and Lynsey Chutel, "South Africa Says Astra-Zeneca's Covid-19 Vaccine Is Not Effective at Stopping Variant," *New York Times*, February 7, 2021, https://www.nytimes.com/2021/02/07/world/south-africa-astrazeneca -vaccine.html; Brenda Goodman, "Where Do COVID Vaccines Stand Against the Variants?," *Medscape*, March 29, 2021, https://www.medscape.com/viewarticle/948335.

8. Corum and Zimmer, "Coronavirus Variants and Mutations."

9. "Total Confirmed Cases of COVID-19," Our World in Data, accessed February 17, 2021, https://ourworldindata.org/grapher/cumulative-covid-cases-region?tab =table&stackMode=absolute&time=2020–09–01.2020–12–31&region=World.

10. "Coronavirus Tracked: See How Your Country Compares: New Confirmed Cases of Covid-19 in European Union," *Financial Times*, accessed February 18, 2021, https://ig.ft.com/coronavirus-chart/?areas=eur&areasRegional=usny&areasRegional =usnj&areasRegional=usaz&areasRegional=usca&areasRegional=usnd&areasRegional =ussd&cumulative=0&logScale=0&per100K=0&startDate=2020–03–01&values=cases.

11. Melissa Eddy, "Across Europe, Reopening Borders in Time for Summer," *New York Times*, May 13, 2020, https://www.nytimes.com/2020/05/13/world/europe/coronavirus -europe-vacation.html.

12. "Covid-19: Ursula von der Leyen defende que projeto europeu não vai collapsar" [Covid-19: Ursula von der Leyen argues that the European project will not collapse], SIC Notícias, April 18, 2020, https://sicnoticias.pt/especiais/coronavirus/2020–04–18 -Covid-19-Ursula-von-der-Leyen-defende-que-projeto-europeu-nao-vai-colapsar.

13. Quoted in Hans von der Burchard, "Germany Eases Border Closures but Checks Remain Until Mid-June," Politico, May 13, 2020, https://www.politico.eu/article /germany-eases-border-checks-but-some-restrictions-will-remain-until-mid-june -coronavirus-covid19/.

14. European Commission, "Coronavirus: Commission Recommends Partial and Gradual Lifting of Travel Restrictions to the EU After 30 June, Based on Common Coordinated Approach," press release, June 11, 2020, https://ec.europa.eu/commission /presscorner/detail/en/ip_20_1035.

15. "China Reports 61 New COVID-19 Cases for Sunday, Highest Daily Domestic In-

fections Since March 6," Reuters, July 26, 2020, https://www.reuters.com/article/us
-health-coronavirus-china-cases/china-reports-61-new-covid-19-cases-for-sunday
-highest-daily-domestic-infections-since-march-6-idUKKCN24S03J; Khanh Vu and
Phuong Nguyen, "Hundreds Jam Airport as Evacuations from Vietnam's Danang Begin," Reuters, July 27, 2020, https://www.reuters.com/article/us-health-coronavirus
-vietnam/vietnam-to-evacuate-80000-people-from-danang-after-virus-outbreak
-idUKKCN24S0C0?edition-redirect=uk; Alice Klein, "Return of Covid-19 to New
Zealand Shows That No One Can Relax," *New Scientist*, August 18, 2020, https://www
.newscientist.com/article/2252136-return-of-covid-19-to-new-zealand-shows-that
-no-one-can-relax/.

16. Ryan Heath and Renuka Rayasam, "The Virus Cancels Its European Vacation,"
    Politico, September 22, 2020, https://www.politico.com/newsletters/politico-nightly
    -coronavirus-special-edition/2020/09/22/the-virus-cancels-its-european-vacation
    -490405; Josh Holder, Matina Stevis-Gridneff, and Allison McCann, "Europe's
    Deadly Second Wave: How Did It Happen Again?," *New York Times*, December
    4, 2020, https://www.nytimes.com/interactive/2020/12/04/world/europe/europe
    -covid-deaths.html.

17. Patrick Kingsley and José Bautista, "'Here We Go Again': A Second Virus Wave
    Grips Spain," *New York Times*, August 31, 2020, https://www.nytimes.com/2020/08
    /31/world/europe/coronavirus-covid-spain-second-wave.html.

18. "Coronavirus Torremolinos cierra de forma cautelar la discoteca en la que un DJ
    escupió al público" [Coronavirus: As a precautionary measure, Torremolinos closes
    the discotheque in which a DJ spat at the public], RTVE, August 3, 2020, https://www
    .rtve.es/noticias/20200803/coronavirus-torremolinos-cierra-discoteca-dj-escupio
    -publico/2036701.shtml.

19. Jessica Bateman, "Coronavirus: Island Isolation Over as Greece Lets Tourists Back,"
    BBC, June 13, 2020, https://www.bbc.com/news/world-europe-53006794.

20. Heath and Rayasam, "The Virus Cancels Its European Vacation."

21. Quoted in Guy Chazan and Anna Gross, "Europe Battles to Contain Surge in
    Covid-19 Cases," *Financial Times*, July 28, 2020, https://www.ft.com/content/bcddc297
    -b7f2-444d-908f-54e8ce6f4f98; Paul Benkimoun and Chloé Hecketsweiler, "Jean-
    François Delfraissy: 'Nous avons une vision à quatre semaines'" [Jean-François
    Delfraissy: "We have a four-week vision"], *Le Monde*, March 20, 2020, https://www
    .lemonde.fr/planete/article/2020/03/20/jean-francois-delfraissy-nous-avons-une
    -vision-a-quatre-semaines_6033854_3244.html.

22. Raphael Minder, "Spain's Reopening Stumbles as Virus Cases Rise Among Young
    People," *New York Times*, July 23, 2020, https://www.nytimes.com/2020/07/23/world
    /europe/spain-coronavirus-reopening.html.

23. "Coronavirus Digest: Younger People Driving COVID-19 Spread, Says WHO,"
    Deutsche Welle, August 18, 2020, https://www.dw.com/en/coronavirus-digest-younger
    -people-driving-covid-19-spread-says-who/a-54603448.

24. Chazan and Gross, "Europe Battles to Contain Surge in Covid-19 Cases."

25. "Coronavirus Tracked: See How Your Country Compares."

26. "Coronavirus Tracked: See How Your Country Compares."

27. Quoted in Sam Fleming, "EU Seeks to Improve Cross-Border Co-ordination as
    Covid-19 Cases Rise," *Financial Times*, September 1, 2020, https://www.ft.com
    /content/989e0a76-058d-46d4-a0ce-876dd5acbfc9.

28. Quoted in Roula Khalaf, "Ursula von der Leyen on European Recovery, Climate
    Change and Life After Brexit," *Financial Times*, December 3, 2020, https://www.ft
    .com/content/6a7a9742-fb94-4430-9ef8-977e32c17be5.

29. Benjamin Mueller, "France and Britain Strike Deal to Reopen Border for Freight

and Some Travel," *New York Times*, December 22, 2020, https://www.nytimes.com /2020/12/22/world/europe/uk-france-covid-19-border.html; FT reporters, "France Reopens Border with UK After Virus Closure," *Financial Times*, December 23, 2020, https://www.ft.com/content/e2d2e680-752a-44a5-b014-60cd837532e7.

30. Amanda Ferguson and Karla Adam, "Ireland Had One of the Lowest Coronavirus Rates in Europe. It's Now Highest in the World," *Washington Post*, January 11, 2021, https://www.washingtonpost.com/world/europe/ireland-covid-curve/2021/01 /11/aeb08592-51cc-11eb-a1f5-fdaf28cfca90_story.html; Rory Carroll, "'Reckless' Christmas Easing of Rules Blamed for Ireland Covid Surge," *The Guardian*, January 11, 2021, https://www.theguardian.com/world/2021/jan/11/reckless-christmas-rule -relaxation-blamed-for-irelands-dire-covid-surge.

31. Valentina Pop, "Dutch Rioters Clash with Police for Third Night over Covid-19 Curfew," *Wall Street Journal*, January 26, 2021, https://www.wsj.com/articles/dutch -rioters-clash-with-police-for-third-night-over-covid-19-curfew-11611664598 ?page=1; Mehreen Khan, "Dutch Extend Covid Curfew Despite Violent Backlash," *Financial Times*, January 26, 2021, https://www.ft.com/content/351fa962-ee98-49d7 -80c8-dfe73a466991.

32. Joshua Posaner and Hanne Cokelaere, "Berlin Bats Away EU Concern over 'Painful' Coronavirus Border Curbs," Politico, February 15, 2021, https://www.politico.eu /article/germany-border-controls-coronavirus-reaction/.

33. Quoted in Matina Stevis-Gridneff, "Virus Variants Deliver Fresh Blow to Europe's Open Borders," *New York Times*, February 21, 2021, https://www.nytimes.com/2021 /02/21/world/europe/european-union-coronavirus-borders.html.

34. "Coronavirus in the U.S.: Map and Latest Case Count," *New York Times*, accessed March 6, 2021, https://www.nytimes.com/interactive/2020/us/coronavirus-us-cases.html.

35. Keith Collins, "Is Your State Doing Enough Coronavirus Testing?," *New York Times*, November 1, 2020, https://www.nytimes.com/interactive/2020/us/coronavirus-testing .html.

36. Mark Mazzetti, Noah Weiland, and Sharon LaFraniere, "Behind the White House Effort to Pressure the C.D.C. on School Openings," *New York Times*, September 28, 2020, https://www.nytimes.com/2020/09/28/us/politics/white-house-cdc-coronavirus -schools.html; Lena H. Sun, "CDC Identifies Public-Health Guidance from the Trump Administration That Downplayed Pandemic Severity," *Washington Post*, March 15, 2021, https://www.washingtonpost.com/health/2021/03/15/cdc-removes -some-trump-era-guidance/.

37. Sheryl Gay Stolberg, "White House Embraces a Declaration from Scientists That Opposes Lockdowns and Relies on 'Herd Immunity,'" *New York Times*, October 13, 2020, https://www.nytimes.com/2020/10/13/world/white-house-embraces -a-declaration-from-scientists-that-opposes-lockdowns-and-relies-on-herd -immunity.html.

38. Victoria Gill, "Coronavirus: Virus Provides Leaps in Scientific Understanding," BBC, January 10, 2021, https://www.bbc.com/news/science-environment-55565284.

39. Hearing of the Senate Committee on Health, Education, Labor, and Pensions, March 3, 2021, https://www.youtube.com/watch?v=zy7id9U7-MI.

40. Nicholas A. Christakis, *Apollo's Arrow: The Profound and Enduring Impact of Coronavirus on the Way We Live* (New York: Little, Brown, 2020), 249–50.

41. Nsikan Akpan, "Why a Coronavirus Vaccine Could Take Way Longer Than a Year," *National Geographic*, April 10, 2020, https://www.nationalgeographic.com/science /article/why-coronavirus-vaccine-could-take-way-longer-than-a-year.

42. "Vaccine Development, Testing, and Regulation," History of Vaccines, accessed

February 15, 2021, https://www.historyofvaccines.org/content/articles/vaccine
-development-testing-and-regulation.

43. Laurie McGinley, "FDA to Require Covid-19 Vaccine to Prevent Disease in 50 Percent of Recipients to Win Approval," *Washington Post,* June 30, 2020, https://www
.washingtonpost.com/health/2020/06/30/coronavirus-vaccine-approval-fda/.

44. U.S. Department of Health & Human Services, "Trump Administration Announces
Framework and Leadership for 'Operation Warp Speed,'" press release, May 15, 2020,
https://www.hhs.gov/about/news/2020/05/15/trump-administration-announces
-framework-and-leadership-for-operation-warp-speed.html.

45. Kavya Sekar, *Funding for COVID-19 Vaccines: An Overview* (Washington, DC: Congressional Research Service, 2021), 2, https://crsreports.congress.gov/product/pdf
/IN/IN11556; John Tozzi, Riley Griffin, and Shira Stein, "Trump Administration
Dips into Protective Gear, CDC Funds to Fund Vaccine Push," Bloomberg, September 23, 2020, https://www.bloomberg.com/news/articles/2020-09-23/how-much-is
-the-trump-administration-spending-on-a-vaccine.

46. "Inside Operation Warp Speed," *The Daily* (podcast), *New York Times,* August 17,
2020, https://www.nytimes.com/2020/08/17/podcasts/the-daily/trump-coronavirus
-vaccine-covid.html; Helen Branswell, Matthew Herper, Lev Facher, Ed Silverman,
and Nicholas Florko, "Operation Warp Speed Promised to Do the Impossible. How
Far Has It Come?," Stat News, September 8, 2020, https://www.statnews.com/2020/09
/08/operation-warp-speed-promised-to-do-the-impossible-how-far-has-it-come/.

47. "Special Issue 4: An Interview with Moncef Slaoui—Delivering on the Promise to Develop COVID Vaccines at Warp Speed," Human Vaccines Project, December 11, 2020,
https://www.humanvaccinesproject.org/covid-post/special-issue-4-an-interview
-with-moncef-slaoui-delivering-on-the-promise-to-develop-covid-vaccines-at-warp
-speed/; Jon Cohen, "Proud of Vaccine Success, Warp Speed's Ex-Science Head Talks
Politics, Presidents, and Future Pandemics," *Science,* January 25, 2021, https://www
.sciencemag.org/news/2021/01/proud-vaccine-success-warp-speed-s-ex-science
-head-talks-politics-presidents-and-future.

48. Noah Weiland and David Sanger, "Trump Administration Narrows Search for Vaccine to Five Companies," *New York Times,* June 3, 2020, https://www.nytimes.com
/2020/06/03/us/politics/coronavirus-vaccine-trump-moderna.html; Noah Weiland,
Denise Grady, and David Sanger, "Pfizer Gets $1.95 Billion to Produce Coronavi-
rus Vaccine by Year's End," *New York Times,* July 22, 2020, https://www.nytimes.com
/2020/07/22/us/politics/pfizer-coronavirus-vaccine.html; Isaac Arnsdorf, "Trump's
Vaccine Czar Refuses to Give Up Stock in Drug Company Involved in His Government Role," ProPublica, September 23, 2020, https://www.propublica.org/article
/trumps-vaccine-czar-refuses-to-give-up-stock-in-drug-company-involved-in
-his-government-role; Peter Loftus and Joseph Walker, "U.S. Commits $2 Billion
for COVID-19 Vaccine, Drug Supplies," *Wall Street Journal,* July 7, 2020, https://
www.wsj.com/articles/u-s-commits-2-billion-for-covid-19-vaccine-drug-supplies
-11594132175.

49. Zimmer, Corum, and Wee, "Coronavirus Vaccine Tracker."

50. *Mission Possible: The Race for a Vaccine* (documentary), National Geographic, March 12,
2021, https://www.nationalgeographic.com/tv/movies-and-specials/mission-possible
-the-race-for-a-vaccine.

51. "Understanding mRNA COVID-19 Vaccines," Centers for Disease Control and
Prevention, March 4, 2021, https://www.cdc.gov/coronavirus/2019-ncov/vaccines
/different-vaccines/mrna.html.

52. Jonathan Corum and Carl Zimmer, "How the Oxford-AstraZeneca Vaccine Works,"

New York Times, last modified March 22, 2021, https://www.nytimes.com/interactive/2020/health/oxford-astrazeneca-covid-19-vaccine.html.

53. Matina Stevis-Gridneff, "Amid Critical Shortage, E.U. Moves to Limit Vaccine Exports," *New York Times*, January 29, 2021, https://www.nytimes.com/2021/01/29/world/europe/EU-AstraZeneca-vaccine-export.html.

54. Corum and Zimmer, "How the Oxford-AstraZeneca Vaccine Works"; Jonathan Corum and Carl Zimmer, "How the Johnson and Johnson Vaccine Works," *New York Times*, March 5, 2021, https://www.nytimes.com/interactive/2020/health/johnson-johnson-covid-19-vaccine.html; Hannah Kuchler, "Novavax Shot Found to Be Highly Effective at Preventing Severe Covid," *Financial Times*, March 11, 2021, https://www.ft.com/content/6546f070-ea07-400b-b6a6-dab47a5e49a5#post-61d07c53-2f51-4235-8b01-933871ce3766.

55. "Special Issue 4: An Interview with Moncef Slaoui," Human Vaccines Project.

56. Cohen, "Proud of Vaccine Success."

57. For an excellent overview of COVAX, see Mark Eccleston-Turner and Harry Upton, "International Cooperation to Ensure Equitable Access to Vaccines for COVID-19: The ACT-Accelerator and the COVAX Facility," *Milbank Quarterly*, March 2, 2021, https://onlinelibrary.wiley.com/doi/full/10.1111/1468–0009.12503; "What Is the ACT-Accelerator," World Health Organization, accessed March 8, 2021, https://www.who.int/initiatives/act-accelerator/about.

58. World Health Organization, "WHO Director-General's Opening Remarks at the Launch of the Access to COVID-19 Tools," April 24, 2020, https://www.who.int/director-general/speeches/detail/who-director-general-s-opening-remarks-at-the-launch-of-the-access-to-covid-19-tools-accelerator.

59. Merkel, the U.S. Mission in Geneva, and Macron quoted in Stephanie Nebehay and Michael Shields, "World Leaders Launch Plan to Speed COVID-19 Drugs, Vaccine; U.S. Stays Away," Reuters, April 24, 2020, https://www.reuters.com/article/us-health-coronavirus-who/world-leaders-launch-plan-to-speed-covid-19-drugs-vaccine-u-s-stays-away-idUSKCN2261M7.

60. World Health Organization, "172 Countries and Multiple Candidate Vaccines Engaged in COVID-19 Vaccine Global Access Facility," August 24, 2020, https://www.who.int/news/item/24-08-2020-172-countries-and-multiple-candidate-vaccines-engaged-in-covid-19-vaccine-global-access-facility; Colin Qian and Stephanie Nebehay, "China Joins WHO-Backed Vaccine Programme COVAX Rejected by Trump," Reuters, October 8, 2020, https://www.reuters.com/article/us-health-coronavirus-china-covax-idUKKBN26U027; "Fact Sheet: President Biden to Take Action on Global Health Through Support of COVAX and Calling for Health Security Financing," The White House, February 18, 2021, https://www.whitehouse.gov/briefing-room/statements-releases/2021/02/18/fact-sheet-president-biden-to-take-action-on-global-health-through-support-of-covax-and-calling-for-health-security-financing/.

61. Jillian Deutsch and Sarah Wheaton, "How Europe Fell Behind on Vaccines," Politico, January 27, 2021, https://www.politico.eu/article/europe-coronavirus-vaccine-struggle-pfizer-biontech-astrazeneca/.

62. Deutsch and Wheaton, "How Europe Fell Behind on Vaccines"; Jacob Funk Kirkegaard, "The European Union's Troubled COVID-19 Vaccine Rollout," Peterson Institute for International Economics, March 15, 2021, https://www.piie.com/blogs/realtime-economic-issues-watch/european-unions-troubled-covid-19-vaccine-rollout.

63. "Committee on Environment Public Health and Food Safety," European Parliament, September 7, 2020, https://multimedia.europarl.europa.eu/en/committee-on-environment-public-health-and-food-safety_20200907-1645-COMMITTEE-ENVI

_vd; Donato Paolo Mancini, "Vaccine Contracts Shrouded in Secrecy Despite Massive Public Funding," *Financial Times*, November 23, 2020, https://www.ft.com/content/95c49b5a-f2c7-49a3-9ac5-3e7a66e3ad6b.

64. Kirkegaard, "The European Union's Troubled COVID-19 Vaccine Rollout."

65. Alexander Freund, "Israel's Clever Coronavirus Vaccination Strategy," Deutsche Welle, February 16, 2021, https://www.dw.com/en/israels-clever-coronavirus-vaccination-strategy/a-56586888; "Pfizer CEO Hails Obsessive CEO for Calling 30 Times to Seal Vaccine Deal," *Times of Israel*, March 11, 2021, https://www.timesofisrael.com/pfizer-ceo-obsessive-netanyahu-called-30-times-in-effort-to-seal-vaccine-deal/; Katy Balls, "Secrets of the Vaccine Task Force's Success," *The Spectator*, February 6, 2021, https://www.spectator.co.uk/article/secrets-of-the-vaccine-taskforces-success.

66. Matt Apuzzo, Selam Gebrekidan, and Monika Pronczuk, "Where Europe Went Wrong in Its Vaccine Rollout and Why," *New York Times*, March 20, 2021, https://www.nytimes.com/2021/03/20/world/europe/europe-vaccine-rollout-astrazeneca.html.

67. Deutsch and Wheaton, "How Europe Fell Behind on Vaccines."

68. "Covid Vaccines Largely Unwanted at First Slowed EU Talks: Report," Deutsche Welle, February 6, 2021, https://www.dw.com/en/covid-vaccines-largely-unwanted-at-first-slowed-eu-talks-report/a-56480023.

69. "AstraZeneca Says Initial EU Delivery Volumes of COVID-19 Vaccine to Fall Short," Reuters, January 22, 2021, https://www.reuters.com/article/health-coronavirus-astrazeneca-eu/astrazeneca-says-initial-eu-delivery-volumes-of-covid-19-vaccine-to-fall-short-idUSL8N2JX4O8; Sam Fleming, Michael Peel, and Guy Chazan, "Redemption Shot: Von der Leyen Begins Fightback on EU Vaccine Rollout," *Financial Times*, March 2, 2021, https://www.ft.com/content/39d31c19-5a3d-4352-9bff-630f7c80e5fa; Alexander Smith, "Germany Has More Than 1 Million Covid-19 Vaccines Unused in Storage," NBC News, February 25, 2021, https://www.nbcnews.com/news/world/germany-has-more-1-million-covid-19-vaccines-unused-storage-n1258855; Sam Jones, "The Best Advert for Brexit: European Press Reacts to EU Covid Vaccine Row," *The Guardian*, January 31, 2021, https://www.theguardian.com/world/2021/jan/31/european-press-reacts-eu-covid-vaccine-row.

70. Steven Erlanger and Matina Stevis-Gridneff, "E.U. Makes a Sudden and Embarrassing U-Turn on Vaccines," *New York Times*, January 20, 2021, https://www.nytimes.com/2021/01/30/world/europe/covid-vaccines-eu.html.

71. Stevis-Gridneff, "Amid Critical Shortage, E.U. Moves to Limit Vaccine Exports."

72. Rym Momtaz, "Macron: AstraZeneca Vaccine Seems 'Quasi-Ineffective' on Older People," Politico, January 29, 2021, https://www.politico.eu/article/coronavirus-vaccine-europe-astrazeneca-macron-quasi-ineffective-older-pe/.

73. European Medicines Agency, "EMA Recommends COVID-19 Vaccine AstraZeneca for Authorisation in the EU," January 29, 2021, https://www.ema.europa.eu/en/news/ema-recommends-covid-19-vaccine-astrazeneca-authorisation-eu.

74. Matina Stevis-Gridneff, "Amid Slow Vaccine Deliveries, Desperate E.U. Nations Hunt for More," *New York Times*, February 26, 2021, https://www.nytimes.com/2021/02/26/world/europe/EU-vaccine-hunt.html.

75. Stevis-Gridneff, "Amid Slow Vaccine Deliveries, Desperate E.U. Nations Hunt for More."

76. Frank Jordans, "Major European Nations Suspend Use of AstraZeneca Vaccine," Politico, March 15, 2021, https://apnews.com/article/germany-suspends-astrazeneca-vaccine-blood-clotting-0ab2c4fe13370c96c873e896387eb92f.

77. Marc Santora and Monika Pronczuk, "Europe's Drug Regulator Says AstraZeneca Vaccine Is Safe," *New York Times*, March 18, 2021, https://www.nytimes.com/2021/03/18/world/europe/astrazeneca-vaccine-europe.html; Roger Cohen, "Trust in AstraZeneca Vaccine Is Shaken in Europe," *New York Times*, March 17, 2021,

https://www.nytimes.com/2021/03/17/world/europe/AstraZeneca-vaccine-trust
-Europe.html.

78. Sam Fleming, "EU Must Prepare for 'Era of Pandemics,' von der Leyen Says," *Finan-cial Times*, February 28, 2021, https://www.ft.com/content/fba558ff-94a5-4c6c-b848
-c8fd91b13c16.

79. James Patton and Riley Griffin, "Warp Speed's Former Adviser Offers to Help Spur EU Vaccine Drive," Bloomberg, February 2, 2021, https://www.bloomberg.com/news
/articles/2021-02-02/warp-speed-s-former-adviser-offers-help-to-spur-eu-vaccine
-drive?sref=bxQtWDnd.

80. Apuzzo, Gebrekidan, and Pronczuk, "Where Europe Went Wrong in Its Vaccine Rollout and Why"; Matine Stevis-Gridneff, "How Europe Sealed a Pfizer Vaccine Deal with Texts and Calls," *New York Times*, April 28, 2021, https://www.nytimes.com
/2021/04/28/world/europe/european-union-pfizer-von-der-leyen-coronavirus
-vaccine.html."

81. Jon Cohen, "Russia's Approval of a COVID-19 Vaccine Is Less Than Meets the Press Release," *Science Magazine*, August 11, 2020, https://www.sciencemag.org/news/2020
/08/russia-s-approval-covid-19-vaccine-less-meets-press-release; Henry Foy, Clive Cookson, and Donato Paolo Mancini, "Russia Vaccine Thrusts Little-Known State Research Unit into Spotlight," *Financial Times*, August 14, 2020, https://www.ft.com
/content/874059a6-da43-4c23-b29d-21ed59152124; "Clinical Trials," Sputnik V, ac-cessed March 10, 2021, https://sputnikvaccine.com/about-vaccine/clinical-trials/;
Ewen Callaway, "Russia's Fast-Track Coronavirus Vaccine Draws Outrage over Safety,"
Nature, August 11, 2020, https://www.nature.com/articles/d41586-020-02386-2;
quoted in Andrew E. Kramer, "Russia Approves Coronavirus Vaccine Before Com-pleting Tests," *New York Times*, August 11, 2020, https://www.nytimes.com/2020/08
/11/world/europe/russia-coronavirus-vaccine-approval.html; Denis Y. Logunov et al.,
"Safety and Efficacy of an rAd26 and rAd5 Vector-Based Heterologous Prime-Boost COVID-19 Vaccine: An Interim Analysis of a Randomised Controlled Phase 3 Trial in Russia," *Lancet* 397, no. 10275 (February 2021): 671–81, https://www.ncbi.nlm.nih.gov
/pmc/articles/PMC7852454/; "Covid: What Do We Know About China's Coronavirus Vaccines?," BBC, January 14, 2021, https://www.statnews.com/2021/02/02/comparing
-the-covid-19-vaccines-developed-by-pfizer-moderna-and-johnson-johnson/.

82. Zimmer, Corum, and Wee, "Coronavirus Vaccine Tracker"; Smriti Mallapaty, "China COVID Vaccine Reports Mixed Results—What Does That Mean for the Pandemic?,"
Nature, January 15, 2021, https://www.nature.com/articles/d41586-021-00094-z; Fa-bian Schmidt, "Coronavirus: How Effective Are the Chinese Vaccines?," Deutsche Welle, February 1, 2021, https://www.dw.com/en/coronavirus-how-effective-are-the
-chinese-vaccines/a-56370802; Scott Neuman, "Chinese Pharmaceutical Makers Seek Approval for New Coronavirus Vaccines," NPR, February 24, 2021, https://
www.npr.org/sections/coronavirus-live-updates/2021/02/24/970915305/chinese
-pharmaceutical-makers-seek-approval-for-new-coronavirus-vaccines.

83. Eric Geller and Betsy Woodruff Swan, "DOJ Says Chinese Hackers Targeted Corona-virus Vaccine Research," Politico, July 21, 2020, https://www.politico.com/news/2020
/07/21/doj-chinese-hackers-coronavirus-research-375855.

84. Jack Stubbs and Christopher Bing, "Exclusive: Iran-Linked Hackers Recently Tar-geted Coronavirus Drugmaker Gilead—Sources," Reuters, May 8, 2002, https://
www.reuters.com/article/us-healthcare-coronavirus-gilead-iran-ex/exclusive
-iran-linked-hackers-recently-targeted-coronavirus-drugmaker-gilead-sources
-idUSKBN22K2EV; Kate Day, "UK: Russian Hackers Attempted to Steal Corona-virus Vaccine Research," Politico, July 16, 2020, https://www.politico.eu/article/uk
-russian-hackers-attempted-to-steal-coronavirus-vaccine-research/; Eric Geller, "Rus-

sia, North Korea Trying to Hack Coronavirus Researchers, Microsoft Says," Politico, November 13, 2020, https://www.politico.com/news/2020/11/13/russia-north-korea -hack-coronavirus-researchers-436423.

85. Loveday Morris, Emily Rauhala, Shibani Mahtani, and Robyn Dixon, "China and Russia Are Using Coronavirus Vaccines to Expand Their Influence. The U.S. Is on the Sidelines," *Washington Post*, November 23, 2020, https://www.washingtonpost .com/world/vaccine-russia-china-influence/2020/11/23/b93daaca-25e5-11eb-9c4a -0dc6242c4814_story.html; Mark Scott, "In Race for Coronavirus Vaccine, Russia Turns to Disinformation," Politico, November 19, 2020, https://www.politico.eu /article/covid-vaccine-disinformation-russia/; Lili Bayer and Jillian Deutsch, "Hungary Issues 6-Month Authorization for Russia's Sputnik Vaccine," Politico, January 20, 2021, https://www.politico.eu/article/hungary-issues-6-month-authorization-for-russias -sputnik-vaccine/; "Hungary Becomes First EU State to Use Russian Vaccine," RFERL, February 12, 2021, https://www.rferl.org/a/hungary-eu-russian-vaccine/31099794 .html; Andrew E. Kramer, "Russia Is Offering to Export Hundreds of Millions of Vaccine Doses, but Can It Deliver?," *New York Times*, February 19, 2021, https://www .nytimes.com/2021/02/19/world/europe/russia-coronavirus-vaccine-soft-power.html.

86. Ryan Dube, "For Covid-19 Vaccines, Latin America Turns to China and Russia," *Wall Street Journal*, February 24, 2021, https://www.wsj.com/articles/for-covid-19 -vaccines-latin-america-turns-to-china-and-russia-11614186599; Joe Parkinson, Chao Deng, and Liza Lin, "China Deploys Covid-19 Vaccine to Build Influence, with U.S. on Sidelines," *Wall Street Journal*, February 21, 2021, https://www.wsj .com/articles/china-covid-vaccine-africa-developing-nations-11613598170; Diego Oré, "Mexico Says China Plans $1 Billion Loan to Ease Latam Access to Virus Vaccine," Reuters, July 22, 2020, https://www.reuters.com/article/us-health-coronavirus -mexico-china/mexico-says-china-plans-1-billion-loan-to-ease-latam-access-to -virus-vaccine-idUSKCN24O08L; Yanzhong Huang, "Vaccine Diplomacy Is Paying Off for China," *Foreign Affairs*, March 11, 2021, https://www.foreignaffairs.com /articles/china/2021-03-11/vaccine-diplomacy-paying-china.

87. Chris Horton and Ken Parks, "Paraguay Says Chinese Vaccine Offers Tied to Dumping Taiwan," Bloomberg, March 24, 2021, https://www.bloomberg.com/news/articles /2021-03-24/paraguay-says-offers-of-chinese-vaccine-tied-to-dumping-taiwan.

88. "Brazil: Coronavirus Pandemic Country Profile," Our World in Data, accessed March 20, 2021, https://ourworldindata.org/coronavirus/country/brazil; "'Covid Is Taking Over': Brazil Plunges into Deadliest Chapter of Its Epidemic," *Guardian*, March 13, 2021, https://www.theguardian.com/world/2021/mar/13/brazil-covid-coronavirus-deaths -cases-bolsonaro-lula; Manuela Andreoni, Ernesto Londoño, and Letícia Casado, "Brazil's Covid Crisis Is a Warning to the Whole World, Scientists Say," *New York Times*, March 3, 2021, https://www.nytimes.com/2021/03/03/world/americas/brazil-covid -variant.html; Ernesto Londoño and Letícia Casado, "A Collapse Foretold: How Brazil's Covid-19 Outbreak Overwhelmed Hospitals," *New York Times*, March 27, 2021, https:// www.nytimes.com/2021/03/27/world/americas/virus-brazil-bolsonaro.html.

89. Quoted in Mauricio Savarese, "Brazil's Bolsonaro Rejects Coronavirus Vaccine from China," *AP News*, October 21, 2020, https://apnews.com/article/virus-outbreak -brazil-state-governments-health-sao-paulo-b7b5b620ba54f402dbf803e26fe6b842.

90. Antonia Noori Farzan and Heloísa Traiano, "U.S. Officials Pushed Brazil to Reject Russia's Coronavirus Vaccine, According to HHS report," *Washington Post*, March 16, 2021, https://www.washingtonpost.com/world/2021/03/16/hhs-brazil-sputnik-russia/.

91. Eduardo Simões, "Exclusive: Brazil to Buy 20 Million More Doses of China's CoronaVac, Governor Says," February 5, 2021, https://www.reuters.com/article/us-health -coronavirus-brazil-vaccines-ex/exclusive-brazil-to-buy-20-million-more-doses-of

-chinas-coronavac-governor-says-idUSKBN2A50EP; Ernesto Londoño and Letícia Casado, "Brazil Needs Vaccines. China Is Benefiting," *New York Times*, March 15, 2021, https://www.nytimes.com/2021/03/15/world/americas/brazil-vaccine-china.html.

92. Mauricio Savarese, "Brazil Reaches Deal for 10 Million Shots of Russian Vaccine," *AP News*, March 12, 2021, https://apnews.com/article/brazil-south-america-coronavirus -pandemic-russia-27f7a6f828cd9a7db8d0b3ed8feed7bc.

93. David Nakamura and Josh Dawsey, "Few Masks, Little Distancing: Trump Celebrates at Crowded White House Party Largely Devoid of Coronavirus Precautions," *Washington Post*, August 27, 2020, https://www.washingtonpost.com/politics/white-house-convention -covid-testing/2020/08/27/44b53cda-e8c4-11ea-bc79-834454439a44_story.html.

94. Larry Buchanan, Lazaro Gamio, Lauren Leatherby, Robin Stein, and Christiaan Triebert, "Inside the White House Event Now Under Covid-19 Scrutiny," *New York Times*, October 5, 2020, https://www.nytimes.com/interactive/2020/10/03/us/rose -garden-event-covid.html; Veronica Rocha, Melissa Macaya, Melissa Mathani, and Fernando Alfonso III, "October 2: Trump's Covid Diagnosis," CNN, October 2, 2020, https://www.cnn.com/politics/live-news/trump-coronavirus-positive/h_cebb891fe9 fe8513948709d5f1793e07.

95. Jeff Mason and Joseph Ax, "Chaotic Clash in Cleveland: Five Takeaways from First U.S. Presidential Debate," Reuters, September 29, 2020, https://www.reuters.com /article/us-usa-election-debate-takeaways-idUSKBN26L03H.

96. Ashley Collman, "2 Days Before His Coronavirus Diagnosis, Trump Mocked Biden for Wearing a Face Mask," *Business Insider*, October 2, 2020, https://www.businessinsider .com/trump-coronavirus-mocked-biden-face-mask-presidential-debate-2020-10.

97. John L. Dorman, "Chris Wallace Said Trump Arrived Too Late to Be Tested for Coronavirus at the First Presidential Debate," *Business Insider*, October 3, 2020, https://www.businessinsider.com/donald-trump-chris-wallace-presidential-debate -coronavirus-2020-10.

98. Peter Baker and Maggie Haberman, "Trump's Symptoms Described as 'Very Concerning' Even as Doctors Offer Rosier Picture," *New York Times*, October 3, 2020, https://www.nytimes.com/2020/10/03/us/politics/trump-covid-updates.html; Noah Weiland, Maggie Haberman, Mark Mazzetti, and Annie Karni, "Trump Was Sicker Than Acknowledged with Covid-19," *New York Times*, February 11, 2021, https:// www.nytimes.com/2021/02/11/us/politics/trump-coronavirus.html.

99. Melissa Quinn, "Trump Says 'Don't Be Afraid of COVID' as U.S. Death Toll Tops 210,000," CBS News, October 6, 2020, https://www.cbsnews.com/news/trump-covid -19-dont-be-afraid-death-toll-210000/.

100. Alexander Burns, "Trump's Closing Argument on Virus Clashes with Science, and Voters' Lives," *New York Times*, October 28, 2020, https://www.nytimes.com/2020/10 /28/us/politics/trump-coronavirus.html.

101. "How Unpopular Is Donald Trump," FiveThirtyEight, January 20, 2021, https:// projects.fivethirtyeight.com/trump-approval-ratings/.

102. Bill Bostock, "Trump Told a Rally Crowd in Swing-State Pennsylvania That He Was Only There Because of How Badly His Campaign Is Going," *Business Insider*, October 21, 2020, https://www.businessinsider.com/trump-pennsylvania-rally-only -there-his-campaign-going-south-votes-2020-10.

103. Quoted in Ashley Parker, Josh Dawsey, Matt Viser, and Michael Scherer, "How Trump's Erratic Behavior and Failure on Coronavirus Doomed His Reelection," *Washington Post*, November 7, 2020, https://www.washingtonpost.com/elections /interactive/2020/trump-pandemic-coronavirus-election/.

104. "Post Election Exit Poll Analysis: 10 Key Target States," Fabrizio, Lee & Associates, https://www.politico.com/f/?id=00000177-6046-de2d-a57f-7a6e8c950000.

105. "National Voter Surveys: How Different Groups Voted," *New York Times*, November 3, 2020, https://www.nytimes.com/interactive/2020/11/03/us/elections/ap-polls-national.html.

106. "Exit Polls," CNN, November 3, 2020, https://www.cnn.com/election/2020/exit-polls/president/national-results.

107. Will Wilkinson, "Why Did So Many Americans Vote for Trump?," *New York Times*, November 27, 2020, https://www.nytimes.com/2020/11/27/opinion/trump-democrats-coronavirus.html.

108. "National Voter Surveys: How Different Groups Voted."

109. "Exit Polls."

110. Jim Rutenberg, Nick Corasaniti, and Alan Feuer, "Trump's Fraud Claims Died in Court, but the Myth of Stolen Elections Lives On," *New York Times*, December 26, 2020, https://www.nytimes.com/2020/12/26/us/politics/republicans-voter-fraud.html.

111. Emily Badger, "Most Republicans Say They Doubt the Election. How Many Really Mean It?," *New York Times*, November 30, 2020, https://www.nytimes.com/2020/11/30/upshot/republican-voters-election-doubts.html; Liz Zhou, "About Half of Republicans Don't Think Joe Biden Should Be Sworn In as President," Vox, January 11, 2021, https://www.vox.com/2021/1/11/22225531/joe-biden-trump-capitol-inauguration.

112. "COVID-19 Virtual Press Conference Transcript—5 January 2021," World Health Organization, January 5, 2021, https://www.who.int/publications/m/item/covid-19-virtual-press-conference-transcript—5-january-2021.

113. "Coronavirus: Trump Accuses WHO of Being a 'Puppet of China,'" BBC, May 19, 2020, https://www.bbc.com/news/health-52679329.

114. World Health Organization (WHO) (@WHO), "They were tested again in #Singapore and were all negative for PCR," Twitter, January 14, 2021, 3:01 a.m., https://twitter.com/WHO/status/1349627669558784002.

115. Damien Cave, "The World in a Vise: Sounding the Alarm on China, Then Running for Shelter," *New York Times*, December 1, 2020, https://www.nytimes.com/2020/12/01/world/australia/china-australia-morrison-tweet.html; Karen DeYoung, "U.S., Australia Call for Global Investigation of Pandemic Response; Pompeo Says WHO Funding Freeze Could Be Permanent," *Washington Post*, April 23, 2020, https://www.washingtonpost.com/national/coronavirus-death-toll-who-trump/2020/04/23/d5c37400-8580-11ea-ae26-989cfce1c7c7_story.html.

116. Jordan Hayne, "Australia 'Hurt the Feelings' of China with Calls for Coronavirus Investigation, Senior Diplomat Says," ABC, August 26, 2020, https://www.abc.net.au/news/2020-08-26/senior-chinese-diplomat-addresses-australia-coronavirus-tensions/12596602.

117. Daniel Hurst, "Top Chinese Diplomat Says Australia's Call for Coronavirus Inquiry Was 'Shocking,'" *The Guardian*, August 26, 2020, https://www.theguardian.com/australia-news/2020/aug/26/top-chinese-diplomat-says-australias-call-for-coronavirus-inquiry-was-shocking; Daniel Hurst, "How Much Is China's Trade War Really Costing Australia?," *The Guardian*, October 27, 2020, https://www.theguardian.com/australia-news/2020/oct/28/how-much-is-chinas-trade-war-really-costing-australia.

118. Gerry Shih, Emily Rauhala, and Josh Dawsey, "China's Xi Backs WHO-Led Review of Covid-19 Outbreak," *Washington Post*, May 18, 2020, https://www.washingtonpost.com/world/asia_pacific/chinas-xi-backs-who-led-review-of-covid-19-outbreak-proposes-aid-for-developing-world/2020/05/18/911a1544-98df-11ea-ad79-eef7cd734641_story.html.

119. Emily Rauhala, Karoun Demirjian, and Toluse Olorunnipa, "Trump Administration Sends Letter Withdrawing U.S. from World Health Organization over Coronavirus Response," *Washington Post*, July 7, 2020, https://www.washingtonpost.com/world

/trump-united-states-withdrawal-world-health-organization-coronavirus/2020/07
/07/ae0a25e4-b550-11ea-9a1d-d3db1cbe07ce_story.html.

120. Javier C. Hernández, "Two Members of W.H.O. Team on Trail of Virus Are Denied
Entry to China," *New York Times*, January 13, 2021, https://www.nytimes.com/2021
/01/13/world/asia/china-who-wuhan-covid.html.

121. Drew Hinshaw and Jeremy Page, "WHO Mission to Look for Answers to Covid-19's
Origin in Wuhan," *Wall Street Journal*, January 14, 2021, https://www.wsj.com/articles
/who-mission-to-look-for-answers-to-covid-19s-origin-in-wuhan-11610566665;
Drew Hinshaw, "WHO Criticizes China for Stymying Investigation into Covid-19
Origins," *Wall Street Journal*, January 6, 2021, https://www.wsj.com/articles/world
-health-organization-criticizes-china-over-delays-in-covid-19-probe-11609883140.

122. Christina Larson, "China's Fox News," *Foreign Policy*, October 31, 2010, https://
foreignpolicy.com/2011/10/31/chinas-fox-news/; "Conspiracy Theories, Smears Rise
Ahead of WHO Experts' China Visit," *Global Times*, January 12, 2021, https://www
.globaltimes.cn/page/202101/1212548.shtml.

123. Jeremy Page and Drew Hinshaw, "China Refuses to Give WHO Raw Data on Early
Covid-19 Cases," *Wall Street Journal*, February 12, 2021, https://www.wsj.com/articles
/china-refuses-to-give-who-raw-data-on-early-covid-19-cases-11613150580.

124. Hernández, "Two Members of W.H.O. Team on Trail of Virus."

125. Sha Hua, "China Floats Covid-19 Theories That Point to Foreign Origins, Frozen Food,"
Wall Street Journal, December 8, 2020, https://www.wsj.com/articles/china-pushes
-alternative-theories-about-origin-of-covid-19-11607445463; Javier C. Hernández,
"China Peddles Falsehoods to Obscure Origin of Covid Pandemic," *New York Times*,
December 6, 2020, https://www.nytimes.com/2020/12/06/world/asia/china-covid-origin
-falsehoods.html.

126. Javier C. Hernández and James Gorman, "On W.H.O. Trip, China Refused to Hand
Over Important Data," *New York Times*, February 12, 2021, https://www.nytimes
.com/2021/02/12/world/asia/china-world-health-organization-coronavirus.html.

127. Jeremy Page, Chao Deng, and Drew Hinshaw, "Coronavirus Likely Came from Animal, Not Leaked from Laboratory, WHO Says," *Wall Street Journal*, February 9, 2021,
https://www.wsj.com/articles/coronavirus-most-likely-spilled-over-to-humans
-through-intermediate-animal-says-who-11612868217.

128. Javier C. Hernández, "China Scores a Public Relations Win After W.H.O. Mission to
Wuhan," *New York Times*, February 9, 2021, https://www.nytimes.com/2021/02/09
/world/asia/wuhan-china-who-covid.html.

129. Page, Deng, and Hinshaw, "Coronavirus Likely Came from an Animal."

130. The White House, "Statement by National Security Advisor Jake Sullivan," February
13, 2021, https://www.whitehouse.gov/briefing-room/statements-releases/2021/02
/13/statement-by-national-security-advisor-jake-sullivan/.

131. *WHO-Convened Global Study of Origins of SARS-CoV-2: China Part*, Joint WHO-
China Study 14 January–10 February, March 30, 2021, 9, https://www.who.int/health
-topics/coronavirus/origins-of-the-virus.

132. Emily Rauhala, "WHO Wuhan Report Leaves Question of Coronavirus Origins Unre-
solved," *Washington Post*, March 29, 2021, https://www.washingtonpost.com/world/who
-wuhan-report-/2021/03/29/cb6ca64e-7778-11eb-9489-8f7dacd51e75_story.html.

133. World Health Organization, "WHO Director-General's Remarks at the Member State
Briefing on the Report of the International Team Studying the Origins of SARS-CoV-2,"
March 30, 2021, https://www.who.int/director-general/speeches/detail/who-director
-general-s-remarks-at-the-member-state-briefing-on-the-report-of-the-international
-team-studying-the-origins-of-sars-cov-2.

134. Jennifer Hansler, "Blinken Suggests US Won't Take Punitive Action Against China

over Coronavirus Outbreak," CNN, March 28, 2021, https://www.cnn.com/2021/03
/28/politics/blinken-china-coronavirus-cnntv/index.html.

135. Office of the Spokesperson, U.S. State Department, "Joint Statement on the WHO-Convened COVID-19 Origins Study," March 30, 2021, https://www.state.gov/joint
-statement-on-the-who-convened-covid-19-origins-study/.

136. European Union External Action Service, "EU Statement on the WHO-Led COVID-19 Origins Study," March 30, 2021, https://eeas.europa.eu/headquarters/headquarters
-homepage/95960/eu-statement-who-led-covid-19-origins-study_en.

137. Author interviews on background with WHO officials, April 2021.

CHAPTER 13: FIGHTING FOR A BETTER FUTURE

1. Joe Biden (@JoeBiden), "We Can't Allow the Good Friday Agreement That Brought Peace to Northern Ireland to Become a Casualty of Brexit," Twitter, September 16, 2020, 4:48 p.m., https://twitter.com/JoeBiden/status/1306334039557586944?s=20.

2. "COVID-19: Boris Johnson to Urge G7 Leaders to Defeat 'Common Foe' with Global Vaccine Effort," Sky News, February 14, 2021, https://news.sky.com/story/covid-19
-boris-johnson-urges-g7-leaders-to-unite-to-defeat-pandemic-12217487.

3. Transcript of Obama's G-20 Press Conference, April 2, 2009, https://www.cbsnews
.com/news/transcript-obamas-g20-press-conference/.

4. G7 Leaders' Statement, February 19, 2021, https://www.consilium.europa.eu/en
/press/press-releases/2021/02/19/g7-february-leaders-statement/.

5. "COVID-19 Vaccination 'Wildly Uneven and Unfair': UN Secretary-General," news release, United Nations, February 17, 2021, https://news.un.org/en/story/2021/02/1084962.

6. "WHO Chief Warns Against 'Catastrophic Moral Failure' in COVID-19 Vaccine Access," news release, United Nations, January 18, 2021, https://news.un.org/en/story
/2021/01/1082362.

7. World Health Organization, "Access to COVID-19 Tools Funding Commitment Tracker," last modified March 26, 2021, https://www.who.int/publications/m/item
/access-to-covid-19-tools-tracker, accessed April 4, 2021.

8. Sinéad Baker, "The US Is Finally Joining the Push for Global Vaccine Access. It's Almost Certainly Not Going to Be Enough," *Business Insider*, February 2, 2021, https://
www.businessinsider.com/us-joins-covax-experts-say-wont-help-poorer-nations
-much-2021-1.

9. Quoted in Roula Khalaf, Ben Hall, and Victor Mallet, "Emmanuel Macron Urges Europe to Send Vaccines to Africa Now," *Financial Times*, February 18, 2021, https://
www.ft.com/content/15853717-af6c-4858-87d4-58b1826895a8.

10. Ben Gittleson, "Biden to Announce US Will Donate $4 Billion for COVID-19 Vaccines for Poor Countries," ABC News, February 18, 2021, https://abcnews.go.com
/Politics/biden-announce-us-donate-billion-covid-19-vaccines/story?id=75978762.

11. "Pandemic Will Not End Until World Is Vaccinated, Merkel Says," Reuters, February 19, 2021, https://www.reuters.com/article/us-germany-politics-g7-merkel/pandemic
-will-not-end-until-world-is-vaccinated-merkel-says-idUSKBN2AJ1WG.

12. The White House, "Fact Sheet: Quad Summit," March 12, 2021, https://www
.whitehouse.gov/briefing-room/statements-releases/2021/03/12/fact-sheet-quad
-summit/; Sheryl Gay Stolberg and Michael Crowley, "Biden Takes First Tentative Steps to Address Vaccine Shortage," *New York Times*, March 12, 2021, https://www
.nytimes.com/2021/03/12/us/politics/covid-19-vaccine-global-shortage.html.

13. Tamara Keith, "Biden Takes First Jab at Vaccine Diplomacy, Sharing Doses with Mexico, Canada," NPR, March 19, 2021, https://www.npr.org/2021/03/19/979279426/biden
-takes-first-jab-at-vaccine-diplomacy-sharing-doses-with-mexico-canada; Denise Lu,

"How Covid Upended a Century of Patterns in U.S. Deaths," *New York Times*, April 23, 2021, https://www.nytimes.com/interactive/2021/04/23/us/covid-19-death-toll.html; Nicky Phillips, "The Coronavirus Is here to Stay—Here's What That Means," *Nature*, February 16, 2021, https://www.nature.com/articles/d41586-021-00396-2.

14. Benjamin Mueller, "As Covid Ravages Poorer Countries, Rich Nations Spring Back to Life," *New York Times*, May 5, 2021, https://www.nytimes.com/2021/05/05/world /europe/coronavirus-covax-vaccination.html?referringSource=articleShare; Aime Williams, Kiran Stacey, Hannah Kuchler, and Donato Paolo Mancini, "US Backs Plan to Suspend Covid Vaccine Patents During Pandemic," *Financial Times*, May 5, 2021, https://www.ft.com/content/eca86f43-7127-4213-948d-3cc8d652805e.

15. Daniel Drezner, *The System Worked: How the World Stopped Another Great Depression* (London: Oxford University Press, 2014).

16. Bill Gates and Melinda Gates, "COVID-19: A Global Perspective," September 2020, https://www.gatesfoundation.org/goalkeepers/report/2020-report/#GlobalPerspective.

17. "Secretary-General's Remarks to the General Assembly Special Session in Response to the COVID-19 Pandemic," December 3, 2020, https://www.un.org/sg/en/content /sg/statement/2020-12-03/secretary-generals-remarks-the-general-assembly-special -session-response-the-covid-19-pandemic-delivered.

18. Hank Paulson, *On the Brink: Inside the Race to Stop the Collapse of the Financial System* (New York: Business Plus, 2010), 160.

19. Laura Silver, Kat Devlin, and Christine Huang, "Unfavorable Views of China Reach Historic Highs in Many Countries," Pew Research Center, October 6, 2020, https://www.pewresearch.org/global/2020/10/06/unfavorable-views-of-china-reach -historic-highs-in-many-countries/.

20. For instance, see Fu Ying, "Fu Ying on Why China and the United States Must Cooperate to Defeat COVID-19," *The Economist*, April 29, 2020, https://www.economist.com /by-invitation/2020/04/29/fu-ying-on-why-china-and-america-must-co-operate-to -defeat-covid-19; Jonathan Cheng, "China's Economy Is Bouncing Back—and Gaining Ground on the U.S.," *Wall Street Journal*, August 24, 2020, https://www.wsj.com/articles /chinas-economy-is-bouncing-backand-gaining-ground-on-the-u-s-11598280917.

21. "France's Macron: 'I Do Believe in NATO,'" Reuters, February 19, 2021, https://www .reuters.com/article/us-germany-security-conference-macron/frances-macron-i-do -believe-in-nato-idUSKBN2AJ24D.

22. Leslie Hook, "The Next Pandemic: Where Is It Coming From and How Do We Stop It?," *Financial Times*, October 29, 2020, https://www.ft.com/content/2a80e4a2-7fb9-4e2c -9769-bc0d98382a5c.

23. Vanda Felbab-Brown, "Preventing the Next Zoonotic Pandemic," Project Syndicate, October 6, 2020, https://www.project-syndicate.org/onpoint/preventing-the-next -zoonotic-pandemic-by-vanda-felbab-brown-2020-10?barrier=accesspaylog.

24. Rupert Beale, "Get the Jab!," *London Review of Books*, December 17, 2020, https:// www.lrb.co.uk/the-paper/v42/n24/rupert-beale/end-in-sight.

25. Interview with Laurie Garrett, *Hell and High Water with John Heileman* (podcast), November 17, 2020, https://www.iheart.com/podcast/1119-hell-and-high -water-with-70854991/episode/laurie-garrett-73985090/.

26. President Joseph R. Biden Jr., *National Strategy for the COVID-19 Response and Pandemic Preparedness*, January 2021, https://www.whitehouse.gov/wp-content /uploads/2021/01/National-Strategy-for-the-COVID-19-Response-and-Pandemic -Preparedness.pdf. See also "National Security Memorandum on United States Global Leadership to Strengthen the International COVID-19 Response to Advance Global Health Security and Biological Preparedness," January 21, 2021, https://www .whitehouse.gov/briefing-room/statements-releases/2021/01/21/national-security

-directive-united-states-global-leadership-to-strengthen-the-international-covid-19
-response-and-to-advance-global-health-security-and-biological-preparedness/.

27. Thomas J. Bollyky, Sawyer Crosby, and Samantha Kiernan, "Fighting a Pandemic Requires Trust," *Foreign Affairs*, October 23, 2020, https://www.foreignaffairs.com /articles/united-states/2020-10-23/coronavirus-fighting-requires-trust.

28. Andrew Green, "Q&A: The Ups and Downs of WHO's Health Emergency Programme," DevEx, October 30, 2019, https://www.devex.com/news/q-a-the-ups-and -downs-of-who-s-health-emergencies-programme-95929.

29. World Health Organization, "Ebola Then and Now: Eight Lessons from West Africa That Were Applied in the Democratic Republic of Congo," April 10, 2020, https:// www.who.int/news-room/feature-stories/detail/ebola-then-and-now.

30. An international debate is just beginning on post-COVID reform of the WHO. See, for example, Carmen Paun, "Countries Plot Changes to World Health Organization Once Pandemic Recedes," Politico, October 2, 2020, https://www.politico.com /news/2020/10/02/countries-plot-changes-at-the-world-health-organization-once -pandemic-recedes-425072. For specific proposals, see France and Germany's "Non-Paper on Strengthening WHO's Leading and Coordinating Role in Global Health," August 2020, http://g2h2.org/wp-content/uploads/2020/08/Non-paper-1.pdf; and the Trump administration's proposals, U.S. Department of Health and Human Services, "Reviewing COVID-19 Response and Strengthening the WHO's Global Emergency Preparedness and Response WHO ROADMAP," September 9, 2020, https://www.hhs.gov/about/agencies/oga/about-oga/what-we-do/international -relations-division/multilateral-relations/who-roadmap-2020.html.

31. Taiwan was an observer state at the World Health Assembly from 2009 to 2015 under the government of Ma Ying-jeou. When Tsai Ing-wen of the DPP party was elected in 2016, Beijing withdrew its support for the existing arrangement and imposed new conditions that Taiwan was unable to meet. As a consequence, Taiwan has been excluded from World Health Assembly meetings. See Jess Macy Yu, "Taiwan Blames China for Absence from U.N. Health Meeting," Reuters, May 8, 2018, https://www .reuters.com/article/us-taiwan-china-health/taiwan-blames-china-for-absence-from -u-n-health-meeting-idUSKBN1I90J0; Mark Leon Goldberg, "What Is the Controversy over Taiwan at the World Health Organization?," *UN Dispatch*, May 18, 2020, https://www.undispatch.com/why-cant-taiwan-join-the-world-health-organization/.

32. Sylvia Mathews Burwell and Francis Fragos Townsend (chairs), Thomas J. Bollyky and Stewart M. Patrick (project directors), "Improving Pandemic Preparedness: Lessons from COVID-19," Council on Foreign Relations, Independent Task Force Report No. 78, October 2020, https://www.cfr.org/report/pandemic-preparedness -lessons-COVID-19/pdf/TFR_Pandemic_Preparedness.pdf, 90.

33. Lisa De Bode, "WHO Wants Sanctions Against Countries for Mishandling Epidemics," Al Jazeera America, October 22, 2015, http://america.aljazeera.com/articles /2015/10/22/health-sanctions-against-countries-misguided.html.

34. *COVID-19 Shows Why United Action Is Needed for More Robust International Health Architecture*, World Health Organization, March 30, 2021, https://www.who.int /news-room/commentaries/detail/op-ed—covid-19-shows-why-united-action-is -needed-for-more-robust-international-health-architecture; "U.S., China Positive on Pandemic Treaty Idea: WHO's Tedros," Reuters, March 30, 2021, https://www.reuters .com/article/us-health-coronavirus-treaty-members-idUSKBN2BM10T.

35. Burwell et al., "Improving Pandemic Preparedness: Lessons from COVID-19," 78–79, 89–92.

36. World Health Organization, "International Health Regulations," http://www.emro .who.int/international-health-regulations/about/ihr-core-capacities.html, accessed

December 13, 2020; Gavin Yamey, Justice Nonvignon, and Cordelia Kenney, "Modernizing Our Public Health Systems to Be Ready for the Next Pandemic," *UN Chronicle*, May 4, 2020, https://www.un.org/en/un-chronicle/modernizing-our-public-health-systems-be-ready-next-pandemic.

37. World Bank, International Working Group on Financing Preparedness, "From Panic and Neglect to Investing in Health Security: Financing Pandemic Preparedness at a National Level," December 2017, http://documents1.worldbank.org/curated/en/979591495652724770/pdf/115271-REVISED-FINAL-IWG-Report-3-5-18.pdf, 6–7.

38. World Bank, "From Panic and Neglect to Investing in Health Security," 4.

39. Vitor Gaspar, W. Raphael Lam, and Mehdi Raissi, "Fiscal Policies for the Recovery from COVID-19," *IMFBlog*, May 6, 2020, https://blogs.imf.org/2020/05/06/fiscal-policies-for-the-recovery-from-covid-19/.

40. Jeff Tollefson, "IPCC Says Limiting Global Warming to 1.5°C Will Require Drastic Action," *Nature*, October 8, 2018, https://www.nature.com/articles/d41586-018-06876-2; Somini Sengupta, "'Bleak' U.N. Report on a Planet in Peril Looms over New Climate Talks," *New York Times*, November 26, 2019, https://www.nytimes.com/2019/11/26/climate/greenhouse-gas-emissions-carbon.html.

41. Global Commission on Adaptation, "Adapt Now: A Global Call for Leadership on Climate Resilience," September 13, 2019, https://gca.org/about-us/the-global-commission-on-adaptation/; OECD, "Making the Green Recovery Work for Jobs, Income and Growth," October 6, 2020, http://www.oecd.org/coronavirus/policy-responses/making-the-green-recovery-work-for-jobs-income-and-growth-a505f3e7/; United Nations Environment Programme, "Emissions Gap Report 2020," December 9, 2020, https://www.unenvironment.org/emissions-gap-report-2020.

42. European Council, "G7 Leaders' Statement, 19 February 2021," https://www.consilium.europa.eu/en/press/press-releases/2021/02/19/g7-february-leaders-statement/.

43. Derek Chollet and James Goldgeier, *America Between the Wars: From 11/9 to 9/11* (New York: PublicAffairs, 2009).

44. Donald J. Trump, *National Security Strategy of the United States of America* (Washington, DC: The White House, December 2017), https://www.whitehouse.gov/wp-content/uploads/2017/12/NSS-Final-12-18-2017-0905.pdf; for a discussion on the strategy, see William Inboden et al., "Policy Roundtable: What to Make of Trump's National Security Strategy," *Texas National Security Review*, December 21, 2017, https://tnsr.org/roundtable/policy-roundtable-make-trumps-national-security-strategy/#essay5; for a perspective on why great-power competition made a return, see Thomas Wright, *All Measures Short of War: The Contest for the 21st Century and the Future of American Power* (New Haven, CT: Yale University Press), 2017.

45. See, for example, Ben Rhodes, "The 9/11 Era Is Over," *The Atlantic*, April 6, 2020, https://www.theatlantic.com/ideas/archive/2020/04/its-not-september-12-anymore/609502/; Stephen Wertheim, "Delusions of Dominance," *Foreign Affairs*, January 25, 2021, https://www.foreignaffairs.com/articles/united-states/2021-01-25/delusions-dominance.

46. O. Hoegh-Guldberg et al., "The Human Imperative of Stabilizing Global Climate Change at 1.5°C," *Science* 365, Issue 6459, September 20, 2019, https://science.sciencemag.org/content/365/6459/eaaw6974.

47. David P. Fidler, "The COVID-19 Pandemic, Geopolitics, and International Law," *Journal of International Humanitarian Legal Studies* 11 (2020): 243, https://www.cfr.org/sites/default/files/pdf/fidler_jihls_covid.pdf.

INDEX